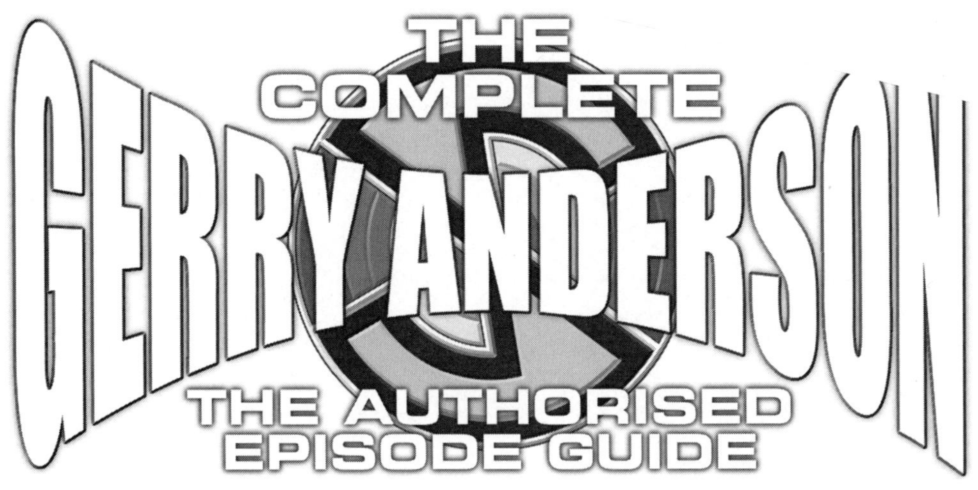
THE
COMPLETE
GERRY ANDERSON
THE AUTHORISED
EPISODE GUIDE

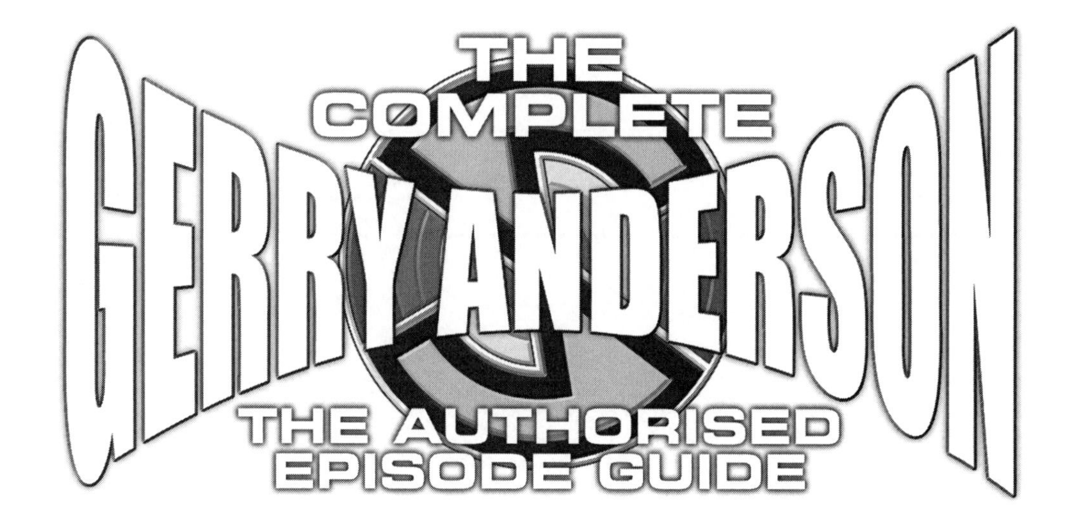

CHRIS BENTLEY

Reynolds & Hearn Ltd
London

Front cover images (clockwise from top left):
Stingray from STINGRAY; Thunderbird 1 from THUNDERBIRDS; Sky One from UFO; Moonbase Alpha from SPACE:1999; the International Rescue team from THUNDERBIRDS; the Mysteron Complex on Mars from CAPTAIN SCARLET AND THE MYSTERONS.

Back cover images:
Gerry Anderson outside Pinewood Studios' M Stage during production of SPACE PRECINCT, 1995; Officer Orrin, Captain Podly and Officer Romek from SPACE PRECINCT.

First published in 2003 by
Reynolds & Hearn Ltd
61a Priory Road
Kew Gardens
Richmond
Surrey TW9 3DH

A CIP catalogue record for this book is available from the British Library.

ISBN 1 903111 41 2

Designed by Chris Bentley.

Printed and bound by Biddles Ltd, Guildford, Surrey.

CONTENTS

C.B.

In memory of
David Watkin
(1961-2003)
who would have loved it
&
Oscar
(1990-2003)
who would have eaten it

G.A.

In memory of
Christine Glanville
(1924-1999)
who was with us right from the start

FOREWORD

To date I have made 17 television series comprising well over 500 episodes, four movies and numerous commercials. Little wonder that when people ask me about a scene in a particular episode my mind goes completely blank. How fortunate I am to be able to consult the appreciation society Fanderson. It was formed over 20 years ago and since then it has grown like topsy. Their chairman is Chris Bentley, a dedicated Anderson aficionado. Sometimes I find it quite spooky when I realise that Chris knows more about me than I do. Who better to write a book about my work?

The Complete Gerry Anderson has been a labour of love for Chris, who spent a great deal of time researching and writing it. He has drawn on his vast knowledge and his huge collection of reference materials to produce what is now, without doubt, the most accurate and informative book that deals with my long career.

Over the years, Chris has become a great friend and has helped me on many occasions to ensure that that my lectures and speeches are accurate. Of course I am able to remember the basic information, but when it comes to specifics like dates and places I have to call Chris, who comes up with the answers in a matter of minutes.

I am delighted that Chris has now turned his hand to writing. I think he has enormous flare and given the right opportunities he will be writing many more books in the future.

There is, however, one subject about which I can say that I know more than Chris – the new series of CAPTAIN SCARLET that has recently commenced production. It is to be a 26-part series with every shot created as a computer generated image. Gone will be the strings, the characters will be able to walk, will have expressions and – finally – they will be able to pick things up without the help of a real hands! The new CAPTAIN SCARLET will be the most advanced and adventurous production I have made.

As I write, there is also a new *Thunderbirds* movie being made here at Pinewood Studios, where my company Anderson Entertainment has its offices. It is being directed by Jonathan Frakes, who directed the *Star Trek* movies *First Contact* and *Insurrection* and of course appeared in the television series as Commander William Riker. Jonathan is a delightful man and I wish him luck with his *Thunderbirds* movie.

CAPTAIN SCARLET and THUNDERBIRDS may be familiar subjects, but they are both about to enter a new era. In the meantime, if you want to discover more about the original versions of these shows and my other productions then you've come to the right place.

Thank you, Chris, and keep up the good work.

Gerry Anderson
Pinewood Studios
March 2003

INTRODUCTION

There cannot be many people still working in the British film and television industry today whose careers in that industry began over half a century ago, and still fewer whose body of work over that time is as prolific and well-loved as that of Gerry Anderson. As a creator and producer of an absolutely unique brand of family entertainment, Gerry changed the face of children's television in the 1960s with a series of programmes that continue to entertain family audiences today and increasing in popularity with every screening. That in itself is remarkable: how many other programmes made in the mid-1960s – of *any* kind – are still being repeated on 21st century British television, let alone ones that can achieve the same kind of viewing figures? What is even more remarkable is that over the last thirty-odd years, Gerry has resolutely refused to rest on his laurels, striving instead to create television programmes that each, in their own way, have pushed back the boundaries of what can be achieved with the medium.

In an industry that notoriously regards anyone over the age of 35 as creatively burnt-out, that Gerry is still working in television production in any capacity is nothing short of miraculous. It is a testament to the man that not only is he working, but he is still pushing back those boundaries in the creation of a new CGI-animated television series of CAPTAIN SCARLET AND THE MYSTERONS (currently the only science-fiction television series in production in this country), embracing the very latest computer animation technology while others of his generation struggle with setting the timer on the video.

On a budget of $30 million, the new 26-episode CAPTAIN SCARLET series will retain all of the characters from the original Supermarionation series, but they will wearing entirely new uniforms, pilot completely redesigned vehicles and be based on a brand new Spectrum Cloudbase. The series will be in production at Pinewood Studios for the next two years and Gerry is quietly confident that it will prove to be his best work yet. Gerry has also recently received very positive interest in REGOR THE RESCUE DOG, a television series idea for younger children, and he is hopeful that he will also be able to bring this programme to our screens in the very near future.

With such a huge body of work behind him – 16 television series totalling 556 individual episodes, four feature films, four television pilot films, a documentary, a music video and over 50 commercials – a single book that covers the output of Gerry Anderson's whole film and television career is long overdue. Previous books have tended to focus on just the four or five most popular series and those that have attempted to spread their net a bit wider have invariably fallen well short of the mark. This book hopes to redress that balance for, despite the emphasis on television implied by the title, between these covers you will find details of all Gerry's screen work – including some films and programmes that didn't quite get off the drawing board.

The guides are broken down into four categories according to the type of production (television series; feature films; television pilots and one-off programmes; miscellaneous projects) and the television series section is then further broken down by era: the pre-ITC series (everything before SUPERCAR), the ITC series (from SUPERCAR to SPACE:1999), and then the post-ITC series (everything after SPACE:1999). The productions are presented in chronological order within the individual sections, but readers who wish to follow the progress of Gerry's career as it developed through all of his various projects may find the Appendix at the back of the book (page 287) useful to navigate their way around.

Each of the series guides begins with an outline of the programme **Format** – all the essential information concerning what the series is actually about and how the main characters fit into it. Certain information in these sections draws on background material developed by the writers and producers during the production of the series but not necessarily revealed on screen in any of the series' episodes. Where conflicts develop between the original background material and what is seen on screen, details appear in the appropriate individual episode entries. A prime example of this is the date in which the events of THUNDERBIRDS take place: the producers' stated intention in the writers' guide and promotional notes was that the television episodes were set in 2065, yet a calendar seen on-screen in the last episode features the date 2026. The 2065 date appears in the 'Format' section while a reference to the 2026 date appears under 'Oops!' in the entry for *Give Or Take A Million*.

In the sidebar next to the 'Format' block is a listing of the series' **Main Characters** and a brief description of their roles. This list includes all named regular characters appearing in the series, including semi-regular or recurring characters. For the purposes of defining which characters are classified as 'regular', I have applied The Harris Rule of Character Recurrence. This rule states that if housekeeper Mrs. Ada Harris can be regarded by the producers (as well as the fans) as a regular character in JOE 90 while only appearing in four of the 30 episodes, then any character who appears in at least four episodes of any given series can also be classed as a regular. For the various puppet series, this must be any puppet which is clearly intended to be the same character in all four episodes, regardless of whether or not the same actor is providing the character's voice on all four occasions – such as the 1st WASP Commander in STINGRAY. For the live-action series, the rule applies to any actor who is clearly intended to be the same character in all four episodes, regardless of whether or not they have any dialogue. Note that this rule is also applied in the 'Regular Cast' listings in the episode entries which include unnamed characters – such as the Main Mission Operatives in SPACE:1999. Some characters may be named in the episode scripts but not on-screen, in which case their scripted names are listed. For example, Anouska Hempel is only credited as 'SHADO Operative' or 'Skydiver Operative' on the end titles of the episodes of UFO in which she appears, but her character is named as Lieutenant Catherine Scott in the script for *Reflections In The Water*. In such cases, space limitations may have prevented me from recognising the specific source of the character's name, but in all instances original production documents have been consulted.

Beneath the 'Format' section, **Production** presents a potted guide to the making of the series with essential behind-the-scenes information such as how the series developed and was commissioned, where and when the episodes were shot, and how much the series cost to make. Notes about the way in which the series was first shown on British television appear in the sidebar alongside or on the next page.

The **Production Credits** section lists all of the production personnel credited on the series' opening, in-show and end titles. The numbers appearing after each credit refer to the individual episodes on which that credit appears, cross-referenced to the **Episode Titles** list in the sidebar. Credits without numbers appear on all episodes of the given series. Some of the 'Production Credits' listings detail members of the production crew whose names are not credited on any of the series' titles, but these are marked with an asterisk. (In the case of SPACE PRECINCT, the availability of full production records presented the unique opportunity to list every member of the production personnel who worked on the series, so those who were not credited on the series' titles appear in a separate **Uncredited Production Personnel** section.)

The episode entries themselves appear in the order in which the episodes were produced, except for those series where the production order is currently unknown, in which case they are presented in the broadcast order recommended by the series' distributor. If even *that* information is not available, the episodes appear in the order in which they were first broadcast on British television.

For each episode entry, the episode title is given as seen on screen, followed by the writer and director credits and a short synopsis of the story. The **Notes** section offers a variety of observations from revelations about the characters or the world they inhabit, to behind-the-scenes information such as alterations to the storyline in different versions of the script, deleted scenes or filming locations. Some entries also include an **Oops!** section which is reserved for continuity errors, production blunders and other kinds of mistakes.

The sidebar next to each episode entry features the **Regular Cast** and **Guest Cast** lists for that episode. For the puppet productions, the 'Regular Voice Cast' list details only the characters who actually have dialogue in that episode. If other main characters appear on-screen without uttering a single word (such as Captain Ochre's very first appearance, in the CAPTAIN SCARLET episode *Winged Assassin*), this will ususally be referred to in the 'Notes' section. For the live-action productions, both cast lists often detail actors who received no credit for their contribution on the end titles.

The **First UK Transmission** date of each episode appears beneath the cast list. As far as it has been possible to verify, these are the premiere transmissions of each *individual* episode as shown around the various ITV regions, rather than the first transmissions of whichever region started to show the series first (as usually listed in other reference works). The difference is very significant as the ITV stations did not always show the episodes in the same order: a station that started screening a particular series months after the others can have ended up screening certain episodes months before them, and some stations even premiered different episodes at the same time. In the most extreme example of this, ATV, Tyne Tees and Border each screened a different new episode of UFO at exactly the same time on the evening of October 7th, 1970, so the broadcast premieres of *Conflict*, *E.S.P.* and *The Sound Of Silence* were simultaneous. UFO is a particular case in point where the previously published broadcast dates from only a single region has led to widely published statements that certain episodes (*The Responsibility Seat* and *The Long Sleep*) were not transmitted until 1973 because of their 'adult' content, yet both episodes were shown as part of Anglia's first run of the series in 1971, and only *The Long Sleep* was considered too 'adult' to be shown before 11.00pm.

For the majority of the Gerry Anderson series, the first UK transmission date is also the world premiere transmission date. However, certain episodes of SPACE:1999 and TERRAHAWKS were shown in the United States or Japan before being seen on British television, so the dates of these transmissions are detailed in the 'Notes' section. All 24 episodes of SPACE PRECINCT were screened in the US before being shown here so those transmission dates are listed separately.

Readers of my two previous books, *The Complete Book of Thunderbirds* (Carlton Books, 2000) and *The Complete Book of Captain Scarlet* (Carlton Books, 2001), will find that much of the information in the THUNDERBIRDS and CAPTAIN SCARLET sections is familiar – the episodes haven't changed since those books were published and the observations I made about them then are still valid. However, I have added quite a bit of new material to those sections that we didn't have room for in the earlier books, including all the **Mysteron Threats** that many readers considered an unfortunate omission from *The Complete Book of Captain Scarlet.* I have also corrected a couple of errors that crept into the episode guides in those earlier books, so where the details don't exactly match up, you can assume that the right information appears here.

Sadly, the sections on THE ADVENTURES OF TWIZZLE, TORCHY THE BATTERY BOY and FOUR FEATHER FALLS are considerably less detailed than those on the later programmes due to the unavailability of a complete set of viewing copies for these three shows. Indeed, only two episodes of THE ADVENTURES OF TWIZZLE are known to be still in existence (*Twizzle And Footso* and *Twizzle Catches Cold*), and while all 39 episodes of FOUR FEATHER FALLS still exist in negative form, prints of all of the episodes do not.

The guides to the feature films, pilot films and miscellaneous projects are presented in much the same way as the television guides with only slight variations that take the different formats into consideration. The feature film guides detail the date of the **UK Premiere** (which is actually the world premiere in all four cases) and the **Aspect Ratio** of each film – the shape of the projected film frame indicated by the width of the picture relative to its height.

What you will not find in the guides is any kind of critical appraisal of the individual productions. I have started from the idea that you have probably come here in search of good, solid information about the programmes you love and really couldn't give a stuff what I personally think of them. Too many guide books of this kind allow the authors to offer their readers the benefit of their opinions, thereby diminishing the book's value as a proper reference work.* Unless the author's opinions tally with yours in every respect (and what are the chances of that happening, eh?), you're inevitably only going to go away infuriated, so we're having none of that nonsense here. If you really want to know which episodes someone you've never met thinks are worth watching and which should never have been committed to celluloid, I'm sure there are plenty of sites on the internet that will adequately satisfy your curiosity.

---

*As the author of just such a guide to SPACE:1999 for *SFX* magazine's free *The Episode Guide to the Galaxy* book, I can hold my hands up and admit that I'm as guilty of it as the next writer, but it was last century and I've learnt my lesson the hard way.

I should perhaps also note that this book limits itself purely to screen projects and as such does not cover any of the spin-off merchandise associated with the various programmes. I mention this only because virtually everyone I have spoken to about the book since it was commissioned seems to have assumed that it would be covering the spin-off novels, comics and records in the same way that my two previous books did, although that was never my intention here. There are occasional references to certain items of merchandise in the programme guides but my apologies if you were also expecting to see something more comprehensive. We had to draw the line somewhere and it seemed that that aspect of Gerry's programmes would perhaps be better served as the subject of an entirely separate book.

Now I'm sure that I've kept you here long enough already, but before I go, I would like to take this opportunity to thank an exceptional bunch of people who were all instrumental in helping to ensure that the material presented in this book is as accurate as possible, namely:

Bob Bailey, Claire Baker and Caroline Raudnitz at Carlton International Media, Ed Bishop, Tim Beddows at Network Video, Kit Bevan, Chris Bowden at Cosgrove Hall Films, Ian Boyce, Stephen Brown, Johnny Byrne, Jonathan Clements, Maxine Cook, Terry Curtis, Jacqueline Dear, Clive Eardley, Cathy Ford, Andrew Frampton, Ian Fryer, Martin Gainsford, Peri Godbold, Peter Gordeno, Neill Gorton, John Hough, Chris King, Stephen La Riviere, Jon Curry, Chris Dale and Elizabeth Gould of *supermarionation.net*, David Lane, Tim Mallett, Dolores Mantez, Don Mead, Zienia Merton, John Needham, David Nightingale, Alan Pattillo, Christopher Penfold, Alan Perry, Andrew Pixley, Michael Prendergast, Arthur Provis, Jonathan Rigby, Adrian Rigelsford, Julie Rogers, Mel Rowlands, Mark Sherwood at Anderson Entertainment, Alan Shubrook, Lynn Simpson, Michelle Skinner of Carlton Visual Entertainment, Andrew Staton, Peter Thomas, Ralph Titterton, Chris Trice, Ken Turner, Jeff Smart, Rowena White, John Wilkinson, Nick Williams, Martin Willey, Keith Wilson, Jaz Wiseman and Dr. Gerard Hutchinson of the Space Science and Technology Department at the Rutherford Appleton Laboratory.

Extra special thanks are due to:

Gerry and Mary Anderson for their friendship, hospitality, support and wonderfully dry sense of humour;

my publishers Marcus Hearn and Richard Reynolds for having sufficient faith in the popularity of Gerry's work to commission the book in the first place as well as the faith in me to write it for them;

and my mother, Joan Bentley, for acting as a sounding board, helping to find obscure nuggets of historical and geographical information, and generally putting up with me over the last six months.

My thanks also to all of the current members of Fanderson who have been patiently waiting for me to finish this so that I can finally get back to concentrating on my club duties again. Now you know why issue 46 of *FAB* magazine was so late!

Chris Bentley
March 2003

GERRY ANDERSON

THE EARLY TELEVISION SERIES

1957-1960

THE ADVENTURES OF TWIZZLE
TORCHY THE BATTERY BOY
FOUR FEATHER FALLS

THE ADVENTURES OF TWIZZLE

Format

Twizzle is a boy doll with red hair, blue trousers and a green wool cap who can 'twizzle' his arms and legs, extending them to any length if he ever wants to reach anything. He lives in a toy shop with his friends but at two shillings and sixpence, he is so expensive that he believes he will never be bought and will stay in the shop forever.

Then one day, a horrid little girl named Sally Cross takes a fancy to Twizzle and bullies the Toy Shop Man into letting her have the toy for only two shillings. Twizzle hides in a Jack-in-the-Box's box where the Toy Shop Man and Sally Cross cannot find him, so the shop-keeper asks the girl to come back the next day. During the night, Twizzle escapes from the shop using his 'twizzling' abilities and runs away. He takes shelter in a dog kennel where he meets Footso, a cat with such big paws that he keeps falling over them. When Twizzle learns that Footso has also run away from home, the two become firm friends and set out to have lots of adventures.

When he saves a doll from a house fire, Twizzle is rewarded with a super racing car but he exchanges it with the Garage Man for a red breakdown truck. With Footso and his new friends Chawky the white-faced golliwog and Jiffy the Broomstick Man, Twizzle decides to use the truck to rescue broken toys, such as Candy Floss the Mama doll, and find them somewhere to live. He and his friends build a town full of log cabins which they name Stray Town and it becomes a sanctuary for all runaway or broken-down toys, including Bouncy the Ball, the Thin Teddy Bear, Jack-in-the-Box and Polly Moppet.

Main Characters

Twizzle
A boy doll who can 'twizzle' his arms and legs to any length

Footso
A black and white cat with enormous paws

Chawky
A white-faced golliwog

Jiffy
The mischievous Broomstick Man who cleans the streets of Stray Town

Candy Floss
A pretty blonde-haired Mama doll who can't say "Mama"

Bouncy
A ball who has lost his bounce and doesn't like being kicked

Sally Cross
A horrid naughty little girl

Production

In 1957, film editor Gerry Anderson and cameraman Arthur Provis established their own film and television production company, AP Films, and set up their fledgling film studios in Islet Park, an Edwardian mansion on the banks of the Thames in Maidenhead, Berkshire. Unfortunately, film production work was unforthcoming and in order to pay the bills, Anderson took on a freelance directorial assignment on the ABC television series MARTIN KANE, PRIVATE INVESTIGATOR, produced by Harry Alan Towers. After six months in business, AP Films was on the verge of bankruptcy when the partners were approached by television merchandising consultant Suzanne Warner, the former publicity director for Howard Hughes. Representing Associated-Rediffusion, Warner invited Anderson and Provis to sub-contract the production of a puppet television series for prolific romantic novelist and children's author Roberta Leigh.

Desperate for work, Anderson and Provis seized the opportunity, resolving to make the best puppet shows that they could. On a meagre budget of £23,400 for 52 thirteen-minute instalments (just £450 per episode), filming began on THE ADVENTURES OF TWIZZLE at the end of July 1957 in the converted ballroom at Islet Park. Anderson set about trying to find puppeteers for the series and was particularly impressed with the work of Joy Laurey, who had television experience operating a character named Mr. Turnip for a live magazine programme. Laurey was employed to make the string puppets for TWIZZLE based on designs by an artist commissioned by Roberta Leigh. She did so by forming the heads from papier mâché, connecting the joints with screw eyes and then stringing them on carpet thread. Laurey also brought on board two puppeteers who had worked for her before, Murray Clark and Christine Glanville.

Although the puppets were made with colourful costumes, the puppet sets built by art director Reg Hill were painted in shades of grey as the series was filmed in black and white. The puppets were operated from above the set on a bridge that was 12 feet off the studio floor. Shooting on 35mm film, the crew filmed from 8.00am to 6.00pm and would then spend the evening rehearsing the action that would be shot the next day. The puppeteers often worked into the night repairing broken strings or repainting and redressing puppets so that everything was ready to film the next morning.

On a schedule that required one episode to be completed every two days, production of THE ADVENTURES OF TWIZZLE took five months. Filming was finally completed early in January 1958, by which time the series had already premiered on Associated-Rediffusion in the London region of the ITV network.

Episode Titles (1-26)

(Listed in broadcast order)

1. **Twizzle And Footso**
2. **Twizzle And Footso Get Caught**
3. **Twizzle Saves The Doll**
4. **The Breakdown Van**
5. **Footso Is Stolen**
6. **Twizzle And The Golliwog**
7. **Jiffy And Chawky Quarrel**
8. **Footso Disappears**
9. **Twizzle And The Broken Down Toy**
10. **Twizzle Builds Stray Town**
11. **A Flag For Stray Town**
12. **Jiffy's New House**
13. **Twizzle And Footso Go Fruit Picking**
14. **Twizzle Has Some Fun**
15. **Twizzle And Candy Floss Open A Cake Shop**
16. **Twizzle Saves The Broken Down Toys**
17. **Twizzle Gets Lost**
18. **Jiffy Opens A Barbers Shop**
19. **Another Racing Car**
20. **Twizzle And His Friends Go To The Circus**
21. **The Toys Go To School**
22. **Bouncy The Ball**
23. **Jack-In-The-Box**
24. **Twizzle Catches Cold**
25. **The Naughty Girl**
26. **Jiffy's New Twigs**

Episode Running Time

13 minutes approx.

PRODUCTION CREDITS

Directed by	**Gerry Anderson**
Produced by	**Roberta Leigh**
Screenplay by	**Roberta Leigh**
Director of Photography	**Arthur Provis**
Art Direction	**Reginald E. Hill**
Puppetry by	**The Laureys**
Editor	**David Elliott**
Lyrics by	**Roberta Leigh**
Music by	**Leslie Clair**
Music Arranged and Conducted by	**Barry Gray**
Camera Operator	**John Read***
Continuity	**Sylvia Thamm***
Voice Artists	**Nancy Nevinson***
	Denise Bryer*
Puppeteers	**Joy Laurey***
	Christine Glanville*
	Murray Clark*
Art Assistant	**Derek Meddings***
Sound Editors	**John Taylor***
	Jean Taylor*

A Banty Books Production
Made by APF
Westrex Recording System

* uncredited

THE EPISODES

TWIZZLE AND FOOTSO — Ep. No. 01

Twizzle, the twizzley toy, runs away from a toy shop and meets Footso, a big black cat with enormous paws. Together they decide to go looking for adventure.
First UK Transmission:
Wednesday, November 13th, 1957, 4.30pm (Associated-Rediffusion)

TWIZZLE AND FOOTSO GET CAUGHT — Ep. No. 02

Twizzle and Footso meet a nasty old man who makes them work for him, but they manage to escape.
First UK Transmission:
Wednesday, November 20th, 1957, 4.30pm (Associated-Rediffusion)

TWIZZLE SAVES THE DOLL — Ep. No. 03

When a doll's house catches fire, Twizzle saves the doll and she gives him a racing car.
First UK Transmission:
Wednesday, November 27th, 1957, 4.30pm (Associated-Rediffusion)

THE BREAKDOWN VAN — Ep. No. 04

Twizzle has an accident with his racing car and exchanges it for a breakdown van.
First UK Transmission:
Wednesday, December 4th, 1957, 4.30pm (Associated-Rediffusion)

FOOTSO IS STOLEN — Ep. No. 05

Footso is stolen by an old woman who makes him drink some magic milk. In the meantime, Twizzle meets a new friend and together they try to save Footso.
First UK Transmission:
Wednesday, December 11th, 1957, 4.30pm (Associated-Rediffusion)

TWIZZLE AND THE GOLLIWOG — Ep. No. 06

Twizzle and Chawky the white-faced golliwog go skating and fall into a lake.
First UK Transmission:
Wednesday, December 18th, 1957, 4.30pm (Associated-Rediffusion)

JIFFY AND CHAWKY QUARREL — Ep. No. 07

Jiffy the Broomstick Man quarrels with Chawky the white-faced golliwog and loses his twigs.
First UK Transmission:
Tuesday, December 31st, 1957, 5.00pm (Associated-Rediffusion)

FOOTSO DISAPPEARS — Ep. No. 08

Footso the cat tries to steal some fish and gets into trouble.
First UK Transmission:
Tuesday, January 7th, 1958, 5.00pm (Associated-Rediffusion)

TWIZZLE AND THE BROKEN DOWN TOY — Ep. No. 09

Twizzle goes to a toy factory and meets Candy Floss, a Mama doll that cannot say "Mama".

First UK Transmission:
Tuesday, January 14th, 1958, 5.00pm (Associated-Rediffusion)

TWIZZLE BUILDS STRAY TOWN — Ep. No. 10

Twizzle builds a town of log cabins so that all of the stray toys in the world can come and live there.

First UK Transmission:
Tuesday, January 21st, 1958, 5.00pm (Associated-Rediffusion)

A FLAG FOR STRAY TOWN — Ep. No. 11

Candy Floss makes a flag and when Twizzle puts it on the flag-pole, something exciting and magical happens.

First UK Transmission:
Tuesday, January 28th, 1958, 5.00pm (Associated-Rediffusion)

JIFFY'S NEW HOUSE — Ep. No. 12

Twizzle builds Jiffy the Broomstick Man a log cabin of his own, but Jiffy does not like it very much.

First UK Transmission:
Tuesday, February 4th, 1958, 5.00pm (Associated-Rediffusion)

TWIZZLE AND FOOTSO GO FRUIT PICKING — Ep. No. 13

Twizzle and Footso the cat have a picnic but Footso swallows a bee.

First UK Transmission:
Tuesday, February 11th, 1958, 5.00pm (Associated-Rediffusion)

TWIZZLE HAS SOME FUN — Ep. No. 14

Footso is so greedy that he eats Twizzle's lunch so Twizzle decides to play a trick on him.

First UK Transmission:
Tuesday, February 18th, 1958, 5.00pm (Associated-Rediffusion)

TWIZZLE AND CANDY FLOSS OPEN A CAKE SHOP — Ep. No. 15

Candy Floss decides to make some toffee but Chawky the white-faced golliwog falls into the mixture.

First UK Transmission:
Tuesday, February 25th, 1958, 5.00pm (Associated-Rediffusion)

TWIZZLE SAVES THE BROKEN DOWN TOYS — Ep. No. 16

Twizzle visits the Toy Inspector and saves all of the broken-down toys. He takes them back with him to live in Stray Town.

First UK Transmission:
Tuesday, March 4th, 1958, 5.00pm (Associated-Rediffusion)

TWIZZLE GETS LOST — Ep. No. 17

Twizzle goes shopping to Tweedle Town and gets lost in the dark, but he is saved by all the broken-down toys.

First UK Transmission:
Tuesday, March 11th, 1958, 5.00pm (Associated-Rediffusion)

JIFFY OPENS A BARBERS SHOP — Ep. No. 18

Jiffy wants to earn money to buy acorns so he decides to open a barbers shop.

First UK Transmission:
Tuesday, March 18th, 1958, 5.00pm (Associated-Rediffusion)

ANOTHER RACING CAR — Ep. No. 19

Twizzle is tired of driving slowly in his breakdown van so he borrows a racing car.

First UK Transmission:
Tuesday, March 25th, 1958, 5.00pm (Associated-Rediffusion)

Regular Voice Cast

Twizzle	**Nancy Nevinson**
Footso	**Denise Bryer**
Narrator	**Nancy Nevinson**

When THE ADVENTURES OF TWIZZLE made its television debut on Associated-Rediffusion in the London region of the ITV network on November 13th, 1957, the AP Films crew were still hard at work filming the series' later episodes. From the eighth episode (*Footso Disappears*) onwards, the series was presented as part of the Tuesday edition of a daily children's programme, JOLLY GOOD TIME, which acted as a frame for each day's individual children's programmes – like an early version of CHILDREN'S ITV. Initially presented by Jimmy Hanley and then by Nevil Whiting from the start of March 1958, the programme's title changed to SMALL TIME from April 15th.

The first run of THE ADVENTURES OF TWIZZLE came to a premature end on November 26th with one episode, *Candy Floss Has A Birthday*, left unscreened. The absence of this episode appears to have been a simple oversight by the programme schedulers and it was finally shown for the first time during a repeat run of the series in 1959.

Episode Titles (27-52)

(Listed in broadcast order)

27. **Twizzle And The Snowman**
28. **Twizzle And The Thin Teddy Bear**
29. **The Lazy Broomstick Man**
30. **Twizzle And Polly Moppet**
31. **Footso And The Magic Seeds**
32. **Footso Has Toothache**
33. **Jiffy And Polly Moppet Quarrel**
34. **Footso Gets A New Tail**
35. **Twizzle Is Naughty**
36. **Twizzle Is Stolen**
37. **Twizzle And The Naughty Breakdown Van**
38. **Twizzle And The Toy Inspector**
39. **Chawky Gets A Present**
40. **Jiffy's Birthday**
41. **The Orange And Banana Tree**
42. **Stray Town Thief**
43. **Footso And The Naughty Girl**
44. **Naughty Polly Moppet**
45. **Polly Moppet Disappears**
46. **Twizzle Goes Fishing**
47. **Twizzle Goes To The Fair**
48. **Twizzle Goes To The Seaside**
49. **Twizzle Goes Camping**
50. **Twizzle Goes To The Zoo**
51. **Twizzle Papers The Cabin**
52. **Candy Floss Has A Birthday**

Episode Running Time

13 minutes approx.

TWIZZLE AND HIS FRIENDS GO TO THE CIRCUS — Ep. No. 20

Twizzle and the toys decide to take a trip to the circus and Footso has a go on the trapeze.
First UK Transmission:
Tuesday, April 1st, 1958, 5.00pm (Associated-Rediffusion)

THE TOYS GO TO SCHOOL — Ep. No. 21

None of the toys can read or write so Twizzle decides to become a teacher.
First UK Transmission:
Tuesday, April 8th, 1958, 5.00pm (Associated-Rediffusion)

BOUNCY THE BALL — Ep. No. 22

Bouncy the ball likes living in Stray Town but he does not like being kicked around.
First UK Transmission:
Tuesday, April 15th, 1958, 4.45pm (Associated-Rediffusion)

JACK-IN-THE-BOX — Ep. No. 23

Twizzle feels jealous when all of the toys make a fuss of Jack-in-the-Box, so he leaves him out in the rain.
First UK Transmission:
Tuesday, April 22nd, 1958, 4.45pm (Associated-Rediffusion)

TWIZZLE CATCHES COLD — Ep. No. 24

Twizzle feels very miserable when he has to go to bed with a cold, but all of the toys cheer him up by bringing him presents.
First UK Transmission:
Tuesday, April 29th, 1958, 4.45pm (Associated-Rediffusion)

THE NAUGHTY GIRL — Ep. No. 25

Twizzle has to rescue the China Doll when she is stolen and locked in a toy cupboard.
First UK Transmission:
Tuesday, May 6th, 1958, 4.45pm (Associated-Rediffusion)

JIFFY'S NEW TWIGS — Ep. No. 26

Jiffy's twigs wear out so the toys go in search of new ones.
First UK Transmission:
Tuesday, May 13th, 1958, 4.45pm (Associated-Rediffusion)

TWIZZLE AND THE SNOWMAN — Ep. No. 27

Twizzle and Footso build a snowman but don't like it when he comes to stay with them.
First UK Transmission:
Tuesday, May 20th, 1958, 4.45pm (Associated-Rediffusion)

TWIZZLE AND THE THIN TEDDY BEAR — Ep. No. 28

Twizzle and Footso decide to find the angry Teddy Bear something to eat.
First UK Transmission:
Tuesday, June 3rd, 1958, 4.45pm (Associated-Rediffusion)

THE LAZY BROOMSTICK MAN — Ep. No. 29

Jiffy refuses to clean the streets of Stray Town until Twizzle thinks of a plan.
First UK Transmission:
Tuesday, June 10th, 1958, 4.45pm (Associated-Rediffusion)

TWIZZLE AND POLLY MOPPET — Ep. No. 30

Twizzle meets a new toy and brings it to Stray Town to help Jiffy the Broomstick Man.
First UK Transmission:
Tuesday, June 17th, 1958, 4.45pm (Associated-Rediffusion)

FOOTSO AND THE MAGIC SEEDS — Ep. No. 31

Chawky the white-faced golliwog doesn't like Footso sleeping in his garden so he plants some magic seeds to give him a fright.
First UK Transmission:
Tuesday, July 8th, 1958, 5.00pm (Associated-Rediffusion)

FOOTSO HAS TOOTHACHE — Ep. No. 32

Footso has a sore tooth, but he doesn't want Twizzle to take him to the dentist.
First UK Transmission:
Tuesday, July 15th, 1958, 5.00pm (Associated-Rediffusion)

JIFFY AND POLLY MOPPET QUARREL — Ep. No. 33

Jiffy the Broomstick Man gets up to mischief once again.
First UK Transmission:
Tuesday, July 22nd, 1958, 5.00pm (Associated-Rediffusion)

FOOTSO GETS A NEW TAIL — Ep. No. 34

When Footso catches his tail in a door, the toys decide to knit him a new one.
First UK Transmission:
Tuesday, July 29th, 1958, 5.00pm (Associated-Rediffusion)

TWIZZLE IS NAUGHTY — Ep. No. 35

Twizzle teases the toys and makes them angry.
First UK Transmission:
Tuesday, August 5th, 1958, 5.00pm (Associated-Rediffusion)

TWIZZLE IS STOLEN — Ep. No. 36

Footso sets out to rescue Twizzle when he is stolen and locked in a bird cage.
First UK Transmission:
Tuesday, August 12th, 1958, 5.00pm (Associated-Rediffusion)

TWIZZLE AND THE NAUGHTY BREAKDOWN VAN — Ep. No. 37

Twizzle decides to build a garage for his breakdown van.
First UK Transmission:
Tuesday, August 19th, 1958, 5.00pm (Associated-Rediffusion)

TWIZZLE AND THE TOY INSPECTOR — Ep. No. 38

Twizzle and Footso make a new friend.
First UK Transmission:
Tuesday, August 26th, 1958, 5.00pm (Associated-Rediffusion)

CHAWKY GETS A PRESENT — Ep. No. 39

Chawky the white-faced golliwog has a surprise when the toys give him a present.
First UK Transmission:
Tuesday, September 2nd, 1958, 5.00pm (Associated-Rediffusion)

JIFFY'S BIRTHDAY — Ep. No. 40

Jiffy the Broomstick Man decides to host a birthday party and all of the broken down toys are invited.
First UK Transmission:
Tuesday, September 9th, 1958, 5.00pm (Associated-Rediffusion)

THE ORANGE AND BANANA TREE — Ep. No. 41

Both oranges and bananas grow on a tree in Stray Town so Twizzle and the toys all have some lovely fruit.
First UK Transmission:
Wednesday, September 17th, 1958, 4.45pm (Associated-Rediffusion)

STRAY TOWN THIEF — Ep. No. 42

There seems to be a thief at large in Stray Town, but the toys manage to clear up the mystery.
First UK Transmission:
Wednesday, September 24th, 1958, 4.45pm (Associated-Rediffusion)

FOOTSO AND THE NAUGHTY GIRL — Ep. No. 43

Footso the cat is in trouble again, but it is not his fault.
First UK Transmission:
Wednesday, October 1st, 1958, 4.45pm (Associated-Rediffusion)

After the 1954 Television Act opened the doors for commercial television broadcasting in the UK, a wealth of opportunities became available for independent television production companies to supply programming for the new ITV service. Controlled and regulated by the Independent Television Authority (ITA), commercial television coverage was divided into regions and sole transmission rights for these regions (franchises) were offered to independent broadcasting companies who paid a levy to the ITA for their licences.

Associated-Rediffusion (A-R) were the very first ITV franchise owners, covering the London area on weekdays. When their programmes went on the air for the first time on September 22nd, 1955, A-R became the UK's first commercial television broadcaster. The weekend franchise for the London area was operated by Lew Grade's Associated TeleVision (ATV) which commenced broadcasting from September 24th, 1955.

In other parts of the country, commercial television viewers had to wait until 1956 for their local franchise holders to start operating. In the Midlands, ATV won the franchise for weekday programming (from February 17th) while ABC Television broadcast at weekends (from February 18th). In Lancashire and Yorkshire, the weekday provider was Granada Television (from May 3rd) with ABC responsible for the weekends (from May 5th). Apart from these regions, the only other area of the country where viewers could receive ITV programmes during the first transmission of THE ADVENTURES OF TWIZZLE was Central Scotland where Scottish Television had begun operating on August 31st, 1957. Other franchises were established over the next five years including TWW and Southern in 1958, Tyne Tees, Anglia and Ulster in 1959, Westward, Border and Grampian in 1961 and Channel Television in 1962.

In 1968, Associated-Rediffusion (or Rediffusion as they were by then known) merged with ABC to resume responsibility for the London weekday franchise as Thames Television.

Roberta Leigh, the creator, writer and producer of THE ADVENTURES OF TWIZZLE and TORCHY THE BATTERY BOY, is a prolific author of children's stories and romantic fiction. Inspired by her ability to create stories and songs to entertain her young son Jeremy, Leigh began her writing career in 1951 with the romance novel *In Name Only* and went on to pen over 100 romance novels over the next 45 years, many of them published under pseudonyms such as Janey Scott and Rachel Lindsay. She has also written 26 books for children, many of them based on her children's television ideas.

After parting company with AP Films and completing work on a second series of TORCHY THE BATTERY BOY, Leigh developed another puppet series for young children, SARA & HOPPITY, in partnership with former AP Films co-founder Arthur Provis as Wonderama Productions. They then went on to make the ambitious puppet science-fiction series SPACE PATROL and a pair of equally ambitious science-fiction pilot films, PAUL STARR and THE SOLARNAUTS, the latter a live-action programme featuring Alex Scott, Derek Fowlds and Jan Leeming.

Neither pilot was commissioned for a full series but in the late Sixties, Leigh went on (without Arthur Provis) to create a pre-school educational series called PICTURE THE WORD and to write and produce two further puppet series, SEND FOR DITHERS and WONDERBOY AND TIGER for ITV before abandoning television production to concentrate on her writing career.

NAUGHTY POLLY MOPPET — Ep. No. 44
Twizzle is angry when Polly Moppet misbehaves.
First UK Transmission:
Wednesday, October 8th, 1958, 4.45pm (Associated-Rediffusion)

POLLY MOPPET DISAPPEARS — Ep. No. 45
Polly Moppet has gone missing, so all the toys go to look for her.
First UK Transmission:
Wednesday, October 15th, 1958, 4.45pm (Associated-Rediffusion)

TWIZZLE GOES FISHING — Ep. No. 46
Twizzle, Footso and Chawky the white-faced golliwog go fishing in the lake, with surprising results.
First UK Transmission:
Wednesday, October 22nd, 1958, 4.45pm (Associated-Rediffusion)

TWIZZLE GOES TO THE FAIR — Ep. No. 47
Twizzle and Candy Floss are glad that Jiffy can fly when they visit the fair.
First UK Transmission:
Wednesday, October 29th, 1958, 4.45pm (Associated-Rediffusion)

TWIZZLE GOES TO THE SEASIDE — Ep. No. 48
Twizzle and Footso go to the beach and Footso gets sand in his whiskers.
First UK Transmission:
Wednesday, November 5th, 1958, 4.45pm (Associated-Rediffusion)

TWIZZLE GOES CAMPING — Ep. No. 49
Twizzle and Footso go off to camp and have some trouble with their tent.
First UK Transmission:
Wednesday, November 12th, 1958, 4.45pm (Associated-Rediffusion)

TWIZZLE GOES TO THE ZOO — Ep. No. 50
Twizzle visits the zoo and the thin Teddy Bear gets into trouble.
First UK Transmission:
Wednesday, November 19th, 1958, 4.45pm (Associated-Rediffusion)

TWIZZLE PAPERS THE CABIN — Ep. No. 51
Twizzle tries his hand at decorating and Jiffy gets into a sticky situation.
First UK Transmission:
Wednesday, November 26th, 1958, 4.45pm (Associated-Rediffusion)

CANDY FLOSS HAS A BIRTHDAY — Ep. No. 52
Twizzle and the broken-down toys help Candy Floss to celebrate her birthday.
First UK Transmission:
Wednesday, June 10th, 1959, 12.47pm (Associated-Rediffusion)

TORCHY THE BATTERY BOY

Format

Children playing in the garden of Mr. Bumble-Drop's house decide to tie their toys to the strings of kites that the old toy-maker has made for them. Then a sudden gust of wind blows the kites away, along with the toys and Bumble-Drop's dog Pom-Pom. Bossy Boots and Bogey Meanymouth insist that Bumble-Drop must find their toys and refuse to play in his garden until he does so. The lonely old man decides to make a toy boy to help find the missing toys and builds a torch battery inside so that he can walk and talk. The toy boy comes to life and Bumble-Drop names him Torchy when he discovers that the torch bulb on his hat has magical properties, projecting a beam that can find any lost object.

Using the magic beam, Torchy soon locates the lost toys and Pom-Pom on a faraway twinkling star. Bumble-Drop builds a rocket out of cardboard and Torchy flies to the star where he discovers Topsy Turvy Land, a magical place where cream buns grow on trees, lollipops grow in fields, puddles are filled with chocolate sauce and everyone can do whatever they please. Torchy soon learns that in Topsy Turvy Land animals can talk and toys can walk when he meets Pom-Pom, Flopsy the rag doll, Pilliwig the clown and Squish the space boy doll.

With the help of his new friends, Torchy builds Frutown, a village in which all of the houses are made out of giant pieces of fruit, and Torchy carves himself a house from an enormous pineapple. He also meets the king of Topsy Turvy Land, the friendly but very dithery King Dithers who lives in a palace made from orange peel. Travelling in the cardboard rocket, Torchy regularly returns to Earth to visit Mr. Bumble-Drop and has many adventures there, in Topsy Turvy Land and on the Moon, helping his friends with their problems and teaching good manners to naughty children.

Production

Roberta Leigh was delighted with the work that Gerry Anderson and Arthur Provis had done on The Adventures Of Twizzle and in October 1958, through her new company, Pelham Films Ltd, she commissioned the production of 26 episodes of a second children's puppet series, Torchy The Battery Boy, at an all-inclusive cost of £27,000. With the budget more than doubled for the production of each episode, Anderson and Provis were able to considerably upgrade the puppets and sets to produce a much more polished television series than Twizzle had been.

Christine Glanville was invited to take charge of the puppets and puppeteers, sculpting the new puppet heads in plasticine and casting them in a mixture of cork dust, glue and methylated spirit which could be treated with sandpaper to get a much smoother finish than had been possible with the rough papier mâché heads of the Twizzle puppets. The puppet bodies were constructed in wood by Glanville's father while her mother made the costumes. The puppet sets also became much more elaborate than the ones used on Twizzle, being entirely three-dimensional, and Reg Hill was assisted in their construction and painting by his new full-time assistant Bob Bell and part-time artist Derek Meddings.

In addition to the budget increase, the AP Films team were also allowed more time in which to make the episodes. The terms of the contract with Roberta Leigh insisted that three episodes should be delivered each month, allowing a full nine months to produce all 26 episodes before the end of June 1959. However, keeping strictly to a filming schedule of one episode in the can each week, Anderson and Provis completed filming before the end of April 1959, by which time Leigh had made it clear that she wanted AP Films to make a further 26 episodes.

However, the partners had already decided to branch out and independently produce their own children's puppet series, so they declined Leigh's commission. As agreed in the contract, she retained sole copyright of Torchy The Battery Boy and ownership of all of the component elements used to make it, including the puppets, sets and music recordings, so the two companies parted amicably and Leigh commissioned Associated British-Pathe to produce the additional 26 episodes under the direction of Vivian Milroy.

Main Characters

Torchy
A boy doll with a torch bulb in his hat that projects a magic beam

Pom-Pom
Mr. Bumble-Drop's poodle, the only poodle in the world with straight hair

Flopsy
A rag doll whose stuffing keeps falling out so that she falls over and cannot remember words properly

Pilliwig
A clown toy who desperately wants to be laughed at

Squish
A mischievous American space boy doll who likes to squirt people with his water pistol

Mr. Bumble-Drop
A kindly old toy-maker who built Torchy and the cardboard rocket

King Dithers
The dithery king of Topsy Turvy Land who lives in the Orange Peel Palace

Bossy Boots
A naughty little girl who likes to tell everyone what to do

Bogey Meanymouth
A naughty little boy who is always up to mischief

The Pollikan Bird
A bird with an enormous beak who is the keeper of King Dithers's crown jewels

The Ting-a-Ling Bird
The most beautiful bird in the world who rings like a bell

Whirly
A humming top who has good ideas when he is spinning

Daffy
The obstinate donkey who pulls King Dithers's royal coach

Sparky
A baby dragon

Ena
A laughing hyena who likes to knit

Clinker
A money box who is always hungry

Gillygolly
A golliwog doll

Pongo the Pirate
A wicked pirate whose sole motive is the acquisition of gold

The Moon Man
The man in the Moon who ensures that the Moon rises every night

Episode Titles (Series One)

(Listed in broadcast order)

1. **Pom-Pom And The Toys**
2. **Topsy Turvy Land**
3. **Torchy And Squish**
4. **The Building Of Frutown**
5. **Torchy And The Broken Rocket**
6. **King Dithers**
7. **Torchy Returns To Earth**
8. **Bossy Boots Goes To Topsy Turvey Land**
9. **Bossy Boots Is Taught A Lesson**
10. **A Bell For The Penny Farthing**
11. **A Trick On Pom-Pom**
12. **Torchy Is Stolen**
13. **King Dithers Loses His Crown**
14. **Pilliwig Gets A Present**
15. **Bad Boy Bogey**
16. **Torchy And The Strange Animal**
17. **Bossy Boots Forgets To Be Good**
18. **The Hungry Money Box**
19. **The Naughty Twins**
20. **The Twins Learn A Lesson**
21. **King Dithers Goes Down To Earth**
22. **Torchy Is Saved At Last**
23. **Torchy And The Man In The Moon**
24. **Bogey And The Statues**
25. **The Moon Falls Asleep**
26. **Torchy's Birthday**

Episode Running Time

13 minutes approx.

PRODUCTION CREDITS (Series One)

Directed by	**Gerry Anderson**
Produced by	**Roberta Leigh**
Screenplay by	**Roberta Leigh**
Director of Photography	**Arthur Provis**
Art Direction	**Reginald E. Hill**
Music & Lyrics by	**Roberta Leigh**
Arranged by	**Barry Gray**
Editorial Supervision	**David Elliott**
Puppetry by	**Christine Glanville**
Operators	**Mary Turner**
	Sam Kemp
	Margaret Carter*
	Murray Clark*
	Buster Stavordale*
Character Voices	**Kenneth Connor**
	Olwyn Griffiths
	Jill Raymond
	Patricia Somerset
Camera Operator	**John Read***
Continuity	**Sylvia Thamm***
Assistant Art Director	**Bob Bell***
Art Assistant	**Derek Meddings***
Sound Editors	**John Taylor***
	Jean Taylor*

Made by APF, Maidenhead
A Pelham Film Production
Sound Westrex System

* uncredited

THE EPISODES

POM-POM AND THE TOYS — Ep. No. 01

When the children's toys and Pom-Pom the poodle are blown away by a gust of wind, Mr. Bumble-Drop makes Torchy the Battery Boy to help him find them. Torchy's magic beam locates Pom-Pom and the missing toys on a twinkling star.
First London Transmission:
Tuesday, February 23rd, 1960, 4.45pm (Associated-Rediffusion)

TOPSY TURVY LAND — Ep. No. 02

Travelling to the twinkling star in the cardboard rocket made by Mr. Bumble-Drop, Torchy arrives in Topsy Turvy Land where animals can talk and toys can walk.
First London Transmission:
Tuesday, March 1st, 1960, 4.45pm (Associated-Rediffusion)

TORCHY AND SQUISH — Ep. No. 03

Torchy meets Squish the space boy toy but is worried in case his battery runs down.
First London Transmission:
Tuesday, March 8th, 1960, 4.45pm (Associated-Rediffusion)

THE BUILDING OF FRUTOWN — Ep. No. 04

Pilliwig the clown helps Torchy and his friends to build some unusual houses to live in.
First London Transmission:
Tuesday, March 15th, 1960, 4.45pm (Associated-Rediffusion)

TORCHY AND THE BROKEN ROCKET — Ep. No. 05

Torchy and Squish meet a new friend called the Ting-a-Ling Bird and together they begin digging for cardboard.
First London Transmission:
Tuesday, March 22nd, 1960, 4.45pm (Associated-Rediffusion)

KING DITHERS — Ep. No. 06

Torchy's search for cardboard to mend his rocket takes him to the Orange Peel Palace where he meets King Dithers, the dithery king of Topsy Turvy Land.
First London Transmission:
Tuesday, March 29th, 1960, 4.45pm (Associated-Rediffusion)

TORCHY RETURNS TO EARTH — Ep. No. 07

Torchy's battery is running low and he cannot operate the rocket to take him back to Earth. Pom-Pom the poodle comes to the rescue.
First London Transmission:
Tuesday, April 5th, 1960, 4.45pm (Associated-Rediffusion)

BOSSY BOOTS GOES TO TOPSY TURVEY LAND — Ep. No. 08

Torchy meets Bossy Boots, a little girl who is rude to grown-ups, who wants her rag doll Flopsy back. Torchy takes her to Topsy Turvy Land in the cardboard rocket.
(Note: The erroneous spelling of 'Turvy' in the title is as seen on screen.)
First London Transmission:
Tuesday, April 12th, 1960, 4.45pm (Associated-Rediffusion)

BOSSY BOOTS IS TAUGHT A LESSON — Ep. No. 09

Bossy Boots is still behaving badly but Flopsy knows just what to do about it.
First London Transmission:
Tuesday, April 19th, 1960, 4.45pm (Associated-Rediffusion)

A BELL FOR THE PENNY-FARTHING — Ep. No. 10

King Dithers gives Torchy a penny-farthing bicycle but he needs to find a bell for it.
First London Transmission:
Tuesday, April 26th, 1960, 4.45pm (Associated-Rediffusion)

A TRICK ON POM-POM — Ep. No. 11

Torchy and Flopsy are so cross at Pom-Pom's conceit when she refuses an invitation to tea that they decide to teach her a lesson and ask Squish and Pilliwig to help them.
First London Transmission:
Tuesday, May 3rd, 1960, 4.45pm (Associated-Rediffusion)

TORCHY IS STOLEN — Ep. No. 12

During a visit to Earth, Torchy is found in the road by Mrs. Meanymouth who takes him home, but Mr. Bumble-Drop and Pom-Pom come to the rescue.
First London Transmission:
Tuesday, May 10th, 1960, 4.45pm (Associated-Rediffusion)

KING DITHERS LOSES HIS CROWN — Ep. No. 13

Torchy and King Dithers search for the King's lost crown and meet a Pollikan Bird.
First London Transmission:
Tuesday, May 17th, 1960, 4.45pm (Associated-Rediffusion)

PILLIWIG GETS A PRESENT — Ep. No. 14

Pilliwig is unhappy because no one will laugh at his jokes. On an island, Torchy and Flopsy meet Ena the laughing hyena who cannot help laughing at Pilliwig.
First London Transmission:
Tuesday, May 24th, 1960, 4.45pm (Associated-Rediffusion)

BAD BOY BOGEY — Ep. No. 15

Torchy learns that Bad Boy Bogey is behaving very badly so Torchy takes him to Topsy Turvy Land where Daffy the donkey helps to give him a lesson in good manners.
First London Transmission:
Tuesday, May 31st, 1960, 4.45pm (Associated-Rediffusion)

TORCHY AND THE STRANGE ANIMAL — Ep. No. 16

Torchy, Flopsy and Pom-Pom meet some toys who are living in fear of a terrible monster but Torchy discovers that it is just a baby dragon called Sparky.
First London Transmission:
Tuesday, June 7th, 1960, 4.45pm (Associated-Rediffusion)

BOSSY BOOTS FORGETS TO BE GOOD — Ep. No. 17

Torchy shines his magic beam down to Earth and finds that Bossy Boots has forgotten how to be good. He decides to teach her a lesson.
First London Transmission:
Tuesday, June 14th, 1960, 4.45pm (Associated-Rediffusion)

THE HUNGRY MONEY BOX — Ep. No. 18

Pongo the pirate steals Clinker's breakfast so Torchy finds him something good to eat.
First London Transmission:
Tuesday, June 21st, 1960, 4.45pm (Associated-Rediffusion)

Regular Voice Cast	
Torchy	**Olwyn Griffiths**
Pom-Pom	**Patricia Somerset**
Flopsy	**Jill Raymond**
Pilliwig	**Kenneth Connor**
Squish	**Patricia Somerset**
Mr. Bumble-Drop	**Kenneth Connor**
King Dithers	**Kenneth Connor**
Bossy Boots	**Jill Raymond**
Pollikan Bird	**Kenneth Connor**
Ting-a-Ling Bird	**Patricia Somerset**
Whirly	**Kenneth Connor**
Daffy	**Kenneth Connor**
Sparky	**Jill Raymond**
Ena	**Patricia Somerset**
Gillygolly	**Kenneth Connor**
Pongo the Pirate	**Kenneth Connor**
Narrator	**Jill Raymond**

Following directly on the heels of a repeat run of THE ADVENTURES OF TWIZZLE, TORCHY THE BATTERY BOY made its debut in the London area of the ITV network in February 1960 as part of the ITV children's programme SMALL TIME. Both series of episodes (26 made by AP Films and 26 by Associated British-Pathe) were screened weekly as a single series of 52 episodes in an entirely unbroken run on the same day at the same time through to February 1961.

Although the earliest of the AP Films episodes had been available for transmission from January 1959, the delayed broadcast of the series by Associated-Rediffusion meant that TORCHY THE BATTERY BOY premiered in the London area just two days before Gerry Anderson's next series FOUR FEATHER FALLS. With TORCHY showing on Tuesdays and FOUR FEATHER FALLS on Thursdays, the two series ran in tandem on Associated-Rediffusion for the next 39 weeks, the only occasion on which two consecutive first-run Gerry Anderson programmes have been screened during the same period in the UK. The local edition of *TV Times* magazine for the week in which both series made their debut (February 21st – 27th, 1960, featuring FOUR FEATHER FALLS on the front cover) carried articles about each programme side by side on a double-page spread.

However, it is understood that TORCHY THE BATTERY BOY was actually shown for the first time in the UK by ABC in the Midlands and Northern regions, bi-weekly from Sunday, January 11th, 1959. Unfortunately, full details of these screenings are not available.

THE NAUGHTY TWINS — Ep. No. 19

The twins, Bobby and Babs, are behaving so badly that Mr. Bumble-Drop sends them to Topsy Turvy Land in the rocket for a lesson in good manners.
First London Transmission:
Tuesday, June 28th, 1960, 4.45pm (Associated-Rediffusion)

THE TWINS LEARN A LESSON — Ep. No. 20

The naughty twins are taught to be good by the Pollikan Bird after they lock King Dithers in the dungeons of the Orange Peel Palace.
First London Transmission:
Tuesday, July 5th, 1960, 4.45pm (Associated-Rediffusion)

KING DITHERS GOES DOWN TO EARTH — Ep. No. 21

King Dithers and the Pollikan Bird set off for Earth to return the rocket to Torchy, but they lose their way and land on the Moon by mistake.
First London Transmission:
Tuesday, July 12th, 1960, 4.45pm (Associated-Rediffusion)

TORCHY IS SAVED AT LAST — Ep. No. 22

Waiting on Earth for King Dithers and the Pollikan Bird to arrive with his rocket, Torchy uses his magic beam to find out why his friends have been delayed.
First London Transmission:
Tuesday, July 19th, 1960, 4.45pm (Associated-Rediffusion)

TORCHY AND THE MAN IN THE MOON — Ep. No. 23

Torchy takes Mr. Bumble-Drop to the Moon and has a very cheesy adventure.
First London Transmission:
Tuesday, July 26th, 1960, 4.45pm (Associated-Rediffusion)

BOGEY AND THE STATUES — Ep. No. 24

Torchy has trouble with Bad Boy Bogey and has to nurse Mr. Bumble-Drop who is in bed with a cold.
First London Transmission:
Tuesday, August 2nd, 1960, 4.45pm (Associated-Rediffusion)

THE MOON FALLS ASLEEP — Ep. No. 25

Torchy and the toys notice that the Moon is not shining. Torchy and Flopsy go to the Moon to find out why but they both have to be rescued by the Moon Man.
First London Transmission:
Tuesday, August 9th, 1960, 4.45pm (Associated-Rediffusion)

TORCHY'S BIRTHDAY — Ep. No. 26

Torchy is upset that he has been left all alone, but the other toys are preparing a special surprise for his birthday with the help of Mr. Bumble-Drop.
First London Transmission:
Tuesday, August 16th, 1960, 4.45pm (Associated-Rediffusion)

PRODUCTION CREDITS (Series Two)

Directed by **Vivian Milroy**
Screenplay, Music & Lyrics by **Roberta Leigh**
Puppetry by **John Wright**, **Jane Tyson**, **Jane Phillips**
Character Voices **Kenneth Connor**, **Olwyn Griffiths**, **Jill Raymond**, **Patricia Somerset**

Music Arranged by **Barry Gray**
Original Production Design by **Reginald E. Hill***
Original Puppets Created by **Christine Glanville***

Produced by Associated British-Pathe for Roberta Leigh

* uncredited

THE EPISODES

The following episodes were not made by Gerry Anderson's AP Films and are primarily included here for completeness. However, many of the elements used in these episodes – such as the puppets, the sets and the music – were created by the AP Films team, and many episodes use footage lifted from the earlier episodes, including the title sequence that appears at the start of each episode.

TORCHY GETS A SURPRISE — Ep. No. 01

Bossy Boots wants to go home to Earth taking Flopsy with her, but Flopsy doesn't want to leave Topsy Turvy Land.
First London Transmission:
Tuesday, August 23rd, 1960, 4.45pm (Associated-Rediffusion)

BANANA BRIDGE — Ep. No. 02

The Orange Juice River overflows its banks, so the toys decide to make a bridge out of a giant banana.
First London Transmission:
Tuesday, August 30th, 1960, 4.45pm (Associated-Rediffusion)

KING DITHERS AND DAFFY — Ep. No. 03

Daffy the donkey is making too much noise, but King Dithers and Torchy think of a good way to keep him quiet.
First London Transmission:
Tuesday, September 6th, 1960, 4.45pm (Associated-Rediffusion)

THE TOYS GET THE COLLYWOBBLES — Ep. No. 04

The toys all get tummy ache, but King Dithers knows just what to do about it.
First London Transmission:
Tuesday, September 13th, 1960, 4.45pm (Associated-Rediffusion)

BOGEY LEARNS ANOTHER LESSON — Ep. No. 05

Bad Boy Bogey is unkind to Flopsy and gets himself into a very strange place.
First London Transmission:
Tuesday, September 20th, 1960, 4.45pm (Associated-Rediffusion)

THE POLLIKAN BIRD IS STOLEN — Ep. No. 06

While holding the Crown Jewels in his beak, the Pollikan Bird is kidnapped by wicked Pongo the pirate.
First London Transmission:
Tuesday, September 27th, 1960, 4.45pm (Associated-Rediffusion)

TORCHY HAS AN ACCIDENT — Ep. No. 07

Torchy accidentally swallows a whistle but Whirly the humming top comes up with an idea to get it out using a magnet.
First London Transmission:
Tuesday, October 4th, 1960, 4.45pm (Associated-Rediffusion)

Episode Titles (Series Two)

(Listed in broadcast order)

1. **Torchy Gets A Surprise**
2. **Banana Bridge**
3. **King Dithers And Daffy**
4. **The Toys Get The Collywobbles**
5. **Bogey Learns Another Lesson**
6. **The Pollikan Bird Is Stolen**
7. **Torchy Has An Accident**
8. **Sparky The Dragon**
9. **Bogey Is Naughty Again**
10. **Pilliwig Cleans The Chimney**
11. **Pongo The Pirate**
12. **King Dithers' Birthday**
13. **Flopsy Goes On A Picnic**
14. **Washing Day In Topsy Turvy Land**
15. **The Gluebell Wood**
16. **Squish Falls Down A Well**
17. **Flopsy In Trouble**
18. **Flopsy Makes A Christmas Pudding**
19. **King Bumble Drop**
20. **A New Suit For Pilliwig**
21. **The Big Storm**
22. **Daffy's Birthday**
23. **Gillygolly In Trouble**
24. **Pom-Pom Gets The Hiccups**
25. **Pongo And The Gold Mine**
26. **The Obstinate Donkey**

Episode Running Time

13 minutes approx.

SPARKY THE DRAGON — Ep. No. 08
When Whirly the humming top has a stiff neck, he finds that Sparky is able to help him.
First London Transmission:
Tuesday, October 11th, 1960, 4.45pm (Associated-Rediffusion)

BOGEY IS NAUGHTY AGAIN — Ep. No. 09
Bad Boy Bogey is nasty to Pom-Pom but after a visit to Topsy Turvy Land, he finds that no-one should ever be unkind to animals.
First London Transmission:
Tuesday, October 18th, 1960, 4.45pm (Associated-Rediffusion)

PILLIWIG CLEANS THE CHIMNEY — Ep. No. 10
Chimney cleaning looks easy enough, but when Pilliwig offers to clean the King's chimney, he gets some unexpected surprises.
First London Transmission:
Tuesday, October 25th, 1960, 4.45pm (Associated-Rediffusion)

PONGO THE PIRATE — Ep. No. 11
When Pongo the pirate kidnaps Flopsy, it is up to Torchy and Sparky to rescue her.
First London Transmission:
Tuesday, November 1st, 1960, 4.45pm (Associated-Rediffusion)

KING DITHERS' BIRTHDAY — Ep. No. 12
All the toys who live in Frutown are invited to the King's birthday party, and have a big surprise when Torchy arrives with his present.
First London Transmission:
Tuesday, November 8th, 1960, 4.45pm (Associated-Rediffusion)

FLOPSY GOES ON A PICNIC — Ep. No. 13
Flopsy decides to go off by herself for a picnic, but she gets a surprise when she opens her picnic basket.
First London Transmission:
Tuesday, November 15th, 1960, 4.45pm (Associated-Rediffusion)

WASHING DAY IN TOPSY TURVY LAND — Ep. No. 14
When Pom-Pom gets washed with the laundry by mistake, the toys try to get her dry again. Sparky's attempt to help only makes matters worse.
First London Transmission:
Tuesday, November 22nd, 1960, 4.45pm (Associated-Rediffusion)

THE GLUEBELL WOOD — Ep. No. 15
Whirly and Sparky plan a big party but find that decorating their cave is not easy. However, a good fairy arrives and they get some unexpected help.
First London Transmission:
Tuesday, November 29th, 1960, 4.45pm (Associated-Rediffusion)

SQUISH FALLS DOWN A WELL — Ep. No. 16
Squish is looking for water and falls into a well in the Magic Wood. Torchy only makes matters worse when he tries to rescue Squish, but Ena and Pilliwig are at hand to help.
First London Transmission:
Tuesday, December 6th, 1960, 4.45pm (Associated-Rediffusion)

FLOPSY IN TROUBLE — Ep. No. 17
Flopsy has a strange accident and as a result is only able to talk backwards. Pom-Pom has a bright idea and finds a way to put things right.
First London Transmission:
Tuesday, December 13th, 1960, 4.45pm (Associated-Rediffusion)

FLOPSY MAKES A CHRISTMAS PUDDING — Ep. No. 18
Torchy brings the King some cheese, but he would rather have Christmas pudding. Flopsy makes a lovely pudding but everyone gets a big surprise when the King cuts it.
First London Transmission:
Tuesday, December 20th, 1960, 4.45pm (Associated-Rediffusion)

Vivian Milroy, the director of the non-AP Films episodes of TORCHY THE BATTERY BOY, was a London-born producer and writer who entered the film industry in 1946. He acted as writer, director and producer of *Don't Say Die* (1950) and wrote the screenplay for *Crow Hollow* (1952), but his work for television was more prolific, scripting plays for the BBC such as EARTHQUAKE IN MACEDONIA and THE INNOCENT CROCODILE. Milroy doubled as both writer and director of THE FISH AND THE ANGEL for the BBC and OUT OF TOUCH for ABC, going on to produce PORTRAIT OF A SCHOOL for Associated-Rediffusion, and DUET FOR TWO HANDS, SIXTY MINUTES TO KILL, THE CAGE and ANN VERONICA for ABC before being chosen to helm the last 26 episodes of TORCHY. He was also the author of the book *Alpine Partisan*, published by Hammond Hammond in 1957.

KING BUMBLE DROP — Ep. No. 19

The toys of Topsy Turvy Land revolt when King Dithers issues some unpopular decrees and the poor King ends up in a dungeon.
First London Transmission:
Tuesday, December 27th, 1960, 4.45pm (Associated-Rediffusion)

A NEW SUIT FOR PILLIWIG — Ep. No. 20

When Pilliwig gets his suit splashed with paint, Ena kindly offers to wash it for him. Somehow the suit is not the same after washing and Flopsy has to come to the rescue.
First London Transmission:
Tuesday, January 3rd, 1961, 4.45pm (Associated-Rediffusion)

THE BIG STORM — Ep. No. 21

A giant hurricane strikes Topsy Turvy Land and the toys seek safety in the mountain caves. But Pom-Pom is missing and when Torchy goes to rescue her, he finds the wind too strong for him and he is whirled away into space.
First London Transmission:
Tuesday, January 10th, 1961, 4.45pm (Associated-Rediffusion)

DAFFY'S BIRTHDAY — Ep. No. 22

When Daffy decides to rest from work on his birthday, Pongo the pirate lures him aboard ship and makes him a prisoner. Torchy and the toys have to think of a way to release their friend.
First London Transmission:
Tuesday, January 17th, 1961, 4.45pm (Associated-Rediffusion)

GILLYGOLLY IN TROUBLE — Ep. No. 23

Gillygolly does not like his curly hair and Pom-Pom wishes her straight hair would curl. She thinks of a way to put matters right, but the scheme is not a success.
First London Transmission:
Tuesday, January 24th, 1961, 4.45pm (Associated-Rediffusion)

POM-POM GETS THE HICCUPS — Ep. No. 24

Poor Pom-Pom has a nasty attack of hiccups after being squirted with water by Squish. The toys think of a way to cure her and it works, but not in the way everyone intended.
First London Transmission:
Tuesday, January 31st, 1961, 4.45pm (Associated-Rediffusion)

PONGO AND THE GOLD MINE — Ep. No. 25

Up to his usual tricks again, Pongo the pirate takes Clinker's money and then imprisons him and Squish in the gold mine. Torchy and the toys come to the rescue and punish the wicked Pongo.
First London Transmission:
Tuesday, February 7th, 1961, 4.45pm (Associated-Rediffusion)

THE OBSTINATE DONKEY — Ep. No. 26

Pongo the naughty pirate appears again and sails away in Daffy's umbrella. Torchy manages to recover the stolen umbrella for Daffy but has to persuade the awkward donkey to pull the King's coach again.
First London Transmission:
Tuesday, February 14th, 1961, 4.45pm (Associated-Rediffusion)

The last 26 episodes of TORCHY THE BATTERY BOY were in production at Associated British-Pathe at the same time as Gerry Anderson's crew at AP Films were making FOUR FEATHER FALLS. The two puppet television series kept actor Kenneth Connor very busy juggling his commitments to providing voices for both series – all of the male characters in TORCHY THE BATTERY BOY, including Mr. Bumble-Drop, Pilliwig and King Dithers, and seven regular characters in FOUR FEATHER FALLS.

Born in London in 1916, Kenneth Connor first appeared on stage at the age of two and performed in revue shows throughout his childhood. After studying to become a professional actor, he made his film debut in *Poison Pen* (1939) but it was the 1950s before he began to appear regularly in films such as Vivian Milroy's *Don't Say Die* (1950), *Miss Robin Hood* (1952), *The Black Rider* (1954) and the classic Ealing comedy *The Ladykillers* (1955). However, at the time of the recording sessions for TORCHY, Connor was best-known for his television appearances in comedy and variety programmes such as A SHOW CALLED FRED, THE CHARLIE FARNSBARNS SHOW, ALFRED MARKS TIME, TWO'S COMPANY and MY PAL BOB.

In 1958, he appeared in the film *Carry On Sergeant* and went on to star in a further 17 films in the long-running 'Carry On...' film series, as well as three CARRY ON CHRISTMAS television specials and the CARRY ON LAUGHING! television series. He also appeared in *Dentist In The Chair* (1960) and its sequel *Dentist On The Job* (1961) and was seen in regular roles in the television sitcoms ROOM AT THE BOTTOM, ON THE HOUSE, RENTAGHOST, HI-DE-HI! and 'ALLO 'ALLO as well as numerous comedy sketch shows. He died in 1993.

FOUR FEATHER FALLS

Main Characters

Sheriff Tex Tucker
The Sheriff of Four Feather Falls, owner of four magic feathers and a fine singing voice

Rocky
Sheriff Tucker's horse who speaks with an English accent by the power of one of Tex's magic feathers

Dusty
Sheriff Tucker's loyal dog, magically endowed with the ability to talk by one of Tex's magic feathers

Grandpa Twink
One of the original pioneers of the American West and the oldest resident of Four Feather Falls

Little Jake
Young grandson of Grandpa Twink

Martha 'Ma' Jones
Elderly proprietor of the Four Feather Falls General Store

Marvin Jackson
Manager of the local bank

Dan Morse
Operator at the Four Feather Falls Telegraph Office

Doc Haggerty
The town's Irish general practitioner

Slim Jim
Owner and bartender of the Denison Saloon

Makooya
A young Indian boy, son of Chief Kallamakooya

Chief Kallamakooya
Chief of a local tribe of friendly Indians who has mysterious magical powers

Pedro
A portly Mexican bandit who often works in collaboration with Fernando

Fernando
A thin Mexican bandit who often works in collaboration with Pedro

Big Ben
A devious horse rustler who wants to take control of Four Feather Falls

Red Scalp
Leader of a tribe of unfriendly Indians who often assists Big Ben in his evil schemes

Format

In Kansas at the end of the 19th century, pioneers of the American West have established a comfortable life in the happy frontier town of Four Feather Falls near Silver City. Wandering cowpoke Tex Tucker is crossing the desert with his horse Rocky and dog Dusty to take up the vacant post of Sheriff in Four Feather Falls when the trio discover a little lost Indian boy. The boy introduces himself as Makooya, son of the powerful Indian Chief Kallamakooya, and Tex decides to take care of the boy and return him to his village.

At sundown, they arrive at a dried-up waterfall and Tex is very concerned that they have no food or drink and a long journey ahead of them. During the night, Makooya calls for his father and Kallamakooya appears in a cloud of smoke, using his mysterious magic powers to replenish the waterfall and make the land around them fertile. When Makooya tells his father how Tex has saved his life, Kallamakooya rewards Tex with four magic feathers: one enables Rocky to talk, another gives Dusty the power of speech and the other two feathers give life to Tex's guns, enabling them to swivel and fire automatically when danger presents itself. Only Tex can hear Rocky and Dusty talking and if he loses the feathers, the animals will lose their voices.

Tex Tucker arrives at Four Feather Falls and becomes Sheriff, protecting the town from horse thieves, cattle rustlers, bank robbers, con men out to swindle the townsfolk of their hard-earned savings, a local tribe of unfriendly Indians and the evil schemes of the desperate Mexican bandits Pedro and Fernando. In return, he is welcomed with open arms by the friendly townsfolk – Grandpa Twink and his grandson Little Jake, General Store owner Ma Jones, bank manager Marvin Jackson, Irish doctor Doc Haggerty, saloon owner Slim Jim and telegraph operator Dan Morse – who can always find the time to listen to one of Tex's songs.

Production

After two years of producing children's television series for Roberta Leigh, Gerry Anderson and Arthur Provis felt that it was time for AP Films to use the profits from the earlier programmes to produce a pilot puppet television episode of their own, and see if they could interest any of the new commercial television companies in commissioning a full series. Developing a concept created by composer Barry Gray, the partners secretly carried out design and construction work on new puppets and sets during filming of the later episodes of TORCHY THE BATTERY BOY, fearing that Leigh might cancel their contract for TORCHY and withhold payment on the completed episodes if she were to get wind of their plans.

FOUR FEATHER FALLS was envisaged as a fantasy Western series which would pioneer the use of a more sophisticated style of puppetry than had previously been seen in TWIZZLE and TORCHY, as Anderson and his team began to experiment with electronics to match dialogue to the puppets' mouth movements. The fibre-glass head of each new puppet was fitted with a solenoid connected to special tungsten wires (with a diameter of 1/5,000th of an inch) on which the puppet was strung. Pulses could then be fed down the wires from a tape recorder running pre-recorded dialogue, and these pulses would trigger the solenoid to operate the puppet's mouth perfectly in sync. This was the embryonic form of the technique which eventually became known as Supermarionation.

On a budget of £6,000, a pilot episode of FOUR FEATHER FALLS was made at Islet Park in April 1959, but then Anderson and Provis parted company, disagreeing over the risky steps that Anderson wanted to take to expand the business. Anderson successfully sold FOUR FEATHER FALLS to Granada Television and in June 1959, AP Films moved into new, larger premises at a unit in Ipswich Road on the Slough Trading Estate, previously owned by visual effects innovator Les Bowie. The puppet soundstage at the new studio premises was four times larger than the ballroom at Islet Park and enabled Reg Hill and Bob Bell to construct a puppet set for the town of Four Feather Falls that was 30 feet long and 15 feet wide. Here, the AP Films crew made a further 38 episodes of the series between June 1959 and April 1960.

PRODUCTION CREDITS (Series One)

Produced by	**Gerry Anderson**
Directed by	**Gerry Anderson**
	David Elliott
	Alan Pattillo
Screenplay by	**Mary Cathcart Borer**
	Phil Wrestler
	Jill Allgood
"Four Feather Falls" is based on an Original Idea by	**Gerry Anderson & Barry Gray**
Director of Photography	**Arthur Provis**
	John Read
Art Director	**Reg Hill**
Special Effects	**John Read**
Music & Lyrics Composed, Arranged & Conducted by	**Barry Gray**
Puppetry by	**Christine Glanville**
	Mary Turner
	Roger Woodburn
Character Voices	**Kenneth Connor**
	Nicholas Parsons
	Denise Bryer
	David Graham
Tex Tucker's Singing Voice by	**Michael Holliday**
Harmonica	**Tommy Reilly**
Editorial Supervision	**David Elliott**
Production Supervisor	**Jim Marsh**
Film Editor	**Bert Rule**
	Alan Pattillo
	David Elliott
Dubbing Editor	**John Kelly**
Assistant Art Director	**Bob Bell**
Continuity	**Sylvia Thamm**
Technical Adviser	**Bob Ledbetter**
Puppet Properties	**Arthur Cripps***
	Peter Cook*
	Jack Whitehead*
Special Effects Assistants	**Derek Meddings***
	Albert Scott*

Made by APF
in association with Granada TV Network
Sound Westrex System

* uncredited

Episode Titles

(Listed in production order)

1. **How It Began**
2. **Kidnapped**
3. **Pedro Has A Plan**
4. **Pedro's Pardon**
5. **A Close Shave**
6. **Indian Attack**
7. **Sheriff For A Day**
8. **Dusty Becomes Deputy**
9. **Gunrunners**
10. **Trouble At Yellow Gulch**
11. **Frame-Up**
12. **Gold Diggers**
13. **Gold Is Where You Find It**
14. **Trapped**
15. **Best Laid Plans**
16. **Escort**
17. **The Toughest Guy In The West**
18. **Ghost Of A Chance**
19. **Gunplay**
20. **A Lawman Rides Alone**
21. **Jailbreak**
22. **A Little Bit Of Luck**
23. **Landgrabbers**
24. **Once A Lawman**
25. **Election Day**
26. **Gunfight On Main Street**
27. **A Bad Name**
28. **Horse Thieves**
29. **The Ma Jones Story**
30. **Bandits Abroad**
31. **A Cure For Everything**
32. **Teething Troubles**
33. **Buffalo Rocky**
34. **Safe As Houses**
35. **First Train Through**
36. **Happy Birthday**
37. **Fancy Shootin'**
38. **Ambush**
39. **Ride 'Em Cowboy**

Episode Running Time

13 minutes approx.

THE EPISODES

HOW IT BEGAN — Prod. No. 01

Wandering cowboy Tex Tucker is crossing the desert with his horse Rocky and dog Dusty when they find a lost Indian boy named Makooya. They look after the boy and his father Kallamakooya rewards Tex with four magic feathers.
First UK Transmission:
Thursday, February 25th, 1960, 5.00pm (ITV Network)

KIDNAPPED — Prod. No. 02

Little Makooya is seriously ill but Doc Haggerty has been kidnapped by Pedro and Fernando. Sheriff Tucker sets out to rescue the Doc before it is too late.
First UK Transmission:
Thursday, October 6th, 1960, 5.00pm (ITV Network)

PEDRO HAS A PLAN — Prod. No. 03

Pedro attempts to outwit Sheriff Tucker by exchanging the magic feathers in his hat with ordinary ones. When Rocky and Dusty discover what has happened, they race to save their master.
First UK Transmission:
Thursday, March 17th, 1960, 5.00pm (ITV Network)

PEDRO'S PARDON — Prod. No. 04

Sheriff Tucker releases Pedro from jail when he promises to behave and become a respectable citizen, but the bandit is soon up to his old tricks.
First UK Transmission:
Thursday, April 14th, 1960, 5.00pm (ITV Network)

A CLOSE SHAVE — Prod. No. 05

Pedro and Red Scalp plan to lure Sheriff Tucker away from town so that they can rob the bank, but Dusty eavesdrops on their conversation and forewarns him.
First UK Transmission:
Thursday, April 7th, 1960, 5.00pm (ITV Network)

Regular Voice Cast

Sheriff Tex Tucker	**Nicholas Parsons**
Rocky	**Kenneth Connor**
Dusty	**Kenneth Connor**
Grandpa Twink	**David Graham**
Little Jake	**Denise Bryer**
Ma Jones	**Denise Bryer**
Marvin Jackson	**Kenneth Connor**
Dan Morse	**Nicholas Parsons**
Doc Haggerty	**Kenneth Connor**
Slim Jim	**Kenneth Connor**
Makooya	**Denise Bryer**
Chief Kallamakooya	**Kenneth Connor**
Pedro	**Kenneth Connor**
Fernando	**David Graham**
Big Ben	**David Graham**
Red Scalp	**David Graham**

FOUR FEATHER FALLS made its television debut on February 25th, 1960 with a broadcast that was fully networked by the various weekday ITV franchise holders in operation at that time: Associated-Rediffusion, ATV (in the Midlands area), Granada, Southern, Scottish, TWW, Tyne-Tees, Anglia and Ulster. Although screenings of some episodes of THE ADVENTURES OF TWIZZLE and TORCHY THE BATTERY BOY were networked as part of the JOLLY GOOD TIME and SMALL TIME strands, the network screening of FOUR FEATHER FALLS was the first time that a Gerry Anderson series received a complete first run network broadcast in the UK.

The next Gerry Anderson series to receive such treatment by a UK broadcaster was LAVENDER CASTLE, 39 years later.

INDIAN ATTACK — Prod. No. 06

Caught red-handed attempting to steal Grandpa Twink's gold watch, Fernando convinces Sheriff Tucker that Indians are about to attack the town.
First UK Transmission:
Thursday, March 31st, 1960, 5.00pm (ITV Network)

SHERIFF FOR A DAY — Prod. No. 07

Sheriff Tucker leaves his magic guns with Little Jake while he investigates a threat to the stagecoach, but Tex is ambushed by Big Ben who plans to take over the town.
First UK Transmission:
Thursday, March 24th, 1960, 5.00pm (ITV Network)

DUSTY BECOMES DEPUTY — Prod. No. 08

Sheriff Tucker appoints Dusty as Deputy Sheriff while he investigates a prairie fire and when Pedro and Fernando arrive to rob the bank, Deputy Dusty races to alert Tex.
First UK Transmission:
Thursday, May 19th, 1960, 5.00pm (ITV Network)

GUNRUNNERS — Prod. No. 09

Sheriff Tucker learns that Big Ben is selling guns to Red Scalp so he sets out to catch them red-handed at a meeting on Dead Man's Hill.
First UK Transmission:
Thursday, April 28th, 1960, 5.00pm (ITV Network)

TROUBLE AT YELLOW GULCH — Prod. No. 10

Pedro and Fernando establish a toll-gate at Yellow Gulch Pass so Ma Jones and Grandpa Twink take an alternative route through Black Boulder Canyon. Sheriff Tucker discovers that the bandits intend to block off the canyon and sets out to stop them.
First UK Transmission:
Thursday, March 3rd, 1960, 5.00pm (ITV Network)

FRAME-UP — Prod. No. 11

After Rocky is stolen by a phantom horse thief, Sheriff Tucker buys a spare horse from Ruff Snyder and realises that he has been framed when the corrupt Sheriff Jameson of Silver City discovers stolen money in the horse's saddle bag.
First UK Transmission:
Thursday, March 10th, 1960, 5.00pm (ITV Network)

GOLD DIGGERS — Prod. No. 12

Pedro and Fernando find a map of buried gold beneath the jail and plan for one of them to be arrested so that they can dig it up, but Sheriff Tucker learns what they are up to.
First UK Transmission:
Thursday, September 15th, 1960, 5.00pm (ITV Network)

GOLD IS WHERE YOU FIND IT — Prod. No. 13

Pedro and Fernando claim that they have found gold at Yellow Gulch and sell worthless shares in the property to the townsfolk. When Sheriff Tucker learns of the scheme, he enlists the help of Dan Morse and Ma Jones to play the bandits at their own game.
First UK Transmission:
Thursday, September 8th, 1960, 5.00pm (ITV Network)

TRAPPED — Prod. No. 14

Little Jake and Makooya discover Red Scalp making counterfeit money in a cave by the creek but the Indian pushes a boulder over the cave entrance, trapping them inside.
First UK Transmission:
Thursday, May 12th, 1960, 5.00pm (ITV Network)

BEST LAID PLANS — Prod. No. 15

Pedro and Fernando find a new ally in Hank Frisbee who takes a room over the bank so that they can cut their way in, but Tex is alerted when Pedro gets stuck in the hole.
First UK Transmission:
Thursday, June 30th, 1960, 5.00pm (ITV Network)

ESCORT — Prod. No. 16

Pedro and Fernando discover that Mr. Huckenbacker is on his way to town with a shipment of gold. They come up with a plan to outwit Sheriff Tucker who is riding escort.
First UK Transmission:
Thursday, June 16th, 1960, 5.00pm (ITV Network)

THE TOUGHEST GUY IN THE WEST — Prod. No. 17

Everyone pokes fun at Grandpa Twink when he boasts of his youthful exploits, but the old timer gets a chance to prove that he can still take on a tribe of Comanches.
First UK Transmission:
Thursday, April 21st, 1960, 5.00pm (ITV Network)

GHOST OF A CHANCE — Prod. No. 18

Marvin Jackson is handling the sale of a gold mine and seeks Sheriff Tucker's help to rid the mine of a pair of ghosts, actually Pedro and Fernando in league with Zeke Harman who wants to purchase the mine at a cheaper price.
First UK Transmission:
Thursday, July 28th, 1960, 5.00pm (ITV Network)

GUNPLAY — Prod. No. 19

Cattle rustlers Johnny Pasto and The Nevada Kid challenge Sheriff Tucker to a shooting match and Tex proves that he doesn't need to rely on his magic guns to uphold the law.
First UK Transmission:
Thursday, June 9th, 1960, 5.00pm (ITV Network)

A LAWMAN RIDES ALONE — Prod. No. 20

Blackie and Whitey Strutt are wanted for robbing the Wells Fargo office in Laredo so Sheriff Tucker rides out alone to bring the brothers to justice.
First UK Transmission:
Thursday, May 26th, 1960, 5.00pm (ITV Network)

JAILBREAK — Prod. No. 21

A $500 reward has been posted for the capture of Zack Morrill, a notorious cattle rustler and horse thief, so Pedro and Fernando plot with Morrill to claim the money.
First UK Transmission:
Thursday, May 5th, 1960, 5.00pm (ITV Network)

A LITTLE BIT OF LUCK — Prod. No. 22

While Tex is out of town, Four Feather Falls is under the protection of the corrupt Marshal Ike Burns who is in league with Big Ben. The townsfolk form a Vigilante Committee to protect a shipment of gold dust, but Burns sets a trap...
First UK Transmission:
Thursday, June 13th, 1960, 5.00pm (ITV Network)

LANDGRABBERS — Prod. No. 23

Morg Fenton has allied himself with Big Ben and Red Scalp to force Abe Weeks to sell his ranch, but Sheriff Tucker cannot intervene as the ranch is not within his territory.
First UK Transmission:
Thursday, August 11th, 1960, 5.00pm (ITV Network)

ONCE A LAWMAN — Prod. No. 24

The bank has been robbed three times in the last two weeks by the Voise Gang and the townsfolk decide that it is time that Four Feather Falls had a new Sheriff. Disgusted, Tex rides out of town and joins the outlaws as they plan to rob the next gold shipment.
First UK Transmission:
Thursday, August 4th, 1960, 5.00pm (ITV Network)

ELECTION DAY — Prod. No. 25

Pedro challenges Tex Tucker for the post of Sheriff when Election Day arrives, planning to rig the election by switching the ballot box with one full of forged votes.
First UK Transmission:
Thursday, July 14th, 1960, 5.00pm (ITV Network)

FOUR FEATHER FALLS developed from Barry Gray's initial idea for a series entitled 'Two Gun Tex Tucker', which would have been set in the early West hick town of Spelltown, Kansas. Even at this early stage, the hero was outlined as Sheriff Tex Tucker, a lawman reputed to be able to hit two flying nickels with a two-gun double draw, but the other characters would have included Tucker's fat assistant Buster, the town's handy man Slim Jim and general store owner Jake Jollymop.

These ideas were refined into a second series concept titled 'Two Gun Tex Of Texas', now set in Four Feather Falls, Kansas, a small happy Western town with a touch of magic about it. Buster became the Sheriff's simple but well-meaning assistant with a tendency towards over-eating while Jake Jollymop transformed into Timothy Twinkle, also known as Ole Twink, the town's oldest resident. The supporting cast would have included Rusty, Tucker's mongrel dog, and Snowy, his horse, both of whom can converse with the Sheriff due to the magical properties of the town. Mrs. Martha Lollipop was to be the owner of the general store who was assisted by Red Feather, an Indian of the Kiowa tribe. The town doctor was to be Doctor Angus McDougall, the series' Scots storyteller, known to the residents as Jock the Doc. Other characters included Ole Twink's grandson Little Jake, the town sourpuss Old Grump, and several undefined characters named Merry Myrtle, Mary Lou, Big Chief Four Feather and Saucy Sal.

The singing voice of Sheriff Tex Tucker in FOUR FEATHER FALLS was provided by Michael Holliday, a popular performer with a voice that listeners often mistook for that of Bing Crosby, although his crooning style was actually closer to that of Perry Como.

Born Michael Miller in Liverpool on November 24th, 1928, the singer changed his name by deed poll to Michael Milne before he eventually adopted the stage name of Michael Holliday for his recording career. He released his first single, 'Sixteen Tons', on the Columbia label in 1956 and followed it up with the Top 20 hits 'Nothin' To Do' and 'Hot Diggity'. He was at the peak of his popularity in 1958 when his tenth single, 'The Story Of My Life' by Burt Bacharach and Hal David, topped the UK chart in January and a follow-up single, 'Stairway Of Love', made it to number three. He had another number one hit in 1959 with 'Starry Eyed' and hosted his own popular television show RELAX WITH MIKE.

Holliday was, therefore, understandably regarded as a major star when Gerry Anderson signed him up to perform songs for FOUR FEATHER FALLS for the princely sum of £2,000, a third of the pilot episode's total budget. He recorded six songs for the series: 'Four Feather Falls', 'The Phantom Rider', 'The Rick-Rick-A-Rackety Train', 'Happy Hearts And Friendly Faces', 'My Home Town' and the end titles song 'Two Gun Tex Of Texas'. 'Four Feather Falls' is often mistaken for the series' theme tune, but it actually only appears as performed by Tex Tucker during various episodes (such as *How It Began* and *Kidnapped*). All six songs were recorded at the Gate Studios in Elstree on May 20th, 1959.

Michael Holliday released over 30 singles between 1956 and 1963, but a loss of popularity and a series of failures in the early 1960s led to depression and he died of a drugs overdose at his home in Croydon, Surrey on October 29th, 1963, aged 34. Two further records, 'Dear Heart' and 'My Last Date (With You)', were released posthumously the following year.

GUNFIGHT ON MAIN STREET — Prod. No. 26

Cass Morgan, an old friend of Sheriff Tucker's, comes to Four Feather Falls in search of two men who robbed a stagecoach and killed his kid brother. Tex warns Morgan that he cannot take the law into his own hands but Morgan is determined to exact his revenge.
First UK Transmission:
Thursday, July 21st, 1960, 5.00pm (ITV Network)

A BAD NAME — Prod. No. 27

Big Ben is framed on a charge of cattle rustling by rancher Lucky Chance and his foreman Matt Ames. Despite Ben's record, Sheriff Tucker decides to investigate and try to prove his innocence.
First UK Transmission:
Thursday, September 29th, 1960, 5.00pm (ITV Network)

HORSE THIEVES — Prod. No. 28

Pedro and Fernando agree to help Big Ben with some horse rustling and take every horse in town, including Rocky. With Dusty's help, Rocky escapes and leads Sheriff Tucker to the villains' hideout.
First UK Transmission:
Thursday, November 10th, 1960, 5.00pm (ITV Network)

THE MA JONES STORY — Prod. No. 29

Two strangers arrive in town with a scheme to put Ma Jones out of business and take over her store. When Sheriff Tucker learns that the heartbroken Ma Jones has left town, he sorts out the crooks before setting out into the desert to find her.
First UK Transmission:
Thursday, July 7th, 1960, 5.00pm (ITV Network)

BANDITS ABROAD — Prod. No. 30

A reward of $200 is offered for the capture of the notorious bandit Pancho Gomez. Pedro comes up with a plan to claim the reward when he notices Fernando's uncanny resemblance to Gomez, but mistaken identity proves to be their undoing.
First UK Transmission:
Thursday, August 25th, 1960, 5.00pm (ITV Network)

A CURE FOR EVERYTHING — Prod. No. 31

Scragg and Wright, a pair of medicine peddlers, arrive in town claiming to have a cure for everything. The townsfolk are so impressed that Doc is soon out of business, until Sheriff Tucker discovers that their curative is nothing but coloured water.
First UK Transmission:
Thursday, August 18th, 1960, 5.00pm (ITV Network)

TEETHING TROUBLES — Prod. No. 32

When Rocky gets toothache, nothing will persuade him to visit a dentist until Sheriff Tucker agrees to have a tooth extracted as well, but the horse's previous visit to an Indian medicine man has unexpected results.
First UK Transmission:
Thursday, October 13th, 1960, 5.00pm (ITV Network)

BUFFALO ROCKY — Prod. No. 33

Rocky uses his horse-sense to help Sheriff Tucker to track down a clever horse thief who is using false buffalo hooves to cover his tracks. Unfortunately, the horse thief steals Rocky as well but Tex is soon hot on his trail.
First UK Transmission:
Thursday, June 2nd, 1960, 5.00pm (ITV Network)

SAFE AS HOUSES — Prod. No. 34

The townsfolk's money is perfectly safe in the bank, but bank manager Marvin Jackson finds it hard to persuade them to keep it there when smart-talking Missouri Mike arrives in town selling safes which come with a free bottle of brandy.
First UK Transmission:
Thursday, September 1st, 1960, 5.00pm (ITV Network)

FIRST TRAIN THROUGH — Prod. No. 35

Sheriff Tucker suspects foul play when an avalanche threatens the new Canyon Railroad line through Four Feather Falls. He discovers that the foreman and a hired hand are in the pay of a rival company to sabotage the project and force Canyon out of business.
First UK Transmission:
Thursday, September 22nd, 1960, 5.00pm (ITV Network)

HAPPY BIRTHDAY — Prod. No. 36

Little Jake and Grandpa Twink head for Silver City to get Sheriff Tucker a pair of gauntlets for his birthday but time is against them and they will probably miss Tex's birthday party. Chief Kallamakooya uses his magic to save the day.
First UK Transmission:
Thursday, November 17th, 1960, 5.00pm (ITV Network)

FANCY SHOOTIN' — Prod. No. 37

Little Jake is thrilled when the fastest gun in the West, Buck Reevers, arrives in town with his shooting circus, but Sheriff Tucker anticipates trouble when a real gunman, Lightnin' Lew, decides to join in the fun.
First UK Transmission:
Thursday, October 20th, 1960, 5.00pm (ITV Network)

AMBUSH — Prod. No. 38

Red Scalp's war party ambush the train from Dallas and steal $10,000, kidnapping bank messenger William Haddon as they make their escape. Sheriff Tucker is soon on their trail and discovers that Haddon is actually in league with Red Scalp.
First UK Transmission:
Thursday, November 3rd, 1960, 5.00pm (ITV Network)

RIDE 'EM COWBOY — Prod. No. 39

The townsfolk present Sheriff Tucker with a new pair of boots to wear while riding in the rodeo. Tex's opponent Bart Stevens, a crack rider from Silver City, is determined to win at any cost and hires Pedro and Fernando to steal Tex's boots.
First UK Transmission:
Thursday, October 27th, 1960, 5.00pm (ITV Network)

FOUR FEATHER FALLS' harmonica player Tommy Reilly was the world's leading classical harmonica performer who perfected his style in German prison camps when he became the first Canadian to be arrested by the Gestapo in the early days of the Second World War. He was also a skilled violinist, juggler and tightrope walker.

Born in Guelph, Ontario on August 21st, 1919, Reilly found fame through concert and radio appearances in the late 1940s, but his recording career was established in 1951 at Parlophone, who teamed him with producer George Martin. Although primarily known for his harmonica recordings of classical works by Heitor Villa-Lobos, Malcolm Arnold and Ralph Vaughan Williams, Reilly also became much in demand to lend his talents to music for films, radio and television productions, including the themes for THE NAVY LARK, DIXON OF DOCK GREEN, LAST OF THE SUMMER WINE, THE SINGING DETECTIVE and the scores for *Those Magnificent Men In Their Flying Machines* (1965) and *Midnight Cowboy* (1969).

Appointed MBE in 1992, Tommy Reilly died in September 2000, aged 81.

THE ITC TELEVISION SERIES

1960-1976

SUPERCAR
FIREBALL XL5
STINGRAY
THUNDERBIRDS
CAPTAIN SCARLET AND THE MYSTERONS
JOE 90
THE SECRET SERVICE
UFO
THE PROTECTORS
SPACE:1999

SUPERCAR

Format

It is the early 1960s and at the remote Black Rock laboratory in the Nevada Desert, a pair of scientists, Professor Rudolph Popkiss and Dr. Horatio Beaker, have spent five years developing Supercar – an incredible futuristic vehicle which can travel on land, in the air, in space and underwater – with the assistance of ace test pilot Mike Mercury. Intended as a multi-purpose vehicle to assist the scientific community, Supercar also quickly proves its worth as a rescue vehicle when the initial test-flight is used to rescue Bill Gibson, his 10 year-old brother Jimmy and chimpanzee Mitch, lost at sea in a life raft. Jimmy and Mitch are invited to join Mike, Popkiss and Beaker at Black Rock and swiftly become valued members of the Supercar team.

Fitted with retractable wings to stabilise the vehicle during flight, Supercar operates on port and starboard engines charged to 1500 rpm at full boost and has vertical take-off and landing capability. The car is equipped with a pressurized cockpit and bullet-proof canopy, a rear-mounted aerial for radio transmission and reception, heating and de-icing systems, a periscope and electromagnetic grabs capable of lifting over 70 tons. Supercar is also equipped with the revolutionary Clear-Vu system which penetrates conditions of poor visibility (low light levels, fog, snow, heavy cloud, etc.) and projects a clear picture on a monitor screen in the cockpit, as well as Videoplan, a navigation aid which plots the car's geographical position and projects its location on a contour map. The car can be fitted with a hood-mounted rocket launcher or ultrasonic gun for demolition or defence.

During flight at high altitude (between 5,000 and 82,000 feet), Supercar is capable of a maximum speed of 4,500 mph but normally travels at a low safe cruising speed of 1,500 mph, particularly on long-distance journeys. The car achieves maximum fuel economy flying at an altitude of 50,000 feet with a safe cruising speed of 2,500 mph. Over land at low altitude (just a few feet above a road surface, for example), Supercar can be driven at a maximum speed of 150 mph, but will normally travel at just over 100 mph for safety. The car can be operated entirely by remote control from a remote console at the Black Rock laboratory. Seating is available for a pilot and three passengers, although there is also room in the trunk to carry a chimpanzee.

Main Characters

Mike Mercury
Fearless and courageous Supercar pilot and leader of the Supercar team

Professor Rudolph Popkiss
Austrian scientist, co-inventor of Supercar and expert cook who emigrated to America in 1929

Dr. Horatio Beaker
English scientist, co-inventor of Supercar, a skilled musician and impersonator, and nephew of the Laird of Inverlachan

Jimmy Gibson
10 year-old younger brother of astronaut Bill Gibson, an apprentice mechanic and skilled musician

Mitch
Mischievous but highly intelligent chimpanzee and Jimmy Gibson's best friend

Bill Gibson
Astronaut, pilot and deep sea diver who operates the Gibson's Transport courier service

Masterspy
Greedy mid-European industrial espionage agent who will stop at nothing to get his hands on Supercar

Zarin
Cowardly and incompetent mid-European assistant to Masterspy

Production

Flush with the success of FOUR FEATHER FALLS, Gerry Anderson approached Granada Television in the spring of 1960 with a new series idea, SUPERCAR, detailed in a lavish brochure produced by Reg Hill. However, Granada executives refused to speak to Anderson so the brochure sat in a drawer until a chance call to Frank Sherwin Green led to a meeting with Lew Grade, head of ATV and its international distribution arm, ITC. Grade was impressed with the AP Films set-up at Ipswich Road in Slough and offered to finance a 26-episode series of SUPERCAR if Anderson could cut the projected budget of £3,000 per episode in half. After working all night tightening the costs, Anderson was forced to admit that he could only reduce the budget by a third, but Grade nonetheless agreed to commission the series at this price, on the condition that the first episodes would be ready to broadcast within six months.

The most expensive single element of the production was the creation of Supercar itself, built at one third scale to accommodate the puppet characters. Designed by Reg Hill and constructed in geleton by Bill James, the seven feet long and three feet wide model weighed 50 lbs and cost the company £1,000. Studio floor effects and model effects were supervised by Derek Meddings, now working for the company full-time, having contributed to the earlier series only on a part-time basis. Extensive use was made of back-projection equipment for the sky backgrounds of both puppet and model sequences, using aerial footage shot by Anderson and director of photography John Read from a twin-engined Airspeed Oxford supplied by Film Aviation Services Ltd.

The initial 26 episodes filmed between September 1960 and May 1961 were a race against time for the AP Films team, as the first episodes began to be broadcast on ATV London at the end of January 1961. A further 13 episodes were commissioned by Grade and filmed in a second production block from October 1961 to January 1962.

Although the two production blocks of SUPERCAR episodes were not intended to constitute two separate seasons, they nonetheless ended up being shown that way during the series' initial UK broadcast in the ATV London region of the ITV network: the first 26 episodes shown between January 28th and August 6th, 1961 and the last 13 between February 4th and April 29th, 1962.

However, in other regions where broadcasts of the series did not commence until September 1961, the 39 episodes were shown in a single run with no break between the two blocks.

Episode Titles

(Listed in production order)

Series One

1. **Rescue**
2. **Amazonian Adventure**
3. **The Talisman Of Sargon**
4. **False Alarm**
5. **What Goes Up**
6. **Keep It Cool**
7. **Grounded**
8. **Jungle Hazard**
9. **High Tension**
10. **A Little Art**
11. **Island Incident**
12. **Ice-Fall**
13. **The Tracking Of Masterspy**
14. **Phantom Piper**
15. **Deep Seven**
16. **Pirate Plunder**
17. **Flight Of Fancy**
18. **Hostage**
19. **The Sunken Temple**
20. **Trapped In The Depths**
21. **Crash Landing**
22. **The Dragon Of Ho Meng**
23. **The Lost City**
24. **The Magic Carpet**
25. **The White Line**
26. **Supercar "Take One"**

Series Two

27. **The Runaway Train**
28. **Precious Cargo**
29. **Operation Superstork**
30. **Hi-Jack**
31. **Calling Charlie Queen**
32. **Space For Mitch**
33. **The Sky's The Limit**
34. **70-B-Lo**
35. **Atomic Witch Hunt**
36. **Jail Break**
37. **The Day That Time Stood Still**
38. **Transatlantic Cable**
39. **King Kool**

Episode Running Time

25 minutes approx.

PRODUCTION CREDITS (Series One: 1 - 26)

Produced by **Gerry Anderson**
Director of Photography **John Read**
Art Director **Reg Hill**
Dialogue Direction **Sylvia Thamm**
From an Original Idea by **Gerry Anderson** & **Reg Hill**
Music Composed, Arranged and Conducted by **Barry Gray**
Editor **Gordon Davie** *(1-8, 11, 13, 15, 19, 21, 23-25)*
Bill Harris *(9, 10, 12, 14, 16-18, 20, 22, 26)*
Sound Editor **Archie Ludski** *(1-10, 12, 14, 17, 23)*
John Peverill *(11, 13, 15, 16, 18-22, 24-26)*
Camera Operator **Julien Lugrin**
Aviation Facilities by **Film Aviation Services Ltd**
Character Voices **David Graham**, **George Murcell**, **Graydon Gould**, **Sylvia Thamm***
Puppets Made and Operated by **Christine Glanville**, **Mary Turner**, **Roger Woodburn**
Second Unit Operator **Cecil Stavordale**
Title Song Performed by **Mike Sammes***

Filmed by APF
at A.P. Film Studios, Slough
Sound – Westrex System
Processing by Kays Laboratories Ltd
In Association with ATV
Associated TeleVision Ltd
An ITC Worldwide Distribution

PRODUCTION CREDITS (Series Two: 27 - 39)

Produced by **Gerry Anderson**
Director of Photography **John Read**
Art Supervisor **Reg Hill**
Production Supervisor **David Elliott**
Lighting Cameraman **Ian Struthers**
Dialogue Direction **Sylvia Anderson**
From an Original Idea by **Gerry Anderson** & **Reg Hill**
Music Composed, Arranged and Conducted by **Barry Gray**
Editor **John Kelly** *(27, 29, 31, 33, 35, 37, 39)*
Gordon Davie *(28, 30, 32, 34, 36, 38)*
Sound Editor **John Peverill**
Camera Operator **Julien Lugrin** *(27, 29, 31, 33, 35, 37, 39)*
Geoff Meldrum *(28, 30, 32, 34, 36, 38)*
Puppetry Supervision **Christine Glanville**, **Mary Turner**
Art Director **Bob Bell**
Special Effects **Derek Meddings**
Character Voices **David Graham**, **Graydon Gould**, **Sylvia Anderson**, **Cyril Shaps**
Title Song Performed by **The Mike Sammes Singers***
Assistant Editor **David Lane***

Filmed in Supermarionation by APF
at A.P. Film Studios, Slough
Sound – Westrex System
Processing by Kays Laboratories Ltd
In Association with ATV
Associated TeleVision Ltd
An ITC Worldwide Distribution

* uncredited

Supermarionation

The term 'Supermarionation' appeared for the first time on the end title credits of the last 13 episodes of Supercar. Pioneered during the production of Four Feather Falls, Supermarionation describes all of the sophisticated puppetry techniques employed by the AP Films/Century 21 production teams (lips that move in synchronisation with speech by feeding electronic pulses converted from the recorded dialogue track down the control wires to solenoids inside the puppets' heads; interchangeable puppet heads with a variety of different expressions; control wires painted to match the background to render them almost invisible and, later, wire-free under-control puppets) combined with the full range of film production facilities normally employed in live-action filming, including 35mm Arriflex film cameras (with Pye industrial cameras in place of the optical viewer), back-projection, front-projection, location filming, state-of-the-art visual effects and full orchestral music scores.

RESCUE — Prod. No. 01

Story by **Martin & Hugh Woodhouse** Directed by **David Elliott**

Bill and Jimmy Gibson and their pet chimpanzee Mitch are stranded in a life raft after their aircraft, Falcon 25, suffers engine failure and ditches into the sea 30 miles from Devil's Point. Bill is injured in the crash and the trio are left without any supplies when Mitch playfully throws them overboard. A heavy fog settles and the Navy rescue helicopter is unable to locate the raft, so Mike Mercury suggests to Professor Popkiss and Dr. Beaker that Supercar be given a test run to rescue the Gibsons and Mitch, using Beaker's Clear-Vu apparatus to find them in the fog. However, Popkiss refuses to jeopardise five years' work on the car by sending it out on a mission without properly completing its test programme...

Notes

This episode has no on-screen title. A number of filming techniques that were subsequently used throughout the series are pioneered here, including the extensive use of back projection in both model and puppet sequences for sea and sky backgrounds, and real hands wearing rubber gloves with painted fingernails (to make them look more 'puppet-like') for close-up shots.

Regular Voice Cast

Mike Mercury	**Graydon Gould**
Prof. Rudolph Popkiss	**George Murcell**
Dr. Horatio Beaker	**David Graham**
Jimmy Gibson	**Sylvia Thamm**
Mitch	**David Graham**
Bill Gibson	**David Graham**

Guest Voice Cast

Hudson Field Rescue	**Graydon Gould**
Navy 49	**George Murcell**
Newsreader	**Graydon Gould**

First UK Transmission

Saturday, January 28th, 1961
5.40pm (ATV London)

AMAZONIAN ADVENTURE — Prod. No. 02

Story by **Martin & Hugh Woodhouse** Directed by **Alan Pattillo**

Mitch is seriously ill and Dr. Beaker diagnoses that he has contracted a form of sleeping sickness which can only be cured by ingesting the leaves of the t'logi, a rare plant which grows in the Amazon Basin. Mike and Beaker set off in Supercar and fly to South America to find the plant but as they search the Amazon jungle they are captured by natives of the Tuaga tribe, identified by Beaker as the last surviving head hunters on the South American continent. The pair are imprisoned in a hut but Mike escapes by cutting through the wall. He then races back to Supercar so that he can use it to scare the natives before their Medicine Man completes his strange ritual by cutting off Beaker's head!

Notes

It is somewhat unusual to see severed heads in a 1960s children's television series.

Oops!

Beaker states that the trip to the Amazon is his first flight in Supercar, so it would be a mistake for this episode to be broadcast after *The Talisman Of Sargon* and *False Alarm* – as it was during the initial ITV transmission run in 1961/62.

Regular Voice Cast

Mike Mercury	**Graydon Gould**
Prof. Rudolph Popkiss	**George Murcell**
Dr. Horatio Beaker	**David Graham**
Jimmy Gibson	**Sylvia Thamm**
Mitch	**David Graham**

Guest Voice Cast

Medicine Man	**George Murcell**
Warrior	**David Graham**

First UK Transmission

Saturday, March 4th, 1961
5.40pm (ATV London)

THE TALISMAN OF SARGON — Prod. No. 03

Story by **Martin & Hugh Woodhouse** Directed by **David Elliott**

Masterspy learns of the whereabouts of the lost Talisman of Sargon the Sumerian, carved from a single priceless emerald and hidden in the burial temple of Sargon at Ka-Kabul. He is hired to find the Talisman by Mustapha Bey who covets the power that the gem is reputed to bring its owner. But the exact location is inscribed on a tablet in cuneiform so Masterspy masquerades as Dr. Julius Mettanik to persuade Beaker to translate it for him. After Beaker realises Mettanik's true identity, he races to the temple in Supercar with Mike, Jimmy and Mitch, but Masterspy and Zarin have already penetrated Sargon's tomb and located the emerald. When the Supercar team arrive and enter the tomb, Masterspy closes the secret entrance, trapping them inside!

Notes

This episode introduces Masterspy and his assistant Zarin, although the dialogue makes it clear that the Supercar team already know them from previous encounters. The characters go on to appear in nine further episodes and are finally detained by the authorities in *Transatlantic Cable*. Sargon was the king of the ancient Babylonian city of Akkad who united the Sumerian cities around 2300 BC.

Regular Voice Cast

Mike Mercury	**Graydon Gould**
Prof. Rudolph Popkiss	**George Murcell**
Dr. Horatio Beaker	**David Graham**
Jimmy Gibson	**Sylvia Thamm**
Mitch	**David Graham**
Masterspy	**George Murcell**
Zarin	**David Graham**

Guest Voice Cast

Mustapha Bey	**David Graham**

First UK Transmission

Saturday, February 18th, 1961
5.40pm (ATV London)

FALSE ALARM

Prod. No. 04

Story by **Martin & Hugh Woodhouse** Directed by **Alan Pattillo**

Regular Voice Cast

Mike Mercury	**Graydon Gould**
Prof. Rudolph Popkiss	**George Murcell**
Dr. Horatio Beaker	**David Graham**
Jimmy Gibson	**Sylvia Thamm**
Mitch	**David Graham**
Masterspy	**George Murcell**
Zarin	**David Graham**

First UK Transmission

Saturday, February 11th, 1961
5.40pm (ATV London)

The Supercar team have just successfully completed tests on an improved remote control system when Popkiss receives a call from Sergeant Petrie of the Nevada State Police requesting his help to rescue a pair of geologists in distress in the mountains. Mike and Beaker set off immediately in Supercar, unaware that Sergeant Petrie is actually Masterspy who has plans to steal Supercar. Arriving in the mountains after dark, Mike and Beaker set up camp to wait until first light before starting to search for the non-existent geologists, but while the pair are sleeping, Masterspy dopes them with ether from their own first aid kit and ties them up. With nobody to stop them, Masterspy and Zarin take control of Supercar and fly away, but they have not counted on Mitch playing with the directional control lever of the new remote control unit...

Oops!

Mike says that the Sierra Nevada mountains are 180 miles north-east of Black Rock, but the only thing 180 miles south-west of the Sierra Nevada mountains is the Californian coast. When Masterspy turns on the Clear-Vu, Popkiss's monitor shows a Videoplan graphic instead of a Clear-Vu picture.

WHAT GOES UP

Prod. No. 05

Story by **Martin & Hugh Woodhouse** Directed by **David Elliott**

Regular Voice Cast

Mike Mercury	**Graydon Gould**
Prof. Rudolph Popkiss	**George Murcell**
Dr. Horatio Beaker	**David Graham**
Jimmy Gibson	**Sylvia Thamm**
Mitch	**David Graham**

Guest Voice Cast

Colonel Lewis	**Graydon Gould**
South Dakota	**David Graham**
Cape Canaveral	**George Murcell**
Patterson Field	**Graydon Gould**

First UK Transmission

Saturday, February 25th, 1961
5.40pm (ATV London)

The Supercar team are assisting Air Force Colonel Lewis with Project Fourth of July, monitoring readings from a canister of new rocket fuel launched into the stratosphere on a balloon. The capsule is too dangerous to attempt a controlled landing so it is to be detonated by remote control, but the remote trigger fails, leaving the capsule in danger of falling to Earth in the middle of the city. Dressed in a foil suit to protect him from cosmic radiation, Mike launches into the stratosphere in Supercar in an attempt to destroy the canister with a rocket launcher mounted on Supercar's bonnet, but the canopy springs a leak and Mike starts losing pressure...

Notes

Colonel Lewis is described as the first person outside the original team to learn of the existence of Supercar. This is the first time that Supercar has travelled to such a high altitude. When Mike talks about the 'Chicago Fire' he is referring to the Great Chicago Fire which swept through the city between the 8th and 10th of October, 1871, leaving 300 people dead, 90,000 homeless and property damage estimated at $200 million. Mike wears Beaker's winter underwear for his journey into the stratosphere.

KEEP IT COOL

Prod. No. 06

Story by **Martin & Hugh Woodhouse** Directed by **Alan Pattillo**

Regular Voice Cast

Mike Mercury	**Graydon Gould**
Prof. Rudolph Popkiss	**George Murcell**
Dr. Horatio Beaker	**David Graham**
Jimmy Gibson	**Sylvia Thamm**
Mitch	**David Graham**
Bill Gibson	**David Graham**
Masterspy	**George Murcell**
Zarin	**David Graham**

First UK Transmission

Saturday, March 25th, 1961
5.40pm (ATV London)

Beaker and Bill Gibson are travelling back to the Black Rock laboratory with a cargo of Beaker's new unstable high octane fuel, crossing the desert at night with the fuel cans in a refrigerator unit as the highly volatile chemical explodes above freezing point. However, Masterspy and Zarin have changed the signposts on their route and Bill and Beaker become hopelessly lost. Then Bill's truck crashes into a rock left in the road by Masterspy, leaving them stranded in the desert with the fridge batteries running down and dawn approaching. Mike races to their location in Supercar with fresh batteries, but Bill and Beaker are captured by Masterspy who steals a sample of the fuel...

Notes

Bill Gibson operates a transport service, Gibson's Transport, which "carries anything anywhere." Masterspy makes an oblique reference to the events of *False Alarm*. Having previously been marked 'Trans-Cambodian Expedition 1933' in *The Talisman Of Sargon*, Masterspy's van now bears a sign for 'Cactus Exterminators Inc.' Voice artist David Graham spends much of the episode talking to himself as both Bill Gibson and Dr. Beaker.

GROUNDED — Prod. No. 07

Story by **Martin & Hugh Woodhouse** Directed by **David Elliott**

Supercar is being fitted with a new portable control unit at JFP Electronics Ltd. in England when disgruntled employee Harper and his assistant Judd break into managing director J. Farleigh Prothero's safe and steal the control unit's printed circuits. When the theft is discovered, the Supercar team dissuade Prothero from calling in the police so as to avoid publicity. Then Harper calls Beaker to admit the theft and inform him that he will be leaving the country in one hour from a flying club at Monk's Norton near Birmingham. Mike prepares to set off in Supercar to intercept the villains, but he discovers that Harper has sabotaged the vehicle's starboard wing leaving Supercar grounded!

Notes

Mitch does not join the rest of the team in England as the weather is too cold for him and he would have to be placed in quarantine for the duration of their visit. This episode introduces secondary regular villains Harper and Judd, who also appear in *Phantom Piper* and *Hostage*. As Mike races to Monk's Norton in Supercar, the back projection footage actually does depict a motorway journey to Birmingham on the M1.

Regular Voice Cast

Mike Mercury	**Graydon Gould**
Prof. Rudolph Popkiss	**George Murcell**
Dr. Horatio Beaker	**David Graham**
Jimmy Gibson	**Sylvia Thamm**
Mitch	**David Graham**

Guest Voice Cast

Harper	**George Murcell**
Ben Judd	**David Graham**
J. Farleigh Prothero	**David Graham**
Secretary	**Sylvia Thamm**

First UK Transmission

Saturday, March 18th, 1961
5.40pm (ATV London)

JUNGLE HAZARD — Prod. No. 08

Story by **Martin & Hugh Woodhouse** Directed by **Alan Pattillo**

Intending to take over a rubber-rich estate at Tinipoor in Malaya that has recently been inherited by Felicity Farnsworth from her late father, Masterspy and Zarin approach Felicity with an offer to purchase the estate. They plan to do away with Felicity if she does not agree to sell, but when she writes to her cousin Dr. Beaker, describing the villainous pair in her letter, he fears the worst and races to the estate with Mike in Supercar. Meanwhile, Masterspy has offered to escort Felicity on a journey to Guam-Husang and they have already set off into the jungle by the time Mike and Beaker arrive. Beaker follows their trail on foot, guiding Mike in Supercar by radio, but Masterspy cuts the ropes on a bridge over a swamp as Felicity is crossing...

Notes

The Felicity Farnsworth puppet is essentially a duplicate of the Beaker puppet with a full wig, lipstick and a dress. We learn that Beaker's forename is Horatio as Felicity calls out to him from the swamp. Felicity makes a second appearance in the series in *Phantom Piper*. It is somewhat unusual for an episode of a 1960s children's television series to end with a lady's knickers falling down.

Regular Voice Cast

Mike Mercury	**Graydon Gould**
Prof. Rudolph Popkiss	**George Murcell**
Dr. Horatio Beaker	**David Graham**
Jimmy Gibson	**Sylvia Thamm**
Mitch	**David Graham**
Masterspy	**George Murcell**
Zarin	**David Graham**

Guest Voice Cast

Felicity Farnsworth	**Sylvia Thamm**
Raman	**David Graham**

First UK Transmission

Saturday, April 1st, 1961
5.40pm (ATV London)

HIGH TENSION — Prod. No. 09

Story by **Martin & Hugh Woodhouse** Directed by **David Elliott**

While shopping in Carson City, Beaker accepts a lift from a pair of strangers looking for the road to Bonneville Flats, unaware that his travelling companions are Masterspy and Zarin. By the time he realises his mistake, Beaker is a prisoner and the trio are well on their way to Ghost Green Wells, a group of craters in the desert where Masterspy intends to offer Beaker in exchange for Supercar. He calls Popkiss with his instructions and Mike sets off in Supercar, planning to land half a mile from the craters and make the rest of the way on foot while Popkiss flies Supercar to the rendezvous on remote control. However, this plan depends upon Mike being able to fly Supercar to a landing in glide mode so as not to alert Masterspy with the sound of the vehicle's motors, but without the vertical thrust motors activated, the operation is a dangerous one...

Notes

As if to make up for their geographical bloomer about the Sierra Nevada mountains in *False Alarm*, script writers Martin & Hugh Woodhouse have clearly checked an atlas for this episode: Beaker tells Masterspy that the Bonneville Salt Flats are 300 miles from Carson City, which they are.

Regular Voice Cast

Mike Mercury	**Graydon Gould**
Prof. Rudolph Popkiss	**George Murcell**
Dr. Horatio Beaker	**David Graham**
Jimmy Gibson	**Sylvia Thamm**
Mitch	**David Graham**
Masterspy	**George Murcell**
Zarin	**David Graham**

First UK Transmission

Saturday, April 8th, 1961
5.40pm (ATV London)

A LITTLE ART

Prod. No. 10

Story by **Martin & Hugh Woodhouse** Directed by **Alan Pattillo**

Dr. Beaker has bought a painting, 'Mexican Plain' by forger Bud Hassler, from art dealer Steindorf who then learns from ex-con Jodie Mellon that the painting shows the exact spot where Hassler buried his counterfeit plates just before he was caught. Steindorf attempts to buy the painting back from Beaker, but the doctor refuses to sell. Steindorf and Mellon break into the laboratory and steal the painting, unaware that Beaker has sprayed the canvas with a solvent to dissolve the top layer in the belief that the artist may have painted over a masterpiece. However, Beaker has kept a photo of the painting, so when Mike recognises the mountain range depicted in it, he and Beaker fly there in Supercar to find out why the painting was stolen.

Notes

Bud Hassler was arrested near the Mexican border on March 5th, 1929, which Steindorf says was 30 years ago. Popkiss recalls the Hassler case being in all the papers just after he came to America in 1929. Mike refers to the events of *Amazonian Adventure* when he recalls flying over the Sleeper Range on the trip to South America. The telephone number of the Black Rock laboratory is Black Rock 1.

Regular Voice Cast

Mike Mercury	**Graydon Gould**
Prof. Rudolph Popkiss	**George Murcell**
Dr. Horatio Beaker	**David Graham**
Jimmy Gibson	**Sylvia Thamm**
Mitch	**David Graham**

Guest Voice Cast

Steindorf	**David Graham**
Jodie Mellon	**Graydon Gould**
Switchboard Operator	**Sylvia Thamm**

First UK Transmission

Saturday, May 13th, 1961
5.40pm (ATV London)

ISLAND INCIDENT

Prod. No. 11

Story by **Martin & Hugh Woodhouse** Directed by **David Elliott**

Called to a rendezvous in Southern California, Mike meets General Sebastian Caprilo de la Festiola LaGuava, President of the islands of Pelota in the Pacific, who has been usurped by his brother Colonel Humberto LaGuava. Humberto has transformed Pelota into a corrupt police state and the General asks for Mike's assistance to restore him to power. With the General aboard, Mike flies Supercar to Pelota, but as they approach the main island seaboard Supercar is spotted by one of Humberto's guards who believes that he has seen a flying saucer. The Colonel orders his army to shoot the craft down and as they open fire, Mike sends Supercar into a dive and crashes into the sea...

Notes

Mike refers to the events of *False Alarm* when he warns about phoney distress calls.

Oops!

Mike says he will mark the location of the rendezvous on Clear-Vu, but the screen shows a Videoplan image. Supercar's canopy is clearly open as it dives into the sea and is still open as the car approaches the island underwater.

Regular Voice Cast

Mike Mercury	**Graydon Gould**
Prof. Rudolph Popkiss	**George Murcell**
Dr. Horatio Beaker	**David Graham**
Jimmy Gibson	**Sylvia Thamm**
Mitch	**David Graham**

Guest Voice Cast

General Sebastian LaGuava	**David Graham**
Colonel Humberto LaGuava	**David Graham**
Guard Pablo	**George Murcell**

First UK Transmission

Saturday, April 15th, 1961
5.40pm (ATV London)

ICE-FALL

Prod. No. 12

Story by **Martin & Hugh Woodhouse** Directed by **Desmond Saunders**

The Supercar team take a short break to picnic in the mountains where Beaker intends to explore an underground cave network in search of a frozen waterfall that he has read about. So as not to get lost, Beaker ties a piece of string to an outcrop at the cave entrance and unwinds the thread from a ball as he makes his way through the tunnels. Unfortunately, Mitch unties the string and follows the doctor, so when Beaker finally finds the ice-fall and Mitch appears tangled in string, the doctor realises that he is completely lost. Examining the ice-fall, Beaker discovers ancient cave drawings behind the ice curtain, but then a sudden cave-in traps him there and without the trail of string, the rest of the team have no way to find him!

Notes

This is the first time that all five members of the Supercar team have travelled in the car at once, as Mitch was absent from the team's trip to England in *Grounded*. This is the only episode to feature no other characters apart from the Supercar team (although there are no other human characters in *Crash Landing*, that episode features an appearance by Mitch's girlfriend).

Regular Voice Cast

Mike Mercury	**Graydon Gould**
Prof. Rudolph Popkiss	**George Murcell**
Dr. Horatio Beaker	**David Graham**
Jimmy Gibson	**Sylvia Thamm**
Mitch	**David Graham**

First UK Transmission

Saturday, April 22nd, 1961
5.40pm (ATV London)

THE TRACKING OF MASTERSPY Prod. No. 13

Story by **Martin & Hugh Woodhouse** Directed by **David Elliott**

Dr. Beaker has just completed work on a new direction-finding apparatus as a navigation aid for Supercar when Mike returns from town to report that he has been approached by a journalist from the Grayburn News Agency and interviewed about Supercar. However, the journalist was Masterspy in disguise and Mike has been tailed by Zarin back to Black Rock, enabling Masterspy to pinpoint the laboratory's secret location. Masterspy arrives in the workshop and threatens to destroy Supercar by igniting leaked aviation spirit unless the team hand over the plans for Supercar and Beaker's new device. Damaging some of the equipment, Masterspy makes his escape, but the device he has taken is a radio transmitter which enables Mike to track him in Supercar...

Notes

Zarin details the location of the Black Rock laboratory to be east of Carson City at a spot some 10 miles east of Walker Lake (the real Black Rock desert is about 150 miles north of this location). The elevator illustrates that the laboratory building has floor levels and the workshop is on the third of these with the gallery on the fourth. Masterspy's office is in room 565 of the Skelton Building on East 49th Street in New York.

Regular Voice Cast

Mike Mercury	**Graydon Gould**
Prof. Rudolph Popkiss	**George Murcell**
Dr. Horatio Beaker	**David Graham**
Jimmy Gibson	**Sylvia Thamm**
Mitch	**David Graham**
Masterspy	**George Murcell**
Zarin	**David Graham**

First UK Transmission

Sunday, July 30th, 1961
5.15pm (ATV London)

PHANTOM PIPER Prod. No. 14

Story by **Martin & Hugh Woodhouse** Directed by **Alan Pattillo**

Felicity Farnsworth calls Beaker to ask the Supercar team to investigate the appearance of the Phantom Piper of Inverlachan at Castle McCrail in Scotland. The phantom is considered to be an ill omen heralding disaster and Beaker fears that Felicity may be in acute danger, so the entire team take off for Scotland. Anticipating foul play, Mike lands the car on the moors away from the castle and while he and Beaker keep watch on the southern battlements, Popkiss and Jimmy meet Beaker's uncle Angus McCrail, the Laird of Inverlachan, and his faithful retainer Campbell. On the stroke of midnight, the piper begins to play, but his visibility on the Clear-Vu screen confirms that he is not a ghost at all and Mike suspects a plot to steal the Laird's priceless Cairngorn of McCrail.

Notes

Inverlachen is 7,000 miles from Black Rock. Harper appears but has no dialogue.

Oops!

The team are happy to take Mitch to Scotland here and yet were so concerned about the weather and quarantine that they left him behind when they visited England in *Grounded*.

Regular Voice Cast

Mike Mercury	**Graydon Gould**
Prof. Rudolph Popkiss	**George Murcell**
Dr. Horatio Beaker	**David Graham**
Jimmy Gibson	**Sylvia Thamm**
Mitch	**David Graham**

Guest Voice Cast

Felicity Farnsworth	**Sylvia Thamm**
Uncle Angus McCrail	**David Graham**
Campbell	**George Murcell**
Ben Judd	**David Graham**

First UK Transmission

Saturday, April 29th, 1961
5.40pm (ATV London)

DEEP SEVEN Prod. No. 15

Story by **Martin & Hugh Woodhouse** Directed by **Desmond Saunders**

To test Supercar's abilities deep underwater, Mike takes the vehicle 400 feet below the surface of the Pacific Ocean to be monitored by Beaker and Bill Gibson on the shore. Beaker has attached a cable connecting Supercar with a transmitting aerial floating on the surface so that Mike remains in constant radio contact. Supercar comes to rest on the sea bed but water starts to leak in through the edge of the canopy and when Mike charges the port engine to return to the surface, it initially fails to fire. A second attempt is successful but as the car rises it becomes fouled in the cable of an acoustic mine and the slightest sound could detonate it. Bill dives to the rescue wearing a deep sea diving suit, but then a vicious monster fish attacks Supercar and Mike realises that if it spots Bill, he won't stand a chance!

Notes

Mike states that Supercar has previously been tested positively at 40 feet underwater, suggesting that the vehicle descended no deeper than this in *Island Incident*. The mine detonation is represented by stock war footage of a real mine detonation and the wake of the minesweeper from which the film was shot is visible on the left of the frame.

Regular Voice Cast

Mike Mercury	**Graydon Gould**
Prof. Rudolph Popkiss	**George Murcell**
Dr. Horatio Beaker	**David Graham**
Jimmy Gibson	**Sylvia Thamm**
Mitch	**David Graham**
Bill Gibson	**David Graham**

First UK Transmission

Saturday, May 27th, 1961
5.40pm (ATV London)

PIRATE PLUNDER

Prod. No. 16

Story by **Martin & Hugh Woodhouse** Directed by **David Elliott**

Modern-day pirate Black Morgan has been terrorising pleasure yachts in the Pacific, but his boat, the *Cuttlefish*, is so fast that the authorities are unable to catch him. Mike decides to pursue Morgan in Supercar so the team rendezvous with the *Argosy*, the private yacht of millionaire Jason Monroe III who agrees to allow his jewel collection to act as bait for Morgan. Mike submerges Supercar to trail the *Argosy* at periscope depth and soon the *Cuttlefish* appears. Destroying the *Argosy*'s radio aerial, Morgan boards the yacht and steals Monroe's jewels. But as he leaves, he threatens to open fire on the Argosy with homing torpedoes if anyone attempts to follow him...

Notes

While underwater, Mike spots the monster fish from *Deep Seven.*

Oops!

Supercar is fitted with the rocket launcher from *What Goes Up* when it is lowered into the water, but the launcher vanishes once Supercar is underwater and only reappears as Mike closes in on the *Cuttlefish.*

Regular Voice Cast

Mike Mercury	**Graydon Gould**
Prof. Rudolph Popkiss	**George Murcell**
Dr. Horatio Beaker	**David Graham**
Jimmy Gibson	**Sylvia Thamm**
Mitch	**David Graham**

Guest Voice Cast

Black Morgan	**George Murcell**
Jason Monroe III	**Graydon Gould**

First UK Transmission

Saturday, May 6th, 1961
5.25pm (ATV London)

FLIGHT OF FANCY

Prod. No. 17

Story by **Martin & Hugh Woodhouse** Directed by **Alan Pattillo**

Before he goes to bed, Jimmy reads about Princess Caroline of Bavania, a central European state where the King is being deposed. Princess Caroline has vanished so Jimmy suggests taking Supercar to find her. He falls asleep and dreams that he and a talking Mitch fly Supercar to Bavania, landing at an old castle where the Princess is being held prisoner by the villainous Marzak and his secretary Hertz. Marzak plans to become the first President of Bavania by denouncing Rudolph's claim to the throne and with Caroline being held hostage, the King will have no choice but to accept Marzak's proclamation. Then Marzak hears Jimmy and Mitch approaching so he sets a trap, locking them in the castle's main hall with no means of escape...

Notes

In Jimmy's dream, Marzak and Hertz bear an uncanny resemblance to Masterspy and Zarin, Mike is a palace guard and Popkiss appears as King Rudolph. This is the first suggestion that Popkiss's forename is Rudolph, later confirmed in *The Day That Time Stood Still*. In the Bavanian language, Marzak means 'The Crow'. This is one of only two episodes in which Dr. Beaker does not appear – the other is *The Dragon Of Ho Meng*.

Regular Voice Cast

Mike Mercury	**Graydon Gould**
Prof. Rudolph Popkiss	**George Murcell**
Jimmy Gibson	**Sylvia Thamm**
Mitch	**David Graham**
Masterspy	**George Murcell**
Zarin	**David Graham**

Guest Voice Cast

Princess Caroline	**Sylvia Thamm**

First UK Transmission

Saturday, May 20th, 1961
5.40pm (ATV London)

HOSTAGE

Prod. No. 18

Story by **Martin & Hugh Woodhouse** Directed by **Desmond Saunders**

While visiting Ireland, Beaker is staying at the Shamrock Inn when Harper and Judd arrive for a drink. The innkeeper's daughter Eileen recognises the pair as agents of the Big Man and his smuggling operation but Harper pulls a gun and takes her hostage to deter her father from calling the police. Beaker calls Mike who races to Ireland in Supercar. In order to locate Harper's hideout, they secrete Beaker's radio transmitter inside a case of money which Judd is unable to resist stealing when he and Harper make their next visit to the inn. Unfortunately, as he and Beaker monitor the villains' position, Mike accidentally throws the 'Talk' switch on the radio receiver. When Harper hears their voices coming from the case, he discovers the transmitter and decides to lay a trap!

Notes

Mike refers to the events of *The Tracking Of Masterspy* when he recalls how the radio transmitter has worked as a tracking device before. This is the first time that Popkiss has been seen flying Supercar. Once again, the team are happy to take Mitch to Ireland despite their concerns about the weather and quarantine that prevented him from joining them in England in *Grounded.*

Regular Voice Cast

Mike Mercury	**Graydon Gould**
Prof. Rudolph Popkiss	**George Murcell**
Dr. Horatio Beaker	**David Graham**
Jimmy Gibson	**Sylvia Thamm**
Mitch	**David Graham**

Guest Voice Cast

Harper	**George Murcell**
Ben Judd	**David Graham**
Eileen O'Farrell	**Sylvia Thamm**
O'Farrell	**George Murcell**
The Big Man	**David Graham**

First UK Transmission

Saturday, June 3rd, 1961
5.25pm (ATV London)

THE SUNKEN TEMPLE — Prod. No. 19

Story by **Martin & Hugh Woodhouse** Directed by **David Elliott**

Archaeologist Professor Terman invites the Supercar team to help in locating the sunken temple of Poseidon the sea god after he finds an ancient vase in the Aegean Sea. Five days later, the team fly out to the Mediterranean and join Terman at his camp, but as they enjoy a barbecue around the camp fire, a gypsy named Antonio appears, claiming to read their fortunes and warning of danger and death if they persist in their search for the temple. The next morning, Mike and Beaker set off to explore the sea bed in Supercar, observed from the cliffs above by Antonio, actually a bandit named Spyros who has hidden a stolen strong box in the temple remains. To prevent the team from finding it, he intends to sabotage the mission by launching home-made depth charges into the sea!

Notes

Elements of this story were later reworked in the STINGRAY episode *In Search Of The Tajmanon* and the THUNDERBIRDS episode *Desperate Intruder*.

Oops!

When Supercar rendezvouses with Terman underwater, the canopy is clearly wide open.

Regular Voice Cast

Mike Mercury	**Graydon Gould**
Prof. Rudolph Popkiss	**George Murcell**
Dr. Horatio Beaker	**David Graham**
Jimmy Gibson	**Sylvia Thamm**
Mitch	**David Graham**

Guest Voice Cast

Professor Terman	**David Graham**
Spyros the Bandit	**George Murcell**

First UK Transmission

Saturday, June 10th, 1961
5.25pm (ATV London)

TRAPPED IN THE DEPTHS — Prod. No. 20

Story by **Martin & Hugh Woodhouse** Directed by **Alan Pattillo**

Off the coast of New Zealand, a Navy attempt to make the deepest ever underwater dive goes badly wrong when bathyscaphe LU-1 is inexplicably damaged and sinks, becoming jammed between rocks 4,000 fathoms down. Telephone contact is severed, but Commander Keefe and scientist John Fraser are able to communicate their situation via their Asdic equipment. With a new ultrasonic gun mounted on Supercar's bonnet, Mike and Beaker set off for New Zealand and dive into the sea, making a swift descent to attempt a rescue but suddenly the car is attacked by a monster fish!

Notes

As a name for underwater radar apparatus, Asdic (anti-submarine detection investigation committee) was superseded by Sonar (sound navigation and ranging) in 1963.

Oops!

Popkiss gives the water pressure at 4,000 feet as 10 psi (pounds per square inch), but the pressure at this depth is actually about 1,797 psi. In any case, Mike needs to know the pressure at 4,000 *fathoms* (24,000 feet) which is about 10,706 psi.

Regular Voice Cast

Mike Mercury	**Graydon Gould**
Prof. Rudolph Popkiss	**George Murcell**
Dr. Horatio Beaker	**David Graham**
Jimmy Gibson	**Sylvia Thamm**
Mitch	**David Graham**

Guest Voice Cast

Cmdr. Phil Keefe	**Graydon Gould**
John Fraser	**George Murcell**
Mistral Control Lt.	**David Graham**
Mistral Commander	**George Murcell**

First UK Transmission

Sunday, June 25th, 1961
5.15pm (ATV London)

CRASH LANDING — Prod. No. 21

Story by **Gerry & Sylvia Anderson** Directed by **Desmond Saunders**

After completing another test in Supercar, Mike, Beaker, Jimmy and Mitch are about to return to Black Rock when the starboard engine fails and the controls become jammed. Mike is forced to make a crash landing in the African jungle but fortunately no one is hurt. Mike and Jimmy set up camp while Mitch helps Beaker to make repairs to Supercar, but after Beaker is attacked by a snake, the team realise that it is too dangerous to continue the repair work in the dark so they turn in, leaving Mitch on guard duty. The next morning, Mitch has disappeared so, while Mike and Jimmy search for him, Beaker completes his repairs. He tests the car at supersonic speed by remote control, but the sonic boom causes a herd of elephants to stampede, heading directly for the camp!

Notes

This was the first television script credited to Gerry and Sylvia Anderson, although Gerry Anderson's new wife continues to be credited for dialogue direction as Sylvia Thamm. Mitch's girlfriend returns with the team to Black Rock at the end of the episode by stowing away aboard Supercar, but we never learn what becomes of her as she is not seen or mentioned again.

Regular Voice Cast

Mike Mercury	**Graydon Gould**
Prof. Rudolph Popkiss	**George Murcell**
Dr. Horatio Beaker	**David Graham**
Jimmy Gibson	**Sylvia Thamm**
Mitch	**David Graham**

First UK Transmission

Sunday, July 23rd, 1961
5.15pm (ATV London)

THE DRAGON OF HO MENG — Prod. No. 22

Story by **Martin & Hugh Woodhouse** Directed by **David Elliott**

Caught in a typhoon, Mike, Jimmy and Mitch land Supercar on a remote Chinese island. There, they find an ancient Chinese temple and are welcomed to the home of Ho Meng and his daughter Lotus Blossom. Ho Meng has mistaken Supercar for a dragon which is a sign of ill fortune, so Mike takes the old man for a ride in the 'mechanical kite' in an attempt to persuade him that the car will not bring bad luck. As they land inside the temple, an evil Chinaman named Mr. Fang appears and announces that he intends to blow up the temple to reveal a legendary treasure hidden within its walls. He takes Ho Meng hostage and locks Mike, Jimmy, Mitch and Lotus Blossom in the temple, but they escape in Supercar along a secret underground tunnel which eventually leads outside. Mike races back to the temple to stop Mr. Fang before he can detonate his explosives!

Notes
Neither Dr. Beaker nor Professor Popkiss appear in this episode. Mike is ambidextrous: although he holds his gun in his left hand in this episode and *Island Incident*, he is later seen holding his gun in his right hand in *The Sky's The Limit* and *Atomic Witch Hunt*. Although Lotus Blossom is invited to visit Black Rock one day, she is not seen again.

Regular Voice Cast

Mike Mercury	**Graydon Gould**
Jimmy Gibson	**Sylvia Thamm**
Mitch	**David Graham**

Guest Voice Cast

Lotus Blossom	**Sylvia Thamm**
Ho Meng	**David Graham**
Mr. Fang	**George Murcell**

First UK Transmission

Sunday, July 2nd, 1961
5.15pm (ATV London)

THE LOST CITY — Prod. No. 23

Story by **Gerry & Sylvia Anderson** Directed by **Alan Pattillo**

Mike, Beaker, Jimmy and Mitch take Supercar on an exploratory mission to the South Pole but the vehicle is forced off course over the Amazon Basin and brought to a controlled landing in the ruins of an ancient city. As Mike and Beaker investigate the ruins, they step onto a hidden elevator panel which takes them underground into a secret complex. There they meet mad scientist Professor Watkins who imprisons them in a steel cell and reveals his plan to target Washington DC with an atomic missile. Jimmy and Mitch attempt to escape in Supercar, which is flown by Popkiss under remote control, but Watkins sends one of his robot servants to stop them...

Notes
Watkins has 30 robots at his disposal according to his control panel. His motive for launching the missile at Washington is never revealed. The robot puppet later appears in the FIREBALL XL5 episode *The Granatoid Tanks*.

Oops!
There is no lettering on the bottom of the puppet-sized Supercar.

Regular Voice Cast

Mike Mercury	**Graydon Gould**
Prof. Rudolph Popkiss	**George Murcell**
Dr. Horatio Beaker	**David Graham**
Jimmy Gibson	**Sylvia Thamm**
Mitch	**David Graham**

Guest Voice Cast

Professor Watkins	**David Graham**
Number 15	**George Murcell**
Number 27	**George Murcell**
Number 30	**George Murcell**

First UK Transmission

Saturday, June 17th, 1961
5.25pm (ATV London)

THE MAGIC CARPET — Prod. No. 24

Story by **Martin & Hugh Woodhouse** Directed by **Desmond Saunders**

Beaker has developed a pocket remote console with engine noise suppressor for Supercar. Just as he and Mike finish testing it, Popkiss sends them on an urgent mission to deliver medical supplies to Karakan in Central Asia where Prince Hassan is dangerously ill after a riding accident. The team fly to the remote city in the desert, but when they arrive at the palace they meet Alif Bey who intends to allow Hassan to die so that he can seize power and marry Hassan's sister, the Princess Medina. The Supercar team are locked in a room on the opposite side of the courtyard from Hassan and Medina, so Beaker uses the pocket remote to send Supercar on a pilotless flight...

Notes
Princess Medina is revamped from the Princess Caroline puppet created for *Flight Of Fancy*. This was voice artist George Murcell's final episode.

Oops!
The knobs on the side of the pocket remote console do not move at all when Mike's close-up hand turns them.

Regular Voice Cast

Mike Mercury	**Graydon Gould**
Prof. Rudolph Popkiss	**George Murcell**
Dr. Horatio Beaker	**David Graham**
Jimmy Gibson	**Sylvia Thamm**
Mitch	**David Graham**

Guest Voice Cast

Alif Bey	**George Murcell**
Princess Medina	**Sylvia Thamm**
Prince Nurid Hassan	**Graydon Gould**
Guard	**David Graham**

First UK Transmission

Sunday, July 9th, 1961
5.15pm (ATV London)

THE WHITE LINE — Prod. No. 25

Story by **Martin** & **Hugh Woodhouse** Directed by **Alan Pattillo**

Chicago gangsters Maxie and Joe Hoyle have organised a series of night-time robberies on Safe T Cars security vehicles in England, laying a false centre line on a sharp bend in the road to lead the drivers over the edge of a cliff. Scotland Yard asks the Supercar team for help so Mike, Beaker, Jimmy and Mitch fly to London where they agree to transport a shipment of gold bullion across the city to the Bank of Kensington. Once there, Mike, Beaker and a Scotland Yard Inspector deliver the gold to the vault, but the Hoyles are waiting inside with machine guns. They lock the trio in the vault and make a clean getaway with the gold!

Notes

Much of the incidental music in this episode was originally composed for the feature film *Crossroads To Crime* (1960). Stop-motion animation is used to illustrate the destruction of Supercar's aerial. This was Martin & Hugh Woodhouse's last script for the series.

Oops!

The team take Mitch to England in violation of the quarantine laws (see *Grounded*).

Regular Voice Cast

Mike Mercury	**Graydon Gould**
Dr. Horatio Beaker	**David Graham**
Jimmy Gibson	**Sylvia Thamm**
Mitch	**David Graham**

Guest Voice Cast

Maxie Hoyle	**Graydon Gould**
Joe Hoyle	**David Graham**
Police Inspector	**David Graham**
Accomplice	**Graydon Gould**

First UK Transmission

Sunday, August 6th, 1961
5.15pm (ATV London)

SUPERCAR "TAKE ONE" — Prod. No. 26

Story by **Gerry** & **Sylvia Anderson** Directed by **Desmond Saunders**

While Popkiss is on holiday at his sister's house in Chicago, Beaker purchases professional film-making equipment in order to make a permanent film record of all of his experiments. Jimmy persuades Beaker to use the equipment to make a film about the Supercar team, but when the negatives are sent to be processed by a laboratory at Satellite Productions in New York, the reels that are returned show US Naval warships and top secret plans of a marine nuclear power unit. Mike realises that a spy ring is operating from the Satellite Productions offices, but when the team fly to New York to investigate, Mike and Beaker fall foul of foreign agent Herman Gredenski and his devious assistant Miss Devenish...

Notes

Popkiss's postcard is simply addressed to 'The Laboratory, Black Rock, Nevada'. Satellite Film Productions is based on the 43rd floor of 34 East 25th Street, New York. Jimmy states that this is the first time he has been to New York. Beaker has a radio transmitter hidden in his bowler hat and a power drill secreted in his umbrella – years before John Steed was seen using similar devices in THE AVENGERS television series!

Regular Voice Cast

Mike Mercury	**Graydon Gould**
Dr. Horatio Beaker	**David Graham**
Jimmy Gibson	**Sylvia Thamm**
Mitch	**David Graham**

Guest Voice Cast

Herman Gredenski	**David Graham**
Olga Devenish	**Sylvia Thamm**
Foreign Dialogue	**David Graham**

First UK Transmission

Sunday, July 16th, 1961
5.15pm (ATV London)

THE RUNAWAY TRAIN — Prod. No. 27

Story by **Gerry** & **Sylvia Anderson** Directed by **David Elliott**

In order to help the Army's Colonel Harris develop a quick, safe method of removing tanks from a war zone, Beaker develops a pair of powerful electromagnetic grabs which he installs on Supercar. The team then join Beaker on a trip to England where the doctor has been invited to operate a prototype diesel train fitted with an atomic engine on its maiden journey from London to Brighton. Unfortunately, Masterspy has been hired by a foreign government to assassinate a VIP who has been causing trouble for them. The VIP will be travelling on the train, so Masterspy sabotages the atomic reactor so that once the train has started on its journey, no one will be able to stop it – the train will continue to accelerate until it crashes into the station at the end of the line!

Notes

This is the first episode to feature the revised recording of the theme song by The Mike Sammes Singers. It is also the first to feature Cyril Shaps providing the voices of Professor Popkiss and Masterspy. The back-projection footage of the atomic train's high-speed journey is taken from the classic, ground-breaking time-lapse photography short film *London To Brighton In Four Minutes* (1952).

Regular Voice Cast

Mike Mercury	**Graydon Gould**
Prof. Rudolph Popkiss	**Cyril Shaps**
Dr. Horatio Beaker	**David Graham**
Jimmy Gibson	**Sylvia Anderson**
Mitch	**David Graham**
Masterspy	**Cyril Shaps**
Zarin	**David Graham**

Guest Voice Cast

Colonel Harris	**Graydon Gould**
Elevator 1	**David Graham**
Receptionist	**Sylvia Anderson**
Radio Announcer	**Cyril Shaps**

First UK Transmission

Sunday, February 4th, 1962
5.20pm (ATV London)

PRECIOUS CARGO

Prod. No. 28

Story by **Gerry & Sylvia Anderson** Directed by **Alan Pattillo**

Regular Voice Cast

Mike Mercury	**Graydon Gould**
Prof. Rudolph Popkiss	**Cyril Shaps**
Dr. Horatio Beaker	**David Graham**
Jimmy Gibson	**Sylvia Anderson**
Mitch	**David Graham**

Guest Voice Cast

Aunt Heidi	**Sylvia Anderson**
Zizi	**Sylvia Anderson**
Monsieur Laval	**David Graham**

First UK Transmission

Sunday, February 11th, 1962
5.20pm (ATV London)

Popkiss and Jimmy visit the Professor's sister Heidi at her home in Chicago. Heidi reveals that she cooks her chicken in wine purchased by mail order from France, so Popkiss makes a note of the vintner's address and sends an order of his own. However, Monsieur Laval is a wicked tyrant who dresses his young ward Zizi in rags, forcing her to do his housework and beating her if she does not meet his unreasonable expectations. Zizi dreams of being rescued by Jimmy in Supercar, so she hides inside the crate of wine that Popkiss has ordered and is delivered to the Black Rock laboratory. She is discovered when the crate is opened but while Mike, Beaker and Popkiss discuss what is to be done with her, Zizi fears that she will be sent back to cruel Monsieur Laval...

Notes

Zizi is revamped from the Princess Caroline puppet created for *Flight Of Fancy*, previously seen as Princess Medina in *The Magic Carpet*. Zizi is seen reading a SUPERCAR comic book, suggesting that the team's exploits are by now well-known to the public (in contrast to earlier episodes such as *What Goes Up*, *Grounded* and *The Tracking Of Masterspy* where maintaining the secrecy of Supercar was paramount).

OPERATION SUPERSTORK

Prod. No. 29

Story by **Gerry & Sylvia Anderson** Directed by **Desmond Saunders**

Regular Voice Cast

Mike Mercury	**Graydon Gould**
Prof. Rudolph Popkiss	**Cyril Shaps**
Dr. Horatio Beaker	**David Graham**
Jimmy Gibson	**Sylvia Anderson**
Mitch	**David Graham**

Guest Voice Cast

Storekeeper Andy	**David Graham**
Shopper	**Sylvia Anderson**
Narrator	**Graydon Gould**

First UK Transmission

Sunday, February 18th, 1962
5.20pm (ATV London)

Beaker is up all night working on his latest project and the constant hammering keeps Popkiss awake. The next morning, Beaker reveals to Mike and Jimmy that he has built a hot air balloon, although he has yet to fit a release valve for the gas which enables the balloon to descend. Unfortunately, Mitch unties the balloon's guy rope while Mike, Beaker and Jimmy are aboard and the balloon floats away with no way for the trio to take it back down. As the balloon rises higher, the air thins and Beaker works out that they have only 90 minutes before the balloon bursts. Furthermore, there is only one parachute on board and the balloon is heading straight for a storm. Popkiss could rescue them in Supercar, but he has been asleep all morning and doesn't know that they are in trouble!

Notes

The nearest town to the Black Rock laboratory is Batesville, where Mike and Jimmy shop for supplies. However, while other American locations referred to in the series have been geographically correct, this location is entirely fictional (there are four towns called Batesville in the USA, but none of them are in Nevada). In a surprisingly early example of televisual postmodernism, Popkiss sings the SUPERCAR theme song as he cooks.

HI-JACK

Prod. No. 30

Story by **Gerry & Sylvia Anderson** Directed by **Bill Harris**

Regular Voice Cast

Mike Mercury	**Graydon Gould**
Prof. Rudolph Popkiss	**Cyril Shaps**
Dr. Horatio Beaker	**David Graham**
Jimmy Gibson	**Sylvia Anderson**
Mitch	**David Graham**
Bill Gibson	**David Graham**

Guest Voice Cast

President Gourmet	**David Graham**
Lieutenant Soir	**Cyril Shaps**
Captain Ross	**Graydon Gould**
Croupier	**Cyril Shaps**
Narrator	**Graydon Gould**

First UK Transmission

Sunday, February 25th, 1962
5.20pm (ATV London)

President Gourmet of Bantonga decides that he should have a new Presidential aircraft to replace his battered old bi-plane, so he sends Lieutenant Soir to America to acquire a Boeing 707 jet airliner. Bill Gibson has been hired by Interstate Airlines to train the crews of their new fleet of Boeing 707s, and Jimmy and Beaker join him on his first training flight, unaware that Bill's pupil, Captain Ross, has been replaced by Soir. Soir forces Bill to change course and the Supercar team soon realise that the plane has been hi-jacked! Meanwhile, Masterspy and Zarin, who arranged the kidnapping of the real Captain Ross, gamble away their fee playing roulette aboard Gourmet's private yacht, but when Masterspy realises that the roulette table was rigged, he vows to get even with Gourmet...

Notes

The (fictional) Bastorga islands are 300 miles west of the Pacific coast of America. The largest island in the group is Bantonga, three miles in length with a population of 4,339. The versatile Bill Gibson has become an astronaut since the last time he appeared in the series (in *Deep Seven*) although he may have always been one: he says that his new job for Interstate Airlines makes "a change from space flight."

CALLING CHARLIE QUEEN — Prod. No. 31

Story by **Gerry & Sylvia Anderson** Directed by **Alan Pattillo**

The Supercar team return from a test flight to receive a mysterious distress call sent to one 'Charlie Queen'. Explaining that Charlie Queen is a general call sign for help from any radio station that intercepts the transmission, Beaker pinpoints the general location of the signal at Petersville, 300 miles away. Mike, Beaker and Mitch fly there in Supercar and arrive at a creepy old house owned by the deranged Professor Karloff who drugs their coffee. When they recover consciousness, the Supercar trio discover that they have been miniaturised along with Karloff's former assistant, Hopkins, who sent the radio message. Hopkins reveals Karloff's plan to contaminate the water supplies of major American cities with a formula that will miniaturise the entire population!

Notes

This episode features the first combination of puppetry and live-action in a Supermarionation series: the characters are miniaturised to 1/3 normal size enabling the puppets to interact with full size props, furniture and live actors. A bottle on the shelf in Karloff's laboratory contains Hydromic Acid, an element used in the construction of STINGRAY's Hydromic Missiles perhaps?

Regular Voice Cast

Mike Mercury	**Graydon Gould**
Prof. Rudolph Popkiss	**Cyril Shaps**
Dr. Horatio Beaker	**David Graham**
Jimmy Gibson	**Sylvia Anderson**
Mitch	**David Graham**

Guest Voice Cast

Professor Karloff	**Cyril Shaps**
Hopkins	**David Graham**

First UK Transmission

Sunday, March 4th, 1962
5.20pm (ATV London)

SPACE FOR MITCH — Prod. No. 32

Story by **Gerry & Sylvia Anderson** Directed by **Desmond Saunders**

The Supercar team are assisting Dr. Harvey with a revolutionary protoptype space rocket which is half the size of a conventional rocket and capable of being launched by only a few people, cutting the cost of sending a man into space by half. After the first test with an unmanned capsule proves successful, a second test is planned with Bill Gibson aboard the capsule. However, Mitch has been looking at pictures of space monkey Ham and, during the night, he sneaks into the rocket wearing Bill's spacesuit and activates the controls to launch himself into space. As the retro rockets are designed to be fired by the astronaut from inside the capsule, there is no way to bring the capsule down by remote control, so Mike launches into space in Supercar on a rescue mission.

Notes

Supercar is fitted with the magnetic grabs that were installed in *The Runaway Train*. Bill Gibson is confirmed to be a fully qualified astronaut working at Cape Canaveral (see *Hi-Jack*). Chimpanzee astronaut Ham flew to a height of 155 miles aboard a Mercury spacecraft on January 31st, 1961. Jimmy says this was "a long time ago" so a couple of years must have passed since *A Little Art* (and Jimmy hardly seems to have aged at all!).

Regular Voice Cast

Mike Mercury	**Graydon Gould**
Prof. Rudolph Popkiss	**Cyril Shaps**
Dr. Horatio Beaker	**David Graham**
Jimmy Gibson	**Sylvia Anderson**
Mitch	**David Graham**
Bill Gibson	**David Graham**

Guest Voice Cast

Dr. Harvey	**Graydon Gould**

First UK Transmission

Sunday, March 11th, 1962
5.20pm (ATV London)

THE SKY'S THE LIMIT — Prod. No. 33

Story by **Gerry & Sylvia Anderson** Directed by **Bill Harris**

Masterspy and Zarin have become obscenely wealthy by printing counterfeit money and now own everything that money can buy – except Supercar. Writing as Joshua T. Zarius III, Masterspy offers Popkiss a billion dollars for the car, but Popkiss writes back to say that it is not for sale. Meanwhile, Beaker has invented a new hard-wearing paint that will resist all attempts to damage it, although it proves to have a strange side-effect, making everything painted with it turn invisible. Then Masterspy hires a pair of gangsters, Jazz and Bud, to help him lay siege to the Black Rock laboratory, cutting the telephone cable and wrecking the radio transmitter before trapping the team inside under machine-gun fire. Mike decides to launch Supercar, but Masterspy has fixed a bomb to the roof doors...

Notes

The workshop at the Black Rock laboratory is seen here to be at ground level, so the two lower floors accessible from the elevator (see *The Tracking Of Masterspy*) must be underground. Mike tells Masterspy that Supercar is at AP Electronics in Slough, England. This company is possibly the manufacturer of Mike's portable radio which features an AP motif (as seen in *The Runaway Train* and *The Day That Time Stood Still*).

Regular Voice Cast

Mike Mercury	**Graydon Gould**
Prof. Rudolph Popkiss	**Cyril Shaps**
Dr. Horatio Beaker	**David Graham**
Jimmy Gibson	**Sylvia Anderson**
Mitch	**David Graham**
Masterspy	**Cyril Shaps**
Zarin	**David Graham**

Guest Voice Cast

Jazz	**David Graham**
Bud	**Graydon Gould**

First UK Transmission

Sunday, April 1st, 1962
5.20pm (ATV London)

70-B-LO

Prod. No. 34

Story by **Gerry & Sylvia Anderson** — Directed by **Alan Pattillo**

Popkiss is rushed to Batesville Hospital with appendicitis but after his appendix is removed, he requires a blood transfusion. Unfortunately, Popkiss has a very rare blood group and the only compatible donor is Professor Karzinsky, currently engaged on a top secret mission at Base 24, 20 miles from the North Pole and cut off from conventional transport by a blizzard. Mike sets off in Supercar with Dr. Maslin to obtain the necessary plasma from Karzinsky, but at Base 24, Karzinsky learns that his unscrupulous assistant Jason intends to sell information about their discovery of rich uranium deposits to the highest bidding superpower. When he hears that Supercar is on its way, Jason sets in motion plans to steal the car and leave Mike, Maslin and Karzinsky stranded...

Notes

This episode opens with a short piece of electronic music that later formed part of the closing title music for UFO. There is another example of early televisual postmodernism here: this time it is Beaker's turn to sing the SUPERCAR theme song (see *Operation Superstork*). To maintain the series' fictional reality, viewers could assume that the Supercar team are now so famous that someone has written a song about them.

Regular Voice Cast

Mike Mercury	**Graydon Gould**
Prof. Rudolph Popkiss	**Cyril Shaps**
Dr. Horatio Beaker	**David Graham**
Jimmy Gibson	**Sylvia Anderson**
Mitch	**David Graham**

Guest Voice Cast

Dr. Clive Maslin	**Cyril Shaps**
Professor Carl Karzinsky	**Cyril Shaps**
Jason	**David Graham**

First UK Transmission

Sunday, March 25th, 1962
5.20pm (ATV London)

ATOMIC WITCH HUNT

Prod. No. 35

Story by **Gerry & Sylvia Anderson** — Directed by **Desmond Saunders**

A foreign power is planting miniature atomic bombs in locations across America and the State Department has been unable to determine how the bombs are being smuggled into the country. Checking through newspapers for the last six months, the Supercar team find reports that unidentified submarines have been sighted off the coast of Temport, so they fly there in Supercar to investigate. As they search the coastline, the team spot an unmarked submarine and follow it to a cave entrance. Leaving Popkiss and Jimmy to set up a radio station on the beach, Mike and Beaker enter the cave in Supercar, surfacing in a cavern where they find the miniature bombs and a powerful transmitter to activate them by remote control. Unfortunately, they have walked into a trap triggered by stepping on a concealed panel in the floor – if they move, they will be cut down by machine gun fire!

Oops!

Supercar is seen here to be capable of flying at 4,500 mph when previously the car has only been able to muster between 1,000 and 1,500 mph, even when flying on emergency missions. The Sheriff of Temport seems to be living in Aunt Heidi's house (as seen in *Precious Cargo* and *The Day That Time Stood Still*).

Regular Voice Cast

Mike Mercury	**Graydon Gould**
Prof. Rudolph Popkiss	**Cyril Shaps**
Dr. Horatio Beaker	**David Graham**
Jimmy Gibson	**Sylvia Anderson**
Mitch	**David Graham**

Guest Voice Cast

Sheriff Elmer P. Jackson	**David Graham**
Rudy	**Cyril Shaps**
Jodie	**Graydon Gould**

First UK Transmission

Sunday, March 18th, 1962
5.20pm (ATV London)

JAIL BREAK

Prod. No. 36

Story by **Gerry & Sylvia Anderson** — Directed by **Bill Harris**

Beaker has developed a new ejector seat for Supercar fitted with retro rockets instead of a parachute. Mike tests it successfully, but ends up landing on a big cactus in the desert. Meanwhile, Red James hires a helicopter from Sam Weston's Helicopter Services Inc., purportedly to take aerial photographs, but when James pulls a gun on Weston and orders him to head for the State Penitentiary, the pilot realises that James intends to use the helicopter to break Joe Anna out of prison. James lowers a winch to pull the bars of Anna's cell window out of the wall with Anna hanging on to them. Then, as the helicopter flies over Black Rock, James comes up with a new escape plan and decides to land near the laboratory. The crooks break into the workshop and threaten Jimmy with a gun unless Mike agrees to fly Anna to Mexico in Supercar, but once they are in the air, Mike opens the canopy and activates his new ejector seat...

Oops!

As he sets off for Mexico with Joe Anna, Mike opens Supercar's canopy, but the canopy is still closed in the next model shot of the car flying along. When the picture cuts back to the puppet-sized car, the canopy is open again.

Regular Voice Cast

Mike Mercury	**Graydon Gould**
Prof. Rudolph Popkiss	**Cyril Shaps**
Dr. Horatio Beaker	**David Graham**
Jimmy Gibson	**Sylvia Anderson**
Mitch	**David Graham**

Guest Voice Cast

Red James	**Graydon Gould**
Joe Anna	**David Graham**
Sam Weston	**Cyril Shaps**
Secretary	**Sylvia Anderson**

First UK Transmission

Sunday, April 8th, 1962
5.30pm (ATV London)

THE DAY THAT TIME STOOD STILL Prod. No. 37

Story by **Gerry & Sylvia Anderson** Directed by **Alan Pattillo**

On Mercurius, the planet of dreams, Planitimus sends Kalmus on a mission to Earth, where a sighting of his flying saucer by Senator Glanville is reported on the radio. Mike doesn't believe a word of it as he listens to the radio before turning in. That night, he dreams that it is his birthday and he is sent in Supercar to collect Aunt Heidi and Zizi from Chicago while the rest of the team prepare a surprise birthday party. Mike is deliberately delayed by Aunt Heidi until the party is ready and the festivities commence as soon as they return to the laboratory. Beaker plays his revolutionary new Beakette organ and Zizi sings a song, but then Kalmus appears and makes time stand still. All but Mike, Beaker and Mitch are frozen in place as Kalmus carries out his assignment...

Notes

Mike's birthday is given here as November 22nd. In the year in which this episode is set, that date is a Thursday, so this must be 1962 (the only year between 1956 and 1973 in which November 22nd fell on a Thursday). This neatly ties in with *The Runaway Train* in which Beaker records his final test on the electromagnet on Tuesday, July 10th, and the only year between 1956 and 1973 in which July 10th fell on a Tuesday was 1962.

Regular Voice Cast

Mike Mercury	**Graydon Gould**
Prof. Rudolph Popkiss	**Cyril Shaps**
Dr. Horatio Beaker	**David Graham**
Jimmy Gibson	**Sylvia Anderson**
Mitch	**David Graham**

Guest Voice Cast

Aunt Heidi	**Sylvia Anderson**
Zizi	**Sylvia Anderson**
Planitimus	**Cyril Shaps**
Kalmus	**David Graham**
Newsreader	**David Graham**
Narrator	**Graydon Gould**

First UK Transmission

Sunday, April 15th, 1962
5.20pm (ATV London)

TRANSATLANTIC CABLE Prod. No. 38

Story by **Gerry & Sylvia Anderson** Directed by **Desmond Saunders**

Masterspy has hired a pair of divers, Foreman and Johnson, to tap the transatlantic telephone cable in order to intercept confidential business information which he can sell to his clients. When Mike is asked by Mr. Bell of the Telecable Corporation to find out who is tampering with the cable, the Supercar team set out on an Atlantic crossing to see if they can find a ship that the culprits could be operating from. As they follow the cable along the sea bed, Jimmy spots a light in a porthole of a sunken merchant vessel, but his colleagues believe that he has imagined it. However, the shipwreck is indeed being used as a base by Foreman and Johnson, who prepare to make another telephone interception...

Notes

In another notable act of postmodernism, Professor Popkiss talks directly to camera when he sits up in bed to complain to viewers that he can never get any sleep when Beaker is working at night. Masterspy and Zarin make their last appearances in the series here, finally apprehended by the police for their part in the telephone tapping operation. However, their previous spell in prison for forgery, assault and property damage (implied by the conclusion of *The Sky's The Limit*) cannot have lasted for very long.

Regular Voice Cast

Mike Mercury	**Graydon Gould**
Prof. Rudolph Popkiss	**Cyril Shaps**
Dr. Horatio Beaker	**David Graham**
Jimmy Gibson	**Sylvia Anderson**
Mitch	**David Graham**
Masterspy	**Cyril Shaps**
Zarin	**David Graham**

Guest Voice Cast

Foreman	**Cyril Shaps**
Johnson	**David Graham**
Mr. Bell	**David Graham**
Freda	**Sylvia Anderson**
Narrator	**Graydon Gould**

First UK Transmission

Sunday, April 22nd, 1962
5.00pm (ATV London)

KING KOOL Prod. No. 39

Story by **Gerry & Sylvia Anderson** Directed by **Bill Harris**

Beaker makes a drum kit so that Jimmy can teach Mitch to play the drums like the famous giant ape jazz drummer King Kool. Then Jimmy reads that King Kool lives on Lincoln Drive in Batesville, so when Beaker goes there to visit his friend Professor Harlow, Mitch sneaks aboard Beaker's truck for the trip into town. Mitch finds King Kool locked in a cage at the house of pianist Bud Hamburger, but when he opens the cage door, King Kool escapes, locks Mitch in the cage in his place and then hides in the back of Beaker's truck. When Beaker returns to the laboratory later that night, King Kool finds Mitch's bed and goes to sleep, but next morning, the Supercar team mistake King Kool for Mitch, thinking that the little chimp has somehow grown to gigantic size!

Notes

The episode title caption appears as the lettering on King Kool's drum kit. Subtitles appear on screen for the dialogue between Mitch and King Kool – Mitch's speech patterns match those of the talking Mitch in Jimmy's dream in *Flight Of Fancy*. The local television station broadcasting The Bud Hamburger Supersoap Show is APF TV. Bud Hamburger appears to be living in Aunt Heidi's house (as seen in *Precious Cargo*).

Regular Voice Cast

Mike Mercury	**Graydon Gould**
Prof. Rudolph Popkiss	**Cyril Shaps**
Dr. Horatio Beaker	**David Graham**
Jimmy Gibson	**Sylvia Anderson**
Mitch	**David Graham**

Guest Voice Cast

Bud Hamburger	**Graydon Could**
Professor Harlow	**David Graham**

First UK Transmission

Sunday, April 29th, 1962
5.00pm (ATV London)

FIREBALL XL5

Format

It is Universal Astronomic Year 2062 and Earth has established colonies on other planets in the solar system and beyond, right across the galaxy. Peaceful contact with intelligent civilisations on other planets has led to the formation of the United Planets Organisation in which the member planets work together to maintain peace and order throughout the universe. Earth's own peace-keeping force is the World Space Patrol, operating from Space City headquarters on an island in the Pacific Ocean off the coast of Chile. Here, Space City chief Commander Zero organises routine space patrols in the various sectors under Earth jurisdiction, and supervises freight deliveries of supplies to the numerous Earth colonies, research bases and space stations.

Although the WSP operates a variety of Light Patrol ships, Space Rescue ships, Q spaceships and cargo freighters, the WSP's primary space vehicles are the XL ships, 300 feet-long interstellar spacecraft. The pride of the XL fleet is *Fireball XL5*, assigned to patrol Sector 25 and piloted by the WSP's top astronaut Colonel Steve Zodiac. Powered by a nutomic reactor, *XL5* can safely travel at speeds of up to Space Velocity 7 with main boosters activated, enabling the ship to reach even the most outlying planets of charted space within a few months. *XL5* is capable of speeds beyond Space Velocity 14 and can even exceed the speed of light, although travelling at these speeds is unhealthy for the crew and can cause them to black out. The ship is equipped with artificial gravity and an automatic pilot in the form of the transparent robot Robert, and is armed with Interceptor blast missiles. *XL5* has a detachable nose-cone, *Fireball Junior*, which is used for planetary surface exploration while the mother ship remains in orbit. *Fireball Junior* houses the ship's main control cabin and a storage bay for three jetmobile vehicles.

Completely self-contained, *Fireball XL5* features living quarters for the crew, an ultra-modernistic lounge, laboratory, navigation bay, space jail, a central control room for piloting the ship while *Fireball Junior* is detached, and an ejection room from which the crew can leave the ship for extra-vehicular exploration with the aid of oxygen pills and thruster packs.

Production

SUPERCAR had proven to be a massive success for ITC, particularly in the United States where the series was screened coast to coast by 107 stations and became the country's top-rated children's television programme. So when Gerry Anderson approached Lew Grade in early 1962 with a proposal for a new science-fiction puppet series entitled 'Century 21', Grade immediately agreed to finance 26 episodes (later followed by a commission for a further 13) on the understanding that the first episodes would be ready for broadcast by the following October.

After a brief period in which it was to be called 'Nova X 100', the series went into production as FIREBALL XL5 at the AP Film Studios in Ipswich Road, Slough in April 1962. In order to cut the series' lengthy production schedule, Anderson established two full-time puppet units with two directors working at once: after a week's main unit photography, filming on each episode would move to the second unit stage to clear up inserts, vacating the main unit stage for the next episode.

XL5 itself was designed by Reg Hill and constructed in a variety of scales for different types of shots: a seven-foot model built by Bill James for close-up shots of sections of the craft and most of the scenes involving *Fireball Junior*, a 24-inch model used for the launching, flying and landing sequences, and even a five-inch model for space scenes shot using back projection. Although back projection had been used extensively on SUPERCAR, FIREBALL XL5 became the first television series to use front projection as well. Using the newly developed Alekan-Gerard Axial Projection system, scenes were shot through a semi-transparent mirror placed at 45° to the optical axis, which reflected the background footage from a projector at right angles to the camera onto a glass-beaded screen. This screen returned the projected image to the film camera with an intensity that nullified any shadows from the foreground elements (puppets or models) as well as any part of the background image projected onto those foreground elements.

Main Characters

Colonel Steve Zodiac
The WSP's youngest Colonel, the courageous commander and pilot of *Fireball XL5*

Dr. Venus
19 year-old French doctor of space medicine and *XL5* medical officer

Professor Matthew Matic
XL5 navigator and engineer, a navigation mathematics and space sciences genius

Commander Wilbur Zero
WSP Commander and Space City chief controller

Lieutenant 90
Space City assistant controller

Robert
Transparent robot and *XL5* automatic pilot invented by Professor Matic

Zoony
Mischievous Lazoon from planet Colevio with telepathic abilities, adopted by Venus

Jock Campbell
No-nonsense Scots engineer who loves haggis and bagpipes

Eleanor Zero
Commander Zero's long-suffering wife and mother of Jonathan Zero

Jonathan Zero
Commander Zero's adventurous 11 year-old son

Griselda Space Spy
Evil co-founder of the Universe Spy Organisation and domineering wife of Boris Space Spy

Boris Space Spy
Evil co-founder of the Universe Spy Organisation and meek husband of Griselda Space Spy

The initial UK broadcast of FIREBALL XL5 on ATV London from October 28th, 1962, comprised only 35 of the 39 episodes as four early episodes were held back until the start of a repeat run in October 1963. The series was also truncated in the Granada region, where the series began on December 26th, 1962, and the same four episodes were held back until a repeat screening in 1964. In other ITV regions, FIREBALL XL5 was not shown until the spring of 1963, but all 39 episodes were screened as a single series - as in the ATV Midlands region where viewers saw the programme for the first time on March 25th, 1963, five months after viewers in London.

PRODUCTION CREDITS

Produced by **Gerry Anderson**
Associate Producer **Reg Hill**
Production Supervisor **David Elliott**
Director of Photography **John Read** *(1, 3, 5, 7, 9, 11, 13, 15, 17, 19, 21, 23, 25, 27, 29, 31, 33, 35, 37, 39)*
Ian Struthers *(2, 4, 6, 8, 10, 12, 14, 16, 18, 20, 22, 24, 26, 28, 30, 32, 34, 36, 38)*
Art Director **Bob Bell**
Special Effects **Derek Meddings**
Script Supervision **Gerry & Sylvia Anderson** *(2-8, 10-39)*
Music Composed, Arranged and Conducted by **Barry Gray**
Title Music Arranged by **Charles Blackwell**
Title Music Vocal **Don Spencer**
Puppetry Supervision **Christine Glanville, Mary Turner**
Puppet Operators **Eddie Hunter*** **Judith Shutt*, Yvonne Hunter***
Sculptors **John Blundall** *(14-31, 33-39)* **John Brown***
Special Effects Lighting **Ted Wooldridge**
Special Effects Camera Operator **Paddy Seale**
Character Voices **David Graham** **Sylvia Anderson, Paul Maxwell** **John Bluthal, Gerry Anderson***
Editor **Gordon Davie** *(1, 4, 7, 10, 13, 16, 19, 22, 25, 28, 31, 32, 34, 37, 39)*
Eric Pask *(2, 5, 8, 11, 14, 17, 20, 23, 26, 29, 35, 38)*
David Lane *(3, 6, 9, 12, 15, 18, 21, 24, 27, 30, 33, 36)*
Sound Editor **John Peverill**
Camera Operator **Julien Lugrin**
Sound Recording **Maurice Askew** **John Taylor**
Special Effects Assistant **Brian Johncock***
Models **Eric Backman*** **Bill James***
Westrex Recording System
Processing by **Kays Laboratories Ltd**
Made in Association with ATV
An ITC World Wide Distribution
An APF Television Production
Filmed in Supermarionation

* uncredited

Original Concept

Gerry Anderson's proposal for the series that eventually became FIREBALL XL5 was presented to Lew Grade in the form of a spiral-bound hand-made brochure prepared by Reg Hill with colour illustrations by Hill and Derek Meddings. Giving the proposed series title as 'Century 21', the brochure presented Grade with two different series formats, both featuring the concept of a small team of adventurers who crew a fantastic spaceship on patrol in outer space.

The first format was virtually identical in every respect to the series that was ultimately produced and presented a story synopsis for the initial episode that made an almost word-for-word transition to the screen as *Planet 46*. The only differences between this 'Century 21' concept and FIREBALL XL5 were that the featured spacecraft was named *Century 21*, the events were set one thousand years in the future in the year 2962, and the main characters were operatives of the United States Space Patrol.

The second format was, perhaps, more unusual and ambitious. This proposed a series made with a combination of live-action and Supermarionation, with the live-action scenes acting as framing sequences for each episode's main story presented in Supermarionation. The live-action scenes would have focused on Little Joe, a young American boy who dreams of being handsome, heroic space pilot Joe 90. The Supermarionation sequences would then have presented Joe's imaginary adventures as Joe 90, pilot of SPV (Space Patrol Vehicle) 1 Zero, and his crew: sister Debbie, brother-in-law Gary, niece Cindy Lou and navigator Professor Matthew Matic. The story of the proposed initial episode had Joe and the SPV1 Zero crew visiting a planet of giants where they become caught in a giant spider's web and then rescue Gary from the giant Goon and his two talking monkey servants. Bernard Braden, Kenneth Connor, Spike Milligan, David Graham and Sylvia Anderson were suggested for the voices of the puppet characters, while Braden and his wife Barbara Kelly were put forward to play Little Joe's parents in the live-action sequences.

Episode Titles

(Listed in production order)

1. **Planet 46**
2. **Hypnotic Sphere**
3. **Planet Of Platonia**
4. **Space Magnet**
5. **The Doomed Planet**
6. **Plant Man From Space**
7. **The Sun Temple**
8. **Space Immigrants**
9. **Space Monster**
10. **Flying Zodiac**
11. **Spy In Space**
12. **XL5 To H_20**
13. **Space Pirates**
14. **The Last Of The Zanadus**
15. **Space Pen**
16. **Convict In Space**
17. **Wings Of Danger**
18. **The Triads**
19. **Sabotage**
20. **Prisoner On The Lost Planet**
21. **Flight To Danger**
22. **Space Vacation**
23. **Mystery Of The TA2**
24. **Robert To The Rescue**
25. **The Forbidden Planet**
26. **The Granatoid Tanks**
27. **Dangerous Cargo**
28. **1875**
29. **The Robot Freighter Mystery**
30. **Drama At Space City**
31. **Whistle For Danger**
32. **Faster Than Light**
33. **The Day The Earth Froze**
34. **Invasion Earth**
35. **Ghosts Of Space**
36. **Trial By Robot**
37. **A Day In The Life Of A Space General**
38. **Space City Special**
39. **The Fire Fighters**

Episode Running Time

25 minutes approx.

The FIREBALL XL5 end titles song 'Fireball' was released as a single by HMV Records in 1963. Performed by Don Spencer, the song entered the UK record chart on March 21st, 1963 and stayed there for 11 weeks, reaching number 32 at its peak. It later re-entered the chart on June 13th, 1963 at number 49.

PLANET 46

Prod. No. 01

Teleplay by **Gerry & Sylvia Anderson** Directed by **Gerry Anderson**

Space City tracks a missile carrying a Planetomic bomb heading for Earth, so Commander Zero contacts Steve Zodiac, aboard *Fireball XL5* on patrol in Sector 25, to intercept the missile. The source of the missile is traced to Planet 46 so Steve sets a course for the planet to investigate and he and Venus take *Fireball Jr.* to the surface. Searching a diamond-filled cave network on their jetmobiles, Steve and Venus are attacked by Subterrains. When Steve recovers from the effects of the Subterrains' coma ray, the Subterrain Leader reveals that Venus has been imprisoned aboard a second Planetomic missile which is to be launched at Earth!

Notes

A Planetomic warhead is said to be a million times more powerful than a hydrogen bomb. It takes the *Fireball* crew several days to travel to Planet 46.

Oops!

At the end of the episode, Steve's dialogue suggests that *XL5* is approaching Earth, but the planet seen through the viewscreen is Planet 46.

Regular Voice Cast

Col. Steve Zodiac	**Paul Maxwell**
Dr. Venus	**Sylvia Anderson**
Prof. Matthew Matic	**David Graham**
Cdr. Wilbur Zero	**John Bluthal**
Lt. 90	**David Graham**
Robert	**Gerry Anderson**

Guest Voice Cast

Subterrain Leader	**John Bluthal**
Subterrain 1	**David Graham**
Subterrain 2	**John Bluthal**
Canaveral Station	**David Graham**
Woomera Rocket Range	**John Bluthal**
Okinawa Station	**Paul Maxwell**
Jodrell Bank	**David Graham**

First UK Transmission

Sunday, October 28th, 1962
4.25pm (ATV London)

HYPNOTIC SPHERE

Prod. No. 02

Teleplay by **Alan Fennell** Directed by **Alan Pattillo**

When the *Fireball* crew discover Earth fuel tanker *EF Z4* in free float near the planet Suventa, Steve and Matt find the ship deserted apart from the pilot, who is in a state of deep hypnosis. This is the fourth such tanker to be found abandoned in the last four weeks, so Steve decides to escort tanker *EF Z5* along the same route. As *XL5* and the tanker approach Suventa, an unmanned spherical craft appears and emits a strange hypnotic light which mesmerises the *Fireball* crew. Fighting the instructions of a disembodied voice, Steve confuses Robert who accidentally knocks him out and sets *XL5* on a collision course with Mirana, the planet of fire!

Notes

All WSP officers must have a regular medical check-up every day during their tour of space duty. Robert keeps a record of everything that happens at all times. Although produced as the series' second episode, *Hypnotic Sphere* was originally broadcast as episode 37. It was one of four episodes held back from the end of the initial run on ATV London to open a repeat screening of the series from October 1963 (the other episodes were *Ghosts Of Space*, *Sabotage* and *Space Magnet*.)

Regular Voice Cast

Col. Steve Zodiac	**Paul Maxwell**
Dr. Venus	**Sylvia Anderson**
Prof. Matthew Matic	**David Graham**
Cdr. Wilbur Zero	**John Bluthal**
Lt. 90	**David Graham**
Robert	**Gerry Anderson**

Guest Voice Cast

Suventan Brain	**John Bluthal**
Tanker Pilot Joe	**David Graham**

First UK Transmission

Sunday, October 13th, 1963
4.00pm (ATV London)

PLANET OF PLATONIA

Prod. No. 03

Teleplay by **Alan Fennell** Directed by **David Elliott**

Planet Platonia is rich in platinum, so the ruler Bizan plans to travel to Earth to engage in trade talks which will secure his position with the Platonian people in the face of opposition from his rival Ginerva. Bizan narrowly avoids a fifth attempt on his life in as many weeks, so Zero sends the *XL5* crew to escort him safely to Earth. Leaving Robert to stand guard on *Fireball Jr.*, Steve and Venus attend a magnificent banquet in their honour at Bizan's palace before being shown to their rooms for the night. But while everyone is asleep, Bizan's assistant Volvo uses a jamming device to incapacitate Robert and plants a bomb inside the robot's body!

Notes

Venus reveals that the effects of the WSP coma ray gun can be countered with an anti-coma serum. *Fireball Jr.* is attached to the main craft with magnetic locks. Ginerva's space fighter is the Subterrain's Planetomic missile seen in footage from *Planet 46*. This episode marks David Lane's first credit on a Gerry Anderson production, although he previously worked as an uncredited assistant editor on SUPERCAR. The editor here, Lane became a director and producer on the later Supermarionation series and UFO.

Regular Voice Cast

Col. Steve Zodiac	**Paul Maxwell**
Dr. Venus	**Sylvia Anderson**
Prof. Matthew Matic	**David Graham**
Cdr. Wilbur Zero	**John Bluthal**
Lt. 90	**David Graham**
Robert	**Gerry Anderson**

Guest Voice Cast

Bizan	**John Bluthal**
Volvo	**David Graham**

First UK Transmission

Sunday, January 20th, 1963
4.50pm (ATV London)

SPACE MAGNET — Prod. No. 04

Teleplay by **Anthony Marriott** — Directed by **Bill Harris**

At Space City, Steve and Lieutenant 90 receive an emergency call from Captain Ross aboard *Fireball XL7,* who reports that his ship has gone out of control. Then all contact is lost and, as the *XL5* crew prepare to set off on a rescue mission, they discover that the Moon has been dragged out of Earth orbit. Trailing the satellite through space, Steve has to apply the ship's main boosters to keep up with it, but then *XL5* accelerates out of control and Steve realises that they have fallen into an ultra-magnetic field. The crew pass out as *XL5* increases speed beyond Space Velocity 14 and, narrowly avoiding collision with the Moon, the ship is drawn to Magneton, the magnetic planet...

Notes
This episode marks the first appearance of Zoony. Steve says that Matt's alarm clock, a 1962 model, is over 100 years old. Matt lives on board *XL5* and has no other home.

Oops!
There is no explanation as to why Earth's Moon will bring light to Magneton: the Moon itself is not a light source and is only capable of reflecting light from the Sun.

Regular Voice Cast

Col. Steve Zodiac	**Paul Maxwell**
Dr. Venus	**Sylvia Anderson**
Prof. Matthew Matic	**David Graham**
Cdr. Wilbur Zero	**John Bluthal**
Lt. 90	**David Graham**
Robert	**Gerry Anderson**
Zoony	**David Graham**

Guest Voice Cast

Super Solar	**David Graham**
Captain Ross	**John Bluthal**

First UK Transmission

Sunday, October 27th, 1963
4.00pm (ATV London)

THE DOOMED PLANET — Prod. No. 05

Teleplay by **Alan Fennell** — Directed by **Alan Pattillo**

The *XL5* crew narrowly avoid a collision with a rogue planet that has broken orbit and Matt calculates that it will collide with planet Membrono in 21 days. To ensure that Membrono is uninhabited, Steve takes *Fireball Jr.* to the surface and confirms that there are no signs of life, although he has a strange feeling that he is being watched. After Steve returns to *XL5*, a saucer-shaped spacecraft lifts off from Membrono and trails *XL5* back to Earth. It is spotted by Steve, Venus and Matt although Zero refuses to take their report seriously. Later, as Venus entertains Steve at her beach house, the saucer lands nearby...

Notes
Venus has had Zoony for three months at this point and Steve hears him speak for the first time here. The disc that Venus plays at the beach house is a track entitled 'Formula 5'. The disc's B-side plays the Bantonga theme from the SUPERCAR episode *Hi-Jack.*

Oops!
When Steve fires Interceptors 2, 3 and 4 at the rogue planet, the detonation occurs before the missiles get there.

Regular Voice Cast

Col. Steve Zodiac	**Paul Maxwell**
Dr. Venus	**Sylvia Anderson**
Prof. Matthew Matic	**David Graham**
Cdr. Wilbur Zero	**John Bluthal**
Lt. 90	**David Graham**
Robert	**Gerry Anderson**
Zoony	**David Graham**

Guest Voice Cast

Saucer Man	**John Bluthal**

First UK Transmission

Sunday, November 4th, 1962
4.25pm (ATV London)

PLANT MAN FROM SPACE — Prod. No. 06

Teleplay by **Anthony Marriott** — Directed by **John Kelly**

A power failure leaves Space City helpless and the Earth undefended. Jock discovers that someone has placed a radioactive retardant capsule in the air intake of the base nuclear reactor, but the only recent visitors to the power plant were Matt and his old friend Dr. Howard Rootes, who has recently returned to Earth after a decade conducting plant experiments in space. Then a missile lands on the beach nearby, releasing alien plant seeds which grow overnight. The next morning, Space City is completely immobilised by Hedera Helix, a particularly virulent form of ivy from planet Hedera...

Notes
This episode introduces engineer Jock Campbell. The elevator used by Matt and Dr. Rootes indicates that there are 63 floors in the Space City tower.

Oops!
The elevator indicates that when Matt and Dr. Rootes leave the power plant, they ascend from the 20th floor to reach the Control Room. But the Control Room is on the 20th floor of the Space City tower (as revealed in *The Granatoid Tanks* and *Invasion Earth).*

Regular Voice Cast

Col. Steve Zodiac	**Paul Maxwell**
Dr. Venus	**Sylvia Anderson**
Prof. Matthew Matic	**David Graham**
Cdr. Wilbur Zero	**John Bluthal**
Lt. 90	**David Graham**
Robert	**Gerry Anderson**
Zoony	**David Graham**
Jock Campbell	**John Bluthal**

Guest Voice Cast

Dr. Howard Rootes	**Paul Maxwell**
The Chlorophon	**David Graham**
Ken Ross	**John Bluthal**
Alarm Service	**Sylvia Anderson**

First UK Transmission

Sunday, November 18th, 1962
4.20pm (ATV London)

THE SUN TEMPLE

Prod. No. 07

Teleplay by **Alan Fennell** Directed by **Bill Harris**

A J17 Warrior rocket is launched from Space City to demolish a meteorite belt that is proving dangerous to space flight. On planet Rajusca in the vicinity of the meteorite belt, the missile is tracked by sun-worshipping priests Kazak and Zodan, who mistake the detonation for an attempt to put another sun in their sky. They perceive this as an insult to their sun-god Miras and decide to take vengeance on Earth, harnessing the power of Miras to project a beam that destroys the rocket launching site at Space City. The *XL5* crew travel to Rajusca to investigate, but Venus is captured by the priests and tied down in the path of the sun-beam in preparation for sacrifice to Miras...

Notes

All creatures on Colevio have telepathic power and Zoony is no exception: he can receive thought waves. He learned to say "Welcome home" months ago and is taught to say "Howdy, folks" and "Follow me" here. The target of the Rajuscan sun beam suggests that Space City is located in the Pacific Ocean somewhere off the coast of Chile. The incidental theme for the Rajuscan temple was originally composed for the SUPERCAR episode *Amazonian Adventure*.

Regular Voice Cast

Col. Steve Zodiac	**Paul Maxwell**
Dr. Venus	**Sylvia Anderson**
Prof. Matthew Matic	**David Graham**
Cdr. Wilbur Zero	**John Bluthal**
Lt. 90	**David Graham**
Robert	**Gerry Anderson**
Zoony	**David Graham**

Guest Voice Cast

Kazak	**John Bluthal**
Zodan	**David Graham**
Warrior Countdown	**David Graham**

First UK Transmission

Sunday, December 2nd, 1962
4.20pm (ATV London)

SPACE IMMIGRANTS

Prod. No. 08

Teleplay by **Anthony Marriott** Directed by **Alan Pattillo**

On planet New Earth, *XL7* pilot Ross has been captured by a pair of tiny Lillispatians, Minotran and Minodor, who eagerly await the arrival of a group of Earth colonists aboard the *Mayflower 3*. Planning to capture the colonists and use them as slaves, the Lillispatians watch preparations for the *Mayflower* launch via Mini Space Videograph. They use a Microwave Transmitter Controller to take control of Robert and force him to dispose of the ship's entire supply of medicine, so when Jock falls ill with appendicitis *en route*, Venus is horrified to learn that there are no anaesthesia tablets aboard the *Mayflower* and cannot perform the emergency surgery that will save his life...

Oops!

Minodor says that Earth is 632 light years from New Earth, but *XL5* only travels at sub-light speeds (the ship breaks the light barrier in *Faster Than Light*), so unless WSP vehicles use some sort of warp technology (that is not referred to in any episode) the *Fireball* crew could not reach the planet within their own lifetime. When the Lillispatians use their MTC, the camera zoom on the Earth model targets Space City in the Atlantic Ocean off the coast of Argentina, which contradicts the location given in *The Sun Temple*.

Regular Voice Cast

Col. Steve Zodiac	**Paul Maxwell**
Dr. Venus	**Sylvia Anderson**
Prof. Matthew Matic	**David Graham**
Cdr. Wilbur Zero	**John Bluthal**
Lt. 90	**David Graham**
Zoony	**David Graham**
Jock Campbell	**John Bluthal**

Guest Voice Cast

Minotran	**John Bluthal**
Minodor	**David Graham**
Captain Ross	**John Bluthal**

First UK Transmission

Sunday, November 11th, 1962
4.25pm (ATV London)

SPACE MONSTER

Prod. No. 09

Teleplay by **Gerry** & **Sylvia Anderson** Directed by **John Kelly**

The *XL5* crew are dispatched to respond to an emergency transmission from *Fireball XL2* pilot Ken Johnson on planet Monotane. Steve and Venus search the surface in *Fireball Jr.* but just as they locate the wreckage of *XL2* something strikes the craft and it goes out of control. Steve manages to land *Fireball Jr.* in one piece but the impact wrecks the radio gear and they lose contact with Matt aboard *XL5*. Hearing what sounds like a storm approaching, Steve and Venus take shelter in a cave where they find Johnson and his co-pilot, but they are now all trapped inside the cave by a huge space monster!

Notes

Venus and Zoony dance to a music track entitled 'This Is The Twist'. The space monster later appears in STINGRAY as the title character in *Loch Ness Monster*.

Oops!

As *XL5* approaches Monotane, the forward viewscreen shows the ship approaching Earth. Later, Matt says that he can see *Fireball Jr.* on his monitor, but the screen actually shows the wreckage of *Fireball XL2*.

Regular Voice Cast

Col. Steve Zodiac	**Paul Maxwell**
Dr. Venus	**Sylvia Anderson**
Prof. Matthew Matic	**David Graham**
Cdr. Wilbur Zero	**John Bluthal**
Lt. 90	**David Graham**
Robert	**Gerry Anderson**
Zoony	**David Graham**

Guest Voice Cast

Captain Ken Johnson	**John Bluthal**
Al Stomper	**David Graham**

First UK Transmission

Sunday, January 6th, 1963
4.50pm (ATV London)

FLYING ZODIAC — Prod. No. 10

Teleplay by **Anthony Marriott** Directed by **Bill Harris**

Steve arranges a special dinner for Venus and Matt to celebrate the 200th anniversary of his great great great grandmother Clara's first circus performance as a clairvoyant. Venus asks Steve to tell them about the Zodiacs who, apart from Clara, were all trapeze artists, but while Steve and Matt are making coffee, Venus falls asleep and dreams that a charity circus is taking place at Space City. Clairvoyant Madame Mivea and Cosmo the Intercosmic Clown are secretly working for a band of Nomadians whose plan to make a permanent camp on Earth involves sabotaging Steve's dangerous trapeze act...

Notes

Venus dreams about Boris and Griselda Space Spy (as Cosmo and Madame Mivea) whom she first meets in *Spy In Space*, so that episode should be seen before this one.

Oops!

The Caravan Leader twice uses light years as a measurement of time (to describe his age and how long his people have been wandering in space), but they are a measurement of distance. Jock mistakes Ken Johnson for Captain Ross.

Regular Voice Cast

Col. Steve Zodiac	**Paul Maxwell**
Dr. Venus	**Sylvia Anderson**
Prof. Matthew Matic	**David Graham**
Cdr. Wilbur Zero	**John Bluthal**
Lt. 90	**David Graham**
Zoony	**David Graham**
Jock Campbell	**John Bluthal**
Griselda Space Spy	**Sylvia Anderson**
Boris Space Spy	**David Graham**

Guest Voice Cast

Caravan Leader	**John Bluthal**
Captain Ken Johnson	**John Bluthal**
Tannoy	**Paul Maxwell**

First UK Transmission

Sunday, December 23rd, 1962
4.40pm (ATV London)

SPY IN SPACE — Prod. No. 11

Teleplay by **Alan Fennell** Directed by **Alan Pattillo**

Fireball XL9 is *en route* to relieve *XL5* in Sector 25 when the ship comes under fire from a pirate spacecraft, the *S.S. Thor*. *XL9* returns to Earth in flames, so Zero diverts *XL5* back to Sector 25 to resume *XL9*'s patrol. Steve sets course for the Companion 12 space station to refuel and finds the *Thor* in free float nearby. Both the *Thor* and the station appear to be deserted, but when Steve, Venus and Matt board Companion 12, they find that they have walked into a trap. The trio are captured by Boris and Griselda Space Spy who intend to take Venus hostage and steal *XL5* as the new headquarters for their Universe Spy Organisation...

Notes

The standard patrol period for the *XL5* crew is three months. Companion 12 is described as one of the first stations to be put in space. The markings on the side of the *S.S. Thor* show (in tiny letters) that S.S. is an acronym for Space Spy. Although Steve clearly knows who Boris and Griselda Space Spy are, the *XL5* crew have not met them before, so this episode should be seen before *Flying Zodiac*, *Convict In Space* and *Space Pen* in which the villains also appear.

Regular Voice Cast

Col. Steve Zodiac	**Paul Maxwell**
Dr. Venus	**Sylvia Anderson**
Prof. Matthew Matic	**David Graham**
Cdr. Wilbur Zero	**John Bluthal**
Lt. 90	**David Graham**
Robert	**Gerry Anderson**
Griselda Space Spy	**Sylvia Anderson**
Boris Space Spy	**David Graham**

Guest Voice Cast

XL9 Pilot	**Paul Maxwell**

First UK Transmission

Sunday, November 25th, 1962
4.20pm (ATV London)

XL5 TO H_2O — Prod. No. 12

Teleplay by **Alan Fennell** Directed by **John Kelly**

On planet Zofeit, the two survivors of an alien civilisation come under fire from a hostile Aquaphibian equipped with a ray gun that spouts poison gas. They send a distress signal to the WSP before taking refuge in an underground shelter, so Zero dispatches the *XL5* crew to Zofeit. Steve and Matt travel to the surface in *Fireball Jr.* but the ship is attacked by the Aquaphibian. Donning gas masks, they return to *XL5* to repair damage to the viewscreen and Matt develops a compound which strengthens the screens against the Aquaphibian's ray gun. Steve and Venus return to the surface, but then their apparently solid landing area gives way and *Fireball Jr.* sinks underwater out of control!

Notes

The Aquaphibian creature that menaces Jenek and Reld inspired the creation of Titan's Aquaphibians in STINGRAY. *Fireball Jr.* is revealed to be equipped with a rocket launcher and can operate underwater like a submarine.

Oops!

As *XL5* approaches Zofeit, the forward viewscreen shows the ship approaching Earth.

Regular Voice Cast

Col. Steve Zodiac	**Paul Maxwell**
Dr. Venus	**Sylvia Anderson**
Prof. Matthew Matic	**David Graham**
Cdr. Wilbur Zero	**John Bluthal**
Lt. 90	**David Graham**
Robert	**Gerry Anderson**

Guest Voice Cast

Jenek	**John Bluthal**
Reld	**David Graham**

First UK Transmission

Sunday, December 9th, 1962
4.25pm (ATV London)

SPACE PIRATES

Prod. No. 13

Teleplay by **Anthony Marriott** Directed by **Bill Harris**

Venus is baby-sitting for Commander Zero, looking after his son Jonathan while he and his wife attend a bingo night at Space City. Jonathan asks Venus to tell him a bedtime story about space pirates, so she tells him of the planet Minera in Sector 25, the richest source of radioactive minerals known to man. Minera is close to Aridan, a barren waterless planet used by space pirate Captain Catt as a base from which to plunder Earth space freighters as they leave Minera. In an attempt to trap the pirates, Steve pilots a disguised Q spaceship along the regular freighter route. Meanwhile, Jock is preparing to leave Minera when his freighter is boarded by Catt and his assistant Patch, who knock Jock out and throw him overboard, stealing the freighter to set a trap for Steve...

Notes

This episode introduces Commander Zero's son Jonathan. His wife Eleanor is heard but not seen. Jonathan has a book about Supercar on the shelf in his bedroom (illustrating that the events of SUPERCAR share the FIREBALL XL5 fictional universe, although it is not clear whether this is in a fictional or historical context). Venus does not reveal if the events of her pirate story actually happened or not.

Regular Voice Cast

Col. Steve Zodiac	**Paul Maxwell**
Dr. Venus	**Sylvia Anderson**
Prof. Matthew Matic	**David Graham**
Cdr. Wilbur Zero	**John Bluthal**
Lt. 90	**David Graham**
Robert	**Gerry Anderson**
Zoony	**David Graham**
Jock Campbell	**John Bluthal**
Eleanor Zero	**Sylvia Anderson**
Jonathan Zero	**Sylvia Anderson**

Guest Voice Cast

Captain Catt	**David Graham**
Patch	**John Bluthal**
XL9 Pilot	**Paul Maxwell**

First UK Transmission

Sunday, December 16th, 1962
4.25pm (ATV London)

THE LAST OF THE ZANADUS

Prod. No. 14

Teleplay by **Anthony Marriott** Directed by **Alan Pattillo**

At Space City, Steve is preparing to host a dinner party in honour of Major Jim Ireland, who is returning to Earth after exploring space for the last decade. Ireland arrives at Space City in his ship *Explorer* and after dinner at Steve's apartment, he shows the WSP team videotapes of the planets that he has visited, including Herbos the jungle planet and Zanadu. Steve and Matt recall that Kudos, the sole surviving inhabitant of Zanadu, has vowed to destroy all Lazoons after the planet was overrun by them. They are unaware that Ireland has become an unwitting agent for Kudos and, during the night, he infects a box of Zoony's favourite Martian Delight with deadly milomytosis virus...

Notes

Steve and Venus listen to 'Formula 5' in Steve's apartment. Steve has a personal intercall device similar to a pager which he attaches to his belt. Following on from similar acts of televisual postmodernism in SUPERCAR, Steve talks directly to camera at one point to tell viewers that women have not changed one bit since the 1960s. He later reveals that Venus has only been with the WSP for five years, while he has been a Patrol operative since before Ireland left Earth 10 years ago.

Regular Voice Cast

Col. Steve Zodiac	**Paul Maxwell**
Dr. Venus	**Sylvia Anderson**
Prof. Matthew Matic	**David Graham**
Cdr. Wilbur Zero	**John Bluthal**
Lt. 90	**David Graham**
Robert	**Gerry Anderson**
Zoony	**David Graham**

Guest Voice Cast

Kudos	**David Graham**
Major Jim Ireland	**John Bluthal**

First UK Transmission

Sunday, January 13th, 1963
4.50pm (ATV London)

SPACE PEN

Prod. No. 15

Teleplay by **Dennis Spooner** Directed by **John Kelly**

Lieutenant 90 receives a request for landing clearance from *Freighter ZX4*, but the ship is occupied by a pair of gangsters, Carmachi and Al, who plan to steal Space City's stock of isotopes. Waiting until nightfall, the gangsters break into Steve's apartment and take his identification papers before cleaning out the isotope store and stealing Zero's uniform. 90 tracks the gangster's ship to Conva, the prison planet, but Zero reports that he cannot send the *XL5* crew there without the approval of Conva's controller General Shan. Determined to bring the gangsters and the mastermind behind their scheme to justice, Steve, Matt and Venus pose as dangerous criminals who have stolen *XL5*...

Notes

Much of the incidental music in this episode was originally composed for SUPERCAR: for example, the track that accompanies the flooding of the pumping chamber was first heard in the SUPERCAR episode *Operation Superstork*. The *S.S. Thor* is shot down by *XL5* and completely destroyed here, so this episode should be seen after *Convict In Space* in which the *Thor* also appears (during the original broadcast run, *Space Pen* was screened before *Convict In Space*).

Regular Voice Cast

Col. Steve Zodiac	**Paul Maxwell**
Dr. Venus	**Sylvia Anderson**
Prof. Matthew Matic	**David Graham**
Cdr. Wilbur Zero	**John Bluthal**
Lt. 90	**David Graham**
Robert	**Gerry Anderson**
Zoony	**David Graham**
Griselda Space Spy	**Sylvia Anderson**
Boris Space Spy	**David Graham**

Guest Voice Cast

Carmachi	**David Graham**
Al	**John Bluthal**
General Shan	**Paul Maxwell**

First UK Transmission

Sunday, December 30th, 1962
4.20pm (ATV London)

CONVICT IN SPACE — Prod. No. 16

Teleplay by **Alan Fennell** Directed by **Bill Harris**

Top secret plans are stolen from WSP's North American research base by Grothan Deblis who escapes in a 37H spaceship. Zero alerts the *XL5* crew and Matt soon spots Deblis's ship, but its course suggests that Deblis has already made a stop-off to hide the plans. Deblis surrenders when Steve targets his ship with a blast missile. Three months later, Deblis is sentenced to 20 years on the prison planet Conva and he is ferried there aboard *XL5*. Boris and Griselda Space Spy plan to rescue Deblis and force him to hand over the top secret papers, so they disguise the *S.S. Thor* and transmit a distress signal to *XL5* which Steve immediately responds to. Matt crosses to the *Thor* to effect engine repairs, but he is captured by Boris and Griselda who then offer to exchange him for Deblis...

Notes

The *XL5* crew are able to recognise the *S.S. Thor* and are aware that it belongs to Boris and Griselda, so this episode should be seen after *Spy In Space* (where they do not know of the *Thor*'s ownership). After Boris and Griselda are captured at the end of this episode, they are presumably incarcerated on Conva where they are seen in *Space Pen*. This was their final appearance in the series.

Regular Voice Cast

Col. Steve Zodiac	**Paul Maxwell**
Dr. Venus	**Sylvia Anderson**
Prof. Matthew Matic	**David Graham**
Cdr. Wilbur Zero	**John Bluthal**
Lt. 90	**David Graham**
Robert	**Gerry Anderson**
Griselda Space Spy	**Sylvia Anderson**
Boris Space Spy	**David Graham**

Guest Voice Cast

Grothan Deblis	**David Graham**
IPN Newsreader	**John Bluthal**
Research Control	**Paul Maxwell**

First UK Transmission

Sunday, February 10th, 1963
4.50pm (ATV London)

WINGS OF DANGER — Prod. No. 17

Teleplay by **Alan Fennell** Directed by **David Elliott**

On Planet 46, the Subterrains plan revenge on Steve Zodiac for the capture of their leader and develop a robot bird which targets a subject with deadly radium capsules. Steve and Venus arrive on the planet to investigate some strange radio signals which have been detected at Space City, so the Subterrains programme the robot bird to follow *XL5* when the crew return to Earth. Steve gives Venus and Zoony a lift to the beach house in his hovercar, but he collapses after the robot bird fires one of its capsules at him and Venus discovers that she must conduct an emergency operation to save his life!

Notes

As the camera moves through the caves of Planet 46, there is a very unusual animated flame effect 'wipe' to the lake of fire. This episode is a direct sequel to *Planet 46* and several of the characters refer to the events of that episode.

Oops!

As the robot bird approaches Earth, the back projection footage of the planet appears in mirror image: South America is the wrong way round.

Regular Voice Cast

Col. Steve Zodiac	**Paul Maxwell**
Dr. Venus	**Sylvia Anderson**
Prof. Matthew Matic	**David Graham**
Cdr. Wilbur Zero	**John Bluthal**
Lt. 90	**David Graham**
Robert	**Gerry Anderson**
Zoony	**David Graham**

Guest Voice Cast

Subterrain 1	**John Bluthal**
Subterrain 2	**David Graham**

First UK Transmission

Sunday, February 3rd, 1963
4.50pm (ATV London)

THE TRIADS — Prod. No. 18

Teleplay by **Alan Fennell** Directed by **Alan Pattillo**

A series of massive planetary explosions in deep space are detected at Space City and Matt traces them to Triad, a planet three times the size of Earth. Zero sends *XL5* across the space frontier to investigate and after a three-week journey, Steve, Venus and Matt take *Fireball Jr.* down to the planet's surface. Steve finds that Triad's gravitational pull is enormous and using the emergency retros to fight it soon exhausts the ship's fuel supply. Crash-landing in the Triad jungle, the trio explore on jetmobiles, but take refuge in a tree when they are attacked by a giant lion. Steve's coma ray gun proves ineffective against the lion, but then they are all suddenly plucked from the tree by a giant man!

Notes

Fireball XL5 travels into uncharted space for the first time, so this episode must be seen before *Prisoner On The Lost Planet* and *Faster Than Light*. Returning to the technique of combining puppets with live actors pioneered in the SUPERCAR episode *Calling Charlie Queen*, *The Triads* even reuses the laboratory bench set and props from that episode. This episode pre-dated the suspiciously similar American television series LAND OF THE GIANTS by six years.

Regular Voice Cast

Col. Steve Zodiac	**Paul Maxwell**
Dr. Venus	**Sylvia Anderson**
Prof. Matthew Matic	**David Graham**
Cdr. Wilbur Zero	**John Bluthal**
Lt. 90	**David Graham**
Robert	**Gerry Anderson**
Zoony	**David Graham**

Guest Voice Cast

Graff	**David Graham**
Snaff	**John Bluthal**

First UK Transmission

Sunday, January 27th, 1963
4.50pm (ATV London)

SABOTAGE
Prod. No. 19

Teleplay by **Anthony Marriott** — Directed by **John Kelly**

Regular Voice Cast

Col. Steve Zodiac	**Paul Maxwell**
Dr. Venus	**Sylvia Anderson**
Prof. Matthew Matic	**David Graham**
Cdr. Wilbur Zero	**John Bluthal**
Lt. 90	**David Graham**
Robert	**Gerry Anderson**

Guest Voice Cast

Arcon Commander	**David Graham**
Ultra Arcon	**John Bluthal**
Kelly	**John Bluthal**

First UK Transmission

Sunday, October 20th, 1963
4.00pm (ATV London)

As the *XL5* crew complete another patrol and return to Earth, the ship is suddenly rocked by the explosion of a neutroni control bomb in the space gyro mechanism, detonated by the Arcon Commander of *Gamma Ship 30* from planet Electra. Steve manages to put out the fire caused by the explosion but contact is lost with Space City and the space gyro mechanism will have to be repaired before the ship can return to Earth. When Matt discovers the remains of the bomb, Steve realises that they are the victims of sabotage and *XL5* is now a sitting duck. The Gamma Ship closes in on *XL5* and the Arcon Commander activates a gamma ray which mesmerises the crew, dragging them out of *XL5* and across space to the Electran craft...

Oops!
Matt says that the Gamma Ships have never been able to venture far from Electra or to reach Earth as they do not have a large enough fuel capacity, but there is no explanation as to how, in that case, the Electrans managed to plant neutroni bombs aboard all of the ships in the WSP fleet. When *Space Rescue 1* lifts off from Space City, the markings on the ship clearly identify it as *Fireball XL5*.

PRISONER ON THE LOST PLANET
Prod. No. 20

Teleplay by **Anthony Marriott** — Directed by **Bill Harris**

Regular Voice Cast

Col. Steve Zodiac	**Paul Maxwell**
Dr. Venus	**Sylvia Anderson**
Prof. Matthew Matic	**David Graham**
Cdr. Wilbur Zero	**John Bluthal**
Lt. 90	**David Graham**
Robert	**Gerry Anderson**

Guest Voice Cast

Aphros	**Sylvia Anderson**

First UK Transmission

Sunday, March 3rd, 1963
4.50pm (ATV London)

When Matt tests a new ultra long-range neutroni receiver, he picks up a transmission from uncharted space which Steve recognises as an old space distress call. Travelling beyond Sector 25, the *XL5* crew brave a flight through a belt of meteorites to reach the uncharted planet that is the source of the signal. Steve, Venus and Matt take *Fireball Jr.* to the surface and Steve explores a cave in the side of a volcano, where he discovers a beautiful woman living in luxurious accommodation. She introduces herself as Aphros, exiled former Queen of the Space Amazons, but when Steve refuses to take her back to Earth, she drugs him and threatens to destroy *Fireball Jr.* with the volcano's molten lava!

Notes
The *XL5* crew travel into uncharted space again so this episode should not be seen before *The Triads*, in which they crossed the frontier of Sector 25 for the first time. Steve reveals that Earth and Amazonia are both members of the United Planets Organisation and are pledged not to interfere in each other's internal affairs. This pre-dated the development of the suspiciously similar United Federation of Planets in the American television series STAR TREK by at least four years.

FLIGHT TO DANGER
Prod. No. 21

Teleplay by **Alan Fennell** — Directed by **David Elliott**

Regular Voice Cast

Col. Steve Zodiac	**Paul Maxwell**
Dr. Venus	**Sylvia Anderson**
Prof. Matthew Matic	**David Graham**
Cdr. Wilbur Zero	**John Bluthal**
Lt. 90	**David Graham**
Robert	**Gerry Anderson**

Guest Voice Cast

Technician	**Paul Maxwell**

First UK Transmission

Sunday, February 24th, 1963
4.50pm (ATV London)

Lieutenant 90 is training to qualify for his astronaut's wings and after he successfully lands *XL5* in one piece, Steve recommends that he should proceed straight to the next stage, piloting *XL1* to blast off from the launch rail. With Robert as co-pilot and Matt as navigator, 90 pilots the ship into space to Zero's satisfaction, so he prepares to undertake a solo orbit of the Moon in a space capsule as the final stage of his training. Launched in a J17 rocket, 90 completes his lunar orbit but the capsule's atomic reactor breaks free and, as he returns to Earth, the Lieutenant discovers that the capsule is on fire!

Notes
Matt's dialogue confirms that Space City is located in the Pacific Ocean.

Oops!
On both of the occasions that *XL5* approaches Earth in this episode, the back projection footage of the planet seen through the forward viewscreen appears in mirror image: South America is the wrong way round. When *XL1* lifts off from Space City, the markings on the ship show that it is actually *XL5*.

SPACE VACATION — Prod. No. 22

Teleplay by **Dennis Spooner** Directed by **Alan Pattillo**

Kanerik, ruler of Kemble, plans to engineer the resettlement of his people on the nearby planet Olympus by poisoning the Olympian ruler's son Ergon with life elixir while visiting the planet for peace talks. Ergon's father Jankel worries that Olympus will become contaminated by aliens and plans to sabotage the peace talks by assassinating Kanerik during Ergon's birthday celebrations. The *XL5* crew become embroiled in the conflict when they arrive on Olympus for a vacation and are invited to Ergon's birthday feast by Jankel. After Ergon falls ill from drinking the poisoned elixir, Venus is taken prisoner by Kanerik to prevent her from treating the young Olympian and Jankel threatens Matt's life unless Steve rescues Venus in time for her to administer a cure!

Notes

The holiday planet Olympus is also seen in *A Day In The Life Of A Space General*.

Oops!

Steve is wearing a patterned shirt when he enters the caves on Kemble but a close-up shot of his hands shows the live actor's arms clothed in the sleeves of a WSP uniform.

Regular Voice Cast	
Col. Steve Zodiac	**Paul Maxwell**
Dr. Venus	**Sylvia Anderson**
Prof. Matthew Matic	**David Graham**
Cdr. Wilbur Zero	**John Bluthal**
Lt. 90	**David Graham**

Guest Voice Cast	
Kanerik	**David Graham**
Jankel	**John Bluthal**
Ergon	**David Graham**

First UK Transmission

Sunday, February 17th, 1963
4.50pm (ATV London)

MYSTERY OF THE TA2 — Prod. No. 23

Teleplay by **Dennis Spooner** Directed by **John Kelly**

Matt picks up a weak signal on the astrascope and when Steve diverts course to investigate, the *XL5* crew discover a piece of wreckage from the *TA2*, an early Space Patrol vessel that disappeared with its pilot, Colonel Harry Denton, 48 years ago. Matt locates the rest of the *TA2* wreckage and on board they learn that one of the ship's atomic motors exploded, causing a fire which destroyed the ship. Examining the ship's charts, Matt realises that Denton planned to try and reach Arctan after he ejected from the ship, so Steve sets a course for the planet to see if they can find him. The trio search the icy surface on jetmobiles, but suddenly Venus falls into a crevasse that opens up beneath her!

Notes

Denton's ice palace is revamped from Kudos's palace in *The Last Of The Zanadus*.

Oops!

There are a series of bad edits as Venus calls for help from the bottom of the crevasse: first she is sitting waist deep in snow, the next second she is trying to climb the ice wall, then she is waist deep in snow again and is finally seen standing in front of the ice wall.

Regular Voice Cast	
Col. Steve Zodiac	**Paul Maxwell**
Dr. Venus	**Sylvia Anderson**
Prof. Matthew Matic	**David Graham**
Cdr. Wilbur Zero	**John Bluthal**
Lt. 90	**David Graham**
Robert	**Gerry Anderson**
Zoony	**David Graham**

Guest Voice Cast	
Col. Harry Denton	**John Bluthal**
Jinco	**David Graham**
2nd Iceman	**John Bluthal**

First UK Transmission

Sunday, March 31st, 1963
4.40pm (ATV London)

ROBERT TO THE RESCUE — Prod. No. 24

Teleplay by **Dennis Spooner** Directed by **Bill Harris**

Matt has built himself a powerful telescope to take up astronomy and he soon spots a new planet that is not shown on the space charts. Naming the planet Matic, Matt reports it to Zero but when Lieutenant 90 checks the position on the radar scanner, there is no sign of it. Despite Zero's scepticism, Matic exists and the next morning it moves into a position which eclipses the Sun. Flying to the planet to investigate, the *XL5* crew are surprised to discover that it is entirely artificial and constructed from metal panels. Suddenly *Fireball Jr.* is pulled inside the planet by an unknown force and when they leave the ship to explore, Steve, Venus and Matt are captured by the planet's Domehead occupants who intend to wipe their memories and keep them as slaves for the rest of their lives!

Notes

The puppets of the Domehead inhabitants of Matic are revamped from the Lillispatian puppets made for *Space Immigrants*. The Domeheads reveal that Robert is made from leadinium. Although their memories return once they are away from the Domeheads' sphere of influence, Steve, Venus and Matt cannot recall what occurred inside the metal planet, so only Robert knows how he saved them all from a life of ignorant servitude.

Regular Voice Cast	
Col. Steve Zodiac	**Paul Maxwell**
Dr. Venus	**Sylvia Anderson**
Prof. Matthew Matic	**David Graham**
Cdr. Wilbur Zero	**John Bluthal**
Lt. 90	**David Graham**
Robert	**Gerry Anderson**
Zoony	**David Graham**

Guest Voice Cast	
Magar	**David Graham**
Proton	**John Bluthal**

First UK Transmission

Sunday, March 17th, 1963
4.55pm (ATV London)

THE FORBIDDEN PLANET — Prod. No. 25

Teleplay by **Anthony Marriott** — Directed by **David Elliott**

At the Interplanetary Astronomers Committee's Space Observatory 1, Matt and Dr. Stamp present an Earth TeleVision broadcast showing the first pictures from a new Ultrascope space probe. The pictures reveal the secrets of Nutopia, reputed to be the most beautiful planet in the universe. But on the planet, two guardians, Privator and Perfectos, are angered by this intrusion. They cut off the transmission to Earth with a protector ray and then journey to the observatory using a travel transmitter to kidnap Matt and Stamp, so when Steve and Venus arrive in *XL5*, the observatory is deserted!

Notes

The ETV announcer gives the date as Universal Astronomic Year 2062. Earth is a member of the Neutral Planets Scientific Organisation. When the ETV transmission from the observatory fails, the programme is replaced by "a short film" – actually footage from the FOUR FEATHER FALLS episode *The Toughest Guy In The West*.

Oops!

Privator uses light years as a measure of time, instead of distance.

Regular Voice Cast

Col. Steve Zodiac	**Paul Maxwell**
Dr. Venus	**Sylvia Anderson**
Prof. Matthew Matic	**David Graham**
Cdr. Wilbur Zero	**John Bluthal**
Lt. 90	**David Graham**
Robert	**Gerry Anderson**
Zoony	**David Graham**

Guest Voice Cast

Privator	**John Bluthal**
Perfectos	**David Graham**
Dr. Stamp	**Paul Maxwell**
Announcer	**John Bluthal**

First UK Transmission

Sunday, March 10th, 1963
4.50pm (ATV London)

THE GRANATOID TANKS — Prod. No. 26

Teleplay by **Alan Fennell** — Directed by **Alan Pattillo**

At a Mineral Research Laboratory on Planet 73, Dr. Baker and Dr. Simpson have just completed six months' work testing the planet's glass soil in preparation for colonisation when they discover that they are in the path of six tanks controlled by Granatoid robots, a hostile intelligence searching for a home and intent on the destruction of all obstacles. The robots can only be repelled by the rare mineral plyton, but Earth's stocks of plyton have run out. Steve and Matt are buying an Electro Orchestra instrument for Venus's birthday at Ma Doughty's music shop when they are alerted to the Granatoid threat. Convinced that she can help against the Granatoids, old Ma Doughty stows away inside the Electro Orchestra's crate when the instrument is delivered to *XL5*...

Notes

One of the Granatoid robot puppets originally appeared in the SUPERCAR episode *The Lost City*. Ma Doughty says that her father was one of the first men to go into space. Steve and Matt listen to 'Formula 5' in the audio lounge at Ma Doughty's shop and then Matt plays 'This Is The Twist' on the Electro Orchestra. The Space City elevator shows that the Control Room is on the 20th floor of the tower.

Regular Voice Cast

Col. Steve Zodiac	**Paul Maxwell**
Dr. Venus	**Sylvia Anderson**
Prof. Matthew Matic	**David Graham**
Cdr. Wilbur Zero	**John Bluthal**
Lt. 90	**David Graham**
Robert	**Gerry Anderson**
Zoony	**David Graham**

Guest Voice Cast

Ma Doughty	**Sylvia Anderson**
Dr. Baker	**David Graham**
Dr. Simpson	**John Bluthal**
Granatoid 1	**Gerry Anderson**

First UK Transmission

Sunday, April 21st, 1963
4.40pm (ATV London)

DANGEROUS CARGO — Prod. No. 27

Teleplay by **Dennis Spooner** — Directed by **John Kelly**

The *XL5* crew conduct a survey of Pharos, the derelict planet, where the strata is so riddled with old Ciluvium mine workings that the surface is collapsing. Returning to Earth, they report that Pharos will have to be destroyed before it falls apart and Zero decides to use Vesivium Nine explosives to completely disintegrate it. Zoony has been expelled from the Space City tower after causing chaos in the Control Room, so Venus begs Steve to let them take him with them to Pharos. Steve agrees on the condition that the Lazoon remains locked in the ship's Space Jail. On Pharos, they place the Vesivium Nine in one of the mine shafts and set the detonator, but a pair of Subterrains block the entrance to the shaft, trapping Steve, Venus and Matt inside with the bomb!

Notes

The Ciluvium mine on planet Pharos was opened in 1998. Vesivium Nine is described as the greatest explosive force in the universe. Steve's coma ray gun contains an atomic capsule which becomes a powerful explosive when removed from the gun. This third appearance of the Subterrains from Planet 46 should not be seen before the episodes *Planet 46* and *Wings Of Danger*.

Regular Voice Cast

Col. Steve Zodiac	**Paul Maxwell**
Dr. Venus	**Sylvia Anderson**
Prof. Matthew Matic	**David Graham**
Cdr. Wilbur Zero	**John Bluthal**
Lt. 90	**David Graham**
Robert	**Gerry Anderson**
Zoony	**David Graham**
Jock Campbell	**John Bluthal**

Guest Voice Cast

Subterrain 1	**David Graham**
Subterrain 2	**John Bluthal**

First UK Transmission

Sunday, March 24th, 1963
4.50pm (ATV London)

1875 — Prod. No. 28

Teleplay by **Anthony Marriott** Directed by **Bill Harris**

After weeks of seclusion in his workshop, Matt finally completes work on a time machine. He tests the machine by sending Robert back to 1875 where the robot surprises the deputy sheriff of a one-horse town. After Robert returns to the 21st century, Matt leaves the workshop key with Lieutenant 90, giving strict instructions that no one is to go in there until his demonstration the next day. But while Matt is sleeping, curiosity impels Steve, Venus and Zero to take the key and explore the workshop. Believing the apparatus to be an artificial gravity rig, the trio step into the time travel booth and when Zoony starts playing with the controls, they are accidentally transported to 1875!

Notes

A bizarre (and unexplained) effect of Matt's time machine is that in 1875, Steve, Venus and Zero forget their true identities and adopt different personas: Steve becomes a travelling gun-for-hire, while Venus (as Frenchie Lil) and Zero become outlaws who are known to Deputy Sheriff Dodgem and Doc, the bank manager. In another odd (and unexplained) twist, the two gentlemen from the Interplanetary Patents Office who arrive in Space City at the end of the episode are identical to Dodgem and Doc.

Regular Voice Cast	
Col. Steve Zodiac	**Paul Maxwell**
Dr. Venus	**Sylvia Anderson**
Prof. Matthew Matic	**David Graham**
Cdr. Wilbur Zero	**John Bluthal**
Lt. 90	**David Graham**
Robert	**Gerry Anderson**
Zoony	**David Graham**

Guest Voice Cast	
Deputy Sheriff Dodgem	**John Bluthal**
Doc	**David Graham**
Sgt. Mahoney	**David Graham**

First UK Transmission

Sunday, April 14th, 1963
4.40pm (ATV London)

THE ROBOT FREIGHTER MYSTERY — Prod. No. 29

Teleplay by **Alan Fennell** Directed by **David Elliott**

An explosion in the Master Robot Console of *Robot Supply Freighter 7* enables unscrupulous salvage operators Slim and Joe Briggs to load the cargo aboard their ship *SCS Valiant* and claim the salvage price from the WSP. This is the third such freighter that the Briggs brothers have 'salvaged' in recent weeks and Zero is certain that they have arranged to sabotage the ships somehow, but he has no proof and cannot arrest them. He orders Jock to make a thorough check of *Freighter 8* before it leaves Space City the next morning but during the night, Jock's assistant Edmundo sneaks into the freighter's Master Control Cabin and plants an incendiary device inside the Master Robot Console...

Notes

Zero tells Slim Briggs that he can recover their money for the 'salvaged' goods from the Pentagon, which seems to suggest that the WSP is financed by the US Department of Defence. The music that accompanies Edmundo's journey from Space City to the Briggs's Space Salvage Company office was originally composed as the main theme for *Crossroads To Crime* (1960) and was previously heard in the SUPERCAR episode *The White Line*.

Regular Voice Cast	
Col. Steve Zodiac	**Paul Maxwell**
Dr. Venus	**Sylvia Anderson**
Prof. Matthew Matic	**David Graham**
Cdr. Wilbur Zero	**John Bluthal**
Lt. 90	**David Graham**
Jock Campbell	**John Bluthal**

Guest Voice Cast	
Slim Briggs	**David Graham**
Joe Briggs	**Paul Maxwell**
Edmundo	**John Bluthal**
Emergency Call Tape	**David Graham**

First UK Transmission

Sunday, April 28th, 1963
4.40pm (ATV London)

DRAMA AT SPACE CITY — Prod. No. 30

Teleplay by **Anthony Marriott** Directed by **Alan Pattillo**

Steve and Venus take a vacation with Steve's Uncle Hans in Switzerland, leaving Zoony in the care of Zero and his family, but when Eleanor goes to visit her sick mother, Zero has to look after Zoony and Jonathan on his own. The pair cause havoc in the Control Room and Zero is at the end of his tether when Jonathan asks if he can have a ride in a spaceship. Disappointed by his father's angry refusal, Jonathan sneaks aboard *XL5* with Zoony during the night to find that Matt has left Robert at the controls while he is sleeping with the help of sedative pills. Unfortunately, Jonathan has taught Zoony to say "Full power" and the Lazoon accidentally orders Robert to launch the ship into space!

Notes

The entries in Steve's diary are accompanied by excerpts from *The Doomed Planet* and *The Triads*. Steve's dialogue implies that the events of this episode take place immediately after those of *The Triads*.

Oops!

When Robert ignites *XL5*'s motors in the middle of the night, it is daylight outside.

Regular Voice Cast	
Col. Steve Zodiac	**Paul Maxwell**
Dr. Venus	**Sylvia Anderson**
Prof. Matthew Matic	**David Graham**
Cdr. Wilbur Zero	**John Bluthal**
Lt. 90	**David Graham**
Robert	**Gerry Anderson**
Zoony	**David Graham**
Eleanor Zero	**Sylvia Anderson**
Jonathan Zero	**Sylvia Anderson**

Guest Voice Cast	
Uncle Hans	**John Bluthal**
Space Control	**Paul Maxwell**

First UK Transmission

Sunday, April 7th, 1963
4.40pm (ATV London)

WHISTLE FOR DANGER — Prod. No. 31

Teleplay by **Dennis Spooner** Directed by **John Kelly**

The *XL5* crew are dispatched to Floran, the jungle planet, to determine what is destroying the plant life there. Steve, Matt and Venus collect samples and Venus discovers traces of Planetoid 3, a virulent plant disease. After decontamination back on Earth, Matt suggests to Zero that they could detonate an Elvium bomb in Floran's atmosphere as the fallout would kill the disease but leave any human life unaffected. Returning to Floran, the *XL5* crew detonate the Elvium warhead and then go down to the surface to observe the effects. Steve, Venus and Matt are welcomed by a pair of Florans who take them to their castle and lay on a feast in their honour, but then the trio discover that their food has been drugged: in the belief that the Elvium bomb was a prelude to an invasion attempt, the Florans plan to execute the WSP officers!

Oops!

As Venus climbs out of the tower window, a shot of Steve watching her is reversed: his hair is parted on the right and the lettering on the XL5 badge on his chest is in mirror image (the shot was deliberately reversed in post-production so that Steve is looking towards the window rather than away from it).

Regular Voice Cast

Col. Steve Zodiac	**Paul Maxwell**
Dr. Venus	**Sylvia Anderson**
Prof. Matthew Matic	**David Graham**
Cdr. Wilbur Zero	**John Bluthal**
Lt. 90	**David Graham**
Robert	**Gerry Anderson**
Zoony	**David Graham**

Guest Voice Cast

Floran 1	**John Bluthal**
Floran 2	**David Graham**
Tannoy	**John Bluthal**

First UK Transmission

Sunday, May 5th, 1963
4.40pm (ATV London)

FASTER THAN LIGHT — Prod. No. 32

Teleplay by **Anthony Marriott** Directed by **Bill Harris**

XL5 is *en route* to Space Station 9 when Steve loses control of the ship. Matt dons a radiation suit to check the nutomic reactor and reports that there is a chain reaction in the main motor which will cause the ship to accelerate continuously until it eventually cuts out. Racing out of control, *XL5* flies into unexplored space at faster than light speed and as the ship breaks the light barrier, the crew pass out. When they recover consciousness, they discover that the ship has been holed by meteorites and most of their air has been lost. Matt calculates that the air supply will only last one more hour and to make matters worse, Zoony has eaten all the oxygen pills...

Notes

A close-up of the ship's speedometer shows that *XL5*'s normal speed is substantially less than light speed (unfortunately, the demarcations shown for 'Sound' and 'Heat' are meaningless for space travel). Some prints of this episode erroneously feature the end titles from *A Day In The Life Of A Space General*, crediting the script to Alan Fennell and direction to David Elliott, while the official ITC publicity information erroneously credits the script to Dennis Spooner.

Regular Voice Cast

Col. Steve Zodiac	**Paul Maxwell**
Dr. Venus	**Sylvia Anderson**
Prof. Matthew Matic	**David Graham**
Cdr. Wilbur Zero	**John Bluthal**
Lt. 90	**David Graham**
Robert	**Gerry Anderson**
Zoony	**David Graham**

Guest Voice Cast

Major Duncan	**John Bluthal**

First UK Transmission

Sunday, June 2nd, 1963
4.40pm (ATV London)

THE DAY THE EARTH FROZE — Prod. No. 33

Teleplay by **Alan Fennell** Directed by **David Elliott**

XL27 makes an emergency landing at Space City on remote control and when Steve, Matt and Zero board the ship, they find that the crew are all unconscious. Steve suspects that a ground-to-space Coma Cannon has been used against the ship and a message in the pilot's hand points to planet Zavia, an uninhabited ice planet in Sector 29, as the source of the attack. The *XL5* crew travel to Zavia while back on Earth, Space City experiences an unseasonal heavy snowfall. On Zavia, Steve, Venus and Matt discover tunnels cut into the ice leading to an underground base constructed by a pair of Jedums, Cardre and Rader, who plan vengeance against Earth by deflecting the sun's rays to freeze the planet!

Notes

The Jedum delegation arrived on Earth three years ago and tried to stir up trouble between Earth's leaders, planning to take over the planet while the Earthmen fought amongst themselves. The plan failed and the Jedums were banished from Earth forever. Venus's comments to Zero at the end of the episode seem to suggest that she has never been to Switzerland, in which case the events of this episode must take place before those of *Drama At Space City*.

Regular Voice Cast

Col. Steve Zodiac	**Paul Maxwell**
Dr. Venus	**Sylvia Anderson**
Prof. Matthew Matic	**David Graham**
Cdr. Wilbur Zero	**John Bluthal**
Lt. 90	**David Graham**
Jonathan Zero	**Sylvia Anderson**

Guest Voice Cast

Cardre	**David Graham**
Rader	**John Bluthal**
Emergency Tannoy	**Paul Maxwell**

First UK Transmission

Sunday, June 9th, 1963
4.40pm (ATV London)

INVASION EARTH — Prod. No. 34

Teleplay by **Dennis Spooner** Directed by **Alan Pattillo**

WSP communications are being disrupted by a strange space cloud and when *XL18* is dispatched to disperse it, the ship inexplicably explodes as it enters the cloud. Meanwhile, the *XL5* crew are on a medical mission, inoculating the members of Colonel Hudson's Space Exploration Team against rystamesia, a virulent space epidemic. As they return to Earth, Zoony falls ill and Venus realises that she has forgotten to inoculate him. Alerted by Zero, they watch on the astrascope as *XL24* approaches the space cloud and explodes, but when they play back the recording in slow motion, Steve notices that the ship was destroyed by a missile fired from inside the cloud. Intercepting an alien transmission, they discover that an invasion fleet is hidden within the cloud and the WSP's weapons are powerless to stop them from conquering the Earth!

Notes

The Zero family watch JUKE BOX JURY on television: one of the panellists is Ma Doughty from *The Granatoid Tanks* and the track they are judging is 'This Is The Twist'. This episode takes its resolution from H.G. Wells's *The War Of The Worlds* and, much like the novel, events are concluded without the protagonists influencing the outcome in any way.

Regular Voice Cast

Col. Steve Zodiac	**Paul Maxwell**
Dr. Venus	**Sylvia Anderson**
Prof. Matthew Matic	**David Graham**
Cdr. Wilbur Zero	**John Bluthal**
Lt. 90	**David Graham**
Robert	**Gerry Anderson**
Zoony	**David Graham**
Eleanor Zero	**Sylvia Anderson**
Jonathan Zero	**Sylvia Anderson**

Guest Voice Cast

Colonel Hudson	**David Graham**
Alien Leader	**David Graham**
Alien Lieutenant	**David Graham**
XL18 Pilot / XL24 Pilot	**Paul Maxwell**

First UK Transmission

Sunday, May 26th, 1963
4.40pm (ATV London)

GHOSTS OF SPACE — Prod. No. 35

Teleplay by **Alan Fennell** Directed by **John Kelly**

XL5 transports geologist James Frazer to planet Electon where he will spend the next 80 days conducting a survey. Expecting a warm welcome from the friendly Electons, Frazer finds the nearest town completely deserted, as if everyone left in a hurry. He discovers a lump of glowing electric rock being used as a light source in the local hotel and the next morning, he locates a plentiful source of the rock. Imagining that it will make him rich, he sets about digging up the rocks to take back to Earth. When the *XL5* crew return 12 weeks later, Venus realises that Frazer is suffering from space melancholia when the man threatens to destroy *Fireball Jr.* unless Steve agrees to transport the rocks to Earth. Then, during the night, objects in the hotel start moving around on their own...

Notes

This is the only episode of FIREBALL XL5 in which Commander Zero and Lieutenant 90 do not appear. The Electon hotel has a packet of Corn Flakes in the store cupboard. The Groverians say that their magnets can do almost anything and, indeed, they can lift a duvet and move a wicker basket, items that would not normally be influenced by a magnet unless they contained traces of iron, cobalt or nickel.

Regular Voice Cast

Col. Steve Zodiac	**Paul Maxwell**
Dr. Venus	**Sylvia Anderson**
Prof. Matthew Matic	**David Graham**
Robert	**Gerry Anderson**
Zoony	**David Graham**

Guest Voice Cast

James Frazer	**John Bluthal**
Halla	**John Bluthal**
Senta	**David Graham**

First UK Transmission

Sunday, October 6th, 1963
4.00pm (ATV London)

TRIAL BY ROBOT — Prod. No. 36

Teleplay by **Alan Fennell** Directed by **Bill Harris**

Four planets have reported that their top robots have vanished and Matt suspects robot expert Professor Al Himber, who visited each planet on his recent lecture tour. Himber is due to lecture at Space City so Matt fits a warning device to Robert in case Himber tries to steal him too. After the lecture, Himber visits Matt's workshop and fixes a control system on Robert, but he discovers the warning device and deactivates it. However, Matt has also added a homing device which Himber does not discover and this enables the *XL5* crew to track Robert when he takes off in *XL1* under Himber's control. Trailing *XL1* to Planet 82, Steve, Venus and Matt follow Robert when he leaves the ship, but they come under fire from a robot tank and are then captured by Himber's robots...

Notes

Two of the jury robots previously appeared as the Granatoid robots in *The Granatoid Tanks* and one of them originally appeared in the SUPERCAR episode *The Lost City*. Zero says that the fourth robot disappeared on May 27th and it is now August. It takes the *XL5* crew three months to get to Planet 82 (or Robotvia as it is renamed by Himber), so it is November when they arrive and will be February before they return to Earth.

Regular Voice Cast

Col. Steve Zodiac	**Paul Maxwell**
Dr. Venus	**Sylvia Anderson**
Prof. Matthew Matic	**David Graham**
Cdr. Wilbur Zero	**John Bluthal**
Lt. 90	**David Graham**

Guest Voice Cast

Prof. Al Himber	**David Graham**
Judge Robot	**Gerry Anderson**
Prosecutor Robot	**Gerry Anderson**
Jury Robot 1	**Gerry Anderson**
Jury Robot 2	**Gerry Anderson**
Jury Robot 3	**Gerry Anderson**

First UK Transmission

Sunday, May 12th, 1963
4.40pm (ATV London)

A DAY IN THE LIFE OF A SPACE GENERAL — Prod. No. 37

Teleplay by **Alan Fennell** — Directed by **David Elliott**

Lieutenant 90 is studying so hard for his Bachelor of Space degree that he has not been getting enough sleep and keeps dozing off while on duty. Zero gives him a dressing down before sending him home to get some rest, but just before he turns in, 90 wishes that he could outrank Zero for just one day. He dreams that he has been promoted to Space General in recognition of his work on a new radar scanner, which Jock has spent all night installing in the Control Room. As Jock has missed his flight to Olympus for his vacation, General 90 orders Steve to fly him there in *XL5*. Then the scanner registers what appear to be unidentified ships in Sector 23 and, assuming them to be hostile invaders, 90 orders Zero to send a task force to intercept them and wipe them out!

Notes

The programme that Jonathan Zero watches on television during breakfast is the FOUR FEATHER FALLS episode *The Toughest Guy In The West*. 90 states that, according to the WSP flight manual, XL pilots must report their position to Space City every two hours. The crash sequence was shot at the end of production on the series, enabling the visual effects team to destroy the 24 inch *Fireball XL5* model and the Space City model set.

Regular Voice Cast

Col. Steve Zodiac	**Paul Maxwell**
Dr. Venus	**Sylvia Anderson**
Prof. Matthew Matic	**David Graham**
Cdr. Wilbur Zero	**John Bluthal**
Lt. 90	**David Graham**
Robert	**Gerry Anderson**
Jock Campbell	**John Bluthal**
Eleanor Zero	**Sylvia Anderson**
Jonathan Zero	**Sylvia Anderson**

Guest Voice Cast

Freighter A14	**David Graham**

First UK Transmission

Sunday, May 19th, 1963
4.40pm (ATV London)

SPACE CITY SPECIAL — Prod. No. 38

Teleplay by **Dennis Spooner** — Directed by **Alan Pattillo**

WSP head General Rossiter is flying to Space City to present Steve with the Astronaut of the Year award. He invites Venus to join him for the journey aboard a new SL6 supersonic airliner as she returns from receiving a diploma in space psychology. At Space City, ETV presenter Johnny Jackson is preparing to cover the event and offers to donate $100,000 to charity if the *XL5* crew and ground staff put on a song and dance show after the presentation. As they wait for their flight, Venus becomes concerned about the mental state of SL6 pilot Major Todd, but it is only after the airliner takes off that she realises he has been brainwashed and intends to crash the plane when it reaches 80,000 feet!

Notes

General Rossiter later appears as Admiral Denver in STINGRAY. The programme for the Astronaut of the Year presentation reveals that it is taking place on June 15th. It features an advert for Ma Doughty's music shop (seen in *The Granatoid Tanks*) and Ma Doughty even joins Jock, Zoony, Eleanor and Jonathan in the theatre box at the end of the episode. The *XL5* crew perform 'I Wish I Was A Spaceman' with Don Spencer providing Steve's singing voice. Uniquely, the end titles run with an instrumental version of the song.

Regular Voice Cast

Col. Steve Zodiac	**Paul Maxwell**
Dr. Venus	**Sylvia Anderson**
Prof. Matthew Matic	**David Graham**
Cdr. Wilbur Zero	**John Bluthal**
Lt. 90	**David Graham**
Zoony	**David Graham**
Jock Campbell	**John Bluthal**

Guest Voice Cast

General Rossiter	**John Bluthal**
Major Todd	**David Graham**
Johnny Jackson	**John Bluthal**
Subterrain Leader	**David Graham**
Subterrain 1	**John Bluthal**
Subterrain 2	**David Graham**

First UK Transmission

Sunday, June 23rd, 1963
4.40pm (ATV London)

THE FIRE FIGHTERS — Prod. No. 39

Teleplay by **Alan Fennell** — Directed by **John Kelly**

Blazing fireballs originating from a strange space cloud are crashing to Earth, the latest setting fire to a forest in Canada and the Hall of Justice in Brazil. The *XL5* crew are sent to analyse the gas cloud which scientists believe is igniting as it comes into contact with oxygen, but the gas sets fire to *XL5*'s tail section. After putting out the blaze, the crew return to Space City where Steve proposes using an old satellite, Skyball 1, to collect the gas cloud and detonate it in space before it can enter Earth's atmosphere. Matt starts work on the necessary modifications, but then a fireball is spotted heading directly for Space City and Venus's beach house!

Notes

Skyball 1 was built 'years ago' as a manned space station, but became obsolete before it was completed. The project was one of Commander Zero's brainwaves and cost him a chance of promotion. Filmed at the end of production on the series, the scenes of the fire at Venus's beach house destroyed both the model beach set and the puppet set of Venus's lounge. The footage of the Warrior 7 rocket launch is lifted from *The Sun Temple*. Zero's final message to the XL fleet indicates that there are at least 30 XL ships.

Regular Voice Cast

Col. Steve Zodiac	**Paul Maxwell**
Dr. Venus	**Sylvia Anderson**
Prof. Matthew Matic	**David Graham**
Cdr. Wilbur Zero	**John Bluthal**
Lt. 90	**David Graham**
Robert	**Gerry Anderson**
Zoony	**David Graham**

Guest Voice Cast

Space Station 9	**David Graham**

First UK Transmission

Sunday, June 16th, 1963
4.40pm (ATV London)

STINGRAY

Format

In the mid-2060s, the World Security Patrol is entrusted with protecting and maintaining world peace from its headquarters in Washington DC. The World Aquanaut Security Patrol is a sub-section of the WSP with responsibility for the security of the Earth's oceans. Based at Marineville, a self-contained town situated 10 miles inland from the Pacific coast of North America, operations are centred in the Main Control Room in Marineville Tower under the command of crippled former naval officer Commander Samuel Shore. The entire Marineville complex is constructed on hydraulic supports which enable it to be submerged into an underground emplacement during emergencies.

The flagship of the World Aquanaut Security Patrol is *Stingray*, an advanced super-submarine capable of speeds of up to 600 knots. 65 feet long and 20 feet wide and powered by an atomic generator, *Stingray* can travel on the surface of the sea as well as underwater, leap from the water in salmon-fashion and withstand immense water pressure. Equipped with Surface Video Scan and automatic boatswain apparatus and a complement of 16 sting missiles, *Stingray* also houses a variety of extra-vehicular equipment: Sea Bug one-man motorised sleds, a pair of Aquasprite two-man mini submarines and three monocopter personal anti-gravity chairs for ship-to-shore transport. Although it requires a crew of just two WASP personnel, *Stingray* is normally manned by a team of three: Captain Troy Tempest and hydrophones operator 'Phones' Sheridan are often joined by Marina, a native of the undersea city of Pacifica who can breathe underwater but is unable to speak.

On patrol in the Pacific Ocean, the Stingray crew explore uncharted territories, investigate unusual occurrences and defend the land masses from hostile undersea races, primarily the forces of Titan, ruler of Titanica, who has sworn the destruction of all terraineans. Titan is assisted by his surface agent X20, a master of disguise based at Primrose Cottage on the remote island of Lemoy, where the lounge hides a complex control room.

Production

In the spring of 1963, STINGRAY became the first production to go before the cameras at AP Films' brand new studio complex on Stirling Road in the Slough Trading Estate, built at a cost of £75,000. Equipped with three shooting stages (two for puppet filming and one for special effects), production offices, preview theatre and 12 cutting rooms with additional offices for the art department nearby in Edinburgh Avenue, the new studios were a considerable improvement over the company's former studios in Ipswich Road.

The special effects stage housed two interior tanks fitted with an artificial horizon system which constantly pumped water over one slightly lower side into an overflow trough. These tanks were used for filming the many water surface sequences required for the series. Underwater sequences were created by 'flying' dry models on wires over a model sea-bed landscape and filming through a long, narrow aquarium filled with hundreds of tiny live tropical fish. The two puppet stages enabled two different episodes to be shot simultaneously by separate film crews using twin puppets of the main characters: although each episode took 11 days to film (as well as an additional 5½ days for visual effects), the whole series of 39 episodes was shot within 10 months. For the first time, the puppets were fitted with 'glass' eyes specially made by an optician, and each main puppet character was given a variety of interchangeable heads to simulate changed expressions.

The budget for STINGRAY was set at £20,000 per episode and enabled the series to be shot entirely in colour on Eastmancolor film, greatly increasing the series' potential for overseas sales to Japan, Canada and North America where colour broadcasts had begun as early as 1954 (colour broadcasts on British television did not start until 1967, and not until 1969 on the ITV network). Although the majority of feature films were by this time being shot in colour, the amount of colour stock required by AP Films was unprecedented for a UK production. As shooting on STINGRAY got underway, APF quickly became the country's largest consumer of colour film.

Main Characters

Captain Troy Tempest
WASP aquanaut, Commander and helmsman of *Stingray*

Lieutenant Phones Sheridan
WASP aquanaut, *Stingray* navigator and hydrophones operator

Marina
A beautiful mute maiden from the undersea city of Pacifica and third member of the *Stingray* crew

Lieutenant Atlanta Shore
Marineville Tower assistant controller and radio communications officer

Commander Sam Shore
Marineville Commander and father of Atlanta, confined to a hoverchair due to injuries received in combat

Sub-Lieutenant John Fisher
Marineville Tower junior assistant controller and aquanaut-in-training

Titan
Evil ruler of the undersea city of Titanica, dedicated to the destruction of the terraineans

Surface Agent X20
Evil scientist, engineer and master of disguise in the employ of Titan to spy on the terraineans

1st WSP Commander
Commander in Chief of the World Security Patrol at Washington HQ

Oink
A friendly and playful seal cub adopted by Marina

Aquaphibians
The members of a strange undersea race in the service of Titan

As far as the AP Films producers and crew were aware, STINGRAY was the first British television series to be filmed entirely in colour and, indeed, the programme was heavily promoted as such by ITC in 1964. However, there is evidence to suggest that several earlier British series were made at least partially in colour, notably THE ADVENTURES OF SIR LANCELOT (1956), AN AGE OF KINGS (1960) and JOURNEY OF A LIFETIME (1961).

Episode Titles

(Listed in production order)

1. **Stingray**
2. **Plant Of Doom**
3. **Sea Of Oil**
4. **Hostages Of The Deep**
5. **Treasure Down Below**
6. **The Big Gun**
7. **The Golden Sea**
8. **The Ghost Ship**
9. **Count Down**
10. **The Ghost Of The Sea**
11. **Emergency Marineville**
12. **Subterranean Sea**
13. **Loch Ness Monster**
14. **The Invaders**
15. **Secret Of The Giant Oyster**
16. **Raptures Of The Deep**
17. **Stand By For Action**
18. **The Disappearing Ships**
19. **The Man From The Navy**
20. **Marineville Traitor**
21. **Tom Thumb Tempest**
22. **Pink Ice**
23. **The Master Plan**
24. **Star Of The East**
25. **An Echo Of Danger**
26. **Invisible Enemy**
27. **Deep Heat**
28. **In Search Of The Tajmanon**
29. **Titan Goes Pop**
30. **Set Sail For Adventure**
31. **Tune Of Danger**
32. **Rescue From The Skies**
33. **The Cool Cave Man**
34. **A Nut For Marineville**
35. **Trapped In The Depths**
36. **Eastern Eclipse**
37. **A Christmas To Remember**
38. **The Lighthouse Dwellers**
39. **Aquanaut Of The Year**

Episode Running Time

25 minutes approx.

PRODUCTION CREDITS

Produced by **Gerry Anderson**
Associate Producer **Reg Hill**
Director of Photography **John Read**
Special Effects Lighting **Ted Wooldridge**
Lighting Cameraman **John Read**
(1, 2, 4, 6, 8, 10, 12, 14, 16, 18, 20, 22, 24, 26, 28, 30, 32, 34, 36, 38)
Julien Lugrin
(3, 7, 11, 15, 19, 23, 27, 31, 35)
Paddy Seale
(5, 9, 13, 17, 21, 25, 29, 33, 37, 39)
Camera Operators **Jimmy Elliott**
Julien Lugrin
(1, 5, 9, 13, 17, 21, 25, 29, 33, 37, 39)
Alan Perry
(2, 4, 6, 8, 10, 12, 14, 16, 18, 20, 22, 24, 26, 28, 30, 32, 34, 36, 38)
Paddy Seale
(3, 7, 11, 15, 19, 23, 27, 31, 35)
Art Director **Bob Bell**
Special Effects Director **Derek Meddings**
Puppetry Supervision
Christine Glanville
(1, 3, 5, 7, 9, 11, 13, 15, 17, 19, 21, 23, 25, 27, 29, 31, 33, 35, 37, 39)
Mary Turner
(1, 2, 4, 6, 8, 10, 12, 14, 16, 18, 20, 22, 24, 26, 28, 30, 32, 34, 36, 38)
Script Supervision
Gerry & Sylvia Anderson *(2-33, 35-38)*
Music Composed, Arranged and Conducted by **Barry Gray**
Title Music Vocal **Gary Miller**
Puppet Operators **Yvonne Hunter**
(1, 3, 5, 7, 9, 11, 13, 15, 17, 19, 21, 23, 25, 27, 29, 31, 33, 35, 37, 39)
Carolyn Turner
(1, 2, 4, 6, 8, 10, 12, 14, 16, 18, 20, 22, 24, 26, 28, 30, 32, 34, 36, 38)
Judith Shutt
(2, 4, 6, 8, 10, 12, 14, 16, 18, 20, 22, 24, 26, 28, 30, 32, 34, 36, 38)
Zena Relph
(3, 5, 7, 9, 11, 13, 15, 17, 19, 21, 23, 25, 27, 29, 31, 33, 35, 37, 39)
Sculptors **John Blundell**
John Brown
Wolfgang Manthey
Wardrobe **Elizabeth Coleman**
Character Voices **Ray Barrett**
Robert Easton, David Graham
Don Mason, Lois Maxwell
Editor **David Lane**
(1, 4, 7, 10, 13, 16, 19, 22, 25, 28, 31, 34, 37, 39)
Eric Pask
(2, 5, 8, 11, 14, 17, 20, 23, 26, 29, 32, 35, 38)
Harry MacDonald
(3, 6, 9, 12, 15, 18, 21, 24, 27, 30, 33, 36)
Sound Editor **John Peverill**
Dialogue Editor **Richard Best Jr.**
Music Editor **Tony Lenny**
Dialogue and Characterisation Supervision **Sylvia Anderson**
Sound **Maurice Askew**
John Taylor
Special Effects Assistant
Brian Johncock*
Models **Eric Backman***
Ezra Deering*, Bill James*

In Association with ATV
Westrex Recording System
An ITC World Wide Distribution
An APF Television Production
in Videocolor
Filmed in Supermarionation

* uncredited

STINGRAY — Prod. No. 01

Teleplay by **Gerry & Sylvia Anderson** — Directed by **Alan Pattillo**

The *Stingray* crew investigate the mysterious destruction of the submarine *Sea Probe* but come under attack from a strange Mechanical Fish. *Stingray* crashes onto the sea bed and Troy and Phones are taken captive by Titan, leader of the undersea city of Titanica. Troy protests that the WASP's function is investigation, not aggression, but Titan subjects him to a strange trial in which he is judged by a huge fish, the sea god Teufel who looks only upon friends of the Titanican people. Teufel turns away from Troy and Titan declares that he and Phones are guilty, sentencing them both to death!

Notes

This episode has no on-screen title. *Stingray*'s maximum safe speed is given as 600 knots (Rate 6, approximately 682 mph). One marine minute is approximately equivalent to two terrainean minutes.

Oops!

Although the 1st WSP Commander is initially voiced by Don Mason, on his second appearance (on the world videophone) he is voiced by Ray Barrett.

Regular Voice Cast

Cpt. Troy Tempest	**Don Mason**
Lt. Phones Sheridan	**Robert Easton**
Lt. Atlanta Shore	**Lois Maxwell**
Cdr. Sam Shore	**Ray Barrett**
Sub-Lt. John Fisher	**Ray Barrett**
Titan	**Ray Barrett**
X20	**Robert Easton**
1st WSP Commander	**Don Mason**

Guest Voice Cast

2nd WSP Commander	**Ray Barrett**
3rd WSP Commander	**Don Mason**
Aquaphibian 1	**Robert Easton**
Aquaphibian 2	**David Graham**

First UK Transmission

Sunday, October 4th, 1964
5.35pm (ATV London)

PLANT OF DOOM — Prod. No. 02

Teleplay by **Alan Fennell** — Directed by **David Elliott**

Titan learns that *Stingray* is bound for the undersea city of Pacifica to meet Marina's people. Dispatching a Mechanical Fish to delay *Stingray*'s journey, Titan sends X20 to Pacifica pretending to be an emissary from Kazu. There, he presents Marina's father Aphony with a Blue Coral flower, a plant that consumes the atmosphere when removed from its glass container. Troy, Phones and Marina arrive at Pacifica where they meet Aphony and are treated to a huge banquet, but when the aquanauts return to Marineville, Marina brings the Blue Coral flower with her as a gift for Atlanta...

Notes

During the pursuit by the Mechanical Fish, *Stingray* performs the salmon-style leap that is seen in the opening title sequence of every episode.

Oops!

Given that the events of this episode follow on directly from the previous one, it would be a mistake for this episode to be broadcast as anything other than episode two, and yet it was shown as episode 34 during the initial ITV transmission run in 1964/65.

Regular Voice Cast

Cpt. Troy Tempest	**Don Mason**
Lt. Phones Sheridan	**Robert Easton**
Lt. Atlanta Shore	**Lois Maxwell**
Cdr. Sam Shore	**Ray Barrett**
Titan	**Ray Barrett**
X20	**Robert Easton**

Guest Voice Cast

Aquaphibian	**David Graham**

First UK Transmission

Sunday, May 23rd, 1965
5.35pm (ATV London)

SEA OF OIL — Prod. No. 03

Teleplay by **Dennis Spooner** — Directed by **John Kelly**

The *Stingray* crew investigate the mysterious destruction of three oil rigs, visiting a fourth rig in the same field to observe operations. During the night, undersea aliens kidnap Atlanta from her cabin, but Marina follows the aliens' vessel to an airlock leading to a city under the sea bed. She returns to *Stingray* and alerts Troy and Phones. Meanwhile, Atlanta discovers that her captors, Bitumites Nefir and Gerit, believed that the drilling operation was an attack on their underwater world. She manages to persuade them otherwise but realises that Troy will take aggressive action to rescue her, so she joins Nefir and Gerit in their craft in an attempt to intercept *Stingray* before Troy destroys the airlock door that will flood the Bitumites' city.

Notes

This episode introduces Oink, the friendly seal cub who stows away on board *Stingray*. He risks his life by removing a sticker bomb that the Bitumites place on *Stingray*'s hull, but is fortunately unhurt when the bomb explodes. He is seen again in *Treasure Down Below*, *The Big Gun*, *The Golden Sea*, *Loch Ness Monster* and *The Invaders*. The destruction of the third rig, Station 472, appears in the opening titles of each episode.

Regular Voice Cast

Cpt. Troy Tempest	**Don Mason**
Lt. Phones Sheridan	**Robert Easton**
Lt. Atlanta Shore	**Lois Maxwell**
Cdr. Sam Shore	**Ray Barrett**
Oink	**David Graham**

Guest Voice Cast

Engineer Preston	**David Graham**
Nefir	**Don Mason**
Gerit	**David Graham**
Base	**Robert Easton**
1st Rigger	**David Graham**
Rigger Jack	**Ray Barrett**

First UK Transmission

Sunday, May 16th, 1965
5.35pm (ATV London)

HOSTAGES OF THE DEEP — Prod. No. 04

Teleplay by **Alan Fennell** Directed by **Desmond Saunders**

Marineville Tower receives a message from retired Admiral Carson on the island of Lull requesting *Stingray*'s aid. But part of the message is a coded warning of a trap, so when Troy and Phones arrive at the Admiral's beach-house, they send a remote-controlled toy fish in first and a massive explosion destroys the building. Carson and his wife Millie have been abducted by Gadus and Maran, undersea aliens who intend to kill Troy and capture *Stingray*. The *Stingray* crew pursue the aliens' underwater craft to a tunnel which is too narrow for the WASP submarine to enter. Marina goes on ahead but is captured and threatened with death unless she talks and reveals WASP secrets.

Notes

The establishing shots of the island of Lull are comprised of stock footage of a real tropical beach which is later used in THUNDERBIRDS as establishing shots of Tracy Island.

Oops!

Troy uses the Surface Video Scan (SVS) but afterwards says "Down *SVC*." Gadus pronounces his name "Gay-dus", but later Maran calls him "Gad-us".

Regular Voice Cast

Cpt. Troy Tempest	**Don Mason**
Lt. Phones Sheridan	**Robert Easton**
Lt. Atlanta Shore	**Lois Maxwell**
Cdr. Sam Shore	**Ray Barrett**

Guest Voice Cast

Admiral Henry Carson	**David Graham**
Millie Carson	**Lois Maxwell**
Gadus	**Ray Barrett**
Maran	**David Graham**
Power Plant	**Ray Barratt**
Toy Fish	**David Graham**

First UK Transmission

Sunday, June 13th, 1965
5.35pm (ATV London)

TREASURE DOWN BELOW — Prod. No. 05

Teleplay by **Dennis Spooner** Directed by **Alan Pattillo**

On leave in Casablanca, Phones purchases a treasure map from an old sea dog and when Marina programmes the automatic boatswain to head for the area shown on the map, *Stingray* is caught in a whirlpool and dragged down to an underwater cavern. There, Troy, Phones and Marina discover a grotto filled with gold and jewels. But a pair of undersea aliens, Ebrun and Trell, claim ownership of the treasure and lock the *Stingray* crew in a cell. They are freed by marooned pirate Captain Black, but when Troy refuses to help him steal the treasure, the pirate betrays them to the aliens...

Notes

Troy and Marina's visit to the restaurant in Casablanca appears in the closing titles of each episode. Ebrun appears to be wearing a candelabra on his head.

Oops!

Stingray's right rear fin is damaged in the whirlpool but when the submarine emerges from the whirlpool, the damage has been fixed! The pilot of *Search Vessel 2* is initially voiced by David Graham but later he responds to Atlanta with the voice of Don Mason.

Regular Voice Cast

Cpt. Troy Tempest	**Don Mason**
Lt. Phones Sheridan	**Robert Easton**
Lt. Atlanta Shore	**Lois Maxwell**
Cdr. Sam Shore	**Ray Barrett**
Oink	**David Graham**

Guest Voice Cast

Captain Black	**Don Mason**
Ebrun	**Ray Barrett**
Trell	**David Graham**
Sea Dog	**Ray Barratt**
Search Vessel 2	**David Graham**
Rescue Launch 8	**Don Mason**

First UK Transmission

Sunday, March 14th, 1965
5.30pm (ATV London)

THE BIG GUN — Prod. No. 06

Teleplay by **Alan Fennell** Directed by **David Elliott**

The *Stingray* crew investigate when San May becomes the third island to be completely obliterated within a week. Phones detects a fast-moving craft which is actually a Missile Ejector vehicle developed by the Solarstar undersea aliens to launch attacks on the terraineans. Troy opens fire and destroys the hostile craft but the pilot, Mauritimus, escapes unhurt and is dispatched by the Solarstar Mighty Leader in a second Missile Ejector to destroy Marineville...

Notes

Marineville is stated to be 10 miles inland of the west coast of the USA. (The STINGRAY Century 21 Mini-Album *A Trip to Marineville* (MA 102) contradicts this, giving a figure of 20 miles.) Oink appears, but has a non-oinking role.

Oops!

Missile Ejector 2 initially has a crab motif on its side, but when we see the vehicle rising to the surface, the crab changes to a fish, as on Missile Ejector 1. In subsequent shots, the motif alternates between the crab and the fish.

Regular Voice Cast

Cpt. Troy Tempest	**Don Mason**
Lt. Phones Sheridan	**Robert Easton**
Lt. Atlanta Shore	**Lois Maxwell**
Cdr. Sam Shore	**Ray Barrett**
Oink	**David Graham**
1st WSP Commander	**Robert Easton**

Guest Voice Cast

Mauritimus	**Ray Barrett**
Mighty Leader	**Don Mason**
Korda	**Robert Easton**
Tracking Station	**Lois Maxwell**

First UK Transmission

Sunday, January 24th, 1965
5.35pm (ATV London)

THE GOLDEN SEA

Prod. No. 07

Teleplay by **Dennis Spooner** Directed by **John Kelly**

WASP assists Professor Darren and his assistant Chuck with their project to extract minute particles of mineral compounds, specifically gold, from sea-water using a bathyscaphe lowered into the Kendrick Trench. Titan is furious when he learns of the plan, claiming the riches of the sea as his own. His chancellor Sculpin has developed a sounding device which attracts the Gargan, a giant swordfish with glowing eyes. He attaches this device to the roof of the bathyscaphe while Phones and Marina are aboard and soon the Gargan begins to attack the vessel!

Notes

Although the *Stingray* Aquasprites were previously mentioned in *Hostages Of The Deep*, this is the only occasion in the series in which we see one. Professor Darren later appears as Professor Alexander Cordo in *Trapped In The Depths*.

Oops!

When the Gargan attacks Titan's vessel, Sculpin has the control device for the sounder so he could just turn off the sounder to get rid of the Gargan, as he did earlier at Titanica.

Regular Voice Cast

Cpt. Troy Tempest	**Don Mason**
Lt. Phones Sheridan	**Robert Easton**
Lt. Atlanta Shore	**Lois Maxwell**
Cdr. Sam Shore	**Ray Barrett**
Titan	**Ray Barrett**
X20	**Robert Easton**
Oink	**David Graham**

Guest Voice Cast

Professor Darren	**Robert Easton**
Chuck	**Ray Barrett**
Sculpin	**Don Mason**

First UK Transmission

Sunday, June 6th, 1965
5.35pm (ATV London)

THE GHOST SHIP

Prod. No. 08

Teleplay by **Alan Fennell** Directed by **Desmond Saunders**

Commander Shore joins Troy, Phones and Marina aboard *Stingray* to investigate the sinking of the jet liner *Arcadia* which reported sighting an ancient galleon in heavy fog just before radio transmissions cut off. Arriving at the *Arcadia*'s last known position, *Stingray* enters a thick fog-bank and the crew see the galleon emerging from the mist. Shore and Phones board the ship but are captured inside by an undersea alien named Idotee who reveals that he has set a trap to destroy the *Stingray* crew for crimes against the advancement of the underwater peoples. Idotee orders Shore to instruct Troy to come aboard the ship, but instead he orders Troy to open fire on the galleon. Troy refuses to obey his orders and takes *Stingray* into a dive only to be pursued by the galleon, but then Idotee contacts Troy and threatens to kill Shore and Phones if he does not join them!

Notes

The highly detailed galleon model built specifically for this episode by Derek Meddings's visual effects model-makers resurfaces as Admiral Denver's galleon in *Set Sail For Adventure*. Similarly, the sets of the galleon's deck designed by Bob Bell were brought out of storage and cleaned up to appear in the same episode.

Regular Voice Cast

Cpt. Troy Tempest	**Don Mason**
Lt. Phones Sheridan	**Robert Easton**
Lt. Atlanta Shore	**Lois Maxwell**
Cdr. Sam Shore	**Ray Barrett**
Sub-Lt. John Fisher	**Ray Barrett**
1st WSP Commander	**David Graham**

Guest Voice Cast

Idotee	**David Graham**

First UK Transmission

Sunday, October 18th, 1964
5.35pm (ATV London)

COUNT DOWN

Prod. No. 09

Teleplay by **Dennis Spooner** Directed by **Alan Pattillo**

Under the guise of one Professor Sanders, X20 arranges to deliver a lecture at Marineville on teaching dumb people to speak as part of a plan to destroy the WASP base. Troy and Phones approach 'Sanders' to help Marina and he agrees to book her into his clinic, telling them that for the treatment to be effective, he requires a recording of the aquanauts speaking simple phrases that Marina has heard many times. They unwittingly provide X20 with recordings of their dialogue with Marineville Tower on approach to the ocean door in *Stingray*, which he then uses to gain access to the *Stingray* pen...

Notes

The Century 21 Mini-Album *Marina Speaks* (MA 104) reveals that Marina *can* speak, but a curse placed on her people by Titan means that one spoken word could mean the death of her father.

Oops!

Although everyone calls the Professor 'Sanders' and his name is given as such on the poster at the main gate, X20's letter from Marineville is addressed to Professor *Saunders*.

Regular Voice Cast

Cpt. Troy Tempest	**Don Mason**
Lt. Phones Sheridan	**Robert Easton**
Lt. Atlanta Shore	**Lois Maxwell**
Cdr. Sam Shore	**Ray Barrett**
Titan	**Ray Barrett**
X20	**Robert Easton**

Guest Voice Cast

Officer- Check Point 1	**David Graham**

First UK Transmission

Sunday, May 9th, 1965
5.35pm (ATV London)

THE GHOST OF THE SEA — Prod. No. 10

Teleplay by **Alan Fennell** — Directed by **David Elliott**

The construction of a new cobalt mining stage in the Pacific reminds Commander Shore of the incident five years before that left him crippled. Pursuing a strange underwater craft which had destroyed the previous mining stage, Shore used his submarine to ram the craft after it opened fire on him. After the collision, Shore was rescued by a mysterious alien man who rowed him back to shore in a life raft. Believing that the new mining stage could be in danger, Shore joins the *Stingray* crew to protect the platform and, detecting an alien craft, they pursue it to an underwater cave. Troy and Marina enter the cave, boarding the craft only to find it deserted, but Troy suddenly realises that it has been set as a booby trap...

Notes

The same piece of footage is used for the explosion of both hydrocharges detonated by Cronson and Loredo, and this explosion also appears at the start of the opening titles of each episode. In the flashback sequence, Shore is wearing World Security Patrol badges and reports to WSP HQ, implying that the World Aquanaut Security Patrol was not in existence at this time.

Regular Voice Cast

Cpt. Troy Tempest	**Don Mason**
Lt. Phones Sheridan	**Robert Easton**
Lt. Atlanta Shore	**Lois Maxwell**
Cdr. Sam Shore	**Ray Barrett**
Sub-Lt. John Fisher	**Ray Barrett**

Guest Voice Cast

Cronson	**David Graham**
Lorado	**Robert Easton**

First UK Transmission

Sunday, January 3rd, 1965
5.35pm (ATV London)

EMERGENCY MARINEVILLE — Prod. No. 11

Teleplay by **Alan Fennell** — Directed by **John Kelly**

The *Stingray* crew investigate an island that is the source of missiles targeting Marineville. Entering an undersea tunnel, Troy and Phones are captured by a pair of Galvanoids named Nucella and Chidora, who threaten Marina with electrocution unless Troy reveals the frequencies that Marineville's Interceptors operate on. Troy realises that this information will enable the Galvanoids to jam the Interceptors and allow their missiles to obliterate Marineville, but he cannot let Marina be killed. After revealing the vital frequencies, Troy is locked in a cell with Phones and Marina as the Galvanoids prepare to launch their next rocket...

Notes

Nucella is one of Titan's guests at the conference in Troy's dream in *Tom Thumb Tempest*, where the events of *Emergency Marineville* are recalled.

Oops!

When the second wave of Spearhead jets is launched, two jets are seen taking off and flying away, but in subsequent shots the two become three and then revert to two again.

Regular Voice Cast

Cpt. Troy Tempest	**Don Mason**
Lt. Phones Sheridan	**Robert Easton**
Lt. Atlanta Shore	**Lois Maxwell**
Cdr. Sam Shore	**Ray Barrett**
Sub-Lt. John Fisher	**Ray Barrett**

Guest Voice Cast

Nucella	**David Graham**
Chidora	**Ray Barrett**
Squadron Leader	**David Graham**
Tracking Station	**David Graham**

First UK Transmission

Sunday, October 11th, 1964
5.35pm (ATV London)

SUBTERRANEAN SEA — Prod. No. 12

Teleplay by **Alan Fennell** — Directed by **Desmond Saunders**

After their vacation is cancelled at the last minute, the *Stingray* crew report to the Undersea Mantle Boring Base to investigate a subterranean ocean that has been discovered by scientists penetrating the Earth's crust. *Stingray* is ferried two miles below the crust on a specially constructed elevator and launched into the new ocean, but the submarine is caught in strong currents, goes out of control and crashes. When Troy, Phones and Marina recover consciousness, they discover that the water has vanished and *Stingray* is beached on the sea-bed.

Notes

Parts of this episode were incorporated with material from *Stingray* and *Plant Of Doom* to create the interactive story on the Century 21 Mini-Album *Into Action With Troy Tempest* (MA 101).

Oops!

There's probably a perfectly reasonable explanation, but it just seems a bit odd that sunglasses are readily to hand in a submarine.

Regular Voice Cast

Cpt. Troy Tempest	**Don Mason**
Lt. Phones Sheridan	**Robert Easton**
Lt. Atlanta Shore	**Lois Maxwell**
Cdr. Sam Shore	**Ray Barrett**

Guest Voice Cast

Prescott	**David Graham**
Andrews	**Ray Barrett**

First UK Transmission

Sunday, October 25th, 1964
5.35pm (ATV London)

LOCH NESS MONSTER — Prod. No. 13

Teleplay by **Dennis Spooner** Directed by **Alan Pattillo**

Commander Shore is sceptical when Admiral Denver reports that he has been attacked by the Loch Ness Monster while on holiday in Scotland, so the Admiral dispatches *Stingray* to explore the Loch. Atlanta joins Troy and Phones on the mission, having arranged for them all to stay at an old castle on the banks of the Loch. They meet their hosts Andy and Jamie McGregor who tell of seeing the "fearful beastie" many times. In the night, the aquanauts are woken by a strange mechanical noise but Andy tells them it is only the ghost of his great, great grandfather Sandy McGregor. The next morning, the *Stingray* crew begin to search the Loch and are astounded when the monster appears!

Notes

This episode introduces Admiral Jack Denver, President of the Undersea Research Programme, who also appears in *Set Sail For Adventure* and *The Cool Cave Man*. The 'monster' was previously seen complete with body and legs as the monster of Monotane in the FIREBALL XL5 episode *Space Monster*. The model of McGregor Castle reappears as Glen Carrick Castle in the THUNDERBIRDS episode *30 Minutes After Noon* and as part of Glen Garry Castle in the CAPTAIN SCARLET AND THE MYSTERONS episode *The Trap*.

Regular Voice Cast

Cpt. Troy Tempest	**Don Mason**
Lt. Phones Sheridan	**Robert Easton**
Lt. Atlanta Shore	**Lois Maxwell**
Cdr. Sam Shore	**Ray Barrett**
Sub-Lt. John Fisher	**Ray Barrett**
Oink	**David Graham**

Guest Voice Cast

Admiral Jack Denver	**David Graham**
Andy McGregor	**David Graham**
Jamie McGregor	**Ray Barrett**

First UK Transmission

Sunday, November 1st, 1964
5.35pm (ATV London)

THE INVADERS — Prod. No. 14

Teleplay by **Dennis Spooner** Directed by **David Elliott**

Troy, Phones and Marina fall into a trap when they answer a distress call from Weather Station 4. The station has been taken over by a pair of Atlanteans, Epayus and Ilium, and adapted to ferry the aquanauts to their subterranean city. There, Troy is questioned about Marineville's security procedures and, although he refuses to answer, his thoughts are translated into pictures via a brain-reading chair. Unaware of this, Troy is puzzled when he and his colleagues are released and returned to *Stingray*. Commander Shore anticipates trouble and withdraws Marineville into the underground emplacement, but this enables the Atlanteans to penetrate the base using a subterranean travel cylinder and take control of Marineville Tower!

Notes

Oink appears but does not oink.

Oops!

After Atlanta fails to make radio contact with Troy, the next shot of *Stingray* shows the exit hatch left open, yet it was shut after the aquanauts boarded the Weather Station.

Regular Voice Cast

Cpt. Troy Tempest	**Don Mason**
Lt. Phones Sheridan	**Robert Easton**
Lt. Atlanta Shore	**Lois Maxwell**
Cdr. Sam Shore	**Ray Barrett**
Sub-Lt. John Fisher	**Ray Barrett**

Guest Voice Cast

Carter	**David Graham**
Epayus	**David Graham**
Ilium	**Ray Barrett**

First UK Transmission

Sunday, April 18th, 1965
5.35pm (ATV London)

SECRET OF THE GIANT OYSTER — Prod. No. 15

Teleplay by **Alan Fennell** Directed by **John Kelly**

In an undersea cave network, amateur divers Mike Bromley and Chick Kingsland discover a giant oyster 20 feet across surrounded by hundreds of little oysters, but they need more up-to-date breathing equipment in order to wait long enough for the oyster to open so that they can collect the pearl inside. Detained by Troy for diving in protected waters, Bromley and Kingsland are taken back to Marineville where Commander Shore agrees to help them as WASP uses crushed pearls to insulate radioactive isotopes. Despite Marina's misgivings, *Stingray* returns to the cave network and Troy enters the tunnel with Bromley, but they are delayed by a rock fall. By the time they reach the oyster, their air is starting to run out...

Notes

The popular incidental track 'March Of The Oysters' was specifically composed by Barry Gray for this episode of STINGRAY although it can be heard in several others, such as *The Man From The Navy*, as well as episodes of THUNDERBIRDS. Gray's commercial recording of the track was released in 1965 as the B-side to Chappell Records' single of the STINGRAY theme (Chappell C957).

Regular Voice Cast

Cpt. Troy Tempest	**Don Mason**
Lt. Phones Sheridan	**Robert Easton**
Lt. Atlanta Shore	**Lois Maxwell**
Cdr. Sam Shore	**Ray Barrett**

Guest Voice Cast

Mike Bromley	**David Graham**
Chick Kingsland	**Robert Easton**

First UK Transmission

Sunday, April 11th, 1965
5.35pm (ATV London)

RAPTURES OF THE DEEP — Prod. No. 16

Teleplay by **Alan Fennell** — Directed by **Desmond Saunders**

A pair of beatnik explorers searching for a legendary undersea gem forest defy Commander Shore's authority and get into trouble when their two-man submarine *Hepcat* fails under pressure and crashes onto the sea-bed. Responding to their SOS, Troy and Phones effect a rescue, pumping air into *Hepcat*'s tanks so that it rises to the surface. On his way back to *Stingray*, Troy spots something shining on the sea-bed but when he goes to investigate, he falls down a crevasse, injuring his leg. As Phones sets out to rescue him, Troy's air runs dry and he passes out. He regains consciousness in a state of euphoria and finds that he can breathe underwater. Then he discovers a gem forest filled with precious stones and becomes the richest man in the world!

Notes

The canopy of the *Hepcat* submarine was originally mounted on the title vehicle in SUPERCAR. Troy's rendition of 'Aqua Marina' is exactly as heard over the end titles of each episode, with additional harp accompaniment by Marina. Sylvia Anderson is uncredited for her role as the voice of Marina. She also provided Marina's voice for the Century 21 Mini-Album *Marina Speaks* (MA 104).

Regular Voice Cast

Cpt. Troy Tempest	**Don Mason**
Lt. Phones Sheridan	**Robert Easton**
Lt. Atlanta Shore	**Lois Maxwell**
Cdr. Sam Shore	**Ray Barrett**

Guest Voice Cast

Marina	**Sylvia Anderson**
Joe	**Ray Barrett**
Frank	**David Graham**

First UK Transmission

Sunday, November 29th, 1964
5.35pm (ATV London)

STAND BY FOR ACTION — Prod. No. 17

Teleplay by **Dennis Spooner** — Directed by **Alan Pattillo**

Goggleheimer Productions have arranged to make a movie about the WASPs on location at Marineville, with all of the personnel playing themselves except for Troy who fails the screen test. He is replaced by heart-throb actor Johnny Swoonara whose name alone is enough to make Atlanta and Marina faint. Then an attempt is made on Troy's life by film producer Goggleheimer, actually a disguised X20 who has set up the movie in an elaborate plan to kill Troy. Troy and Phones pursue X20 as he escapes in a hovercar, but lose him when he disappears into an underground hangar on Lemoy. Filming continues the next day aboard *Stingray* with Swoonara joining Phones at the helm. Suddenly X20 attacks from his underwater craft and *Stingray* sinks out of control to the sea-bed!

Notes

The visual effects footage of *Stingray* destroying a Mechanical Fish that appears as part of the movie rushes is taken from *Plant Of Doom*. Johnny Swoonara was previously seen as Colonel Steve Zodiac in FIREBALL XL5 and his arrival at Marineville is accompanied by music composed for the FIREBALL XL5 episode *Flying Zodiac*. The puppet of film director Marty was based on ITC's American distribution executive Abe Mandell.

Regular Voice Cast

Cpt. Troy Tempest	**Don Mason**
Lt. Phones Sheridan	**Robert Easton**
Lt. Atlanta Shore	**Lois Maxwell**
Cdr. Sam Shore	**Ray Barrett**
Sub-Lt. John Fisher	**Ray Barrett**
Titan	**Ray Barrett**
X20	**Robert Easton**

Guest Voice Cast

Johnny Swoonara	**Ray Barrett**
Marty	**David Graham**

First UK Transmission

Sunday, March 21st, 1965
5.35pm (ATV London)

THE DISAPPEARING SHIPS — Prod. No. 18

Teleplay by **Alan Fennell** — Directed by **David Elliott**

Three old freighter ships due for demolition at sea with explosives set on timed detonators mysteriously disappear and the *Stingray* crew are dispatched to investigate. They discover a cluster of shipwrecked galleons on the sea-bed and the missing freighters nearby. Troy and Phones are ambushed by Parasitica, leader of a race of Hermit Nomads who inhabit the derelict ships. He ushers them through an airlock into one of the freighters, where Troy explains that the three ships the Nomads have chosen for their new homes are due to explode at any moment. Parasitica refuses to believe him until the first freighter blows up, but the blast jams the airlock door, leaving the trio trapped inside!

Notes

If Commander Shore's estimate of how long it would take Troy to pay what he owes after their poker game is reasonably accurate, Troy's salary must be somewhere in the region of $14,600 per annum. It is unfortunate that while Parasitica's understanding of English enables him to locate the freighter's automatic boatswain and sluice valve, it does not extend to recognising the significance of 'Danger High Explosive' marked in big letters on the hull of each ship.

Regular Voice Cast

Cpt. Troy Tempest	**Don Mason**
Lt. Phones Sheridan	**Robert Easton**
Lt. Atlanta Shore	**Lois Maxwell**
Cdr. Sam Shore	**Ray Barrett**
Sub-Lt. John Fisher	**Ray Barrett**

Guest Voice Cast

Parasitica	**David Graham**

First UK Transmission

Sunday, April 4th, 1965
5.35pm (ATV London)

THE MAN FROM THE NAVY

Prod. No. 19

Teleplay by **Alan Fennell** Directed by **John Kelly**

During tests of a new World Navy marine missile, a feud develops between Troy and the arrogant World Navy Captain Jacques Jordan, who insists that the Navy is the superior service. Their argument ruins Marina's dinner party as Jordan is unable to resist slighting the WASPs every time he opens his mouth and Troy eventually storms out. The next morning, the tests continue with *Stingray* as the target for the unarmed prototype missiles, but Jordan's submarine is boarded by two Aquaphibians under instructions from Titan to sabotage the operation. Held at gunpoint, Jordan is forced to arm the first missile but, fortunately, Troy manages to evade it, and when it explodes he realises that it has not been charged by accident. Warning Jordan that his craft has been classified as a hostile vessel, Troy closes in to attack...

Notes

The record playing on Marina's music centre at the dinner party is an instrumental version of 'I've Got Something To Shout About', the song performed by Duke Dexter in *Titan Goes Pop*. The puppet-sized version of Troy's car was previously seen as X20's hovercar in *Stand By For Action*, although in long shot, Troy's car has wheels.

Regular Voice Cast

Cpt. Troy Tempest	**Don Mason**
Lt. Phones Sheridan	**Robert Easton**
Lt. Atlanta Shore	**Lois Maxwell**
Cdr. Sam Shore	**Ray Barrett**
Sub-Lt. John Fisher	**Ray Barrett**
Titan	**Ray Barrett**
X20	**Robert Easton**

Guest Voice Cast

Captain Jacques Jordan	**David Graham**
Aquaphibian 1	**David Graham**
Aquaphibian 2	**David Graham**

First UK Transmission

Sunday, November 15th, 1964
5.35pm (ATV London)

MARINEVILLE TRAITOR

Prod. No. 20

Teleplay by **Alan Fennell** Directed by **Desmond Saunders**

The new air/sea hydroprobe, a vital piece of the long-range warning system, is stolen from Marineville Tower and an incriminating recording points to Commander Shore as the prime suspect. Then top secret plans are stolen from the Tower safe and Shore is found unconscious on the control desk, although security reports that he was the only person to enter the Tower. Shore claims he was struck down from behind, but when Troy overhears him making contact with the mysterious 'Zero Red' using a hidden transmitter, he becomes convinced that the Commander has turned traitor...

Notes

This is the only episode in which *Stingray* does not actually appear (outside the main and closing title sequences). The music that Atlanta plays in her apartment is 'Formula 5', originally composed for the FIREBALL XL5 episode *The Granatoid Tanks*.

Oops!

Having been voiced by Don Mason, Robert Easton and David Graham in previous episodes, this time the WSP HQ Commander is voiced by Robert Easton.

Regular Voice Cast

Cpt. Troy Tempest	**Don Mason**
Lt. Phones Sheridan	**Robert Easton**
Lt. Atlanta Shore	**Lois Maxwell**
Cdr. Sam Shore	**Ray Barrett**
Sub-Lt. John Fisher	**Ray Barrett**
1st WSP Commander	**Robert Easton**

Guest Voice Cast

Lt. Misen	**David Graham**
Zero Red	**David Graham**
Radio Voice	**David Graham**

First UK Transmission

Sunday, June 20th, 1965
5.35pm (ATV London)

TOM THUMB TEMPEST

Prod. No. 21

Teleplay by **Alan Fennell** Directed by **Alan Pattillo**

While waiting on stand-by for a dangerous mission, Troy falls asleep and wakes with a start as Commander Shore sounds launch stations. He sets off with Phones and Marina in *Stingray* following the Commander's instructions, but the submarine suddenly collides with an invisible obstacle which turns out to be the glass of an aquarium in a giant room. Leaving *Stingray*, the miniaturised aquanauts find a giant table set for dinner with names on the placemats and top secret plans which reveal that Titan is preparing for an assault on Marineville in league with WASP's deadliest undersea enemies!

Oops!

At the start of the episode, the clock in the Stand-by Lounge shows the time at 8.54 but only one minute later it reads 9.01. Phones is seen reading a magazine with blank pages inside for over two hours. Troy pronounces Gadus's name as "Gad-us" but Gadus introduced himself as "Gay-dus" in *Hostages Of The Deep*. When Phones unrolls the Marineville plans, a puppeteer's hands are visible holding the puppet's arms. Troy dreams of a telephone with the number Lemoy X20000 when he should have no idea that X20 lives on Lemoy.

Regular Voice Cast

Cpt. Troy Tempest	**Don Mason**
Lt. Phones Sheridan	**Robert Easton**
Lt. Atlanta Shore	**Lois Maxwell**
Cdr. Sam Shore	**Ray Barrett**
X20	**Robert Easton**

Guest Voice Cast

Newsreader	**David Graham**
Aquaphibian	**David Graham**

First UK Transmission

Sunday, February 28th, 1965
5.35pm (ATV London)

PINK ICE
Prod. No. 22

Teleplay by **Alan Fennell** Directed by **David Elliott**

When the Northwest Pacific is frozen over by a strange pink ice that has also covered the other oceans around the globe, the *Stingray* crew are dispatched to investigate. Surfacing through a hole in the ice, Troy and Phones examine the strange pink landscape and when he tastes it, Troy discovers that the ice has been produced chemically. Commander Shore recognises a pattern to the freezing which suggests an undersea craft touring the world's oceans and he predicts that the Northeast Pacific will be hit next. *Stingray* arrives in the area but becomes trapped by ice when the undersea craft releases its ice generator. Hydromic missiles are launched from Marineville to break up the ice field, but if the missile targeting is off by only a few degrees, the *Stingray* crew could be killed!

Oops!
A shot of *Stingray* trapped in the ice appears just before the commercial break, but at this point in the story the ship is actually clear of ice, having surfaced through a hole in the ice field – as we see after the break when *Stingray* submerges again. The 1st WSP Commander has a different voice again from any of the ones he has had in previous episodes – he now sounds like Jacques Jordan (from *The Man From The Navy*).

Regular Voice Cast

Cpt. Troy Tempest	**Don Mason**
Lt. Phones Sheridan	**Robert Easton**
Lt. Atlanta Shore	**Lois Maxwell**
Cdr. Sam Shore	**Ray Barrett**
Sub-Lt. John Fisher	**Ray Barrett**
1st WSP Commander	**David Graham**

Guest Voice Cast

2nd WSP Commander	**Robert Easton**
3rd WSP Commander	**Ray Barrett**
Tracking Station	**David Graham**

First UK Transmission
Sunday, March 28th, 1965
5.35pm (ATV London)

THE MASTER PLAN
Prod. No. 23

Teleplay by **Alan Fennell** Directed by **John Kelly**

In order to recover his standing amongst the undersea races, Titan develops a master plan to recapture Marina and make her his slave again. He sends a Mechanical Fish to damage *Stingray* during a patrol and when Troy leaves the ship to make repairs, an Aquaphibian uses a jet gun to spray him with a purple liquid and then swims away. Returning to Marineville, Troy collapses and the Doc diagnoses that he has been poisoned with an unknown substance for which there is no known antidote – he will die within hours. Then Titan contacts Commander Shore, offering the antidote in exchange for Marina. Shore refuses but Marina swims to Titanica to give herself up and a delighted Titan forwards the antidote inside an unarmed missile. Titan expects to capture both Troy and *Stingray* when the aquanaut attempts to rescue Marina, but Troy has a master plan of his own...

Oops!
Stingray is on half power as it returns to Marineville after the Mechanical Fish attack, yet the submarine is still able to muster Rate 6. It is odd that Troy and Phones set out to rescue Marina in an unarmed facsimile Mechanical Fish built by WASP engineers when they could have used the genuine Mechanical Fish that they captured in the first episode.

Regular Voice Cast

Cpt. Troy Tempest	**Don Mason**
Lt. Phones Sheridan	**Robert Easton**
Lt. Atlanta Shore	**Lois Maxwell**
Cdr. Sam Shore	**Ray Barrett**
Titan	**Ray Barrett**
X20	**Robert Easton**

Guest Voice Cast

Doc	**David Graham**
Tracking Station	**David Graham**

First UK Transmission
Sunday, May 30th, 1965
5.35pm (ATV London)

STAR OF THE EAST
Prod. No. 24

Teleplay by **Alan Fennell** Directed by **Desmond Saunders**

As visiting dignitary El Hudat, President of the island state of Hudatvia, signs agreement papers to join the WSP, news arrives that there has been a revolt in his country and the new government, led by El Hudat's brother, does not wish to join World Security. El Hudat accuses the WSP of sponsoring the revolt and then insults Atlanta, so Shore demands that he leave Marineville first thing in the morning. El Hudat swears vengeance and kidnaps Marina, holding her prisoner aboard his gunboat, the *Wadi*, as he sets sail for Monte Carlo. When he learns that Marina is missing, Troy realises what has happened and sets out in *Stingray* to rescue her...

Oops!
A peculiar edit during the gunboat trials makes the *Wadi* appear to vanish in the middle of a turn when the scene cuts to show aircraft flying overhead from the same camera position. The 1st WSP Commander is voiced again by David Graham but he has lost the French accent he adopted during the *Pink Ice* affair. As *Stingray* dives following the *Wadi*'s attack (in footage of *Stingray* caught in the whirlpool lifted from *Treasure Down Below*), the sub's rear right fin is bent, but later shows no sign of damage.

Regular Voice Cast

Cpt. Troy Tempest	**Don Mason**
Lt. Phones Sheridan	**Robert Easton**
Lt. Atlanta Shore	**Lois Maxwell**
Cdr. Sam Shore	**Ray Barrett**
Sub-Lt. John Fisher	**Ray Barrett**
1st WSP Commander 1	**David Graham**

Guest Voice Cast

El Hudat	**David Graham**
Abu	**Robert Easton**

First UK Transmission
Sunday, February 14th, 1965
5.35pm (ATV London)

AN ECHO OF DANGER — Prod. No. 25

Teleplay by **Dennis Spooner** Directed by **Alan Pattillo**

Stingray is escorting a tug vessel towing a vast quantity of crude oil sealed inside a tube when Phones picks up a sounding on his hydrophones. The aquanauts submerge *Stingray* to investigate but find nothing as the sounding is generated by an echo transmitter planted by X20 to decoy *Stingray* while he destroys the oil tube. An enquiry into the incident calls Phones's judgement into question. He is relieved of duty and ordered to submit to a full medical check-up, but the psychiatrist that Phones visits is a disguised X20 who uses his concealed control room on Lemoy to convince Phones that he really *is* ill!

Notes

This episode features Lieutenant Fisher's first trip out to sea in *Stingray*, so the events of this episode must take place before those of *Rescue From The Skies*.

Oops!

After Phones says, "I could have sworn the room was different before," the cut to a wide shot of X20's control room shows a painting still moving back into place over one of the control panels.

Regular Voice Cast

Cpt. Troy Tempest	**Don Mason**
Lt. Phones Sheridan	**Robert Easton**
Lt. Atlanta Shore	**Lois Maxwell**
Cdr. Sam Shore	**Ray Barrett**
Sub-Lt. John Fisher	**Ray Barrett**
Titan	**Ray Barrett**
X20	**Robert Easton**

Guest Voice Cast

Tow Vessel	**David Graham**

First UK Transmission

Sunday, November 22nd, 1964
5.35pm (ATV London)

INVISIBLE ENEMY — Prod. No. 26

Teleplay by **Alan Fennell** Directed by **David Elliott**

Responding to an SOS signal, Troy and Phones rescue a man named Thompson whom they find lying in the bottom of a fishing boat, apparently in a coma. At the Marineville Hospital, Doc is baffled by the man's condition: he appears to be suffering from a form of paralysis, but he can find no cause for it. Then a nurse is found in the same condition and, suspecting a contagion, Shore places the ward under quarantine. But the real culprit is Thompson who periodically comes out of his coma to activate a hypno-wave wrist-watch device that induces a trance-like condition in his victims. Soon all of Marineville is effected, but Marina is immune to the hypno-waves and she contacts Troy and Phones on patrol in *Stingray*. Returning to find the base like a ghost town, the aquanauts discover that Thompson is the cause and set a trap for him with Phones as the bait!

Notes

This is the first episode with a revamped main title sequence featuring the explosion, APF and Videcolor logos in colour as well as a new Commander Shore puppet. The invading alien craft previously appeared as the Ghost's craft in *The Ghost Of The Sea* and all footage of it here is lifted from that episode.

Regular Voice Cast

Cpt. Troy Tempest	**Don Mason**
Lt. Phones Sheridan	**Robert Easton**
Lt. Atlanta Shore	**Lois Maxwell**
Cdr. Sam Shore	**Ray Barrett**
Sub-Lt. John Fisher	**Ray Barrett**
1st WSP Commander	**David Graham**

Guest Voice Cast

Thompson	**David Graham**
Doc	**David Graham**
Tracking Station	**David Graham**

First UK Transmission

Sunday, February 21st, 1965
5.35pm (ATV London)

DEEP HEAT — Prod. No. 27

Teleplay by **Alan Fennell** Directed by **John Kelly**

When the Sea Probe remote survey probe is drawn into an extinct undersea volcano, the *Stingray* crew are sent to investigate, but *Stingray* is also pulled down into the crater, coming to rest on a paved floor 2½ miles down. Menaced by missile launchers in the crater wall, the aquanauts are forced to enter an airlock with an elevator which takes them to a control room deep beneath the sea. There they meet Torata and Fragil, the sole survivors of Centralius, whose people constructed the city of Voldana in the shaft of the volcano. Voldana was destroyed when the volcano erupted and only the control room remains, sealed off from the lava by a protective door. Desperate to escape in *Stingray*, the Centralians take the aquanauts' breathing gear, leaving Troy and Phones behind...

Notes

The Wasps Jazz Band are seen here playing at the Blue Lagoon nightspot prior to their featured appearance in *Tune Of Danger*. As seen on all the 20th century television broadcasts, the original prints of this episode start with the revised all-colour version of the main title sequence (not the partial-monochrome version which appears on the digital transfer prepared for the UK and USA DVD releases and the BBC transmission in 2001).

Regular Voice Cast

Cpt. Troy Tempest	**Don Mason**
Lt. Phones Sheridan	**Robert Easton**
Lt. Atlanta Shore	**Lois Maxwell**
Cdr. Sam Shore	**Ray Barrett**
Sub-Lt. John Fisher	**Ray Barrett**

Guest Voice Cast

Torata	**David Graham**
Fragil	**Ray Barrett**
Tracking Station	**David Graham**

First UK Transmission

Sunday, February 7th, 1965
5.35pm (ATV London)

IN SEARCH OF THE TAJMANON Prod. No. 28

Teleplay by **Dennis Spooner** Directed by **Desmond Saunders**

The legendary Tajmanon Palace has inexplicably disappeared since it was submerged beneath the surface of a dam 35 years ago, so Troy, Phones and Atlanta join archaeologist Professor Graham to find out what has happened to it. Searching the dam, Graham finds several distinctive tribal spears, but he and Troy narrowly escape injury when dynamite is detonated in the dam by Sheikh Hassan El-Hamrah whose family lay claim to the Tajmanon. The team take *Stingray* into Central Africa to find the tribe who made the spears but Troy, Phones and Atlanta are captured and taken to the Tajmanon, now relocated in the jungle. Bound and gagged in a sarcophagus with a spiked lid suspended overhead, the aquanauts meet Sheikh Hassan, who believes they have come to destroy the Palace. Sentencing them to death, he activates the descent of the sarcophagus lid...

Notes

This is the only episode of STINGRAY in which Marina does not appear (aside from her usual appearance in the end title sequence that is). Much of the incidental music in this episode was originally composed for the SUPERCAR episodes *Amazonian Adventure* and *The Talisman Of Sargon.*

Regular Voice Cast

Cpt. Troy Tempest	**Don Mason**
Lt. Phones Sheridan	**Robert Easton**
Lt. Atlanta Shore	**Lois Maxwell**
Cdr. Sam Shore	**Ray Barrett**
Sub-Lt. John Fisher	**Ray Barrett**

Guest Voice Cast

Professor Graham	**David Graham**
Hassan El-Hamrah	**David Graham**
Supply Lieutenant	**David Graham**
Africa 28	**David Graham**

First UK Transmission

Sunday, December 13th, 1964
5.35pm (ATV London)

TITAN GOES POP Prod. No. 29

Teleplay by **Alan Fennell** Directed by **Alan Pattillo**

X20 is intrigued by the extent of the security arrangements in place at Marineville for a visit by pop star Duke Dexter and informs Titan that he must be the most important person ever to visit the base. Titan decides he wants Dexter brought to Titanica so X20 poses as Special Security agent 'X' in order to make contact with Dexter's agent Sandy Gibson. Troy is set up as a decoy for the hundreds of screaming fans surrounding the base as Dexter arrives by helicopter. Gibson is delighted when 'X' arranges for Dexter to stay on Lemoy during his visit, but after Gibson leaves the island to return to Marineville with Troy and Phones in *Stingray*, X20 drugs Dexter's food. Later, Gibson becomes concerned for his client when he tries to call 'X' and gets no reply. Demanding immediate action, he joins Troy and Phones as they return to Lemoy, but there is no sign of Dexter or 'X'!

Oops!

The security pass that X20 flashes at the sergeant is actually Sandy Gibson's pass, which was seen only moments before (X20's thumb obscures the picture, but Gibson's name is visible on the left side).

Regular Voice Cast

Cpt. Troy Tempest	**Don Mason**
Lt. Phones Sheridan	**Robert Easton**
Lt. Atlanta Shore	**Lois Maxwell**
Cdr. Sam Shore	**Ray Barrett**
Sub-Lt. John Fisher	**Ray Barrett**
Titan	**Ray Barrett**
X20	**Robert Easton**
1st WSP Commander	**Robert Easton**

Guest Voice Cast

Duke Dexter	**Ray Barrett**
Sandy Gibson	**David Graham**
2nd WSP Commander	**Ray Barrett**
3rd WSP Commander	**David Graham**
Announcer / Main Gate	**Don Mason**
Security Point 1 Sergeant	**Don Mason**

First UK Transmission

Sunday, December 6th, 1964
5.35pm (ATV London)

SET SAIL FOR ADVENTURE Prod. No. 30

Teleplay by **Dennis Spooner** Directed by **David Elliott**

To settle an argument with Commander Shore, Admiral Denver arranges to borrow an old galleon from the Maritime Museum, planning to sail across the Pacific and back with a crew of WASP officers to prove whether today's sailors are as tough as those in the past. Dressed in authentic period costume, Denver, Phones and Lieutenant Fisher set off in the galleon but during a bad storm, lightning strikes a mast and Denver is struck on the head by falling debris. When he regains consciousness, Denver finds he has amnesia but he convinces himself that he is genuinely a galleon captain in the 18th century. Phones realises something is wrong when Denver appears on deck brandishing a pistol and shouting orders in the style of Captain Bligh. Fisher tries to disarm him but Denver charges the aquanauts with mutiny and casts them adrift in an open boat!

Notes

This episode has no on-screen title and is incorrectly listed by some sources as 'Set Sail For Danger'. Admiral Denver's old film is a mixture of stock footage from a film library and newly shot miniatures. Atlanta plays Duke Dexter's latest record: 'I've Got Something To Shout About' as performed by the character in *Titan Goes Pop.*

Regular Voice Cast

Cpt. Troy Tempest	**Don Mason**
Lt. Phones Sheridan	**Robert Easton**
Lt. Atlanta Shore	**Lois Maxwell**
Cdr. Sam Shore	**Ray Barrett**
Sub-Lt. John Fisher	**Ray Barrett**

Guest Voice Cast

Admiral Jack Denver	**David Graham**

First UK Transmission

Sunday, November 8th, 1964
5.35pm (ATV London)

TUNE OF DANGER — Prod. No. 31

Teleplay by **Alan Fennell** Directed by **John Kelly**

The Wasps jazz trio and their manager Lieutenant Lawrence Gray meet Marina at a party hosted by Atlanta and decide to arrange a special concert at Pacifica for Aphony. Leaving the party early, Troy detects a radio signal coming from the guest quarters and overhears Gray making a report to X20 in which he reveals that he is secretly an agent of Titanica. He has sabotaged the radio in the band's submarine, the *Downbeat*, and planted a bomb inside bass player Vic Steigo's instrument. Troy confronts Gray but is overcome by knockout gas and taken to a forest shack 100 miles from Marineville. The next morning, Phones, Marina and Atlanta are unaware of the danger as they join the Wasps aboard the *Downbeat*, and Troy is left tied up inside the shack while Gray starts a fire in the forest!

Notes

The Wasps' jazz sessions were performed by Gordon Langford (piano), Alan Ganley (drums) and Joe Mundele (bass). The villainous Lawrence (Larry) Gray is named after composer Barry Gray, as is the pianist's piano: a 'Graystein.' In the audience at the Marineville Theatre concert are the three WSP Commanders and Sandy Gibson, Duke Dexter's manager from *Titan Goes Pop*.

Regular Voice Cast	
Cpt. Troy Tempest	**Don Mason**
Lt. Phones Sheridan	**Robert Easton**
Lt. Atlanta Shore	**Lois Maxwell**
Cdr. Sam Shore	**Ray Barrett**
Sub-Lt. John Fisher	**Ray Barrett**
X20	**Robert Easton**

Guest Voice Cast	
Lt. Lawrence Gray	**David Graham**
Vic Steigo	**Don Mason**
Wasps Pianist	**Robert Easton**
Wasps Drummer	**Ray Barrett**
Gate Sergeant	**David Graham**
Tracking Station	**David Graham**

First UK Transmission

Sunday, December 27th, 1964
5.35pm (ATV London)

RESCUE FROM THE SKIES — Prod. No. 32

Teleplay by **Dennis Spooner** Directed by **Desmond Saunders**

After Lieutenant Fisher passes a test in the simulator at the WASP Training Unit, he is ready to captain the real *Stingray* for the last stage of his aquanaut training. Commander Shore discusses Fisher's training exercise with Troy, but their conversation is overheard by X20 concealed inside a packing case. Planning to sabotage the training exercise and destroy *Stingray*, X20 places explosives on one of the targets at the WASP Missile Range, so when Fisher strikes the target with a sting missile, *Stingray* is caught in the blast and crashes to the sea-bed, leaving Phones and Fisher trapped inside!

Notes

At the end of the training simulation, there is a quick shot of the real back projection equipment at the AP Film Studios in operation: Ernemann X equipment with automatic camera phasing, supplied to AP Films by Walterdaw Limited of Kingston-on-Thames.

Oops!

After Troy's Arrowhead jet crashes into the sea and explodes, the model of the jet can be seen intact, floating on the surface of the water.

Regular Voice Cast	
Cpt. Troy Tempest	**Don Mason**
Lt. Phones Sheridan	**Robert Easton**
Lt. Atlanta Shore	**Lois Maxwell**
Cdr. Sam Shore	**Ray Barrett**
Sub-Lt. John Fisher	**Ray Barrett**
X20	**Robert Easton**

Guest Voice Cast	
Simulator Sergeant	**David Graham**
Gate Sergeant	**David Graham**
Truck Driver Joe	**David Graham**
Security Guard	**David Graham**

First UK Transmission

Sunday, January 10th, 1965
5.35pm (ATV London)

THE COOL CAVE MAN — Prod. No. 33

Teleplay by **Alan Fennell** Directed by **Alan Pattillo**

Commander Shore places Troy and Phones on stand-by in case anything should go wrong with the *Shenandoah*, a freighter carrying radioactive isotopes. Hoping that he will not have to miss Atlanta's fancy dress party, Troy looks through a pictorial history book for costume ideas and falls asleep looking at a picture of some cavemen. He is woken by the alarm signal and joins Phones aboard *Stingray* to recover an isotope canister that has fallen into the sea after the *Shenandoah* hit some rocks and broke apart. Just as they locate the canister, it is found by three underwater cavemen. The aquanauts follow the men as they take it into a subterranean cave network, but fall into a deep pit set as a trap. The oldest of the cavemen falls sick after opening the canister and Troy tries to persuade the other two that he can save the old man's life with anti-radiation pills. The cavemen agree to allow Troy to help, with the proviso that if he fails, both aquanauts will die!

Notes

Among the guests at Atlanta's party are Admiral Denver (in his *Set Sail For Adventure* period costume) and, oddly, the villainous Lieutenant Gray from *Tune Of Danger*, disguised with Lieutenant Fisher's false nose and moustache.

Regular Voice Cast	
Cpt. Troy Tempest	**Don Mason**
Lt. Phones Sheridan	**Robert Easton**
Lt. Atlanta Shore	**Lois Maxwell**
Cdr. Sam Shore	**Ray Barrett**
Sub-Lt. John Fisher	**Ray Barrett**

Guest Voice Cast	
Old Caveman	**David Graham**
Caveman 1	**David Graham**
Caveman 2	**David Graham**

First UK Transmission

Sunday, January 31st, 1965
5.35pm (ATV London)

A NUT FOR MARINEVILLE

Prod. No. 34

Teleplay by **Gerry & Sylvia Anderson** Directed by **David Elliott**

After a pair of undersea aliens, Grupa and Noctus, approach Marineville in an underwater craft made of a metal able to withstand all WASP armaments, leading scientist Professor Burgoyne is assigned to Marineville to develop a missile nose-cone that can penetrate the alien craft's hull. Burgoyne insists on being isolated in a laboratory as far from the Tower as possible, so when the laboratory building explodes and is completely destroyed, the Professor is assumed to have been killed. However, he turns up alive and well to announce that he has been successful. The new nose-cone is fitted to a missile which is loaded aboard *Stingray* and Burgoyne joins Troy and Phones as they race to intercept the aliens' craft...

Oops!

It doesn't make sense that instead of pressing home their attack on Marineville after *Stingray*'s missiles prove ineffective against their craft, Grupa and Noctus retreat to their base, a full 24 hours' travel time away, and then come all the way back again. Nor does it make sense that, given the emergency situation, only *one* scientist is assigned to WASP to develop a new metal for the missile nose-cone rather than a team of experts.

Regular Voice Cast

Cpt. Troy Tempest	**Don Mason**
Lt. Phones Sheridan	**Robert Easton**
Lt. Atlanta Shore	**Lois Maxwell**
Cdr. Sam Shore	**Ray Barrett**
Sub-Lt. John Fisher	**Ray Barrett**

Guest Voice Cast

Professor Burgoyne	**David Graham**
Grupa	**Ray Barrett**
Noctus	**David Graham**
Tracking Station	**David Graham**
Missile Unit	**Don Mason**
Philippine Station 178	**Robert Easton**

First UK Transmission

Sunday, April 25th, 1965
5.35pm (ATV London)

TRAPPED IN THE DEPTHS

Prod. No. 35

Teleplay by **Alan Fennell** Directed by **John Kelly**

While studying operations at the Nuclear Fish Farm, Atlanta stumbles on a plan by her tutor, Professor Cordo, to kill Troy and steal *Stingray* using a full-size model of the WASP submarine. Cordo reveals he has sworn to help an undersea race that his father discovered, restoring them to their former glory by destroying Marineville. When the *Stingray* crew visit the farm and join Atlanta and the Professor for a meal, Atlanta is prevented from warning her friends of Cordo's plans as he targets Troy with a gun hidden under the table. Meanwhile, Grupa and Noctus, the undersea aliens working with Cordo, tow *Stingray* away and replace it with the model. When Troy, Phones and Marina leave the farm and swim back to *Stingray*, they discover the mock-up. With nowhere else to go, they return to the farm but are trapped outside when Cordo closes the airlock!

Notes

Professor Cordo is named after the prolific Hungarian film producer-director Alexander Korda (1893-1956), who revived the flagging British film industry in the 1930s and 40s. Either the events of this episode take place before those of *A Nut For Marineville*, or Grupa and Noctus did not receive much of a jail sentence after the previous episode.

Regular Voice Cast

Cpt. Troy Tempest	**Don Mason**
Lt. Phones Sheridan	**Robert Easton**
Lt. Atlanta Shore	**Lois Maxwell**
Cdr. Sam Shore	**Ray Barrett**
Sub-Lt. John Fisher	**Ray Barrett**

Guest Voice Cast

Professor Alexander Cordo	**David Graham**
Grupa	**Ray Barrett**
Noctus	**David Graham**
Weather Tower 7	**David Graham**

First UK Transmission

Sunday, May 2nd, 1965
5.20pm (ATV London)

EASTERN ECLIPSE

Prod. No. 36

Teleplay by **Alan Fennell** Directed by **Desmond Saunders**

Ali Khali, twin brother of El Hudat, arrives at Marineville aboard an old bi-plane which crashes into Marineville Tower after the pilot, a disguised X20, bails out. X20 has arranged a counter-revolution in Hudatvia which has overthrown Ali Khali's presidency, leaving the way clear for El Hudat to return to power and help Titan overthrow the land masses in gratitude – once X20 has rescued El Hudat from Marineville jail. Posing as a legal advisor, X20 gains access to El Hudat's cell and plans his escape. When Ali Khali arrives to visit his brother, X20 knocks him out and El Hudat walks free, masquerading as his twin...

Notes

This episode takes place 12 months after the events of *Star Of The East* (X20 states that El Hudat has been imprisoned in the Marineville jail for the last year).

Oops!

Troy cannot know that Ali Khali has the same 'line of patter' as his brother as he was not aboard the *Wadi* to hear El Hudat boasting of his achievements in *Star Of The East*.

Regular Voice Cast

Cpt. Troy Tempest	**Don Mason**
Lt. Phones Sheridan	**Robert Easton**
Lt. Atlanta Shore	**Lois Maxwell**
Cdr. Sam Shore	**Ray Barrett**
Sub-Lt. John Fisher	**Ray Barrett**
Titan	**Ray Barrett**
X20	**Robert Easton**

Guest Voice Cast

Ali Khali	**David Graham**
El Hudat	**David Graham**
Abu	**Robert Easton**
Aquaphibians	**David Graham**

First UK Transmission

Sunday, March 7th, 1965
5.35pm (ATV London)

A CHRISTMAS TO REMEMBER — Prod. No. 37

Teleplay by **Dennis Spooner** Directed by **Alan Pattillo**

Visiting young Barry Byrne at the WASP Orphanage, Troy relates a slightly exaggerated version of his latest mission, in which he apparently boarded a hostile underwater craft by being fired from *Stingray* using the sting missile launcher. The craft was apparently deserted, so it has been towed back to Marineville for examination. Troy arranges for Barry to visit Marineville over Christmas and the boy joins him aboard *Stingray* when the aquanauts re-enact their battle with the alien vessel, hoping to learn what became of the crew. Phones takes the helm of the alien vessel but the vehicle's pilot emerges from a secret compartment and overpowers him. Opening the vessel's entry hatch, the alien plans to lure Troy into the open and shoot him down as he swims across from *Stingray*!

Notes
Like *Stingray* and *Set Sail For Adventure*, this episode has no on-screen title.

Oops!
The Marineville scientists who searched the alien vessel must have been a bit short-sighted not to notice the rather obvious hinges on the door to the 'secret' compartment.

Regular Voice Cast

Cpt. Troy Tempest	**Don Mason**
Lt. Phones Sheridan	**Robert Easton**
Lt. Atlanta Shore	**Lois Maxwell**
Cdr. Sam Shore	**Ray Barrett**
Sub-Lt. John Fisher	**Ray Barrett**

Guest Voice Cast

Barry Byrne	**Sylvia Anderson**
Alien	**David Graham**
Shore's Drinking Buddy	**David Graham**

First UK Transmission

Sunday, December 20th, 1964
5.35pm (ATV London)

THE LIGHTHOUSE DWELLERS — Prod. No. 38

Teleplay by **Alan Fennell** Directed by **David Elliott**

After 175 years, the lighthouse at Arago Rock is closed down as the beacon would confuse aircraft on approach to the new Arago Point Air Base. Keeper Frank Lincoln shuts down the beam and leaves his beloved lighthouse for the last time, but the beacon suddenly comes back on, causing Sky Eagle 127 to fly too low and crash. When the *Stingray* crew investigate, Troy and Phones are captured by an undersea alien, Lorif, and taken in an elevator to the undersea city of Prisma. There, another alien, Cromer, explains that their power source relies on the opening and closing of thousands of sea anemones as they react to the revolving lighthouse beam. Troy assures Cromer that he will ensure the light stays on until they can provide an alternative energy source, but at that very moment, Commander Shore cuts the power to the lighthouse and the beacon goes out!

Notes
The date of the episode is given on the lighthouse dedication plaque as 2065. If the events of the series are assumed to occur in the order in which the episodes were produced, the earlier episodes (at least up to and including the events of *Star Of The East*, which were stated to have taken place a year before in *Eastern Eclipse*) are set in 2064.

Regular Voice Cast

Cpt. Troy Tempest	**Don Mason**
Lt. Phones Sheridan	**Robert Easton**
Lt. Atlanta Shore	**Lois Maxwell**
Cdr. Sam Shore	**Ray Barrett**
Sub-Lt. John Fisher	**Ray Barrett**

Guest Voice Cast

Frank Lincoln	**David Graham**
Admiral Frendor	**David Graham**
Cromer	**David Graham**
Lorif	**David Graham**
Sky Eagle Pilot	**Don Mason**
Arago Point	**Lois Maxwell**
Rescue Launch 8	**Ray Barrett**

First UK Transmission

Sunday, January 17th, 1965
5.35pm (ATV London)

AQUANAUT OF THE YEAR — Prod. No. 39

Teleplay by **Gerry & Sylvia Anderson** Directed by **Alan Pattillo**

After a party celebrating his presentation with a medallion as 'Aquanaut of the Year', Troy is surprised to find a TV camera crew on his doorstep at 7.00 in the morning. Troy is the subject of a This Is Your Life programme being broadcast live from his apartment and he is joined by his colleagues as the presenter invites them to recall some of Troy's most daring exploits.

Notes
This episode features 16 minutes of footage from *Emergency Marineville*, *Raptures Of The Deep* and *Subterranean Sea*. The This Is Your Life theme was originally composed to accompany the launch of the title vehicle in Supercar.

Oops!
In close-up, the hour hand of Troy's bedside clock is missing. As the rippling flashback effect takes us into Troy's reminiscence of *Raptures Of The Deep*, the edit leaves several frames of Phones's face in the cross-fade. Somehow Troy manages to shave and change into his uniform while relating the events of *Raptures Of The Deep*.

Regular Voice Cast

Cpt. Troy Tempest	**Don Mason**
Lt. Phones Sheridan	**Robert Easton**
Lt. Atlanta Shore	**Lois Maxwell**
Cdr. Sam Shore	**Ray Barrett**
Sub-Lt. John Fisher	**Ray Barrett**

Guest Voice Cast

Presenter	**David Graham**
Nucella	**David Graham**

First UK Transmission

Sunday, June 27th, 1965
5.35pm (ATV London)

Regular Voice Cast

Cpt. Troy Tempest	**Don Mason**
Lt. Phones Sheridan	**Robert Easton**
Lt. Atlanta Shore	**Lois Maxwell**
Cdr. Sam Shore	**Ray Barrett**

Guest Voice Cast

Admiral Jack Denver	**David Graham**

Additional Voice Cast (Flashback Sequences)

Sub-Lt. John Fisher	**Ray Barrett**
Titan	**Ray Barrett**
X20	**Robert Easton**
1st WSP Commander	**Don Mason**
2nd WSP Commander	**Ray Barrett**
3rd WSP Commander	**Don Mason**
Aquaphibian 1	**Robert Easton**
Aquaphibian 2	**David Graham**
Tow Vessel	**David Graham**
Marina	**Sylvia Anderson**
Joe	**Ray Barrett**
Frank	**David Graham**
Nucella	**David Graham**
Chidora	**Ray Barrett**
Squadron Leader	**David Graham**
Tracking Station	**David Graham**

First UK Transmission

Unscreened to date

Episode Running Time

99 minutes approx.

STINGRAY (Feature Presentation)

Teleplay by **Alan Pattillo** Directed by **Alan Pattillo**

Admiral Denver joins Commander Shore in his apartment to review taped records of *Stingray*'s most hazardous missions. Troy and Phones arrive to escort Atlanta and Marina to a reunion dinner, but join the viewing session while they wait for the girls to finish putting on their make-up. They recall the attempt to discredit Phones with phoney radio signals and Troy's strange experience during the rescue of the *Hepcat* crew. Atlanta and Marina appear as Shore and Denver are arguing over whether the records could be falsified and Atlanta runs the tape of the Galvanoids' missile attack on Marineville. Troy decides that it is time they were leaving, but Atlanta reminds him that he has forgotten something – the song.

Notes

This feature-length episode of STINGRAY was prepared by the AP Films team as a presentation for Japanese television executives who visited the studios in 1963. Rather than simply screen four complete episodes of STINGRAY for the executives, Lew Grade and Gerry Anderson decided to turn the selected episodes into a feature film by shooting 4½ minutes of additional footage to link the four stories together. The film begins with the standard opening title sequence and the whole of the first episode, *Stingray*, but then cuts to the first section of linking footage (revealing Commander Shore and Admiral Denver, who have just finished watching the events of that episode projected on a screen in Shore's apartment) instead of the end titles. The three subsequent episodes – *An Echo Of Danger*, *Raptures Of The Deep* and *Emergency Marineville* – are then shown without title sequences as if presented as part of the characters' review of taped records of *Stingray* missions. The film concludes with a final section of linking material in which Atlanta provides the cue for 'Aqua Marina' before the standard closing title sequence. Forgotten for nearly 40 years, the framing sequences for the film were rediscovered in 2001 and released as a special feature on Carlton Visual Entertainment's STINGRAY Volume 3 DVD the same year.

Oops!

Apparently the World Aquanaut Security Patrol has equipment so sophisticated that it can make an audio-visual record of Troy's oxygen-starved hallucinations from *Raptures Of The Deep*.

THUNDERBIRDS

Format

In the year 2065, millionaire former astronaut Jeff Tracy has established an independent privately funded rescue organisation with an array of sophisticated rescue machines and equipment able to offer assistance in a wide range of disaster situations where conventional rescue methods have proved inadequate. Operating in secret from Tracy Island near the island of Moyla in the Southern Pacific, International Rescue maintains a fleet of five Thunderbird primary rescue vehicles designed by genius scientist Brains, each with a specific function and manned by Tracy's five sons:

Thunderbird 1, the spearhead craft of International Rescue with a top speed of 15,000 mph. Piloted by Scott Tracy, the vehicle's principal role is to get to the danger zone as fast as possible to enable Scott to direct the rescue operation.

Thunderbird 2, a heavy-duty freighter which carries the organisation's auxiliary rescue equipment aboard one of six interchangeable pods. Capable of speeds up to 5,000 mph, Thunderbird 2 is piloted by Virgil Tracy who also operates many of the auxiliary rescue vehicles, including the Mole boring machine and the Firefly fire-fighting vehicle.

Thunderbird 3, a massive space rocket used for rescues in Earth orbit and outer space. Piloted by Alan Tracy, the rocket is also used for ferrying personnel and equipment to the Thunderbird 5 space station.

Thunderbird 4, a compact submarine used for underwater and sea surface rescues. Piloted by Gordon Tracy, the craft is usually carried to and from the danger zone aboard Thunderbird 2 Pod 4.

Thunderbird 5, a massive space station packed with sophisticated scanning equipment which monitors all radio transmissions for SOS signals. Manned by John Tracy and Alan Tracy on alternating tours of duty, the station is maintained in a secret geostationary orbit.

The International Rescue team are often assisted in their operations by London agent Lady Penelope Creighton-Ward and her manservant Parker, based at stately Creighton-Ward Mansion in southern England. Lady Penelope owns a striking pink Rolls-Royce, FAB 1, which is fitted with an array of hidden equipment and armoury and can travel at speeds in excess of 200 mph.

Production

STINGRAY was massively successful in Britain and netted ITC over £3 million in overseas sales when the series was syndicated in the United States. As a result, Lew Grade was more than happy to back Gerry Anderson's next television series proposal, initially entitled 'International Rescue' and inspired by news reports of a difficult rescue operation at the Lengede iron mine in Lower Saxony, West Germany in late October 1963. With a budget of £25,000 per episode, filming began on 26 half-hour episodes of THUNDERBIRDS in the late summer of 1964, following five months of pre-production.

As with STINGRAY, two sets of the main puppet characters were created to enable different episodes to be shot simultaneously on the separate puppet stages and maintain a schedule of filming two episodes every fortnight. By mid-December 1964, nine episodes had been completed when the opening episode, *Trapped In The Sky*, was screened for Lew Grade. Grade was so impressed that he decided to double the length of each instalment and increase the budget to £38,000 per episode. New footage had to be shot that could be incorporated into each of the already filmed episodes, new scenes had to be written for the scripts waiting to be filmed, and while this material was being prepared to go before the cameras, the puppet and effects crews continued shooting half-hour episodes. Eventually settling into a schedule of filming two episodes every four weeks, the initial 26 episodes were finally completed in December 1965, by which time the earlier episodes were already being screened on British television to phenomenal public response and winning £350,000 in sales to overseas markets.

Lew Grade commissioned a further six episodes which were shot in tandem with a £250,000 feature film, *Thunderbirds Are Go* (1966), from March to August 1966. However, Grade's failure to secure a network sale in the US ultimately prompted his decision to terminate production of further THUNDERBIRDS episodes.

Main Characters

Jeff Tracy
Founder of International Rescue and patriarch of the Tracy family, formerly a USAF Colonel and astronaut

Scott Tracy
26-year-old eldest son of Jeff Tracy and pilot of Thunderbird 1, formerly USAF pilot

Lady Penelope Creighton-Ward
International Rescue's aristocratic London agent, formerly a Federal Agents Bureau operative

Virgil Tracy
24-year-old son of Jeff Tracy and pilot of Thunderbird 2

Alan Tracy
21-year-old youngest son of Jeff Tracy, pilot of Thunderbird 3 and a former champion racing-car driver

Brains
25-year-old scientist and genius inventor of all International Rescue vehicles and support equipment

Aloysius Parker
Lady Penelope's faithful butler and chauffeur, formerly one of the world's finest safe-crackers and cat burglars

Tin-Tin Kyrano
22-year-old daughter of Kyrano, International Rescue's maintenance technician and laboratory assistant

Gordon Tracy
22-year-old son of Jeff Tracy and pilot of Thunderbird 4, an expert oceanographer and former aquanaut

John Tracy
25-year-old son of Jeff Tracy and Thunderbird 5 space monitor, an electronics and communications expert and former astronaut

Kyrano
The Tracys' faithful family retainer, an expert botanist and chef, father of Tin-Tin and half-brother of The Hood

Grandma Tracy
Jeff Tracy's mother, the Tracy Villa housekeeper and an excellent cook

The Hood
Evil half-brother of Kyrano, a master of the black arts determined to obtain the secrets of International Rescue

Commander Norman
Chief controller at London Airport

Captain Hanson
Chief pilot of Air Terranean's Fireflash passenger aircraft

Episode Titles

(Listed in production order)

Series One

1. **Trapped In The Sky**
2. **Pit Of Peril**
3. **City Of Fire**
4. **Sun Probe**
5. **The Uninvited**
6. **The Mighty Atom**
7. **Vault Of Death**
8. **Operation Crash-Dive**
9. **Move – And You're Dead**
10. **Martian Invasion**
11. **Brink Of Disaster**
12. **The Perils Of Penelope**
13. **Terror In New York City**
14. **End Of The Road**
15. **Day Of Disaster**
16. **Edge Of Impact**
17. **Desperate Intruder**
18. **30 Minutes After Noon**
19. **The Impostors**
20. **The Man From MI.5**
21. **Cry Wolf**
22. **Danger At Ocean Deep**
23. **The Duchess Assignment**
24. **Attack Of The Alligators!**
25. **The Cham-Cham**
26. **Security Hazard**

Series Two

27. **Atlantic Inferno**
28. **Path Of Destruction**
29. **Alias Mr. Hackenbacker**
30. **Lord Parker's 'Oliday**
31. **Ricochet**
32. **Give Or Take A Million**

Episode Running Time

50 minutes approx.

F.A.B. *interjection British informal* an expression of agreement to, or acknowledgement of, a command. [from British television series, *Thunderbirds*]
Collins Dictionary (2002)

PRODUCTION CREDITS

Produced by *(1-26)* / Executive Producer *(27-32)* **Gerry Anderson**
Associate Producer *(1-26)* / Produced by *(27-32)* **Reg Hill**
Director of Photography *(1-26)* / Associate Producer *(27-32)* **John Read**
Character Visualisation *(1-26)* / Characters Created by *(27-32)* **Sylvia Anderson**
Lighting Cameraman **Paddy Seale** *(1, 4, 6, 9, 11, 12, 14, 16, 18, 19, 21, 24, 31)*
Julian Lugrin *(2, 3, 5, 7, 8, 10, 13, 15, 17, 20, 22, 23, 25-30, 32)*
Special Effects Lighting *(1)* / Special Effects Lighting Cameraman *(2-32)* **Michael Wilson**
Camera Operators **Jimmy Elliott**
Alan Perry *(1, 4, 6, 9, 11, 12, 14, 16, 18, 19, 21, 24)*
Geoff Meldrum *(2, 3, 5, 7, 8, 13, 15, 17, 20, 22, 23)*
Noel Rowland *(10, 25-30, 32)*
Gary Coxall *(27-32)*
Ted Cutlack *(31)*
Art Director *(1-26)* / Supervising Art Director *(27-32)* **Bob Bell**
Special Effects Director *(1)* / Supervising Special Effects Director *(2-32)* **Derek Meddings**
Puppetry Supervision **Christine Glanville** *(1, 4, 6, 9, 11, 12, 14, 16, 18, 19, 21, 24, 25, 27-32)*
Mary Turner *(1-3, 5, 7, 8, 10, 13, 15, 17, 20, 22, 23, 26-32)*
Script Supervision **Gerry & Sylvia Anderson** *(2-32)*
Music Composed and Directed by **Barry Gray**
Puppet Operators **Yvonne Hunter** *(1)*
Wanda Webb *(1, 4, 6, 9, 11, 12, 14, 16, 18, 19, 21, 24, 25, 27-32)*
Carolyn Turner *(4, 6, 9, 11, 12, 14, 16, 18, 19, 21, 24, 25)*
Judith Shutt *(2, 3, 5, 7, 8, 10, 13, 15, 17, 20, 22, 23, 26-32)*
Ernest Shutt *(2, 3, 5, 7, 8, 10, 13, 15, 17, 20, 22, 23, 26)*
Sculptors **John Brown, John Blundall, Tim Cooksey*, Terry Curtis*, Peter Hayward*, Mike Richardson***
Sculpting Supervision **John Brown** *(27-32)*
Wardrobe **Elizabeth Coleman**
Assistant Art Director *(1-26)* / Art Director *(27-32)* **Grenville Nott**

Character Voices **Sylvia Anderson**
Ray Barrett, Peter Dyneley, Christine Finn, David Graham, David Holliday *(1-26)*
Paul Maxwell*, Shane Rimmer, John Tate*, Charles Tingwell*, Jeremy Wilkin *(27-32)*
Matt Zimmerman
Special Effects Director **Jimmy Elliott** *(27-30, 32)*
Shaun Whittacker-Cook *(31)*
Designer **Keith Wilson** *(27-32)*
John Lageu *(27-32)**
Script Editor **Alan Pattillo** *(2-26)*
Supervising Editor **Len Walter** *(2-32)*
Editors **Len Walter** *(1)*
David Lane *(1)*
Harry MacDonald *(2, 5, 9, 11, 14, 17, 20, 21, 22, 26, 27-30, 32)*
Harry Ledger *(3, 6, 8, 12, 15, 18, 23-25, 31)*
Peter Elliott *(4, 7, 10, 13, 16, 19)*
Supervising Sound Editor **John Peverill**
SPECIAL EFFECTS 2nd UNIT
Director **Brian Johncock** *(1-9, 12-23)*
Ian Scoones *(10, 11, 24)*
Shaun Cook *(25, 26)*
Lighting Cameraman **Harry Oakes**
Camera Operator **John Foley** *(2, 4, 12-18)*
Garry Coxall *(3, 5-11, 19-26)*

Sound Editor **Brian Hickin** *(1, 2, 4, 12-18)*
John Beaton *(3, 5, 7, 20, 22-25)*
Tony Lenny *(6, 8, 9-11, 19, 21, 26)*
Norman Cole *(27-30)*
Peter Pennell *(31, 32)*
Dialogue Editor **Roy Lafbery** *(2-32)*
Special Effects Assistant **Brian Johncock** *(1)*
Richard Conway*, Peter Wragg*
Puppet Properties **Eddie Hunter** *(1)*
Tony Dunsterville*
Stewart Osborn*
Property Master **Arthur Cripps**
Sound **Maurice Askew** *(1-28)*
John Taylor *(1-26)*
Ken Scrivener *(28-32)*
2nd Assistant Art Director **Ken Turner***
Special Effects Designer **Mike Trim***
Models **Peter Aston*, Eric Backman*, Ray Brown*, Charlie Bryant*, Ezra Deering*, Roger Dicken*, Arthur 'Wag' Evans*, Bill James*, Brian Smithies*, Mike Trim***

An APF Television Production *(1-26)*
in association with ATV
Westrex Sound System
An ITC World Wide Distribution
Filmed in Videcolor and Supermarionation

* uncredited

TRAPPED IN THE SKY — Prod. No. 01

Teleplay by **Gerry & Sylvia Anderson** Directed by **Alan Pattillo**

Through a psychic rapport with his half-brother Kyrano, The Hood learns that International Rescue is ready to begin operations. Plotting to lure the International Rescue craft, he straps a bomb to the landing gear of the atomic-powered airliner Fireflash on its maiden flight from London to Tokyo so that if the crew attempts a landing by conventional means, the bomb will detonate. Although the airliner's atomic motors enable the Fireflash to stay in the air for six months, the passengers and crew will receive fatal doses of radiation when the anti-radiation shield on the reactor fails. On board is Kyrano's daughter Tin-Tin, *en route* to Tracy Island to join International Rescue. The Fireflash crew attempt to dislodge the bomb with aerobatics, without success. Then, an attempt is made to winch a man to the landing gear from a TX 204 target-carrying aircraft, but this also fails, so Jeff dispatches Scott and Virgil in Thunderbirds 1 and 2 to London Airport. International Rescue are in business!

Notes

This episode has no on-screen title but is referred to in all production documentation by the title of the shooting script – *Trapped In The Sky*. The arrangement of the music on the main titles and end credit sequences is unique to this episode and sound effects are heard in the episode montage during the opening titles. Alan is voiced by Ray Barrett as Matt Zimmerman had not been employed when the dialogue recording session took place.

Oops!

Several shots from beneath Thunderbird 1 show the 'T' of 'Thunderbird' painted on the nose cone, yet the nose cone is free of markings in all other shots of the craft. At the end of the episode, Operation Cover-Up replaces the portraits of the brothers in uniform with pictures of them in civilian clothing, but when the doctor enters the room, the uniformed portraits are still clearly visible in shots of Scott, Gordon and Jeff.

Regular Voice Cast

Jeff Tracy	**Peter Dyneley**
Scott Tracy	**Shane Rimmer**
Lady Penelope	**Sylvia Anderson**
Virgil Tracy	**David Holliday**
Alan Tracy	**Ray Barrett**
Brains	**David Graham**
Aloysius Parker	**David Graham**
Tin-Tin Kyrano	**Christine Finn**
Gordon Tracy	**David Graham**
John Tracy	**Ray Barrett**
Kyrano	**David Graham**
The Hood	**Ray Barrett**
Commander Norman	**Peter Dyneley**
Captain Hanson	**David Graham**

Guest Voice Cast

Fireflash Co-Pilot	**Ray Barrett**
Assistant Controller	**Ray Barrett**
Lt. Bob Meddings	**David Graham**
Harris	**Ray Barrett**
TX 204 Pilot (Target One)	**Ray Barrett**
TX 204 Co-Pilot	**Shane Rimmer**
Interceptor One	**Peter Dyneley**
Air Terrainean Guide	**Sylvia Anderson**
Doctor	**David Graham**
Fireflash Passenger	**David Graham**

First UK Transmission

Thursday, September 30th, 1965
7.00pm (ATV Midlands)

PIT OF PERIL — Prod. No. 02

Teleplay by **Alan Fennell** Directed by **Desmond Saunders**

In the African jungle, the US Army is testing a new all-terrain Sidewinder vehicle when the ground gives way and it falls into a blazing pit with a three man crew trapped inside – 300 feet below ground. Lieutenant Mead, a member of the relief crew, is lowered into the pit from a helijet to assess the situation; he is badly burned but able to report the condition of the vehicle. A second man, Sergeant Reynolds, tries to attach a line to one of the Sidewinder's legs to haul it upright, but he too is badly burned and the line slips off during the attempt. General Peters calls in International Rescue and Scott, Virgil and Brains are soon speeding to the scene in Thunderbirds 1 and 2. Thunderbird 1's remote camera reveals that the pit was once an open-cast mine used as a military equipment dump after World War II. A crust of earth has formed over the top and the International Rescue team realise that they must remove the remainder of the crust before the 500-ton Sidewinder can be dragged up the side of the pit...

Notes

Pit Of Peril features the smallest number of regular characters seen in any THUNDERBIRDS episode and no female characters whatsoever. The episode introduces the Mole which is later seen in *City Of Fire*, *Cry Wolf* and *The Duchess Assignment*. The vehicle appears for the first time in the end title sequence, having been absent from the end titles of *Trapped In The Sky*. Colonel Sweeney previously appeared as Fireflash pilot Captain Hanson in *Trapped In The Sky* and one of his subordinates was Hanson's co-pilot in that episode.

Oops!

When the Mole returns to the surface with Scott and Virgil on board, dust and sand can be seen pouring *up* from the ground onto the Mole's tracks (footage of the Mole tunnelling into the ground has simply been reversed). Thunderbird 1 sets fire to a dead tree trunk when Scott lifts off at the end of the episode.

Regular Voice Cast

Jeff Tracy	**Peter Dyneley**
Scott Tracy	**Shane Rimmer**
Virgil Tracy	**David Holliday**
Brains	**David Graham**
John Tracy	**Ray Barrett**

Guest Voice Cast

Colonel Sweeney	**David Graham**
Ralph	**Peter Dyneley**
General Peters	**David Graham**
Captain	**Matt Zimmerman**
Lieutenant Mead	**Ray Barrett**
Sergeant Reynolds	**David Graham**
Frank	**David Graham**
Johnny	**Shane Rimmer**
Helijet Pilot Charlie	**Matt Zimmerman**

First UK Transmission

Thursday, October 7th, 1965
7.00pm (ATV Midlands)

CITY OF FIRE

Prod. No. 03

Teleplay by **Alan Fennell** Directed by **David Elliott**

A car crash in the underground parking lot of the newly opened Thompson Tower maxi-mall causes a raging inferno which soon consumes the building when the sprinkler system fails. Unseen by the security cameras, the Carter family – Joe, Blanche and their son Tommy – is trapped by sealed fire doors in the access corridors beneath the Tower. By the time that they are spotted, it is too late to effect a rescue by normal means. The Tower Controller calls International Rescue and Scott and Virgil race to the scene in Thunderbirds 1 and 2, despite having only just recovered from the side-effects of experiments with new cutting equipment fuelled by oxyhydnite gas. As Thunderbird 1 arrives, the Tower collapses, raising doubts as to how long the ceiling of the underground corridor can last before caving in. Scott and Virgil realise that the only way to reach the Carters in time is to cut through the fire doors with the oxyhydnite equipment, whatever the risks from the side-effects...

Notes

The Thompson Tower has 350 floors on which every single commercial item produced throughout the entire world can be obtained. Half a mile wide and two miles deep, the Tower houses 12 hotels and features a massive sub-basement with parking for 10,000 vehicles linked to the store by a monorail four miles long. The Firefly is seen again in *Terror In New York City* and *Cry Wolf* while the Tracy brothers' hoverbikes (the THUNDERBIRDS equivalent of FIREBALL XL5's jetmobiles and STINGRAY's monocopters) reappear in *Vault Of Death*, *Martian Invasion*, *Cry Wolf* and *Attack Of The Alligators!*

Oops!

Although the Thompson Tower is clearly situated in the United States, a sign on the wall of the Control Centre uses the British spelling of 'Centre' instead of the American 'Center'.

Regular Voice Cast

Jeff Tracy	**Peter Dyneley**
Scott Tracy	**Shane Rimmer**
Virgil Tracy	**David Holliday**
Alan Tracy	**Matt Zimmerman**
Brains	**David Graham**
Tin-Tin Kyrano	**Christine Finn**
John Tracy	**Ray Barrett**

Guest Voice Cast

Joe Carter	**Ray Barrett**
Blanche Carter	**Sylvia Anderson**
Tommy Carter	**Sylvia Anderson**
Tower Controller	**Matt Zimmerman**
Tower Control Assistant	**David Graham**
WTV Reporter	**Matt Zimmerman**
Woman Driver	**Christine Finn**
Woman Driver's Husband	**David Graham**
Fire Chief	**Peter Dyneley**

First UK Transmission

Thursday, January 6th, 1966
7.00pm (ATV Midlands)

SUN PROBE

Prod. No. 04

Teleplay by **Alan Fennell** Directed by **David Lane**

The Sun Probe, a rocket designed to ferry three solarnauts to the Sun and return with a piece of solar matter, is launched from Cape Kennedy and within a week has arrived at its destination. The mission goes according to plan but as the solarnauts prepare to return to Earth, high radiation levels prevent the Probe's control systems from firing the retro rockets and the solarnauts find themselves on a collision course with the Sun. Brains realises that a powerful radio beam is needed to fire the Probe's retros and Jeff decides to mount a two-pronged rescue: Thunderbird 3, with Alan, Scott and Tin-Tin on board, is launched into space whilst Virgil and Brains head for Mount Arkan in Thunderbird 2 with a powerful mobile transmitter. But Alan's first attempt to reach the Probe with the safety beam fails and he and Scott realise that Thunderbird 3 must go much closer to the Sun than originally planned...

Notes

Jeff states that this is Tin-Tin's first mission and the episode also marks the first appearance of Brains's robot Braman, who is later seen in *Edge Of Impact* and *The Cham-Cham*. Although we do not see Grandma, Jeff tells Virgil that she will organise auxiliary clothing for the trip to Mount Arkan.

Oops!

During the television report about the Sun Probe, a diagram shows the solarnauts' control cabin within the Probe Module, but the control cabin is within the body of the Probe Rocket when the Module is fired into the solar prominence. Alan and Scott manage to swap seats during their journey to Thunderbird 3 on the sofa, but are in their original positions when the sofa arrives on board the spacecraft. When Thunderbird 2 leaves the hangar on Tracy Island, it appears that Pod 3 has been selected, yet when Virgil and Brains arrive at Mount Arkan, the Transmitter Truck emerges from Pod 6.

Regular Voice Cast

Jeff Tracy	**Peter Dyneley**
Scott Tracy	**Shane Rimmer**
Virgil Tracy	**David Holliday**
Alan Tracy	**Matt Zimmerman**
Brains	**David Graham**
Tin-Tin Kyrano	**Christine Finn**
Gordon Tracy	**David Graham**
Kyrano	**David Graham**

Guest Voice Cast

Colonel Harris	**Ray Barrett**
Solarnaut Asher	**David Graham**
Solarnaut Camp	**John Tate**
Colonel Benson	**Ray Barrett**
Prof. Heinz Bodman	**Peter Dyneley**
TV Reporter	**Matt Zimmerman**
Braman	**David Graham**

First UK Transmission

Thursday, December 9th, 1965
7.00pm (ATV Midlands)

THE UNINVITED

Prod. No. 05

Teleplay by **Alan Fennell** Directed by **Desmond Saunders**

As Scott returns from the scene of a fire in Tokyo, Thunderbird 1 is shot down in the Sahara Desert by three unidentified fighter planes. Scott cracks his head as Thunderbird 1 crashes into the sand dunes, but he is able to open the cabin hatch before passing out. He is found by two archaeologists, Wilson and Lindsey, who administer first aid. They radio International Rescue and Virgil, Brains and Tin-Tin soon arrive in Thunderbird 2. After the International Rescue group return to Tracy Island, the archaeologists continue their search for the lost pyramid of Khamandides, but their supplies trailer breaks loose from their jeep and explodes, leaving the pair stranded without water. Their SOS call is picked up by Alan on Thunderbird 5 and Scott is soon on his way in Thunderbird 1. Meanwhile, Wilson and Lindsey discover the pyramid of Khamandides but the door through which they enter the pyramid swings shut behind them, trapping them inside!

Notes

The working title of this episode was 'Desert Of Danger'. Although the pyramid people are named as 'Zombites' in the script and the symbol on their helmets is a stylised 'Z', they are never actually referred to as 'Zombites' in the episode.

Oops!

When Tin-Tin responds to news of Scott's disappearance, a floor puppeteer's hand (with dirty fingernails) can be seen in the bottom of the screen lifting Tin-Tin from her seat. Between arriving on board Thunderbird 3 and climbing into the elevator to travel up to the control room, Alan completely changes his clothes from a purple suit to green checked shirt and beige trousers. Similarly, Scott returns from Thunderbird 3 wearing different clothes from those that he left in, swapping a yellow suit and orange shirt for his usual blue roll-neck and checked jacket. The symbols on the walls of the Zombites' control room are the reverse of the symbol on their helmets.

Regular Voice Cast	
Jeff Tracy	**Peter Dyneley**
Scott Tracy	**Shane Rimmer**
Virgil Tracy	**David Holliday**
Alan Tracy	**Matt Zimmerman**
Brains	**David Graham**
Tin-Tin Kyrano	**Christine Finn**
Gordon Tracy	**David Graham**
John Tracy	**Ray Barrett**
Grandma Tracy	**Christine Finn**

Guest Voice Cast	
Wilson	**Ray Barrett**
Lindsey	**Matt Zimmerman**
Zombite Leader	**David Graham**
Zombite Controller	**Matt Zimmerman**
Zombite Guard	**Ray Barrett**
Zombite Flight Leader	**David Graham**

First UK Transmission

Thursday, December 2nd, 1965
7.00pm (ATV Midlands)

THE MIGHTY ATOM

Prod. No. 06

Teleplay by **Dennis Spooner** Directed by **David Lane**

Attempting to film the secrets of an atomic irrigation plant in Eastern Australia, The Hood accidentally causes a fire which leads to the explosion of the plant's nuclear reactor. The resulting atomic cloud drifts towards Melbourne, but a strong wind blows it away. A year later, The Hood attends a demonstration of a remarkable surveillance device, the Mighty Atom. Disguised as a mouse, the Mighty Atom can photograph control systems by focusing on technicians' faces as they monitor their control panels, so The Hood steals the device and uses it to photograph the control room of a new irrigation plant which has been built in the Sahara Desert. He then sparks a fire similar to the one at the Australian plant, planning to lure International Rescue and use the Mighty Atom to photograph the control cabins of the Thunderbird vehicles...

Notes

Penelope makes her first visit to Tracy Island since International Rescue became operational and also takes part in her first rescue mission. It is stated that International Rescue were not operating when the Australian plant exploded 12 months ago. The rescue plane that evacuates the personnel of the Australian plant is the TX 204 target-carrying aircraft from *Trapped In The Sky*. This is the only episode to feature the entire regular cast and all five Thunderbird craft.

Oops!

The Mighty Atom is programmed only to photograph the profiles of human faces, yet it is seen taking photographs of the control panels at the Saharan plant when no one is in the room. An edition of the *Melbourne Herald* newspaper is seen to be dated Friday, December 24, 1964. This date is also seen on newspapers in *Edge Of Impact*, *The Impostors* and *Cry Wolf* but was not intended to be legible to television viewers. (Oddly, December 24th, 1964 was actually a Thursday.)

Regular Voice Cast	
Jeff Tracy	**Peter Dyneley**
Scott Tracy	**Shane Rimmer**
Lady Penelope	**Sylvia Anderson**
Virgil Tracy	**David Holliday**
Alan Tracy	**Matt Zimmerman**
Brains	**David Graham**
Aloysius Parker	**David Graham**
Tin-Tin Kyrano	**Christine Finn**
Gordon Tracy	**David Graham**
John Tracy	**Ray Barrett**
Kyrano	**David Graham**
Grandma Tracy	**Christine Finn**
The Hood	**Ray Barrett**

Guest Voice Cast	
Controller Wade	**Ray Barrett**
Controller Collins	**David Graham**
General Speyer	**Ray Barrett**
Professor Holden	**Peter Dyneley**
Control Assistant	**Shane Rimmer**
Press Officer	**Matt Zimmerman**
Plant Tour Guide	**David Graham**
1st Reporter	**Peter Dyneley**
2nd Reporter	**Matt Zimmerman**
Fire Chief	**Ray Barrett**
Guard	**Ray Barrett**

First UK Transmission

Thursday, December 30th, 1965
7.00pm (ATV Midlands)

VAULT OF DEATH

Prod. No. 07

Teleplay by **Dennis Spooner** Directed by **David Elliott**

Lady Penelope and Parker are invited to break into the vault of the Bank of England to illustrate that improved security is required. A new vault is fitted which can only be opened with an electronic key carried by the Bank's President, Lord Silton, in a briefcase which, he boasts, never leaves his side. But while Lord Silton dines with Lady Penelope at Creighton-Ward Mansion, the workaholic accountant Lambert is accidentally trapped inside the vault when it is closed for the next two years. The air is automatically pumped out to keep everything sterile, but with no manual shutdown Lambert will soon suffocate. Then Parker discovers that an old cell-mate, 'Light-Fingered' Fred, has just escaped from Parkmoor Scrubs. He recalls Fred's intention to break into the Bank of England when he got out, so when Penelope and Lord Silton learn of the emergency at the bank, Parker sabotages their attempts to get there in the mistaken belief that Fred is responsible...

Notes

This episode features the only appearance of a real human face (or, at least, part of one) in the series: when Penelope peeps through a spyhole in the door of the bank during the opening scene. The City of London Heliport is partially constructed from the remains of STINGRAY's Marineville Tower. Grandma remembers her grandmother talking about the London subway when she was a little girl, suggesting that the Underground has been out of use since the late 20th century.

Oops!

When Lovegrove realises that Lambert is still in the vault, Carter is initially voiced by Shane Rimmer but then by David Graham. Virgil and Alan arrive at Bank station via a tunnel from Piccadilly Circus, although the two stations are on different lines of the Underground: Piccadilly Circus is on the Piccadilly and Bakerloo lines, while Bank is on the Central, Northern, Waterloo & City and Docklands Light Railway lines.

Regular Voice Cast

Jeff Tracy	**Peter Dyneley**
Scott Tracy	**Shane Rimmer**
Lady Penelope	**Sylvia Anderson**
Virgil Tracy	**David Holliday**
Alan Tracy	**Matt Zimmerman**
Brains	**David Graham**
Aloysius Parker	**David Graham**
Tin-Tin Kyrano	**Christine Finn**
John Tracy	**Ray Barrett**
Grandma Tracy	**Christine Finn**

Guest Voice Cast

Lord Silton	**Peter Dyneley**
Lovegrove	**Ray Barrett**
Lambert	**David Graham**
Lil	**Sylvia Anderson**
Light-Fingered Fred	**David Graham**
Taylor	**David Graham**
Carter	**Shane Rimmer**
Moore	**David Graham**
Longman	**Peter Dyneley**
Barrett	**David Graham**
Policeman	**David Graham**

First UK Transmission

Thursday, December 23rd, 1965
7.00pm (ATV Midlands)

OPERATION CRASH-DIVE

Prod. No. 08

Teleplay by **Martin Crump** Directed by **Desmond Saunders**

Fireflash 3 crashes into the sea soon after taking off from London Airport and Air-sea Rescue can find no trace of the wreckage. A test Fireflash is launched and this too experiences difficulties and crashes into the sea. However, on this occasion, the flight has been monitored by Alan on Thunderbird 5 and he is able to report that the craft is actually some 180 miles north west of the position given by the crew. As Thunderbirds 1 and 2 are launched, the Fireflash sinks and the crew are trapped in the cabin when the emergency exit becomes jammed. In Thunderbird 4, Gordon locates the downed Fireflash and uses a laser cutter to remove the airliner's heavy engines, enabling the Fireflash to float to the surface where the crew escape in Thunderbird 2's rescue capsule. In an attempt to determine the cause of the crashes, Scott joins Captain Hanson during the next Fireflash test, but again the aircraft loses power and goes into a crash-dive...

Notes

Author Martin Crump's original script of this episode was titled 'The Test Crew'. The events of *Trapped In The Sky* are mentioned by a TV reporter who was previously seen in *Sun Probe*. After the second Fireflash crash, the saboteur escapes in an EJ2 jet, later seen as the bogus Thunderbird 2 in *The Impostors*. Lieutenant Burroughs, Commander Norman's assistant at London Airport, was previously seen as Solarnaut Asher in *Sun Probe*. An insert shot of a pile of newspapers and magazines shows that *The Daily Telegraph*, *Daily Mail*, *Life* and *Mad* are still being published in 2065.

Oops!

While Gordon searches for Fireflash on the sea-bed, the parting in his hair keeps changing sides. When he returns to Thunderbird 4 after making contact with the trapped crew, the configuration of the puppet-sized Thunderbird 4 doesn't match the model seen in long-shot.

Regular Voice Cast

Jeff Tracy	**Peter Dyneley**
Scott Tracy	**Shane Rimmer**
Virgil Tracy	**David Holliday**
Alan Tracy	**Matt Zimmerman**
Brains	**David Graham**
Tin-Tin Kyrano	**Christine Finn**
Gordon Tracy	**David Graham**
John Tracy	**Ray Barrett**
Grandma Tracy	**Christine Finn**
Commander Norman	**Peter Dyneley**
Captain Hanson	**David Graham**

Guest Voice Cast

Lt. Burroughs	**Ray Barrett**
Air Minister	**Peter Dyneley**
Patterson	**David Graham**
Fireflash Pilot	**David Graham**
Fireflash Co-Pilot Bob	**Ray Barrett**
Fireflash 3 Pilot	**David Graham**
TV Reporter	**Matt Zimmerman**
Seahawk Pilot	**Matt Zimmerman**
Farmer	**David Graham**
Radar Operator	**Shane Rimmer**
Saboteur	**Ray Barrett**
Newsreader	**David Holliday**

First UK Transmission

Thursday, December 16th, 1965
7.00pm (ATV Midlands)

MOVE - AND YOU'RE DEAD — Prod. No. 09

Teleplay by **Alan Pattillo** Directed by **Alan Pattillo**

Alan and Grandma are trapped high on the girders of a suspension bridge over the San Miguel River with a sonic wave generator positioned nearby. If either of them makes any move, the sonic wave device will register the movement and detonate a bomb attached to the underside of the bridge. Alan manages to use his personal intercall wrist communicator to call Tracy Island and Scott, Virgil and Brains set off in Thunderbirds 1 and 2. Grandma faints and in order to keep Alan from passing out too, Jeff makes him explain how they got into this fix. Alan tells how he took part in the Parola Sands Race to test a new engine designed by Brains and fitted into a BR2 racing car. On arrival at Parola Sands, Alan met his friend, engineer Kenny Malone, and an old race track rival, Victor Gomez, but Gomez and his partner Johnnie Gillespie proved to be desperate for the prize money and prepared to go to any lengths to win the race...

Notes
Grandma Tracy leaves her home to join the International Rescue team on Tracy Island for the first time, suggesting that the events of this episode take place before those of all the other episodes she appears in (including *Sun Probe*, *The Uninvited*, *The Mighty Atom*, *Vault Of Death* and *Operation Crash-Dive).*

Oops!
When Jeff is first contacted by Alan, he is sat behind his desk, but when the picture cuts back to him after a quick shot of Alan, he is suddenly perched on the front of the desk reading a magazine. As Alan makes his telecall to Grandma, the close-up of his hand dialling her number shows the push-button dial panel with letters on the left and numbers on the right, but on the puppet-sized telecall unit, the numbers are on the left and the letters are on the right. For a blond 21-year-old, Alan's close-up (ie. live action) hand is remarkably hirsute with very dark hair.

Regular Voice Cast

Jeff Tracy	**Peter Dyneley**
Scott Tracy	**Shane Rimmer**
Virgil Tracy	**David Holliday**
Alan Tracy	**Matt Zimmerman**
Brains	**David Graham**
Tin-Tin Kyrano	**Christine Finn**
Grandma Tracy	**Christine Finn**

Guest Voice Cast

Victor Gomez	**David Graham**
Johnny Gillespie	**Ray Barrett**
Kenny Malone	**Ray Barrett**
Billy Billoxi	**Matt Zimmerman**
Parola Sands Announcer	**Ray Barrett**
Timekeeper	**David Holliday**
Parola Sands Page	**Sylvia Anderson**

First UK Transmission

Thursday, February 10th, 1966
7.00pm (ATV Midlands)

MARTIAN INVASION — Prod. No. 10

Teleplay by **Alan Fennell** Directed by **David Elliott**

Two policemen, responding to a flying saucer report, find themselves attacked by Martians and trapped in a cave. However, this is just part of a movie script to be filmed by B-movie director Goldheimer under the supervision of The Hood in a devious plan to capture the secrets of International Rescue on film for sale to General Strond. Exerting his psychic control, The Hood forces Kyrano to switch off the automatic camera detector in Thunderbird 1 and then sets his plan in motion. Filming begins in the Nevada Desert using automatic camera equipment. The first scenes involve the two policemen becoming trapped in the cave by the Martians, but The Hood sabotages a pyrotechnic effects sequence and the resulting explosion brings down the whole cliff face. The two actors are trapped inside the cave, which begins to fill up with water from an underground river...

Notes
Although he is only called General 'X' on screen, The Hood's customer is named Strond in the script. Up to this point, The Hood has never been referred to by any name on screen – not even 'The Hood'. Here he calls himself Agent 79 in his radio transmissions to General Strond. His price for the secrets of International Rescue is $200 million. The film's special effects technician Brian, who operates the smoke machine for the cave scenes, is a puppet of THUNDERBIRDS special effects director Brian Johncock.

Oops!
In its hangar, Thunderbird 2 selects Pod 5, but when the cliff face drops down, Pod 2 is on the right of Thunderbird 2 instead of Pod 4. When Thunderbird 1 arrives at the danger zone, it descends with wheels on the end of the landing gear, but lands with skids. There are no markings down the length of the vehicle when it lands, but lettering appears after Scott calls for help with his equipment. This lettering is in a completely different font to that seen on the vehicle during the launch sequence.

Regular Voice Cast

Jeff Tracy	**Peter Dyneley**
Scott Tracy	**Shane Rimmer**
Virgil Tracy	**David Holliday**
Alan Tracy	**Matt Zimmerman**
Tin-Tin Kyrano	**Christine Finn**
Gordon Tracy	**David Graham**
John Tracy	**Ray Barrett**
Kyrano	**David Graham**
The Hood	**Ray Barrett**

Guest Voice Cast

Goldheimer	**Ray Barrett**
Bletcher	**David Graham**
General Strond	**Matt Zimmerman**
Maguire	**David Graham**
Slim	**Matt Zimmerman**
Martian Pete	**Peter Dyneley**
Martian Ray	**Ray Barrett**
Director of Photography	**Shane Rimmer**
Production Manager	**David Graham**
Make-Up Girl	**Sylvia Anderson**
Brian	**Ray Barrett**

First UK Transmission

Thursday, March 17th, 1966
7.00pm (ATV Midlands)

BRINK OF DISASTER — Prod. No. 11

Regular Voice Cast

Jeff Tracy	**Peter Dyneley**
Scott Tracy	**Shane Rimmer**
Lady Penelope	**Sylvia Anderson**
Virgil Tracy	**David Holliday**
Alan Tracy	**Matt Zimmerman**
Brains	**David Graham**
Aloysius Parker	**David Graham**
Tin-Tin Kyrano	**Christine Finn**
John Tracy	**Ray Barrett**

Guest Voice Cast

Warren Grafton	**David Graham**
Harry Malloy	**David Graham**
Doolan	**Matt Zimmerman**
Selsden	**Ray Barrett**
Hugo	**Peter Dyneley**
2nd Investor	**Ray Barrett**
Joe (Patrol 304)	**Ray Barrett**
Stan (Patrol 538)	**Matt Zimmerman**
Patrol Base	**Matt Zimmerman**
Crook with Machine Gun	**Ray Barrett**

First UK Transmission

Thursday, February 24th, 1966
7.00pm (ATV Midlands)

Teleplay by **Alan Fennell** Directed by **David Lane**

Lady Penelope is visited by American businessman Warren Grafton, who explains that he is looking for investors in his Pacific Atlantic Monorail company. Parker suspects a scam when he recognises Grafton's chauffeur as a crook named Harry Malloy, so Penelope puts Grafton in touch with Jeff Tracy, who investigates the operation posing as an interested investor. Grafton takes Jeff, Brains and Tin-Tin for a ride aboard the totally automated Pacific Atlantic monotrain, along the 500 miles of track that have already been completed. Grafton assures them of complete safety, although Jeff spots a number of flaws in the design which could endanger the monotrain passengers. Then a patrolling helijet is struck by lightning in a storm and crashes into a monorail bridge, bringing down part of the bridge and cutting off the automatic signals. The monotrain is out of control and heading for disaster!

Notes

Lady Penelope's driving in this episode – as she evades the crooks in the opening scenes – is very proficient and in complete contrast to the atrocious driving that she exhibited in *Vault Of Death*. The bogus telegram that Penelope receives from Parker reveals the location of Creighton-Ward Mansion to be Foxleyheath.

Oops!

Just as the villains' car goes out of control in the opening sequence, a huge lump of greenery falls out of the sky in the background. When Selsden and Malloy try to open Penelope's safe, the bulb in Malloy's torch gets so hot that the prop torch begins to smoulder. The broken section of monorail track that is attached to the top of the centre coach when Thunderbird 2 lifts it away from the bridge is significantly longer when Virgil sets the coach down on the mountainside. Incidentally, the inland telegram service was withdrawn in the UK in 1982.

THE PERILS OF PENELOPE — Prod. No. 12

Regular Voice Cast

Jeff Tracy	**Peter Dyneley**
Scott Tracy	**Shane Rimmer**
Lady Penelope	**Sylvia Anderson**
Virgil Tracy	**David Holliday**
Alan Tracy	**Matt Zimmerman**
Aloysius Parker	**David Graham**
Tin-Tin Kyrano	**Christine Finn**
Gordon Tracy	**David Graham**

Guest Voice Cast

Sir Jeremy Hodge	**Peter Dyneley**
Professor Borender	**David Graham**
Dr. Godber	**Ray Barrett**
Albert	**Matt Zimmerman**
Roache	**David Graham**
Waiter	**David Graham**
Colonel Benson	**David Graham**

First UK Transmission

Thursday, October 14th, 1965
7.00pm (ATV Midlands)

Teleplay by **Alan Pattillo** Directed by **Alan Pattillo & Desmond Saunders**

Professor Borender, creator of a new rocket fuel produced from sea water, used to power the Sun Probe on its historic solar flight, disappears from a monotrain during a journey from Paris to Anderbad. International Rescue's Sir Jeremy Hodge calls in Lady Penelope to help find his friend and they meet in a Parisian café where Penelope narrowly avoids drinking poisoned Pernod. The culprit leaves behind a matchbook emblazoned with a heraldic crest, but when they try to locate the crest in the Heraldic Archive, Penelope and Sir Jeremy are trapped in the basement by the evil Dr. Godber as gas is pumped in. Rescued by Parker in FAB 1, Penelope and Sir Jeremy retrace Borender's steps by taking the express monotrain to Anderbad, but Godber arranges a power failure as the train enters the Anderbad Tunnel and kidnaps them both. Taking them to his tunnel hideout, he tries to force Sir Jeremy and Borender to reveal the secret of their process by tying Penelope to a ladder and lowering her into the path of the Anderbad Express!

Notes

This episode has no on-screen title but is referred to in all production documentation by the title of the shooting script – *The Perils Of Penelope*. The launch of the Sun Probe at the start of this episode is the same event that was seen in flashback at the start of *Sun Probe*. The events of that episode occurred one week after the launch, so the events of *The Perils Of Penelope* must take place immediately before those of *Sun Probe*. The Anderbad Express monotrain was previously seen as the Pacific Atlantic monotrain in *Brink Of Disaster*. Godber's Anderbad Tunnel Control Chart unit is revamped from the Marineville Tower launch tunnel scanner unit seen in STINGRAY.

Oops!

As it bears down on Penelope's perilous position, the leading car on the Anderbad Express monotrain keeps changing colour, from white and red to silver and blue.

TERROR IN NEW YORK CITY Prod. No. 13

Teleplay by **Alan Fennell** Directed by **David Elliott & David Lane**

Returning from a rescue operation at an oil well fire, Thunderbird 2 strays into a Naval test area and is attacked by missiles launched from the *USN Sentinel*. Virgil pilots the damaged Thunderbird 2 to a crash-landing on Tracy Island and although he is not badly injured, Thunderbird 2 will be out of action for weeks. From his sick bed, Virgil watches a television report from New York on an ingenious operation to move the Empire State Building for redevelopment of the surrounding area. Suddenly, the ground gives way beneath the building and as it comes crashing down, television reporter Ned Cook and his cameraman, Joe, fall into a deep cavern. The Empire State Building collapses over the hole and the men are trapped with water seeping into their hollow from an uncharted underground river. Thunderbird 4 is their only hope of rescue, but with Thunderbird 2 out of commission there seems to be no way to get the submarine to New York in time!

Notes

The red scaffolding supporting the damaged Thunderbird 2 in the Tracy Island hangar reappears only a few minutes later as part of the Empire State Building atomic gantry tractor. It was previously seen as the Sun Probe rocket gantry in *Sun Probe* and *The Perils Of Penelope*. Among the members of the audience at The Ned Cook Show are Dr. Godber from *The Perils Of Penelope* and film producer Bletcher from *Martian Invasion*.

Oops!

The back of cameraman Joe's head flies off as he falls into the cavern. As Thunderbird 4 is shaken by the shockwave from the collapse of the Fulmer Finance building, water can be seen running down the outside of the aquarium positioned in front of the model set. At The Ned Cook Show, Dr. Godber is initially seen sitting in front of Bletcher with at least three rows of seats behind him, but he then appears two rows from the back sat in front of Jeff.

Regular Voice Cast

Jeff Tracy	**Peter Dyneley**
Scott Tracy	**Shane Rimmer**
Virgil Tracy	**David Holliday**
Alan Tracy	**Matt Zimmerman**
Brains	**David Graham**
Tin-Tin Kyrano	**Christine Finn**
Gordon Tracy	**David Graham**
Kyrano	**David Graham**

Guest Voice Cast

Ned Cook	**Matt Zimmerman**
Joe	**David Graham**
Sentinel Commander	**Ray Barrett**
First Officer Clayton	**David Graham**
Scanners	**Shane Rimmer**
1st Policeman – Site Control	**Ray Barrett**
2nd Policeman – Site Control	**David Graham**
Police Patrol	**David Graham**
Newsreader	**Ray Barrett**
Washington	**Shane Rimmer**
Garner	**David Graham**
TV Compere	**Ray Barrett**

First UK Transmission

Thursday, October 21st, 1965
7.00pm (ATV Midlands)

END OF THE ROAD Prod. No. 14

Teleplay by **Dennis Spooner** Directed by **David Lane**

The Gray & Houseman Construction Company are building a road through a mountain range in South-East Asia using an amazing road building vehicle, but they have to complete their contract before the monsoon season. Eddie Houseman successfully blasts a pathway through the mountains but, while he is visiting his old friend Tin-Tin Kyrano on Tracy Island, the mountain range starts to crumble into the pathway and his business partner Bob Gray realises that it will not survive the monsoon. Eddie immediately returns to the site and recklessly sets off in an explosives tractor to plant charges on an unstable peak which will cause it to fall away from the road. With the peak about to collapse, Eddie fires the charges while still too close and the blast leaves his tractor teetering on the edge of the mountain trail. But there's worse to come: he still has a case of unstable nutomic charges aboard and if he goes over the edge, he will be blown sky high!

Notes

The model of the Gray & Houseman Road Construction Vehicle is given a new coat of yellow paint for its reappearance in the series as the Road Construction Vehicle in *Atlantic Inferno*. Eddie's explosives tractor is later revamped to appear as an International Rescue fire-fighter truck in the opening scenes of *Security Hazard*. The front section of the tractor is identical to that of the International Rescue Transmitter Truck seen in *Sun Probe* (and later in *Cry Wolf*), albeit a different colour. Project manager Bob Gray is seen again as Cravitz in *Atlantic Inferno*. The framed portrait of Eddie that Tin-Tin keeps on her dressing table later turns up on a bench in the Williams homestead in *Cry Wolf*. Brains appears only in a non-speaking role, playing Gordon at chess.

Oops!

The raindrops on the faces of Eddie Houseman and his colleagues during the storm are disproportionately large.

Regular Voice Cast

Jeff Tracy	**Peter Dyneley**
Scott Tracy	**Shane Rimmer**
Virgil Tracy	**David Holliday**
Alan Tracy	**Matt Zimmerman**
Tin-Tin Kyrano	**Christine Finn**
Gordon Tracy	**David Graham**
John Tracy	**Ray Barrett**
Kyrano	**David Graham**
Grandma Tracy	**Christine Finn**

Guest Voice Cast

Eddie Houseman	**Ray Barrett**
Bob Gray	**David Graham**
Cheng	**David Graham**
J.B. Lester	**Ray Barrett**
Chuck Taylor	**Matt Zimmerman**
Engineer	**David Graham**

First UK Transmission

Thursday, November 25th, 1965
7.00pm (ATV Midlands)

DAY OF DISASTER — Prod. No. 15

Teleplay by **Dennis Spooner** Directed by **David Elliott**

A Martian Space Probe rocket is being transported to its launch site over the Allington Suspension Bridge when the suspension cables snap and the bridge collapses, tipping the MSP from its transport vehicle into the Allington River. The rocket lands on the river bed in an upright launch position, covered in debris from the bridge. The impact sets off the automatic launch countdown which will blow the rocket to pieces, killing two engineers who are trapped in the command module. Brains is visiting Lady Penelope and they both watch the disaster taking place on television. They rush to the bridge in FAB 1 and while Lady Penelope and Parker arrange a diversion, Brains makes his way to the bridge control centre. However, the Bridge Controller refuses to acknowledge the need for more sophisticated rescue equipment so Brains contacts John on his personal intercall wrist communicator and directs the International Rescue operation himself...

Notes

The music accompanying the journey of the MSP is the track 'March Of The Oysters', originally composed by Barry Gray for the STINGRAY episode *Secret Of The Giant Oyster*. The piece is also heard in *30 Minutes After Noon*, *The Impostors* and *The Cham-Cham*. Dave Clayton was previously seen as a reporter in *The Mighty Atom*. He reappears later in the series as Eddie Kerr in *The Impostors* and Chip Morrison's father in *Security Hazard*. During the edible transmitter incident, Jeff's wall map of the Tracy Villa reveals that the house contains six bedrooms, two guest rooms, laboratory and workshop in addition to the lounge, patio and Thunderbird 1 bay. Dr. R.G. Korda has a statue in his office that is identical to one in The Hood's temple. Korda is named after the psychiatrist Dr. Roger Corder, the lead character in the popular ABC television series THE HUMAN JUNGLE which originally aired in the UK between March 1963 and May 1965. Corder was played in the series by Herbert Lom, later seen as Dr. Kurt Hassler in Gerry Anderson's *Doppelgänger* (1968) feature film.

Regular Voice Cast

Jeff Tracy	**Peter Dyneley**
Scott Tracy	**Shane Rimmer**
Lady Penelope	**Sylvia Anderson**
Virgil Tracy	**David Holliday**
Alan Tracy	**Matt Zimmerman**
Brains	**David Graham**
Aloysius Parker	**David Graham**
Tin-Tin Kyrano	**Christine Finn**
Gordon Tracy	**David Graham**
John Tracy	**Ray Barrett**
Grandma Tracy	**Christine Finn**

Guest Voice Cast

Bridge Controller	**Ray Barrett**
Dave Clayton	**David Graham**
Kirby	**Ray Barrett**
Chuck	**David Graham**
Bill Craddock	**Matt Zimmerman**
Frank	**David Graham**
Professor Wingrove	**Peter Dyneley**
NTBS Reporter	**Peter Dyneley**
2nd NTBS Reporter	**Matt Zimmerman**
Policeman	**David Graham**
Dr. R. G. Korda	**Ray Barrett**
Crane Chief	**Peter Dyneley**

First UK Transmission

Thursday, November 4th, 1965
7.00pm (ATV Midlands)

EDGE OF IMPACT — Prod. No. 16

Teleplay by **Donald Robertson** Directed by **Desmond Saunders**

The Hood is hired by General Bron to sabotage the new Red Arrow fighter plane, ensuring that the plane crashes into the launch site on its test flight. World Space Control project supervisor Colonel Tim Casey is replaced for the test programme on Red Arrow 2, so he decides to pay an unexpected call on his old friend Jeff Tracy at Tracy Island. Brains suspects that the Red Arrow was sabotaged and provides Red Arrow 2 pilot Goddard with a diversion detector before he returns to base, but The Hood plants a homing device on an international television relay tower so that when Red Arrow 2 makes its test flight, it is drawn off course. Goddard ejects safely but the Red Arrow crashes into the tower, trapping a pair of operatives, Jim and Stan, in the control cabin. The men call International Rescue as the tower disintegrates, but with Colonel Casey still on the island, Jeff cannot risk launching Thunderbirds 1 and 2...

Notes

The TX 204 target-carrying aircraft originally seen in *Trapped In The Sky* appears briefly in an establishing shot of the airfield. A WASP Spearhead bomber from STINGRAY is also visible in the background. Tim Casey previously appeared as a bank executive in the opening scenes of *Vault Of Death*. The Hood's North Pole Laundry truck is revamped from Ned Cook's broadcast truck seen in *Terror In New York City*. Braman from *Sun Probe* can be seen in Brains's laboratory. Jeff's comment about their unexpected visitors being "some more of Tin-Tin's admirers" refers to the events of *End Of The Road*. In a startling prediction of the future, the television relay tower is seen to be owned by British Telecommunications Ltd: the formation of the real-life British Telecommunications (aka BT) did not take place until 1980, 16 years after this episode was made.

Oops!

Tim Casey is a Colonel, but Scott refers to him as a General in one scene.

Regular Voice Cast

Jeff Tracy	**Peter Dyneley**
Scott Tracy	**Shane Rimmer**
Virgil Tracy	**David Holliday**
Alan Tracy	**Matt Zimmerman**
Brains	**David Graham**
Tin-Tin Kyrano	**Christine Finn**
Gordon Tracy	**David Graham**
The Hood	**Ray Barrett**
Commander Norman	**Peter Dyneley**

Guest Voice Cast

Colonel Tim Casey	**David Graham**
General Bron	**David Graham**
Goddard	**Matt Zimmerman**
Jim	**David Graham**
Stan	**Ray Barrett**
Race	**David Graham**
Control Tower Lt.	**Ray Barrett**
Captain	**Matt Zimmerman**
1st Policeman	**David Graham**
2nd Policeman	**Ray Barrett**
Police Radio	**Christine Finn**

First UK Transmission

Thursday, October 28th, 1965
7.00pm (ATV Midlands)

DESPERATE INTRUDER — Prod. No. 17

Teleplay by **Donald Robertson** Directed by **David Lane**

Brains and Tin-Tin mount an expedition to find treasure in a temple on the bed of Lake Anasta in the Middle East, but The Hood learns of their plans through his psychic link with Kyrano. Ferried to the desert in Thunderbird 2, Brains and Tin-Tin make the final leg of their journey in a desert jeep towing a pair of caravans, rendezvousing with archaeologist Professor Blakely before completing the journey. Arriving at Lake Anasta, Brains and Tin-Tin use scuba gear to dive in and take a first look at the lost temple. Brains takes a rock sample from the central column for later examination but The Hood, observing from a mini-submarine hidden in the lake, believes that they have found the treasure already. That night, disguised as a Bedouin tribesman, he steals into the expedition caravans and hypnotises the three team members. The next morning, Brains regains consciousness to find himself buried up to his neck in the desert sand...

Notes

In a nicely understated piece of continuity, Tin-Tin has an Air Terrainean flight bag (presumably acquired during her trip on the Fireflash in *Trapped In The Sky*) with her on board Thunderbird 2 as they fly out to the Middle East. Tin-Tin points out the Pyramids during the flight: her next visit there is seen in *Thunderbird 6* (1968). Brains's desert jeep is revamped from the archaeologists' jeep seen in *The Uninvited*. Tin-Tin wears the same diving outfit that she sported in *Edge Of Impact*. This episode has the smallest guest cast of all of the THUNDERBIRDS episodes, with only two characters other than the regular cast.

Oops!

When Brains falls under The Hood's influence, he collapses and between shots his glasses simply disappear. They are subsequently shown to have fallen off but the action is not seen on screen: one moment the glasses are on his face and the next they have vanished.

Regular Voice Cast

Character	Voice
Jeff Tracy	**Peter Dyneley**
Scott Tracy	**Shane Rimmer**
Virgil Tracy	**David Holliday**
Brains	**David Graham**
Tin-Tin Kyrano	**Christine Finn**
Gordon Tracy	**David Graham**
John Tracy	**Ray Barrett**
Kyrano	**David Graham**
Grandma Tracy	**Christine Finn**
The Hood	**Ray Barrett**

Guest Voice Cast

Character	Voice
Professor Blakely	**Peter Dyneley**
Hassan Ali	**David Graham**

First UK Transmission

Thursday, November 18th, 1965
7.00pm (ATV Midlands)

30 MINUTES AFTER NOON — Prod. No. 18

Teleplay by **Alan Fennell** Directed by **David Elliott**

Driving home late at night, Tom Prescott picks up a hitch-hiker who locks a bracelet made of hydrochromatised steel to his wrist. He is told that the key is in his office at the Hudson Building in Spoke City, so Prescott races back to the building and unlocks the bracelet before the explosive device set into it detonates. Unfortunately, he is still descending in the elevator when the device left in his office explodes. The elevator plunges into the basement and Prescott is trapped at the bottom of the lift shaft as fire rages through the building. The local fire department is unable to contain the blaze, so Jeff dispatches Thunderbirds 1 and 2 to the scene. Virgil and Alan descend into the lift shaft in a specially cooled dicetylene cage fitted with grabs, recovering the elevator car and rescuing Prescott. Police Commissioner Garfield suspects that the Erdman gang are behind the incident so he turns the case over to the British Security Service...

Notes

The 'March Of The Oysters' track from STINGRAY's *Secret Of The Giant Oyster* episode is heard coming from Gladys Saltzman's television, while the Highland theme from STINGRAY's *Loch Ness Monster* accompanies the scenes at Glen Carrick Castle. The castle itself previously appeared as Castle McGregor in *Loch Ness Monster*. The puppet previously seen as Braman in *Sun Probe* plays all four of the plutonium store security robots. The Leader's helijet also appears as the World TV helijet at the start of *The Impostors*.

Oops!

When Jeff Tracy contacts Lady Penelope, it is 10.00am in England, yet it is already daylight on Tracy Island in the South Pacific and Alan, Gordon and Tin-Tin have been out fishing for some time. (It is later established in *Thunderbirds Are Go* that there is a five hour time difference between Tracy Island and England.)

Regular Voice Cast

Character	Voice
Jeff Tracy	**Peter Dyneley**
Scott Tracy	**Shane Rimmer**
Lady Penelope	**Sylvia Anderson**
Virgil Tracy	**David Holliday**
Alan Tracy	**Matt Zimmerman**
Brains	**David Graham**
Aloysius Parker	**David Graham**
Tin-Tin Kyrano	**Christine Finn**
Gordon Tracy	**David Graham**
John Tracy	**Ray Barrett**

Guest Voice Cast

Character	Voice
Southern	**Ray Barrett**
Sir William Frazer	**David Graham**
Tom Prescott	**Matt Zimmerman**
Commissioner Garfield	**David Graham**
The Leader	**David Graham**
Dempsey	**Peter Dyneley**
Kenyon	**David Graham**
Officer Flanagan	**Ray Barrett**
Officer Jones	**Peter Dyneley**
Stranger	**Ray Barrett**
Sam Saltzman	**David Graham**
Gladys Saltzman	**Sylvia Anderson**
Frank Forrester	**Matt Zimmerman**
BSS Assistant	**David Graham**
Erdman Gang Member	**Peter Dyneley**

First UK Transmission

Thursday, November 11th, 1965
7.00pm (ATV Midlands)

THE IMPOSTORS

Prod. No. 19

Teleplay by **Dennis Spooner** Directed by **Desmond Saunders**

A fake International Rescue team apparently rescues a man from an underground well, but when it is discovered that they have stolen top secret plans from the nearby Aeronautical Centre, General Lambert launches a worldwide search to track down International Rescue and bring them to justice. The Tracys have no choice but to shut down operations while the hunt is on but Jeff contacts International Rescue agents around the world to help them to find the impostors. Lady Penelope flies to America to interview a reporter who covered the 'rescue' at the well, while hillbilly agent Jeremiah Tuttle finds aircraft tracks in the woods near his shack which lead to an old mine. Meanwhile at the Space Observatory 3 scanning satellite, a technician is stranded in space when his jet pack goes haywire. Only International Rescue can save him, but launching Thunderbird 3 will reveal the organisation's location to Lambert's search team!

Notes

The photographer who takes the picture of the impostor Jenkins at the start of the episode was previously seen as Colonel Tim Casey in *Edge Of Impact*. Also among the crowd at the bogus rescue is Blanche Carter from *City Of Fire*. World Television reporter Eddie Kerr has a statue in his office that previously appeared in Dr. Korda's office in *Day Of Disaster*, a statue that is usually seen in The Hood's temple.

Oops!

When the Tracy brothers board Thunderbird 3, Alan does another quick change into different clothes before climbing into the elevator (as in *The Uninvited*). This time, Scott does a quick change too: initially he is wearing a yellow suit and orange shirt, but just before blast-off we see him in his blue roll-neck sweater and checked jacket. After he is rescued, Elliott tells Scott and Alan that it is great that they have been cleared and Scott replies, "You can say that again," without moving his lip.

Regular Voice Cast

Jeff Tracy	**Peter Dyneley**
Scott Tracy	**Shane Rimmer**
Lady Penelope	**Sylvia Anderson**
Virgil Tracy	**David Holliday**
Alan Tracy	**Matt Zimmerman**
Aloysius Parker	**David Graham**
Tin-Tin Kyrano	**Christine Finn**
Captain Hanson	**David Graham**

Guest Voice Cast

General Lambert	**Ray Barrett**
Elliott	**David Graham**
Eddie Kerr	**Matt Zimmerman**
Jeremiah Tuttle	**Peter Dyneley**
Ma Tuttle	**Sylvia Anderson**
Jenkins	**Ray Barrett**
Carela	**David Graham**
Hale	**Ray Barrett**
Fireflash Co-Pilot	**Ray Barrett**
Fireflash Stewardess	**Sylvia Anderson**
Colonel	**Ray Barrett**
Wakefield	**Matt Zimmerman**
Air Force Officer	**Peter Dyneley**
Air Force Lt.	**Peter Dyneley**
Speed Merchant	**Matt Zimmerman**
Helijet Pilot	**David Graham**
Search Control	**David Graham**
Jack	**David Graham**

First UK Transmission

Thursday, January 13th, 1966
7.00pm (ATV Midlands)

THE MAN FROM MI.5

Prod. No. 20

Teleplay by **Alan Fennell** Directed by **David Lane**

When top secret papers are stolen from Captain Blacker's ship anchored in harbour on the French Riviera, MI.5 agent Bondson contacts International Rescue, warning of the destruction of the world. Penelope agrees to meet Bondson in the Forest of Digne, where he reveals that the stolen papers are plans for a nuclear device. The recovery of the plans is vital so Penelope sets herself up as a target for the thieves, posing as model Gayle Williams, newly arrived on the French Riviera to expose those who blew up Blacker's boat. Penelope decides to give Parker the night off so she is alone on her luxury yacht FAB 2 when Carl, the leader of the crooks, kidnaps her. She is tied up in a lonely boathouse where Carl plants a radio-controlled bomb, explaining that the explosion will create a diversion for the harbour patrol, thereby enabling Carl and his cronies to escape into the open sea in their mini-submarine...

Notes

Reporter Eddie Kerr from *The Impostors* appears on board Fireflash as Lady Penelope flies to the South of France. Penelope wears the big orange hat that she sports in her picture caption in the opening titles of every episode. Brains's test submarine is a small model of The Hood's 3E Submarine as seen in *Desperate Intruder*. This episode features the first full Thunderbird 4 launch sequence shown from inside Pod 4 – prior to this, Thunderbird 4 has only been seen emerging down the ramp outside the pod door. This is also the only occasion in which Thunderbird 2 gently rests the pod on the surface of the water and then rises clear of the pod with lifting jets (normally, the pod is simply dropped on to the water). During the production of this episode in late 1965, the world was in the grip of Bondmania in anticipation of the December release of *Thunderball* (1965), the fourth James Bond 007 feature, and MI.5 agent Bondson was intended to be THUNDERBIRDS' own version of the character. Bondson also made a guest appearance in the 'Lady Penelope' strip in *Lady Penelope* comic (issue 44).

Regular Voice Cast

Jeff Tracy	**Peter Dyneley**
Scott Tracy	**Shane Rimmer**
Lady Penelope	**Sylvia Anderson**
Virgil Tracy	**David Holliday**
Alan Tracy	**Matt Zimmerman**
Brains	**David Graham**
Aloysius Parker	**David Graham**
Tin-Tin Kyrano	**Christine Finn**
Gordon Tracy	**David Graham**
John Tracy	**Ray Barrett**

Guest Voice Cast

Bondson	**Ray Barrett**
Carl	**David Graham**
Ritter	**Ray Barrett**
Third Man	**Matt Zimmerman**
MI.5 Agent Tidman	**David Graham**
Fireflash Stewardess	**Sylvia Anderson**

First UK Transmission

Thursday, January 20th, 1966
7.00pm (ATV Midlands)

CRY WOLF — Prod. No. 21

Teleplay by **Dennis Spooner** Directed by **David Elliott**

Two young boys, Tony and Bob Williams, unwittingly call out International Rescue on their walkie-talkies while playing in the Australian desert near their home at Charity Springs in the Northern Territory. To explain how their games are dangerous to International Rescue, Scott takes the boys back to Tracy Island for a guided tour, but the story makes headlines in the local newspapers which worries their father: under the guise of a weather station, he runs a satellite tracking station and is engaged in top security research for the military. Realising the true nature of the weather station, The Hood encourages Tony and Bob to play in the old Charity Springs tin mine at Dunsley Hill. Once the boys are inside, he fires a grenade into the mine entrance, causing a cave-in and trapping the boys. Tony and Bob call International Rescue on their walkie-talkies but their rescue plea is assumed to be another of the boys' games, and no action is taken...

Notes

Tony and Bob's tour of Tracy Island takes in the hangar for the Thunderbird 2 pod vehicles: they see the Mole (used in *Pit Of Peril*, *City Of Fire* and *The Duchess Assignment*), the Firefly (from *City Of Fire* and *Terror In New York City*), the Transmitter Truck (from *Sun Probe*), the Excavator (*Martian Invasion*) and the Monobrake (*The Perils Of Penelope*) as well as a civilian fire truck and a yellow fire vehicle first seen in *City Of Fire*. Colonel Jameson was previously General Lambert in *The Impostors.* Satellite HQ and the tracker satellite were also seen in that episode. Other tracking stations marked on Lansfield's console are at Cranston, Kangaroo (East) and Spring Hill.

Oops!

The characters all refer to Williams's station as Dunsley Tracker and it is labelled as such on Lansfield's console on the puppet-sized set, but in a close-up of the console (a large-scale section of the same set), the caption above the alert light reads '*Densley* Tracker'.

Regular Voice Cast

Jeff Tracy	**Peter Dyneley**
Scott Tracy	**Shane Rimmer**
Virgil Tracy	**David Holliday**
Alan Tracy	**Matt Zimmerman**
Brains	**David Graham**
Tin-Tin Kyrano	**Christine Finn**
Gordon Tracy	**David Graham**
John Tracy	**Ray Barrett**
Grandma Tracy	**Christine Finn**
The Hood	**Ray Barrett**

Guest Voice Cast

Williams	**Ray Barrett**
Bob Williams	**Sylvia Anderson**
Tony Williams	**Christine Finn**
Colonel Jameson	**David Graham**
Lt. Lansfield	**Matt Zimmerman**
Sergeant	**David Graham**

First UK Transmission

Thursday, January 27th, 1966
7.00pm (ATV Midlands)

DANGER AT OCEAN DEEP — Prod. No. 22

Teleplay by **Donald Robertson** Directed by **Desmond Saunders**

Ocean Pioneer I, an automated tanker carrying liquid alsterene, sails into a mysterious sea mist and explodes. Six months later, Lady Penelope launches *Ocean Pioneer II*, having thoroughly searched the ship beforehand for signs of sabotage. Meanwhile, International Rescue respond to a distress call from Oahu in the Pacific, which has been hit by a typhoon, but suddenly all radio transmissions are blacked out, leaving the organisation blind and deaf. Brains traces the cause of the interference to a reaction between OD60, a sea fungus used in the production of dog food, and liquid alsterene fuel in close proximity: bringing them even closer together results in a huge explosion. Jeff realises that this reaction must be the cause of the destruction of *Ocean Pioneer I*. Then Lady Penelope learns that there are large deposits of active OD60 in the Mediterranean and *Ocean Pioneer II* is heading straight for the area loaded with liquid alsterene!

Notes

This episode features the only occasion in which John is seen taking an active part in a rescue. Much of the music in this episode was originally composed for STINGRAY, including the *Ocean Pioneer* theme in the opening scene. Lord Worden was originally seen as Sir Jeremy Hodge in *The Perils Of Penelope* while the Mayor to Penelope's right at the Clydeside launching of *Ocean Pioneer II* is Professor Holden from *The Mighty Atom*. Tony Williams (from *Cry Wolf*), MI.5 agent Tidman (from *The Man From MI.5*) and Lovegrove (from *Vault Of Death*) are also visible in the crowd, as is the Commander of *Ocean Pioneer I*, oddly. Lieutenant Jensen is portrayed by Dave Clayton from *Day Of Disaster*. John admits that he has only been on about a dozen rescue missions, while Scott says that he has taken part in every single one. However, Scott was not involved in saving the kidnapped Lady Penelope in *The Perils Of Penelope*, so unless he has forgotten all about that mission, the events of this episode must take place before those of *The Perils Of Penelope*.

Regular Voice Cast

Jeff Tracy	**Peter Dyneley**
Scott Tracy	**Shane Rimmer**
Lady Penelope	**Sylvia Anderson**
Virgil Tracy	**David Holliday**
Alan Tracy	**Matt Zimmerman**
Brains	**David Graham**
Aloysius Parker	**David Graham**
Tin-Tin Kyrano	**Christine Finn**
Gordon Tracy	**David Graham**
John Tracy	**Ray Barrett**
Kyrano	**David Graham**

Guest Voice Cast

Lord Worden	**Peter Dyneley**
Ocean Pioneer II Captain	**John Tate**
Ocean Pioneer II No. 2	**David Graham**
Lt. Jensen	**Matt Zimmerman**
Captain Johnson	**Ray Barrett**
Collins	**David Graham**
Stevens	**John Tate**
Ocean Pioneer I Cdr.	**John Tate**
Sir Arthur	**Ray Barrett**
TV Reporter	**Ray Barrett**
Scottish Onlooker	**John Tate**
Pioneer Base	**Ray Barrett**

First UK Transmission

Thursday, February 3rd, 1966
7.00pm (ATV Midlands)

THE DUCHESS ASSIGNMENT

Prod. No. 23

Teleplay by **Martin Crump** Directed by **David Elliott**

Lady Penelope finds her old friend Deborah, the Duchess of Royston, playing roulette in a French casino. When the Duchess tells Penelope that she has lost everything except for her precious Braquasso painting 'Portrait Of A Gazelle', their conversation is overheard by a pair of gangsters, Chandler and Brophy. Penelope realises that the roulette table is fixed but she and Parker are unable to prevent the crooked casino owner from escaping with Deborah's money. Later, Penelope learns that the Duchess has been forced to put her home up for sale so, to help her, she and Jeff arrange a meeting with Wilbur Dandridge III, head of Gazelle Automations Inc. in New York. Deborah agrees to loan the Braquasso painting to Dandridge on a rental basis, taking the picture to New York herself. But on her arrival in America, the Duchess is kidnapped by Chandler and Brophy who steal the painting and leave her tied up in the basement of an old house...

Notes

The Duchess of Royston (both the puppet itself and Ray Barrett's voice for the character) was based on the distinguished British stage actress Dame Edith Evans (1888-1976), best known for her role as Lady Bracknell in *The Importance Of Being Earnest* (1951). Lady Penelope's cook Lil (from *Vault Of Death*) is seen here at the Duchess's table in the casino at the start of the episode and also in the Art Gallery admiring 'Portrait Of A Gazelle'. Other paintings on display in the Exhibition of 20th Century Art at the gallery are several splatter paintings by designer Keith Wilson and Virgil's abstract portrait of Alan from *Move – And You're Dead*. The Hood makes a non-speaking cameo appearance in his *Martian Invasion* disguise behind Jeff at the London Air Display. The Domo is revamped from the Excavator seen in *Martian Invasion* and *Cry Wolf*. The Empire State Building is clearly visible in an establishing shot of New York so the events of this episode must take place before those of *Terror In New York City*. Wilbur Dandridge previously appeared as Warren Grafton in *Brink Of Disaster*.

Regular Voice Cast

Jeff Tracy	**Peter Dyneley**
Scott Tracy	**Shane Rimmer**
Lady Penelope	**Sylvia Anderson**
Virgil Tracy	**David Holliday**
Alan Tracy	**Matt Zimmerman**
Aloysius Parker	**David Graham**
Tin-Tin Kyrano	**Christine Finn**
John Tracy	**Ray Barrett**
Grandma Tracy	**Christine Finn**
Captain Hanson	**David Graham**

Guest Voice Cast

Duchess of Royston	**Ray Barrett**
Wilbur Dandridge III	**David Graham**
Chandler	**Peter Dyneley**
Brophy	**Ray Barrett**
Mrs. Godolphin	**Sylvia Anderson**
Casino Owner	**Peter Dyneley**
1st Croupier	**Peter Dyneley**
2nd Croupier	**Matt Zimmerman**
Fireflash Co-Pilot	**Ray Barrett**
Hendricks	**Matt Zimmerman**
Percy	**David Graham**
Percy's Friend	**Ray Barrett**
Customs Officer	**David Graham**
Air Hostess	**Sylvia Anderson**
Hotel Receptionist	**Christine Finn**
Elevator Voice	**David Graham**

First UK Transmission

Thursday, February 17th, 1966
7.00pm (ATV Midlands)

ATTACK OF THE ALLIGATORS!

Prod. No. 24

Teleplay by **Alan Pattillo** Directed by **David Lane**

Blackmer visits Dr Orchard and his assistant Hector McGill at a lonely house on the Ambro River to see the effects of a new food additive called theramine, developed by Orchard from a rare plant that only grows in this area. Theramine greatly increases the size of animals fed with it, offering a solution to the world food shortage and even greater financial potential. These revelations are overheard by the boatman Culp, who later steals a sample of theramine from the laboratory, accidentally spilling some of the drug into the sink. He washes the spillage away into the river where it immediately affects the growth of three alligators. When Culp ferries Blackmer down the river the next morning, they are attacked by one of the alligators, now grown to enormous size. Blackmer is rescued by McGill but when they take refuge in the house with Orchard and his housekeeper Mrs. Files, they are surrounded by all three of the giant creatures...

Notes

This episode was inspired by the H.G. Wells novel *The Food Of The Gods* and director Paul Leni's 1927 classic silent film *The Cat And The Canary* (remade with Bob Hope in 1939 and with Honor Blackman in 1977). The production team hired baby crocodiles to double as the giant alligators on the model set and this was the first time that live animals were used in the filming of the Supermarionation productions. Visual effects director Brian Johncock refused to be involved as he did not agree with the use of electricity to encourage the crocodiles to move as required, although these scenes were supervised by an RSPCA inspector. The episode's events take place on March 10th and 11th (the next day is Alan's birthday, given as March 12th in the series' promotional information).

Oops!

The camera and camera operator can be seen reflected in the glass during a shot of Mrs. Files at the window of Orchard's house in the opening sequence.

Regular Voice Cast

Jeff Tracy	**Peter Dyneley**
Scott Tracy	**Shane Rimmer**
Virgil Tracy	**David Holliday**
Alan Tracy	**Matt Zimmerman**
Brains	**David Graham**
Tin-Tin Kyrano	**Christine Finn**
Gordon Tracy	**David Graham**
John Tracy	**Ray Barrett**
Grandma Tracy	**Christine Finn**

Guest Voice Cast

Dr. Orchard	**Ray Barrett**
Culp	**David Graham**
Blackmer	**John Tate**
Hector McGill	**Matt Zimmerman**
Mrs. Files	**Sylvia Anderson**

First UK Transmission

Thursday, March 10th, 1966
7.00pm (ATV Midlands)

Above: Tex Tucker supervises the filming of another exciting adventure in FOUR FEATHER FALLS.

Above: The AP Films crew shoot a scene with the puppets of Little Jake, Makooya and Big Ben for the FOUR FEATHER FALLS episode *Trapped*.

Top: Harper, Judd, Felicity Farnsworth, Colonel LaGuava and Pablo with the regular cast of SUPERCAR at the AP Films Studios.
Above: Professor Popkiss plans to use the Supercar jets to rescue Dr. Beaker in SUPERCAR – *Ice Fall*.

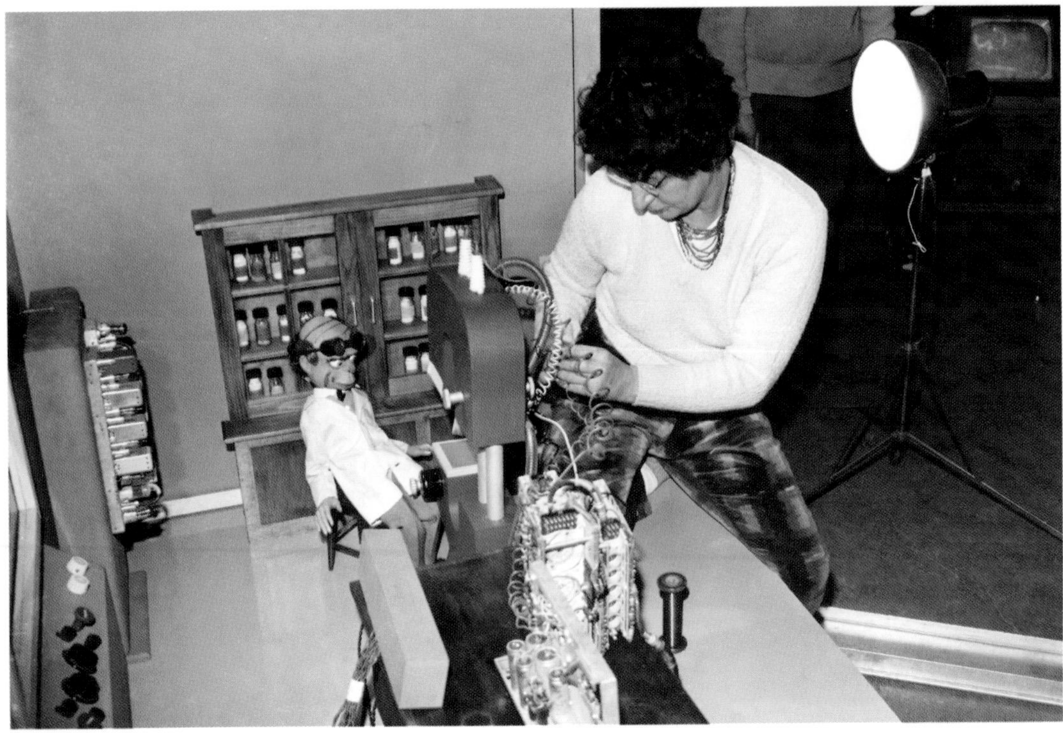

Top: A floor puppeteer corrects Mike Mercury's posture during filming of an episode of SUPERCAR.
Above: Puppeteer Christine Glanville makes an adjustment to one of Dr. Beaker's experiments during filming on SUPERCAR.

Top: Dr. Venus treats Zoony the Lazoon to his favourite sweets, Martian Delight, in FIREBALL XL5.
Above: *Fireball XL5* on the launch rail of the Space City model at the AP Films Studios during filming on FIREBALL XL5.

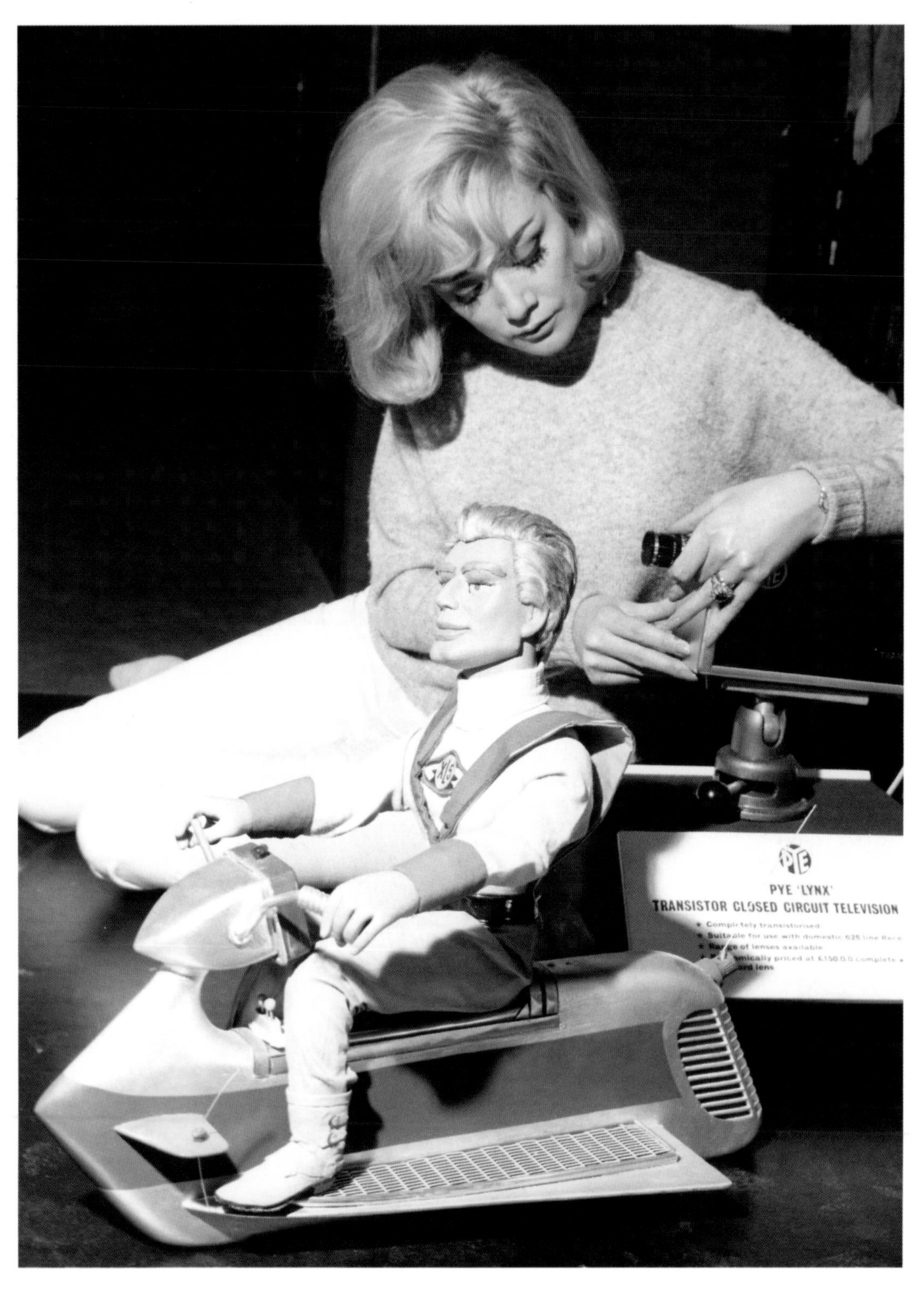

Above: Colonel Steve Zodiac helps a model to demonstrate the use of the Pye 'Lynx' transistor closed circuit television camera during the filming of Fireball XL5 in 1962.

Top: *Stingray* visits Tracy Island, a promotional photo taken for *TV Century 21* comic.
Above: Gerry and Sylvia Anderson pictured with Captain Troy Tempest from STINGRAY in their office at the AP Films Studios.

Above: A member of the art department makes an adjustment to Atlanta's control console on the Marineville Tower set during filming on STINGRAY.

Top: Alan arrives at Grandma's house in the BR2 racing car in the THUNDERBIRDS episode *Move – And You're Dead*.
Above: Lighting cameraman Paddy Seale takes a light reading before filming a scene for THUNDERBIRDS – *The Impostors*.

Top: IR agent Jeremiah (centre) with other guest puppets during production of the THUNDERBIRDS episode *The Impostors*.
Above: The crew of World Navy atom sub *Reaper* unwittingly cause trouble for Seascape in THUNDERBIRDS – *Atlantic Inferno*.

Above: Art director Bob Bell assists the puppet of Wilbur Dandridge III with a miniature prop, observed by Jeff Tracy on the set of the Gazelle Corporation office in THUNDERBIRDS – *The Duchess Assignment*.

Top: A technician wires up the Trans American TV Network building model for *Thunderbirds Are Go*.
Above: The model as it would have appeared in *Thunderbirds Are Go* (1966) had the sequence not been deleted.

Top: The Shadows' Brian Bennett and Hank Marvin admire the puppets of themselves made for *Thunderbirds Are Go*.
Above: Lady Penelope and Alan dine at the real Swinging Star nightspot in *Thunderbirds Are Go* (1966).

Top: Scarlet is assigned to the protection of President Roberts in Captain Scarlet And The Mysterons – *The Launching*.
Above: The Cloudbase model ready for filming on the visual effects stage for Captain Scarlet And The Mysterons.

Top: The Spectrum Saloon Car, a five-seater patrol vehicle capable of speeds up to 200 mph.
Above: The disgraced Scarlet meets with Kramer and Steele in CAPTAIN SCARLET AND THE MYSTERONS – *Special Assignment*.

Top: Ace pilot Joan Hughes flies Tiger Moth G-ANFM over Buckinghamshire during filming on *Thunderbird 6*.
Above: Parker observes Alan's Tiger Moth from the roof of Creighton-Ward Mansion in *Thunderbird 6* (1968).

THE CHAM-CHAM — Prod. No. 25

Teleplay by **Alan Pattillo** Directed by **Alan Pattillo**

An RTL2 transporter plane is attacked and shot down by three enemy fighter jets while on a secret missile delivery mission. This is the third such attack and Alan has noticed that each time a transporter is shot down, the Cass Carnaby Five have been giving a live performance of their hit tune 'Dangerous Game', broadcast by Radio Maxwell. The group are currently performing at Paradise Peaks, a deluxe hotel in the Alps, so Jeff sends Penelope to investigate, posing as torch singer Wanda Lamour. Penelope is joined by Tin-Tin and they secretly film the band's manager Olsen working at a complex computer board. Brains realises that Olsen is using a Cham-Cham, a device that is sensitive to ultrasonic harmonics and microtones, to encode information about the rocket transporters into the broadcast musical arrangements of 'Dangerous Game'. Only Penelope's next performance with the band can prevent the destruction of another transporter plane!

Notes

The artists' agent Maxie previously appeared as film producer Bletcher in *Martian Invasion*. The photos on the wall in his office include portraits of Bletcher, Goldheimer and a Martian (all from *Martian Invasion*), Lieutenant Jensen and Allpets chairman Sir Arthur (both from *Danger At Ocean Deep*), Frank Hooper (from *Atlantic Inferno*) and the Duchess of Royston (from *The Duchess Assignment*). Cass Carnaby also has a picture of the Duchess on the wall of his dressing room and the Duchess herself can be seen dancing nearby as Penelope dances with Olsen. When Penelope and Tin-Tin go ski-ing, their journey to Olsen's chalet is accompanied by a track entitled 'Happy Flying' that was first heard in the SUPERCAR episode *Amazonian Adventure*.

Oops!

When Penelope and Tin-Tin pause to turn on their ski thrusts as they return to the hotel from Olsen's chalet, it starts to snow, but it has stopped when they set off seconds later.

Regular Voice Cast	
Jeff Tracy	**Peter Dyneley**
Scott Tracy	**Shane Rimmer**
Lady Penelope	**Sylvia Anderson**
Virgil Tracy	**David Holliday**
Alan Tracy	**Matt Zimmerman**
Brains	**David Graham**
Aloysius Parker	**David Graham**
Tin-Tin Kyrano	**Christine Finn**
John Tracy	**Ray Barrett**
Grandma Tracy	**Christine Finn**

Guest Voice Cast	
Cass Carnaby	**Ray Barrett**
Olsen	**David Graham**
Matthews Field Cdr.	**Ray Barrett**
Maxie	**John Tate**
Banino	**Matt Zimmerman**
Captain Savidge	**David Graham**
Scheiler	**John Tate**
Hitchins	**David Graham**
Macklin	**Matt Zimmerman**
Foreign Colonel	**John Tate**
Foreign Lt.	**Matt Zimmerman**
Radio Maxwell DJ	**Ray Barrett**

First UK Transmission

Thursday, March 24th, 1966
7.00pm (ATV Midlands)

SECURITY HAZARD — Prod. No. 26

Teleplay by **Alan Pattillo** Directed by **Desmond Saunders**

While Scott, Virgil and Alan are fighting a fire in an English mine, young Chip Morrison stows away inside Thunderbird 2 Pod 1. When Thunderbird 2 arrives back at Tracy Island, the intruder alert goes off and the Tracys find themselves with a security hazard on their hands. While Jeff tries to think of a solution to their problem, Chip is looked after by each of the brothers in turn. The boy exhibits a rare talent for encouraging the brothers to expose International Rescue secrets, as each recalls past rescues which highlight the importance of their individual rescue vehicles. Realising too late what they have all done, the brothers are concerned about what their father will say when he finds out, but they are surprised to discover Jeff giving Chip a full run-down of the importance of his own position in the organisation! Somehow they must prevent Chip from innocently leaking the secrets of International Rescue...

Notes

This episode features extensive flashback footage from *End Of The Road*, *Sun Probe*, *Trapped In The Sky* and *Day Of Disaster* and only 17 minutes of new material. The International Rescue Fire Truck seen during the mine fire rescue in the opening sequence is revamped from the Gray & Houseman explosives tractor seen in *End Of The Road*. Chip Morrison previously appeared as Bob Williams in *Cry Wolf*.

Oops!

The puppet which portrays Chip's father is also seen as Dave Clayton in the sequence from *Day Of Disaster*. When Thunderbird 2 returns to its hangar, smoke can be seen flowing back down into units inside the hangar, revealing that this is reversed footage of the regular Thunderbird 2 launch sequence (this sequence appears again in *Ricochet*). Once inside the hangar, Thunderbird 2 unloads Pod 1 but the numeral on the puppet-sized pod door in the close-up shots doesn't match the one on the model pod seen in long-shot.

Regular Voice Cast	
Jeff Tracy	**Peter Dyneley**
Scott Tracy	**Shane Rimmer**
Lady Penelope	**Sylvia Anderson**
Virgil Tracy	**David Holliday**
Alan Tracy	**Matt Zimmerman**
Brains	**David Graham**
Tin-Tin Kyrano	**Christine Finn**
Gordon Tracy	**David Graham**
Commander Norman	**Peter Dyneley**
Captain Hanson	**David Graham**

Guest Voice Cast	
Chip Morrison	**Sylvia Anderson**
Morrison	**David Graham**
Eddie Houseman	**Ray Barrett**
Bob Gray	**David Graham**
J.B. Lester	**Ray Barrett**
Colonel Harris	**Ray Barrett**
Solarnaut Asher	**David Graham**
Solarnaut Camp	**John Tate**
TV Reporter	**Matt Zimmerman**
Fireflash Co-Pilot	**Ray Barrett**
Assistant Controller	**Ray Barrett**
Bill Craddock	**Matt Zimmerman**
Frank	**David Graham**
Bridge Controller	**Ray Barrett**
Dave Clayton	**David Graham**

First UK Transmission

Thursday, March 31st, 1966
7.00pm (ATV Midlands)

ATLANTIC INFERNO

Prod. No. 27

Teleplay by **Alan Fennell** Directed by **Desmond Saunders**

Jeff reluctantly accepts an invitation to holiday with Lady Penelope at her farm in Bonga Bonga, Australia, leaving Scott in temporary command of International Rescue. Meanwhile, the World Navy is testing gyropedoes in the Atlantic but one of their missiles goes wild, exploding on the sea-bed and igniting a gas field beneath the crust, throwing up a huge column of fire which endangers the crew of the drilling rig Seascape. Scott dispatches Gordon in Thunderbird 4 to cap the escaping gas with a sealing device, putting out the flame, but Jeff is furious as he does not believe that the situation warranted International Rescue's involvement. However, the gas field remains ignited beneath the sea-bed and another burst fractures one of the rig's legs. Crewmen Hooper and O'Shea submerge in a diving bell to check the damage, but a third explosion causes the the rig to slip further and the diving bell crashes to the sea-bed trapping Hooper and O'Shea inside!

Notes

This was the first episode of the series' second production block, originally screened as part of a repeat run of the earlier episodes in 1966 (it was preceded only by *Trapped In The Sky*). In some areas (including ATV Midlands), this and the following five episodes were first broadcast as two-part episodes in 25-minute instalments. The Road Construction Vehicle seen in the opening sequence previously appeared as the Gray & Houseman Road Construction Vehicle in *End Of The Road*, although it has been repainted yellow for its appearance here. The World Navy Commander was last seen as the Commander of Matthews Field in *The Cham-Cham*. This is the only episode in which anyone other than Scott is seen piloting Thunderbird 1, namely Alan.

Oops!

Lady Penelope's sheep-counting meter is useless to her as it only counts to five digits. She needs six digits to count all of her 200,007 sheep.

Regular Voice Cast

Jeff Tracy	**Peter Dyneley**
Scott Tracy	**Shane Rimmer**
Lady Penelope	**Sylvia Anderson**
Virgil Tracy	**Jeremy Wilkin**
Alan Tracy	**Matt Zimmerman**
Brains	**David Graham**
Aloysius Parker	**David Graham**
Tin-Tin Kyrano	**Christine Finn**
Gordon Tracy	**David Graham**
John Tracy	**Ray Barrett**

Guest Voice Cast

Frank Hooper	**John Tate**
Dick O'Shea	**Jeremy Wilkin**
World Navy Cdr.	**Peter Dyneley**
Atlantic Captain	**David Graham**
Sir Harry	**John Tate**
Atom Sub Reaper Captain	**Ray Barrett**
Atom Sub Reaper Lt.	**Matt Zimmerman**
Cravitz	**Jeremy Wilkin**
TV Reporter	**Ray Barrett**

First UK Transmission

Thursday, October 2nd, 1966
5.05pm (ATV London/Anglia)

PATH OF DESTRUCTION

Prod. No. 28

Teleplay by **Donald Robertson** Directed by **David Elliott**

Crablogger One, a huge tree-felling machine, arrives at base camp in South America in preparation for its first mission. The base commander, Jansen, takes the crew for a meal at a local restaurant in nearby San Martino and all but Jansen have the 'special'. The next morning, when the Crablogger sets off from the camp, both of the two-man crew collapse, victims of food poisoning, and the Crablogger veers off course, heading straight for San Martino. To make matters worse, the vehicle has to be constantly relieved of the supplies of wood pulp that it produces whilst in motion, for if the machinery jams the resulting explosion of the Superon-fuelled atomic reactor would lay waste to everything within a 50-mile radius. The only way to stop the huge machine is to activate the secret reactor shut-down procedure from inside the control cabin, which can only be accessed through the roof of the vehicle. Jansen calls International Rescue...

Notes

Base camp operative Simms previously appeared as Dave Clayton in *Day Of Disaster*. Dam site manager Manuel was originally seen as General Bron in *Edge Of Impact*. The incidental theme for the Crablogger was originally composed as the theme for the Sidewinder in *Pit Of Peril*. A live mouse appears with Maria on the puppet set of the restaurant kitchen. Director David Elliott decided that he had had enough of working with puppets and left the company after completing this episode, bringing to an end a working relationship with Gerry Anderson that had started in the editing rooms at Pinewood Studios 13 years earlier.

Oops!

Crablogger designer Jim Lucas lives at 75 Sunnigale Road, Eppington Wood East, Somerset according to the card that Penelope finds in the personnel files at Robotics International, but she reads it out to Parker as "20 Hazlemere Gardens, Iresham".

Regular Voice Cast

Jeff Tracy	**Peter Dyneley**
Scott Tracy	**Shane Rimmer**
Lady Penelope	**Sylvia Anderson**
Virgil Tracy	**Jeremy Wilkin**
Brains	**David Graham**
Aloysius Parker	**David Graham**
Tin-Tin Kyrano	**Christine Finn**
John Tracy	**Ray Barrett**

Guest Voice Cast

Jansen	**Ray Barrett**
Simms	**David Graham**
McColl	**John Tate**
Jim Lucas	**David Graham**
Peterson	**Jeremy Wilkin**
Franklin	**Matt Zimmerman**
Sanchos	**David Graham**
Maria	**Sylvia Anderson**
Gutierrez	**Matt Zimmerman**
Manuel	**David Graham**
Security Guard	**John Tate**
Mrs. Lucas	**Christine Finn**

First UK Transmission

Thursday, October 9th, 1966
5.05pm (ATV London/Anglia)

ALIAS MR. HACKENBACKER — Prod. No. 29

Teleplay by **Alan Pattillo** Directed by **Desmond Saunders**

Using the alias Hiram K. Hackenbacker, Brains has designed a revolutionary new airliner for Atlantic Airlines, the Skythrust, which incorporates a top secret design feature to make it the safest craft in the skies. Penelope believes that the vehicle's maiden flight from Paris to London will be ideal for the unveiling of a new fashion collection designed by her friend François Lemaire. Lemaire has developed an incredible new fibre, Penelon, which can fold up so compactly that a complete outfit will fit into a cigarette box without creasing, but the secret formula for Penelon is highly sought-after by his competitors. Skythrust takes off, the fashion show begins and Penelon is a huge success with the invited guests, but Lemaire's assistant Madeline hi-jacks the plane, giving Captain Ashton instructions to head for the Sahara Desert. Assisted by her co-conspirator Mason, Madeline plans to steal Lemaire's entire collection!

Notes

This episode features the largest cast of characters (in speaking roles) seen in any THUNDERBIRDS episode. Uncredited guest voice artist Paul Maxwell (Captain Ashton) previously voiced Colonel Steve Zodiac in FIREBALL XL5. He is also heard as Captain Paul Travers in *Thunderbirds Are Go* (1966) and later voiced Captain Grey in CAPTAIN SCARLET AND THE MYSTERONS. The 1st Reporter at the press conference is Frank Hooper from *Atlantic Inferno*. Hiram Hackenbacker is clearly a pseudonym adopted by Brains and is not his real name. Brains's London Airport security pass is signed by series props maker Tony Dunsterville. The roof of the airport building also appears as the floor of the meeting room of the Space Exploration Center in *Thunderbirds Are Go* (1966).

Oops!

At the end of the episode, Penelope says that 1993 is the best year for champagne, but retrospect tells us that 1993 actually wasn't a particularly good year for champagne at all.

Regular Voice Cast

Jeff Tracy	**Peter Dyneley**
Scott Tracy	**Shane Rimmer**
Lady Penelope	**Sylvia Anderson**
Virgil Tracy	**Jeremy Wilkin**
Alan Tracy	**Matt Zimmerman**
Brains	**David Graham**
Aloysius Parker	**David Graham**
Tin-Tin Kyrano	**Christine Finn**
Gordon Tracy	**David Graham**
Commander Norman	**Peter Dyneley**

Guest Voice Cast

Captain Ashton	**Paul Maxwell**
François Lemaire	**Ray Barrett**
Madeline	**Sylvia Anderson**
Mason	**Jeremy Wilkin**
Dierdre	**Christine Finn**
Captain Saville	**Ray Barrett**
Skythrust Co-Pilot	**David Graham**
Control Tower Lt.	**Ray Barrett**
D103 Pilot	**Jeremy Wilkin**
1st Reporter	**Jeremy Wilkin**
2nd Reporter	**Paul Maxwell**
Airport Officer	**David Graham**
Saville's Secretary	**Christine Finn**
Telephone Operator	**Sylvia Anderson**
Waiter	**David Graham**
1st Fashion Buyer	**David Graham**
2nd Fashion Buyer	**David Graham**
Ross	**David Graham**
Co-Conspirator	**Ray Barrett**

First UK Transmission

Thursday, October 16th, 1966
5.05pm (ATV London/Anglia)

LORD PARKER'S 'OLIDAY — Prod. No. 30

Teleplay by **Tony Barwick** Directed by **Brian Burgess**

Professor Lungren has developed a solar generator which will, as its first test, power the sleepy Mediterranean town of Monte Bianco from a vantage point on a mountain overlooking the town. Penelope and Parker are among the invited guests at the hotel to witness this historic event, which all goes according to plan until a violent storm hits the surrounding area. The solar reflector dish is repeatedly struck by lightning and eventually buckles, crashing down the mountainside and lodging half-way with the reflector pointing directly at the village. The village is plunged into darkness as the solar power cuts off but then, as the storm clears, Monte Bianco is bathed in moonlight reflected by the huge dish. Everyone enjoys the spectacle, but Penelope suddenly realises the potential disaster: as the sun rises in the morning, the sunlight will be magnified and reflected on to the town, which will burn under the intense heat!

Notes

The incidental music that opens this episode is a track entitled 'Pleasant Theme', first heard in the SUPERCAR episode *Amazonian Adventure*. Professor Lungren's assistant Mitchell previously appeared as Captain Ashton in *Alias Mr. Hackenbacker*. Uncredited guest voice artist Charles Tingwell (Mitchell and Bruno) also provides the voice of Zero X scientist Dr. Tony Grant in *Thunderbirds Are Go* (1966) and later voiced Dr. Fawn in CAPTAIN SCARLET AND THE MYSTERONS. The jazz track 'Blues Pacifica', composed for the STINGRAY episode *Tune Of Danger*, is heard playing on the radio in FAB 1. It appears that Señor Faccini has hired Cass Carnaby to perform at his hotel on this prestigious occasion, as the pianist from *The Cham-Cham* is seen in a brief clip from that episode. Other guests at the hotel include Madeline, Mason and Dierdre from *Alias Mr. Hackenbacker* and a female puppet who later appears as Nurse Nimmo in *Give Or Take A Million*. FAB 1 is revealed to be equipped with hydrofoils which enable the car to travel on water at high speed.

Regular Voice Cast

Jeff Tracy	**Peter Dyneley**
Scott Tracy	**Shane Rimmer**
Lady Penelope	**Sylvia Anderson**
Virgil Tracy	**Jeremy Wilkin**
Alan Tracy	**Matt Zimmerman**
Brains	**David Graham**
Aloysius Parker	**David Graham**
Grandma Tracy	**Christine Finn**

Guest Voice Cast

Professor Lungren	**Peter Dyneley**
Mitchell	**Charles Tingwell**
Señor Faccini	**Jeremy Wilkin**
Bruno	**Charles Tingwell**
Party Goer	**David Graham**

First UK Transmission

Thursday, October 23rd, 1966
5.05pm (ATV London/Anglia)

RICOCHET
Prod. No. 31

Teleplay by **Tony Barwick** Directed by **Brian Burgess**

Telsat 4 is launched from Sentinel Base, but the second stage fails to separate, even under manual control. International Space Control are contacted to allocate safe co-ordinates for the destruction of the rocket but, unknown to ISC, the co-ordinates they provide are dangerously close to those of unlicensed pirate television satellite KLA with DJ Rick O'Shea and his engineer Loman on board. The explosion of the rocket damages the satellite and Loman realises that they are headed for re-entry. Then he discovers that the breaking parachutes will not operate, so he goes outside to assess the damage but becomes trapped in the airlock when the inner door fails to open on his return. Unfortunately, Thunderbird 5 is non-operational as Gordon and John are fitting a new component, so when O'Shea uses the KLA transmitter to signal for help, his call goes unheard on the International Rescue space station...

Notes
The song 'Flying High' that O'Shea plays as a request from Tin-Tin is an unused end titles song recorded for the series, performed by Gary Miller with backing vocals by Fred Datchler, Ken Barrie and Eddie Lester. The main theme from *The Man From MI.5* is also heard on Rick's show and Little Luther's 'Shram-Shram' is an instrumental version of 'I've Got Something To Shout About' from the STINGRAY episode *Titan Goes Pop*. The ISC building previously appeared as the Satellite HQ tracking station seen in *The Impostors* and *Cry Wolf*. Professor Marshall is portrayed by Madeline from *Alias Mr. Hackenbacker*.

Oops!
As Gordon and John fit the new component on Thunderbird 5, John is seen speaking with Gordon's voice for the line, "It looks like we'll be another two hours before we're back in business. In the meantime, International Rescue is non-operational."

Regular Voice Cast

Jeff Tracy	**Peter Dyneley**
Scott Tracy	**Shane Rimmer**
Virgil Tracy	**Jeremy Wilkin**
Alan Tracy	**Matt Zimmerman**
Brains	**David Graham**
Tin-Tin Kyrano	**Christine Finn**
Gordon Tracy	**David Graham**
Grandma Tracy	**Christine Finn**

Guest Voice Cast

Rick O'Shea	**Ray Barrett**
Loman	**David Graham**
Professor Marshall	**Sylvia Anderson**
Power	**Jeremy Wilkin**
International Space Control	**Charles Tingwell**
DJ Tom	**Jeremy Wilkin**
Sentinel Base Computer	**David Graham**

First UK Transmission
Thursday, November 6th, 1966
5.05pm (ATV London/Anglia)

GIVE OR TAKE A MILLION
Prod. No. 32

Teleplay by **Alan Pattillo** Directed by **Desmond Saunders**

In conjunction with Harman's Department Store, the directors of the Coralville Children's Hospital arrange for a container full of presents to be launched by rocket from the roof of the store and dropped in the hospital grounds on Christmas Day. By arrangement with Jeff, one of the gift boxes will contain an invitation for one of the Coralville children to visit Tracy Island and spend Christmas with International Rescue. As the rocket is being packed with presents on Christmas Eve, two crooks, Scobie and Straker, break into the Second National Bank from the toy department of Harman's, which is just next door. Using a harness on a pulley to lift him clear of the touch-sensitive vault floor, Scobie steals the gold reserves stacked on the shelves of the vault, but he accidentally dislodges a pencil from a table and it falls on to the floor, setting off the alarm. The two crooks hide in the container of toys, just as it is loaded on to the rocket...

Notes
The Thunderbird 3 launch footage seen in this episode is lifted from *Thunderbirds Are Go* (1966). Jeff tells Nicky that Thunderbird 3 is 287 feet high. During the Tracys' Christmas preparations, various calendars are seen which indicate that Christmas Day is a Sunday, which it actually will be in 2067, the year that the producers intended this episode to be set in. Dr. Pringle previously appeared as the Commander of Matthews Field in *The Cham-Cham*, Dr. Lang is portrayed by François Lemaire from *Alias Mr. Hackenbacker* and toy packer Tanner was seen as Frank Hooper in *Atlantic Inferno*.

Oops!
Tin-Tin tears a page off a calendar which shows the date as 2026, but other calendars indicate that Christmas Day falls on a Sunday this year and December 25th, 2026 will be a Friday. It is supposed to be the middle of the night when Virgil sets off in Thunderbird 2 for Coralville Hospital, but the Thunderbird 2 launch takes place in full daylight.

Regular Voice Cast

Jeff Tracy	**Peter Dyneley**
Scott Tracy	**Shane Rimmer**
Lady Penelope	**Sylvia Anderson**
Virgil Tracy	**Jeremy Wilkin**
Alan Tracy	**Matt Zimmerman**
Brains	**David Graham**
Tin-Tin Kyrano	**Christine Finn**
Gordon Tracy	**David Graham**
John Tracy	**Ray Barrett**
Kyrano	**David Graham**
Grandma Tracy	**Christine Finn**

Guest Voice Cast

Nicky	**Sylvia Anderson**
Scobie	**Ray Barrett**
Straker	**David Graham**
Dr. Pringle	**Jeremy Wilkin**
Dr. Lang	**Charles Tingwell**
Nurse Nimmo	**Sylvia Anderson**
Harman	**Ray Barrett**
Saunders	**Jeremy Wilkin**
TV Reporter	**Jeremy Wilkin**
Santa 1	**Jeremy Wilkin**
Santa 2 (Leo)	**David Graham**
Tanner	**Charles Tingwell**
Preston	**Peter Dyneley**
Security Chief Joe	**Ray Barrett**

First UK Transmission
Thursday, December 25th, 1966
5.05pm (ATV London/Anglia)

CAPTAIN SCARLET AND THE MYSTERONS

Format

In the year 2068, peace on Earth is maintained by the Spectrum organisation, a super-efficient security organisation headquartered in the vast floating aircraft carrier Cloudbase, hovering on the edge of Earth's atmosphere and manned by agents recruited from various World Government services, each assigned colour codenames to protect their true identities. Under the command of Colonel White, Spectrum has become the supreme peace-keeping force, maintaining a fleet of sophisticated vehicles for use by Spectrum field agents including the Angel Interceptor strike aircraft, Spectrum Pursuit Vehicle, Spectrum Saloon Car, Spectrum Passenger Jet and Spectrum Helicopter.

But then an ill-fated mission to locate the source of alien signals originating on Mars unleashed the power of the Mysterons, ruthless sentient computers created by an alien race to protect their Martian Complex. When a Zero X exploration team, led by Spectrum's Captain Black, discovered the Mysteron Complex on Mars, they mistook the friendly intentions of the Mysteron computers for a hostile offensive and opened fire, completely destroying the complex. Using their incredible power of retrometabolism, the ability to recreate matter, the sentient computers reconstructed the complex and declared war against the people of Earth for their unprovoked attack. This has taken the form of a war of nerves, with the Mysteron computers issuing cryptic warnings of their next offensive, and then using their amazing powers to influence people, vehicles and inanimate objects to fall under their control. The Mysterons' primary Earth agent is Captain Black, recreated from the body of the original Spectrum agent.

Spectrum's personnel and facilities are now mobilised solely to combat the threat of the Mysterons. Leading the fight is one man fate has made indestructible – Captain Scarlet. Killed during Earth's initial conflict with the Mysterons, Scarlet was retrometabolised and became a Mysteron agent for a time, but the Mysterons' hold over him was inexplicably broken after he fell 800 feet from the London Car-Vu. Retaining the original man's memories, personality and loyalties, the new Captain Scarlet also retains the ability to survive injuries that would prove fatal to any other person, making him Spectrum's greatest weapon in their unceasing war against the menace from Mars.

Production

In 1966, Lew Grade's failure to sell THUNDERBIRDS to American network television prompted him to cancel that series and commission Gerry Anderson to make an entirely new programme. Inspired by a live-action series proposal that he had previously put forward in which the lead character would be killed off after half of the episodes, Anderson developed a series concept entitled 'The Mysterons'. Here, the lead character would be the first casualty in a war with mysterious invisible aliens, but he would be replaced by an indestructible mechanical duplicate who would then go on to combat the aliens each week. Slightly modified to make the duplicate a flesh and blood reconstruction, this idea evolved into CAPTAIN SCARLET AND THE MYSTERONS.

The new series presented the Century 21 team with the opportunity to abandon the disproportionate caricatured puppets that had been used on the previous series in favour of new, perfectly proportioned 1/3 scale marionettes with the voice mechanism solenoids relocated from the head to the chest. Aside from the puppets of the regular characters, a full repertory cast of more than 50 revamp puppets were created to appear in guest character roles or as background 'extras', and the puppet workshop team also constructed a number of 'under-control' puppets that could be operated from beneath the puppet set like sophisticated hand puppets, rather than from above on wires.

With a budget of £1,500,000 (just over £45,000 per episode), filming on CAPTAIN SCARLET AND THE MYSTERONS began on Monday, January 2nd, 1967. As with STINGRAY and THUNDERBIRDS, two puppet units each shot separate episodes in 11 working days so that filming of the 32 episodes could be completed in eight months. However, the complications of filming the series back to back with a second THUNDERBIRDS feature film, *Thunderbird 6* (1967), caused various delays and the last episodes were not completed until the end of October 1967.

Main Characters

Captain Scarlet (Paul Metcalfe)
Spectrum's leading agent, a former World Army Air Force officer replaced by a virtually indestructible Mysteron doppelgänger

Captain Blue (Adam Svenson)
Top Spectrum field agent, formerly a World Aeronautic Society test pilot and security agent

Colonel White (Charles Grey)
Spectrum commander-in-chief, formerly a decorated World Navy officer and Universal Secret Service agent

Destiny Angel (Juliette Pontoin)
Angel Interceptor pilot, formerly a World Army Air Force intelligence officer

Symphony Angel (Karen Wainwright)
Angel Interceptor pilot, formerly a Universal Secret Service agent

Lieutenant Green (Seymour Griffiths)
Communications specialist and Spectrum chief controller

Captain Black (Conrad Turner)
Leading Spectrum agent replaced by an indestructible doppelgänger in the service of the Mysterons

Captain Ochre (Richard Fraser)
Spectrum field agent, formerly an officer of the World Government Police Corps

Captain Grey (Bradley Holden)
Spectrum field agent, formerly a World Navy submarine commander

Captain Magenta (Patrick Donaghue)
Spectrum field agent, formerly the boss of a New York crime syndicate, pardoned by the World Government

Rhapsody Angel (Dianne Simms)
Angel Interceptor pilot, formerly chief security officer for European Charter airlines

Melody Angel (Magnolia Jones)
Angel Interceptor pilot, formerly a World Army Air Force test pilot

Harmony Angel (Chan Kwan)
Angel Interceptor pilot, formerly manager of Peking Taxi Corps flying taxi service

Dr. Fawn (Edward Wilkie)
Spectrum chief medical officer, formerly an administrator for the World Medical Organisation

The Mysterons
Ruthless sentient computers created by an alien race, bent on vengeance for an unprovoked attack on their Martian Complex

Episode Titles

(Listed in production order)

1. **The Mysterons**
2. **Winged Assassin**
3. **Big Ben Strikes Again**
4. **Point 783**
5. **Manhunt**
6. **Operation Time**
7. **Renegade Rocket**
8. **White As Snow**
9. **Seek And Destroy**
10. **Spectrum Strikes Back**
11. **Avalanche**
12. **Shadow Of Fear**
13. **The Heart Of New York**
14. **Fire At Rig 15**
15. **The Launching**
16. **Lunarville 7**
17. **The Trap**
18. **Model Spy**
19. **Dangerous Rendezvous**
20. **Special Assignment**
21. **Traitor**
22. **Crater 101**
23. **Place Of Angels**
24. **Flight 104**
25. **Codename Europa**
26. **Flight To Atlantica**
27. **Noose Of Ice**
28. **Treble Cross**
29. **Expo 2068**
30. **Attack On Cloudbase**
31. **Inferno**
32. **The Inquisition**

Episode Running Time

25 minutes approx.

PRODUCTION CREDITS

Executive Producer **Gerry Anderson**
Produced by **Reg Hill**
Format **Gerry & Sylvia Anderson**
Director Supervising Series **Des Saunders**
Supervising Visual Effects Director **Derek Meddings**
Associate Producer **John Read**
Characters Created by **Sylvia Anderson**
Lighting Cameraman **Julien Lugrin** *(1, 4, 6, 8, 10, 12, 14, 16, 18, 20, 22, 23, 25, 27, 29)*
Paddy Seale *(2, 3, 5, 7, 9, 11)*
Ted Catford *(13, 15, 17, 19, 21, 24, 26, 28, 30-32)*
Visual Effects Lighting Cameraman **Harry Oakes** *(1, 3, 5, 7, 9)*
Bert Mason *(2, 4, 6, 8, 10, 11, 14, 16, 18, 20, 22, 25, 27, 29)*
Derek Black *(12)*
Les Paul *(13, 15, 17, 19, 23, 21, 24, 26, 28, 30-32)*
Camera Operators **Tom Fletcher** *(1)*
Ron Gallifant *(1, 3, 5, 7, 9, 12, 13)*
Les Paul *(12)*
Alan McDonald *(2, 3, 5, 7, 9, 11, 13, 15, 17, 19, 21, 24, 26, 28, 30-32)*
Nick Procopides *(2, 4, 6, 8, 10, 11, 14, 16, 18, 20, 22, 25, 27, 29)*
Derek Black *(4, 6, 8, 10, 14, 16, 18, 20, 22, 23, 25, 27, 29)*
Ted Cutlack *(15, 17, 19, 21, 23, 24, 26, 28, 30-32)*
Supervising Art Director **Bob Bell**
Script Editor **Tony Barwick**
Music Composed and Directed by **Barry Gray**
Puppetry Co-ordination **Mary Turner**
Production Manager **Frank Hollands**
Assistant Director **Leo Eaton** *(1, 4, 7, 9, 10, 14, 16)*
Peter Anderson *(2, 5, 23, 26, 29-32)*
Keith Lund *(3, 6, 8, 11, 13, 15, 17, 18, 22)*
Ian Griffiths *(12, 20, 21, 24, 27)*
Ray Atcheler *(19)*
Ian Spurrier *(25, 28)*
Puppetry Supervision **Christine Glanville** *(1, 4, 6, 8-32)*
Wanda Webb *(2, 3, 5, 7)*
Operators **Peter Johns** *(1, 4, 6, 8, 10, 12, 14, 16, 18, 22, 23, 25, 27, 29)*
Mel Cross *(1, 4, 6, 8, 10, 12, 14, 16, 18, 22, 23, 25, 27, 29)*
Judith Morgan *(2, 3, 5, 7, 9, 11, 13, 15, 17, 19-21, 24)*
John Lane *(2, 3, 5, 7)*
Wanda Webb *(26, 28, 30-32)*
Jan King *(9, 11, 13, 15, 17, 19, 20, 21, 24, 26, 28, 30-32)*
Character Voices **Sylvia Anderson**
Edward Bishop, **Gary Files** *(13-32)*
Cy Grant, **Donald Gray**
David Healy *(13-32)*, **Janna Hill**
Martin King *(13-32)*, **Francis Matthews**
Paul Maxwell, **Neil McCallum***, **Liz Morgan**
Shane Rimmer*, **Lian Shin** *(13-32)*
Charles Tingwell, **Jeremy Wilkin**
Visual Effects Director **Shaun Whittacker-Cook** *(1, 3, 5, 7, 9, 12, 13, 15, 17, 19, 21, 22, 25, 26, 28, 30-32)*
Jimmy Elliott *(2, 4, 6, 8, 10, 11, 14, 16, 18, 20, 23, 24, 27, 29)*
Art Director **Grenville Nott**
Designer **Keith Wilson** *(1-21)*
John Lageu *(1-21)*
Production Designer **Keith Wilson** *(22-32)*
Sculpting Supervision **John Brown** *(1-8)*
Sculptors **Tim Cooksey** *(9-32)*
Terry Curtis *(9-32)*
Plugg Shutt *(9-32)*
Visual Effects Production Manager **Harry Ledger** *(1-17, 19)*
Brian Burgess *(18, 20-32)*
Wardrobe **Iris Richens**
Dialogue Synchronisation **Ian Spurrier** *(1, 4, 6, 8)*
James Cowan *(2, 3, 5, 7, 9, 11, 13, 15, 17, 19, 20, 21, 24, 26, 28, 30-32)*
Antony Bell *(10, 12, 14, 16, 18, 22, 23, 25, 27, 29)*
Editor **Len Walter** *(1)*
Harry McDonald *(2, 5, 8, 11, 14, 17, 20, 23, 26, 29)*
John Beaton *(3, 6, 9, 12, 15, 18, 22, 25, 28)*
Bob Dearberg *(4, 7, 10, 13, 16, 19, 21, 24, 27, 30-32)*
Supervising Editor **Len Walter** *(2-32)*
Supervising Sound Editor **Peter Pennell**
Music Editor **George Randall**
Dialogue Editor **Don Brill**
Property Master **Arthur Cripps**
Sound **Anvil Films Ltd**
VISUAL EFFECTS – 2nd UNIT
Director **Peter Wragg**
Lighting Cameraman **Les Paul** *(1-10, 27)*
Ted Wooldridge *(11-26, 28-32)*
Camera Operator **Ted Cutlack** *(1-11, 27)*
John Shann *(12-17)*
Noel Rowlands (18-26, 28-32)
Assistant **Alan Berry***
Designer **Mike Trim***
Models **Peter Aston***, **Eric Backman***
Ray Brown*, **Alan Shubrook***,
Brian Smithies*
Electronic Development **Jack Kensley**
Electronic Collaboration **Standard Telecommunication Laboratories, Harlow** *(16)*
Captain Scarlet Sung by **The Spectrum** *(15-32)*

A Gerry Anderson
Century 21 Television Production
An ITC World Wide Distribution
Filmed in Supermarionation

* uncredited

THE MYSTERONS — Prod. No. 01

Teleplay by **Gerry & Sylvia Anderson** Directed by **Desmond Saunders**

During a mission to Mars to investigate the source of extra-terrestrial signals, Captain Black and the crew of a Martian Exploration Vehicle discover a strange alien complex inhabited by the Mysterons. Mistaking a sensor device for a weapon, Black opens fire, completely destroying the complex, but it is miraculously restored by the Mysterons using the power of retrometabolism. Seeking revenge for this act of aggression, the Mysterons threaten the life of the World President so Spectrum's Captain Brown and Captain Scarlet are assigned to escort him to New York, but their car is sabotaged by the Mysterons and crashes. Both men are killed instantly and reconstructed as Mysteron doppelgängers. Undetected as a Mysteron agent, Brown then accompanies the World President to the Spectrum Maximum Security Building, but after they arrive in the President's luxury suite deep underground, Captain Brown spontaneously explodes, totally destroying the building!

Notes

This episode has no on-screen title but is referred to in all production documentation by the title of Gerry & Sylvia Anderson's shooting script – *The Mysterons*. The Zero X MEV was previously seen in *Thunderbirds Are Go* (1966) and a foreword to the shooting script indicated that the producers intended for this to be seen as the same vehicle.

Mysteron Threat

"This is the voice of the Mysterons. We know that you can hear us, Earthmen. Our retaliation will be slow but nonetheless effective. It will mean the ultimate destruction of life on Earth. It will be useless for you to resist, for we have discovered the secret of reversing matter, as you have just witnessed. One of you will be under our control. You will be instrumental in avenging the Mysterons. Our first act of retaliation will be to assassinate your World President."

Regular Voice Cast

Captain Scarlet	**Francis Matthews**
Captain Blue	**Edward Bishop**
Colonel White	**Donald Gray**
Destiny Angel	**Liz Morgan**
Lieutenant Green	**Cy Grant**
Captain Black	**Donald Gray**
Rhapsody Angel	**Liz Morgan**
Harmony Angel	**Liz Morgan**
Voice of the Mysterons	**Donald Gray**

Guest Voice Cast

World President	**Paul Maxwell**
Captain Brown	**Charles Tingwell**
Captain Black (Original)	**Jeremy Wilkin**
Lieutenant Dean	**Charles Tingwell**
Delta Garage Attendant	**Jeremy Wilkin**
Helicopter A42 Pilot	**Charles Tingwell**
Spectrum HQ, London	**Charles Tingwell**
Radio Voice	**Jeremy Wilkin**

First UK Transmission

Friday, September 29th, 1967
5.25pm (ATV Midlands)

WINGED ASSASSIN — Prod. No. 02

Teleplay by **Tony Barwick** Directed by **David Lane**

After the Mysterons announce that they intend to assassinate the Director General of the United Asian Republic, Spectrum is assigned to his protection as he travels from his London hotel to the airport. Captain Blue is placed in charge of the operation and he is joined by Captain Scarlet, now free of Mysteron control but having retained the ability of retrometabolism. As the pair requisition a Spectrum Pursuit Vehicle and head for London Airport, Intercontinental Airlines Stratojet DT19 suddenly loses all power and crashes into the sea. The passenger jet is reconstructed by the Mysterons and completes the journey to London under Mysteron control. The Director General arrives at the airport under Spectrum escort and boards his personal jet, but when the DT19 is discovered to be completely empty of passengers and crew just seconds before it moves away from the terminal building, Blue realises that the plane is a Mysteron booby trap!

Notes

This episode follows on from the events of *The Mysterons* and should, therefore, always be screened as episode two. Unfortunately, during the first BBC screening of digitally remastered episodes produced by Carlton in 2001, the scheduled broadcast of *Winged Assassin* on Monday, September 17th, 2001 was postponed following the previous Tuesday's terrorist attack on the World Trade Center in New York. The episode was eventually screened much later in the run. The flashback footage of the car crash from *The Mysterons* is presented in full colour here, although in *The Mysterons* it appeared partly in blue monotone. Captain Ochre is seen for the first time but does not speak.

Mysteron Threat

"This is the voice of the Mysterons. We know that you can hear us, Earthmen. You will pay for your unprovoked attack on our complex on Mars. We will be avenged. We will assassinate the Director General of the United Asian Republic."

Regular Voice Cast

Captain Scarlet	**Francis Matthews**
Captain Blue	**Edward Bishop**
Colonel White	**Donald Gray**
Destiny Angel	**Liz Morgan**
Lieutenant Green	**Cy Grant**
Captain Grey	**Paul Maxwell**
Rhapsody Angel	**Liz Morgan**
Melody Angel	**Sylvia Anderson**
Dr. Fawn	**Charles Tingwell**
Voice of the Mysterons	**Donald Gray**

Guest Voice Cast

Director General	**Jeremy Wilkin**
Captain Brown	**Charles Tingwell**
Airport Chief	**Neil McCallum**
Airport Operator	**Charles Tingwell**
Agent 042	**Charles Tingwell**
DT19 Pilot	**Neil McCallum**
Director General's Double	**Jeremy Wilkin**
Intercontinental Airlines Tannoy	**Janna Hill**

First UK Transmission

Friday, October 6th, 1967
5.25pm (ATV Midlands)

BIG BEN STRIKES AGAIN

Prod. No. 03

Teleplay by **Tony Barwick** Directed by **Brian Burgess**

Transporter driver Macey is ferrying a nuclear device intended for civil use through London when his vehicle suddenly falls under Mysteron control, evading its police escort and racing through the narrow streets until it finally comes to rest in an underground car park. Macey is knocked unconscious and when he comes round, he switches on the radio to check the time and hears Big Ben strike 13 times. Checking his cargo, Macey is horrified to find the trigger mechanism on the atomic device activating itself, but he is struck down from behind before he can do anything to stop it. Responding to the latest Mysteron threat, Spectrum begins a full-scale search for the missing transporter and Captain Scarlet soon finds Macey lying in the road. The driver is taken to Cloudbase where he relates every detail of his story, but he doesn't know where the underground car park is situated and there are about 2,000 car parks in London that fit his description! With time running out, Blue suddenly realises that Macey's report of hearing Big Ben strike 13 holds the solution.

Oops!

At the start of the episode, a shot of Big Ben shows that the time is 11.45 pm and, shortly after, the transporter is taken over by the Mysterons. Colonel White then states that the search for the missing transporter has been going on for 2½ hours, so by this time it must be at least 2.15 am. Yet when Macey recovers consciousness, his watch reads 11.58 pm and he hears Big Ben strike midnight.

Mysteron Threat

"This is the voice of the Mysterons. We know that you can hear us, Earthmen. You attacked our complex on Mars and you will pay a heavy price. Our next act of retaliation will be to destroy the city of London. Do you hear, Earthmen? We will destroy the city of London."

Regular Voice Cast

Captain Scarlet	**Francis Matthews**
Captain Blue	**Edward Bishop**
Colonel White	**Donald Gray**
Destiny Angel	**Liz Morgan**
Lieutenant Green	**Cy Grant**
Captain Ochre	**Jeremy Wilkin**
Captain Grey	**Paul Maxwell**
Melody Angel	**Sylvia Anderson**
Voice of the Mysterons	**Donald Gray**

Guest Voice Cast

Macey	**Charles Tingwell**
1st Policeman	**Paul Maxwell**
3rd Policeman	**Jeremy Wilkin**
4th Policeman	**Neil McCallum**
5th Policeman	**Jeremy Wilkin**
Radio Announcer	**Jeremy Wilkin**

First UK Transmission

Friday, October 13th, 1967
5.25pm (ATV Midlands)

POINT 783

Prod. No. 04

Teleplay by **Peter Curran** & **David Williams** Directed by **Robert Lynn**

After the Mysterons threaten the life of the Supreme Commander of Earth Forces, he is escorted by Scarlet and Blue to SHEF Headquarters in New York to chair a briefing on the new Unitron computer-controlled tank. Unfortunately, the Supreme Commander's personal aide, Major Brooks, becomes a Mysteron agent after his car is involved in a head-on collision with a Mysteron-controlled tanker. When smoke begins to pour from his neck at the Unitron briefing, Scarlet activates security shields which fall into place just as Brooks explodes. Later, Blue escorts the Supreme Commander to Point 783, a command post in the Sahara Desert which is being used as a base for the Unitron test programme. Blue is introduced to General Cope, who explains that the Unitron can be programmed to seek and destroy a pre-ordained target automatically, but as the Unitron tests begin, it soon becomes apparent that the vehicle has been pre-programmed by a Mysteron agent to target the command post!

Notes

This episode features the first appearance of the revamp puppet that later became WIN agent Sam Loover in JOE 90. Seen here as the Supreme Commander of Earth Forces, the Loover puppet also appears as Dr. Harrison in *Operation Time*, President Roberts in *The Launching*, the Lunar Controller in *Lunarville 7*, Dr. Denton in *Place Of Angels*, Rhodes in *Noose Of Ice* and Colgan in *The Inquisition*. *Point 783* was later remade as *Recall To Service*, an episode of THE SECRET SERVICE in which the Unitron became the computer-controlled Aquatank targeting a World Army observation blockhouse.

Mysteron Threat

"This is the voice of the Mysterons. We know you can hear us, Earthmen. We have not forgotten. We will destroy the Supreme Commander of Earth Forces within the next 24 hours. Supreme Commander, you have only 24 more hours to live."

Regular Voice Cast

Captain Scarlet	**Francis Matthews**
Captain Blue	**Edward Bishop**
Colonel White	**Donald Gray**
Destiny Angel	**Liz Morgan**
Lieutenant Green	**Cy Grant**
Captain Black	**Donald Gray**
Melody Angel	**Sylvia Anderson**
Harmony Angel	**Liz Morgan**
Voice of the Mysterons	**Donald Gray**

Guest Voice Cast

Supreme Commander	**Paul Maxwell**
General Cope	**David Healy**
Colonel Storm	**Jeremy Wilkin**
Major Brooks	**David Healy**
Captain Hassel	**Charles Tingwell**
MCA Tanker Driver Pete	**Charles Tingwell**
MCA Tanker Driver's Mate	**Martin King**
Arab	**Martin King**
Security Bank Voice	**Martin King**
Robot Voice	**Jeremy Wilkin**

First UK Transmission

Friday, December 22nd, 1967
5.25pm (ATV Midlands)

MANHUNT

Prod. No. 05

Teleplay by **Tony Barwick** Directed by **Alan Perry**

When Captain Black is discovered breaking into the Culver Atomic Centre, he hides from security guards in a radioactive area where he is exposed to a short life atomic isotope. After he escapes, Black's exposure to the radioactivity enables Spectrum to track him with directional long-range Geiger counters and a manhunt is launched. Scarlet and Blue head for Stone Point Village to requisition a Spectrum Pursuit Vehicle, but Black arrives ahead of them, killing a mechanic at the local garage and taking the SPV. When Scarlet and Blue arrive at the garage, the Mysteronised mechanic pulls a gun on them, but Scarlet shoots him down. Symphony makes visual contact with the SPV in a clearing and lands her Angel Interceptor, but she is captured by Captain Black and taken back to the Atomic Centre where he exposes her to a deadly dose of radiation!

Notes

The music being played on the radio in the Delta garage where Black murders a mechanic was composed for the main titles of *Crossroads To Crime* (1960).

Oops!

Scarlet's grammar and punctuation leave something to be desired: his written report of an investigation in Sydney, Australia ends, "We must conclude from our enquiries that there *was* no Mysteron activities and it was in fact a false alarm." After Colonel White thanks Scarlet and Blue, the pair are seen speaking with each other's voices.

Mysteron Threat

"This is the voice of the Mysterons. We will continue to take our revenge. You started the shockwave with your unprovoked attack on our Martian Complex. This act of aggression will be avenged. Our retaliation will be slow but nonetheless effective. You will pay in full."

Regular Voice Cast

Captain Scarlet	**Francis Matthews**
Captain Blue	**Edward Bishop**
Colonel White	**Donald Gray**
Symphony Angel	**Janna Hill**
Lieutenant Green	**Cy Grant**
Captain Black	**Donald Gray**
Captain Ochre	**Jeremy Wilkin**
Captain Grey	**Paul Maxwell**
Voice of the Mysterons	**Donald Gray**

Guest Voice Cast

Harris	**Charles Tingwell**
Richards	**Martin King**
Geiger Operator	**David Healy**
Garage Mechanic	**Martin King**
Guard	**Paul Maxwell**
Guard Voice 1	**Jeremy Wilkin**
Guard Voice 2	**David Healy**

First UK Transmission

Friday, October 20th, 1967
5.25pm (ATV Midlands)

OPERATION TIME

Prod. No. 06

Teleplay by **Richard Conway** & **Stephen J. Mattick** Directed by **Ken Turner**

The latest Mysteron threat to "kill time" leaves the Spectrum officers baffled. While Colonel White dispatches his top officers to key cities, in London, top neurosurgeon Dr. Magnus visits General Tiempo, the Commander of Western Region World Defence, at the Westbourne Clinic to confirm that his operation is scheduled for the next day. As Magnus leaves the clinic, his car is targeted by Captain Black and skids out of control over the edge of a cliff. Magnus is killed when the car explodes on impact but he is recreated by the Mysterons with orders to kill time. When Captain Magenta realises that the General is the Mysterons' target as *tiempo* is the Spanish word for time, Colonel White decides to relocate the operation to Cloudbase. The operation gets under way in Sick Bay using Magnus's revolutionary cerebral pulsator, but then a radiographer discovers that an X-ray of Tiempo's head also shows a normal view of Magnus's hand...

Notes

The events of this episode mark a turning point in Spectrum's battle against the Mysterons and have a direct impact later in the series, leading to the development of the Mysteron Detector and Mysteron Gun introduced in *Spectrum Strikes Back*. The revamp puppet which is seen for the first time here as General Tiempo is one of the most often used repertory puppets in the three Century 21 Supermarionation series, with appearances as 11 separate characters in Captain Scarlet alone. It has the unique distinction of appearing as three different characters in *The Inquisition* and is best-known for its role as Igor Sladek in the Joe 90 episode *International Concerto*.

Mysteron Threat

"This is the voice of the Mysterons. We know that you can hear us, Earthmen. We will continue to take our revenge. You will pay for your act of aggression. Our next act of retaliation will be to kill time. We will kill time."

Regular Voice Cast

Captain Scarlet	**Francis Matthews**
Captain Blue	**Edward Bishop**
Colonel White	**Donald Gray**
Lieutenant Green	**Cy Grant**
Captain Black	**Donald Gray**
Captain Ochre	**Jeremy Wilkin**
Captain Grey	**Paul Maxwell**
Captain Magenta	**Gary Files**
Dr. Fawn	**Charles Tingwell**
Voice of the Mysterons	**Donald Gray**

Guest Voice Cast

Dr. Magnus	**Martin King**
General J.F. Tiempo	**Paul Maxwell**
Dr. Turner	**Gary Files**
Morgan	**Charles Tingwell**
1st Student	**Gary Files**
2nd Student	**Jeremy Wilkin**
Porter Benson	**Jeremy Wilkin**
Radiographer	**Jeremy Wilkin**
Nurse	**Liz Morgan**

First UK Transmission

Friday, November 17th, 1967
5.25pm (ATV Midlands)

RENEGADE ROCKET

Prod. No. 07

Teleplay by **Ralph Hart** Directed by **Brian Burgess**

Space Major Reeves is travelling by power launch to the Base Concord rocket base when he is targeted by Captain Black and falls from the deck into the sea. Caught in the wake of the launch, Reeves drowns and is reconstructed by the Mysterons. Arriving at Base Concord, Reeves reprogrammes the telemetry of an experimental Variable Geometry Rocket and launches it before escaping in an interceptor jet with the flight programme unit. The Angels are dispatched to track down Major Reeves and Melody soon makes visual contact with Reeves's jet. Meanwhile, Scarlet and Blue arrive at Base Concord where they discover that the VGR is flying on an absolutely vertical flight path and has been programmed to come straight down on Base Concord itself. As evacuation procedures are put into practice, a new flight programme unit is fitted to the VGR control board, but without the destruct code the rocket cannot be prematurely detonated. Scarlet and Blue learn that the destruct code is based on four-letter words, but there are 10,000 possible combinations of letters in the codebook!

Regular Voice Cast

Captain Scarlet	**Francis Matthews**
Captain Blue	**Edward Bishop**
Colonel White	**Donald Gray**
Lieutenant Green	**Cy Grant**
Rhapsody Angel	**Liz Morgan**
Melody Angel	**Sylvia Anderson**
Harmony Angel	**Liz Morgan**
Voice of the Mysterons	**Donald Gray**

Guest Voice Cast

Major Reeves	**Gary Files**
Base Commander	**Paul Maxwell**
Base Controller	**Charles Tingwell**
Sergeant	**Martin King**
Boat Captain	**Jeremy Wilkin**
Security Captain	**Jeremy Wilkin**
Airstrip Voice	**Martin King**

First UK Transmission

Friday, January 19th, 1968
5.25pm (ATV Midlands)

Notes

The Yellow Fox Security Tanker employed by Spectrum in *Winged Assassin* and *Dangerous Rendezvous* is involved here in the evacuation of Base Concord.

Oops!

Major Reeves normally has two gold stars on his uniform, but when his Mysteron reconstruction appears for the first time, he has only one star on his chest.

Mysteron Threat

"This is the voice of the Mysterons. We know that you can hear us, Earthmen. We are going to launch one of your own incendiary rockets and you will have no way of knowing its target. We have not forgotten. We will continue our war of nerves."

WHITE AS SNOW

Prod. No. 08

Teleplay by **Peter Curran** & **David Williams** Directed by **Robert Lynn**

Manned communications satellite TVR-17 is destroyed when Captain Black takes over the Control Centre on Earth and brings the satellite into a premature re-entry. The satellite is reconstructed by the Mysterons and set on a collision course with Cloudbase but Colonel White recognises the satellite as a Mysteron booby trap and dispatches Symphony to shoot it down. As the target of the latest Mysteron threat, the Colonel leaves Cloudbase for a secret destination so as not to place other members of Spectrum in jeopardy. He charters a helijet to fly him to a rendezvous with the atomic submarine *USS Panther II* and introduces himself to the crew as Robert Snow, so that only the Captain of the ship is aware of his true identity. The submarine prepares to dive, but Ensign Soames traps his foot in a chain on the deck and drowns when the vessel submerges. Now acting as a Mysteron agent, Soames is assigned by the ship's Captain to act as Colonel White's personal steward...

Regular Voice Cast

Captain Scarlet	**Francis Matthews**
Captain Blue	**Edward Bishop**
Colonel White	**Donald Gray**
Destiny Angel	**Liz Morgan**
Symphony Angel	**Janna Hill**
Lieutenant Green	**Cy Grant**
Rhapsody Angel	**Liz Morgan**
Harmony Angel	**Liz Morgan**
Voice of the Mysterons	**Donald Gray**

Guest Voice Cast

Captain, USS Panther II	**Paul Maxwell**
Lt. Belmont	**Charles Tingwell**
Ensign Soames	**Jeremy Wilkin**
DJ Bob Lynn	**Gary Files**
TVR-17 Control	**Martin King**
Pilot	**Jeremy Wilkin**

First UK Transmission

Friday, November 3rd, 1967
5.25pm (ATV Midlands)

Notes

The script for this episode originally started with the Mysterons simply using their influence to take control of the TVR communications satellite: the scenes of Captain Black engineering the satellite's destruction were all late additions. TVR-17 DJ Bob Lynn is named after episode director Robert Lynn. The tune broadcast by the TVR-17 satellite is a composition by Barry Gray entitled 'White As Snow'. It can be heard again in *Special Assignment* and also turns up in episodes of JOE 90 and THE SECRET SERVICE.

Mysteron Threat

"This is the voice of the Mysterons. We know you can hear us, Earthmen. We also know of your pathetic attempts to defend yourselves. Our next act of retaliation will be to kill the Commander in Chief of Spectrum, Colonel White. Do you hear, Earthmen? We will kill Colonel White."

SEEK AND DESTROY — Prod. No. 09

Teleplay by **Peter Curran** & **David Williams** Directed by **Alan Perry**

When the Mysterons threaten to kill one of the Spectrum Angels, Captain Blue suspects that Destiny, on vacation in Paris, is the most likely target. Colonel White agrees and dispatches Scarlet and Blue to Paris to escort Destiny back to Cloudbase. Destiny is out shopping but the Captains track her to the Café de la Paix where Scarlet explains the situation and the three Spectrum agents are soon *en route* for the airport in a Spectrum Saloon Car. However, Captain Black has engineered a fire at a local warehouse which has destroyed three new Angel Interceptors awaiting delivery to Spectrum. Now reconstructed by the Mysterons, the three Angel jets target the Saloon Car and Scarlet, Blue and Destiny take cover in a ditch as the fighter planes make their final approach...

Notes

The operation of the transporter picking up the crate containing an Angel Interceptor is described in the shooting script as "...like Thunderbird II picking up a pod." A short scene deleted from the end of the finished episode featured Destiny discovering that her bottle of perfume is miraculously unbroken after the destruction of the Saloon Car.

Oops!

When the second Mysteronised Angel Interceptor shot down by Rhapsody crashes, the explosion visibly shakes the foreground of the model countryside set. Melody's hands are white in the close-up shots of real hands operating her Angel Interceptor controls.

Mysteron Threat

"This is the voice of the Mysterons. We will continue to take our revenge. You started the shockwave with the attack on our Martian Complex. This act of aggression will be avenged. We intend to kill one of the Spectrum Angels. Spectrum Angels, one of you will die."

Regular Voice Cast

Captain Scarlet	**Francis Matthews**
Captain Blue	**Edward Bishop**
Colonel White	**Donald Gray**
Destiny Angel	**Liz Morgan**
Lieutenant Green	**Cy Grant**
Captain Black	**Donald Gray**
Rhapsody Angel	**Liz Morgan**
Melody Angel	**Sylvia Anderson**
Harmony Angel	**Liz Morgan**
Voice of the Mysterons	**Donald Gray**

Guest Voice Cast

Fairfield	**Charles Tingwell**
Jackson	**Jeremy Wilkin**
Fire Chief	**Paul Maxwell**

First UK Transmission

Friday, January 5th, 1968
5.25pm (ATV Midlands)

SPECTRUM STRIKES BACK — Prod. No. 10

Teleplay by **Tony Barwick** Directed by **Ken Turner**

Scarlet and Blue rendezvous with Colonel White, the World President, Space General Peterson and Captain Indigo for a briefing by Spectrum Intelligence Agency scientist Dr. Giadello at a hunting lodge in Africa, where the entire building acts as an elevator to a secret SIA conference room hidden underground. As Giadello demonstrates Spectrum's new devices for use against the Mysterons, a Mysteron Gun and a Mysteron Detector, Captain Black arrives at the lodge building above and shoots Captain Indigo, who is then reconstructed by the Mysterons. A demonstration of the Mysteron Detector reveals that Indigo is a Mysteron agent, but he locks the lift mechanism in the down position and takes the master key as he makes his escape. Scarlet races after the Mysteron agent to recover the key before the lift crushes the men trapped in the conference room below...

Notes

The working title of this episode was the grammatically incorrect 'Spectrum *Strike* Back'. Colonel White refers to the events of *Operation Time* to explain the development of the Mysteron Detector and, although Dr. Giadello doesn't say so, the creation of the Mysteron Gun was inspired by the death of Dr. Magnus in the same episode. The Captain Indigo puppet was previously seen as Macey in *Big Ben Strikes Again.*

Oops!

Captain Blue fires 14 shots into the descending ceiling, although only eight bullet holes appear in it.

Mysteron Threat

"This is the voice of the Mysterons. We know that you can hear us, Earthmen. We know of your pathetic attempts to discover our secrets. But you will never succeed. You will never solve the mystery of the Mysterons."

Regular Voice Cast

Captain Scarlet	**Francis Matthews**
Captain Blue	**Edward Bishop**
Colonel White	**Donald Gray**
Destiny Angel	**Liz Morgan**
Symphony Angel	**Janna Hill**
Lieutenant Green	**Cy Grant**
Captain Black	**Donald Gray**
Rhapsody Angel	**Liz Morgan**
Voice of the Mysterons	**Donald Gray**

Guest Voice Cast

World President	**Paul Maxwell**
General Peterson	**Charles Tingwell**
Captain Indigo	**Gary Files**
Dr. Giadello	**Jeremy Wilkin**
1st Warden (Post 14)	**Gary Files**
2nd Warden (Post 28	**Martin King**

First UK Transmission

Friday, November 24th, 1967
5.25pm (ATV Midlands)

AVALANCHE

Prod. No. 11

Teleplay by **Shane Rimmer** | Directed by **Brian Burgess**

Regular Voice Cast

Captain Scarlet	**Francis Matthews**
Captain Blue	**Edward Bishop**
Colonel White	**Donald Gray**
Destiny Angel	**Liz Morgan**
Lieutenant Green	**Cy Grant**
Voice of the Mysterons	**Donald Gray**

Guest Voice Cast

General Ward	**Paul Maxwell**
Eddie	**Gary Files**
Marshall	**Charles Tingwell**
Lieutenant Burroughs	**Jeremy Wilkin**
Trapper	**Gary Files**
1st Sentry (Joe)	**Martin King**
2nd Sentry	**Martin King**
3rd Sentry	**Gary Files**
Radio	**Jeremy Wilkin**

First UK Transmission

Friday, October 27th, 1967
5.25pm (ATV Midlands)

In Northern Canada, maintenance engineer Eddie is making a regular tour of the Frost Line Outer Space Defence system bases when he loses control of his vehicle and crashes down the mountainside. Reconstructed by the Mysterons, Eddie arrives at Red Deer Base and shortly afterwards, the Frost Line Command Base receives an emergency signal from Red Deer before losing all contact. Colonel White sends Scarlet and Green to investigate and, wearing respirators, they enter Red Deer's hermetically sealed dome. The Spectrum officers find all the base personnel dead, but there is no explanation of what killed them. Then contact is lost with Cariboo Base and Frost Line commander-in-chief General Ward warns Colonel White that if Big Bear, the next base on the Frost Line, is similarly targeted, he will order a retaliatory missile strike on Mars!

Notes

Shane Rimmer's shooting script for this episode opens with a description of the Frost Line Command Base that was partially lost in the translation from script to screen:

We are in Northern Canada. Deep snow surrounds the plexiglass domes that make up the Command Base of the Frost Line Outer Space Defence system. This stretches in a number of similar bases three thousand miles across Northern Canada. From the large central dome acting as a hub, avenues run off in eight directions. At the end of each spoke at varying distances from the centre are smaller domes. Each dome is air-tight and serviced by an artificial atmosphere from an air-conditioning dome.

Mysteron Threat

"This is the voice of the Mysterons. We know that you can hear us, Earthmen. Our next strike is imminent. We will show you how weak you really are. Within the next four hours, we will destroy key links in your Frost Line Outer Space Defence system. We will be avenged."

SHADOW OF FEAR

Prod. No. 12

Teleplay by **Tony Barwick** | Directed by **Robert Lynn**

Regular Voice Cast

Captain Scarlet	**Francis Matthews**
Captain Blue	**Edward Bishop**
Colonel White	**Donald Gray**
Lieutenant Green	**Cy Grant**
Captain Grey	**Paul Maxwell**
Melody Angel	**Sylvia Anderson**
Voice of the Mysterons	**Donald Gray**

Guest Voice Cast

Breck	**Paul Maxwell**
Carter	**Charles Tingwell**
Angelini	**Jeremy Wilkin**

First UK Transmission

Friday, February 2nd, 1968
5.25pm (ATV Midlands)

After a decoy satellite is destroyed by the Mysterons, Spectrum successfully lands Mini-Sat 5 on the Martian moon Phobos where it will transmit close-up pictures of Mars back to the K14 Observatory in the Himalayas. As Scarlet and Blue wait at the observatory for the pictures to be received, one of the astronomers, Dr. Breck, is killed by the Mysterons and reconstructed as a Mysteron agent. When it is discovered that Breck is missing, Colonel White dispatches Captain Grey in a Spectrum Helicopter to search the area while Scarlet and Blue set out on foot. They finally locate Breck hiding in the rocks above the observatory but as the Mini-Sat 5 transmission countdown begins, Breck tells Scarlet that he has attached a bomb to the radio telescope's rotation gear – when the dish is moved into position to receive the signals from Phobos, the observatory will be blown to pieces!

Notes

Captains Blue and Grey use Mysteron Detectors to track down Breck, so this episode must be set after the events of *Spectrum Strikes Back* where the devices are introduced.

Oops!

Colonel White reveals that the Mini-Sat 5 mission is part of Operation Sword, a much larger plan that will go ahead as scheduled even though the K14 Observatory has been destroyed. Possibly this was intended to be a story thread that could have been picked up in later episodes, but it is never mentioned again so viewers never learn what Operation Sword is actually all about.

Mysteron Threat

"This is the voice of the Mysterons. We know that you can hear us, Earthmen. The eye that dares to look upon our planet has been destroyed. You will never succeed. You will never discover the secret of the Mysterons. We will be avenged."

THE HEART OF NEW YORK — Prod. No. 13

Teleplay by **Tony Barwick** Directed by **Alan Perry**

A trio of crooks, Kruger, Doig and Carl, steal Grade A Security documents from the Spectrum Security Vaults and when Kruger reads about the Mysterons' power of retrometabolism, he devises a plan to get the Mysterons to work for them. Faking their own deaths by staging a car crash for the benefit of a fire warden at a lookout tower in the hills, the three men then pretend to have been Mysteronised, telling the warden that they intend to rob the Second National Bank in New York. New York is evacuated and Spectrum roadblocks are established at the city limits, but Kruger, Doig and Carl gain access to the city posing as FBI agents. Querying how these 'Government agents' appeared to be aware of information that was only circulated to Spectrum personnel, Scarlet figures out the crooks' plan and he and Blue race into the city to stop them.

Notes

This is the first episode in which the Mysterons are seen to exhibit powers of dematerialisation, here used to help Black evade capture. Later, in *Model Spy*, *Expo 2068* and *Inferno* it appears that Black is able to control this power himself, giving him the ability to also make inanimate objects appear and disappear at will. The revamp puppet which is seen here as Kruger is one of the most often used repertory puppets in the three Century 21 Supermarionation series with appearances as 10 separate characters in CAPTAIN SCARLET alone. First seen as the Assassin in *Winged Assassin*, the puppet later appears as Commander Kovac in the JOE 90 episode *Arctic Adventure* and the Dreisenberg Ambassador in the THE SECRET SERVICE episode *A Case For The Bishop*.

Mysteron Threat

"This is the voice of the Mysterons. We know that you can hear us, Earthmen. We've seen the greed and corruption of the world in which you live and will take our revenge upon it. We will destroy the heart of New York. We have not forgotten."

Regular Voice Cast

Captain Scarlet	**Francis Matthews**
Captain Blue	**Edward Bishop**
Colonel White	**Donald Gray**
Lieutenant Green	**Cy Grant**
Captain Black	**Donald Gray**
Captain Ochre	**Jeremy Wilkin**
Captain Magenta	**Gary Files**
Voice of the Mysterons	**Donald Gray**

Guest Voice Cast

Kruger	**David Healy**
Doig	**Gary Files**
Carl	**Martin King**
Lookout	**Jeremy Wilkin**
Guard	**Martin King**

First UK Transmission

Friday, December 8th, 1967
5.25pm (ATV Midlands)

FIRE AT RIG 15 — Prod. No. 14

Teleplay by **Bryan Cooper** Directed by **Ken Turner**

In the Middle East, ultra-sonic drilling Rig 15 strikes oil, but the Mysterons use their powers to open the master valve and the oil explodes, turning Rig 15 into a column of fire 1,000 feet high. As the oil is needed at Spectrum's Bensheba refinery to produce a specialised fuel used by all Spectrum vehicles, Scarlet and Blue fly out to Bensheba. There they meet fire control expert Jason Smith, who has been hired to put out the Rig 15 blaze. Smith enters the raging inferno in a specially equipped tractor to place explosives which will blow out the flames, but Captain Black uses Mysteron powers to mesmerise him and he is killed when the explosives detonate. Reconstructed as an agent of the Mysterons, Smith receives his instructions from Captain Black: he is to drive his truck to the Bensheba refinery and blow it to pieces!

Notes

The revamp puppet that is seen here as Jason Smith first appeared as the TVR-17 Controller in *White As Snow* and then as the Fire Chief in *Seek And Destroy*. It is later seen as Major Stone in *Traitor* and a guard at Hotspot Tower in *Noose Of Ice*. The puppet can also be seen as Dr. Emil Kados in the JOE 90 episode *Operation McClaine* and the Dreisenberg Ambassador's Aide in the THE SECRET SERVICE episode *A Case For The Bishop*. Bryan Cooper's original script sets the location of the Spectrum refinery at Bethsheba rather than Bensheba. This was the last episode to feature Barry Gray's original arrangement of the end titles music before it was replaced by a version recorded by The Spectrum.

Mysteron Threat

"This is the voice of the Mysterons. We know that you can hear us, Earthmen. We have observed the pathetic attempts of Spectrum to combat us and we have decided to render them powerless. We intend to immobilise the whole of Spectrum."

Regular Voice Cast

Captain Scarlet	**Francis Matthews**
Captain Blue	**Edward Bishop**
Colonel White	**Donald Gray**
Lieutenant Green	**Cy Grant**
Melody Angel	**Sylvia Anderson**
Voice of the Mysterons	**Donald Gray**

Guest Voice Cast

Jason Smith	**David Healy**
Charlie Hansen	**Gary Files**
Kinley	**Jeremy Wilkin**
Oil Worker	**Martin King**

First UK Transmission

Friday, February 16th, 1968
5.25pm (ATV Midlands)

THE LAUNCHING — Prod. No. 15

Teleplay by **Peter Curran** & **David Williams** — Directed by **Brian Burgess**

Regular Voice Cast

Captain Scarlet	**Francis Matthews**
Captain Blue	**Edward Bishop**
Colonel White	**Donald Gray**
Destiny Angel	**Liz Morgan**
Symphony Angel	**Janna Hill**
Lieutenant Green	**Cy Grant**
Captain Black	**Donald Gray**
Captain Ochre	**Jeremy Wilkin**
Harmony Angel	**Lian Shin**
Voice of the Mysterons	**Donald Gray**

Guest Voice Cast

President Roberts	**David Healy**
Mervin Brand	**Gary Files**
Vice President	**Martin King**
Vice President's Wife	**Sylvia Anderson**
Operator, Tribune Control	**Jeremy Wilkin**

First UK Transmission

Tuesday, April 2nd, 1968
5.00pm (ATV Midlands)

Reporter Mervin Brand is killed instantly when his jet is struck by lightning and crashes, but he is reconstructed as a Mysteron agent. When the Mysterons threaten to destroy President Roberts, Scarlet is assigned to the President's protection while Blue and Ochre impose a security cordon around the Presidential Residence. Roberts insists on holding his weekly press conference so all attendees are screened with a Mysteron Detector, but Blue becomes suspicious of Brand's car parked nearby and when Ochre points the Mysteron Detector at the reporter, Brand suddenly drives off, almost running Blue down. Then Roberts reveals that a new atomic liner is about to be named after him at a launching ceremony and Scarlet realises that the ship is actually the Mysterons' target!

Notes

A short scene deleted from the finished episode featured Harmony and Symphony discussing how President Roberts comes from Symphony's home town. Scarlet refers to the events of *Winged Assassin* when he reminds Roberts of the assassination of the Director General of the United Asian Republic. Although voice artist Lian Shin is credited on 20 episodes of the series, this episode features her only vocal appearance as Harmony Angel and she does not portray any other characters. For all of Harmony's previous speaking roles, her voice was provided by Liz Morgan, who also plays the character on the Century 21 Mini-Album *Introducing Captain Scarlet* (MA 131). Harmony is seen in a number of later episodes, but this is the last time that she speaks.

Mysteron Threat

"This is the voice of the Mysterons. We know that you can hear us, Earthmen. You continue your futile defence against us even though you must know that you cannot succeed. In order to show you your ineffectiveness, we will deal you yet another crippling blow. We will destroy *President Roberts* within the next 12 hours."

LUNARVILLE 7 — Prod. No. 16

Teleplay by **Tony Barwick** — Directed by **Robert Lynn**

Regular Voice Cast

Captain Scarlet	**Francis Matthews**
Captain Blue	**Edward Bishop**
Colonel White	**Donald Gray**
Lieutenant Green	**Cy Grant**
Captain Magenta	**Gary Files**
Voice of the Mysterons	**Donald Gray**

Guest Voice Cast

Lunar Controller	**David Healy**
Orson	**Martin King**
Control	**Jeremy Wilkin**
Pilot	**Gary Files**

First UK Transmission

Friday, December 15th, 1967
5.25pm (ATV Midlands)

After the Lunar Controller announces that he has come to a peaceful settlement with the Mysterons, Colonel White sends Scarlet, Blue and Green to Lunarville 7 to find out how the Controller has contacted the Mysterons and also to investigate reports of a strange complex under construction in the Humboldt Sea. On arrival, the Spectrum officers are equipped with recognition discs which enable them to be identified by the base control computer SID. The Controller's aide Orson then takes them in a Moonmobile to view Lunarville 4 but he refuses Scarlet's request to go on to the Humboldt Sea as he says that it is getting late. Back at Lunarville 7, Scarlet finds that their quarters are bugged and rips out the microphone, but in response, the Controller declares a state of emergency, sealing the base and programming SID to accept only his authorisation...

Notes

A talking computer called SID also appears in UFO where the name is an acronym for Space Intruder Detector rather than Speech Intelligence Decoder. The design of the Lunarville Moonmobiles formed the basis of the SHADO Moon Mobiles in UFO.

Oops!

Scarlet's and Green's seat belts change colour between shots during their journey to the Humboldt Sea in the Moonmobile. When the Spectrum agents return to Lunarville 7 from Crater 101, SID identifies Scarlet re-entering the complex although he is actually wearing the Lunar Controller's recognition disc.

Mysteron Threat

"This is the voice of the Mysterons. We know that you can hear us, Earthmen. We have no quarrel with the Moon and we accept their offer of friendship. But we will continue to take our revenge against the Earth. We will be avenged."

THE TRAP

Prod. No. 17

Teleplay by **Alan Pattillo** Directed by **Alan Perry**

World Air Force staff plane XQR is *en route* to Cloudbase when it is struck by lightning and crashes, but the plane and its passengers, Commodore Goddard and his aide Holt, are reconstructed by the Mysterons. Goddard arrives on Cloudbase to discuss security arrangements for the International Air Conference and announces that he has changed its location to Glen Garry Castle in Scotland. Scarlet accompanies Goddard to the castle and Colonel White informs the Captain that he will wait for his final clearance before allowing the the delegates' Magnacopter transport to land there. Then Scarlet discovers Holt concealed in an alcove behind a painting in the conference room, operating a machine gun aimed at the conference table, but he is captured by Goddard who impersonates his voice to give the all-clear for the Magnacopter...

Notes

The ten revamp puppets which portray the conference delegates previously appeared in the series as Lieutenant Dean (*The Mysterons*), Space Navigator Conway (*The Mysterons*), the Director General of the United Asian Republic (*Winged Assassin*), the London Airport Control Tower operator (*Winged Assassin*), General Tiempo (*Operation Time*), Dr. Magnus (*Operation Time*), Eddie (*Avalanche*), Kruger (*The Heart Of New York*), an oilworker (*Fire At Rig 15*) and the Vice-President of Trans-Pacific Shipping (*The Launching*). The latter two puppets are better-known for their appearances as Kramer and Steele in *Special Assignment*.

Mysteron Threat

"This is the voice of the Mysterons. We know that you can hear us, Earthmen. We are transmitting on all your radio and television frequencies. We will continue to strike when and where you least expect it. At the appointed hour, as the clock is chiming, the wings of the world will be clipped."

Regular Voice Cast

Captain Scarlet	**Francis Matthews**
Captain Blue	**Edward Bishop**
Colonel White	**Donald Gray**
Symphony Angel	**Janna Hill**
Lieutenant Green	**Cy Grant**
Melody Angel	**Sylvia Anderson**
Voice of the Mysterons	**Donald Gray**

Guest Voice Cast

Commodore Goddard	**David Healy**
Holt	**Gary Files**
Morton	**Jeremy Wilkin**
Attendant	**Jeremy Wilkin / Martin King**

First UK Transmission

Friday, November 10th, 1967
5.25pm (ATV Midlands)

MODEL SPY

Prod. No. 18

Teleplay by **Bill Hedley** Directed by **Ken Turner**

Top fashion models Gabrielle and Helga are killed when the monotrain on which they are travelling crashes, but both girls are reconstructed as Mysteron agents. Scarlet and Blue are puzzled as to why the latest Mysteron threat should target a fashion designer until Colonel White explains that André Verdain is secretly the controller of the European Area Intelligence Service. Suspecting that the attempt on Verdain will be made at a fashion show in Monte Carlo, the Colonel assigns Destiny and Symphony to go undercover as models, with Scarlet and Blue as press relations officer and photographer respectively. The four agents join Verdain and his models, Gabrielle and Helga, on his cabin cruiser, but Scarlet discovers a fire in the engine room. Ordering everyone to jump overboard, Scarlet takes the helm to get the boat away from them before it explodes...

Notes

Scarlet and Blue's true identities are revealed here as Paul Metcalfe and Adam Svenson.

Oops!

When the four Spectrum agents meet Verdain, Scarlet decides that they will drop their Spectrum code names so as to maintain their cover, but everyone just carries on calling the two Angels Destiny and Symphony. After they have kidnapped Verdain, Captain Black tells Helga that they need Verdain alive, but there is no explanation for this change of heart: the Mysterons threatened to assassinate Verdain, so it just doesn't make sense that Black simply throws Verdain out of the car without killing him first.

Mysteron Threat

"This is the voice of the Mysterons. We know you can hear us, Earthmen. We will continue to take our revenge. You should never have attacked our Martian Complex. We are about to attack the House of Verdain. André Verdain will die."

Regular Voice Cast

Captain Scarlet	**Francis Matthews**
Captain Blue	**Edward Bishop**
Colonel White	**Donald Gray**
Destiny Angel	**Liz Morgan**
Symphony Angel	**Janna Hill**
Lieutenant Green	**Cy Grant**
Captain Black	**Donald Gray**
Voice of the Mysterons	**Donald Gray**

Guest Voice Cast

André Verdain	**Jeremy Wilkin**
Helga	**Liz Morgan**
Gabrielle	**Sylvia Anderson**
Commissionaire	**Jeremy Wilkin**

First UK Transmission

Friday, December 29th, 1967
5.25pm (ATV Midlands)

DANGEROUS RENDEZVOUS — Prod. No. 19

Teleplay by **Tony Barwick** — Directed by **Brian Burgess**

Dr. Kurnitz of the Nash Institute of Technology has been studying the Mysteron pulsator recovered by Scarlet from the complex in Crater 101, and under his instructions Spectrum have constructed a transmission device that will enable Colonel White to speak directly to the Mysterons for the first time. He transmits a message to the Mysterons in which he admits and apologises for the error made by the Zero X team, offering the hand of friendship in the hope of finally ending the war of nerves. Two hours later, the Mysterons respond by allowing one member of Spectrum to meet with their representative, under the condition that he carries no weapons or communications equipment. The rendezvous is set for a desolate volcanic area in Greenland and Scarlet takes up the challenge, even though he knows he may be walking into a trap...

Notes

Dangerous Rendezvous is the final part of a story that began with *Lunarville 7* and continued in *Crater 101*, although this conclusion was actually shot in advance of *Crater 101*. During Colonel White's message to the Mysterons, flashback footage from the opening sequence of *The Mysterons* reminds viewers how the war of nerves began. The central section of the episode, where Colonel White explains various Spectrum facilities to Dr. Kurnitz, is clearly padding which plays very much like the early Century 21 Mini-Albums *A Trip to Marineville* (MA 102) and *Introducing Thunderbirds* (MA 103), where a visitor is given a tour of the secret base in a story designed to explain to new viewers how the organisation works.

Mysteron Threat

"This is the voice of the Mysterons. We know that you can hear us, Earthmen. Our next act of retaliation will be to destroy Cloudbase. Do you hear? Spectrum's headquarters Cloudbase will be destroyed at midnight."

Regular Voice Cast

Captain Scarlet	**Francis Matthews**
Captain Blue	**Edward Bishop**
Colonel White	**Donald Gray**
Destiny Angel	**Liz Morgan**
Lieutenant Green	**Cy Grant**
Captain Black	**Donald Gray**
Captain Ochre	**Jeremy Wilkin**
Voice of the Mysterons	**Donald Gray**

Guest Voice Cast

Dr. Kurnitz	**Jeremy Wilkin**
Receptionist	**Sylvia Anderson**
Captain Black (Original)	**Jeremy Wilkin**
Lieutenant Dean	**Charles Tingwell**

First UK Transmission

Friday, February 9th, 1968
5.25pm (ATV Midlands)

SPECIAL ASSIGNMENT — Prod. No. 20

Teleplay by **Tony Barwick** — Directed by **Robert Lynn**

Captain Black engineers the deaths of gangsters Steele and Kramer who are then reconstructed as Mysteron agents. When the Mysterons announce their intention to destroy North America, Colonel White sends Scarlet on a special assignment based on a report from Spectrum Intelligence, but the Captain seems intent on ruining his Spectrum career by gambling away all his money at a casino in Arizona. As gambling is a serious breach of the Spectrum code of conduct, Colonel White asks for Scarlet's resignation. Then Scarlet is contacted by Kramer and Steele who offer to pay off his debts if he will requisition a Spectrum Pursuit Vehicle for them. They take Scarlet to an old ranch house where he learns that their plans are being co-ordinated by Captain Black. Kramer and Steele intend to use the SPV to carry an atomic device into Nuclear City, Nevada, and detonate it, starting a chain reaction which will completely obliterate North America!

Notes

The original version of the script for this episode opened with Scarlet losing all his money at the casino. This script was then revised to add the scenes with Kramer and Steele's car accident (a genuine accident in this version), their reconstruction by the Mysterons, and Colonel White's briefing after receiving the Mysterons' threat. The scenes with Captain Black murdering the garage attendant, and the attendant then sabotaging Steele's car, were all later additions. The 'White As Snow' incidental track composed for *White As Snow* can be heard playing in the garage at Mason's Autos when Black backs his car over the attendant.

Mysteron Threat

"This is the voice of the Mysterons. We know that you can hear us, Earthmen. We will deal another crushing blow. We told you we intend to obliterate the sub-continent of North America. We will be avenged."

Regular Voice Cast

Captain Scarlet	**Francis Matthews**
Captain Blue	**Edward Bishop**
Colonel White	**Donald Gray**
Lieutenant Green	**Cy Grant**
Captain Black	**Donald Gray**
Captain Ochre	**Jeremy Wilkin**
Melody Angel	**Sylvia Anderson**
Voice of the Mysterons	**Donald Gray**

Guest Voice Cast

Steele	**Martin King**
Kramer	**Gary Files**
Croupier	**Gary Files**
Barman	**Jeremy Wilkin**
Mason	**Shane Rimmer**
Security Chief	**Gary Files**
Attendant	**Martin King**

First UK Transmission

Friday, December 1st, 1967
5.25pm (ATV Midlands)

TRAITOR

Prod. No. 21

Teleplay by **Tony Barwick** Directed by **Alan Perry**

After the malfunction of a third hovercraft at the Spectrum cadet school at Koala Base in Australia, sabotage is suspected, possibly from inside the Spectrum organisation itself in light of the latest Mysteron threat. Scarlet and Blue are sent to Koala Base under the pretext of giving a series of lectures to the new recruits, in order to investigate the sabotage claims without alerting the base commander, Major Stone. Cadet Phil Machin begins to suspect that Scarlet might still be working for the Mysterons and, during the night, Scarlet and Blue awake to find their room on fire, although they manage to escape unharmed. The next day, the Spectrum officers are accompanying Machin and fellow cadet Joe Johnson on a hovercraft exercise when the vehicle loses control and starts to overheat. Machin pulls a gun on Scarlet, threatening to shoot him unless he reveals how the vehicle has been sabotaged!

Regular Voice Cast

Captain Scarlet	**Francis Matthews**
Captain Blue	**Edward Bishop**
Colonel White	**Donald Gray**
Destiny Angel	**Liz Morgan**
Lieutenant Green	**Cy Grant**
Captain Black	**Donald Gray**
Voice of the Mysterons	**Donald Gray**

Guest Voice Cast

Major Stone	**David Healy**
Phil Machin	**Gary Files**
Joe Johnson	**Jeremy Wilkin**
Helicopter A42 Pilot	**Charles Tingwell**

First UK Transmission

Sunday, January 14th, 1968
5.30pm (ATV London)

Notes

Five minutes of footage from *The Mysterons* helps Captain Blue to explain to the cadets (and new viewers) how Captain Scarlet became indestructible. In his script for *Traitor*, Tony Barwick noted of this sequence that no scenes from *The Mysterons* would be used in the composite flashback script that he was planning for episode 32 (*The Inquisition*). The scheduled premiere screening of this episode on ATV Midlands was postponed from January 12th, 1968, so *Traitor* was actually first broadcast on ATV London two days later. The episode was not screened on ATV Midlands until Tuesday, April 23rd, 1968 by which time it had already also been seen in the Granada and Anglia regions.

Mysteron Threat

"This is the voice of the Mysterons. We know that you can hear us, Earthmen. The Spectrum organisation will be torn apart from within. The traitor among you will create havoc and destroy morale."

CRATER 101

Prod. No. 22

Teleplay by **Tony Barwick** Directed by **Ken Turner**

Scarlet, Blue and Lieutenant Green volunteer for a mission to enter the Mysteron Complex in Crater 101 on the Moon to remove its power source, preventing the complex from reconstructing itself after it is destroyed by a low-yield atomic device. Arriving at Lunarville 6, the trio are briefed by Neptune Probe veteran Linda Nolan, who explains that they will have just four hours to penetrate the complex, remove the power source and get clear before the atomic device, ferried by Nolan's colleague Frazer in a Lunar Tank, is detonated at midnight. Driving a Lunar Tractor, the Spectrum officers fight their way past robot construction vehicles to access the complex, but then Nolan learns that Frazer has been replaced by a Mysteron agent who has set the detonator on the atomic device to explode two hours earlier than planned!

Regular Voice Cast

Captain Scarlet	**Francis Matthews**
Captain Blue	**Edward Bishop**
Colonel White	**Donald Gray**
Lieutenant Green	**Cy Grant**
Captain Magenta	**Gary Files**
Voice of the Mysterons	**Donald Gray**

Guest Voice Cast

Linda Nolan	**Sylvia Anderson**
Frazer	**David Healy**
Shroeder	**Jeremy Wilkin**

First UK Transmission

Friday, January 26th, 1968
5.25pm (ATV Midlands)

Notes

Although it is intended to be read as *Crater 101*, each of the two '1' numerals has been replaced by a letter 'I' in the episode title caption at the start of this episode, as shown in the heading above. In the typeface used for the series' title captions (Microgramma Bold Extended), the number '1' almost looks like a number '7' (as in the title caption for *Fire At Rig 15*) so the substitution was made for clarity. The same substitution appears on the title caption for *Flight 104*. Linda Nolan's lucky charm details that the first Neptune Probe was launched from the Moon on July 10th, 2058. When Frazer sets off from Lunarville 6 in the Lunar Tank, part of the base can be seen to be constructed from Mini-Sat 5 (*Shadow Of Fear*) and the Frost Line Command Base domes (*Avalanche*).

Mysteron Threat

"This is the voice of the Mysterons. We know that you can hear us, Earthmen. Although you have discovered our Complex on the Moon, it will never reveal its secrets. Anyone who dares to enter will be destroyed. You have been warned. We have not forgotten."

PLACE OF ANGELS

Prod. No. 23

Teleplay by **Leo Eaton** Directed by **Leo Eaton**

Captain Black causes the death of biological research assistant Judy Chapman in a road accident, and she is reconstructed by the Mysterons to steal a phial of deadly K14 virus from Biological Research Station 'D' near Manchester. Responding to a call for assistance, Scarlet and Blue arrive at the Research Station, where project co-ordinator Dr. Denton tells them of the theft and reveals that as there is no known antidote for the virus, it could wipe out a city of ten million people if the phial is broken. Chapman is sighted by Spectrum Security in New York, so Scarlet and Blue fly there and trail her car in a Spectrum Pursuit Vehicle, but Chapman is warned by Captain Black that she is being followed, so she abandons the car and pushes it off the road down an embankment. By the time Scarlet and Blue arrive, Chapman has vanished, but broken glass found in the car could be the remains of the phial and the Spectrum officers fear that the K14 virus has been released into the atmosphere!

Notes

The original title of Leo Eaton's script for this episode was 'The City of Angels'. In this script, the Mysterons' threat was to "destroy the population of the City of Angels". Judy Chapman is portrayed by a revamp puppet which was previously seen in the series as a nurse in *Operation Time*, the Vice President's wife in *The Launching* and Gabrielle in *Model Spy*. The BBC2 UK television network premiere of this episode on Friday, April 29th, 1994 was delayed by ten minutes when live coverage of the 1994 World Snooker Championship semi-final between Stephen Hendry and Steve Davis overran.

Mysteron Threat

"This is the voice of the Mysterons. We know that you can hear us, Earthmen, and we have not forgotten your unprovoked attack. To prove how useless it is for you to resist, we will destroy the Place of the Angels."

Regular Voice Cast

Captain Scarlet	**Francis Matthews**
Captain Blue	**Edward Bishop**
Colonel White	**Donald Gray**
Destiny Angel	**Liz Morgan**
Symphony Angel	**Janna Hill**
Lieutenant Green	**Cy Grant**
Captain Black	**Donald Gray**
Voice of the Mysterons	**Donald Gray**

Guest Voice Cast

Judith Chapman	**Sylvia Anderson**
Dr. Denton	**Jeremy Wilkin**
Captain	**Martin King**
Engineer	**Gary Files**
Security Guard	**Gary Files**
Spectrum, New York	**Jeremy Wilkin**

First UK Transmission

Friday, March 8th, 1968
5.25pm (ATV Midlands)

FLIGHT 104

Prod. No. 24

Teleplay by **Tony Barwick** Directed by **Robert Lynn**

Travelling incognito, Scarlet and Blue escort leading astrophysicist, Dr. Conrad, to a conference with the World President at Lake Toma in Switzerland, where they will determine the method and purpose of Earth's return to Mars. During a stopover at the Adelphi Hotel, they incite the curiosity of a news reporter, Harry, and his photographer, Joe, who then tail them to Novena Airport. There, Scarlet, Blue and Conrad meet security chief Bill Williams who reports that all the seats on their plane, Flight 104 to Geneva, have been booked by Spectrum. When Harry and Joe attempt to reserve seats on the flight, Scarlet tells Williams to let the men board the plane so as not to arouse further suspicion. Meanwhile, Captain Black has drugged the flight crew and locked them in a storage room, so that when Flight 104 leaves Novena, it is under Mysteron control...

Notes

This episode opens with incidental music that was originally composed for *Avalanche*. When the plane makes its approach to Geneva Airport, footage from the THUNDERBIRDS episode *Trapped In The Sky* shows crash tenders moving into position.

Oops!

When Angel One is launched, the normal launch sound appears on the soundtrack but the aircraft stays exactly where it is. It only starts to move as the scene cuts to a shot of Angel One flying off the end of the flight deck. After Scarlet and Blue break into the cockpit of the passenger jet, Destiny reports to Cloudbase speaking with Rhapsody's voice.

Mysteron Threat

"This is the voice of the Mysterons. We know that you can hear us, Earthmen. The conference at Lake Toma will be sabotaged. We know what you are trying to do, but you will not succeed."

Regular Voice Cast

Captain Scarlet	**Francis Matthews**
Captain Blue	**Edward Bishop**
Colonel White	**Donald Gray**
Destiny Angel	**Liz Morgan**
Symphony Angel	**Janna Hill**
Lieutenant Green	**Cy Grant**
Captain Ochre	**Jeremy Wilkin**
Voice of the Mysterons	**Donald Gray**

Guest Voice Cast

Dr. Conrad	**David Healy**
Reporter Harry	**Jeremy Wilkin**
Photographer Joe	**Gary Files**
Bill Williams	**Martin King**
Flight Desk	**Gary Files**
Airport Tannoy	**Liz Morgan**

First UK Transmission

Friday, March 1st, 1968
5.25pm (ATV Midlands)

CODENAME EUROPA — Prod. No. 25

Teleplay by **David Lee** Directed by **Alan Perry**

Electronics genius Professor Gabriel Carney is assassinated by Captain Black and reconstructed as a Mysteron agent with instructions to kill John L. Henderson, Conrad Olafson and Joseph Meccini, the three joint presidents of the Congress of Europe who are the targets of the latest Mysteron threat. Colonel White activates an operation to protect the presidents by sending them to three different places of maximum security, but Carney makes an attempt on the life of Conrad Olafson while he is under the protection of Captain Ochre at Vandon Maximum Security Base. Intelligence reports lead Scarlet and Blue to Carney's bungalow where they find evidence that the Professor is working for the Mysterons. They also discover a hand-written note which suggests that his next assassination attempt will target President Henderson at the Maximum Security Centre...

Notes

The script for this episode featured additional scenes in which the Mysteron Carney disposed of the body of the original Carney using a remote-controlled lawn mower. The script also reveals that Carney was the chief designer of the electronic security systems at Spectrum's maximum security bases.

Oops!

For a top security installation, the Maximum Security Base at Vandon is very clearly signposted. Scarlet is fully aware that Carney is a Mysteron agent, yet he shoots him with his regular pistol rather than a Mysteron Gun and, somehow, this kills Carney.

Mysteron Threat

"This is the voice of the Mysterons. We know that you can hear us, Earthmen. We will continue to take our revenge and deal yet another devastating blow. We will destroy the Triumvirate of Europe. The Triumvirate of Europe will be destroyed."

Regular Voice Cast

Captain Scarlet	**Francis Matthews**
Captain Blue	**Edward Bishop**
Colonel White	**Donald Gray**
Destiny Angel	**Liz Morgan**
Lieutenant Green	**Cy Grant**
Captain Black	**Donald Gray**
Captain Ochre	**Jeremy Wilkin**
Voice of the Mysterons	**Donald Gray**

Guest Voice Cast

Professor Gabriel Carney	**Neil McCallum**
Conrad Olafson	**Gary Files**
Security Base Guard 1	**Martin King**
Security Base Guard 2	**Martin King**
Security Centre Guard	**Neil McCallum**

First UK Transmission

Thursday, March 21st, 1968
5.00pm (Granada)

FLIGHT TO ATLANTICA — Prod. No. 26

Teleplay by **Tony Barwick** Directed by **Leo Eaton**

The Spectrum officers celebrate the first anniversary of the formation of Spectrum with the help of some anonymously donated non-alcoholic champagne, but their party comes to an abrupt end when Colonel White discovers what is going on. Then Cloudbase receives the latest Mysteron threat which targets the World Navy Complex at Atlantica, so Colonel White assigns Blue and Ochre to take charge of an Air Force operation to bomb a wreck that is being carried by heavy currents towards Atlantica. However, at the mission briefing at Maxwell Base, both officers are oddly off-hand and rude, failing to recognise Captain Black when he substitutes a different target plan in their bombing orders. After the other Spectrum officers become erratic and irresponsible, Scarlet and Colonel White realise that they are the only ones who are unaffected by the strange ailment and capable of intercepting Blue and Ochre before they can bomb Atlantica!

Notes

Flight To Atlantica is one of only two CAPTAIN SCARLET AND THE MYSTERONS episodes in which all the members of the regular cast appear (although they do not all have speaking roles). The other such episode is *Attack On Cloudbase*. Colonel White reveals that Spectrum was formed in July 2067 with the inaugural charter drawn up on July 7th and signed by the World President on July 10th. A jazz track composed for the STINGRAY episode *Tune Of Danger* can be heard playing at the party in the conference room at the start of the episode. Later, in the cockpit of the V17 bomber, Blue and Ochre listen to the radio playing 'Dangerous Game', a track originally composed for the THUNDERBIRDS episode *The Cham-Cham*.

Mysteron Threat

"This is the voice of the Mysterons. We know that you can hear us, Earthmen. We intend to destroy the World Navy Complex at Atlantica. Atlantica will be annihilated."

Regular Voice Cast

Captain Scarlet	**Francis Matthews**
Captain Blue	**Edward Bishop**
Colonel White	**Donald Gray**
Symphony Angel	**Janna Hill**
Lieutenant Green	**Cy Grant**
Captain Ochre	**Jeremy Wilkin**
Voice of the Mysterons	**Donald Gray**

Guest Voice Cast

Williams	**Gary Files**
Sergeant	**Shane Rimmer**

First UK Transmission

Sunday, March 24th, 1968
5.30pm (ATV London)

NOOSE OF ICE

Prod. No. 27

Teleplay by **Tony Barwick**

Directed by **Ken Turner**

The Hotspot mining base in the North Pole provides the only natural supply of Tritonium, which will be used to construct the rocket nose casings of the Space Administration's vital new space fleet. Suspecting that the base is the most likely target of the Mysterons' latest threat, Scarlet and Blue travel to Hotspot Tower, crossing a bridge that spans a ring of water around the tower and entering a lift that takes them 1,000 feet below the ice to the base control centre. The station commander, Rhodes, explains that the Tritonium mining operation relies on huge heating elements, fed by 100,000 volts from the booster station, which keep the temperature of the water around the tower above freezing. Unfortunately, maintenance man Neilson has become a Mysteron agent and he cuts off the power from the booster station. With the heating elements out of action, the sea will freeze within half an hour and the expanding ice will crush the tower!

Notes

Much of the incidental music featured in this episode was originally composed for STINGRAY, as heard during Neilson's death in the snow storm and when the temperature drops around Hotspot Tower. The Space Administration Headquarters building originally appeared as the SHEF Headquarters building in *Point 783*. Maintenance man Neilson is portrayed by a revamp puppet that originally appeared as Captain Brown in *The Mysterons*. The puppet has also been seen in the series as Major Reeves in *Renegade Rocket*, Charlie Hansen in *Fire At Rig 15*, Dr. Conrad in *Flight 104* and Professor Carney in *Codename Europa*.

Mysteron Threat

"This is the voice of the Mysterons. We know that you can hear us, Earthmen. You are powerless to defeat us. Your much-boasted new space fleet is doomed to failure. We will make certain you never return to our planet Mars."

Regular Voice Cast

Captain Scarlet	**Francis Matthews**
Captain Blue	**Edward Bishop**
Colonel White	**Donald Gray**
Lieutenant Green	**Cy Grant**
Captain Black	**Donald Gray**
Voice of the Mysterons	**Donald Gray**

Guest Voice Cast

General Rebus	**David Healy**
Neilson	**Gary Files**
Rhodes	**Jeremy Wilkin**
Hotspot Control	**Martin King**
Guard	**Martin King**

First UK Transmission

Tuesday, March 12th, 1968
5.00pm (ATV Midlands)

TREBLE CROSS

Prod. No. 28

Teleplay by **Tony Barwick**

Directed by **Alan Perry**

Captain Black engineers an accident in which the car transporting chief test pilot Major Gravener to Slaton Air Base crashes into a lake. Gravener drowns and is reconstructed as a Mysteron agent, but a pair of doctors recover Gravener's body from the water and connect him to a resuscitator. Gravener is taken to Slaton Hospital where he is placed in a recovery unit and revived two hours later. At Slaton Air Base, Gravener's Mysteron doppelgänger commandeers an XK107 fighter with a live nuclear warhead, but when the authorities learn that the real Gravener is in the hospital, they realise that the pilot of the XK107 is an impostor and block the runway, causing the plane to crash on take-off. Scarlet and Blue visit Gravener at Slaton Hospital and persuade him to find out how the Mysterons intend to carry out their latest threat – by impersonating his Mysteron double!

Notes

Dr. Mitchell is portrayed by a revamp puppet that went on to become Matthew Harding in THE SECRET SERVICE. The puppet was briefly seen as an airline passenger in *Place Of Angels* and can also be seen in four different roles in JOE 90. A montage of footage from *Manhunt* illustrates the Spectrum ground forces closing in on Weston Airstrip.

Oops!

The events of this episode are predominantly set on July 10th, 2068, the same date as the events of *Winged Assassin* and the closing scenes of *Flight To Atlantica* according to dialogue in all three episodes.

Mysteron Threat

"This is the voice of the Mysterons. We know that you can hear us, Earthmen. We intend to deal another devastating blow. We will destroy the world capital Futura City. Futura will be razed to the ground."

Regular Voice Cast

Captain Scarlet	**Francis Matthews**
Captain Blue	**Edward Bishop**
Colonel White	**Donald Gray**
Destiny Angel	**Liz Morgan**
Lieutenant Green	**Cy Grant**
Captain Black	**Donald Gray**
Voice of the Mysterons	**Donald Gray**

Guest Voice Cast

Major Gravener	**Jeremy Wilkin**
Mitchell	**David Healy**
Baxter	**Martin King**
Nurse	**Liz Morgan**
Sergeant	**Gary Files**

First UK Transmission

Friday, February 23rd, 1968
5.25pm (ATV Midlands)

EXPO 2068 — Prod. No. 29

Teleplay by **Shane Rimmer** Directed by **Leo Eaton**

A transporter truck is ferrying a new core reactor to the Manicougan Power Complex when it is diverted by Captain Black on to a route which sends it crashing into a gorge. The driver, his transporter and the core reactor are all reconstructed by the Mysterons. When Spectrum receives the latest Mysteron threat, Scarlet and Blue are dispatched to escort the transporter to the Manicougan Dam, but Black instructs the transporter driver to remove the reactor's thermic safety valve before transferring it to a hi-jacked supply helicopter. A lumberjack witnesses the transfer but he is shot down. Tracking the transporter, Scarlet and Blue find both the injured man and the safety valve, and the reactor project controller confirms that without the valve in place, the temperature of the missing reactor will rise above 200 degrees, causing a nuclear explosion!

Notes

Scenes deleted from the *Expo 2068* script featured Scarlet and Blue collecting SPV 442 from a village store managed by a Spectrum agent wearing a nightgown and baseball cap.

Oops!

There is no explanation as to why Black positions the Seneca helicopter directly above the Expo Tower if the Mysterons' target is the Manicougan Power Complex as suggested by Colonel White. In fact, a vital line of dialogue which was cut from the finished episode would have made it clear that the Mysterons actually planned to "deal a heavy blow to the prestige of the world" by crashing the core reactor into the Expo 2068 site.

Mysteron Threat

"This is the voice of the Mysterons. We know that you can hear us, Earthmen. Disaster will strike the Atlantic seaboard of North America. We will deal a heavy blow to the prestige of the world. We will continue to take our revenge."

Regular Voice Cast

Captain Scarlet	**Francis Matthews**
Captain Blue	**Edward Bishop**
Colonel White	**Donald Gray**
Destiny Angel	**Liz Morgan**
Lieutenant Green	**Cy Grant**
Captain Black	**Donald Gray**
Voice of the Mysterons	**Donald Gray**

Guest Voice Cast

Dr. Sommers	**Jeremy Wilkin**
Raynor	**Neil McCallum**
Driver	**Gary Files**
Captain	**Martin King**
Lumberjack	**Gary Files**
Operator	**Martin King**

First UK Transmission

Tuesday, March 26th, 1968
5.00pm (ATV Midlands)

ATTACK ON CLOUDBASE — Prod. No. 30

Teleplay by **Tony Barwick** Directed by **Ken Turner**

While on routine patrol, Symphony apparently comes under enemy fire. She loses control of her aircraft and is forced to eject, landing in the desert where she collapses and passes out. Then the Mysterons issue a warning that Cloudbase is their next target, so all personnel are placed on red alert and the base is sealed from all external contact. The Angels are recalled while ground forces are mobilised to search for Symphony, but Captain Blue is denied permission to join them. Night falls and Captain Magenta tracks a large UFO which takes up a position 25 miles from Cloudbase. Rhapsody is sent to investigate but as she makes visual contact, her Interceptor is attacked by the spacecraft and she is blown out of the sky. Colonel White realises that there is only one explanation: the Mysterons themselves have come to Earth to annihilate Cloudbase!

Notes

The original script for this episode introduced a new Spectrum agent, Lieutenant Sienna, but he was replaced by Captain Magenta before filming began so as to save on the cost of creating an additional Spectrum uniform. This is the only episode in which no other characters appear apart from all of the regular characters.

Oops!

The Mysteron attack on Cloudbase is revealed to be just a nightmare dreamt by Symphony while she is stranded in the desert, but there is no explanation for what caused the explosion that made her Angel Interceptor crash in the first place.

Mysteron Threat

"This is the voice of the Mysterons. We know that you can hear us, Earthmen. Spectrum's headquarters Cloudbase is our next objective. We will spare no effort to ensure that Cloudbase is totally destroyed."

Regular Voice Cast

Captain Scarlet	**Francis Matthews**
Captain Blue	**Edward Bishop**
Colonel White	**Donald Gray**
Destiny Angel	**Liz Morgan**
Symphony Angel	**Janna Hill**
Lieutenant Green	**Cy Grant**
Captain Magenta	**Gary Files**
Rhapsody Angel	**Liz Morgan**
Voice of the Mysterons	**Donald Gray**

First UK Transmission

Sunday, May 5th, 1968
5.30pm (ATV London)

INFERNO — Prod. No. 31

Teleplay by **Tony Barwick & Shane Rimmer** — Directed by **Alan Perry**

Regular Voice Cast

Captain Scarlet	**Francis Matthews**
Captain Blue	**Edward Bishop**
Colonel White	**Donald Gray**
Destiny Angel	**Liz Morgan**
Symphony Angel	**Janna Hill**
Lieutenant Green	**Cy Grant**
Captain Ochre	**Jeremy Wilkin**
Captain Magenta	**Gary Files**
Rhapsody Angel	**Liz Morgan**
Voice of the Mysterons	**Donald Gray**

Guest Voice Cast

Major Moran	**David Healy**
Pilot	**Shane Rimmer**
Navigator	**Martin King**
Sergeant	**Gary Files**

First UK Transmission

Tuesday, April 16th, 1968
5.00pm (ATV Midlands)

An SKR4 recovery craft is involved in a collision with a meteorite and is totally obliterated, but the craft is reconstructed by the Mysterons. The latest Mysteron threat targets the Najama Complex, a giant de-salination plant in the foothills of the Andes mountains, so Scarlet and Blue are assigned to surveillance duties at an ancient Aztec temple on the rim of the Najama valley overlooking the complex. They note that the complex contains a number of large liquid oxygen tanks and one explosion could start a chain reaction that would turn the whole valley into a blazing inferno. During the night, Captain Black plants a homing device in the mouth of a huge Sun-god statue which dominates the main chamber of the temple. The next morning, the SKR4 is on its final orbital approach but refuses to answer calls from the Euro-Space Tracker Station. Blue realises that the craft is homing in on a transmission from the temple but with only five minutes to go before impact, it will be impossible to locate the transmitter and stop it!

Oops!

When the Angels are launched, Destiny sets off in Angel One and then Harmony and Melody are seen boarding Angels Two and Three, but when they arrive at Najama, Angels Two and Three are piloted by Rhapsody and Symphony. Many of the shots of the Angel Interceptors approaching the temple are flopped, with the Spectrum emblem reversed. After Scarlet reveals that "The statue is the only thing left standing," the next scene shows that this is indeed the case, although only seconds before (in the previous shot) the temple was still mostly intact.

Mysteron Threat

"This is the voice of the Mysterons. We know that you can hear us, Earthmen. It is useless for you to persist in futile attempts to defend yourselves. Our next act of retaliation will be to destroy the complex at Najama. Najama will be destroyed."

THE INQUISITION — Prod. No. 32

Teleplay by **Tony Barwick** — Directed by **Ken Turner**

Regular Voice Cast

Captain Scarlet	**Francis Matthews**
Captain Blue	**Edward Bishop**
Symphony Angel	**Janna Hill**
Lieutenant Green	**Cy Grant**
Voice of the Mysterons	**Donald Gray**

Guest Voice Cast

Colgan	**David Healy**
Waiter	**Gary Files**
Macey	**Charles Tingwell**
1st Policeman	**Paul Maxwell**
3rd Policeman	**Jeremy Wilkin**
2nd Policeman	**Neil McCallum**
Linda Nolan	**Sylvia Anderson**
Frazer	**David Healy**
Shroeder	**Jeremy Wilkin**
Commodore Goddard	**David Healy**
Holt	**Gary Files**

First UK Transmission

Sunday, May 12th, 1968
5.30pm (ATV London)

While dining in a restaurant with Scarlet, Blue starts to feel strange after drinking his coffee. Scarlet goes to fetch their coats, but when he returns to their table, Blue has disappeared. Blue recovers consciousness in the Cloudbase Control Room, where a stranger sitting behind Colonel White's desk introduces himself as Colgan of Spectrum Intelligence. Colgan explains that Blue has been missing for three months and must now prove to his satisfaction that he truly is Captain Blue by revealing the Spectrum cipher codes. Reluctant to disclose top security information, Blue attempts to prove who he is by detailing various Spectrum assignments, but he soon begins to smell a rat.

Notes

Only 11 minutes of new material was filmed for this episode as the remainder comprises excerpts from *Big Ben Strikes Again*, *Crater 101* and *The Trap*. During the *Crater 101* sequence, the continuity of the original episode is altered by the insertion of an additional flashback scene (a flashback within a flashback!) as Scarlet recalls the inscription on Linda Nolan's lucky charm.

Oops!

The General Tiempo revamp puppet appears as three different characters here: a pianist in the framing sequence, Shroeder in the footage from *Crater 101*, and a delegate in the footage from *The Trap*. When Blue makes his escape from the fake Cloudbase, the arm of a puppeteer is visible in two separate shots hurling the puppet through the window.

Mysteron Threat

"This is the voice of the Mysterons. We know that you can hear us, Earthmen. We have observed the Spectrum organisation's attempts to counter us, but one of the members of Spectrum will betray you all. We will be avenged."

JOE 90

Format

In 2012, the World Intelligence Network has united the world's secret services into a vast, single intelligence organisation in the interest of maintaining global peace. Operating primarily from offices in Washington, Moscow and London but with bureaus and offices in every corner of the world manned by the top agents of the CIA, the KGB and MI.5, WIN faces its major opposition in the form of the Eastern Alliance, an ill-organised conglomerate of member states governed by dictatorships and military juntas, but the Network also serves to combat gun-runners, saboteurs, extortionists, power-seeking scientists and fraudulent businessmen.

Nine-year-old Joe McClaine is WIN's Most Special Agent. His father, noted electronics expert Professor Ian 'Mac' McClaine, has developed the BIG RAT (Brain Impulse Galvanascope Record And Transfer), an amazing computer which stores the recorded brain impulses of specialists in a variety of fields and transfers them to Joe, who is then able to draw on the knowledge and experience of the experts whose brain patterns he has received when he wears special glasses with built-in electrodes.

With these brain patterns and the codename Joe 90, Joe carries out dangerous assignments for WIN directed by WIN operatives Sam Loover and Shane Weston. To assist him on his missions, Joe carries a special agent's case with the outward appearance of an ordinary school case but concealing an automatic pistol, a two-way radio-communicator, a WIN agent's badge, the electrode glasses and other items of special equipment, all camouflaged as toys in the event of discovery by the enemy.

The BIG RAT remains a closely guarded secret, known only to Joe, Mac, Sam and Shane. It is hidden in Mac's secret laboratory constructed in ancient sea tunnels beneath his beautiful old Tudor cottage situated on the cliffs of Culver Bay, Dorset. To receive the brain patterns, Joe sits in a chair inside the Rat Trap, a spinning spherical cage, and relaxes with the aid of a Psychedelic Traumascope which prepares Joe's mind for the induction of the recorded electronic impulses.

Mac's favourite mode of transport is his own hand-built Jet Air Car, an amazing vehicle that can travel on land, in the air and on water. With the wheels in the down position and wings fitted into the undercarriage, the vehicle is capable of a maximum road speed of 200 mph, but with the wheels retracted and wings extended, it becomes an aircraft capable of travelling at 300 mph. It can also travel on water at 70 knots.

Production

JOE 90 was something of a departure from the established Gerry Anderson series format, placing much more emphasis on character than hardware, and with stories that were more in the spy thriller genre than science fiction. The puppets created for CAPTAIN SCARLET AND THE MYSTERONS were so lifelike that Anderson felt it was now possible for the characters to carry the action without much assistance from futuristic hardware, and as all of the previous Supermarionation series were receiving constant repeat screenings, it was important for JOE 90 to be a significantly different type of show.

With the puppet crew able to draw on the large cast of revamp puppets constructed for CAPTAIN SCARLET, very few new puppets were created for JOE 90. Although the puppets of Joe, Mac and Mrs. Harris were made especially for the series, Sam Loover and Shane Weston were both revamp puppets that had previously appeared in CAPTAIN SCARLET: the Sam puppet most notably as the Lunar Controller in *Lunarville 7* and Colgan in *The Inquisition*, and the Shane puppet as Dr. Kurnitz in *Dangerous Rendezvous*. In both cases, new heads with a variety of different expressions were created for JOE 90 and the Shane puppet was rewigged, replacing his original blond locks with dark brown hair.

Filming began on Monday, November 13th, 1967 (just a few weeks after principal photography was completed on CAPTAIN SCARLET) and continued until early-August 1968. Gerry Anderson was less hands-on in his role as producer than he had been on the earlier programmes as he was initially supervising post-production on *Thunderbird 6* (1967) and then became closely involved with the live-action feature film *Doppelgänger* (1968), so the role of producer on JOE 90 was entrusted to director David Lane.

Main Characters

Joe McClaine
Nine-year-old adopted son of Professor McClaine and WIN's Most Special Agent

Professor Ian 'Mac' McClaine
Electronics and aerodynamics expert and creator of the BIG RAT computer

Sam Loover
Deputy Head of the WIN London office and close personal friend of Professor McClaine

Shane Weston
WIN Deputy Head and London office Supreme Commander

Mrs. Ada Harris
Housekeeper at Professor McClaine's Culver Bay Cottage

In comparison with its predecessors, JOE 90 received a chequered initial screening on the ITV network in the UK. The series debuted on ATV Midlands and Tyne-Tees at the end of September 1968 and began to appear shortly after in the LWT, Southern and Anglia regions, but it was late November before JOE 90 started in the Harlech and Channel regions and Christmas Day when the series first appeared on Granada (bizarrely starting with *The Unorthodox Shepherd*; *The Most Special Agent* was not screened until several weeks later!). Other regions, notably Yorkshire, did not show the series at all until 13 years later. This was, perhaps, an indication of the shape of things to come for Supermarionation.

Episode Titles

(Listed in production order)

1. **The Most Special Agent**
2. **Hi-Jacked**
3. **Splashdown**
4. **Operation McClaine**
5. **Three's A Crowd**
6. **International Concerto**
7. **Big Fish**
8. **The Unorthodox Shepherd**
9. **Relative Danger**
10. **Business Holiday**
11. **King For A Day**
12. **Double Agent**
13. **Most Special Astronaut**
14. **Arctic Adventure**
15. **The Fortress**
16. **Colonel McClaine**
17. **Project 90**
18. **The Race**
19. **The Professional**
20. **Lone-Handed 90**
21. **Attack Of The Tiger**
22. **Talkdown**
23. **Breakout**
24. **Mission X-41**
25. **Test Flight**
26. **Child Of The Sun God**
27. **Trial At Sea**
28. **See You Down There**
29. **The Birthday**
30. **Viva Cordova**

Episode Running Time

25 minutes approx.

PRODUCTION CREDITS

Produced by **David Lane**
Format by **Gerry** and **Sylvia Anderson**
Production Controller **Desmond Saunders**
Supervising Visual Effects Director **Derek Meddings**
Characters Created by **Sylvia Anderson**
Music Composed and Directed by **Barry Gray**
Lighting Cameraman **Julien Lugrin** *(1, 3, 5, 7, 9, 11, 13, 15, 16, 19, 20, 23, 24, 27-29)*
Paddy Seale *(2, 4, 6, 8, 10, 12, 14, 17, 18, 21, 22, 25, 26, 30)*
Art Directors **Gren Nott**
Keith Wilson
Camera Operator **Derek Black** *(1, 3, 5, 7, 9, 11, 13, 15, 16, 19, 20, 23, 24, 27-29)*
Peter Nash *(2, 4)*
Ian Vinson *(6, 8, 10, 12, 14, 17, 18, 21, 22, 25, 26, 30)*
Script Editor **Tony Barwick**
Supervising Film Editor **Len Walter** *(1-23)*
Alan Killick *(24-30)*
Supervising Sound Editor **John Peverill**
Production Manager **Frank Hollands**
Puppet Co-ordinator **Mary Turner**
Puppet Supervisor **Christine Glanville** *(1-4)*
Visual Effects Production Manager **John Jelly** *(1, 3, 5-30)*
Puppet Operators **Christine Glanville** *(5, 7, 9, 11, 13, 15, 16, 19, 20, 23, 24, 27-29)*
Mel Cross *(1-15, 17, 18)*
Peter Johns *(1, 2, 4, 6, 8, 10, 12)*
Wanda Webb *(2, 4, 6, 8, 10, 12, 14, 17, 18, 21, 22, 25, 26, 30)*
Jan King *(3, 5, 7, 9, 11, 13, 15, 16, 19, 20, 23, 24, 27-29)*
Rowena White *(21, 22, 25, 26, 30)*
Charmaine Wood *(21-30)*
Sculptors **Tim Cooksey**
Plugg Shutt
Terry Curtis*
Wardrobe **Iris Richens**

VISUAL EFFECTS – MAIN UNIT
Director **Jimmy Elliott** *(1, 3)*
Shaun Whittacker-Cook *(2, 4, 6, 9, 10, 12, 14, 17, 19, 21, 22, 24, 25, 26, 30)*
Bill Camp *(5, 7, 8, 11, 13, 15, 16, 18, 20, 23, 27-29)*
Lighting Cameraman
Bert Mason *(1, 3, 5, 7, 8)*
Harry Oakes *(2, 4, 6, 9, 10, 12, 14, 17)*
Les Paul *(11, 13, 15, 16, 18, 20, 23, 27-29)*
Eric Cross *(19, 21, 22, 24, 25, 26, 30)*
Camera Operator **Nick Procopides** *(1, 3, 5, 7, 8, 11, 13, 15, 16, 18, 20, 23, 27-29)*
Ted Cutlack *(2, 4, 6, 9, 10, 12, 14, 17, 19, 21, 22, 24, 25, 26, 30)*

VISUAL EFFECTS – 2nd UNIT
Director **Peter Wragg** *(1-13)*
Alan Berry *(14-30)*
Lighting Cameraman **Ted Wooldridge**
Camera Operator **Noel Rowlands**

Senior Visual Effects Director **Jimmy Elliott** *(2, 4, 5-30)*
Designer **Mike Trim**
Models **Ray Brown** *(1-7)*
Peter Aston *(8-30)*
Alan Shubrook*, **Brian Smithies***
BIG RAT by **Century 21 Film Props**
Film Editor **Harry MacDonald** *(1, 3, 8)*
Bob Dearberg *(2, 4, 7)*
Len Cleal *(5, 10, 12, 13, 15, 18, 19, 23, 25, 27, 29)*
Alan Killick *(6, 9, 11, 14, 16, 17, 20, 21, 22)*
Norman A. Cole *(24, 26, 28, 30)*
Assistant Director **Peter Anderson** *(1)*
Ian Spurrier *(2, 5, 8, 11, 14, 17, 20, 23)*
Brian Heard *(3, 6, 9, 12, 15, 18, 21, 24)*
Antony Bell *(4, 7, 10, 13, 16, 19, 22, 25, 26)*
Tony Harding *(27)*
John Jelly *(28, 29)*
Geoff Pitman *(30)*
Dialogue Synchronisation **Antony Bell** *(1)*
James Cowan *(2, 4, 6, 8, 10, 12, 14, 17-19, 22, 28-30)*
John Drake *(3, 5, 7, 9, 11, 13, 15, 16, 20, 21, 23-27)*
Property Master **Peter Holmes**
Sound Editor **John Beaton** *(1)*
Alan Killick *(2)*
Peter Pennell *(3-24, 26, 28, 29)*
Tony Roper *(25, 27, 30)*
Music Editor **George Randall**
Dialogue Editor **Don Brill** *(1-13)*
Peter Dobson *(14-30)*
Sound Re-recording **Anvil Films Ltd.**
Character Voices **Keith Alexander**
Sylvia Anderson
Rupert Davies
Gary Files
David Healy
Len Jones
Martin King
Liz Morgan*
Shane Rimmer*
Jeremy Wilkin
Executive Producer **Reg Hill**

An ITC World Wide Distribution
Filmed in Supermarionation
A Gerry Anderson
Century 21 Television Production

* uncredited

THE MOST SPECIAL AGENT — Prod. No. 01

Teleplay by **Gerry & Sylvia Anderson** Directed by **Desmond Saunders**

Professor Ian 'Mac' McClaine gives a demonstration of his revolutionary BIG RAT computer to his friend Sam Loover of the World Intelligence Network. Impressed by the computer's abilities to transfer Mac's knowledge and experience to his son Joe, Loover invites the McClaines to WIN HQ in London. There, WIN chief Shane Weston proposes to buy the BIG RAT and recruit Joe as WIN's Most Special Agent. By way of example, he outlines a scenario in which Joe might use the brain patterns of a Russian pilot to steal a Mig 242 fighter plane during a display at an airbase in Moscow...

Notes

In the initial draft script for this episode, Joe was to become the CIA's Most Special Agent. An additional scene was filmed for the episode but deleted from the final edit: during their flight to Moscow, Mac explains to Joe why the Soviet authorities have invited Western aviation experts to visit the Mig 242 factory. All that remains of this scene in the finished episode is a brief shot of Mac and Joe on board the plane. The Mig 242s are revamped from CAPTAIN SCARLET's Angel Interceptors. The footage of the destruction of the missile base is taken from the climax of *Thunderbird 6* (1967).

Regular Voice Cast

Joe McClaine	**Len Jones**
Prof. Ian McClaine	**Rupert Davies**
Sam Loover	**Keith Alexander**
Shane Weston	**David Healy**

Guest Voice Cast

Commander	**David Healy**
Director	**Keith Alexander**
Red Leader	**Gary Files**
Guard	**Gary Files**
Manston Controller	**Gary Files**
John Woodburn	**Gary Files**
Russian Pilot	**Keith Alexander**
Farmer	**Gary Files**

First UK Transmission

Sunday, September 29th, 1968
5.30pm (ATV Midlands)

HI-JACKED — Prod. No. 02

Teleplay by **Tony Barwick** Directed by **Alan Perry**

Joe receives the brain pattern of Ed Johnson, one of WIN's top agents, in order to infiltrate the organisation of international gun-runner Mario Coletti. Hiding inside a rifle case, Joe is on board an armaments truck when it is hi-jacked by Coletti's men and taken to a secret underground headquarters. Leaving the truck, Joe explores the complex but trips security sensors which alert Coletti's men. He is captured and taken before Coletti who believes that while the boy appears to be just playing a child's game, he has seen and heard too much of the operation and must be disposed of. Joe is locked in the boot of a car without his special glasses...

Notes

The Hudson Armaments transporter truck was originally seen as the truck ferrying an atomic device through London in the CAPTAIN SCARLET AND THE MYSTERONS episode *Big Ben Strikes Again*. In *The Birthday*, we learn that this was Joe's very first assignment as WIN's Most Special Agent, so *Hi-Jacked* should be seen as episode two (not episode four as it was during the first transmission of the series in 1968). The nearest conurbation to Culver Bay is Weyford – Mac gives his telephone number as Weyford 238.

Regular Voice Cast

Joe McClaine	**Len Jones**
Prof. Ian McClaine	**Rupert Davies**
Sam Loover	**Keith Alexander**

Guest Voice Cast

Mario Coletti	**David Healy**
Ed Johnson	**Martin King**
Gregson	**Keith Alexander**
Davis	**Martin King**
Carter	**Martin King**
Policeman	**Martin King**
Radio	**Keith Alexander**
Police Radio	**David Healy**

First UK Transmission

Sunday, October 20th, 1968
5.30pm (ATV Midlands)

SPLASHDOWN — Prod. No. 03

Teleplay by **Shane Rimmer** Directed by **Leo Eaton**

When the bodies of leading electronics experts Professor Brunowski and Dr. Frank Adams are the only ones not recovered from the wreckage of two fatal air crashes, WIN suspects that the scientists were kidnapped before each plane crashed. To determine how and why, Joe receives the brain patterns of a US Army Air Force test pilot and joins his father on a flight to Istanbul, with Mac acting as bait for the kidnappers. As the plane approaches Athens, hi-jackers knock out the flight crew and force Mac at gun-point into the plane's escape unit. After the escape unit ejects, Joe discovers that the plane is out of control and losing height rapidly. Locking himself in on the flight deck, Joe puts on his special glasses, takes the controls and manages to pull the plane out of the dive, but meanwhile Mac is being taken by speedboat to a rendezvous with a submarine...

Oops!

Tony Barwick is credited as the author of this episode on the end titles, but the script was actually written by Shane Rimmer (the voice of Scott Tracy in THUNDERBIRDS). When the co-pilot is shot by Kramer, the pilot refers to him as Bill, but the co-pilot's name is later revealed to be Frank, while the pilot's name is Bill.

Regular Voice Cast

Joe McClaine	**Len Jones**
Prof. Ian McClaine	**Rupert Davies**
Sam Loover	**Keith Alexander**
Shane Weston	**David Healy**

Guest Voice Cast

Anton	**Keith Alexander**
Kramer	**David Healy**
Captain Barry	**Keith Alexander**
Co-Pilot Frank Casper	**Gary Files**
Stewardess	**Sylvia Anderson**
Mrs. Mary Rose	**Sylvia Anderson**
Watson	**Martin King**
Bates	**David Healy**

First UK Transmission

Sunday, November 24th, 1968
5.30pm (ATV Midlands)

OPERATION McCLAINE — Prod. No. 04

Teleplay by **Gerry Anderson** & **David Lane** — Directed by **Ken Turner**

Specialist brain surgeon Dr. Emil Kados is severely injured when his passenger jet crashes in a storm. Kados is the only surgeon capable of performing a vital operation on Maurice Estoral, one of the world's greatest writers and a Nobel Prize winner, so Joe and Mac fly to Switzerland to record Kados's brain pattern enabling it to be transferred to Joe. In Dr. Kados's absence, Dr. Blakemore has no choice but to proceed with the operation himself, but Mac adopts the brain pattern of a top WIN agent in order to force Blakemore's surgical team to allow Joe to perform the delicate procedure.

Notes

An additional scene was filmed for this episode but deleted from the final edit: after his brain transfer, Mac expresses concerns that it might not work – although Joe's brain is still highly receptive to learning and knowledge, it isn't as easy for Mac to learn at his age. Dr. Sherman is portrayed by the puppet that was previously seen as the World President in CAPTAIN SCARLET AND THE MYSTERONS, while Dr. Blakemore is played by Captain Brown from *The Mysterons*. CAPTAIN SCARLET's Symphony and Rhapsody Angels are also seen here, as a stewardess and nurse respectively.

Regular Voice Cast

Joe McClaine	**Len Jones**
Prof. Ian McClaine	**Rupert Davies**
Sam Loover	**Keith Alexander**

Guest Voice Cast

Dr. Blakemore	**Jeremy Wilkin**
Dr. Sherman	**Keith Alexander**
Dr. Emil Kados	**David Healy**
Maurice Estoral	**Keith Alexander**
Nurse Linda	**Sylvia Anderson**
Nurse John	**Jeremy Wilkin**
Stewardess	**Sylvia Anderson**
Nurse	**Sylvia Anderson**
Tannoy	**Jeremy Wilkin**

First UK Transmission

Sunday, December 15th, 1968
5.30pm (ATV Midlands)

THREE'S A CROWD — Prod. No. 05

Teleplay by **Tony Barwick** — Directed by **Peter Anderson**

When Mac begins to spend time in the company of attractive American reporter Angela Davis, Sam becomes concerned that the security of Project 90 might be compromised. Mac is furious when he learns that Sam is prying into his private life, but Joe tells Sam that there is something about Miss Davis that he doesn't like. Sam secretly records Miss Davis's brain pattern and as soon as the pattern is transferred to Joe, he discovers that Miss Davis is acting as an agent for a foreign power – she intends to break into Mac's laboratory and steal the plans of the BIG RAT!

Notes

Tony Barwick's original title for this episode was 'Think Of A Number'. Mrs. Harris appears briefly in a non-speaking role. The footage of the monorail leaving the station is lifted from the THUNDERBIRDS episode *The Perils Of Penelope*.

Oops!

World Airways Passenger Jet AV21 changes its markings to CV9 whilst in the air, and then back to AV21 when it lands.

Regular Voice Cast

Joe McClaine	**Len Jones**
Prof. Ian McClaine	**Rupert Davies**
Sam Loover	**Keith Alexander**
Shane Weston	**David Healy**

Guest Voice Cast

Angela Davis	**Sylvia Anderson**
Carlson	**David Healy**
Andrews	**Gary Files**
General	**Keith Alexander**
Condemned Man	**Keith Alexander**

First UK Transmission

Sunday, January 19th, 1969
5.30pm (ATV Midlands)

INTERNATIONAL CONCERTO — Prod. No. 06

Teleplay by **Tony Barwick** — Directed by **Alan Perry**

Renowned concert pianist Igor Sladek is also an undercover agent for WIN, but his cover is broken during an international tour after he secretly records vital information about plans for a new military airbase while performing at the Russian embassy. Recognising that his arrest is imminent, Sladek transmits a coded message to WIN just before he is imprisoned by Colonel Malner. However, in order to avoid an international incident, Malner allows Sladek to perform in a scheduled live radio broadcast, so Joe receives Sladek's brain patterns as part of a daring plan to rescue the pianist right in the middle of the recital and enable him to escape across the border before the performance ends.

Notes

A scene in which Colonel Malner and Major Kloss retrieve Sladek's pen from the piano and discover that it is a recording device was filmed for the episode but deleted from the final edit. The footage of Sladek's monorail train is lifted from the CAPTAIN SCARLET episode *Model Spy* while the shot of the Trans American TV Network building is an unused scene filmed for *Thunderbirds Are Go* (1966). The hands seen in the close-up shots of Joe's hands playing the piano belong to composer Barry Gray's son Simon.

Regular Voice Cast

Joe McClaine	**Len Jones**
Prof. Ian McClaine	**Rupert Davies**
Sam Loover	**Keith Alexander**

Guest Voice Cast

Igor Sladek	**Keith Alexander**
Major Kloss	**David Healy**
Colonel Malner	**Jeremy Wilkin**
Senator Casper	**David Healy**
Kelly	**Shane Rimmer**
Diplomat	**Keith Alexander**
Clerk	**Shane Rimmer**
Technician	**Shane Rimmer**

First UK Transmission

Sunday, November 17th, 1968
5.30pm (ATV Midlands)

BIG FISH

Prod. No. 07

Teleplay by **Shane Rimmer** Directed by **Leo Eaton**

Joe takes on the brain pattern of a top aquanaut to recover a U85 advanced two-man atomic submarine that has sunk in hostile Porto Guavan territorial waters. The discovery of the U85 by military dictator Juan Chaves could jeopardise forthcoming free elections in Porto Guava, so Mac and Joe put out to sea in a rented motor launch to give the appearance of an innocent fishing trip. Joe locates the U85 but as he struggles to force open the missile hatch which is his only access to the submarine, his foot becomes trapped in the jaws of a giant clam, while back on the surface Mac is arrested for murder!

Notes

The footage of the McClaines' hotel in Porto Guava is lifted from the THUNDERBIRDS episode *Lord Parker's 'Oliday* where it appeared as the hotel in Monte Bianco.

Oops!

The U85's jammed missile tube is on the starboard side when it sinks, but when Joe dives down to the vessel, the jammed tube is on the port side. As Joe approaches the U85, the markings on the hull are reversed in long shot.

Regular Voice Cast

Joe McClaine	**Len Jones**
Prof. Ian McClaine	**Rupert Davies**
Sam Loover	**Keith Alexander**
Shane Weston	**David Healy**

Guest Voice Cast

Miguel Umberto dos Passos Francesca	**Gary Files**
El Capitain	**David Healy**
Lieutenant	**Keith Alexander**
U85 Captain	**David Healy**
Gardner	**Shane Rimmer**

First UK Transmission

Sunday, December 1st, 1968
5.30pm (ATV Midlands)

THE UNORTHODOX SHEPHERD

Prod. No. 08

Teleplay by **Tony Barwick** Directed by **Ken Turner**

With the brain pattern of a World Bank Vice-President, Joe confirms that a $10 bill paid into a bank by the Reverend Shepherd is a perfect forgery, printed from the original plates which should have been destroyed 17 years ago. Joe, Mac and Sam question Shepherd but the vicar's hearing deficiency makes conversation very difficult. However, Shepherd is feigning deafness and eventually reveals that forgers are holding his verger hostage to guarantee his co-operation while they print their money in the church crypt. To catch the counterfeiters and save the verger's life, Joe becomes the Angel of Vengeance...

Notes

Exteriors and interiors of St. David's Church were filmed on location at the Church of St. Mary the Virgin in Harefield, Buckinghamshire.

Oops!

Clem Mason's tombstone details that he died in 1996, which we are told was 17 years ago. This dates the episode to 2013, contrary to the producers' intentions that the series is set in 1998 (as stated in the JOE 90 writers' guide).

Regular Voice Cast

Joe McClaine	**Len Jones**
Prof. Ian McClaine	**Rupert Davies**
Sam Loover	**Keith Alexander**

Guest Voice Cast

Reverend Joseph Shepherd	**Gary Files**
Mason	**Martin King**
Kline	**David Healy**
Constable Lewis	**Gary Files**

First UK Transmission

Sunday, December 22nd, 1968
5.30pm (ATV Midlands)

RELATIVE DANGER

Prod. No. 09

Teleplay by **Shane Rimmer** Directed by **Peter Anderson**

Sam's father, Dr. Willie Loover, is leading a geological team to search for Uranium 534 in a disused silver mine in the Pueblo Mountains when explosives cause a rock fall and the three men are trapped in the tunnels. Joe receives the brain pattern of a leading underground explorer and flies out to the mine with Sam and Mac to help with the rescue operation. Then Sam reveals that his father needs regular serum injections and by the time the rescue team have drilled down to his position, it will be too late to save him. A small opening at the old mine entrance allows access to the tunnels, so Joe dons his potholing gear and glasses – the rescue operation has now become a Joe 90 mission!

Notes

In Shane Rimmer's script for this episode, Sam explains that Dr. Loover's team are setting up tunnels for rainwater to run off the desert into underground aquifers. Sam also reveals in the script that his father is diabetic, an explanation for Dr. Loover's condition that does not appear in the finished episode. The Colonel White puppet from CAPTAIN SCARLET AND THE MYSTERONS portrays Dr. Loover while his colleague Banning is played by the Captain Ochre puppet.

Regular Voice Cast

Joe McClaine	**Len Jones**
Prof. Ian McClaine	**Rupert Davies**
Sam Loover	**Keith Alexander**
Shane Weston	**David Healy**

Guest Voice Cast

Dr. Willie Loover	**Gary Files**
Banning	**Martin King**
Selkirk	**Gary Files**
Johnson	**Keith Alexander**
Rollins	**David Healy**
Charlie	**Martin King**

First UK Transmission

Sunday, December 8th, 1968
5.30pm (ATV Midlands)

BUSINESS HOLIDAY — Prod. No. 10

Teleplay by **Tony Barwick** Directed by **Alan Perry**

Sam suggests that Joe should adopt the brain pattern of an aquanaut to help him enjoy the vacation that Mac has planned, but he secretly substitutes the brain pattern of a military vehicle expert when Joe gets 'brained up'. Sam also suggests their holiday destination, the coastal resort of Borova where the new government has taken over the World Army Base at Beneleta. The McClaines begin their holiday but after Joe's swimming trunks are stolen, they discover that Sam and Shane have followed them to Borova in an attempt to persuade Joe to take on a mission to destroy Beneleta Base...

Notes

The brain pattern library list seen here includes Major Charles Taylor (*Splashdown*), Dr. Emil Kados (*Operation McClaine*), Igor Sladek (*International Concerto*), Angela Davis (*Three's A Crowd*), Bill Frazer (*Big Fish*) and Clive Brinker (*Relative Danger*).

Oops!

The list gives Bill Frazer's brain pattern number as Q8, but it was Q14 in *Big Fish*. Metallurgist and Optician are both misspelled on the list (as *Metalurgist* and *Opticion*).

Regular Voice Cast

Joe McClaine	**Len Jones**
Prof. Ian McClaine	**Rupert Davies**
Sam Loover	**Keith Alexander**
Shane Weston	**David Healy**

Guest Voice Cast

Colonel Henderson	**Shane Rimmer**
Major	**David Healy**
Lieutenant	**Keith Alexander**
Clerk	**Sylvia Anderson**
Taxi Driver	**Shane Rimmer**
Assistant	**Keith Alexander**

First UK Transmission

Sunday, December 29th, 1968
5.30pm (ATV Midlands)

KING FOR A DAY — Prod. No. 11

Teleplay by **Shane Rimmer** Directed by **Leo Eaton**

The Sultan of Ardaji is murdered by his Regent, Ben Shazar, who then arranges the kidnapping of the Sultan's heir, Prince Kahib, from his school in England. The Regent is empowered to declare himself King if the Prince does not appear in Ardaji for his coronation, so Joe takes on the brain patterns of the Prince's former tutor in order to impersonate the Prince for 24 hours and give WIN time to track down and free the real Prince. Realising that the boy must be an impostor, Ben Shazar attempts to trick Joe into revealing ignorance of the customs of succession, but Joe's impersonation is so good that the Regent comes to believe that he is the real Prince after all and makes plans to have him eliminated...

Notes

Prince Kahib and Joe's impersonation of him are both portrayed by the same duplicate Joe puppet modified with brown skin and black hair, although for its appearances as Kahib the puppet is fitted with a Plasticine appliance to make the nose bigger. The stewardess on the charter jet who questions Joe is portrayed by the Destiny Angel puppet from CAPTAIN SCARLET AND THE MYSTERONS.

Regular Voice Cast

Joe McClaine	**Len Jones**
Prof. Ian McClaine	**Rupert Davies**
Sam Loover	**Keith Alexander**
Shane Weston	**David Healy**

Guest Voice Cast

Ben Shazar	**Gary Files**
Vizier	**Gary Files**
Salim	**Keith Alexander**
Stewardess	**Sylvia Anderson**
Driver	**Gary Files**
Radio	**Keith Alexander**

First UK Transmission

Sunday, November 10th, 1968
5.30pm (ATV Midlands)

DOUBLE AGENT — Prod. No. 12

Teleplay by **Tony Barwick** Directed by **Ken Turner**

After three top WIN couriers are killed, Shane Weston believes that there must be a double agent in the courier department. Joe is given the brain pattern of department head Harry Sloane in order to undertake a vital mission to ferry the new codes and ciphers for the whole of WIN's Eastern Network to Tehran, but when he puts on his special glasses at the airport, Joe tells Mac that he is boarding a flight to Paris instead. Later Joe is reported to be *en route* to Copenhagen, but he slips past WIN agents at the airport and disappears. Then Mac realises that Harry Sloane is the double agent and Joe is using Sloane's brain pattern to track down his contacts, but WIN HQ in Washington has already issued a C48 red priority order to shoot Joe on sight!

Notes

The character of Dr. Newman was originally written as Dr. Nieuwenhoff in Tony Barwick's script. Mac is seen reading a newspaper that previously appeared in the THUNDERBIRDS episode *Edge Of Impact* (the headline on the front cover reads "Red Arrow Test Flight Cancelled"). The establishing shot of the airport is also from THUNDERBIRDS – it is London Airport as seen in *Trapped In The Sky*.

Regular Voice Cast

Joe McClaine	**Len Jones**
Prof. Ian McClaine	**Rupert Davies**
Sam Loover	**Keith Alexander**
Shane Weston	**David Healy**
Mrs. Ada Harris	**Sylvia Anderson**

Guest Voice Cast

Harry Sloane	**Jeremy Wilkin**
Dr. Newman	**Keith Alexander**
Miller	**Jeremy Wilkin**
Sherman	**Keith Alexander**
Courier A14	**Keith Alexander**
Radio Control	**Shane Rimmer**

First UK Transmission

Sunday, January 12th, 1969
5.30pm (ATV Midlands)

MOST SPECIAL ASTRONAUT — Prod. No. 13

Teleplay by **Tony Barwick** Directed by **Peter Anderson**

The failure of two supply rockets leaves astronauts Brodie and Kent trapped aboard an OTC space station with only three days' air supply left, and when the second rocket is destroyed by remote control, debris crashes onto the OTC Astronaut Quarters injuring four astronauts. Joe takes on the brain pattern of one of the injured astronauts while Shane makes arrangements for Joe to pilot a third rocket. Further faults delay the launch, but Joe finally blasts off with less than two hours before the astronauts' air runs out. Brodie and Kent pass out before Joe arrives so they are unable to activate the rendezvous adaptor and docking lights, but Joe refuses to abort the mission and decides to try and complete the difficult docking manoeuvre without assistance...

Oops!

Although the letters 'OTC' are clearly marked on the outside of the space station, the characters constantly refer to the company as "OCT". This inconsistency originated in Tony Barwick's script where the first page details that OTC is an abbreviation for the Orbital Telecommunications Company, but this abbreviation is then erroneously typed as 'OCT' throughout the rest of the script.

Regular Voice Cast

Joe McClaine	**Len Jones**
Prof. Ian McClaine	**Rupert Davies**
Sam Loover	**Keith Alexander**
Shane Weston	**David Healy**

Guest Voice Cast

Dr. Nagel	**Gary Files**
Kent	**Shane Rimmer**
Brodie	**David Healy**
Crawford	**Jeremy Wilkin**
Dobson	**Gary Files**
Astronaut	**Gary Files**

First UK Transmission

Sunday, October 6th, 1968
5.30pm (ATV Midlands)

ARCTIC ADVENTURE — Prod. No. 14

Teleplay by **Tony Barwick** Directed by **Alan Perry**

A World Air Force bomber strays off course in a storm and crashes in Eastern Sector territory in the Arctic Circle. Three of the bomber's nuclear devices are recovered but the fourth is missing under the pack ice. Dr. Kelvin is the only man with the knowledge and ability to recover the device but he is too old to participate in the mission, so Joe receives his brain pattern and sets out in a mini-sub to locate the device. He finds it lodged amongst rocks close to the Eastern Alliance Vostula underwater research centre, but as he attempts to dislodge it, he is detected by Vostula operatives and base commander Colonel Kovac dispatches a pair of U18 killer submarines with orders to seek and destroy!

Notes

The working title of this episode was 'The Search'. Mac is again seen reading the newspaper with the "Red Arrow Test Flight Cancelled" headline from the THUNDERBIRDS episode *Edge Of Impact*. The underwater theme composed by Barry Gray for this episode later became Arra's theme in the SPACE:1999 episode *Collision Course*. Part of the underwater section of Vostula Base incorporates the London Car-Vu from the CAPTAIN SCARLET AND THE MYSTERONS episode *The Mysterons*.

Regular Voice Cast

Joe McClaine	**Len Jones**
Prof. Ian McClaine	**Rupert Davies**
Sam Loover	**Keith Alexander**
Shane Weston	**David Healy**
Mrs. Ada Harris	**Sylvia Anderson**

Guest Voice Cast

Commander Kovac	**David Healy**
Dr. William Kelvin	**Gary Files**
B107 Pilot	**Gary Files**
B107 Co-Pilot Hal	**Jeremy Wilkin**
1st Russian	**Gary Files**
2nd Russian	**Jeremy Wilkin**
Captain	**Keith Alexander**

First UK Transmission

Sunday, January 5th, 1969
5.30pm (ATV Midlands)

THE FORTRESS — Prod. No. 15

Teleplay by **Shane Rimmer** Directed by **Leo Eaton**

WIN agent Roger Fleming is captured in Santa Marina, South America by Captain Trang and his soldiers. The agent is imprisoned in a virtually unapproachable fortress and interrogated to reveal the whereabouts of top secret microfilm that he managed to hide before he was detained. Joe receives the brain pattern of Fleming's WIN colleague Mike Laramie and negotiates the Lareno River on a compact hovercraft which enables him to clear the river mines around the fortress. He penetrates the fortress and locates Fleming, but when Fleming insists on telling him the location of the microfilm in case one of them is unable to escape, Trang overhears and takes a motor launch to recover the microfilm. Joe and Fleming shoot their way out of the fortress and set off in desperate pursuit...

Notes

Deleted scenes in the original script feature Joe, Mac and Sam being fired upon in the helijet by auto-rocket batteries as they make their way to the boat house on the Lareno River, and the race to the microfilm coming to an end when both vehicles negotiate a sudden bend in the river and Trang's launch crashes into an islet. One of the soldiers at the fortress is portrayed by the Captain Magenta puppet from CAPTAIN SCARLET.

Regular Voice Cast

Joe McClaine	**Len Jones**
Prof. Ian McClaine	**Rupert Davies**
Sam Loover	**Keith Alexander**
Shane Weston	**David Healy**

Guest Voice Cast

Roger Fleming	**Gary Files**
Trang	**David Healy**
Mike Laramie	**Keith Alexander**
Lieutenant	**Keith Alexander**
Soldier	**Keith Alexander**
Soldier Voice	**Gary Files**

First UK Transmission

Sunday, November 3rd, 1968
5.30pm (ATV Midlands)

COLONEL McCLAINE

Prod. No. 16

Teleplay by **Tony Barwick** — Directed by **Ken Turner**

Helijets ferrying supplies of highly volatile U114 liquid explosives to the construction site of the new Kuchunga tunnel are being sabotaged *en route*, so Joe receives the brain patterns of an explosives expert and a top Army driver in order to lead a convoy of three transporter trucks 200 miles overland to the Kuchinga mountains. With the rank of Colonel, Joe takes charge of the convoy, braving sand-storms, river crossings and a heavy rainstorm that causes a landslide, blocking the road into the mountains. Two of the trucks are lost while attempting to winch them up the mountainside and then, as Joe drives the last truck on the final leg of the journey through the mountains, Sam discovers that the U114 containers have been fixed to detonate when they rise above 5,000 feet!

Notes

Deleted scenes filmed for the episode included the dangerous operation of injecting U114 into bore holes in the Kuchunga tunnel wall, and the engineers explaining that U114 is the only explosive that will destroy 1000 feet of tunnel with a single blast. Other scenes dropped from the script featured Joe test-driving the truck at a World Army Base under the watchful eye of a Colonel who does not know that the driver is a nine-year-old boy.

Regular Voice Cast

Joe McClaine	**Len Jones**
Prof. Ian McClaine	**Rupert Davies**
Sam Loover	**Keith Alexander**
Shane Weston	**David Healy**

Guest Voice Cast

Private Johnson	**Keith Alexander**
Lieutenant Pierce	**Keith Alexander**
Sergeant	**Gary Files**
King	**Keith Alexander**
Kopal	**Gary Files**
Preston	**Gary Files**
Radio	**Keith Alexander**

First UK Transmission

Sunday, October 27th, 1968
5.30pm (ATV Midlands)

PROJECT 90

Prod. No. 17

Teleplay by **Tony Barwick** — Directed by **Peter Anderson**

Dr. Conrad Darota runs an international espionage ring from the cover of his Darota Clinic high in the Swiss Alps. Surveillance of WIN HQ has revealed the existence of WIN File 90 and Darota is determined to discover the secrets of the BIG RAT, so he arranges to kidnap Mac and imprison him in the clinic until he reveals the computer's function. He is surprised when Mac proves quite willing to talk about his invention, but Darota doesn't believe him when he tells how the BIG RAT is used to transfer brain patterns to his nine-year-old son. What Darota doesn't know is that Sam and Shane have been tracking his every move and now, with his father's brain patterns giving him the knowledge and experience of a top balloonist, Joe is already on his way to rescue Mac, travelling to the clinic by hot air balloon...

Notes

An establishing shot of Kurson's boat in Culver Bay shows the back of Mac's cottage (the chimney is on the left of the building) on the cliffs above, illustrating how close to the sea the cottage is situated. As this is the Dorset coast, the cottage faces north while the back of the house has a view of the English Channel.

Regular Voice Cast

Joe McClaine	**Len Jones**
Prof. Ian McClaine	**Rupert Davies**
Sam Loover	**Keith Alexander**
Shane Weston	**David Healy**

Guest Voice Cast

Dr. Conrad Darota	**Jeremy Wilkin**
Kurson	**Keith Alexander**
Agent	**David Healy**
Receptionist	**David Healy**
Secretary	**Jeremy Wilkin**
Driver	**Jeremy Wilkin**

First UK Transmission

Sunday, October 13th, 1968
5.30pm (ATV Midlands)

THE RACE

Prod. No. 18

Teleplay by **Tony Barwick** — Directed by **Alan Perry**

Joe receives Mac's brain pattern in an experiment to see if the BIG RAT also transfers the pattern of the subconscious, and when Joe goes to sleep wearing his special glasses, he has the same dream as his father. In the dream, Shane Weston accepts a challenge from General Tempest of the World Army to test the initiative, speed and endurance of their respective organisations with an extended paper chase from London to Monte Carlo. Tempest recruits a ringer as the driver of his U87 vehicle, but Joe adopts the brain pattern of a Monte Carlo rally driver to lead the WIN team in Mac's Jet Air Car. As the two vehicles race to the coast, it soon becomes apparent that Tempest will stop at nothing to ensure victory over the WIN team...

Notes

The opening scenes with Joe and Mac did not originally form part of Tony Barwick's script. Instead, the episode began with Shane Weston and General Tempest at WIN HQ. Lieutenant Burns is portrayed by the puppet that previously appeared as Captain Grey in CAPTAIN SCARLET AND THE MYSTERONS. The French Officer is played by Grey's Spectrum colleague Captain Magenta.

Regular Voice Cast

Joe McClaine	**Len Jones**
Prof. Ian McClaine	**Rupert Davies**
Sam Loover	**Keith Alexander**
Shane Weston	**David Healy**

Guest Voice Cast

General Tempest	**Jeremy Wilkin**
Private Cloony	**Gary Files**
Lieutenant Burns	**Keith Alexander**
Colonel	**Jeremy Wilkin**
French Officer	**David Healy**

First UK Transmission

Sunday, February 2nd, 1969
5.30pm (ATV Midlands)

THE PROFESSIONAL — Prod. No. 19

Teleplay by **Donald James** — Directed by **Leo Eaton**

The new military dictatorship of a middle-European country refuses to return a $10 million grant for a hospital building programme to the Kramer Foundation, after Foundation chairman Hugo Waddington learns that the money is being spent by General Heppel on developing Spider riot control vehicles. Prototype Spider vehicles guard the remaining portion of the grant secured in Langallo Castle, so Joe takes on the brain pattern of a professional safe-breaker to penetrate the castle, armed with a proton lance which fries the Spiders' circuity. Joe locates the castle vault and breaks into it to recover the Foundation's gold but as he makes his escape, Heppel issues a full security alert and multiple Spiders close in on Joe's position...

Oops!

Mac tells Joe that they will move in on the castle as soon as it gets dark, but when they synchronise their watches just before Joe sets off it is 0131 hours. It isn't clear why the countryside starts exploding beneath the Jet Air Car as Mac and Joe make their escape: the script details that this is the conventional weaponry of Heppel's army being trained on the vehicle, but there is no dialogue to explain this to viewers.

Regular Voice Cast

Joe McClaine	**Len Jones**
Prof. Ian McClaine	**Rupert Davies**
Sam Loover	**Keith Alexander**
Shane Weston	**David Healy**

Guest Voice Cast

General Heppel	**Jeremy Wilkin**
Hugo Waddington	**Gary Files**
Engineer	**Gary Files**
Scientist	**Keith Alexander**
Henry Summerfield	**Jeremy Wilkin**
Warder	**Gary Files**
1st Guard	**Gary Files**
2nd Guard	**Jeremy Wilkin**

First UK Transmission

Sunday, January 26th, 1969
5.30pm (ATV Midlands)

LONE-HANDED 90 — Prod. No. 20

Teleplay by **Desmond Saunders** & **Keith Wilson** — Directed by **Ken Turner**

A breakdown has put the BIG RAT out of service and while Mac, Sam and Shane argue about how long it will take to repair, Joe falls asleep in front of the television. In his dream, Mac, Sam and Shane are the members of the notorious WIN Gang, who stage a robbery at the bank in Spoke City and then head for Joesville where they plot the theft of a consignment of gold from the mail train at Altuna. After a shoot-out in the saloon of the Palace Hotel, Sheriff Joe arrests the trio and imprisons them in the town jail, but while he is away dealing with trouble at the Cripple Creek rodeo, the gang stage a break-out...

Notes

The incidental music on Joe's TV programme was composed for the THUNDERBIRDS episode *Trapped In The Sky*. The pianist and barmaid in the saloon are named Gerry and Sylvia respectively.

Oops!

Joe sees Shane as a cowboy and a sign for Joesville on his television programme *before* he falls asleep.

Regular Voice Cast

Joe McClaine	**Len Jones**
Prof. Ian McClaine	**Rupert Davies**
Sam Loover	**Keith Alexander**
Shane Weston	**David Healy**

Guest Voice Cast

Doc	**Gary Files**
Bank Teller	**Gary Files**
Slim	**Jeremy Wilkin**
Hank	**Gary Files**
Barman	**Jeremy Wilkin**
Sylv	**Sylvia Anderson**

First UK Transmission

Sunday, March 9th, 1969
5.30pm (ATV Midlands)

ATTACK OF THE TIGER — Prod. No. 21

Teleplay by **Tony Barwick** — Directed by **Peter Anderson**

A top WIN agent discovers that the Eastern Alliance has completed work on a secret rocket base hidden inside a cliff face which will be used to put a nuclear device into Earth orbit in 10 days' time, thereby holding the world to ransom. Joe adopts the brain patterns of an Eastern Alliance defence expert and a top World Air Force pilot to fly the VG 104, the WAF's fastest, most heavily armed fighter bomber, on a dangerous mission to destroy the base. The rocket is already fuelled and ready for launch as Joe approaches the base, but the Alliance targets the VG 104 with ground-to-air missiles...

Notes

The incidental music for this episode draws heavily on material originally composed for SUPERCAR, STINGRAY and THUNDERBIRDS. The Eastern Alliance theme which is heard throughout was originally composed for the SUPERCAR episode *The Talisman Of Sargon*.

Oops!

The Eastern Alliance soldiers wear the same motif on their caps as the World Army officers seen in *Colonel McClaine*.

Regular Voice Cast

Joe McClaine	**Len Jones**
Prof. Ian McClaine	**Rupert Davies**
Sam Loover	**Keith Alexander**
Shane Weston	**David Healy**

Guest Voice Cast

Agent 26 ('Fez')	**Gary Files**
General	**Jeremy Wilkin**
Officer	**Jeremy Wilkin**
Lieutenant	**Jeremy Wilkin**
Private	**Gary Files**
Fearless Foley	**Gary Files**
Control	**Gary Files**
Tanker	**Jeremy Wilkin**

First UK Transmission

Sunday, March 16th, 1969
5.30pm (ATV Midlands)

TALKDOWN — Prod. No. 22

Teleplay by **Tony Barwick** Directed by **Alan Perry**

Regular Voice Cast	
Joe McClaine	**Len Jones**
Prof. Ian McClaine	**Rupert Davies**
Sam Loover	**Keith Alexander**
Shane Weston	**David Healy**

Guest Voice Cast	
Jim Grant	**Gary Files**
Flight Controller Colman	**David Healy**
Doctor	**Keith Alexander**
General	**Gary Files**
Operator	**Gary Files**

First UK Transmission

Sunday, February 9th, 1969
5.30pm (ATV Midlands)

Top test pilot Jim Grant runs into difficulty as he attempts to land the experimental F116 hypersonic fighter jet. He manages to eject just before the plane crashes and later blames the problem on an electrical failure. A second prototype plane is checked and prepared for a presentation to the World Air Force top brass, but with Grant injured with a broken foot and unable to fly the plane, Joe adopts his brain pattern and flies the F116 during the demonstration. Then Sam and Mac learn that Grant suffered a mental blackout during his test flight which caused him to forget the F116 landing procedure, and as his brain pattern was recorded after the blackout, Joe has no knowledge of how to land the plane!

Notes

The revamp puppet that portrays Jim Grant was first seen as Major Brooks in the CAPTAIN SCARLET AND THE MYSTERONS episode *Point 783* and also appeared as Commodore Goddard in *The Trap*. This episode is the puppet's last JOE 90 appearance, having previously taken the roles of the condemned man in *Three's A Crowd*, Dr. Newman in *Double Agent*, Roger Fleming in *The Fortress*, General Tempest in *The Race* and the Air Force General in *Attack Of The Tiger*.

BREAKOUT — Prod. No. 23

Teleplay by **Shane Rimmer** Directed by **Leo Eaton**

Regular Voice Cast	
Joe McClaine	**Len Jones**
Prof. Ian McClaine	**Rupert Davies**

Guest Voice Cast	
Captain Pat Moran	**Gary Files**
Real	**David Healy**
Marney	**Keith Alexander**
Prime Minister MacCormack	**Keith Alexander**
Guard Eddie	**Gary Files**
Robbins	**Gary Files**
Warden	**David Healy**
Guard Pierre	**Gary Files**
Gun Captain	**Keith Alexander**

First UK Transmission

Sunday, February 16th, 1969
5.30pm (ATV Midlands)

As preparations are being made for a ceremonial gun salute in honour of Canadian Prime Minister MacCormack, a pair of convicts, Real and Marney, escape from a work detail and overpower the soldiers manning the gun on Monument Hill. They target the opposite ends of a railway bridge just as MacCormack's monotrain is crossing, trapping the train on the remaining middle section. Contacting Captain Moran of the Royal Canadian Mounted Police at Fort Cherook, the convicts threaten to shell the train unless their ransom demands for a helijet and a million dollars are met. Mac and Joe are holidaying with Moran at Fort Cherook and Joe offers to act as the ransom courier, confident that he has the necessary abilities to capture the convicts even though his special glasses only enable him to access the brain pattern of an Olympic bob sleigh champion...

Notes

The Cherook Penitentiary truck model was previously seen as one of the transporter trucks in *Colonel McClaine*, but is painted red for its appearance here. Cherook Penitentiary itself previously appeared as Langallo Castle in *The Professional*. Prime Minister McCormack is portrayed by the World President puppet from CAPTAIN SCARLET.

MISSION X-41 — Prod. No. 24

Teleplay by **Pat Dunlop** Directed by **Ken Turner**

Regular Voice Cast	
Joe McClaine	**Len Jones**
Prof. Ian McClaine	**Rupert Davies**
Sam Loover	**Keith Alexander**
Shane Weston	**David Healy**

Guest Voice Cast	
General Kwan	**Jeremy Wilkin**
Dr. Chang	**Gary Files**
Professor Baxter	**Gary Files**
Hawkins	**Keith Alexander**
Doctor	**Jeremy Wilkin**
Agent 84	**Gary Files**
Pilot	**David Healy**

First UK Transmission

Sunday, March 30th, 1969
5.30pm (ATV Midlands)

The Eastern Alliance has succeeded in isolating X-41, a virus that breaks down the molecular structure of everything it touches. WIN scientist Professor Baxter is searching for an antibody when he is infected by the virus and collapses, so the only hope of obtaining the antibody is to steal the formula from Dr. Chan's laboratory at an Eastern Alliance base. Joe is given the brain patterns of Professor Baxter and a top WIN agent and then dropped near the base in a pressurised canister, but he is captured by guards and taken before the base commander General Kwan...

Notes

The original title of Pat Dunlop's script was 'Mission X-14'. Captain Ochre from CAPTAIN SCARLET plays Agent 84 while Captain Grey is Baxter's assistant Hawkins.

Oops!

The pilot of the transport jet tells Sam to eject the canister on the red light, but Sam has only green and yellow lights on his control panel and he pulls the eject lever when the yellow one lights up.

TEST FLIGHT — Prod. No. 25

Teleplay by **Donald James** Directed by **Peter Anderson**

During the test flight of a new Orbital Glide Transport plane, a fault develops in the motors and the plane crashes onto the Launch Control building, trapping the flight controller Dr. Slade inside along with a concealed monitoring computer that will reveal whether the fault was due to a design flaw or sabotage. The rescue drill can only cut a bore hole that is not wide enough for a man, but Joe *can* fit through so he receives the brain pattern of project controller Brad Johnson and descends into the Launch Control building to rescue Slade and recover the computer. However, once inside, he discovers that it is Slade himself who has sabotaged the project...

Notes

Donald James's script details that the OGT Test Base is located in Cornwall.

Oops!

There are three launch control operators, all of whom are reported to be injured in the OGT crash, but only two are seen using the escape capsule. In Shane's office, Sam and Mac both refer to the OGT as "OGC" due to typing errors in the script.

Regular Voice Cast

Joe McClaine	**Len Jones**
Prof. Ian McClaine	**Rupert Davies**
Sam Loover	**Keith Alexander**
Shane Weston	**David Healy**

Guest Voice Cast

Brad Johnson	**Jeremy Wilkin**
Dr. Slade	**Gary Files**
Engineer	**Keith Alexander**
1st Operator	**Keith Alexander**
2nd Operator	**Gary Files**
3rd Operator	**David Healy**
Countdown	**Jeremy Wilkin**

First UK Transmission

Sunday, April 6th, 1969
5.30pm (ATV Midlands)

CHILD OF THE SUN GOD — Prod. No. 26

Teleplay by **John Lucarotti** Directed by **Alan Perry**

Four world leaders are struck down within 24 hours by the same type of poison-tipped dart which archaeologist Dr. Aston identifies as originating with the supposedly extinct Amaztec Indians of South America. Aston surmises that the Amaztec culture has been revived at an old Amaztec temple in the foothills of the Andes, so Joe adopts Aston's brain pattern to go in search of an antidote for the poison. Joe lands by parachute near the temple, but a ruthless extortionist who has set himself up as the high priest of Huitzilopoctli encourages the Amaztecs to capture Joe and offer him as a sacrifice to the God of Darkness...

Notes

The scene in which Ataka brings the bowl of poison as an offering to Huitzilopoctli was originally shot as the opening of the episode, but was repositioned during post-production. A scene filmed for the episode but deleted from the final edit featured Joe in Amaztec dress masquerading as the Child of the Sun God to tell the Indians that Quetzalcoatl brings them peace and happiness. This would have appeared between the death of the High Priest and the closing scene in Shane's office.

Regular Voice Cast

Joe McClaine	**Len Jones**
Prof. Ian McClaine	**Rupert Davies**
Sam Loover	**Keith Alexander**
Shane Weston	**David Healy**

Guest Voice Cast

High Priest	**David Healy**
Dr. Aston	**Jeremy Wilkin**
Ataka	**Jeremy Wilkin**
Proctl	**Gary Files**
President	**Keith Alexander**
Servant	**Gary Files**
Amaztec Warrior	**Jeremy Wilkin**

First UK Transmission

Sunday, February 23rd, 1969
5.30pm (ATV Midlands)

TRIAL AT SEA — Prod. No. 27

Teleplay by **Donald James** Directed by **Brian Heard**

A bomb explodes on the dockside during preparations for the maiden voyage of the hoverliner *HL Friendship*, but shipping company president Sir George Harris refuses to postpone the launch. With a hundred VIPs among the passengers, WIN takes charge of security and Shane joins the voyage to New York, but as the hoverliner reaches mid-Atlantic, Sir George receives a second bomb threat. The culprit, Johnston Webb, is tracked down using WIN's voice print analysis computer and when Joe receives Webb's brain pattern he is able to confirm that there *is* a bomb on board the hoverliner, concealed inside a presentation model and fitted with a motion-sensitive detonator!

Notes

The Colonel White puppet from CAPTAIN SCARLET AND THE MYSTERONS appears as Sir George Harris, while his Spectrum colleague Dr. Fawn appears as a photographer.

Oops!

Joe refers to the hoverliner as the *SS Friendship* but the markings on the crew uniforms and the base of the presentation model give the name as the *HL Friendship*.

Regular Voice Cast

Joe McClaine	**Len Jones**
Prof. Ian McClaine	**Rupert Davies**
Sam Loover	**Keith Alexander**
Shane Weston	**David Healy**

Guest Voice Cast

Sir George Harris	**Jeremy Wilkin**
Johnston Webb	**Gary Files**
Jack Cope	**Gary Files**
Captain	**Jeremy Wilkin**
Miller	**Gary Files**
Launch Controller	**Keith Alexander**
WIN Pager	**Gary Files**

First UK Transmission

Saturday, April 5th, 1969
5.30pm (ATV London)

SEE YOU DOWN THERE

Prod. No. 28

Teleplay by **Tony Barwick** Directed by **Leo Eaton**

With the brain pattern of a financial expert, Joe discovers that Clayton Enterprises is manipulating share prices to engineer take-overs of small businesses. One of the companies affected by the fraud supplies specialised components to WIN, so the Project 90 team embark on a plan to convince managing director Ralph Clayton that he has swallowed a hallucinogenic drug and will only receive the antidote if he calls off his next take-over. Joe adopts the brain patterns of a jazz trumpeter, a power-pack specialist and the world's leading mimic to persuade Clayton that the drug is taking effect...

Notes

Joe is seen reading a copy of *TV21* issue 183 (with the headline "Scarlet Captured"). Ralph Clayton is portrayed by the Colonel White puppet from Captain Scarlet And The Mysterons. Clayton's meeting with Harris was originally intended to appear immediately after the scene in Shane's office but was repositioned during post-production (the scene with Mac arriving in Clayton's office as the new tea boy is actually the end of that sequence). The 'see you down there' phrase and hand signal is a pastiche of the 'be seeing you' farewell from the 1967 ITC series The Prisoner.

Regular Voice Cast

Joe McClaine	**Len Jones**
Prof. Ian McClaine	**Rupert Davies**
Sam Loover	**Keith Alexander**
Shane Weston	**David Healy**

Guest Voice Cast

Ralph Clayton	**Jeremy Wilkin**
Jim Molineaux	**Gary Files**
Stewart	**Keith Alexander**
Harris	**Gary Files**
Doorman	**Keith Alexander**
TV Commentator	**Keith Alexander**

First UK Transmission

Sunday, February 23rd, 1969
5.30pm (Anglia)

THE BIRTHDAY

Prod. No. 29

Teleplay by **Tony Barwick** Directed by **Leo Eaton**

It is Joe's tenth birthday, but he is bitterly disappointed when his father leaves the cottage first thing in the morning and then Mrs. Harris tells him that he hasn't received any cards. It seems that everyone has forgotten his birthday, but later he finds that Mac, Sam and Shane have laid on a special surprise birthday tea. The group recall Joe's most memorable assignments of his first year as WIN's Most Special Agent, including the mission to locate the headquarters of Mario Coletti's illegal arms export organisation and the expedition to transport U114 to the construction site of the Kuchunga tunnel.

Notes

This episode features only four minutes of new material as the remaining 18½ minutes comprise footage from *The Most Special Agent*, *Hi-Jacked* and *Colonel McClaine*. Tony Barwick's script also included a flashback sequence recalling Joe's dream in *Lone-Handed 90*. The calendar by Joe's bedside marks his birthday as the 7th of an unnamed month which has 31 days and follows a 31-day month. The condition of the trees outside suggests August rather than January, although this conflicts with the official promotional information for the series which lists Joe's birthdate as April 1st.

Regular Voice Cast

Joe McClaine	**Len Jones**
Prof. Ian McClaine	**Rupert Davies**
Sam Loover	**Keith Alexander**
Shane Weston	**David Healy**
Mrs. Ada Harris	**Sylvia Anderson**

Guest Voice Cast

Guard	**Gary Files**
Red Leader	**Gary Files**
Gregson	**Keith Alexander**
Carter	**Martin King**
Mario Coletti	**David Healy**
Private Johnson	**Keith Alexander**
Sergeant	**Gary Files**

First UK Transmission

Sunday, April 20th, 1969
5.30pm (ATV Midlands)

VIVA CORDOVA

Prod. No. 30

Teleplay by **Tony Barwick** Directed by **Peter Anderson**

After a failed attempt on the life of Juan Cordova, the new democratically elected President of a South American state, his wife Dorina contacts WIN to arrange security for him. Cordova refuses to accept any kind of conventional bodyguard, so Joe receives the brain pattern of a top WIN agent to masquerade as Dorina Cordova's cousin visiting from England. He accompanies Cordova and his wife on a car journey to a ski resort in the mountains, unaware that Cordova's opponent General Valdes has arranged an ambush. Following in a helijet, Mac and Sam spot the roadblock ahead and warn Joe, but Cordova's driver Garancia suddenly jumps out, leaving the car speeding out of control...

Notes

General Valdes is portrayed by the Captain Black puppet from Captain Scarlet And The Mysterons while various Spectrum personnel also appear as onlookers at the election (Captain Grey and Dr. Fawn), Valdes's truck driver (Captain Ochre) and one of Valdes's frogmen (Dr. Fawn again). A scene filmed for the climax of the episode but deleted from the final edit featured General Valdes attempting to escape through the bushes but being cornered by Joe and Sam.

Regular Voice Cast

Joe McClaine	**Len Jones**
Prof. Ian McClaine	**Rupert Davies**
Sam Loover	**Keith Alexander**
Shane Weston	**David Healy**

Guest Voice Cast

Dorina Cordova	**Liz Morgan**
President Juan Cordova	**Gary Files**
General Valdes	**Jeremy Wilkin**
Garancia	**David Healy**
Waiter	**Keith Alexander**
Frogman	**Keith Alexander**
Operator	**Keith Alexander**

First UK Transmission

Sunday, March 23rd, 1969
5.30pm (ATV Midlands)

THE SECRET SERVICE

Format

In the late 1960s, the brilliant and dedicated scientist Professor Humbolt completed work on the Minimiser, a device with the capacity to shrink a person or object to about one-third normal size and then reverse the process, restoring the subject to full size again. Fearing that the device might fall into the wrong hands, Humbolt concealed the Minimiser inside a large book and, on his death, bequeathed it to a close friend, the parish priest Father Stanley Unwin.

Entrusting knowledge of the existence of the Minimiser to British Intelligence, Unwin leads a double life as a special agent for BISHOP, British Intelligence Service Headquarters Operation Priest, acting on assignments issued by The Bishop from his office in Whitehall, London. A top Intelligence agent, Matthew Harding, has been assigned to assist Father Unwin, often as the focus of the Minimiser which shrinks him to a height of two feet, enabling him to gain access to strategic sites undetected. While miniaturised, Matthew is transported inside a specially converted suitcase equipped with a chair and periscope, as well as drawers and compartments housing miniature tools and instruments that he might need on a mission. Matthew can open and close the case himself from the inside, and communicates with Father Unwin via linked radio transceivers disguised as hearing aids. Between assignments, Matthew acts as the gardener at Unwin's Vicarage, adopting the persona of a slow-thinking country boy.

Father Unwin's favoured mode of transport is Gabriel, a beautifully maintained vintage 1917 coupelet Model T Ford. Gabriel's normal top speed is only a little over 40 mph, but with the assistance of the boffins at British Intelligence, Unwin has made modifications under Gabriel's bonnet which allow the car to reach speeds in excess of 50 mph. Gabriel has a closed valve type engine (20 brake horse power at 1600 rpm) and is equipped with magneto-powered electric headlamps and horn. Originally painted black with black fenders, Gabriel sports yellow bodywork with imitation leather upholstery.

Main Characters

Father Stanley Unwin
57-year-old country vicar and BISHOP secret agent on permanent assignment to Operation Priest

Matthew Harding
28-year-old BISHOP agent on permanent assignment to Operation Priest working undercover as a Vicarage gardener

The Bishop
52-year-old senior member of British Intelligence in charge of Operation Priest

Mrs. Appleby
55-year-old housekeeper at Father Unwin's Vicarage who knows nothing of Unwin's Intelligence activities

Agent Blake
Bespectacled junior BISHOP agent

Production

A chance meeting between Gerry Anderson and popular raconteur Stanley Unwin at Pinewood Studios during production of *Doppelgänger* (1968) inspired the development of THE SECRET SERVICE as an espionage series featuring Unwin himself as the lead character. Mary Turner sculpted a puppet of Unwin who not only provided the voice of the character, but also wrote his own 'double-talk' dialogue and appeared in live-action location footage. The decision to film the series with a blend of Supermarionation puppetry and live-action was the ultimate solution to the problem of making the puppets appear to walk convincingly, and the present-day setting of the series also enabled a second unit team to go on location and shoot inserts of Unwin driving around the countryside, arriving at his destination or involved in car chases.

Filming on THE SECRET SERVICE began on Tuesday, August 20th, 1968, just two weeks after principal photography had concluded on JOE 90. By this stage, the puppet workshop had constructed such a large number of revamp puppets that the series could be entirely populated by existing puppets modified to suit the characters required. Indeed, much as with Sam and Shane in JOE 90, the puppet of Matthew was developed from an existing revamp that had previously appeared as Dr. Mitchell in the CAPTAIN SCARLET episode *Treble Cross*, his formerly grey hair now replaced by a blond wig. Even so, new puppets were created for the main characters of The Bishop and Mrs. Appleby, the latter sculpted by Christine Glanville and modelled after her own mother.

Ten episodes were already in the can with another three at various stages of production when the first episode was screened for Lew Grade in December 1968. As soon as Father Unwin began speaking in gobbledegook, Grade stopped the screening and cancelled the series on the grounds that American viewers would not be able to understand what Unwin was saying – entirely missing the point that no one was supposed to understand him. The last three episodes were completed but no new Supermarionation productions were commissioned and the puppet stages at the Century 21 Studios finally closed on Friday, January 24th, 1969.

THE SECRET SERVICE was only broadcast by three regions of the ITV network in the UK: ATV Midlands, Granada and Southern. All three regions screened repeat runs of the 13 episodes through to 1972 and Granada were still showing episodes as late as 1975, but the series has not been broadcast by any station in the UK (terrestrial or satellite) since then.

Episode Titles

(Listed in production order)

1. **A Case For The Bishop**
2. **A Question Of Miracles**
3. **The Feathered Spies**
4. **To Catch A Spy**
5. **Last Train To Bufflers Halt**
6. **Errand Of Mercy**
7. **Recall To Service**
8. **Hole In One**
9. **School For Spies**
10. **The Cure**
11. **The Deadly Whisper**
12. **May-Day, May-Day!**
13. **More Haste Less Speed**

Episode Running Time

25 minutes approx.

PRODUCTION CREDITS

Executive Producer **Reg Hill**
Produced by **David Lane**
Format by **Gerry & Sylvia Anderson**
Production Supervisor **Des Saunders**
Supervising Visual Effects **Derek Meddings**
Characters Created by **Sylvia Anderson**
Music Composed and Directed by **Barry Gray**
Vocal Title Music by **The Mike Sammes Singers**
Lighting Cameraman **Paddy Seale** *(1, 3, 5, 7, 9, 11)*
Julien Lugrin *(2, 4, 6, 8, 10, 12, 13)*
Script Editor **Tony Barwick**
Supervising Editor **Alan Killick**
Art Director **Keith Wilson**
Production Manager **Frank Rowlands**
Puppet Co-ordinator **Mary Turner**
Puppet Operators **Wanda Webb** *(1, 3, 5, 7, 9, 11)*
Rowena White *(1, 2, 4, 6, 8, 10, 12, 13)*
Charmaine Wood *(1, 3, 5, 7, 9, 11)*
Christine Glanville *(2, 4, 6, 8, 10, 12, 13)*
Sculptors **Tim Cooksey**
Plugg Shutt
Wardrobe **Iris Richens**
Film Editor **Alan Killick** *(1, 3, 7, 10, 12, 13)*
Len Cleal *(2, 5, 8, 9, 11)*
Norman A. Cole *(4, 6)*
Camera Operator **Ian Vinson** *(1, 3, 5, 7, 8, 9)*
Derek Black *(2, 4, 6, 10, 11, 12, 13)*
Assistant Director **Geoff Pittman** *(1, 4, 7, 12)*
John Jelly *(2, 5, 8, 10, 11)*
Tony Harding *(3, 6)*
Ian Spurrier *(9, 13)*
Dialogue Synchronisation **John Drake** *(1, 4, 5, 10, 11, 12, 13)*
James Cowan *(2, 3, 6, 7, 8, 9)*
Senior Visual Effects Director **Jimmy Elliott**

Visual Effects Designer **Mike Trim**
Models **Peter Aston**
Alan Shubrook*
Brian Smithies*
Property Master **Peter Holmes**

VISUAL EFFECTS UNIT
Director **Bill Camp** *(1, 3, 5, 7, 9, 11, 13)*
Shaun Whittacker-Cook *(2, 6, 8, 10, 12)*
Alan Berry *(4)*
Lighting Cameraman **Les Paul** *(1, 7)*
Eric Cross *(2, 4, 6, 8)*
Bert Mason *(3, 5, 9, 11, 13)*
Harry Oakes *(10, 12)*
Camera Operator **Nick Procopides** *(1, 3, 5, 7, 9, 11, 13)*
Mike Rainer *(2, 4, 6, 8, 10, 12)*

LOCATION UNIT
Director **Ken Turner**
Lighting Cameraman **Ted Wooldridge**
Camera Operator **Noel Rowlands**
Manager **Gren Nott**

Supervising Sound Editor **Peter Pennell**
Sound Editor **Tony Roper**
Music Editor **George Randall**
Sound Re-Recording **Anvil Films Limited**
Character Voices **Keith Alexander**
Sylvia Anderson
Gary Files
David Graham*
David Healy
Stanley Unwin
Jeremy Wilkin

A Gerry Anderson
Century 21 Television Production
An ITC World Wide Distribution
Filmed in Supermarionation

* uncredited

Regular Voice Cast

Father Stanley Unwin **Stanley Unwin**
Matthew Harding **Gary Files**
The Bishop **Jeremy Wilkin**
Mrs. Appleby **Sylvia Anderson**

Guest Voice Cast

Dreisenberg Ambassador **David Healy**
Ambassador's aide **Keith Alexander**
Patterson **Jeremy Wilkin**
Saunders **Keith Alexander**
Captain **Keith Alexander**
Policeman **Jeremy Wilkin**
Tower Controller **Keith Alexander**
Co-Pilot **Gary Files**

First UK Transmission

Sunday, September 21st, 1969
5.30pm (ATV Midlands)

A CASE FOR THE BISHOP — Prod. No. 01

Teleplay by **Gerry & Sylvia Anderson** Directed by **Alan Perry**

Healey Automation's KX20 mini-computer has been stolen by Dreisenberg agents and will be smuggled out of the country by the Dreisenberg Ambassador under the protection of diplomatic immunity. Assigned to recover the computer, Father Unwin takes a miniaturised Matthew to the Dreisenberg hangar at London Airport where Matthew hides inside an engine cowling of the Ambassador's plane. When the airliner takes off with the Ambassador and his aide aboard, Matthew causes an engine failure, forcing the pilot to turn back for a landing at Oakington Airfield. But *en route* to rendezvous with the plane when it lands, Unwin is stopped by the police for speeding...

Notes

Healey Automation is named after voice artist David Healy, while British Intelligence head Saunders is named after series production supervisor Desmond Saunders.

Oops!

The mini-computer is referred to throughout the episode as the KX20 (as written in the script) but the computer itself is actually labelled XK20.

A QUESTION OF MIRACLES — Prod. No. 02

Teleplay by **Donald James** — Directed by **Leo Eaton**

British-designed desalination plants in North Africa and Burgossa have exploded as they approach 250 hours of operation and The Bishop suspects sabotage. He assigns Father Unwin to prevent the last remaining plant at Port Trennick from being destroyed. From a beach near Port Trennick, the miniaturised Matthew swims out to the plant's seawater inlet to find it has been breached by saboteurs who intend to fire a torpedo into the plant through the inlet. Matthew stretches a net over the inlet to catch the torpedo, but then is unable to pull it free. The torpedo will explode unless Unwin can gain access to the plant's control building and persuade the authorities to turn off the pumps...

Notes

BISHOP agent Blake makes the first of four appearances in the series here. The character is portrayed by the Captain Scarlet puppet from CAPTAIN SCARLET AND THE MYSTERONS, now with brown hair and wearing glasses. Several of Scarlet's colleagues also appear in this episode: Colonel White is Brooks, the controller of the North African desalination plant, and Captain Grey is Tom Williams, the plant designer. When he arrives at Port Trennick, Blake is driving Sam Loover's car from JOE 90.

Regular Voice Cast

Father Stanley Unwin	**Stanley Unwin**
Matthew Harding	**Gary Files**
The Bishop	**Jeremy Wilkin**
Mrs. Appleby	**Sylvia Anderson**
Agent Blake	**Keith Alexander**

Guest Voice Cast

Hartley	**Keith Alexander**
Tom Williams	**Jeremy Wilkin**
Shaw	**David Healy**
Doctor	**Keith Alexander**
Nielson	**David Healy**
Brooks	**Keith Alexander**
Green	**Gary Files**

First UK Transmission

Sunday, September 28th, 1969
5.30pm (ATV Midlands)

THE FEATHERED SPIES — Prod. No. 03

Teleplay by **Tony Barwick** — Directed by **Ian Spurrier**

The Bishop learns that aerial photos of the new XK4 fighter plane are being offered on the black market by industrial spy De Groot, so he assigns Father Unwin to find out how the photos are being taken, as overhead access to the XK4's airbase at Crayfield is restricted. Unwin and Matthew discover that pigeon fancier John Masden is being blackmailed by De Groot into photographing the airbase using pigeons fitted with miniature cameras. Searching Masden's house, Unwin and Matthew find explosives which have been given to Masden disguised as special film for the cameras, and realise that De Groot intends to use the pigeons to bomb the airbase and destroy the XK4!

Notes

Pigeon fancier John Masden is portrayed by the Captain Ochre puppet from CAPTAIN SCARLET AND THE MYSTERONS which previously appeared in THE SECRET SERVICE as the co-pilot of the Dreisenberg Ambassador's plane in *A Case For The Bishop*. The De Groot puppet was previously seen as Kramer in CAPTAIN SCARLET's *Special Assignment* episode. The Matthew puppet is seen interacting with a live animal for the first time as he encounters Masden's Great Dane Kruger in the garden of Masden's house.

Regular Voice Cast

Father Stanley Unwin	**Stanley Unwin**
Matthew Harding	**Gary Files**
The Bishop	**Jeremy Wilkin**
Mrs. Appleby	**Sylvia Anderson**

Guest Voice Cast

John Masden	**Jeremy Wilkin**
De Groot	**David Healy**
Carl	**Keith Alexander**
Agent	**Keith Alexander**
Officer	**Jeremy Wilkin**
Operator	**Gary Files**

First UK Transmission

Sunday, October 12th, 1969
5.30pm (ATV Midlands)

TO CATCH A SPY — Prod. No. 04

Teleplay by **Pat Dunlop** — Directed by **Brian Heard**

Mercenaries engineer a break-out at North Exmanston prison and prisoner George Grey is flown by helijet to the country residence of the influential Sir Humphrey Burton. The Bishop assigns Father Unwin to confirm that Grey is in hiding at the estate and is being assisted in his escape by Sir Humphrey. Unwin smuggles the miniaturised Matthew into Burton's house and the agent discovers that Sir Humphrey has arranged to transport Grey out of the country on board a submarine the next morning. Matthew stows away on the helijet that ferries Grey off the estate, relaying directions to Unwin who follows in Gabriel. Sir Humphrey and Grey transfer to a car and Unwin tails them to Kew Gardens where he confronts Sir Humphrey armed only with the Minimiser...

Notes

Sir Humphrey Burton is portrayed by the Colonel White puppet from CAPTAIN SCARLET AND THE MYSTERONS. The helijet was previously seen in the JOE 90 episode *Breakout* but the model's tail section was turned upside-down for its appearance here. Hall Barn in Beaconsfield was used for location filming of Sir Humphrey's house while the gates of nearby Cliveden House in Beaconsfield doubled for the entrance to Kew Gardens.

Regular Voice Cast

Father Stanley Unwin	**Stanley Unwin**
Matthew Harding	**Gary Files**
The Bishop	**Jeremy Wilkin**
Mrs. Appleby	**Sylvia Anderson**

Guest Voice Cast

Sir Humphrey Burton	**Keith Alexander**
George Grey	**Jeremy Wilkin**
Saunders	**Keith Alexander**
Patterson	**Jeremy Wilkin**
Manservant	**Gary Files**
Skipper	**Gary Files**
Pilot	**Gary Files**
1st Guard	**Keith Alexander**

First UK Transmission

Sunday, October 5th, 1969
5.30pm (ATV Midlands)

LAST TRAIN TO BUFFLERS HALT — Prod. No. 05

Teleplay by **Tony Barwick** — Directed by **Alan Perry**

After a security van carrying £1 million in used bank notes manages to evade an ambush, Father Unwin and Matthew are assigned to protect the bank notes on the second leg of their journey to London on board an express train. Security official Reed was behind the attempted robbery and he now arranges for the train to be diverted to the disused Buffler's Halt station, where Reed and his colleagues imprison Unwin and the security guards in the stationmaster's office. Assisted by old stationmaster Albert Hobson, Unwin escapes and locks the hi-jackers in the guard's van while they are distracted by the miniaturised Matthew. Hobson starts the train up and they set off back to the main line, but with the train travelling towards London at 80 mph, Hobson confesses to Unwin that he doesn't know how to stop it!

Notes

The working title of this episode was simply 'The Train'. The character of Reed was originally written as Price in Tony Barwick's script. Although the name of the station is given as Bufflers Halt (no apostrophe) in the episode title caption, a sign on the platform identifies it as Buffler's Halt (as in the script).

Regular Voice Cast

Father Stanley Unwin	**Stanley Unwin**
Matthew Harding	**Gary Files**
The Bishop	**Jeremy Wilkin**
Agent Blake	**Keith Alexander**

Guest Voice Cast

Reed	**Keith Alexander**
Albert Hobson	**Gary Files**
Calow	**Jeremy Wilkin**
Jackie	**Sylvia Anderson**
Guard	**Jeremy Wilkin**
McGrath	**Gary Files**
Agent	**Keith Alexander**
Signalman	**Keith Alexander**

First UK Transmission

Sunday, October 19th, 1969
5.30pm (ATV Midlands)

ERRAND OF MERCY — Prod. No. 06

Teleplay by **Tony Barwick** — Directed by **Leo Eaton**

Suffering from sunstroke, Father Unwin is retired to bed and Dr. Brogan prescribes sleeping pills, but just before he falls asleep, Unwin reads in the newspaper about a plague in Africa. Soon he is dreaming that he and Matthew have been assigned to collect medical supplies and fly them in Gabriel to Bishopsville for a rendezvous with Dr. Purple. The pair have tea with Mrs. Appleby at a petrol station in the desert before being captured by hostile jungle natives and prepared for sacrifice. Matthew tries to explain their mission to the natives but the only language they understand is gobbledegook. Fortunately, Unwin is able to converse with them and once they understand the situation, the natives set them free and fetch the medical supplies. The agents take off again bound for Bishopsville, but suddenly Gabriel comes under fire from mercenary fighter jets!

Oops!

Father Unwin is seen sitting up in bed reading his newspaper which can clearly be seen to be a copy of *The Times*, but then the close-up shot of the newspaper's cover identifies it as the *Universal News*. The cover of the newspaper gives the date as Friday, February 3rd, 1969, an unlikely time of year for anyone to collapse from sunstroke!

Regular Voice Cast

Father Stanley Unwin	**Stanley Unwin**
Matthew Harding	**Gary Files**
The Bishop	**Jeremy Wilkin**
Mrs. Appleby	**Sylvia Anderson**

Guest Voice Cast

Officer	**Keith Alexander**
General	**Keith Alexander**
Operator	**Jeremy Wilkin**
Pilot (Mercenary 1)	**Jeremy Wilkin**
1st Native	**Jeremy Wilkin**
2nd Native	**Gary Files**
3rd Native	**Keith Alexander**

First UK Transmission

Sunday, November 9th, 1969
5.30pm (ATV Midlands)

RECALL TO SERVICE — Prod. No. 07

Teleplay by **Pat Dunlop** — Directed by **Peter Anderson**

Sabotage is suspected when a control failure occurs during tests of the Aquatank, a new computer-controlled military vehicle. Father Unwin and Matthew are assigned to investigate in advance of a demonstration to NATO heads of defence at a World Army base. Introducing himself as the new chaplain, Unwin meets Colonel Blair, Captain Mitchell and computer scientist Professor Graham, who reveals that the person responsible for the sabotage must be someone in authority. Matthew sneaks aboard the Aquatank but as the demonstration begins, Captain Mitchell forces Graham to change the tank's programme so that it targets the observation blockhouse with the Colonel and the NATO chiefs trapped inside.

Notes

The working title of this episode was 'You're In The Army Now'. The aircraft that attack the Aquatank during the test run are Angel Interceptors from CAPTAIN SCARLET AND THE MYSTERONS, seen in footage lifted from episodes of that series. Professor Graham is portrayed by the Captain Blue puppet from CAPTAIN SCARLET, now with brown hair. Blue's colleague Captain Grey appears again here, this time portraying Colonel Blair.

Regular Voice Cast

Father Stanley Unwin	**Stanley Unwin**
Matthew Harding	**Gary Files**
The Bishop	**Jeremy Wilkin**
Mrs. Appleby	**Sylvia Anderson**

Guest Voice Cast

Colonel Blair	**Jeremy Wilkin**
Captain Mitchell	**Gary Files**
Professor Graham	**Keith Alexander**
Sergeant Walsh	**Gary Files**
French General	**Keith Alexander**

First UK Transmission

Sunday, November 2nd, 1969
5.30pm (ATV Midlands)

HOLE IN ONE — Prod. No. 08

Teleplay by **Shane Rimmer** Directed by **Brian Heard**

When plans to correct the orbit of the crucial G9 early warning satellite are sabotaged, British Intelligence discovers that vital information about the rescue operation is being leaked by General Brompton at his golf club. Father Unwin joins the General for a round of golf and passes bogus information about a tracker sub-station operating from a caravan at a specific location. Later, Unwin and Matthew observe saboteurs Kromer and Blake as they destroy the caravan and Matthew stows away aboard Kromer's car. He is taken to the saboteur's base near the golf course where he discovers that the General's golf balls have been rigged with mini tape-recorders. Now the success of the final attempt to correct the G9's orbit hinges on Unwin's ability to play a very special hole in one!

Notes

Kromer was previously seen as De Groot in *The Feathered Spies* and as Kramer in Captain Scarlet's *Special Assignment* episode. Captain Magenta from Captain Scarlet and Angela Davis from Joe 90's *Three's A Crowd* episode are visible in the background at the golf club. The Western Early Warning System Tracking Station later appears as a SHADO Tracking Station in UFO.

Regular Voice Cast

Father Stanley Unwin	**Stanley Unwin**
Matthew Harding	**Gary Files**
The Bishop	**Jeremy Wilkin**
Mrs. Appleby	**Sylvia Anderson**

Guest Voice Cast

General Brompton	**Keith Alexander**
Kromer	**Jeremy Wilkin**
Forrester	**Gary Files**
Dr. Hawthorn	**Jeremy Wilkin**
Blake	**Keith Alexander**
Operator	**Keith Alexander**

First UK Transmission

Sunday, October 26th, 1969
5.30pm (ATV Midlands)

SCHOOL FOR SPIES — Prod. No. 09

Teleplay by **Donald James** Directed by **Ken Turner**

The destruction of an experimental weapons station is the latest in a series of acts of sabotage and Father Unwin discovers that a vicar was seen in the vicinity of each attack. A vicar was also involved in a car accident near the site of an attack on an army truck, so Unwin visits the injured Brother Gregory in hospital, enabling a miniaturised Matthew to stow away in a holdall belonging to another visitor, Brother Thomas. Matthew is taken to Pennyridge Seminary where he learns that the bogus vicars are mercenaries led by the mysterious Archdeacon. Unwin infiltrates the group by posing as their replacement demolitions expert, but Brother Gregory recognises him as an impostor...

Notes

Wexham Park Hospital in Stoke Green near Slough, Buckinghamshire doubled for Stonehouse Hospital where Unwin visits Brother Gregory. The vehicle destroyed in Operation Roadway is an explosives truck from Joe 90's *Colonel McClaine* episode. The radio in Brother Gregory's room plays the 'White As Snow' track composed for the Captain Scarlet episode *White As Snow*. The piano concerto played by the Archdeacon was originally performed by Igor Sladek in the Joe 90 episode *International Concerto*.

Regular Voice Cast

Father Stanley Unwin	**Stanley Unwin**
Matthew Harding	**Gary Files**
The Bishop	**Jeremy Wilkin**

Guest Voice Cast

Brother Thomas	**Keith Alexander**
Brother Gregory	**Jeremy Wilkin**
Archdeacon	**Keith Alexander**
Brother Simon	**Gary Files**
Brother Jess	**Gary Files**
5th Brother	**Jeremy Wilkin**

First UK Transmission

Sunday, November 30th, 1969
5.30pm (ATV Midlands)

THE CURE — Prod. No. 10

Teleplay by **Pat Dunlop** Directed by **Leo Eaton**

Notorious international agent Sakov books himself into the Greenways health farm, so The Bishop assigns Father Unwin to find out what he's up to. Unwin meets the chief therapist Dr. Klam, who explains that Sakov is receiving treatment on the Klam Recliner, a gyroscope device designed to facilitate a greater blood flow to the head, thus relieving tension. However, Sakov has left the clinic via an air duct, making his way to a nearby racetrack to sabotage tests on a new additive, GK2, which produces a liquid equivalent to high octane petrol when mixed with distilled water. Matthew secretes himself aboard the test car unaware that Sakov has replaced the GK2 with a highly volatile chemical which will explode when the driver switches from regular fuel to the GK2 tank...

Notes

One of Unwin's fellow guests at Greenways is a Mrs. Dunlop, named after the episode's author, Pat Dunlop. The Captain Ochre puppet from Captain Scarlet And The Mysterons appears again, this time as GK2 test scientist Burrows. Sakov was previously seen as Igor Sladek in Joe 90's *International Concerto* and Dr. Klam originally appeared as Miguel in Joe 90's *Big Fish*.

Regular Voice Cast

Father Stanley Unwin	**Stanley Unwin**
Matthew Harding	**Gary Files**
The Bishop	**Jeremy Wilkin**
Mrs. Appleby	**Sylvia Anderson**
Agent Blake	**Keith Alexander**

Guest Voice Cast

Dr. E.H. Klam	**Gary Files**
Sakov	**David Healy**
Burrows	**Keith Alexander**
Pete Mackintosh	**Jeremy Wilkin**
Kalin	**Gary Files**
Dave Marden	**Keith Alexander**
Minister	**Jeremy Wilkin**

First UK Transmission

Sunday, November 23rd, 1969
5.30pm (ATV Midlands)

THE DEADLY WHISPER — Prod. No. 11

Teleplay by **Donald James** — Directed by **Leo Eaton**

Father Unwin is concerned when his friend Professor Soames, creator of a new sonic rifle capable of projecting ultrasonic vibration with the power to destroy a tank, tells him that he will be entering dahlias in this year's flower show, when Unwin knows that he only grows roses. Unwin smuggles a miniaturised Matthew into Soames's house, where the agent discovers that the Professor's daughter Anne is being held hostage by Mark Slater and his associates, who plan to sabotage tests of a prototype aircraft using the sonic rifle. Unwin visits Soames again on the pretence of collecting the dahlias for the flower show, but Slater recognises the deception and takes Unwin prisoner. With Matthew's assistance, Unwin and Soames escape and race to stop Slater before he can destroy the aircraft.

Notes

Professor Soames gives the date as May 24th. The Captain Black puppet from CAPTAIN SCARLET AND THE MYSTERONS portrays Kroner while Captain Ochre is the Controller at the ECA Flight Research Establishment. Agent Blake appears briefly in a non-speaking role. The Mach 3 aircraft used to repel the force of the sonic rifle was previously seen as the XK4 fighter in *The Feathered Spies*.

Regular Voice Cast

Father Stanley Unwin	**Stanley Unwin**
Matthew Harding	**Gary Files**
The Bishop	**Jeremy Wilkin**
Mrs. Appleby	**Sylvia Anderson**

Guest Voice Cast

Kroner	**Keith Alexander**
Mark Slater	**David Healy**
Anne Soames	**Sylvia Anderson**
Professor Soames	**Keith Alexander**
Eastman	**Jeremy Wilkin**
Controller	**Jeremy Wilkin**
Pilot	**Gary Files**

First UK Transmission

Sunday, November 16th, 1969
5.30pm (ATV Midlands)

MAY-DAY, MAY-DAY! — Prod. No. 12

Teleplay by **Bob Kesten** — Directed by **Alan Perry**

The Bishop assigns Father Unwin and Matthew to protect the King of Muldovia when he visits London to sign an oil rights agreement which will bring benefits to his country. The agents take turns watching the King but during the night an assassin hired by the Prince of Muldovia makes an attempt on the King's life. Fortunately, he is frightened by the sight of the miniaturised Matthew and falls from the window to his death. Unwin and Matthew join the King's retinue on a flight to New York, but The Bishop is warned that the Prince has planted a bomb on board, hidden inside a teddy bear for the King's four-year-old son and set to detonate at noon!

Notes

The Captain Blue puppet from CAPTAIN SCARLET AND THE MYSTERONS portrays toolmaker Joe while his Spectrum colleague Captain Grey appears as the Captain of the Muldovian plane RM1. The Century 21 Studios buildings doubled as the factory and workshops of NS Precision Instruments. Toolmaker Joe is shot down at Windsor End in Beaconsfield, Buckinghamshire. Footage of the Palace of Ardaji is lifted from the JOE 90 episode *King For A Day* to appear here as the Royal Palace of Muldovia.

Regular Voice Cast

Father Stanley Unwin	**Stanley Unwin**
Matthew Harding	**Gary Files**
The Bishop	**Jeremy Wilkin**

Guest Voice Cast

Prince of Muldovia	**Gary Files**
Achmed	**Jeremy Wilkin**
King of Muldovia	**David Graham**
Joe	**Keith Alexander**
Joe's Father	**Jeremy Wilkin**
Assassin	**Keith Alexander**
Captain	**Gary Files**
Co-Pilot	**Keith Alexander**
Air Traffic Controller	**David Graham**

First UK Transmission

Sunday, December 7th, 1969
5.30pm (ATV Midlands)

MORE HASTE LESS SPEED — Prod. No. 13

Teleplay by **Tony Barwick** — Directed by **Ken Turner**

Lord Edward and Lady Martha Hazlewell have inherited one of a pair of counterfeit printing plates for a one dollar bill from their late father, but their father's accomplice, Mullins, hid the other plate before he was arrested. The Bishop assigns Unwin and Matthew to tail Mullins on his release from prison until he leads them to the plates. In a miniaturised Gabriel, the pair follow Mullins to Hazlewell Manor where he reveals that his plate is hidden at Greenacre Farm, just outside Eastford. Lady Martha locks Mullins, her brother and their accomplice Spiker in the dungeon and sets off for the farm in her car closely followed by Unwin and Matthew in Gabriel. Escaping from the dungeon, Edward and Mullins give chase in an old bi-plane that neither knows how to fly, while Spiker flags down an ambulance to join the wacky race.

Notes

The model of Lord Hazlewell's bi-plane was previously seen as Alan Tracy's Tiger Moth, the title vehicle of *Thunderbird 6* (1967). The race through the woods was filmed in Burnham Beeches in Buckinghamshire and Abbey Park Farm near Littleworth Common, just outside Burnham Beeches, doubled as the finish line at Greenacre Farm.

Regular Voice Cast

Father Stanley Unwin	**Stanley Unwin**
Matthew Harding	**Gary Files**
The Bishop	**Jeremy Wilkin**
Mrs. Appleby	**Sylvia Anderson**

Guest Voice Cast

Lady Martha	**Keith Alexander**
Lord Hazlewell	**David Graham**
Spiker	**Gary Files**
Mullins	**Jeremy Wilkin**
Charlie	**Gary Files**
Pete	**David Graham**
Attendant	**Gary Files**

First UK Transmission

Sunday, December 14th, 1969
5.30pm (ATV Midlands)

UFO

Format

It is the early 1980s and Earth is being visited in secret by the humanoid members of a dying race from Alpha Centauri, who are searching for fresh donor organs that they can use in transplant surgery and complete host bodies in which to implant their consciousness. Earth is defended from these aliens by SHADO (Supreme Headquarters Alien Defence Organisation), a covert organisation operating under the auspices of the United Nations Special Committee and funded by the UN through the International Astrophysical Commission. Under the command of former USAF Colonel Ed Straker, SHADO HQ is concealed in a vast underground emplacement beneath the Harlington-Straker Film Studios in Harlington West, Wessex, England.

Moonbase is SHADO's first line of defence against the aliens. Located in the Sea of Tranquillity on Earth's satellite, the base is equipped with a fleet of Interceptor spacecraft, each armed with a powerful computer-assisted low-yield atomic missile. When SID, SHADO's Space Intruder Detector advance warning satellite, tracks incoming alien craft, the Interceptors are launched from their crater housings to target and destroy the UFOs before they can enter Earth atmosphere. Should any UFOs manage to evade the Interceptors, SHADO's main line of defence within Earth's atmosphere is the *Skydiver* fleet, nuclear-powered submarines on constant patrol beneath the surface of the world's oceans. Alerted by SHADO control, a *Skydiver* races to the UFO's estimated trajectory termination and launches the detachable front section, Sky One, a powerful jet fighter aircraft capable of supersonic speeds.

SHADO also maintains a variety of other vehicles and aircraft for use by operatives in the field: SHADO Mobiles, amphibious track vehicles used to transport personnel to the site of UFO landings; Moonmobiles for transportation over the lunar surface; the Lunar Transporter to ferry personnel, equipment and supplies between Earth and the Moon, comprising the Lunar Module spacecraft and the Lunar Carrier Earth atmosphere launching and landing unit; custom-designed cars with gull-wing doors equipped with built-in radar and detection gear; and the SHADAIR fleet which includes Mobile Transporter aircraft for heavy duty equipment transport, Seagull supersonic passenger transport jets and Albatross long-range rescue aircraft.

Production

Gerry Anderson's first live-action television series was filmed over an 18-month period utilising the facilities of three different film studios. Gerry and Sylvia Anderson began work on developing the format with Reg Hill in the late autumn of 1968 while production of THE SECRET SERVICE was still ongoing. At the time, Anderson was also completing post-production work on *Doppelgänger* (1968) and preparing a second live-action science-fiction feature entitled *Youth Is Wasted On The Young*, planned to be shot on location in Portugal. This project ultimately collapsed, but Lew Grade agreed to finance UFO with a budget of £100,000 per episode and five months of pre-production began in December 1968.

Principal photography commenced at the end of April 1969 on Stages 6 and 7 at the giant 114-acre MGM British Studios in Borehamwood, Hertfordshire, the former Amalgamated Studios originally constructed in 1937. Visual effects photography took place at the Century 21 Studios in Slough where the two puppet soundstages were transformed into additional effects stages. Neptune House at the ATV Elstree Studios (now BBC Elstree) in Borehamwood doubled as the main administration block of the Harlington-Straker Film Studios in location photography.

Towards the end of 1969, it became apparent that the MGM British Studios were to be closed down, enforcing the suspension of production on UFO after the completion of principal photography on episode 17, *Sub-Smash*, at the end of November. New studio space was found at the 92-acre Pinewood Studios in Iver Heath, Buckinghamshire, built in 1936. Anderson had previously shot the principal photography for *Doppelgänger* (1968) at Pinewood and filming on UFO resumed on J & K Stages there in May 1970, with the last of the series' 26 episodes finally completed that October.

Main Characters

Commander Ed Straker
SHADO Commander in Chief, formerly a USAF Colonel

Colonel Alec Freeman
SHADO 2nd in Command, formerly a combat pilot and intelligence agent

Colonel Paul Foster
Moonbase Commander and field operative, formerly a test pilot

Colonel Virginia Lake
Electronics expert, later promoted to SHADO 2nd in Command

Captain Peter Carlin
Skydiver Captain and Sky One pilot

Lieutenant Gay Ellis
Moonbase Commander

Lieutenant Nina Barry
Moonbase space tracker, later promoted to Moonbase Commander

Lieutenant Joan Harrington
Moonbase space tracker

Lieutenant Keith Ford
Communications operative, SHADO Control

Lieutenant/Captain Lew Waterman
Interceptor pilot, later promoted to Skydiver Captain and Sky One pilot

General James Henderson
Head of the International Astrophysical Commission

Dr. Doug Jackson
Medical and psychological specialist

Miss Ealand
Commander Straker's secretary

Lieutenant Mark Bradley
Interceptor pilot

Lieutenant John Masters
Skydiver engineer

Lieutenant Gordon Maxwell
Skydiver navigator

Lieutenant Ayshea Johnson
Operative, SHADO Control

Lieutenant Sylvia Howell
Operative, Skydiver

Dr. Shroeder
Medical and psychological specialist

Dr. Frazer
Medical specialist

Captain Steve Minto
Interceptor pilot

Lieutenant Catherine Scott
Operative, SHADO Control and Skydiver

SID (Space Intruder Detector)
SHADO computerised advance tracking and space communication satellite

Episode Titles

(Listed in production order)

1. **Identified**
2. **Computer Affair**
3. **Flight Path**
4. **Survival**
5. **Exposed**
6. **Conflict**
7. **The Dalotek Affair**
8. **A Question Of Priorities**
9. **Ordeal**
10. **The Responsibility Seat**
11. **The Square Triangle**
12. **Court Martial**
13. **Close Up**
14. **Confetti Check A-O.K.**
15. **E.S.P.**
16. **Kill Straker!**
17. **Sub-Smash**
18. **The Sound Of Silence**
19. **The Cat With Ten Lives**
20. **Destruction**
21. **The Man Who Came Back**
22. **The Psychobombs**
23. **Reflections In The Water**
24. **Timelash**
25. **Mindbender**
26. **The Long Sleep**

Episode Running Time

50 minutes approx.

The first run of UFO on British television began in the ATV Midlands, Tyne-Tees and Border regions on September 16th, 1970 although the episodes were not always screened in the same order in each region (on October 7th, 1970, each premiered a different episode at the same time). Due to low ratings, the series was curtailed on ATV in February 1971 after 18 episodes and relaunched in a new timeslot, starting again with the first episode on February 27th.

By this time, other ITV regions were starting to show the series: Anglia from October 2nd, 1970 Southern from February 20th, 1971 Yorkshire from April 17th, 1971 and Granada and Grampian from July 17th, 1971. LWT, however, did not start screening the series until September 18th, 1971, a full year after ATV Midlands, Tyne-Tees and Border .

PRODUCTION CREDITS

Executive Producer **Gerry Anderson** *(1-17)*
Produced by **Reg Hill**
Gerry Anderson *(18-26)*
Format **Gerry & Sylvia Anderson** with **Reg Hill**
Century 21 Fashions by **Sylvia Anderson**
Visual Effects Supervisor *(1-5)* / Special Effects *(6-26)* **Derek Meddings**
Art Director **Bob Bell**
Production Supervisor **Norman Foster**
Assistant to Producer *(1-17)* / Post Production Executive *(18-26)* **Des Saunders**
Lighting Cameraman *(1-17)* / Director of Photography *(18-26)* **Brendan J. Stafford BSC**
Music Composed and Directed by **Barry Gray**
Script Editor **Tony Barwick**

VISUAL EFFECTS *(1-5)* /
SPECIAL EFFECTS *(6-26)*
Senior Director **Jim Elliott** *(6-17)*
Director **Bill Camp** *(1, 3, 5, 7, 9, 11, 15, 17, 19, 21, 23, 26)*
Shaun Whittacker-Cook *(2, 4, 6, 8, 10, 13, 16)*
Derek Meddings *(18, 20, 22, 24, 25)*
Production Manager **Frank Hollands** *(1-9)*
Ken Holt *(10-26)*
Lighting Cameraman **Harry Oakes**
Camera Operator **Mike Rainer** *(1-17)*
Alan Perry *(18-26)*
Assistant to Supervisor **Jim Elliott** *(1-5)*
Designer **Mike Trim**

Supervising Editor **Lee Doig** *(19, 22, 24, 26)*
Editor **Alan Killick** *(1, 4, 7, 14)*
Harry MacDonald *(2, 5, 8, 10, 11, 13, 17, 18)*
Len Walter *(3, 6, 9, 12, 16, 20, 23)*
Lee Doig *(15)*
Mike Campbell *(21, 25)*
Sound Editors **John Peverill**
Jim Hopkins *(1)*
Peter Pennell *(2-26)*
Music Editor **George Randall** *(1-22)*
Mike Campbell *(23-26)*
Instrumentation **Don Fagan**, Century 21 Film Props
Sound Recordists **Ken Rawkins** *(1-9, 11, 12, 14-17)*
J.B. Smith *(1-6, 19-26)*
Sash Fisher *(10, 13)*
Ken Barker *(18, 19)*
John Streeter *(18)*
Ted Karnon *(20-26)*
Dubbing Mixer **J.B. Smith** *(7-17)*
Assistant Director **Leo Eaton** *(1, 3, 5, 7, 9, 11, 13)*
Ron Appleton *(2, 4, 6, 8, 10)*
Frank Hollands *(12, 14, 16, 18, 20, 22, 25, 26)*
Ken Baker *(15, 17)*
Gino Marotta *(19, 21, 23, 24)*
Camera Operator **Derek Black** *(1-17)*
Jack Lowin *(18-26)*
Continuity **Doreen Soan**
Chief Make-up Artist **Alex Garfath** *(18-26)*
Make-up **Cliff Sharp** *(1, 2)*
Robert L. Alexander *(3)*
Basil Newall *(4-17)*
Chief Hairdresser **Alice Holmes** *(18-26)*
Hairdressing **Alice Holmes** *(1-3, 14)*
Henry Montsash *(4-13)*
Stephanie Kaye *(15-17)*
Wardrobe Supervisor **Jean Fairlie** *(18-26)*
Wardrobe **Kim Martin** *(1-17)*
Iris Richens *(1-4)*
Processed by **Rank Film Laboratories**
Casting Director **Rose Tobias Shaw** *(1-17)*
Assistant Art Director **Keith Wilson**
Unit Manager **Roger Connolly** *(1-17)*
Location Manager **Ray Frift** *(18-26)*
Construction Manager **Fred Gunning**
Production Buyer **Harry Solomons** *(1-17)*
Bill MacIlraith *(18-26)*
Stunt Arranger **Jack Silk** *(1-3, 5, 9-12, 14, 16, 17)*
Fight Arranger **Gerry Crampton** *(19, 21)*
Roy Vincente *(22-26)*
Barnard Sports Cars **Overton, Challis Associates** *(24)*
Models **David Palmer***
Alan Shubrook*
Brian Smithies*
Special Effects Assistants **Alan Berry***
Ian Wingrove*
Peter Wragg*
Optical Effects **Ray Capel***

Made at
MGM British Studios, Borehamwood *(1-17)*
Pinewood Studios, London, England *(18-26)*
and **Century 21 Studios, Slough, England**
and on Location
A Gerry Anderson
Century 21 Television Production
An ITC World Wide Distribution

* uncredited

IDENTIFIED — Prod. No. 01

Teleplay by **Gerry & Sylvia Anderson** with **Tony Barwick**
Directed by **Gerry Anderson**

1970: Peter Carlin, his sister Leila and their friend Jean discover a UFO in the woods but they come under fire from the UFO's occupant. Jean is killed, Carlin is severely injured and Leila is cornered by the alien. USAF Colonel Ed Straker and General James Henderson arrive in England for a meeting with the Prime Minister to present conclusive evidence of UFO landings but their Rolls-Royce is attacked by an alien craft. Ten years later, Straker is commander-in-chief of SHADO, a secret defence network with headquarters sited 80 feet below the Harlington-Straker Film Studios. He assigns his second-in-command, Colonel Alec Freeman, to safeguard SHADO's new Utronic tracking equipment and its design team during a flight from the United States, but a UFO evades the Moonbase Interceptors and targets Freeman's Seagull X-Ray aircraft!

Notes

Writer Donald James made various contributions to the script for *Identified*, but received no on-screen credit for his work. A couple of scenes filmed for the episode were dropped from the final cut: Alec Freeman arriving at the Harlington-Straker Film Studios and flirting with the receptionist Janis (Penny Spencer), and Peter Carlin discussing the disappearance of his sister with Gordon Maxwell. Alan Killick's original edit of the opening sequence in the woods was considerably more violent – the bloodletting was toned down in the final edit to make it more suitable for a family audience. The Model T Ford (T42) that appeared as Father Unwin's car Gabriel in the live-action sequences of THE SECRET SERVICE makes a cameo appearance in the grounds of the Harlington-Straker Film Studios during the episode credits. Gary Myers (as astronaut Lew Waterman) is dubbed here by Jeremy Wilkin but his own voice is heard throughout the rest of the series. The shooting script sets the events on June 23rd, 1980, although Virginia Lake's *Daily Express* newspaper in the completed episode is dated August 24th, 1980.

Regular Cast

Cdr. Ed Straker	**Ed Bishop**
Col. Alec Freeman	**George Sewell**
Dr. Virginia Lake	**Wanda Ventham**
Capt. Peter Carlin	**Peter Gordeno**
Lt. Gay Ellis	**Gabrielle Drake**
Lt. Nina Barry	**Dolores Mantez**
Lt. Joan Harrington	**Antonia Ellis**
Lt. Keith Ford	**Keith Alexander**
Lt. Lew Waterman	**Gary Myers**
Gen. James Henderson	**Grant Taylor**
Miss Ealand	**Norma Ronald**
Lt. Mark Bradley	**Harry Baird**
Lt. John Masters	**Jon Kelley**
Lt. Gordon Maxwell	**Jeremy Wilkin**
Lt. Sylvia Howell	**Georgina Moon**
Lt. Ayshea Johnson	**Ayshea Brough**
Dr. Shroeder	**Maxwell Shaw**
Voice of SID	**Mel Oxley**

Guest Cast

Cabinet Minister	**Basil Dignam**
Lt. Bill Johnson	**Shane Rimmer**
Lt. Ken Matthews	**Michael Mundell**
Dr. Harris	**Matthew Robertson**
Kurt Mahler	**Paul Gillard**
Phil Wade	**Gary Files**
Nurse	**Annette Kerr**
Alien	**Gito Santana**

First UK Transmission

Wednesday, September 16th, 1970
8.00pm (ATV/Tyne Tees/Border)

COMPUTER AFFAIR — Prod. No. 02

Teleplay by **Tony Barwick**
Directed by **David Lane**

Astronaut Ken Matthews is killed during a UFO alert when the alien craft collides with his Interceptor. Freeman believes that Lieutenant Ellis may have been in error when she relayed course instructions to the pilots, so Straker recalls Ellis and the two surviving astronauts, Mark Bradley and Lew Waterman, to Earth to undergo computer tests supervised by Dr. Shroeder. His report suggests that Ellis was influenced in her actions by an emotional attachment to Bradley, so Straker orders the pair to be given separate assignments. Meanwhile, the UFO has been damaged in the collision with the Interceptor and SID tracks the craft when it emerges from hiding in northern Canada. The craft is intercepted by Carlin in Sky One and crash-lands in a forest near Lexfield Air Base. Freeman is assigned to secure the craft and as he is unconvinced by the validity of the computer tests, he decides that Ellis and Bradley will accompany him. Coordinating the operation from a Control Mobile, Ellis selects Mobile 1, commanded by Bradley, to make the final assault on the UFO...

Notes

Tony Barwick's original outline for the episode had the events starting on July 10th, 1985, but his script sets the date as November 4th, 1981 – Mark Bradley's 29th birthday. However, at the end of the episode, Mark Bradley and Gay Ellis share a bottle of champagne that is apparently of 1984 vintage. As filmed for the episode, Freeman's inspection of Moonbase was originally more extensive, but trimmed to reduce the running time of the episode. The inspection ended with a scene in which the Moonbase personnel celebrate Bradley's birthday with a cake and non-alcoholic champagne brought by Freeman. Only the very end of this scene appears in the finished episode: we see Lieutenant Ellis stepping forward to kiss Bradley as Lieutenant Barry announces the UFO sighting (Freeman has a drink in his hand and Lieutenant Harrington has joined the others in the Leisure Sphere).

Regular Cast

Cdr. Ed Straker	**Ed Bishop**
Col. Alec Freeman	**George Sewell**
Capt. Peter Carlin	**Peter Gordeno**
Lt. Gay Ellis	**Gabrielle Drake**
Lt. Nina Barry	**Dolores Mantez**
Lt. Joan Harrington	**Antonia Ellis**
Lt. Keith Ford	**Keith Alexander**
Lt. Lew Waterman	**Gary Myers**
Miss Ealand	**Norma Ronald**
Lt. Mark Bradley	**Harry Baird**
Lt. John Masters	**Jon Kelley**
Lt. Gordon Maxwell	**Jeremy Wilkin**
Lt. Sylvia Howell	**Georgina Moon**
Dr. Shroeder	**Maxwell Shaw**
Voice of SID	**Mel Oxley**

Guest Cast

Dr. Murray	**Peter Burton**
Lt. Ken Matthews	**Michael Mundell**
Operative Chris Granger	**Nigel Lambert**
Lt. Bill Johnson	**Shane Rimmer**
Mobile 1 Personnel	**Hein Viljoen / Dennis Plenty**
Mobile 3 Officer	**Hugh Armstrong**
Operative	**Rosemary Donnelly**
Alien	**Hugo Panczak**

First UK Transmission

Wednesday, December 9th, 1970
8.00pm (Tyne Tees/Border)

FLIGHT PATH

Prod. No. 03

Teleplay by **Ian Scott Stewart** Directed by **Ken Turner**

Regular Cast

Cdr. Ed Straker	**Ed Bishop**
Col. Alec Freeman	**George Sewell**
Capt. Peter Carlin	**Peter Gordeno**
Lt. Gay Ellis	**Gabrielle Drake**
Lt. Nina Barry	**Dolores Mantez**
Lt. Joan Harrington	**Antonia Ellis**
Lt. Keith Ford	**Keith Alexander**
Lt. John Masters	**Jon Kelley**
Lt. Gordon Maxwell	**Jeremy Wilkin**
Lt. Sylvia Howell	**Georgina Moon**
Lt. Ayshea Johnson	**Ayshea Brough**
Dr. Shroeder	**Maxwell Shaw**
Voice of SID	**Mel Oxley**

Guest Cast

Paul Roper	**George Cole**
Carol Roper	**Sonia Fox**
Medic Dawson	**Keith Grenville**
SHADO Guard	**David Daker**

First UK Transmission

Wednesday, January 20th, 1971
8.00pm (ATV/Anglia)

Computer technician Paul Roper ends his current tour of duty on Moonbase and returns to his home on Earth, where he discovers that his wife Carol has been menaced by an unseen visitor. Blackmailed by a mystery caller, Roper promises to pass confidential information to the aliens. Next morning at SHADO HQ, Roper completes a debriefing test which indicates that his decision-making is impaired and he has become a security risk, so Straker assigns Freeman to check him out. Using a directional microphone, Freeman records Roper's telephone conversation when he passes a series of coordinates to his contact later that night. Under interrogation, Roper admits that he was given programme numbers for SID, told to feed in certain information and memorise the results, but he doesn't know the significance of the figures. However, SID deduces that they are a series of navigation coordinates in three dimensions, possibly a flight path for a UFO...

Notes

Author Ian Scott Stewart's original title for this episode, as detailed in his story outline, was 'The Sun Always Rises' and Roper was originally written as 'Paul Bridges'. Just over four minutes of scenes filmed for the start of the episode were deleted from the final edit, including a scene in which Joan Harrington attempts to help Roper pack his belongings in the Moonbase Sleep Sphere, and another in which Roper passes through a Radiation and Documentation check at Earth Spaceport. The character of SHADO medical technician Dawson did not appear in the shooting script: originally, Roper was contacted directly by the aliens and it was an alien who later arrived at the Roper house to kill Carol. Maxwell Shaw (Dr. Shroeder) was the husband of UFO casting director Rose Tobias Shaw. After filming his role in this episode, he underwent major surgery for a heart condition which prevented him from continuing as a member of the series' regular cast for nearly five months (he returned for only one further appearance in *E.S.P.*).

SURVIVAL

Prod. No. 04

Teleplay by **Tony Barwick** Directed by **Alan Perry**

Regular Cast

Cdr. Ed Straker	**Ed Bishop**
Col. Alec Freeman	**George Sewell**
Col. Paul Foster	**Michael Billington**
Lt. Nina Barry	**Dolores Mantez**
Lt. Joan Harrington	**Antonia Ellis**
Lt. Mark Bradley	**Harry Baird**

Guest Cast

Tina Duval	**Suzan Farmer**
Bill Grant	**Robert Swann**
Alien	**Gito Santana**
Rescuers	**Ray Armstrong**
	David Weston

First UK Transmission

Wednesday, January 6th, 1971
8.00pm (ATV/Anglia)

Meteorites play havoc with the Moonbase tracking systems enabling a UFO to land undetected on the lunar surface. One of the vehicle's occupants fires a projectile through the observation port of the Leisure Sphere and astronaut Bill Grant is killed when the sphere undergoes rapid decompression. Colonel Paul Foster realises that the meteorite interference did not last long enough to allow the UFO to depart and Straker sees this as an opportunity to capture a UFO intact. Aerial photos show the UFO in a nearby crater, so Foster and Bradley take a pair of Moonmobiles to investigate. But as they close in on the craft on foot, the UFO opens fire. Foster attempts to return to his Moonmobile but he twists his ankle and falls against a rock outcrop, damaging his radio. When the UFO takes off, it is shot down by the Interceptors and crash-lands on Foster's Moonmobile. As he is out of radio contact, Foster is assumed to have been killed in the explosion. Stranded on the lunar surface, he starts to make his way back to Moonbase but he is found and held at gunpoint by the alien assassin...

Notes

Scenes filmed for *Survival* but deleted from the final edit included an after-dinner scene with Foster and Tina at her apartment in which they discussed their future together, and a later scene in which Freeman broke the news of Foster's death to Tina. Although captions on *Identified* suggest that the events of that episode take place in 1980, this is the only episode of UFO to be specifically dated on screen when Foster announces at Grant's funeral that it is April 12th, 1981.

Oops!

Oddly, Foster uses Straker's car (A21-384) to visit Tina Duval, leaving his own car (A4-215) in the studio car park. The cast seem unable to decide how to pronounce 'Moonmobile': at first it is "moon-mow-beel" but later it becomes "moon-mow-byle".

EXPOSED — Prod. No. 05

Teleplay by **Tony Barwick** — Directed by **David Lane**

During a UFO alert, an XV-104 civilian test aircraft from the Ventura Aircraft Corporation enters the area of the UFO's trajectory termination. The pilot, Paul Foster, sights the UFO and violates orders to leave the area. But when Sky One intercepts the UFO, the XV-104 is damaged and falls to Earth out of control. Foster manages to eject just in time but his co-pilot is killed when the vehicle crashes. After making a full recovery from his injuries, Foster meets with Ventura president William Kofax, who dismisses Foster's UFO story and warns him that if he pursues the matter any further he will never fly again. Foster calls for a hearing into the incident and is taken aboard a military jet to be interviewed by Dr. Jackson, a military intelligence officer. Jackson shows Foster the reconnaissance film from the test plane, but the footage shows nothing out of the ordinary and Foster realises that the film has been doctored. Later, his apartment is trashed by a pair of thugs, but with the help of his co-pilot's sister, Janna Wade, Foster discovers that the cover-up leads to Ed Straker...

Notes

Although filmed after *Survival*, *Exposed* was written to introduce the character of Paul Foster and the producers intended that *Exposed* should follow *Identified* as episode two for transmission. The character's induction to SHADO in *Exposed* would explain why he had not appeared in the opening episode while his absence from *Computer Affair* and *Flight Path* would be due to the rigorous training course that Straker tells Foster he must undergo before qualifying as a SHADO operative. Several scenes filmed for this episode were trimmed in the final edit, including Foster's meeting with Kofax and his hearing with Jackson aboard the military jet. The voice of Matt Zimmerman (Foster's XV-104 co-pilot) is dubbed here by Jeremy Wilkin. The location footage of Paul Foster's apartment building (actually one of a series of flats in Fellows Road, Swiss Cottage, London) was originally shot for the *Handicap Dead* episode of the 1968 ITC series DEPARTMENT S.

Regular Cast

Cdr. Ed Straker	**Ed Bishop**
Col. Alec Freeman	**George Sewell**
Col. Paul Foster	**Michael Billington**
Capt. Peter Carlin	**Peter Gordeno**
Lt. Nina Barry	**Dolores Mantez**
Lt. Joan Harrington	**Antonia Ellis**
Lt. Keith Ford	**Keith Alexander**
Lt. Lew Waterman	**Gary Myers**
Dr. Doug Jackson	**Vladek Sheybal**
Miss Ealand	**Norma Ronald**
Lt. Mark Bradley	**Harry Baird**
Lt. Ayshea Johnson	**Ayshea Brough**
Dr. Frazer	**Basil Moss**
Voice of SID	**Mel Oxley**

Guest Cast

Janna Wade	**Jean Marsh**
William Kofax	**Robin Bailey**
Tsi Chan	**Paula Li Schiu**
Louis Graham	**Arthur Cox**
Co-Pilot Jim	**Matt Zimmerman**
Nurse	**Sue Gerrard**

First UK Transmission

Wednesday, September 23rd, 1970
8.00pm (ATV/Tyne Tees/Border)

CONFLICT — Prod. No. 06

Teleplay by **Ruric Powell** — Directed by **Ken Turner**

Straker puts forward a proposal to the International Astrophysical Commission for a total space clearance programme. Space junk poses a threat to SHADO operations and could be used by the aliens to crack SHADO defences but General Henderson, head of the IAC, balks at the cost. However, a small Limpet UFO is already using debris from Apollo 8 as cover from which to strike against SHADO's space vehicles. Attaching itself to Lunar Module 32, piloted by Steve Maddox, the UFO dramatically alters the Module's re-entry angle and the vehicle burns up on orbit insertion. Suspecting that Maddox might have been involved in a re-entry collision with space debris, Straker pressures Henderson to consider his space clearance report before making a final decision, but the General only agrees to do so if Straker suspends all flights between Earth and the Moon. Straker agrees to the orbital flight ban, but Foster is determined to prove Maddox innocent of error and takes off in Lunar Module 29 to follow the same route as Maddox's craft, ignoring Straker's orders to turn back...

Notes

This episode was filmed under the title of 'Ambush' and did not become *Conflict* until after principal photography was completed. Ruric Powell's shooting script details that the International Astrophysical Commission is part of a larger United Space organisation, created in 1980 when the nations of the world combined their space programmes. Henderson's role in *Conflict* was originally written for a different character, 'James L. Douglas', but his dialogue was not significantly altered when the name was changed.

Oops!

The first shot of the Limpet UFO shows it nestling into the side of Apollo 8 with the dome pointing downwards, but when the shot cuts to a close-up (overlaid by the UFO logo caption), the Limpet UFO has suddenly flipped the other way up.

Regular Cast

Cdr. Ed Straker	**Ed Bishop**
Col. Alec Freeman	**George Sewell**
Col. Paul Foster	**Michael Billington**
Capt. Peter Carlin	**Peter Gordeno**
Lt. Nina Barry	**Dolores Mantez**
Lt. Joan Harrington	**Antonia Ellis**
Lt. Keith Ford	**Keith Alexander**
Lt. Lew Waterman	**Gary Myers**
Gen. James Henderson	**Grant Taylor**
Miss Ealand	**Norma Ronald**
Lt. Ayshea Johnson	**Ayshea Brough**

Guest Cast

Captain Steve Maddox	**Drewe Henley**
Pilot – Space Ship	**Gerald Norman**
Navigator – Space Ship	**Alan Tucker**
Lunar Module Crewman Stevens	**David Courtland**
Joe Steiner	**Michael Kilgarriff**

First UK Transmission

Wednesday, October 7th, 1970
8.00pm (ATV)

THE DALOTEK AFFAIR

Prod. No. 07

Regular Cast

Cdr. Ed Straker	**Ed Bishop**
Col. Alec Freeman	**George Sewell**
Col. Paul Foster	**Michael Billington**
Lt. Nina Barry	**Dolores Mantez**
Lt. Joan Harrington	**Antonia Ellis**
Lt. Keith Ford	**Keith Alexander**
Lt. Lew Waterman	**Gary Myers**
Lt. Ayshea Johnson	**Ayshea Brough**
Voice of SID	**Mel Oxley**

Guest Cast

Jane Carson	**Tracy Reed**
Mark Tanner	**Clinton Greyn**
Phil Mitchell	**David Weston**
Dr. Frazer	**Basil Moss**
Blake	**Philip Latham**
Dr. Charles Reed	**John Breslin**
Lunar Module Pilot	**Alan Tucker**
Moonmobile Captain	**John Cobner**
Moonmobile Lt.	**Richard Poore**
Dr. Frank E. Stranges	**himself**

First UK Transmission

Wednesday, February 10th, 1971
8.00pm (ATV/Anglia)

Teleplay by **Ruric Powell** Directed by **Alan Perry**

Three UFOs approach Moonbase and then veer off, heading back the way they came. But as they return to deep space, one of the UFOs ejects a small object which makes its way back to the Moon. Assumed to be a meteorite, the object is tracked to its termination point near the Dalotek installation, base of a three-man geological expedition funded by a private corporation which has agreed to use limited radio frequencies so as not to interfere with SHADO operations. Then Moonbase experiences a complete communications breakdown, apparently the result of outside interference, so Foster visits the Dalotek unit and demands that they shut down their geo-scanner. Jane Carson, the geologist in charge of the geo-scanner, assures him that it has not been operating outside the guidelines, but when a second blackout occurs, a Lunar Module is cut off from computer control for landing and it crashes onto the lunar surface, killing the crew!

Notes

The working title of this episode was 'Crater 236', the designation assigned to the new crater created by the alien jamming device. In Ruric Powell's original script, the name of Blake's company was the 'Calotex' Corporation. Early in production, it was planned that David Weston (Mitchell) would appear irregularly in the series as astronaut Gary North, but the role did not materialise. The restaurant favoured by Foster and Freeman is the same one frequented by Gay Ellis and Mark Bradley in *Computer Affair*, although the interior has been completely refurbished. During filming of this episode in July 1969, Apollo 11 landed on the Moon and Neil Armstrong became the first man to walk on the lunar surface.

Oops!

During Straker's initial conversation with Blake, there are a number of papers on his desk pad, but when the camera angle changes the papers have completely vanished!

A QUESTION OF PRIORITIES

Prod. No. 08

Regular Cast

Cdr. Ed Straker	**Ed Bishop**
Col. Alec Freeman	**George Sewell**
Capt. Peter Carlin	**Peter Gordeno**
Lt. Gay Ellis	**Gabrielle Drake**
Lt. Nina Barry	**Dolores Mantez**
Lt. Keith Ford	**Keith Alexander**
Lt. Lew Waterman	**Gary Myers**
Miss Ealand	**Norma Ronald**
Lt. John Masters	**Jon Kelley**
Lt. Gordon Maxwell	**Jeremy Wilkin**
Lt. Ayshea Johnson	**Ayshea Brough**
Lt. Sylvia Howell	**Georgina Moon**
Voice of SID	**Mel Oxley**

Guest Cast

Mary Rutland	**Suzanne Neve**
Mrs. O'Connor	**Mary Merrall**
John Rutland	**Barnaby Shaw**
Steven Rutland	**Philip Madoc**
Dr. Segal	**Peter Halliday**
Dr. Green	**Russell Napier**
Alien	**Richard Aylen**
Nurse	**Andrea Allen**
Car Driver	**David Cargill**
SHADO Operative	**Penny Spencer**

First UK Transmission

Wednesday, October 14th, 1970
8.00pm (ATV/Tyne Tees)

Teleplay by **Tony Barwick** Directed by **David Lane**

Straker's son John is badly injured in a car accident after spending the day with his father at the film studios. He is rushed to hospital where Dr. Segal informs Straker and his ex-wife Mary that John is haemorrhaging and his allergy to antibiotics means that his only hope is a new anti-allergenic drug from the USA. Fortunately, Straker is able to arrange for the drug to be flown over on a Mobile Transporter. Meanwhile, an alien enters the home of a blind old lady, Mrs. O'Connor, and sets up a transmitter to broadcast a powerful signal which is picked up at SHADO HQ. Straker realises that the alien could be a defector on the run from his own people and seeking sanctuary but to locate the source of the transmission, Mobiles are needed to triangulate from the ground. Freeman diverts the nearest Mobile Transporter to Ireland, unaware that this is the very aircraft that is ferrying the vital drug that will save John's life!

Notes

The story for this episode was devised by Gerry Anderson and then developed into a full script by Tony Barwick. In the script, Straker and Mary are described as having been divorced for just three years. The original ending filmed for the episode featured Straker visiting Mrs. O'Connor at her cottage where the old lady offers Straker some absolution by telling him that she senses he is a good man. Suzanne Neve (Mary) wears a costume that was originally made for Loni Von Freidl as Lise Hartman in *Doppelgänger* (1968). Straker and John are seen driving the Model T Ford (T42) that previously appeared as Gabriel in THE SECRET SERVICE.

Oops!

Dr. Segal talks authoritatively about an 'anti-allergeretic drug' when what he really means is an anti-*allergenic* drug. Philip Madoc is incorrectly credited as 'Phillip' Madoc on the end titles.

ORDEAL

Prod. No. 09

Teleplay by **Tony Barwick** Directed by **Ken Turner**

While the Moonbase personnel respond to a UFO sighting, Paul Foster arrives at the SHADO Research Centre to take part in a mandatory fitness programme. Tired and hung-over from an all-night party, he undergoes a gruelling exercise regime supervised by Dr. Frazer and then falls asleep in the sauna bath, but when he wakes up and tries to leave, he finds the door jammed and the temperature control turned up to 130º F. He collapses from the heat and is unable to defend himself when a pair of aliens burst in, drag him from the sauna and beat him senseless. The aliens take him to their craft where he is kitted out in an alien space suit and helmet filled with green liquid. When Freeman finds everyone dead at the Research Centre, he realises that Foster has been kidnapped by the aliens, but Straker gives orders for the escaping UFO to be destroyed on sight!

Notes

Tony Barwick's original script for *Ordeal* focussed on Peter Carlin as the subject of the alien abduction – the party sequence at the start of the episode was specifically written to highlight Peter Gordeno's dancing talents. Scenes of Freeman arriving at the party and chatting with Foster and Sylvia Graham were filmed for the episode but cut from the final edit. The set for the reception area of the SHADO Research Centre is a revamp of the hospital reception set built for *A Question Of Priorities*.

Oops!

When Foster arrives at the Research Centre, the face of a crew member can be seen reflected in the window of the car's gull-wing door as Foster climbs out. Everything that happens before Foster passes out in the sauna is 'real', yet the threat of the approaching UFO is left unresolved when Foster recovers. On the end credits, Basil Moss's character is captioned as 'Dr. Harris' instead of Dr. Frazer, while Peter Burton's character is captioned as 'Perry' instead of Dr. Murray.

Regular Cast

Cdr. Ed Straker	**Ed Bishop**
Col. Alec Freeman	**George Sewell**
Col. Paul Foster	**Michael Billington**
Lt. Gay Ellis	**Gabrielle Drake**
Lt. Nina Barry	**Dolores Mantez**
Lt. Joan Harrington	**Antonia Ellis**
Lt. Keith Ford	**Keith Alexander**
Capt. Lew Waterman	**Gary Myers**
Dr. Doug Jackson	**Vladek Sheybal**
Lt. John Masters	**Jon Kelley**
Lt. Gordon Maxwell	**Jeremy Wilkin**
Lt. Ayshea Johnson	**Ayshea Brough**
Lt. Sylvia Howell	**Georgina Moon**
Dr. Frazer	**Basil Moss**
Voice of SID	**Mel Oxley**

Guest Cast

Sylvia Graham	**Quinn O'Hara**
Joe Franklin	**David Healy**
Dr. Murray	**Peter Burton**
Medic	**Joseph Morris**
Interceptor Pilot	**Mark Hawkins**

First UK Transmission

Wednesday, January 20th, 1971
8.00pm (Tyne Tees)

THE RESPONSIBILITY SEAT

Prod. No. 10

Teleplay by **Tony Barwick** Directed by **Alan Perry**

In his role as a film studio executive, Straker is interviewed by reporter Josephine Fraser of the Global Press Agency. She records the interview using a microphone in the front of her purse, but when she leaves the purse in Straker's office while he walks her to her car, the microphone records Ford's voice on the intercom referring to him as "Commander Straker". While Straker tours the studio lot, Jo returns to the office to collect her bag and when he learns what has happened, Straker realises that they may have a security leak. Leaving Freeman in charge, he sets off to track down Jo and recover the tape. Meanwhile, Moonbase tracks the erratic course of a Russian mobile rig, a commercial mining vehicle used by the Sovatek company. Sovatek Commander Dudzinski admits that he has been unable to establish radio contact with the crew and the rig is driving out of control on a course that will eventually lead it to a collision with Moonbase!

Notes

Jane Merrow (Jo Fraser) wears a costume that was originally worn by Loni Von Freidl in *Doppelgänger* (1968). The bar visited by Straker and Jo is the restaurant previously seen in *Computer Affair* and *The Dalotek Affair* although the interior decor has changed again.

Oops!

While Straker tracks down Jo Fraser, his suit repeatedly changes colour between cream and grey. As Foster is waiting on the lunar surface to board the Sovatek Rig, an alien can be seen reflected in his helmet faceplate (the footage is actually lifted from *Survival*). Sovatek is written in Russian characters as 'COBATEK' on the interior wall of the mobile rig, but the company logo (as seen on Dudzinski's uniform) is a stylised 'S'. The condition of the rig crew is repeatedly referred to (both on-screen and in the script) as 'inoxia' – it should be *anoxia*. As the rig approaches Moonbase, the colour of Ellis and Harrington's space helmets repeatedly changes between white and yellow.

Regular Cast

Cdr. Ed Straker	**Ed Bishop**
Col. Alec Freeman	**George Sewell**
Col. Paul Foster	**Michael Billington**
Lt. Gay Ellis	**Gabrielle Drake**
Lt. Nina Barry	**Dolores Mantez**
Lt. Joan Harrington	**Antonia Ellis**
Lt. Keith Ford	**Keith Alexander**
Capt. Lew Waterman	**Gary Myers**
Miss Ealand	**Norma Ronald**
Lt. John Masters	**Jon Kelley**
Lt. Gordon Maxwell	**Jeremy Wilkin**
Lt. Ayshea Johnson	**Ayshea Brough**
Lt. Sylvia Howell	**Georgina Moon**
Voice of SID	**Mel Oxley**

Guest Cast

Josephine Fraser	**Jane Merrow**
Commander Dudzinski	**Patrick Jordan**
Russian Astronauts	**Janos Kurucz**
	Paul Tamarin
Film Director	**Ralph Bell**
Stuntman	**Royston Rowe**
Interceptor Pilot	**Mark Hawkins**
SHADO Operative	**Penny Spencer**

First UK Transmission

Wednesday, March 3rd, 1971
8.00pm (Anglia)

THE SQUARE TRIANGLE

Prod. No. 11

Teleplay by **Alan Pattillo** Directed by **David Lane**

When a UFO on Earth approach is confirmed to have a trajectory termination in southern England, Straker decides to allow the craft to pass through the SHADO defences. The UFO lands in woods between Clare Cross and Lingbury, so Straker has the area cordoned off and assigns Foster to lead a search team in the Mobiles. Meanwhile, at a cottage near Lingbury, Liz Newton and her lover Cass Fowler are preparing an elaborate plan to murder her husband Jack in such a way that it will appear to be an accident. She phones a friend to explain that she is staying at the cottage alone while Jack is away on business, so that when her husband arrives at midnight and she shoots him as he comes through the door, it will appear that she believed he was an intruder and shot him in self defence!

Notes

Alan Pattillo's original script for *The Square Triangle* featured an additional scene at the start of the episode: set in Jack Newton's office, this scene established that Newton has been having an affair with his secretary Miss Cadwell. Adrienne Corri (Liz Newton) wears a costume that was originally made for Loni Von Freidl in *Doppelgänger* (1968). The closing scene in the churchyard was a late unscripted addition. Filmed at the Church of St. Mary the Virgin in Harefield, Buckinghamshire (previously seen as St. David's Church in the Joe 90 episode *The Unorthodox Shepherd*) this sequence replaces the regular UFO end title sequence.

Oops!

Lieutenant Ford's voice is dubbed throughout by another actor whose tone and delivery is entirely unlike that of Keith Alexander (unfortunately, Alexander was unavailable for post-sync work on this episode). Straker recalls the Interceptors without firing on the UFO, but the Interceptors are nonetheless seen returning to Moonbase without their missiles (the footage was shot for *Computer Affair*).

Regular Cast

Cdr. Ed Straker	**Ed Bishop**
Col. Alec Freeman	**George Sewell**
Col. Paul Foster	**Michael Billington**
Lt. Gay Ellis	**Gabrielle Drake**
Lt. Nina Barry	**Dolores Mantez**
Lt. Joan Harrington	**Antonia Ellis**
Lt. Keith Ford	**Keith Alexander**
Capt. Lew Waterman	**Gary Myers**
Miss Ealand	**Norma Ronald**
Lt. Ayshea Johnson	**Ayshea Brough**
Voice of SID	**Mel Oxley**

Guest Cast

Liz Newton	**Adrienne Corri**
Cass Fowler	**Patrick Mower**
Jack Newton	**Allan Cuthbertson**
Alien	**Anthony Chinn**
Game Warden Mitchell	**Godfrey James**
SHADO Mobile Navigator Clyde	**Hugo Panczak**

First UK Transmission

Wednesday, November 11th, 1970
8.00pm (Tyne Tees/Border)

COURT MARTIAL

Prod. No. 12

Teleplay by **Tony Barwick** Directed by **Ron Appleton**

Information about a *Skydiver* rendezvous with a supply ship has been leaked to the press and Straker traces the leak back to Foster. The Colonel denies the accusation, but when there is a second leak, this time of a Moonbase mission authorised by Foster, Henderson convenes a military court martial indicting Foster under Section 8 of SHADO security procedures. Dr. Jackson, acting as prosecution counsel, calls several of Foster's colleagues as witnesses, forcing them to admit that the only possible source of the leaks is Foster. Then Jackson questions Foster about $10,000 that was recently deposited by an unknown subscriber into his bank account, but Foster denies all knowledge of it. Despite the damning evidence, Straker is convinced that Foster is innocent but the jury finds him guilty and as this is a military court, the sentence is death!

Notes

The working title of this episode was 'Shoot To Kill'. Tony Barwick's script included a UFO sighting and successful interception at the start of the episode, as well as an additional scene in which Straker and Freeman coerce information from surveillance device manufacturer Singleton by dousing him in petroleum solvent and threatening to set light to him with a blow lamp. The pre-credits sequence which previews the verdict of the court from later in the episode was a late addition which did not appear in the shooting script. The footage of the IAC headquarters building is lifted from *Conflict* while the footage of Foster's apartment building is taken from *Exposed*.

Oops!

The picture is flipped horizontally on Freeman's line "But who is it?" in Straker's office (the parting in Freeman's hair suddenly moves to the opposite side of his head). The agent's protégée is clearly named Diana on-screen, but on the end titles she is captioned as 'Diane'.

Regular Cast

Cdr. Ed Straker	**Ed Bishop**
Col. Alec Freeman	**George Sewell**
Col. Paul Foster	**Michael Billington**
Lt. Keith Ford	**Keith Alexander**
Capt. Lew Waterman	**Gary Myers**
Gen. James Henderson	**Grant Taylor**
Dr. Doug Jackson	**Vladek Sheybal**
Miss Ealand	**Norma Ronald**
Lt. John Masters	**Jon Kelley**

Guest Cast

Webb	**Jack Hedley**
Jane Grant	**Georgina Cookson**
Carl Mason	**Neil McCallum**
Artist's Agent	**Noel Davis**
Assistant Director	**Paul Greenhalgh**
Guard	**Michael Glover**
A.G. Singleton	**Tutte Lemkow**
Miss Scott	**Louise Pajo**
Diana	**Pippa Steel**

First UK Transmission

Saturday, May 1st, 1971
5.15pm (ATV)

CLOSE UP — Prod. No. 13

Teleplay by **Tony Barwick** Directed by **Alan Perry**

A test transmission from a satellite fitted with an electronic telescope results in detailed photographs of the Earth's surface, convincing Straker to champion Project Discovery, a plan to launch a modified B142 space probe fitted with the electronic telescope and programmed to follow a UFO back to its homeworld. The project is approved by Henderson's finance committee and a launch date is set with NASA. The launch goes as scheduled and the probe takes up orbit around the Moon. Phase One of Project Discovery is reasonably straightforward: Foster and Masters rendezvous with the probe in the Lunar Module, spacewalking between the two craft to fit the specialised equipment. However, Phase Two of the operation, manoeuvring a UFO into a position where the probe can be locked onto its flight pattern, proves to be much more dangerous...

Notes

The entire sequence with *Skydiver* at the start of the episode was a late addition to Tony Barwick's script, designed to add three minutes to an episode that was running short. Another sequence written to pad out the episode was dropped from the final edit: set in the Sleep Sphere on Moonbase it featured Nina Barry and Joan Harrington discussing the male visitors to Moonbase, revealing that Nina fancies Foster and Masters while Joan thinks that Straker is 'minty'. Lieutenant Ayshea Johnson was originally going to be the focus of Kelly's close-up photography at the end of the episode. The spacewalk sequence is accompanied by incidental music originally composed for *Doppelgänger* (1968).

Oops!

Both Kelly and Henderson refer to the International Astrophysical Commission as the 'Astro Space Commission'. Joan Harrington reveals that the UFO is travelling at speed SOL 8.35, but SID then announces the UFO's speed as SOL *minus* 8.35 which Ford confirms is constant.

Regular Cast

Cdr. Ed Straker	**Ed Bishop**
Col. Alec Freeman	**George Sewell**
Col. Paul Foster	**Michael Billington**
Lt. Gay Ellis	**Gabrielle Drake**
Lt. Nina Barry	**Dolores Mantez**
Lt. Joan Harrington	**Antonia Ellis**
Lt. Keith Ford	**Keith Alexander**
Capt. Lew Waterman	**Gary Myers**
Gen. James Henderson	**Grant Taylor**
Lt. John Masters	**Jon Kelley**
Lt. Gordon Maxwell	**Jeremy Wilkin**
Lt. Ayshea Johnson	**Ayshea Brough**
Lt. Sylvia Howell	**Georgina Moon**
Voice of SID	**Mel Oxley**

Guest Cast

Dr. Joseph Kelly	**Neil Hallett**
Dr. Young	**James Beckett**
Tracking Operative	**Alan Tucker**
Launch Controller	**Frank Mann**
Interceptor Pilots	**Mark Hawkins**
	John Levene
Launch Operative 1	**Robert Sherman**
Launch Operative 2	**Robert Howay**
Launch Control Harry	**Clive Endersby**

First UK Transmission

Wednesday, December 16th, 1970
8.00pm (ATV/Anglia)

CONFETTI CHECK A-O.K. — Prod. No. 14

Teleplay by **Tony Barwick** Directed by **David Lane**

The birth of Lieutenant Grey's twins brings back uncomfortable memories for Straker as his mind goes back to his wedding day. It is 1970 and Straker and his new wife Mary plan to honeymoon in Greece, but the holiday is cancelled when Straker is called to an urgent meeting with Henderson, recovering in hospital after the UFO attack on their Rolls-Royce. On Henderson's instructions, Straker flies to New York to make a presentation to the special committee of the United Nations, proposing the formation of an international organisation to defend the Earth from an extra-terrestrial threat. His passionate plea earns unanimous approval and Straker is appointed Commander in Chief of SHADO. But over the next few months, the long hours working in total secrecy to set up the organisation begin to take their toll on Straker's marriage...

Notes

An introductory scene for Lieutenants Ford and Barry was filmed for the episode but cut from the final edit. In it, Straker watches the taping of a television programme in which Ford interviews William Lloyd, a man who claims to have seen a UFO in his garden, and Nina Barry, an electronics expert from London University who is called upon to examine and disprove Lloyd's photographs. After the interview concludes, Straker approaches Ford and invites him to join SHADO. This is one of only two UFO episodes that do not feature the regular title sequence (the other is *The Psychobombs*). A calendar on the wall by the reception desk at the Caledonian Hotel shows a snowy scene, which would seem to indicate that the Strakers were married in December 1970. The Jensen Interceptor driven by Straker here was actually owned by producer Reg Hill.

Oops!

In 1971, Straker and Freeman arrive at the IAC headquarters building in Straker's SHADO car.

Regular Cast

Cdr. Ed Straker	**Ed Bishop**
Col. Alec Freeman	**George Sewell**
Lt. Nina Barry	**Dolores Mantez**
Lt. Joan Harrington	**Antonia Ellis**
Lt. Keith Ford	**Keith Alexander**
Gen. James Henderson	**Grant Taylor**
Lt. John Masters	**Jon Kelley**
Lt. Gordon Maxwell	**Jeremy Wilkin**
Lt. Ayshea Johnson	**Ayshea Brough**

Guest Cast

Mary Straker	**Suzanne Neve**
Mary's Father	**Michael Nightingale**
English Delegate	**Jack May**
Monsieur Duval	**Jeffrey Segal**
German Delegate	**Gordon Sterne**
US Delegate	**Alan Tilvern**
Lt. David Grey	**Julian Grant**
CIA Man	**Shane Rimmer**
Hotel Clerk	**Geoffrey Hinsliff**
Estate Agent	**Donald Pelmear**
Porter	**Frank Tregear**
Doctor	**Tom Oliver**
Nurse	**Penny Jackson**

First UK Transmission

Saturday, July 10th, 1971
5.15pm (ATV)

E.S.P. — Prod. No. 15

Teleplay by **Alan Fennell** Directed by **Ken Turner**

Regular Cast

Cdr. Ed Straker	**Ed Bishop**
Col. Alec Freeman	**George Sewell**
Col. Paul Foster	**Michael Billington**
Lt. Gay Ellis	**Gabrielle Drake**
Lt. Nina Barry	**Dolores Mantez**
Lt. Joan Harrington	**Antonia Ellis**
Lt. Keith Ford	**Keith Alexander**
Miss Ealand	**Norma Ronald**
Lt. Mark Bradley	**Harry Baird**
Dr. Shroeder	**Maxwell Shaw**

Guest Cast

John Croxley	**John Stratton**
Dr. Ward	**Douglas Wilmer**
Stella Croxley	**Deborah Stanford**
SHADO Security Man	**Stanley McGeagh**
Gate-Man	**Donald Tandy**

First UK Transmission

Wednesday, October 7th, 1970
8.00pm (Tyne Tees)

After an appointment with a psychiatrist to discuss his unusually strong telepathic abilities, accountant John Croxley has a premonition that his wife Stella is about to have a visitor. Meanwhile, SHADO tracks a UFO that is following an odd flight pattern, banking and weaving as if it is trying to find something. Damaged by the Interceptors, the UFO heads for southern England, but as it heads for a landing, the vehicle crashes through the upper floor of Croxley's house, killing Stella. On his way home, Croxley experiences the disaster in his mind before passing out. Foster is badly injured when he arrives at the ruined house just as the UFO explodes. He is taken to hospital while Straker expresses his condolences to Croxley, but the man blames Straker for his wife's death. A month later, Straker receives a personally addressed package in the mail which contains a film script written by Croxley detailing the entire SHADO set-up...

Notes

In the original script, Freeman says that the largest piece of the destroyed UFO was found in Foster's left side, rather than embedded in Mobile 2 as in the completed episode. In the climax of this earlier version, Croxley shoots Foster in the shoulder when he arrives in the driveway of the ruined house and continues to fire on him as Foster takes cover. The gun's reports cause part of the building to collapse, half-burying Straker and Freeman, but Croxley escapes and pursues Foster into the drive. Reacting without consciously thinking about it, Foster shoots Croxley dead, and then rescues Straker and Freeman from the rubble just before the entire house collapses.

Oops!

Although Douglas Wilmer's character is named Dr. Ward in both the script and on the episode credits, his name appears as Dr. A. Brünner on the name plaque outside his office. Stanley McGeagh is mis-credited as Stanley 'McGeogh' on the end titles.

KILL STRAKER! — Prod. No. 16

Teleplay by **Donald James** Directed by **Alan Perry**

Regular Cast

Cdr. Ed Straker	**Ed Bishop**
Col. Alec Freeman	**George Sewell**
Col. Paul Foster	**Michael Billington**
Lt. Gay Ellis	**Gabrielle Drake**
Lt. Nina Barry	**Dolores Mantez**
Lt. Joan Harrington	**Antonia Ellis**
Lt. Keith Ford	**Keith Alexander**
Gen. James Henderson	**Grant Taylor**
Dr. Doug Jackson	**Vladek Sheybal**
Lt. Mark Bradley	**Harry Baird**
Lt. Ayshea Johnson	**Ayshea Brough**
Voice of SID	**Mel Oxley**

Guest Cast

Captain Frank Craig	**David Sumner**
Moonbase Guard	**Steve Cory**
Nurse	**Louise Pajo**

First UK Transmission

Wednesday, September 30th, 1970
8.00pm (Border)

SID confirms a UFO sighting just as a Lunar Module piloted by Colonel Foster and Captain Frank Craig is approaching re-entry. Straker orders Craig to make an emergency re-entry but the UFO closes in on the Module and Craig and Foster are bathed in hypnotic coloured lights while unearthly voices urge them to "kill Straker". The Lunar Module is recovered 16 hours later but Foster has become belligerent, blaming Straker for the re-entry accident which caused the Lunar Module to bounce off the Earth's atmosphere, and questioning Straker's motives in requesting funding for the construction of four automated Moonbases. That night, while Straker is asleep, Craig enters his quarters and attempts to inject an air bubble into his blood stream but fortunately, Straker wakes and fights him off. Evading capture, Craig steals a detonation pack and leaves the base, intending to destroy Moonbase's vital air purifying and water recovery installation...

Notes

The working title of this episode was 'The Inside Man'. Donald James's script included a scene in which Straker mourns Foster's apparent death in the Lunar Module accident with a drinking binge in a local bar, but the scene was dropped as it was considered to be a contradiction of Straker's character to behave in this way.

Oops!

Lieutenant Barry confirms the UFO's speed as SOL 0.4 (zero decimal four), but Lieutenant Ellis relays the speed to SHADO HQ as SOL 4.0 (four decimal zero) and Ford then announces that the UFO's speed has increased to SOL 0.6 (zero decimal six). As the Lunar Module makes its steep re-entry, the Limpet UFO from *Conflict* can clearly be seen attached to the underside (the footage is lifted from the earlier episode). The three Interceptor pilots seen jumping down the chutes to board their vehicles are all Caucasian but seconds later, one of them has turned into Mark Bradley.

SUB-SMASH — Prod. No. 17

Teleplay by **Alan Fennell** — Directed by **David Lane**

After the *Atlantica 4* tanker ship is attacked by an Unidentified Submarine Object, Straker decides to make a detailed search of the area in *Skydiver*, accompanying a crew of four field experts despite his claustrophobia. As *Skydiver* begins a radar sweep of the search area, Straker and Foster discuss how it would be much easier for the aliens to take human bodies from the middle of the ocean, where there would be no witnesses. Suddenly, *Skydiver* comes under attack from the USO, which damages the submarine's rear section and port motor, preventing it from surfacing. Waterman launches in Sky One and pursues the USO into the atmosphere, successfully destroying the craft, but *Skydiver* sinks as the turbines fail and the submarine comes to rest on a rock ledge. A marker beacon is launched but with radio communications down, the crew are completely cut off from SHADO Control...

Notes

A different opening scene, featuring Straker and Nina facing death alone in *Skydiver*, was filmed for the episode but dropped in the final edit. It was originally intended that the rest of the episode would then appear in flashback to explain how they arrived in this predicament. In this opening scene, the pair observed that they have known each other for 12 years (thereby dating the episode to 1984 as *Confetti Check A-O.K.* established that they met in 1972). Only Straker's log recording from the end of this scene was retained in the completed episode, although relocated to the end of the story. Flashback footage from *A Question Of Priorities* and *Confetti Check A-O.K.* appears as Straker hallucinates. During the first broadcast of this episode, many viewers would have been confused by these sequences as *Confetti Check A-O.K.* had not been shown before *Sub-Smash* was transmitted, and viewers in the Anglia region had not seen *A Question Of Priorities* either. For this episode alone, Freeman's hair is brushed from the right. This was the last episode of UFO to be filmed at the MGM British Studios in Borehamwood.

Regular Cast

Cdr. Ed Straker	**Ed Bishop**
Col. Alec Freeman	**George Sewell**
Col. Paul Foster	**Michael Billington**
Lt. Nina Barry	**Dolores Mantez**
Lt. Keith Ford	**Keith Alexander**
Capt. Lew Waterman	**Gary Myers**

Guest Cast

Lt. Jim Lewis	**Paul Maxwell**
Lt. Chin	**Anthony Chinn**
Holden	**John Golightly**
Albatross Pilot Turner	**Burnell Tucker**
SHADO Diver Ross	**Alan Haywood**
Mary Rutland	**Suzanne Neve**
John Rutland	**Barnaby Shaw**

First UK Transmission

Wednesday, November 11th, 1970
8.00pm (ATV/Anglia)

THE SOUND OF SILENCE — Prod. No. 18

Teleplay by **David Lane** and **Bob Bell** — Directed by **David Lane**

A UFO takes up a position two miles from GSP 4, a manned NASA probe, and follows it back to Earth, using the probe as protection from the Moonbase Interceptors which cannot risk making an attack. The UFO lands somewhere in a thickly wooded area so Straker alerts the Mobiles to make a ground search. Meanwhile, at nearby Stone Dean Farm, international show-jumper Russell Stone is having some trouble with an itinerant hippy, Ben Culley. Stone warns the hippy off the estate but Culley lusts after Stone's sister Anne and that night, he sneaks into the stables where he is attacked and dragged away by an alien. The next morning, Stone is practising in the show paddock when he is thrown by his horse and knocked unconscious. The horse returns to the farmhouse alone but when Anne and her father go looking for Stone, there is no sign of him. Pa Stone searches the woods but finds only the horribly mutilated body of Culley's dog...

Notes

This was the first episode of UFO to be filmed at Pinewood Studios in Buckinghamshire. A short additional scene in which another hippy, Joe, informs Culley of their group's decision to banish him from their company for being "a bad scene" was filmed for the episode but dropped from the final edit. The script by director David Lane and production designer Bob Bell reveals the name of Ayshea Brough's SHADO Operative character, previously referred to in the series' scripts only as 'Ayshea' or 'Aisha': she is Lieutenant Johnson (Straker is actually seen speaking to her with this name on-screen, but as the character is on the other end of Straker's intercom at the time, it is not entirely clear who he is talking to). Bob Bell specifically wrote this episode around the setting of the real Stone Dean Farm in the Quaker village of Jordans in Buckinghamshire, which was not far from his home. He was also instrumental in securing permission for the UFO production crew to film on location at the farm. Music composed for the Joe 90 episode *Hi-Jacked* accompanies the scene in which Russ chases Culley through the woods.

Regular Cast

Cdr. Ed Straker	**Ed Bishop**
Col. Paul Foster	**Michael Billington**
Lt. Nina Barry	**Dolores Mantez**
Lt. Ayshea Johnson	**Ayshea Brough**
Dr. Frazer	**Basil Moss**
Voice of SID	**Mel Oxley**

Guest Cast

Russell Stone	**Michael Jayston**
Anne Stone	**Susan Jameson**
Pa Stone	**Richard Vernon**
Ben Culley	**Nigel Gregory**
Alien	**Gito Santana**
GSP 4 Pilot Hudson	**Craig Hunter**
GSP 4 Co-Pilot Scott	**Burnell Tucker**
1st Technician	**Tom Oliver**
2nd Technician	**Malcolm Reynolds**
Moonbase Operative	**Andrea Allen**
Voice of Interceptor Pilot	**Keith Alexander**
Animal Noises	**Percy Edwards**

First UK Transmission

Wednesday, October 7th, 1970
8.00pm (Border)

THE CAT WITH TEN LIVES — Prod. No. 19

Teleplay by **David Tomblin** — Directed by **David Tomblin**

Following a UFO attack on Moonbase in which the Interceptors successfully destroy three of the alien spacecraft, Interceptor pilot Jim Regan returns home for a well-earned vacation only to find that his wife Jean has arranged for them to visit his cousin Albert Thompson and wife Muriel for dinner. On their way home, Jim stops the car to avoid hitting a Siamese cat in the road and they are suddenly attacked by aliens who render the couple unconscious, taking them back to their craft. Regan is subjected to a barrage of lights and sounds but then finds himself back in the car, powerless to stop the UFO lifting off with Jean aboard. Back at SHADO HQ, Regan is assigned to escort the Venus Probe as it returns to Earth, but the astronaut has fallen under the influence of an alien consciousness implanted in the mind of the Siamese cat!

Notes

Wanda Ventham makes her first appearance in the series as a member of the regular cast, reprising her guest role from *Identified* (made over 12 months previously). Her role in this episode was scripted simply as '2nd in Command' as the producers had not decided upon a replacement character for Alec Freeman when the script was written. Dr. Jackson's role was originally written as a character named 'Dr. Zradowski'. When Foster leaves SHADO HQ for Moonbase, he exits from what was, at the time, the UFO production offices at Pinewood Studios' J&K Stage administration block.

Oops!

It doesn't seem quite right that Regan has the personal use of Foster's car (A4-215). As the UFO leaves Earth and the Interceptors attack, Captain Minto fires his missile control but his missile (seen through the cockpit window) stays where it is. In several close-up shots of the cat at the end of the episode, it is more than obvious that the animal is being held up to the camera and is actually clear of the ground.

Regular Cast

Cdr. Ed Straker	**Ed Bishop**
Col. Paul Foster	**Michael Billington**
Col. Virginia Lake	**Wanda Ventham**
Lt. Nina Barry	**Dolores Mantez**
Dr. Doug Jackson	**Vladek Sheybal**
Lt. Ayshea Johnson	**Ayshea Brough**
Capt. Steve Minto	**Steven Berkoff**
Voice of SID	**Mel Oxley**

Guest Cast

Lt. Jim Regan	**Alexis Kanner**
Jean Regan	**Geraldine Moffatt**
Albert Thompson	**Colin Gordon**
Muriel Thompson	**Eleanor Summerfield**
Miss Holland	**Lois Maxwell**
Morgan	**Windsor Davies**
Lt. Andy Conroy	**Al Mancini**

First UK Transmission

Wednesday, September 30th, 1970
8.00pm (ATV/Tyne Tees)

DESTRUCTION — Prod. No. 20

Teleplay by **Dennis Spooner** — Directed by **Ken Turner**

When a Navy Cruiser in the Atlantic scores a direct hit on a UFO, a naval investigation supervised by Admiral Sheringham concludes that the UFO was a prototype aircraft. Suspecting a cover-up to preserve the security of the Cruiser's operations, Straker decides to conduct his own investigation and assigns Foster to make contact with Sheringham's secretary Sarah Bosanquet. Following a dinner date, Sarah takes Foster to her apartment where he is surprised to find that she has a powerful telescope pointing out through a skylight. Colonel Lake keeps watch on the apartment and witnesses Sarah using the telescope to transmit the coordinates of the Navy Cruiser to a UFO in deep space. Then Straker learns that the Cruiser is on a mission to dump 1000 gallons of a virtually indestructible experimental nerve gas – if the aliens attack the ship and destroy the gas containers it will mean the end of all life on Earth!

Notes

As in *The Cat With Ten Lives*, Wanda Ventham's role in this episode simply appeared as '2nd in Command' in Dennis Spooner's script. Sarah Bosanquet was originally written as 'Virginia Bosanquet' but her name was changed when the producers decided to reintroduce the character of Virginia Lake. It was originally intended that the UFO interception mentioned by Foster on the golf course would be seen on-screen. The footage of Admiral Sheringham's Rolls-Royce being escorted to SHADO HQ is lifted from *Identified* while the footage of its arrival at the studio is taken from *Conflict*.

Oops!

Captain Steven looks through standard binoculars with round eyepieces, but the image he sees appears as if through the futuristic binoculars used by Colonel Lake. The aliens' plan doesn't seem to make sense (a race that requires transplantable organs and living host bodies are attempting to destroy all life on Earth) but is not rationalised on screen.

Regular Cast

Cdr. Ed Straker	**Ed Bishop**
Col. Paul Foster	**Michael Billington**
Col. Virginia Lake	**Wanda Ventham**
Lt. Nina Barry	**Dolores Mantez**
Gen. James Henderson	**Grant Taylor**
Lt. John Masters	**Jon Kelley**
Lt. Ayshea Johnson	**Ayshea Brough**
Capt. Steve Minto	**Steven Berkoff**
Voice of SID	**Mel Oxley**

Guest Cast

Sarah Bosanquet	**Stephanie Beacham**
Admiral Sheringham	**Edwin Richfield**
Captain Steven	**Philip Madoc**
2nd Officer Cooper	**Peter Blythe**
Skydiver Captain	**David Warbeck**
Skydiver Engineer	**Barry Stokes**
Rating	**Jimmy Winston**
Radar Technician	**Michael Ferrand**
Radar Officer	**Robert Lloyd**

First UK Transmission

Wednesday, December 2nd, 1970
8.00pm (ATV/Anglia)

THE MAN WHO CAME BACK — Prod. No. 21

Teleplay by **Terence Feely** — Directed by **David Lane**

As Colonel Craig Collins approaches Earth re-entry aboard *Ship 534*, Moonbase confirms a sighting of three UFOs, one of which suddenly changes course and opens fire on SID, seriously damaging the satellite. Collins apparently fails to effect re-entry and is certified dead, but he later turns up alive and well on an island in the South Pacific. Collins returns to SHADO HQ and Straker assigns him to the SID repair project under Colonel John Grey. On Moonbase, Collins attempts to resume his relationship with Lake, but she is now involved with Foster and finds his advances repulsive. Collins asks for Foster to partner him on the repair mission and Grey agrees to the request although he suspects that there is something wrong with Collins. Then Collins accidentally injures Foster during a weight-lifting session and the only qualified substitute who can join Collins on the SID repair mission is Straker...

Notes

Additional sequences filmed for this episode but dropped from the final edit included Grey more closely questioning Sir Esmond about Collins on the set of his latest film, and Collins attacking Dr. Jackson in SHADO Medical Centre with a hypodermic of SHADO's amnesia drug. Foster's warning to Straker as Collins is about to attack him was a late addition in post-production: as filmed, Grey was sedated before he could call SHADO and it was only by chance that Straker turned in time to fend off Collins. Nancy Nevinson, who provided the voice for Twizzle in THE ADVENTURES OF TWIZZLE, is seen here as the housekeeper who finds Grey's unconscious body in Collins's apartment. Mike Stevens, who appears as Sir Esmond's chauffeur, has the distinction of being the only member of the SPACE:1999 regular cast to appear in UFO. Although uncredited, Stevens portrayed a Main Mission operative throughout SPACE:1999's first season. Rona Newton-John is the sister of singer Olivia Newton-John. The sequences of the SID 2 rocket launch and module separation are both lifted from *Doppelgänger* (1968).

Regular Cast

Cdr. Ed Straker	**Ed Bishop**
Col. Paul Foster	**Michael Billington**
Col. Virginia Lake	**Wanda Ventham**
Lt. Nina Barry	**Dolores Mantez**
Dr. Doug Jackson	**Vladek Sheybal**
Lt. Ayshea Johnson	**Ayshea Brough**
Lt. Catherine Scott	**Anouska Hempel**
Voice of SID	**Mel Oxley**

Guest Cast

Colonel Craig Collins	**Derren Nesbitt**
Colonel John Grey	**Gary Raymond**
Sir Esmond	**Roland Culver**
Miss Holland	**Lois Maxwell**
Moonbase Doctor	**Robert Grange**
Moonbase Operative	**Andrea Allen**
Hospital Doctor	**David Savile**
Housekeeper	**Nancy Nevinson**
Porter	**Fred Real**
Chauffeur	**Mike Stevens**
Nurse	**Rona Newton-John**

First UK Transmission

Wednesday, February 3rd, 1971
8.00pm (ATV/Anglia)

THE PSYCHOBOMBS — Prod. No. 22

Teleplay by **Tony Barwick** — Directed by **Jeremy Summers**

A UFO penetrates the SHADO defences and lands in southern England. Secretary Linda Simmons, bank clerk Daniel Clark and construction manager Clem Mason are drawn to the vehicle by a pulsating green light on its dome and come under the aliens' control. The next morning, Straker is driving to SHADO HQ and stops to give a lift to Clark, but the man attacks him, knocking him out. When he recovers, he finds a message from Clark left in his coat pocket which threatens the destruction of the Fairfield Tracker Station, *Skydiver 3* and then SHADO HQ unless SHADO surrenders all of its forces. Moonbase is evacuated and all *Skydivers* are brought to the surface. Then Clark is caught breaking through the perimeter fence of the Fairfield Tracker Station and is taken inside by the guards. Once there, he breaks free and grasps the cables inside the main electrical switch panel, causing a massive explosion that destroys the station...

Notes

Like *Confetti Check A-O.K.*, *The Psychobombs* does not include the regular UFO title sequence due to the length of the pre-credits sequence which is the series' longest, running seven minutes and 20 seconds. Much of the incidental music used in this episode was originally composed for STINGRAY. This is the first time in the series that mention is made of more than one *Skydiver* in the SHADO fleet. Although *Skydiver 2* is not specifically referred to, the inference is that SHADO has at least four *Skydiver* vehicles – at least until the destruction of *Skydiver 3*.

Oops!

As Clark breaks through the fence at the Fairfield Tracker Station, the shadow of a crew member running past off-camera can be seen crossing the fence. Foster goes to Straker's rescue in SHADO Jeep A51-623, but shortly afterwards the same jeep is seen being used by the guards at the Fairfield Tracker Station.

Regular Cast

Cdr. Ed Straker	**Ed Bishop**
Col. Paul Foster	**Michael Billington**
Col. Virginia Lake	**Wanda Ventham**
Dr. Doug Jackson	**Vladek Sheybal**
Lt. Ayshea Johnson	**Ayshea Brough**

Guest Cast

Linda Simmons	**Deborah Grant**
Clem Mason	**Mike Pratt**
Daniel Clark	**David Collings**
Captain Lauritzen	**Tom Adams**
The Executive	**Alex Davion**
Skydiver 3 Captain	**Robin Hawdon**
Skydiver 3 Navigator	**Christopher Timothy**
Lieutenant Blythe	**Peter Blythe**
Plain Clothes Officer	**Oscar James**
Room 22 Guard	**Aiden Murphy**
Tracker Station Guards	**Peter Davies**
	Derek Steen
Police Motorcyclist	**Gavin Campbell**
Security Men	**Nigel Gregory**
	Hans de Vries
Skydiver 3 Engineers	**Peter Dolphin**
	Mark York

First UK Transmission

Wednesday, December 30th, 1970
8.00pm (ATV/Anglia)

REFLECTIONS IN THE WATER — Prod. No. 23

Teleplay by **David Tomblin** Directed by **David Tomblin**

A UFO travelling underwater attacks the freighter *Kingston* as it passes an uninhabited volcanic island in the Atlantic. Deep Space Probe 87 reports a concentration of 25 UFOs in Area NML 12 but then comes under attack and is destroyed. An underwater cameraman reports warm water populated by tropical fish off the coast of Cornwall and is then found dead with his airline cut. Straker realises that these incidents are connected in some way so he orders *Skydiver* to the area where the *Kingston* went down. The Captain finds an undersea power cable leading from an energy plant under the volcano all the way to Cornwall, and when he tracks the cable along the sea-bed, he discovers a huge undersea dome. Joining the *Skydiver* crew, Straker and Foster use sea-sleighs to ferry them to the dome but neither man is prepared for what they find inside...

Notes

The character of Lieutenant Anderson was designed to become a permanent replacement for Lieutenant Ford and was listed as part of the regular cast in the script for this episode. Anderson was originally written as 'Lieutenant Johnson' but this was changed to avoid confusion with Ayshea's character (and it should go without saying who the character was named after!). The UFO attack on Moonbase is lifted from *The Cat With Ten Lives*.

Oops!

Straker says that the aliens plan to take over SHADO Control, when he surely means that they plan to take over *from* SHADO Control (the aliens clearly intend to override SHADO's transmissions to Moonbase and *Skydiver* and broadcast their own messages from the duplicate SHADO Control, not invade the real SHADO Control and replace the staff with the duplicates). The alien duplicate who attacks Straker as he leaves the dome has two large holes in the seam under his right arm. During the final battle, three Interceptors are launched, but four are seen to make successful strikes.

Regular Cast

Cdr. Ed Straker	**Ed Bishop**
Col. Paul Foster	**Michael Billington**
Col. Virginia Lake	**Wanda Ventham**
Lt. Nina Barry	**Dolores Mantez**
Dr. Doug Jackson	**Vladek Sheybal**
Lt. Ayshea Johnson	**Ayshea Brough**
Capt. Steve Minto	**Steven Berkoff**
Lt. Catherine Scott	**Anouska Hempel**
Voice of SID	**Mel Oxley**

Guest Cast

Lt. Anderson	**James Cosmo**
Skydiver Captain	**David Warbeck**
Skydiver Engineer	**Barry Stokes**
Skipper	**Conrad Phillips**
Film Producer	**Richard Caldicott**
Helmsman Ellis	**Gordon Sterne**
Film Director	**Keith Bell**
Insurance Man	**Gerald Cross**
Underwater Cameraman	**Mark Griffith**

First UK Transmission

Saturday, July 24th, 1971
5.15pm (ATV)

TIMELASH — Prod. No. 24

Teleplay by **Terence Feely** Directed by **Cyril Frankel**

Straker suddenly appears in SHADO Control and starts smashing up the equipment. Pursued by Foster, he escapes into the studio complex and climbs onto the roof of an outbuilding where Colonel Lake lies unconscious. Foster finally apprehends him and Dr. Jackson discovers that Straker is in a state of severe mental and physical shock. On Henderson's instructions, Jackson injects Straker with a drug that unlocks his mind and he recalls the events of five hours previously... Straker and Lake are returning to the studio when their car is attacked by a UFO, freezing them in a strange light. After the UFO leaves the area, they continue their journey to the studios, but are surprised when night suddenly become day as they pass through the gates. Straker and Lake find everything and everyone completely motionless both on the studio lot and in SHADO Control, and they soon realise that the aliens have frozen time!

Notes

Terence Feely's script for *Timelash* clearly specified that it should be night-time outside during the scenes at the start in which Straker is chased by Foster and the guards (see *Oops!* below). Straker sets up the MOLLY on the roof of the J&K Stage administration block at Pinewood Studios where the UFO production offices were based. Many of the scenes on the studio lot in this episode were shot in the surrounding area.

Oops!

In the scene in SHADO Control at the start of the episode, Straker has just released the aliens' localised hold on time so when he runs outside, it should be night (just as it was before he and Lake arrived at the studio) yet it is still broad daylight. It also doesn't really make sense that none of the SHADO personnel realise that they have suddenly skipped a few hours. The 'motionless' stool that Straker hits with a piece of wood actually wobbles a bit. Actor Ron Pember is mis-credited as Ron 'Bember' on the end titles.

Regular Cast

Cdr. Ed Straker	**Ed Bishop**
Col. Paul Foster	**Michael Billington**
Col. Virginia Lake	**Wanda Ventham**
Lt. Nina Barry	**Dolores Mantez**
Gen. James Henderson	**Grant Taylor**
Dr. Doug Jackson	**Vladek Sheybal**
Miss Ealand	**Norma Ronald**
Lt. Ayshea Johnson	**Ayshea Brough**

Guest Cast

Turner	**Patrick Allen**
Casting Agent	**Ron Pember**
Actor	**Jean Vladon**
Actress	**Kirsten Lindholm**
SHADO Maintenance Engineer	**Douglas Nottage**
Studio Guard	**John Lyons**
Studio Security Man	**John C. Carney**

First UK Transmission

Wednesday, February 17th, 1971
8.00pm (ATV/Anglia)

MINDBENDER — Prod. No. 25

Teleplay by **Tony Barwick** — Directed by **Ken Turner**

After a UFO inexplicably explodes over the lunar surface, Lieutenant Conroy discovers a large Moon diamond at the crash site. Back at Moonbase, he goes on a rampage, attacking Lieutenant Barry, shooting Lieutenant Dale and exchanging gun-fire with Straker and Foster in the belief that he is fighting off Mexican bandits. He is finally shot down and killed. Then Captain Beaver James shoots a guard and takes Colonel Lake hostage in SHADO Control, seeing his SHADO colleagues only as aliens who have invaded the complex. Realising that he is beyond reason, Foster shoots him down. Later, Straker examines Conroy's personal effects and picks up the Moon diamond as he wonders about the nature of Conroy's hallucinations, but then Henderson arrives and provokes an argument. Straker is about to strike Henderson when, suddenly, he finds that he is no longer in his office but standing on a film set in the middle of acting out a scene!

Notes

The script for this episode was written as a cost-saving exercise, utilising only standing sets, studio locations, stock visual effects footage and material from earlier episodes. The role of Lieutenant Conroy was originally written as a new character, 'Lieutenant Tranter', but this was changed when it was decided that Al Mancini would reprise his character from *The Cat With Ten Lives*. Beaver James was originally written as 'Beaver Jones'. Conroy's gunfight with Straker and Foster in a Mexican village was an unscripted additional scene. During filming of this scene on a standing set at Pinewood Studios, Michael Billington accidentally stepped on Ed Bishop's ankle and broke it, halting production until Bishop recovered. The film footage that Straker watches in Theatre 7 is lifted from *Identified* and *A Question Of Priorities*. *Mindbender* features Grant Taylor's final performance. He was very ill with cancer during filming and his physical deterioration since first appearing as Henderson in *Identified* is highlighted by the footage from that episode. He did not work again and died the following year, aged 54.

Regular Cast

Cdr. Ed Straker	**Ed Bishop**
Col. Paul Foster	**Michael Billington**
Col. Virginia Lake	**Wanda Ventham**
Lt. Nina Barry	**Dolores Mantez**
Capt. Lew Waterman	**Gary Myers**
Gen. James Henderson	**Grant Taylor**
Miss Ealand	**Norma Ronald**
Lt. Ayshea Johnson	**Ayshea Brough**
Captain Steve Minto	**Steven Berkoff**
Lt. Catherine Scott	**Anouska Hempel**

Guest Cast

Howard Byrne	**Stuart Damon**
Beaver James	**Charles Tingwell**
Lt. Andy Conroy	**Al Mancini**
Lt. Dale	**Craig Hunter**
Film Director	**Stephan Chase**
1st Assistant Director	**Norton Clarke**
2nd Assistant Director	**Paul Greaves**
Mexican Bandits	**Larry Taylor**
	Richard Montez / Bill Morgan
SHADO Operative	**James Marcus**
SHADO Guards	**Stanley McGeagh**
	John Lyons

First UK Transmission

Wednesday, January 13th, 1971
8.00pm (ATV/Anglia)

THE LONG SLEEP — Prod. No. 26

Teleplay by **David Tomblin** — Directed by **Cyril Frankel**

Catherine Frazer has awoken from a coma that she has been in since she was accidentally knocked down by Straker ten years ago. As she was the main witness to a UFO sighting, Straker re-opens the enquiry and visits Catherine at Harville Hospital, where he encourages her to remember how she was taken to a farmhouse in the country by a young man called Tim. While under the influence of hallucinogenic drugs, they discovered aliens burying a device in the cellar of the farmhouse. Catherine removed a cylinder from the device and hid it while the aliens chased Tim onto the roof, but Tim apparently fell to his death. The aliens knocked Catherine out and when she recovered consciousness, she saw the aliens carrying Tim away. Realising that the alien device was probably a bomb similar to one that devastated Turkey in 1970, Straker desperately urges Catherine to recall where the farmhouse is and what became of the cylinder...

Notes

In David Tomblin's original script for this episode, Straker went to the farmhouse in 1970 to investigate reports of a UFO in the area, but he has since forgotten its location. As he arrived there, he saw Catherine running away and gave chase, trailing her to London. He saved Catherine from being raped by a lorry driver and gave the man his just desserts, but Catherine ran off, boarding the Underground. She dropped the cylinder from the bridge over Little Venice but then ran into the road and was knocked down by a bus. Realising that Straker has fallen in love with Catherine, Foster hides the true circumstances of her death from him, and Straker never sees the body. Catherine's surname was originally written as 'Ross' and Tim was originally 'Tom'.

Oops!

Straker refers to Catherine as 'Miss Ross' as he leaves his office (someone forgot to change the name on that page of Ed Bishop's script).

Regular Cast

Cdr. Ed Straker	**Ed Bishop**
Col. Paul Foster	**Michael Billington**
Col. Virginia Lake	**Wanda Ventham**
Dr. Doug Jackson	**Vladek Sheybal**
Lt. Catherine Scott	**Anouska Hempel**

Guest Cast

Catherine Frazer	**Tessa Wyatt**
Tim Redman	**Christian Roberts**
Bomb Disposal Expert	**Christopher Robbie**
Van Driver	**John Garrie**

First UK Transmission

Thursday, April 1st, 1971
11.00pm (Anglia)

THE PROTECTORS

Main Characters

Harry Rule
American private detective based in London and co-founder of The Protectors Organisation

Contessa Caroline di Contini
English private detective based in Rome, formerly Lady Caroline FitzTempest and widow of the Count di Contini

Paul Buchet
French private detective based in Paris and co-founder of The Protectors Organisation

Chino
The Contessa di Contini's loyal Oriental chauffeur and bodyguard

Suki
Harry Rule's coolly efficient Oriental secretary and Judo expert

The first ITV region to start screening THE PROTECTORS in the UK was Granada, who began their initial run of the series on July 7th, 1972. This was a full two months before the other regions, who decided to delay broadcast in order to herald the show as part of the new autumn season, starting on September 15th, 1972 in the ATV London region and on September 29th in the ATV Midlands region.

However, Granada's first run came to an end with *It Could Be Practically Anywhere On The Island* on December 15th, 1972, leaving two episodes, *The First Circle* and *A Case For The Right*, unscreened. These were finally shown by Granada at the start of a repeat run of the series from April 14th, 1973, by which time both episodes had already been broadcast by ATV London and ATV Midlands.

Despite their initial enthusiasm, Granada were slow to broadcast the second series, opting instead to continue with their repeat run of the first series throughout 1973. ATV London picked up the ball and premiered the second season on April 7th, 1973 just four weeks after the end of their run of the first season, although the episodes were scheduled very irregularly. ATV Midlands broadcast the second series from September 21st, 1973 and, due to the nature of the ATV London broadcasts, ended up showing five episodes in advance of the London franchise holder.

Format

After many years as a successful private detective operating from New York and then London, Harry Rule recognised the need for a professional protection service which could draw upon the talents of agents around the globe. His ideas became a reality when he met French private detective Paul Buchet in Marseilles while they were both working on the same case from different angles. Buchet shared Rule's thoughts and they went into partnership to establish The Protectors, a private international organisation comprising a network of members of the world's finest detective agencies, unrestricted by the legal technicalities that hamper many police investigations, and dedicated to the protection of those in peril.

The most important cases are handled by Rule and Buchet in association with the Protectors' Rome-based agent Contessa Caroline di Contini, an English aristocrat and wealthy widow of the Count di Contini. These three main agents can call upon the assistance and expertise of top private detectives in every major city in the world, such as the Greek Protector Yanos, American Protector Carter and Czech Protector Emil Markov. All members of The Protectors Organisation are connected by an innovative communications network in the form of a computer communications console installed in each Protectors' home. Filled with sophisticated, state-of-the-art computer equipment, this communications centre enables every Protector to be in immediate contact with their colleagues and instantly transfer photographs and documentation between them.

Each of the three primary operatives has their own preferred mode of transport. While on the continent, Harry Rule drives a Ford Mustang (4112 BA92) or a Mercedes Convertible (Roma E3 4646), but in London he drives his prized Jensen Interceptor (BEA 898J). The Contessa di Contini owns a fleet of cars but she principally uses a blue Citroen SM (2905 ITA 75) fitted with a Maserati engine, a white Ford Capri (MYW 277L) or a magnificent black Rolls-Royce (CON 1) driven by her Oriental chauffeur and bodyguard Chino. Paul Buchet has a particular penchant for fast cars but is equally at home behind the wheel of a Citroen Dyane, a Ford Escort (LMV 360K) or his powerful transverse twin-engined BMW motorcyle.

Production

After production on UFO came to an end, Gerry Anderson and his business partners Reg Hill and Sylvia Anderson established a new independent production company called Group Three which would provide television productions to ITC on commission. However, the partners were surprised when their first commission from Lew Grade was presented to them as a brief proposal for a contemporary detective thriller series. Grade also signed the series' main leads, Robert Vaughn and Nyree Dawn Porter, although the casting of the third lead, Tony Anholt, was left to Anderson and Hill.

Benefiting from a co-finance deal between ITC and Fabergé, the budget for THE PROTECTORS allowed for 12 of the initial 26 episodes to be filmed on location abroad, lending the series genuine international settings – part of a general initiative for ITC adventure programmes that Grade was also instigating with THE PERSUADERS!, JASON KING and THE ADVENTURER. However, THE PROTECTORS was shot on 16mm film which, while economic on the budget, was a noticeable degradation in picture and sound quality in comparison with Anderson's previous series.

After shooting in Paris, Rome, Malta and on the Costa Brava near Barcelona throughout the summer of 1971, the crew returned to the series' production base at the EMI/MGM Elstree Studios in Borehamwood, Hertfordshire to film the remaining episodes. The first series became a ratings hit in the UK and this was sufficiently boosted by international sales to encourage Grade to commission a further 26 episodes. Fourteen of these episodes were shot on location in Madrid, Venice, Salzburg and Copenhagen during the summer of 1972 and filming was completed on the remaining episodes in early 1973. With this second season, THE PROTECTORS became Anderson's most successful series since THUNDERBIRDS and a third season was in preparation when Fabergé suddenly withdrew their funding.

PRODUCTION CREDITS (Series One)

Producers **Gerry Anderson**
Reg Hill
Script Editor **Tony Barwick** *(1-11, 13, 14, 16-22, 24-26)*
Executive in Charge of Ferdporqui Productions **Sherwood Price**
Music Composed and Directed by **John Cameron**
Theme "Avenues and Alleyways"
Music by **Mitch Murray**
Lyrics by **Peter Callender**
Sung by **Tony Christie**
Director of Photography **Brendan J. Stafford BSC** *(1-14, 16-26)*
Frank Watts BSC *(15)*
Production Manager **Norman Foster**
Post Production Supervisor **Desmond Saunders**
Art Director **Bob Bell**
Supervising Editor **David Lane**
Miss Porter's Wardrobe Designed by **Germinal Rangel**
Editor **David Lane** *(1, 7, 10, 11, 13, 16, 18, 25)**
Mike Campbell *(2, 3, 5, 6, 8, 14, 15, 19, 23, 24, 26)*
John S. Smith *(4, 9, 12, 17, 20, 21, 22)*
Assistant Director **Frank Hollands** *(1, 3, 5, 6, 8, 9, 13, 14, 17-19, 21, 22, 25)*
David Bracknell *(2, 4, 7, 10-12, 15, 16, 20, 23, 26)*
Gino Marotta *(24)*
Sound Editor **Peter Pennell** *(1, 10, 12, 14, 17, 19, 20)*
Brian Holland *(2, 3, 5, 6, 9)*
John Beaton *(8, 11, 13, 16, 21, 22)*
Music Editor **Alan Willis**
Sound Recordists **J.B. Smith** *(1-14, 16-26)*
Len Abbott *(1, 2, 7, 10, 12, 13, 15, 16)*
Dennis Whitlock *(3-6, 8, 9, 11, 17-22, 24-26)*
Bill Rowe *(14, 23)*
Dave Bowen *(15)*
Casting **Mary Selway**
Processed by **Rank Film Laboratories**
Camera Operator **Ray Sturgess** *(1-14, 16-26)*
Jack Lowen *(15)*
Continuity **Marjorie Lavelly** *(1-14, 16-26)*
Sally Ball *(15)*
Make-Up **Eddie Knight**
Hairdressing **Betty Sheriff**
Wardrobe Supervisor **James Smith**
Stunt Director **Roy Vincente** *(4, 6-23)*
Fred Haggarty *(24-26)*
Title Sequence Directed by **John Hough***
Second Unit Director **David Lane***
Assistant Art Director **Keith Wilson***

A Group Three Production
for ITC World Wide Distribution
Made on Location and at
EMI/MGM Studios, London, England

* uncredited

Episode Titles (Series One)

(Listed in ITC recommended screening order)

1. **2000 ft To Die**
2. **Brother Hood**
3. **Disappearing Trick**
4. **Your Witness**
5. **The Quick Brown Fox**
6. **The Numbers Game**
7. **Triple Cross**
8. **A Kind Of Wild Justice**
9. **One And One Makes One**
10. **See No Evil**
11. **Balance Of Terror**
12. **King Con**
13. **The Big Hit**
14. **Thinkback**
15. **The First Circle**
16. **Chase**
17. **...With A Little Help From My Friends**
18. **For The Rest Of Your Natural...**
19. **The Bodyguards**
20. **Talkdown**
21. **A Case For The Right**
22. **A Matter Of Life And Death**
23. **It Could Be Practically Anywhere On The Island**
24. **Vocal**
25. **It Was All Over In Leipzig**
26. **Ceremony For The Dead**

Episode Running Time

25 minutes approx.

Original Concept

The brief for THE PROTECTORS that Gerry Anderson received from Lew Grade began with the simple statement that, "There is a small group of private detectives who are able to work more efficiently since they are operating outside the constraints of the law." From this, Anderson and Reg Hill developed the concept of a brotherhood of the world's top private investigators led by London-based American agent Craig Bradford. He would be assisted by German investigator Kurt Neilson, an adventurous bohemian based in Hamburg, and the coolly beautiful Rome-based Contessa di Contini, formerly Lady Caroline of England, clearly modelled as a present-day incarnation of THUNDERBIRDS icon Lady Penelope Creighton-Ward complete with Rolls-Royce and loyal manservant.

For the role of Craig Bradford, Anderson and his colleagues were considering actors such as Paul Burke, Chuck Connors, Frank Converse, Robert Culp, Vince Edwards, Ben Gazzara, Robert Goulet, Harry Guardino, William Shatner and James Whitmore before Lew Grade telephoned to inform them that he had signed Robert Vaughn as the series' star. The roles of second and third lead were switched after Grade told Anderson at a Screen Writers' Guild dinner that he had also signed Nyree Dawn Porter as Vaughn's co-star. With the casting of Tony Anholt, Kurt Neilson became Paul Dubois in all of the first season scripts: the surname was changed to Buchet just before filming commenced.

Although previous (and subsequent) Gerry Anderson series included sequences filmed on location, none made location filming such a prominent feature of the production as THE PROTECTORS. Not only is this the only Anderson-produced series (to date) to feature overseas location photography, but also the only one to include episodes filmed entirely on location with no studio interiors. The series' main filming location, Harry Rule's apartment building, was a house at 2 Courtfield Mews in South Kensington, London which remains virtually unchanged from its appearance in 1971/72.

2000 ft TO DIE — Ep. No. 01

Screenplay by **Terence Feely** Directed by **John Hough**

The Protectors are retained by scientist Freddie Reiwald after five of his colleagues from the Cranston Research Centre have died in odd circumstances within the last six months, including project leader Sir John Ackland. Harry liberates a document from a safe at Cranston which confirms that the team's abandoned research into the molecular structure of metals came close to creating synthetic gold. Then Harry and Caroline learn from Captain Carozza that a new gold-smuggling operation has appeared in Italy, so they visit a waterfront warehouse at Ostia to find a consignment of ersatz gold waiting for delivery. Someone has completed Reiwald's research and Harry suspects that they will make an attempt on Reiwald's life when he takes part in a dangerous sky-diving stunt...

Notes

Haberdashers' Aske's School in Elstree, Hertfordshire doubled for Cranston Research Centre in the pre-credits sequence while Booker Airfield near High Wycombe in Buckinghamshire provided the location for Reiwald's flying club. The music playing in the nightclub where Harry and the Contessa meet Reiwald is the CSC cover version of Led Zeppelin's 'Whole Lotta Love', better known as the theme from TOP OF THE POPS.

Regular Cast

Harry Rule	**Robert Vaughn**
Contessa di Contini	**Nyree Dawn Porter**
Paul Buchet	**Tony Anholt**
Chino	**Anthony Chinn**
Suki	**Yasuko Nagazumi**

Guest Cast

Freddie Reiwald	**Harvey Hall**
Ransome	**Nicholas Jones**
Susan	**Jacqueline Stanbury**
Captain Carozza	**Paul Stassino**
Civil Servant	**John Scott**

First UK Transmission

Friday, July 7th, 1972
8.00pm (Granada)

BROTHER HOOD — Ep. No. 02

Screenplay by **John Goldsmith** Directed by **Don Chaffey**

Reclusive industrial magnate Bela Karoleon offers Harry $250,000 to break his brother Sandor out of a prison on a Mediterranean island where he is being held on bogus charges to silence his outspoken political views. Posing as her cousin Lady Margaret Mandeville, Caroline visits the prison on the pretext of making a survey for the British Red Cross and during an 'interview' with Sandor in his cell, she wires the bars with explosives. When they detonate, Sandor escapes and is airlifted off the island by Harry and Paul in a helicopter. But Sandor is less than pleased to discover that his brother has paid for his liberation as it was Bela who arranged to have him imprisoned...

Notes

Location filming in Spain for this episode took the cast and crew to Girona Airport in Catalonia among other locations on the Costa Brava near Girona and Barcelona.

Oops!

When the frogmen are forced off the Contessa's yacht, the legs of the second diver to jump overboard reappear in shot as he rolls on a crash-mat in the bottom of the frame.

Regular Cast

Harry Rule	**Robert Vaughn**
Contessa di Contini	**Nyree Dawn Porter**
Paul Buchet	**Tony Anholt**

Guest Cast

Sandor Karoleon	**Vladek Sheybal**
Bela Karoleon	**Patrick Troughton**
Maria Karoleon	**Jill Balcon**
Heller	**John Cazabon**
Governor	**Robert Brown**
Sgt. Pannides	**Leon Lissek**
Yanos	**Antony Stamboulieh**
Police Inspector	**Stefan Gryff**

First UK Transmission

Friday, July 14th, 1972
8.00pm (Granada)

DISAPPEARING TRICK — Ep. No. 03

Screenplay by **Brian Clemens** Directed by **Jeremy Summers**

Harry and Caroline are approached by Brad Huron, son of shipping billionaire Carl Huron, to help him disappear without trace in order to win a bet with a friend. Harry appears reluctant to accept the job but, still smarting from Harry's earlier suggestion that she doesn't take their work seriously, Caroline agrees to Brad's request and uses every technique she knows to enable them to drop out of sight and head for Spain. However, Harry and Paul learn from Carl Huron that his son is a homicidal maniac who has escaped from care, putting one of his guards in hospital. They realise that once she has succeeded in making him disappear, Caroline will become Brad's next victim...

Notes

Location photography in Paris for this episode was shot at the Champ-de-Mars near the Eiffel Tower and the Quai de la Tournelle on the Left Bank near Notre-Dame Cathedral. The Contessa has a private underground car park in Paris full of her own cars.

Oops!

Michael da Costa is incorrectly credited as Michael 'de' Costa on the end titles.

Regular Cast

Harry Rule	**Robert Vaughn**
Contessa di Contini	**Nyree Dawn Porter**
Paul Buchet	**Tony Anholt**

Guest Cast

Carl Huron	**David Bauer**
Brad Huron	**Derren Nesbitt**
Malloy	**Chris Malcolm**
Walters	**Don Henderson**
Café Owner	**Michael da Costa**
Garage Mechanic	**David Calderisi**
Joe Lomax	**Roy Evans**

First UK Transmission

Friday, July 28th, 1972
8.00pm (Granada)

YOUR WITNESS — Ep. No. 04

Screenplay by **Donald James** Directed by **Jeremy Summers**

The Protectors have been retained by nightclub owner George Dixon to safeguard his ward Christie on her return to Paris from Bermuda. After an attempt is made on Christie's life at Le Bourget Airport, Dixon explains that she is the only witness to the murder of gang leader Henri Cartier by Sacha Besson, leader of another gang with whom Cartier was in partnership. Christie agrees to remain hidden at Paul's apartment until she can testify at Besson's trial in three days' time, but during the night, Paul is attacked and Christie is apparently kidnapped. Then Caroline learns from Inspector Bayard that the two gang leaders were in league with a third to organise a successful $700,000 bullion robbery, but the identity of the third man remains a mystery...

Notes

Location filming in Paris for this episode took the cast and crew to Le Bourget Airport for the pre-credits sequence, the Avenue Foch for scenes of Caroline and Bayard horse-riding near the Arc de Triomphe, and the Champs-Élysées for the closing scenes of the Contessa's Rolls-Royce. Robert Vaughn's business partner Sherwood Price makes an uncredited appearance as American Protector Carter in the pre-credits sequence.

Regular Cast

Harry Rule	**Robert Vaughn**
Contessa di Contini	**Nyree Dawn Porter**
Paul Buchet	**Tony Anholt**
Chino	**Anthony Chinn**

Guest Cast

George Dixon	**George Baker**
Christie	**Stephanie Beacham**
Monique	**Judith Arthy**
Inspector Bayard	**Georges Lambert**
Barman	**Gordon Sterne**
Croupier	**Hugo de Vernier**
Carter	**Sherwood Price**

First UK Transmission

Friday, December 8th, 1972
7.50pm (Granada)

THE QUICK BROWN FOX — Ep. No. 05

Screenplay by **Donald James** Directed by **Don Chaffey**

The Protectors are commissioned by the West German government to locate the source of payments being made to various former Nazi officers living in luxury around the world. Harry and Caroline investigate Hans Keller, formerly a high-ranking officer in Hitler's SS Panzer Lehr Division, and intercept a letter he has sent to one H. Gratz at a Poste Restante address in Geneva. The typed message features a date and the phrase 'The quick brown fox jumps over the lazy dog', which Harry recognises is simply a device for the recipient to identify that the message is genuine. The date, however, reveals part of a Swiss bank account number, so they arrange to send a forgery with a different date...

Notes

Location filming near Barcelona for this episode once again took the cast and crew to Girona Airport in Catalonia, previously seen in the pre-credits sequence of *Brother Hood*.

Oops!

Just before the fade-out at the end of the episode, Robert Vaughn can be seen making a very rude gesture to Nyree Dawn Porter with the middle finger of his left hand.

Regular Cast

Harry Rule	**Robert Vaughn**
Contessa di Contini	**Nyree Dawn Porter**
Paul Buchet	**Tony Anholt**
Chino	**Anthony Chinn**

Guest Cast

Hans Keller	**Morris Perry**
Osuna	**Mark Malicz**
Helga Gratz	**Anna Matisse**
Monica	**Angie Grant**
Banker	**Christopher Benjamin**
Spanish Official	**Kenneth Hendal**

First UK Transmission

Friday, August 18th, 1972
8.00pm (Granada)

THE NUMBERS GAME — Ep. No. 06

Screenplay by **Ralph Smart** Directed by **Don Chaffey**

On assignment in Spain to persuade young Susan Crediton to return home to her father in England, Harry and Caroline discover that Susan is being paid to pass lists of numbers to unseen agents during pre-arranged telephone calls. Intercepting the latest list, Harry learns that it details the registration number of a Bentley belonging to heart surgeon Lawrence Savage, and his arrival time back in England from a holiday on the continent. Tailing the Bentley from Dover, Harry and Caroline catch a man named Luigi removing a package of heroin from under the car after Savage returns home, and realise that they have stumbled upon an international drug-smuggling operation...

Notes

Sherwood Price makes a second uncredited appearance as American Protector Carter. Although part of this episode was filmed on location on the Costa Brava in Spain, the Edgwarebury Hotel in Elstree, Hertfordshire doubles for Dr. Savage's house while other scenes were shot at the Eastern Docks Car Ferry Terminal and Hoverport in Dover, Kent, and on the A1 at Borehamwood, Hertfordshire. CSC's version of 'Whole Lotta Love' can be heard in the background as Harry and Caroline wait outside Pepe's Bar in Cabañas.

Regular Cast

Harry Rule	**Robert Vaughn**
Contessa di Contini	**Nyree Dawn Porter**

Guest Cast

Susan Crediton	**Margareta Lee**
Frank	**Henry McGee**
Sir Walter Crediton	**Frederick Treves**
Luigi	**George Innes**
Dr. Lawrence Savage	**Richard Easton**
Giocovetti	**Peter Arne**
Carter	**Sherwood Price**

First UK Transmission

Friday, September 29th, 1972
8.00pm (Granada)

TRIPLE CROSS — Ep. No. 07

Screenplay by **Lew Davidson** Directed by **John Hough**

A hitch-hiker pulls a gun on Harry and forces him to drive to a deserted farmhouse where he is introduced to a confidence trickster named Charlie who has kidnapped Caroline and Paul. Leaving Paul tied up at the farmhouse with a time bomb set to explode in eight hours, Charlie forces Harry and Caroline to take him to a meeting with shipping magnate Gregor Kofax, who retains the Protectors to safeguard a shipment of jewels as they arrive in Britain from Amsterdam. At the airport, Harry has no choice but to switch the consignment for a duplicate package and Charlie makes his escape with the jewels...

Notes

Location photography around Elstree in Hertfordshire took the crew to Deeves Hall Cottage near Ridge (the deserted farm) and High Canons at Well End (Kofax's house). Other scenes were shot on the A1 at Borehamwood. Harry's black Jaguar (MVC 2040) previously appeared as Sir John Ackland's car (MAN 3) in *2000 ft To Die*. To achieve the effect of the bust thrown by Kofax smashing in Del Henney's face, the actor was protected with a sheet of perspex placed between him and the camera: the bust smashes against the camera side of the perspex and Henney reacts as if hit.

Regular Cast

Harry Rule	**Robert Vaughn**
Contessa di Contini	**Nyree Dawn Porter**
Paul Buchet	**Tony Anholt**
Suki	**Yasuko Nagazumi**

Guest Cast

Charlie	**John Neville**
Gregor Kofax	**Peter Bowles**
Linda	**Angharad Rees**
Detective	**Del Henney**
Gem Setter	**John Barrard**
Garage Attendant	**Bill Stewart**

First UK Transmission

Friday, September 22nd, 1972
7.30pm (Granada)

A KIND OF WILD JUSTICE — Ep. No. 08

Screenplay by **Donald James** Directed by **Jeremy Summers**

A late-night meeting with a mystery caller leaves Harry with broken ribs after his female contact guns him down. She makes a second attempt on his life while he is recovering in hospital and Paul manages to note the registration number of her car when she escapes. Harry discharges himself from hospital and he and Caroline trace the driver to a room in Jordan's Hotel off Hyde Park. Harry confronts her and she reveals that she is Kate Lindeman, daughter of a man who was jailed on Harry's evidence and recently died in prison. She believes that Harry framed her father, so Harry sets out to prove that her father was a vicious gangster by introducing her to some of his business associates...

Notes

In a scene cut from the final edit, Kate's second attempt on Harry's life in the hospital would have involved her trying to inject strychnine into his veins.

Oops!

Driving to Jordan's Hotel, Harry makes two different approaches to Parliament Square in consecutive shots, first south along Whitehall and then west across Westminster Bridge.

Regular Cast

Harry Rule	**Robert Vaughn**
Contessa di Contini	**Nyree Dawn Porter**
Paul Buchet	**Tony Anholt**
Chino	**Anthony Chinn**
Suki	**Yasuko Nagazumi**

Guest Cast

Reagan	**Patrick O'Connell**
Kate Lindeman	**Anna Palk**
Jill	**Kubi Chaza**
Soaper	**Barry Stanton**
Mechanic	**Paul Freeman**
Turf Accountant	**Brian Jackson**
Health Clinic Proprietor	**Lewis Jones**

First UK Transmission

Friday, September 8th, 1972
7.30pm (Granada)

ONE AND ONE MAKES ONE — Ep. No. 09

Screenplay by **Jesse & Pat Lasky** Directed by **Don Chaffey**

The Protectors are assigned to find missing Canadian agent Bennett, held captive by foreign agents, before he is forced to reveal the names of six operatives of the top secret Anglo-American Sky project. Paul learns that Bennett is being held in an upstairs room in a house on the Rue de l'Église in Paris, so they plan a rescue attempt. However, Bennett's interrogators, Shkoder and Maria Ghardala, believe that the man they are questioning is one of their own agents, Alexi Kosneff, a double who replaced Bennett in order to learn his secrets, and that a head injury has left him thinking that he is the real Bennett. Harry, Caroline and Paul gain access to the house but can find no sign of Bennett. Instead, they are captured by Shkoder and his men...

Notes

Filming on location in Paris for this episode took the cast and crew to the Place du Tertre and Sacré-Coeur Basilica in Montmartre, the Pont de Tournelle near Notre-Dame Cathedral, the Left Bank at St. Michel and Napoleon's tomb at the Église du Dôme in the Invalides. Previously seen in *Brother Hood*, Antony Stamboulieh (mis-credited as 'Anthony' Stamboulieh) makes a second appearance as Greek Protector Yanos.

Regular Cast

Harry Rule	**Robert Vaughn**
Contessa di Contini	**Nyree Dawn Porter**
Paul Buchet	**Tony Anholt**
Suki	**Yasuko Nagazumi**

Guest Cast

Shkoder	**Michael Gough**
Maria Ghardala	**Georgia Brown**
Yanos	**Antony Stamboulieh**
Alexi Kosneff	**Neil McCallum**
Kramer	**Christopher Dunham**

First UK Transmission

Friday, November 3rd, 1972
7.30pm (Granada)

SEE NO EVIL — Ep. No. 10

Screenplay by **Donald Jonson** Directed by **Jeremy Summers**

The Protectors are assigned to safeguard Senator Gordini, who plans to present a report to the Senate on organised crime in Rome, but Harry and Caroline lose him when they tail him to a rendezvous with an anonymous informant in the Piazza Navona. The next morning, the Senator is found unconscious in the mens' room of a café on the Via Veneto and Harry realises that he has been drugged and photographed consorting with well-known racketeers to discredit him. The Senator recognises the work of organised crime head Lucello, the 'Bird Man', but when Harry and Caroline set out to find him, they soon discover that Lucello's identity is the best-kept secret in Rome...

Notes

This episode's location photography in Rome was filmed at the church of Sant'Agnese in Agone and the Fontana dei Fiumi, both on the Piazza Navona, as well as on the Via Veneto. In the original script, Lucello was written as El Gufo, 'the Owl'. For his role as one of Mario's 'heavies', Anthony Haygarth is dubbed throughout by Robert Rietty. Roger Lloyd Pack (Trigger in ONLY FOOLS AND HORSES and Owen in THE VICAR OF DIBLEY) appears in an uncredited non-speaking role as a pappagalli photographer.

Regular Cast

Harry Rule	**Robert Vaughn**
Contessa di Contini	**Nyree Dawn Porter**
Chino	**Anthony Chinn**

Guest Cast

Max Toller	**James Bolam**
Lucello	**Alan Webb**
Senator Gordini	**Leonard Sachs**
Mario	**Phillip Hinton**
Waiter	**Al Mancini**
Driver	**Anthony Haygarth**
Photographer	**Roger Lloyd Pack**

First UK Transmission

Friday, July 21st, 1972
8.00pm (Granada)

BALANCE OF TERROR — Ep. No. 11

Screenplay by **John Goldsmith** Directed by **Don Chaffey**

Harry and the Contessa are assigned by Colonel Krassinkov of the KGB to locate Nobel Prize-winning scientist Alexander Schelpin, the Soviet Union's top biochemist, who has disappeared in London with a phial of deadly botulinus toxin alpha beta which could wipe out the population of a major city. Then Schelpin appears at the International Scientific Forum and announces that mankind will not be safe from germ warfare until the full effects of it are made evident. Harry and Paul track Schelpin back to his hotel room and confront him, but he threatens to release the toxin if they try to stop him...

Notes

Harry's calendar shows the date as Monday, August 6th so the year must be 1973 (the only year between 1962 and 1979 in which August 6th fell on a Monday).

Oops!

A crucial plot point hinges on Harry's statement that the 'Little Boy' nuclear bomb was dropped on Hiroshima at 9.00am on August 6th, 1945, but it was actually dropped at 8.15am on that day.

Regular Cast

Harry Rule	**Robert Vaughn**
Contessa di Contini	**Nyree Dawn Porter**
Paul Buchet	**Tony Anholt**
Suki	**Yasuko Nagazumi**

Guest Cast

Col. Vassily Krassinkov	**Nigel Green**
Prof. Alexander Schelpin	**Laurence Naismith**
KGB Man	**Janos Kurucz**
Prof. Grodny	**Angus Lennie**
Russian Diplomat	**Milos Kirek**
Hotel Receptionist	**Barry Warren**

First UK Transmission

Friday, September 15th, 1972
7.30pm (Granada)

KING CON — Ep. No. 12

Screenplay by **Tony Barwick** Directed by **Jeremy Summers**

The Contessa purchases a 12th century Novgorod icon at auction for £75,000 and returns it to her friend Irena Gleskova in Prague. Caroline enlists the help of Harry and Paul to help her recover the outlay from Alan Sutherland, a confidence trickster who swindled the icon from Irena, by setting herself up as Sutherland's next victim. She meets Sutherland at a car showroom and he recognises her from the auction as a wealthy widow worth pursuing. He and his colleague Cribbs arrange a car accident so that he can inveigle himself into the Contessa's company as she visits Royal Ascot. There, Caroline introduces him to Harry, who poses as a millionaire on a remarkable winning streak...

Oops!

Sutherland's black Jaguar (MVC 2040) was previously seen to be owned by Harry in *Triple Cross*. When Chino goes to meet Paul in the car park at Ascot, Paul is sitting in a right-hand drive car in long shot, but then in a left-hand drive car in close-up as the film is erroneously flopped (this error was corrected for the digitally remastered episode released on Region 2 DVD by Carlton Visual Entertainment in 2002). As Harry is being tailed by Cribbs, Robert Vaughn's shadow is visible on the back projection screen.

Regular Cast

Harry Rule	**Robert Vaughn**
Contessa di Contini	**Nyree Dawn Porter**
Paul Buchet	**Tony Anholt**
Chino	**Anthony Chinn**
Suki	**Yasuko Nagazumi**

Guest Cast

Alan Sutherland	**Anton Rodgers**
Cribbs	**Ronald Lacey**
Irena Gleskova	**Izabella Telezynska**
Emil Markov	**Michael da Costa**
Auctioneer	**Peter Cellier**
Salesman	**Brian Worth**

First UK Transmission

Friday, August 25th, 1972
8.00pm (Granada)

THE BIG HIT — Ep. No. 13

Screenplay by **Donald James** — Directed by **Roy Ward Baker**

An assassin makes an attempt on the Contessa's life at her villa in Rome and then a girl named Suzanne tries to poison Paul at his apartment in Paris. Questioning the girl leads Caroline and Paul to London, where they discover that Harry has been kidnapped and Caroline realises that someone is systematically targeting the members of The Protectors Organisation. Imprisoned in a packing crate suspended from a crane, Harry is questioned by Jason Howard, managing director of Howard Swimwear, who wants a complete list of every operative in the organisation. Harry refuses to talk so Howard orders the crate to be repeatedly slammed into a wall until it breaks...

Notes

The EMI/MGM Elstree Studios doubled for the offices of Howard Swimwear and the street outside Finlay's nightclub in location photography: Howard's henchman attempts to run Paul down outside the studios' Stage 3. Shortly after filming his role in this episode, henchman Carl Rigg was cast in the regular role of Dr. Gregory Knight in ITV's GENERAL HOSPITAL and then appeared as Detective Constable Dukes in the BBC's TARGET series with Patrick Mower and Philip Madoc.

Regular Cast

Harry Rule	**Robert Vaughn**
Contessa di Contini	**Nyree Dawn Porter**
Paul Buchet	**Tony Anholt**
Chino	**Anthony Chinn**
Suki	**Yasuko Nagazumi**

Guest Cast

Jason Howard	**Derek Smith**
Suzanne	**Morag Hood**
Señor Vitello	**Arthur Howell**
Barman	**Tony Bateman**
Howard's Henchmen	**Carl Rigg**
	Phil Woods
Assassin	**Bob Anderson**

First UK Transmission

Friday, October 27th, 1972
7.30pm (Granada)

THINKBACK — Ep. No. 14

Screenplay by **Brian Clemens** — Directed by **Cyril Frankel**

Harry and Caroline are apparently involved in a car accident and when Harry recovers consciousness in hospital to be told by Dr. Page that he was found alone by his car, he becomes concerned for Caroline's safety. CID Inspector Wilson asks Harry about his current assignment, keeping Frank Dilling in protective custody until he can testify before an international committee and expose a network of official corruption. Wilson suggests that Harry should reveal Dilling's whereabouts, but Harry notices that his nurse is wearing high-heeled shoes and realises that the whole thing is an elaborate set-up...

Notes

The EMI/MGM Elstree Studios doubled for the disused film studios in location photography: the final scenes were shot on the empty Stage 3.

Oops!

Wilson's Jaguar (MVC 2040) was previously seen to be owned by Harry in *Triple Cross* and Sutherland in *King Con*. At the studios, Wilson parks next to a wooden fence, but from inside the car it looks like a white brick wall.

Regular Cast

Harry Rule	**Robert Vaughn**
Contessa di Contini	**Nyree Dawn Porter**
Paul Buchet	**Tony Anholt**
Suki	**Yasuko Nagazumi**

Guest Cast

Inspector Wilson	**Ian Hendry**
Sergeant Peters	**Keith Bell**
Dr. Page	**Donald Burton**
Ginter	**James Culliford**
Frank Dilling	**Geoffrey Morris**
Nurse	**Penny Sugg**

First UK Transmission

Friday, September 1st, 1972
7.30pm (Granada)

THE FIRST CIRCLE — Ep. No. 15

Screenplay by **Tony Barwick** — Directed by **Don Chaffey**

Former USAF Colonel John Hunter has suffered a mental breakdown and gone to ground in a disused US airbase outside London where he relives his experiences as commander of an airbase in Vietnam. When he mistakes a security guard for a North Vietnamese soldier and shoots him dead, the base is surrounded by police and the officer in charge, Slade, decides to play a waiting game until Hunter can be targeted by police marksmen. Harry is hired by Hunter's wife Karen to try and talk him back to reality, but when Harry approaches Hunter in the base control tower, the Colonel believes that he is a North Vietnamese infiltrator and opens fire on him. Rescued by Slade, Harry decides to try another tactic, masquerading as Hunter's USAF colleague Bill Roberts...

Notes

In Tony Barwick's original script, Hunter had been involved in the Korean War (1950-1953) rather than the Vietnam War (1956-1975). Nyree Dawn Porter is credited on the end titles although she does not appear in the episode. This is one of only three episodes of THE PROTECTORS in which Robert Vaughn is the only member of the regular cast to appear: the others are *It Could Be Practically Anywhere On The Island* and *Shadbolt*.

Regular Cast

Harry Rule	**Robert Vaughn**

Guest Cast

Col. John Hunter	**Ed Bishop**
Slade	**John Collin**
Karen Hunter	**Sally Bazely**
Policeman	**George Roubicek**
Security Man	**Frederick Bennett**

First UK Transmission

Friday, March 2nd, 1973
7.00pm (ATV London)

CHASE Ep. No. 16

Screenplay by **Brian Clemens** Directed by **Harry Booth**

Harry joins Caroline for a holiday at an old family hunting lodge where they plan to celebrate Harry's birthday. Caroline presents Harry with one of her father's shotguns as a birthday gift before leaving to stock up on drinks at the local store. While she is gone, Harry receives an unexpected visit from missing diplomat Douglas Perston, who is being pursued by the ruthless Garder. When Garder arrives at the lodge, Harry fights off his henchman Kurt but is shot by Garder in the arm as he escapes into the woods. Capturing Perston, Garder sets his team of hunters and their dogs onto Harry's trail. When she returns to the lodge, Caroline discovers that Harry is missing and sets off to find him...

Notes

The Bridgewater Monument at Aldbury in Hertfordshire doubled for Bobby's Tower in location photography, while the (now demolished) Norwegian Barn at the Edgwarebury Hotel in Elstree, Hertfordshire took the place of Caroline's family hunting lodge. Isabella Telezynska (Garder's secretary Ingrid) previously appeared as the Contessa's friend Irena Gleskova in *King Con*. Tony Anholt is credited on the end titles, but does not appear in the episode.

Regular Cast

Harry Rule	**Robert Vaughn**
Contessa di Contini	**Nyree Dawn Porter**

Guest Cast

Garder	**Patrick Magee**
Kurt	**Keith Buckley**
Douglas Perston	**Donald Eccles**
Ingrid	**Isabelle Telezynska**
Vent	**Tom Chadbon**
Gromeld	**Gertan Klauber**

First UK Transmission

Friday, December 1st, 1972
7.50pm (Granada)

...WITH A LITTLE HELP FROM MY FRIENDS Ep. No. 17

Screenplay by **Sylvia Anderson** Directed by **Jeremy Summers**

Harry's ex-wife Laura arrives at his apartment in a state of distress: their son Johnny has been kidnapped and she has been given instructions to take Harry to a meeting with the culprits. Currently assigned to the protection of President Ali during his stay in London, Harry leaves a taped message for Caroline and Paul, warning them that the President's life is in danger and that they are to follow the plan that they used in the Conroy case. Then Harry and Laura meet Ali's main opponent Kahan, who wants Harry to assassinate the President, threatening the lives of Laura and Johnny to ensure his co-operation...

Notes

Neptune House at the ATV Elstree Studios in Borehamwood, Hertfordshire (previously seen as the Harlington-Straker Film Studios in UFO) doubled for the Hotel Excelsior in location photography, while Aldenham Grange near Letchmore Heath, Hertfordshire appeared as Kahan's house. The sign on the wall outside the hospital mortuary giving directions to various wards was previously seen at the end of the bogus hospital corridor in *Thinkback*. Henchman Marc Zuber later appeared in SPACE:1999 as a Main Mission operative in *Black Sun* and a security Lieutenant in *Brian The Brain*.

Regular Cast

Harry Rule	**Robert Vaughn**
Contessa di Contini	**Nyree Dawn Porter**
Paul Buchet	**Tony Anholt**
Chino	**Anthony Chinn**
Suki	**Yasuko Nagazumi**

Guest Cast

Kahan	**Jeremy Brett**
Laura	**Hannah Gordon**
President Ali	**Martin Benson**
President's Aide	**Saeed Jaffrey**
Pursuer	**Roshan Seth**
Doctor	**Desmond Jordan**
Butler	**John Gatrell**
Kahan's Henchmen	**Julian Sherrier**
	Marc Zuber
Johnny	**Daron Barnham**

First UK Transmission

Friday, November 24th, 1972
7.50pm (Granada)

FOR THE REST OF YOUR NATURAL... Ep. No. 18

Screenplay by **Tony Barwick** Directed by **John Hough**

Caroline is staying in Harry's apartment for a few days while he is away on business, but while Suki is out walking Gus, the house is broken into by the psychopathic escaped murderer Colin Grant, who attacks the Contessa, knocking her out with chloroform and driving off with her in Harry's Jaguar. Caroline recovers consciousness to find herself tied up in a surreal mock-up of a courtroom that Grant has constructed in his flat. Acting as prosecuting counsel, the deranged Grant accuses Caroline of destroying his life by testifying against him at his trial and calls for the ultimate punishment for her 'crime'...

Notes

Anthony Chinn is credited on the end titles, but does not appear in the episode.

Oops!

After the Contessa tries to use the phone, Grant furiously knocks the head off a ginger-haired ventriloquist's dummy in his 'jury'. Seconds later, a shot of the 'jury' shows the dummy's head still intact when Grant asks for their verdict, but the head is back on the floor when Grant attacks Caroline shortly after.

Regular Cast

Harry Rule	**Robert Vaughn**
Contessa di Contini	**Nyree Dawn Porter**
Paul Buchet	**Tony Anholt**
Suki	**Yasuko Nagazumi**

Guest Cast

Colin Grant	**Norman Rodway**
Designer	**Damien Thomas**
Detective	**Kenneth Gilbert**
Mary Cooper	**Susan Travers**

First UK Transmission

Friday, October 6th, 1972
8.00pm (Granada)

THE BODYGUARDS

Ep. No. 19

Screenplay by **Dennis Spooner** Directed by **Don Chaffey**

When the Protectors are retained by Inspector Jack Newman to guard the body of the late Ralph Corder at his country house, Corder's former partners Mason and Robard question whether Corder might have faked his own death and actually be alive and well. Robard tells Mason to stay calm while he conducts his own investigation, sending Harry an invitation to meet 'George' at a pub opposite Battersea Power Station. But with a vested interest in recovering his share of the hidden proceeds from a series of bank robberies, Mason takes matters into his own hands, breaking into Corder's house to make absolutely sure that he is dead...

Notes

Location filming on this episode took the cast and crew to the Edgwarebury Hotel in Elstree, Hertfordshire (Corder's house, previously seen as The Old Barn in *The Numbers Game*), the church at Ridge in Hertfordshire, the King William IV pub on Grosvenor Road in Pimlico, London, and Vauxhall Bridge and Vauxhall Station in Vauxhall, London. The view from the window of Robard's office is the same as the view from Jason Howard's office in *The Big Hit*.

Regular Cast

Harry Rule	**Robert Vaughn**
Contessa di Contini	**Nyree Dawn Porter**
Paul Buchet	**Tony Anholt**
Chino	**Anthony Chinn**
Suki	**Yasuko Nagazumi**

Guest Cast

Robard	**Freddie Jones**
Alan Mason	**Manning Redwood**
Inspector Jack Newman	**Ken Watson**
Butler	**Harry Hutchinson**

First UK Transmission

Friday, October 13th, 1972
8.00pm (Granada)

TALKDOWN

Ep. No. 20

Screenplay by **Jesse** & **Pat Lasky** Directed by **Jeremy Summers**

Harry is abandoned at the controls of a light aircraft when deranged criminal Colin Foster jumps out and parachutes to safety. With no knowledge of how to fly the plane, Harry is coached via radio by Paul, who tells him to circle for an hour to use up his fuel. While he does so, Harry recalls how Foster visited him at his apartment and threatened to frame him for the murder of police informant Harry Farr. Then Farr turned up dead at the firing range while Harry was practicing there with Caroline and Paul, and Harry realised that he had become the target of an elaborate plan to frame him for Foster's murder as well...

Notes

Location photography for this episode was filmed at the Tower of London and at Elstree Aerodrome in Elstree, Hertfordshire.

Oops!

Foster drives the Jaguar (MVC 2040) that was previously seen to be owned by Harry in *Triple Cross*, Sutherland in *King Con* and Wilson in *Thinkback*. William Moore is erroneously credited as 'Willian' Moore on the end titles.

Regular Cast

Harry Rule	**Robert Vaughn**
Contessa di Contini	**Nyree Dawn Porter**
Paul Buchet	**Tony Anholt**
Chino	**Anthony Chinn**
Suki	**Yasuko Nagazumi**

Guest Cast

Colin Foster	**Derren Nesbitt**
Inspector Hill	**John Nettleton**
Rifle Range Supervisor	**William Moore**
Air Traffic Control	**John Joyce**

First UK Transmission

Friday, November 10th, 1972
7.30pm (Granada)

A CASE FOR THE RIGHT

Ep. No. 21

Screenplay by **Jesse** & **Pat Lasky** Directed by **Michael Lindsay-Hogg**

At a meeting on board the *Silver Mare* cruising down the Thames, Harry is retained by an anonymous Italian to deliver a locked briefcase to the Villa Bianca on the Via Appia Antica in Rome. Harry is attacked by the two-man crew of the boat who try to wrest the briefcase from him, so he jumps overboard. The next day, he meets Caroline in Rome but they are stopped by a pair of bogus motorcycle policemen who also try to grab the case. Fighting them off, they return to the Contessa's villa where she learns that the Villa Bianca is a love-nest owned by megalomaniac millionaire Prince Carpiano. They find the villa deserted, but a note left for Harry gives the combination to open the case, which is then revealed to contain a bomb set to explode at any minute!

Notes

Location filming in Rome for this episode took the cast and crew to the Colosseum, the Baths of Caracalla during preparations for the 1971 summer season of the Teatro dell'Opera, and the terrace restaurant of the four-star Hotel Forum on the Via Tor de Conti with its view of the Vittoriano Monument in the Piazza Venezia. Tony Anholt is credited on the end titles, but does not appear in the episode.

Regular Cast

Harry Rule	**Robert Vaughn**
Contessa di Contini	**Nyree Dawn Porter**
Chino	**Anthony Chinn**
Suki	**Yasuko Nagazumi**

Guest Cast

Prince Carpiano	**Milo O'Shea**
Fabrizzio	**Jacques Sernas**
Extremist Officer	**Jeffrey Segal**

First UK Transmission

Friday, March 9th, 1973
7.00pm (ATV London)

A MATTER OF LIFE AND DEATH — Ep. No. 22

Screenplay by **Donald James** Directed by **Don Chaffey**

The Protectors are retained by the solicitors of English hippy Peter Hendricks, heir to a small fortune, to find out how he came to die in a car accident in North Africa. Dozens of other hippies have recently died in similar accidents and all were involved in a smuggling racket run by a man named Goran. Harry's investigation leads to Malta where Goran's latest shipment will be delivered to the wealthy James Leroy Mallory. Caroline arranges a meeting with Mallory and offers to outbid his American buyer for the shipment, but he becomes suspicious when he learns that Harry and Paul have been asking questions about his operations and issues instructions to have them shot...

Notes

On location in Malta for this episode, scenes were filmed at Malta International Airport at Luqa, Marsamxett Harbour in Valletta, the 'Silent City' of Mdina (where the Contessa is seen travelling by horse-drawn *karrozin* through the main city gate), the Blue Grotto near Wied iz-Zurrieq (where Harry and Paul are shot at), the fishing village of Marsaxlokk (Harry fights Baruna) and Marsaxlokk Bay. Blood plasma expert Cyril Shaps provided the voice for Professor Popkiss in the last 13 episodes of SUPERCAR.

Regular Cast

Harry Rule	**Robert Vaughn**
Contessa di Contini	**Nyree Dawn Porter**
Paul Buchet	**Tony Anholt**

Guest Cast

James Leroy Mallory	**Patrick Allen**
Baruna	**Maxwell Shaw**
Goran	**Barrie Houghton**
Doctor	**Cyril Shaps**
Mallory's Girl	**Julie Crossthwaite**

First UK Transmission

Friday, October 20th, 1972
8.00pm (Granada)

IT COULD BE PRACTICALLY ANYWHERE ON THE ISLAND — Ep. No. 23

Screenplay by **Tony Barwick** Directed by **Robert Vaughn**

Harry comes to the aid of Arkansas millionairess Rita McCall when she arrives at the Grand Hotel Verdala in Malta and someone snatches her Muffin, a tiny poodle puppy. The dog has been taken by industrial espionage agents Felix Costa and Mary Laroche, who plan to smuggle microfilm out of the country hidden inside the dog's collar. Unfortunately, their contact, Joe Flynn, has been delayed and the hypochondriac Costa's attempt to find out from Rita what the dog will eat attracts Harry's attention. Then Muffin accidentally swallows the microfilm and escapes from Costa's hotel room...

Notes

On this episode alone, Big Ben does not appear at the start of the opening titles. Instead, the first chimes of the theme play over a freeze-frame of Harry and Rita. Linda Staab (Rita) became Mrs. Robert Vaughn in 1974.

Oops!

Linda Staab's character is erroneously captioned as 'Linda' McCall on the in-show titles and end credits: she is referred to as "Miss Rita" several times during the episode.

Regular Cast

Harry Rule	**Robert Vaughn**

Guest Cast

Felix Costa	**Sherwood Price**
Rita McCall	**Linda Staab**
Mary Laroche	**Madeline Hinde**
Gail	**Michael da Costa**
Joe Flynn	**Vernon Dobtcheff**
Jonathan P. Hacket	**Dervis Ward**
Bartender	**Peter Fontaine**
Doctor	**David Glover**
Mrs. Jonathan P. Hacket	**Wendy Hutchinson**

First UK Transmission

Friday, December 15th, 1972
7.50pm (Granada)

VOCAL — Ep. No. 24

Screenplay by **Brian Clemens** Directed by **Cyril Frankel**

During an operation at the Pine Vale Country Club to catch drugs dealers Azon and Gregg, Paul is temporarily blinded by powder burns when Gregg's gun goes off in his face. While he recovers, Paul is kept under protection in a London hotel as he is the only person who can identify Azon. Harry leaves for Beirut to investigate the other end of Azon's operation, but when Caroline drives him to the airport, Gregg plants a transmitter on her Rolls-Royce so that expert mimic Vickers can record Harry's voice, enabling him to produce a perfect imitation. With Vickers pretending to be Harry, Azon gains access to Harry's apartment, planning to coerce information he needs from Paul...

Notes

This episode was specifically written to minimise Robert Vaughn's involvement so that he could prepare to direct the filming in Malta on *It Could Be Practically Anywhere On The Island*. The closing scene with Harry in the Middle East was scripted to be shot in Malta during production on that episode. Shane Rimmer (Vickers) provided the voice for Scott Tracy in THUNDERBIRDS. He is seen again in THE PROTECTORS as Zeke Daley in *Zeke's Blues*, which he also wrote.

Regular Cast

Harry Rule	**Robert Vaughn**
Contessa di Contini	**Nyree Dawn Porter**
Paul Buchet	**Tony Anholt**
Suki	**Yasuko Nagazumi**

Guest Cast

John Azon	**David Buck**
Gregg	**Ian Hogg**
Vickers	**Shane Rimmer**

First UK Transmission

Friday, November 17th, 1972
7.50pm (Granada)

IT WAS ALL OVER IN LEIPZIG — Ep. No. 25

Regular Cast

Harry Rule	**Robert Vaughn**
Contessa di Contini	**Nyree Dawn Porter**
Paul Buchet	**Tony Anholt**

Guest Cast

Jim Palmer	**Ron Randell**
Adam Markos	**Phil Brown**
Lintar	**Paul Weston**
Maria	**Diane Mercer**
Girl with Pram	**Tanya Bayona**

First UK Transmission

Friday, August 11th, 1972
8.00pm (Granada)

Screenplay by **Donald James** Directed by **Don Chaffey**

On her yacht *Dolphin*, at anchor in the harbour of a small Mediterranean island, Caroline is reunited with her old friend Jim Palmer. She explains that the Protectors have been enlisted by the island's government to expose whoever is behind an armed coup that they suspect is being planned. Palmer assists Harry, Caroline and Paul to track down a red-panelled truck used as a getaway vehicle after an incident at a roadblock and uncovers a string of evidence that incriminates restaurateur Adam Markos. But Harry suspects that they are being deliberately misled...

Notes

The scene with the pram full of grenades rolling down the stepped streets of Valletta in Malta is a deliberate homage to the massacre scene on the Odessa Steps in Eisenstein's silent masterpiece *The Battleship Potemkin* (1925). Paul Weston (Lintar) later became stunt co-ordinator on SPACE:1999 and also appeared as a guard in several episodes.

Oops!

A large crowd of spectators are watching as Harry shoots at Lintar's getaway truck.

CEREMONY FOR THE DEAD — Ep. No. 26

Regular Cast

Harry Rule	**Robert Vaughn**
Contessa di Contini	**Nyree Dawn Porter**
Paul Buchet	**Tony Anholt**

Guest Cast

Madame Rue	**Toby Robins**
Medina	**Stanley Lebor**
Police Inspector	**Charles Thake**
Skipper	**Robert Sessions**
Julie	**Jenny Lee Wright**

First UK Transmission

Friday, August 4th, 1972
8.00pm (Granada)

Screenplay by **Donald James** Directed by **Jeremy Summers**

Harry interrupts Caroline's holiday and pulls a few strings to have her brought 3,000 miles to a Mediterranean island so that she can impersonate Madame Rue, the wife of a foreign President who suspects that her husband might be kidnapped when he arrives on the island for vital surgery. Caroline takes Madame Rue's place at the airport, where Harry stages a fake ambush with a bogus President as a red herring for the real kidnappers. But then the ambulance that Harry has arranged to collect the real President from his charter yacht is hi-jacked...

Notes

Paul Weston (Lintar in *It Was All Over In Leipzig*) has a non-speaking role as the guy who is shot by the fake nurse at the Marina and falls off a boat into the water.

Oops!

When the motor launch rescues the Contessa from the sea in the pre-credits sequence, the person in the launch wearing a red crash helmet who is supposed to be the Contessa quite clearly isn't even female.

PRODUCTION CREDITS (Series Two)

Producers **Gerry Anderson**
Reg Hill
Script Editor **Tony Barwick**
(1-9, 11-12, 15-18, 20, 21, 23-26)
Executive in Charge of Ferdporqui Productions
Sherwood Price
Music Composed and Directed by
John Cameron
Theme "Avenues and Alleyways"
Music by **Mitch Murray**
Lyrics by **Peter Callender**
Sung by **Tony Christie**
Associate Producer **Des Saunders**
Director of Photography
Brendan J. Stafford BSC *(1-24, 26)*
Frank Watts BSC *(25)*
Production Manager
Malcolm Christopher
Art Director **Bob Bell**
Supervising Editor **David Lane**
Miss Porter's Wardrobe Designed by
Germinal Rangel
Editor **Bert Rule**
(1, 4, 6, 7, 9, 13-15, 18, 20, 22, 24)
Mike Campbell
(2, 3, 8, 10, 11, 17, 21, 23, 25, 26)
David Lane *(5, 12, 19)*
Geoffrey Mackrill *(16)*
Assistant Director **Gino Marotta**
(1, 2, 4, 5, 8-11, 14, 16, 18-26)
Frank Hollands
(3, 6, 7, 12, 15, 17)
Victor Tourjansky *(13)*
Sound Editor **Peter Pennell**
(1, 3-6, 8, 10, 13, 14, 19, 20, 24)
John Beaton
(2, 7, 9, 11, 12, 15-18, 21-23, 25, 26)
Music Editor **Alan Willis**
Sound Recordists **J.B. Smith**
(1, 3-6, 8-24, 26)
Dennis Whitlock *(1-21, 23-26)*
Bob McPhee *(2, 7)*
Ray Merrin *(22)*
David Bowen *(25)*
Casting **Michael Barnes**
Assistant Art Director **Keith Wilson**
(1-18, 23-26)
Michael Ford *(19-22)*
Processed by **Rank Film Laboratories**
Camera Operator **John Winbolt**
(1-24, 26)
John Drake *(25)*
Location Manager **Arnold Ross**
(1-9, 12, 13, 17, 26)
Brian Heard
(14, 16, 18, 21, 24)
Peter Carter
(10, 11, 15, 19, 20, 22, 23, 25)
Continuity **Doreen Soan**
(1, 4, 5, 13)
Marjorie Lavelly
(2, 3, 6-12, 14-19, 21-26)
June Randall *(20)*
Make-Up **Basil Newall**
(1-9, 12, 13, 17, 26)
Eddie Knight
(10, 11, 14-16, 18-25)
Hairdressing **Betty Sheriff**
Wardrobe **Frank Vinall**
Jean Fairlie *(1-17, 26)*
Special Effects Supervisor
Brian Johnson*
Title Sequence Directed by **John Hough***
Second Unit Director **David Lane***

A Group Three Production
for ITC World Wide Distribution
Made on Location and at
EMI/MGM Studios, London, England

* uncredited

Second Season Changes

A number of small changes were made to the format of THE PROTECTORS for the second season, although these were primarily cosmetic and went largely unnoticed by viewers. The main change was the loss of first season regular actors Anthony Chinn and Yasuko Nagazumi as, respectively, Chino and Suki. Both characters had appeared throughout the series' first season but were not felt to have made a substantial impact so they were dropped, although Chino continued to be seen in the opening titles of each instalment. The concept of the The Protectors Organisation itself was played down in the second series episodes, and no other Protectors were seen apart from the three leads. Indeed, the computer communications console that had been a prominent part of the lounge set in Harry's apartment during the first season vanished altogether in the general refurbishment of the apartment set, which now incorporated a brown leather sofa in place of the previous black one.

Episode Titles (Series Two)

(Listed in ITC recommended screening order)

1. **Bagman**
2. **The Bridge**
3. **Fighting Fund**
4. **Quin**
5. **Lena**
6. **Goodbye George**
7. **Implicado**
8. **The Last Frontier**
9. **Baubles Bangles And Beads**
10. **Petard**
11. **Burning Bush**
12. **Border Line**
13. **WAM Part One**
14. **WAM Part Two**
15. **Dragon Chase**
16. **Zeke's Blues**
17. **Decoy**
18. **A Pocketful Of Posies**
19. **Shadbolt**
20. **Sugar And Spice**
21. **Blockbuster**
22. **Wheels**
23. **The Tiger And The Goat**
24. **The Insider**
25. **Trial**
26. **Route 27**

Episode Running Time

25 minutes approx.

The popular theme song of THE PROTECTORS, 'Avenues And Alleyways' performed by Tony Christie, was especially written for the series by prolific composers Mitch Murray and Pete Callender, writers and producers of Christie's 1971 chart hit 'I Did What I Did For Maria'. A full three-minute recording of the song, produced by Murray and Callender and featuring an orchestra conducted by Lew Warburton, was released as a 7" vinyl single by MCA Records (MKS 5101) at the end of 1972 backed by 'I Never Was A Child', another song written by Murray and Callender. The record entered the UK charts on February 10th, 1973 where it stayed for four weeks, reaching number 37 at its zenith. The theme song was also released in stereo on Christie's 1973 LP *With Loving Feeling* (MCA Records, MUPS 468).

BAGMAN — Ep. No. 01

Screenplay by **Terry Nation** Directed by **John Hough**

Wealthy widow Gudren Andersen contacts Harry and Caroline when she receives a call from Christian Janson demanding one million krone in return for her daughter Evi, being held hostage in a disused island fort. Harry and Caroline take the ransom money to an arranged rendezvous at a derelict house on the coast road to Elsinore, but the exchange is interrupted when a policeman named Hansen arrives asking what they are doing on private property. After he leaves, Harry and Caroline find a note left on their car giving the location of a new rendezvous and Harry realises that Janson plans to send them running all over Copenhagen so that they are unable to set a trap for him...

Notes

Location filming in Copenhagen for this episode took the cast and crew to the Fredericksholms Kanal and the Ridebanen on Slotsholmen (Castle Island). Stephan Chase (Christian Janson) was previously seen as the film director in Straker's hallucination in the UFO episode *Mindbender*. He is erroneously credited as 'Stephen' Chase on the in-show titles at the start of the episode. Lalla Ward (Evi Andersen) went on to become the second Romana in the BBC's DOCTOR WHO series.

Regular Cast

Harry Rule	**Robert Vaughn**
Contessa di Contini	**Nyree Dawn Porter**
Paul Buchet	**Tony Anholt**

Guest Cast

Christian Janson	**Stephan Chase**
Gudren Andersen	**Patricia Haines**
Evi Andersen	**Lalla Ward**
Hansen	**Oliver Ford-Davies**
Davidson	**Paul Dawkins**
Beck	**Karl Ahlefeldt**
Waiter	**Gert Thynov**

First UK Transmission

Saturday, May 12th, 1973
5.45pm (ATV London)

THE BRIDGE — Ep. No. 02

Screenplay by **Tony Barwick** Directed by **Jeremy Summers**

Anna De Santos has been abducted by David Mitchell, the son of one of her father's closest friends. Señor De Santos calls in the Contessa who meets Mitchell at a cuevas in Madrid, where she learns that his ransom demands are $10 million plus explosives and someone who knows how to handle them. Masquerading as a ruthless mercenary and explosives expert, Harry delivers the ransom and is taken to a villa outside Madrid where Anna is being held captive. There, Harry learns that Mitchell plans to assassinate America's special envoy during a fact-finding tour by detonating the explosives under the bridge at Diaganda while the envoy's car is crossing it...

Notes

This episode's location photography in Spain was filmed at Barajas Airport in Madrid and various locations in the surrounding countryside. At the time of filming, Richard Morant (David Mitchell) had recently completed his role as Flashman in the BBC's fondly remembered 1972 adaptation of TOM BROWN'S SCHOOLDAYS. Within 18 months of appearing as Juan in this episode, Christopher Mitchell was cast as Gunner Nigel Parkin in the long-running BBC sitcom IT AIN'T HALF HOT MUM.

Regular Cast

Harry Rule	**Robert Vaughn**
Contessa di Contini	**Nyree Dawn Porter**

Guest Cast

David Mitchell	**Richard Morant**
De Santos	**Michael Goodliffe**
Mitchell	**James Maxwell**
Anna De Santos	**Diana Quick**
Juan	**Christopher Mitchell**
Carlos	**David Mayberry**

First UK Transmission

Friday, September 14th, 1973
7.00pm (ATV London)

FIGHTING FUND — Ep. No. 03

Screenplay by **John Kruse** Directed by **Jeremy Summers**

The Marquesa Visconti and her antiquities preservation society have received film of an audacious art theft by the members of Red Army Group C. The thieves have issued instructions for an auction of the art treasures, threatening that the lots will be destroyed if the police are informed. Harry and Caroline attend the auction at the address detailed in the instructions, only to find that they must bid by radio, competing against bidders at addresses all over Rome. Caroline joins the bidding to stall the auction long enough for Harry and the police to pinpoint the source of the auctioneer's signal, but as they close in on an apartment at the Calle di Santa Monica, the auction is suddenly terminated...

Notes

Location filming in Venice for this episode took the cast and crew to the Piazza San Marco (St. Mark's Square) for shots of the Palazzo Ducale (Doges' Palace), the Basilica di San Marco (St. Mark's Basilica), the Libreria Vecchia and scenes on the roof of the Torre dell'Orologio (Clock Tower). Filming also took place at the Ponte di Rialto (Rialto Bridge) on the Grand Canal. Shane Rimmer can be heard as the voice of the auction bidder at Riva Angeli.

Regular Cast

Harry Rule	**Robert Vaughn**
Contessa di Contini	**Nyree Dawn Porter**
Paul Buchet	**Tony Anholt**

Guest Cast

Marquesa Visconti	**Lisa Daniely**
Leo	**David Suchet**
Vincenzo	**Ben Howard**
Dr. Bianco	**Mischa De La Motte**
Bishop	**Hugh Morton**
Professor Williams	**Jack Lynn**
Principessa Lilli	**Gladys Spencer**
Police Captain	**Gino Melvazzi**
Bank Manager	**Sal Pantelone**

First UK Transmission

Saturday, June 16th, 1973
6.35pm (ATV London)

QUIN — Ep. No. 04

Screenplay by **Trevor Preston** Directed by **Don Leaver**

The Protectors have been retained by Laura Sutton to find her missing brother Jimmy, recruited in Marseilles 19 months ago by Quin, an international mercenary who has made a fortune out of war, genocide and political expediency. After two months, their search for Quin has brought them to Madrid where Harry is taken to a meeting with Quin's associate Garcia at Las Ventas bullring. Explaining that he has a proposition for Quin, Harry is later taken to a deserted cuevas beneath the Plaza Mayor where another of Quin's associates, Allen, bundles him into a car. Caroline attempts to follow in a taxi, but she loses him when the road is suddenly blocked by a truck...

Notes

This episode's location filming in Madrid took the cast and crew to the Plaza Mayor, the El Rastro flea-market on the Ribera de Curtidores, the massive Las Ventas bullring and the Eurobuilding hotel on Padre Damian. The answer to the question that Harry asks the waiter is that the equestrian statue of Philip III in the Plaza Mayor was the work of Giovanni da Bologna and Pietro Tacca. Simon & Garfunkel's 'Scarborough Fair' can be briefly heard on the soundtrack when the Contessa visits the El Rastro flea-market.

Regular Cast

Harry Rule	**Robert Vaughn**
Contessa di Contini	**Nyree Dawn Porter**
Paul Buchet	**Tony Anholt**

Guest Cast

Quin	**Peter Vaughan**
Allen	**Brian Glover**
Paco	**Henry Woolf**
Garcia	**Anthony Langdon**
Maxwell	**Tristan Rogers**
Waiter	**Jesus Suzman**
Taxi Driver	**Luis Bar Boo**

First UK Transmission

Saturday, April 7th, 1973
5.45pm (ATV London)

LENA — Ep. No. 05

Screenplay by **Trevor Preston** Directed by **Don Leaver**

Caroline's friend Lena Haydon is a journalist intent on exposing Italian politician Mauro Carpiano as a man so ruthless that he murdered his own father, Antonio, in order to inherit his wealth. Lena is trying to track down Antonio's close friend Paolo Morleiter, whom she believes is in hiding after faking his own death. Her contact Russi is badly beaten up by Carpiano's men but he agrees to help her find Morleiter and sends word for her to meet a man named Carlo in a disused glass factory on the island of Murano. During a trip to Torcello with Harry and Caroline, Lena stops off at Murano, but she finds Carlo dead and Harry is attacked by the assassin in the factory shower room...

Notes

Location photography in Venice for this episode was shot at the Palazzo Ducale in the Piazza San Marco, the Ponti dei Sospiri (Bridge of Sighs) by the Piazzetta San Marco, the terrace restaurant of the Hotel Regina on the Grand Canal opposite the church of Santa Maria della Salute, the Riva di Schiavoni, the Cimitero on St. Michele, the Pescheria (fish market) on the Grand Canal and the quay at S. Pietro in Volta on the Lido. Roger Lloyd Pack (Russi) was previously seen as a photographer in *See No Evil*.

Regular Cast

Harry Rule	**Robert Vaughn**
Contessa di Contini	**Nyree Dawn Porter**

Guest Cast

Lena Haydon	**Judy Parfitt**
Mauro Carpiano	**John Thaw**
Russi	**Roger Lloyd Pack**
Maria Russi	**Judi Bloom**
Paolo Morleiter	**Frederick Peisley**
Helena Morleiter	**Miki Iveria**
Pursuer	**Mario Depita**
Gunman	**Terry Plummer**
Vendor	**Alexander Bron**
Barman	**Leo Dolan**

First UK Transmission

Friday, October 5th, 1973
7.00pm (ATV London)

GOODBYE GEORGE — Ep. No. 06

Screenplay by **Brian Clemens** Directed by **Michael Lindsay-Hogg**

American millionaire Cedric Parton retains Caroline to find out why his son Caspar, living as an artist in Venice, has suddenly started drawing large sums of money from an account that his late mother left him. Suspecting that Caspar is being blackmailed, she masquerades as an interested art buyer to question him about his close friend George Milworth who seems to have gone missing, but Caspar denies any knowledge of George's whereabouts. Then Caroline trails Caspar as he makes another cash withdrawal from his account and passes it to a woman at a meeting in the Piazza San Marco...

Notes

This episode's location filming in Venice took the cast and crew to the Basilica di San Marco and Palazzo Ducale in the Piazza San Marco while the closing scenes were shot at the Ponte S. Barnaba. To preserve the surprise of the final twist for viewers, Paul Jones is credited with playing 'Caspar' on the in-show titles (and also, oddly, on the end titles after the character's true identity has been revealed). Jones later appeared as Mike Ryan in the SPACE:1999 episode *Black Sun*. Geraldine Moffatt (Maria) was previously seen as Jean Regan in the UFO episode *The Cat With Ten Lives*.

Regular Cast

Contessa di Contini	**Nyree Dawn Porter**

Guest Cast

George Milworth	**Paul Jones**
Maria Milworth	**Geraldine Moffatt**
Barney Mailer	**Barry Keegan**
Cedric Parton	**Lionel Murton**
Policeman	**Arnold Diamond**
Bank Teller	**Paul McDowell**
Intruder	**Malcolm Hayes**

First UK Transmission

Saturday, July 7th, 1973
6.05pm (ATV London)

IMPLICADO — Ep. No. 07

Screenplay by **Tony Barwick** Directed by **Jeremy Summers**

Teenager Stephen Douglas waits in the car while his friend Raphael Santana receives a consignment of drugs on a building site in Madrid. Later, Santana plants the drugs in Stephen's bag during a police raid at the Cafeteria Palma Real and Stephen is imprisoned on possession charges. Stephen's mother asks Caroline to investigate the case and Stephen protests his innocence when she visits him in prison. Paul learns from the waiter at the café that Santana is the true culprit but when he introduces himself to Santana as a friend of Stephen's, he comes under fire from Santana and his colleagues...

Notes

Location photography for this episode was shot in Spain at Barajas Airport in Madrid and Manzanares el Real, north of the city. Caroline visits Mrs. Douglas at Barnet General Hospital in Barnet, Greater London. Later seen as MI5 boss Harry Pearce in the BBC spy drama SPOOKS, Peter Firth was best known at the time for his role as Scooper in HERE COME THE DOUBLE DECKERS! His DOUBLE DECKERS co-star Debbie Russ (Tiger) appears as Vicky Standish in *Sugar And Spice*. Policeman Stephen Greif can also be seen as Eric Volker in the SPACE PRECINCT episode *Two Against The Rock.*

Regular Cast

Harry Rule	**Robert Vaughn**
Contessa di Contini	**Nyree Dawn Porter**
Paul Buchet	**Tony Anholt**

Guest Cast

Raphael Santana	**Patrick Mower**
Stephen Douglas	**Peter Firth**
Mrs. Douglas	**Ruth Trouncer**
Dr. Dove	**Neil Hallett**
Patron	**Pat La Touche**
Jacques	**Aldo Sanbrell**
Waiter	**Carl Forgione**
Policeman at Café	**Stephen Greif**
Assassin	**Ron Eagleton**

First UK Transmission

Saturday, August 11th, 1973
6.05pm (ATV London)

THE LAST FRONTIER — Ep. No. 08

Screenplay by **Jean Morris** Directed by **Charles Crichton**

Dr. Irena Gayevska, the USSR's leading nuclear scientist, has been selected to chair the first international conference of Medicine for Peace in Salzburg. British junior minister John Eastbrook hires the Protectors to facilitate Irena's defection to London where she can marry him, so Harry develops an elaborate escape plan. During an official party for the conference delegates at Anif Castle, Paul distracts the guards by appearing to escape across the castle moat with Irena in a motor boat, thereby enabling Caroline and Irena to simply walk out through the main gate. But as they catch a flight to London, Harry suspects that Eastbrook may not have told them the whole truth about Irena's defection...

Notes

The working title of this episode was 'Beyond The Last Frontier'. Oddly, script-writer Jean Morris receives no on-screen credit for her work. The scenes of Irena's escape from the conference party were shot at Anif Castle, a 16th century neo-Gothic moated castle at Anif, three miles south of Salzburg in Austria. Scenes were also filmed on location at Salzburg International Airport in Himmelreich, Salzburg. Hildegard Neil later appeared as Elizia in the SPACE:1999 episode *Devil's Planet.*

Regular Cast

Harry Rule	**Robert Vaughn**
Contessa di Contini	**Nyree Dawn Porter**
Paul Buchet	**Tony Anholt**

Guest Cast

Dr. Irena Petrovna Gayevska	**Hildegard Neil**
John Eastbrook	**William Lucas**
Zhukov	**Yuri Borienko**
Jones	**Peter Cellier**
British Delegate	**Dennis Clinton**
Magda	**Manuela Renard**

First UK Transmission

Saturday, June 23rd, 1973
6.35pm (ATV London)

BAUBLES BANGLES AND BEADS — Ep. No. 09

Screenplay by **Terry Nation** Directed by **Jeremy Summers**

A gang of jewel thieves are double-crossed when their colleague Bergen makes off with the Malvern collection after staging an ambush outside Copenhagen. The collection's insurers receive an offer to return the jewels for ten per cent of the insurance value so Harry and Caroline are retained to deliver the payoff. Bergen has been badly injured by gunfire but is assisted by his daughter Katie, who meets Harry and Caroline at Kronborg Castle to issue instructions for the exchange. When she returns to the house where her father is in hiding, Katie is followed by one of the members of Bergen's gang...

Notes

Location filming in Copenhagen took the cast and crew to the main entrance of the Tivoli Gardens on Vesterbrogade and the north bank of the Nyhavn canal. Scenes were also shot at Kronborg Castle in Elsinore. Gang members Peter Porteous, Martin Grace and Robert Russell all went on to appear in SPACE:1999. Russell plays Hadin in *Mission Of The Darians*, stuntman Martin Grace appears as a security guard in a number of Year One episodes and Peter Porteous can be seen as Petrov in several Year Two episodes. Jacqueline Stanbury previously appeared as Susan in *2000 ft To Die.*

Regular Cast

Harry Rule	**Robert Vaughn**
Contessa di Contini	**Nyree Dawn Porter**

Guest Cast

Bergen	**Frederick Jaeger**
Katie Bergen	**Yvonne Antrobus**
Insurance Executive	**John Barron**
Motorcyclist	**Andrew Bradford**
Gang	**Peter Porteous** **Martin Grace / Robert Russell**
Car Hire Receptionist	**Jacqueline Stanbury**
Miss Hansen	**Paula Patterson**

First UK Transmission

Saturday, June 30, 1973
6.35pm (ATV London)

PETARD — Ep. No. 10

Screenplay by **Tony Barwick** Directed by **Cyril Frankel**

Industrial espionage has already cost the IMA company over £2 million and managing director Wyatt is determined to prevent details of their new detergent being leaked to rival company Universal before the product is launched. Harry joins the company as a consultant with Caroline acting as his secretary. They bring in electronics expert Ludo Jones, who quickly discovers that the IMA offices are being bugged. He traces the source of the signals to a nearby office block, but industrial spies Scudder and Conway have vacated the premises by the time Paul gets there...

Notes

Lee House in the Barbican, London doubled for the offices of IMA during location filming while the nearby Royex House in Aldermanbury Square appeared as the office block used by Scudder for surveillance. RSC actor Mark Jones (Scudder) was, at the time of production, making a name for himself as the male lead in British sex comedies such as *Layout For 5 Models* (1972), *Keep It Up Jack!* (1973) and *The Sexplorer* (1975). Basil Dignam and Clinton Greyn had both previously appeared in UFO, Dignam in *Identified* and Greyn in *The Dalotek Affair*.

Regular Cast

Harry Rule	**Robert Vaughn**
Contessa di Contini	**Nyree Dawn Porter**
Paul Buchet	**Tony Anholt**

Guest Cast

Wyatt	**Iain Cuthbertson**
Alec Weston	**Cyril Luckham**
Scudder	**Mark Jones**
Ludo Jones	**John Kane**
Charles Engleton	**Basil Dignam**
Linda Grant	**Angela Douglas**
David Lee	**Ralph Bates**
David Cameron	**Clinton Greyn**
Conway	**Milton Johns**
Cleaner	**Carmel McSharry**
Night Security Man	**Lewis Wilson**

First UK Transmission

Saturday, June 9th, 1973
6.35pm (ATV London)

BURNING BUSH — Ep. No. 11

Screenplay by **Trevor Preston** Directed by **Don Leaver**

Retained by millionaire Adam Ferris to find his daughter Anne, Harry and Paul have discovered that she has joined a religious community in London led by the mysterious Mrs. Apsimon, a medium and spiritualist preacher. Ferris goes to the order's premises but Anne begs him to leave her alone and Ferris becomes convinced that she has been brainwashed so that she will sign a will leaving all her money to Mrs. Apsimon. To find out if this is so, Harry poses as a homeless alcoholic who is taken in as a probationary member of the community. Once inside, he witnesses a strange ceremony in which Mrs. Apsimon appears to become possessed by the spirit of Anne's dead mother...

Notes

Adam Ferris's burgundy Rolls-Royce (NM 777) was previously seen being used by Engleton in *Petard*. Ken Hutchison (Mark) also appears in the SPACE:1999 episode *The Seance Spectre* as a deranged individual dabbling in a form of occult spiritualism. This is the only episode of THE PROTECTORS to feature any kind of fantasy element as Mrs. Apsimon's possession by the spirit of Anne's mother and the circumstances of Mark's comeuppance in the chapel are presented as genuine spiritual manifestations.

Regular Cast

Harry Rule	**Robert Vaughn**
Paul Buchet	**Tony Anholt**

Guest Cast

Anne Ferris	**Sinead Cusack**
Mark Jenner	**Ken Hutchison**
Mrs Apsimon	**Madge Ryan**
Adam Ferris	**Anthony Steel**

First UK Transmission

Friday, October 12th, 1973
7.00pm (ATV London)

BORDER LINE — Ep. No. 12

Screenplay by **Anthony Terpiloff** Directed by **Charles Crichton**

Actress Ilona Tabori has been refused permission to bury her father Janos, a Hungarian freedom fighter, in his home country so she turns to the Protectors to help her smuggle the body into Hungary for a private ceremony. Harry agrees only on the condition that there will be no publicity or political speeches at the burial service, as this could jeopardise their safe return. After they arrive in Salzburg, Tabori's coffin is hidden in the boot of the Contessa's new Mercedes and Harry and Caroline meet Tabori's old friend Zoltan Kolas, who initially misunderstands their intentions for Tabori's body. The next morning, Harry and Ilona set off for the Hungarian border but when they get there, the border guards insist on seeing inside the boot of the Mercedes...

Notes

The original title of the script for this episode was 'Patriot's Game'. Location photography in Austria was shot at Salzburg International Airport in Himmelreich and other locations in the countryside surrounding Salzburg. Georgia Brown (Ilona Tabori) previously appeared as Maria Ghardala in *One And One Makes One*. Jon Laurimore (Gerald Marks) is also seen as Smitty in the SPACE:1999 episode *Black Sun*.

Regular Cast

Harry Rule	**Robert Vaughn**
Contessa di Contini	**Nyree Dawn Porter**
Paul Buchet	**Tony Anholt**

Guest Cast

Ilona Tabori	**Georgia Brown**
Zoltan Kolas	**Oscar Homolka**
Gerald Marks	**Jon Laurimore**
Customs Official	**David Allister**
Hungarian Border Guards	**Gabor Vernon / Petar Vidovic**
Hungarian Peasant Woman	**Elizabeth Balogh**

First UK Transmission

Saturday, July 21st, 1973
6.05pm (ATV London)

WAM Part One — Ep. No. 13

Screenplay by **Tony Barwick** Directed by **Jeremy Summers**

Monica Davies's father believes that she has fallen in with bad company and is involved in some sort of racket after she has told him that she will soon have all the money she will ever need. Paul follows Monica to Victoria Station where she changes into hippy clothes before boarding a train to Vienna. Then Harry tails her from Vienna as she hitch-hikes to Salzburg and checks into the city's most expensive hotel. While Paul follows Monica to a shop where she buys a tape recorder, Caroline searches her hotel room and finds a note that reads, "Thanks for the goodies – WAM is on." But what is WAM?

Notes

Location filming in Austria for this story took the cast and crew to the Residenzplatz and the Mirabell Gardens in Salzburg, the cable car terminus at St. Leonhard, and the Geiereck mountain refuge and Hochalm restaurant on the 6,078-feet high plateau of the Untersberg mountain. Earlier scenes in the episode were shot on location at Victoria Station in London. The events of this story begin on September 4th, 1972 (the purchase date shown on Monica's ticket to Vienna) therefore preceding the events of the series one episode *Balance Of Terror*. The return rail fair to Vienna costs Monica £35.40.

Regular Cast

Harry Rule	**Robert Vaughn**
Contessa di Contini	**Nyree Dawn Porter**
Paul Buchet	**Tony Anholt**

Guest Cast

William Arthur McKay	**Prentis Hancock**
Monica Davies	**Jill Townsend**
Davies	**Michael Glover**
Attendant	**Rudolf Barry**
Official	**John Herrington**
Manager	**Bert Fortell**

First UK Transmission

Saturday, July 28th, 1973
6.05pm (ATV London)

WAM Part Two — Ep. No. 14

Screenplay by **Tony Barwick** Directed by **Jeremy Summers**

Unknown to those at the base of the mountain, the appearance of armed hi-jackers holding tourists at gunpoint on the plateau is being cleverly faked by one man, William Arthur McKay, who makes a ransom demand for $10 million. Commissioner Braun suspects that the whole thing is a bluff, but McKay uses Monica's taped performance as a frightened hostage to convince him to pay the ransom. After the money is collected by Monica, McKay reveals the con and the tourists are released, but Harry realises that the hi-jacker must be among those on board the cable car when it arrives at the terminus...

Notes

As Darwin King in *Dragon's Domain*, Michael Sheard was the fourth cast member of this story to later appear in SPACE:1999, following Jill Townsend (Sahala in *Dorzak*) and 1999 regulars Prentis Hancock (Paul Morrow) and Tony Anholt (Tony Verdeschi).

Oops!

When Braun arrives at the Untersberg cable car terminus, the external appearance of the building suddenly looks like the EMI/MGM Elstree Studios in Borehamwood.

Regular Cast

Harry Rule	**Robert Vaughn**
Contessa di Contini	**Nyree Dawn Porter**
Paul Buchet	**Tony Anholt**

Guest Cast

William Arthur McKay	**Prentis Hancock**
Monica Davies	**Jill Townsend**
Commissioner Braun	**Olaf Pooley**
Inspector Luhrs	**Michael Sheard**
Attendant / Official	**Rudolf Barry**

First UK Transmission

Saturday, August 4th, 1973
6.05pm (ATV London)

DRAGON CHASE — Ep. No. 15

Screenplay by **John Kruse** Directed by **Charles Crichton**

London publisher Lockier has smuggled Russian writer Nickolai Ivanov into Britain to enable him to write his new book about Soviet politics free from interference. Harry is safeguarding Nickolai at Lockier's country house Dragon Chase when a group of students, led by their Marxist political science tutor Devlin, barge in and kidnap them both, imprisoning them aboard a barge. Caroline arrives at the house the next morning to find it deserted but when Lockier returns and realises what has happened, he throws her out. However, she recognises that Lockier deduced who was responsible as soon as he saw that his dog had been fed, so she and Paul tail him to Oxford...

Notes

Shenley Lodge (now Manor Lodge School) in Shenley, Hertfordshire doubled for Lockier's house Dragon Chase during location filming. Bruce Robinson (Peter Lockier) has gone on to become the highly acclaimed script-writer of *The Killing Fields* (1984) and writer/director of the comedy films *Withnail & I* (1986) and *How To Get Ahead In Advertising* (1989). Richard Marner (credited as 'First Russian') went on to appear as Colonel Kurt Von Strohm in the long-running BBC sitcom 'ALLO 'ALLO.

Regular Cast

Harry Rule	**Robert Vaughn**
Contessa di Contini	**Nyree Dawn Porter**
Paul Buchet	**Tony Anholt**

Guest Cast

Lockier	**Donald Houston**
Nickolai Ivanov	**William Dexter**
Devlin	**Kenneth Colley**
Peter Lockier	**Bruce Robinson**
KGB Agent	**Richard Marner**
Jennie Rowan	**Mary Larkin**
Jasper Pollard	**Jack Galloway**
Mike	**Gary Hamilton**
Stage Door Keeper	**Norman Atkyns**

First UK Transmission

Friday, October 19th, 1973
7.00pm (ATV London)

ZEKE'S BLUES — Ep. No. 16

Screenplay by **Shane Rimmer** Directed by **Jeremy Summers**

Harry collects Caroline from the Cunter Hotel to go and see his old college friend Zeke Daley, who is performing as the pianist at the Condor Club off Old Compton Street in London. As they leave the club after Zeke's final set, a car tries to run Zeke down in the street, but he brushes the incident off as an accident. Harry invites Zeke to stay with him at his apartment, but something is clearly preying on Zeke's mind. The owner of the Condor Club, Kasankas, has paid off a large debt for Zeke, so the pianist is obliged to cooperate when Kasankas orders him to place a homing device on Harry's Jensen, leading Kasankas to where his former book-keeper Bradley is in hiding...

Notes

Shenley Hall in Shenley, Hertfordshire doubled for Bradley's house in location filming, while the buildings of the EMI/MGM Elstree Studios in Borehamwood appear as the streets outside the Condor Club. Shane Rimmer (Zeke) previously appeared as Vickers in *Vocal* and scripted both this episode and *Blockbuster*. He later appeared in SPACE:1999 as Kelly in *Space Brain* and provided the narration for DICK SPANNER. Ray Lonnen (Patrick) went on to star as Willie Caine in Yorkshire Television's THE SANDBAGGERS.

Regular Cast

Harry Rule	**Robert Vaughn**
Contessa di Contini	**Nyree Dawn Porter**

Guest Cast

Zeke Daley	**Shane Rimmer**
Kasankas	**Paul Curran**
Patrick	**Ray Lonnen**
Fred	**Jackie Leapman**
George	**Donald Webster**
Max	**Graham Weston**
Bradley	**James Ottaway**

First UK Transmission

Friday, September 28th, 1973
7.00pm (ATV London)

DECOY — Ep. No. 17

Screenplay by **Brian Clemens** Directed by **Michael Lindsay-Hogg**

Harry receives a coded message from private investigator Jerry Butler, inviting Harry to join him in Venice. During the flight to Italy, Harry explains to Caroline that Butler is on the trail of the Mulhaney diamonds, stolen in an armed raid in 1967 by Butler's best friend Nick Archer, who was killed in an explosion during the raid. However, by the time they arrive at his hotel, Butler has been assassinated. Then Harry is approached by a man named Marcus who claims to have information about who killed Butler and why, but he leads Harry to a derelict house where he is attacked and left for dead...

Notes

Location filming in Venice took the cast and crew to the Piazza San Marco, the Rialto Bridge and the Hotel Regina on the Grand Canal. Bruce Montague (Police Captain) is best known for his role as Leonard Dunn in the BBC sitcom BUTTERFLIES.

Oops!

The Contessa tells the Police Captain that Archer was killed during the Mulhaney raid in 1967, but later Harry says that Archer was believed to have been killed in 1970.

Regular Cast

Harry Rule	**Robert Vaughn**
Contessa di Contini	**Nyree Dawn Porter**

Guest Cast

Jerry Butler	**Ronald Radd**
Nick Archer	**Mark Damon**
Marcus	**George Innes**
Police Captain	**Bruce Montague**
Conyapepi	**Stephen Sheppard**
Hotel Porter	**Pierre Bedenes**
Desk Clerk	**George Little**
Airline Steward	**George Von Moos**
Girlfriend	**Erika Bergmann**

First UK Transmission

Saturday, July 14th, 1973
6.05pm (ATV London)

A POCKETFUL OF POSIES — Ep. No. 18

Screenplay by **Terry Nation** Directed by **Cyril Frankel**

As she prepares for an important comeback performance, international singing star Carrie Blaine is terrorised in her own home by a series of strange incidents which appear to be some sort of hallucinations. Her husband Mario Toza fears that she is losing her sanity and this appears to be confirmed when Harry fails to find any evidence that Carrie is in any physical danger. Then Harry notices that the contents of Carrie's coffee cup have solidified into a gel and when he has them analysed, he discovers that Carrie has been drugged by stimulants which can induce hallucinations...

Notes

The working title of this episode was 'There's Someone Outside'. Terry Nation's script was written specifically for Shirley Bassey in the role of Carrie Blaine and would have been the Welsh international recording artist's acting debut. However, Bassey backed out shortly before filming and director Cyril Frankel quickly cast Eartha Kitt in the role, based on her previous acting work in episodes of I SPY, BATMAN and MISSION: IMPOSSIBLE and the feature film *Up The Chastity Belt* (1971). Bernard Kay later appeared as a Humanoid creature in the SPACE:1999 episode *New Adam New Eve*.

Regular Cast

Harry Rule	**Robert Vaughn**
Paul Buchet	**Tony Anholt**

Guest Cast

Carrie Blaine	**Eartha Kitt**
Mario Toza	**Kieron Moore**
Philip Bentley	**Bernard Kay**
Sara Trent	**Kate O'Mara**
Joe	**Terry Cantor**
Nelly Baxter	**Gretchen Franklin**
Theatre Doctor	**John Law**
Consultant	**Michael Lees**
Reporter	**Jon Croft**

First UK Transmission

Friday, February 22nd, 1974
7.00pm (ATV Midlands)

SHADBOLT — Ep. No. 19

Regular Cast

Harry Rule	**Robert Vaughn**

Guest Cast

Shadbolt	**Tom Bell**
Amelia Benwell	**Georgina Hale**
Police Inspector	**Stanley Stewart**
Attendant	**Neville Barber**

First UK Transmission

Friday, November 16th, 1973
7.00pm (ATV London)

Screenplay by **Tony Barwick** — Directed by **John Hough**

Professional hitman Shadbolt receives notification of his next contract together with a train ticket. His target is Harry Rule, who is travelling on the same train from Waverley Station, Edinburgh to King's Cross, London. Shadbolt strikes up a conversation with Amelia Benwell, a librarian travelling in his first-class compartment, but she rejects his advances and leaves the train at Retford. There, Shadbolt finds an envelope waiting for him which contains his payment and instructions to proceed with the contract. As the train sets off again, he joins Harry in his compartment and holds him at gunpoint...

Notes

Unusually, this episode features UK location photography shot away from the vicinity of the series' production base in Borehamwood, Hertfordshire. The early scenes were filmed in Edinburgh at Holyrood Park, the Forth Bridge, High Street, Horse Wynde, a newsagents on the corner of Princes Street and South Charlotte Street, Calton New Burial Ground and Waverley Station. Scenes were also filmed at Neville Street Station in Newcastle, Tyne and Wear. Nyree Dawn Porter and Tony Anholt are credited on the end titles but do not appear in the episode.

SUGAR AND SPICE — Ep. No. 20

Regular Cast

Harry Rule	**Robert Vaughn**
Contessa di Contini	**Nyree Dawn Porter**
Paul Buchet	**Tony Anholt**

Guest Cast

Vicky Standish	**Debbie Russ**
Manning	**Derek Anders**
Colson	**Phil Woods**
Sir Charles Standish	**Norman Ettlinger**
Brian Dukes	**John Normington**
Headmistress	**Cicely Paget-Bowman**
Kruger	**Shane Shelton**
Barnes	**Gerry Crampton**

First UK Transmission

Friday, September 21st, 1973
7.00pm (ATV London)

Screenplay by **David Butler** — Directed by **Charles Crichton**

Industrialist Sir Charles Standish hires the Protectors to safeguard his ten-year-old daughter Vicky for six days, as his competitors have threatened her life if he proceeds with a series of international mergers. Vicky must not know that she is in danger, so Harry takes her out of school on the pretext of providing her with special history tuition. With Harry posing as a tutor, Paul as a chauffeur and Caroline as the housekeeper, Vicky is taken to a remote farmhouse, but the Contessa discovers a homing device attached to Vicky's bag and the farmhouse soon comes under siege from a group of assassins...

Notes

High Canons at Well End in Hertfordshire, previously seen in *Triple Cross*, doubles for the Radcliffe School for Girls in location photography, while the safehouse is Summerswood Farm at Ridge in Hertfordshire. Caroline's housekeeper persona Mrs. MacGillicuddy is a reference to the American sitcom I LOVE LUCY (1951-1961), in which MacGillicuddy was the maiden name of the character portrayed by Lucille Ball. Derek Anders can also be seen as Wayland in the SPACE:1999 episode *Space Brain*. Debbie Russ is best known for her role as Tiger in HERE COME THE DOUBLE DECKERS!

BLOCKBUSTER — Ep. No. 21

Regular Cast

Harry Rule	**Robert Vaughn**
Contessa di Contini	**Nyree Dawn Porter**
Paul Buchet	**Tony Anholt**

Guest Cast

Police Inspector	**Peter Jeffrey**
Birch	**Stanley Meadows**
Glen Bailey	**Christopher Neame**
Slater	**Maurice O'Connell**
Doyle	**Eric Dodson**
Barney	**Raymond Skipp**
Workman	**Ron Pember**
Policeman	**Paul Antrim**

First UK Transmission

Friday, March 15th, 1974
7.00pm (ATV Midlands)

Screenplay by **Shane Rimmer** — Directed by **Jeremy Summers**

Harry accepts an assignment from Ben Doyle whose security firm faces bankruptcy after a series of van hi-jackings in which the thieves have escaped with shipments of platinum. After the latest robbery the previous day, the police have cordoned off the entire area, but there is no sign of Doyle's distinctive blue van. Harry visits Bailey's Car Breakers on Thames Street and although owner Glen Bailey is uncooperative, Harry learns that a van was crushed there the previous day, although it was white, not blue. Then the Police Inspector in charge of the case confirms that a witness saw the van being resprayed white after the robbery, but there is still no indication as to what has become of the platinum...

Notes

The Saunders Chemical Works are named after associate producer Desmond Saunders. Location photography in London for this episode was shot at Wembley Stadium, Tower Bridge, Bankside Jetty and the Bankside Power Station in North Southwark and St. Margaret Street by the Houses of Parliament. Workman Ron Pember was previously seen as a casting agent in the UFO episode *Timelash*. Policeman Paul Antrim later appeared as Bill Lowry in the SPACE:1999 episode *Mission Of The Darians*.

WHEELS — Ep. No. 22

Screenplay by **Tony Barwick** Directed by **David Tomblin**

A dispatch case containing confidential details of numbered Swiss bank accounts has been obtained by Manning who offers to return it for $2 million. To enable a consortium of Swiss banks to confirm which accounts are affected and then expose Manning's contact in Switzerland, the Protectors are assigned to acquire the case and photograph the contents without Manning's knowledge. Harry plans to break into Manning's safe, switch the case with an identical one and then replace the original in Manning's car as he drives to a rendezvous with consortium representative Sneider, but this plan relies on split-second timing and a hair-raising cross-country rally drive against the clock...

Notes

High Canons at Well End in Hertfordshire, previously seen in *Triple Cross* and *Sugar And Spice*, doubles for Manning's house in location photography, while Brewhouse Farm at Wildhill near Essenden, Hertfordshire is the base for Harry and Paul's rally car. Sudbury House on Newgate Street (previously seen as the IAC offices in UFO) appears as Sneider's bank. Shortly after appearing in this episode, British-born Robert Coleby emigrated to Australia where he starred in THE YOUNG DOCTORS and CHOPPER SQUAD.

Regular Cast

Role	Actor
Harry Rule	**Robert Vaughn**
Contessa di Contini	**Nyree Dawn Porter**
Paul Buchet	**Tony Anholt**

Guest Cast

Role	Actor
Manning	**Dinsdale Landen**
Sneider	**George Pravda**
Anton	**Robert Coleby**

First UK Transmission

Friday, March 1st, 1974
7.00pm (ATV Midlands)

THE TIGER AND THE GOAT — Ep. No. 23

Screenplay by **Trevor Preston** Directed by **Jeremy Summers**

Drawn to a derelict house under false pretences, Caroline meets Commander Whiting of British Intelligence, who questions her about her old friend David Barsella. She tells him that she has not seen Barsella for some time and has no idea where he is. Whiting eventually reveals that Barsella has been working for British Intelligence for the last 12 years and is believed to be the next target of a psychotic assassin who has killed eight experienced agents in the last 20 months. Whiting intends to leak information that Barsella has renewed his relationship with the Contessa so that Caroline can act as bait for the assassin at Harry's apartment...

Notes

Douglas Wilmer and Drewe Henley both also appear in UFO and SPACE:1999. Wilmer can be seen in UFO's *E.S.P.* episode and SPACE:1999's *Dragon's Domain* while Henley appears in UFO's *Conflict* and both parts of SPACE:1999's *The Bringers Of Wonder*. Max Faulkner can be seen in SPACE:1999 too, as Ted Clifford in *Ring Around The Moon*. Location photography was shot at Elstree Lawns on Barnet Lane in Elstree, Hertfordshire, which doubled for the derelict house where Caroline meets Whiting.

Regular Cast

Role	Actor
Contessa di Contini	**Nyree Dawn Porter**
Paul Buchet	**Tony Anholt**

Guest Cast

Role	Actor
Commander Whiting	**Douglas Wilmer**
David Barsella	**Derek Godfrey**
Reece	**Derek Newark**
Clark	**Drewe Henley**
Ibbett	**Neville Hughes**
Jarman	**Max Faulkner**
Tom Watt	**Doug Fisher**

First UK Transmission

Friday, October 26th, 1973
7.00pm (ATV London)

THE INSIDER — Ep. No. 24

Screenplay by **Trevor Preston** Directed by **Don Leaver**

When the master negatives of a new movie are stolen from a film studio and the only print is destroyed by a fire in the editing room, the producer Chambers calls in Harry. As Chambers briefs Harry, a man who calls himself Smith walks into the office, hands over one of the reels and demands £10,000 for each of the ten remaining reels. Harry tries to tail Smith as he leaves, but the man seems to vanish after boarding the elevator. Harry puts together a photo-fit picture of Smith so that Caroline, Paul and other agents can watch for him when he returns for the first instalment of the ransom, but no-one sees him either arrive or leave again after he collects the money from Chambers...

Notes

Neptune House at the ATV Elstree Studios in Borehamwood, Hertfordshire (previously seen as the Harlington-Straker Film Studios in UFO) doubled for Chambers's film studios in location photography, although the scenes on the roof of the building were shot on the roof of the now demolished Sudbury House on Newgate Street, near St. Paul's Cathedral in London. Stuart Wilson can also be seen as Vindrus in the SPACE:1999 episode *A Matter Of Balance*.

Regular Cast

Role	Actor
Harry Rule	**Robert Vaughn**
Contessa di Contini	**Nyree Dawn Porter**
Paul Buchet	**Tony Anholt**

Guest Cast

Role	Actor
Smith	**Stuart Wilson**
Chambers	**Donald Hewlett**
Editor	**Tim Pearce**
Secretary	**Alison Griffin**
Chauffeur	**Alf Costa**
Taxi Driver	**Alf Joint**

First UK Transmission

Friday, March 8th, 1974
7.00pm (ATV Midlands)

TRIAL Ep. No. 25

Screenplay by **Robert Banks Stewart** Directed by **Charles Crichton**

Anne Gordon retains the Protectors to find her husband Arthur, who has gone missing. She fears he may be suffering from stress induced by the trial of their son John, who is accused of murder. The trial judge, Justice Cronin, collapsed before his summing-up and is recuperating at a nursing home when Gordon turns up and attacks him. Harry locates Gordon in his local pub where the man reveals his belief that Cronin has been unfairly biased during the trial, but when Harry follows him back to the office of his building firm, Gordon knocks him out and goes into hiding again. Then Harry discovers that Gordon has taken components from the office that will enable him to build a time bomb...

Notes

Kendal's Hall (now Radlett Prep School) on Watling Street in Radlett, Hertfordshire doubled for the Clyde Nursing Home in location photography. Shortly after appearing as Arthur Gordon's apple-munching secretary in this episode, Sally James became one of the presenters of the ground-breaking ATV Saturday morning children's show TISWAS. The scene with Gordon speaking to Harry in the pub is accompanied by the haunting incidental theme from the earlier *Border Line* episode.

Regular Cast

Harry Rule	**Robert Vaughn**
Contessa di Contini	**Nyree Dawn Porter**
Paul Buchet	**Tony Anholt**

Guest Cast

Arthur Gordon	**Joss Ackland**
Anne Gordon	**Gwen Cherrell**
Justice Cronin	**Richard Hurndall**
Prosecuting Council	**John Ringham**
John Gordon	**Paul Kelly**
Nurse	**Margaret John**
Gardener	**Fred McNaughton**
Secretary	**Sally James**
Police Inspector	**Graham Ashley**

First UK Transmission

Friday, November 9th, 1973
7.00pm (ATV London)

ROUTE 27 Ep. No. 26

Screenplay by **Terry Nation** Directed by **Don Leaver**

After being found shot and left for dead on a rubbish tip, Harry recovers in hospital, his life saved by a bullet-proof jacket. In the morgue, he identifies the body of drugs courier Leo Cléman and explains to Inspector Bergen how he tailed Cléman from Marseilles along Route 27, a favoured route for smugglers that ends in Copenhagen. Cléman was carrying 40 lbs of pure heroin, but shooting broke out when he met the buyer. However, Cléman hid the heroin beforehand and as Harry is the only person who knows where it is, he realises that he must set himself up as a target to learn the identity of the buyer...

Notes

Establishing shots of Copenhagen for this episode were filmed by David Lane's 2nd Unit on location at the Rådhuspladsen (City Hall Square) and Københavns Rådhus (City Hall). Tony Anholt is credited on the end titles but does not appear in the episode.

Oops!

During Harry's fight with the chauffeur at the lager storage depot, Norman Beaton suddenly turns into a white stunt-man wearing a wild afro wig and Mexican moustache.

Regular Cast

Harry Rule	**Robert Vaughn**
Contessa di Contini	**Nyree Dawn Porter**

Guest Cast

Sandven	**Michael Coles**
Inspector Lars Bergen	**Jeremy Wilkin**
Nurse	**Virginia Wetherell**
Doctor	**Christopher Masters**
Revell	**Carl Bohun**
Lendrop	**Dan Meaden**
Detective	**Terry Richards**
Chauffeur	**Norman Beaton**
Bell Boy	**Andrew Burleigh**

First UK Transmission

Friday, February 1st, 1974
7.00pm (ATV Midlands)

SPACE:1999

Format

In 1999, Moonbase Alpha is a self-contained community located in the crater Plato near the Sea of Showers on Earth's Moon. A marvel of modern engineering, Alpha is constructed of quarried rock and ores, a base some 2½ miles in diameter extending up to two thirds of a mile below the lunar surface. Designed as a base for scientific research and deep space exploration, Alpha acquired a secondary function as a nuclear waste monitoring station following the thermonuclear war of 1987 when all nuclear weapons were broken down and their waste material buried on the far side of the Moon.

On September 13th, 1999, an increase in magnetic radiation detonated the nuclear waste stored in Nuclear Disposal Area 2, causing a chain reaction which blasted the Moon out of Earth orbit, hurling it into outer space. Shortly after, the Moon was drawn into a black sun, emerging from the other side hundreds of light years from Earth. Further encounters with space warps and time warps have left the Moon hopelessly lost in unknown regions of space where few of the established laws of science and astrophysics apply. On Alpha, the survivors of the disaster are powerless to control the flight of their runaway Moon, hoping only that their travels will eventually bring them to a habitable planet on which they can settle and start a new life.

Under the command of John Koenig, Moonbase Alpha is totally self-sustaining, a scientific community of 311 men and women serviced by a fleet of Eagle spacecraft. Each service section is identified by the colour of the uniform sleeve: black for Command, white for Medical, flame for Main Mission, yellow for Services, orange for Reconnaissance, rust for Technical and purple for Security.

Operation of Alpha is primarily controlled from Main Mission, located in a tower at the hub of the wheel-shaped base. This central point links all sections of Alpha from Medical Center and the Recreation Complex to the Hydroponics Farm and Nuclear Generating Facilities. However, after nearly a year in deep space, the decision was made to close down Main Mission and all surface stations in favour of the less vulnerable sub-stations below the lunar surface, with operations centralised in Command Center on Alpha's lowest construction level.

Production

Late in 1972, Lew Grade commissioned Gerry Anderson to produce a second season of UFO following promising ratings for syndicated screenings of the series on American television that autumn. After months of design and research which focused on developing SHADO Moonbase as a much larger complex, ITC ultimately abandoned the project, but Anderson re-developed the UFO second season pre-production work into a brand new television series which would combine serious science-fiction concepts with realistic human-interest drama and spectacular visual effects.

With a budget of £3 million (£125,000 per episode), part of which was funded by the Italian television company RAI, principal photography on SPACE:1999 began at Pinewood Studios in Buckinghamshire on December 3rd, 1973 although visual effects filming had already been underway since November 5th at Bray Studios near Windsor in Berkshire. Heavily influenced by the atmosphere and design of the Moon-based section of *2001: A Space Odyssey* (1968), each episode was scheduled for 12 days of principal photography, allowing 14 months to make 24 episodes so that transmission could begin in January 1975. However, production problems delayed completion of principal photography until February 28th, 1975, so transmission was postponed until the following autumn.

The series was a massive success overseas and a second season was commissioned, but ITC's New York office insisted that Anderson employ an American head writer to restructure the format in an attempt to secure a network sale. Under the influence of former STAR TREK producer Fred Freiberger, the series was reworked as an action-adventure show in the STAR TREK mould. With significant changes to the regular cast and a budget increased to £160,000 per episode, filming on the second season's 24 episodes began on January 26th, 1976 and was finally completed on December 23rd.

Main Characters

Commander John Koenig
Commander of Moonbase Alpha, a dedicated and experienced astronaut and Eagle pilot previously involved in missions to Venus and Ultra

Dr. Helena Russell
Chief Medical Officer and a leading expert in the field of space medicine, involved in a close relationship with John Koenig

Professor Victor Bergman
Professor of Technology at the International Space Academy, a civilian advisor visiting Alpha at the time of the Breakaway disaster

Maya
Alien transmorph who becomes Alpha's Science Officer following the destruction of her homeworld Psychon

Tony Verdeschi
Italian Chief of Security who develops a close relationship with Maya

Captain Alan Carter
Australian Chief Eagle Pilot, previously involved in missions to Mars and Venus

Paul Morrow
British Main Mission Controller and second in-command of Alpha

Sandra Benes
Asian Data Analyst involved in a close relationship with Paul Morrow

David Kano
Jamaican Head of Technical Department who shares an unusual rapport with Main Computer

Dr. Bob Mathias
Jamaican Assistant Medical Officer and psychiatric specialist

Bill Fraser
British Eagle pilot, married to Services Section operative Annette

Dr. Ben Vincent
Assistant Medical Officer

Tanya Alexander
German Main Mission Operative

Yasko
Asian Command Center Operative

Operative Kate
British Main Mission and Command Center Operative

Ken Johnson
Eagle pilot

Operative Lee
Main Mission Operative

Operative June
Main Mission Operative

Operative Peter
Command Center Operative

Episode Titles (Year One)

(Listed in production order)

1. **Breakaway**
2. **Matter Of Life And Death**
3. **Black Sun**
4. **Ring Around The Moon**
5. **Earthbound**
6. **Another Time, Another Place**
7. **Missing Link**
8. **Guardian Of Piri**
9. **Force Of Life**
10. **Alpha Child**
11. **The Last Sunset**
12. **Voyager's Return**
13. **Collision Course**
14. **Death's Other Dominion**
15. **The Full Circle**
16. **End Of Eternity**
17. **War Games**
18. **The Last Enemy**
19. **The Troubled Spirit**
20. **Space Brain**
21. **The Infernal Machine**
22. **Mission Of The Darians**
23. **Dragon's Domain**
24. **The Testament Of Arkadia**

Episode Running Time

50 minutes approx.

PRODUCTION CREDITS (Year One)

Executive Producer **Gerry Anderson**
Producer **Sylvia Anderson**
Story Consultant **Christopher Penfold** *(1-9, 12-16)*
Script Editor **Edward di Lorenzo** *(1, 2, 5, 6, 8)*
Johnny Byrne *(3, 4, 7, 10, 11, 13-15, 17, 18, 20, 21, 23)*
Moon City Costumes Designed by **Rudi Gernreich**
Series Created by **Gerry** and **Sylvia Anderson**
Music by **Barry Gray**
Associate **Vic Elms**
Special Effects **Brian Johnson**
Production Designer **Keith Wilson**
Production Manager **Ron Fry**
Director of Photography **Frank Watts BSC**
Casting Director **Michael Barnes**
Supervising Editor **Dave Lane**
Camera Operator **Tony White** *(1)*
Neil Binney *(2-24)*
Assistant Director **Ken Baker**
Sound Recordist **David Bowen**
Editor **Derek Hyde Chambers** *(2, 4, 6, 8, 10, 12, 14, 16, 18, 20, 22, 24)*
Mike Campbell *(3, 5, 7)*
Alan Killick *(9, 11, 13, 15, 17, 19, 21, 23)*
Sound Editor **Peter Pennell** *(1, 3, 5, 7, 9, 11, 13, 15-18, 22-24)*
Roy Lafbery *(2, 4, 6, 8, 10, 12, 14, 19-21)*
Music Editor **Alan Willis**
Continuity **Gladys Goldsmith** *(1-7, 9-24)*
Phyllis Townshend *(8)*
Processed by **Rank Film Laboratories**
Make-up **Basil Newall** *(1, 3, 4, 6-9, 12, 13, 16, 18, 19, 21, 23)*
Ann Cotton *(2, 3, 5, 10, 11, 14, 15, 17, 20, 22, 24)*
Hair Designer **Helene Bevan**
Wardrobe **Eileen Sullivan**
SPECIAL EFFECTS
Director **Nick Allder**
Lighting Cameraman **Harry Oakes**
Camera Operator **Frank Drake**
Electronics **Michael S.E. Downing**

Made at Pinewood Studios,
Buckinghamshire, England
An ITC/RAI Co-Production
Produced by Group Three
for World-Wide Distribution

Original Concept

Starting with just the idea of a vast Moon-based complex completely cut off from Earth, the development of the format for SPACE:1999 evolved through a variety of initial concepts. Agreeing to back a series set on the Moon, the only stipulation made by American ITC executive Abe Mandell was that Earth should never be seen. After dismissing an early idea that Earth could be destroyed in the opening episode, Anderson put forward a series proposal that met with Mandell's blessing, one which was promoted to television executives at an international television conference in 1973 as follows:

"1999: At the dawn of the 21st Century, 300 men and women from Earth maintain an early-warning system on the Moon. Aliens launch a devastating thermonuclear attack on the far side of the Moon redistributing critical force-fields. The gravitational relationship of Earth and Moon is abruptly negated and the Moon is violently thrust out of orbit, marooning the 300 Earth men on a world adrift in outer space – on an endless odyssey to the infinite regions of the furthest galaxies."

The promotion went on to describe the environs of Moon City as highly sophisticated and complex representations of space technology, including geodesic domes, domestic and industrial structures, surface and sub-surface installations, a Control Sector and a Spaceport. Amongst the hardware available to the Moon City personnel would be Lunarmobiles, Hoverhoppers, Moon Buggies, Explorers, Reconnaissance Rockets, Interceptors and Interplanetary Multiple Transport Units (MTUs).

The pilot script for what was envisaged as a half-hour series was written by Gerry & Sylvia Anderson. Titled 'Zero G', this script followed Commander Steve Maddox, Head of Operations at Moon City, his Science Officer Marc Miller, Head of Reconnaissance Lieutenant Caron and female Medical Officer Dr. Gordon as they attempted to combat an attack by aliens determined to prevent Earthmen from exploiting and colonising other planets. The aliens eventually use a green light beam to nullify the Moon's gravitational pull, causing the satellite to break out of Earth orbit and leave the Solar System.

Although SPACE:1999 premiered on British television (with broadcasts in the ATV and Yorkshire regions preceding those on London Weekend Television) five days in advance of transmissions in the USA, the American screening order departed dramatically from the order adopted by the British stations. As a result, eight first season episodes were screened in the USA in advance of the British broadcasts: *Matter Of Life And Death, Another Time, Another Place, Alpha Child, Guardian Of Piri, End Of Eternity, The Testament Of Arkadia, The Last Enemy* and *Ring Around The Moon* (in order of transmission). The American broadcast dates for these episodes are noted in the individual episode entries.

BREAKAWAY — Prod. No. 01

Screenplay by **George Bellak** Directed by **Lee H. Katzin**

Commander John Koenig arrives at Moonbase Alpha to supervise a manned probe mission to the newly discovered planet Meta, but nine astronauts have died from a mysterious illness and Dr. Helena Russell is convinced that radiation is the cause. An investigation of the nuclear waste disposal areas on the far side of the Moon reveals no radiation leakage, although intense heat is registered and Professor Victor Bergman suggests that increased magnetic output, not radiation, is the real threat. Koenig recommends that Luna Commissioner Simmonds should delay the launch of the Meta Probe and cease shipments of nuclear waste until their investigations are completed and a solution is found, but Simmonds is embroiled in political intrigue and refuses Koenig's requests. Then, one of the nuclear waste areas explodes and Bergman reports that unless the waste canisters are dispersed over a wider area, there is going to be a major disaster...

Notes

Although George Bellak receives sole screenplay credit for this episode, his original script, titled 'The Void Ahead', was entirely rewritten by Christopher Penfold as 'Turning Point'. Principal photography on this episode took a full 25 days, 13 days over the original schedule. Director Lee H. Katzin's initial cut ran for over two hours, prompting Gerry Anderson to rewrite a number of scenes which he directed himself in an additional three-day shoot after filming was completed on *Black Sun*. These scenes were then integrated with the original footage to bring the running time down to 50 minutes.

Oops!

The visor on Nordstrom's spacesuit helmet flies open as he throws Steiner. Nordstrom's name is written on his helmet as 'Nordstom'. Koenig's Eagle arrives on Alpha with the port side to the boarding tube, but Koenig exits the ship through the starboard side. The style of Koenig's spacesuit collar keeps changing as he flies over NDA-1.

Regular Cast

Cdr. John Koenig	**Martin Landau**
Dr. Helena Russell	**Barbara Bain**
Prof. Victor Bergman	**Barry Morse**
Paul Morrow	**Prentis Hancock**
Capt. Alan Carter	**Nick Tate**
Sandra Benes	**Zienia Merton**
Dr. Bob Mathias	**Anton Phillips**
Tanya Alexander	**Suzanne Roquette**
Operative Lee	**Loftus Burton**
Guards	**Tony Allyn / Quentin Pierre**
Voice of Computer	**Barbara Kelly**

Guest Cast

Commissioner Simmonds	**Roy Dotrice**
Commander Gorski	**Philip Madoc**
Benjamin Ouma	**Lon Satton**
Eddie Collins	**Eric Carte**
GTV Newsreader	**Don Fellows**
Jim Nordstrom	**Roy Scammell**
Steiner	**Alf Joint**
Operatives	**Chai Lee / Paul Weston / Norma West / Valerie Van Ost**
Eagle Stewardess	**Laurie Davis**
Voice of Eagle Pilot	**Shane Rimmer**

First UK Transmission

Thursday, September 4th, 1975
7.00pm (ATV/Yorkshire)

MATTER OF LIFE AND DEATH — Prod. No. 02

Screenplay by **Art Wallace** & **Johnny Byrne** Directed by **Charles Crichton**

An Eagle returns from a reconnaissance flight to planet Terra Nova with the pilots unconscious and an extra man on board. Helena identifies him as her husband, Lee Russell, the pilot of *Astro 7* lost in the vicinity of Jupiter in 1994. However, examination of Russell shows peculiarities in his life signs and Professor Bergman determines that he is gradually turning into anti-matter. In obvious distress, Russell warns the Alphans to stay away from the planet, but is unable to explain why they should do so. Inexplicably, the man dies and his body disappears. Disregarding Russell's warnings, Koenig and Helena lead a landing party to Terra Nova where they find a paradise environment, perfect for habitation by the Alphans. Suddenly, disaster strikes: their Eagle blows up with Carter aboard and Morrow's laser explodes, killing him and blinding Sandra. Then a massive explosion destroys the Moon...

Notes

Although writer Art Wallace receives the primary credit for the screenplay, his original script, titled 'Siren Planet', did not suit the series' revised format and had to be completely re-written by Johnny Byrne. In 'Siren Planet', Helena's husband was named Telford. He was revealed to be the creation of the alien inhabitants of Homeland II who made the Alphans' thoughts and fears a reality, conjuring images of their dead relatives to dissuade the Alphans from settling on the planet. Due to production problems with *Breakaway*, *Matter Of Life And Death* was the first episode of the series to be completed in post-production. The episode was initially broadcast in North America (as episode two) on September 16th, 1975, six weeks before it was transmitted in the UK (as episode 13). Contracted as a replacement for Lon Satton who had appeared as Benjamin Ouma in *Breakaway*, Clifton Jones makes his first appearance in the series here as David Kano. His role was written for Ouma in the script. Part of the incidental music used in the episode was originally recorded for *Thunderbirds Are Go* (1966).

Regular Cast

Cdr. John Koenig	**Martin Landau**
Dr. Helena Russell	**Barbara Bain**
Prof. Victor Bergman	**Barry Morse**
Paul Morrow	**Prentis Hancock**
Capt. Alan Carter	**Nick Tate**
Sandra Benes	**Zienia Merton**
David Kano	**Clifton Jones**
Dr. Bob Mathias	**Anton Phillips**
Tanya Alexander	**Suzanne Roquette**
Operative Lee	**Loftus Burton**
Operatives	**Andy Dempsey / Mike Stevens**
Guards	**Tony Allyn / Quentin Pierre**
Voice of Computer	**Barbara Kelly**

Guest Cast

Lee Russell	**Richard Johnson**
Parks	**Stuart Damon**
Bannion	**John Oxley**
Operatives	**Jeremy Anthony / Chai Lee / Christopher Matthews**
Medics	**Saad Ghazi / Christopher Williams**
Voice of Eagle Pilot	**Shane Rimmer**

First UK Transmission

Thursday, November 27th, 1975
7.00pm (ATV)

BLACK SUN

Prod. No. 03

Screenplay by **David Weir** Directed by **Lee H. Katzin**

Regular Cast

Cdr. John Koenig	**Martin Landau**
Dr. Helena Russell	**Barbara Bain**
Prof. Victor Bergman	**Barry Morse**
Paul Morrow	**Prentis Hancock**
Capt. Alan Carter	**Nick Tate**
Sandra Benes	**Zienia Merton**
David Kano	**Clifton Jones**
Dr. Bob Mathias	**Anton Phillips**
Tanya Alexander	**Suzanne Roquette**
Operative Lee	**Loftus Burton**
Operatives	**Andy Dempsey**
	Mike Stevens
Guards	**Tony Allyn / Quentin Pierre**
Voice of Computer	**Barbara Kelly**

Guest Cast

Mike Ryan	**Paul Jones**
Smitty	**Jon Laurimore**
Toshira Fujita	**Vincent Wong**
Operatives	**Chai Lee / Marc Zuber**

First UK Transmission

Thursday, November 6th, 1975
7.00pm (ATV/Yorkshire)

The Moon is drawn inexorably towards a black sun, an area of intense gravitational pull that is the remains of a collapsed stellar mass. A reconnaissance Eagle piloted by Mike Ryan is torn apart by the phenomenon and Koenig estimates that the Alphans have only three days before they suffer the same fate. Bergman designs a force shield based on a ring of towers erected around the base, which offers a slim chance for the Alphans, but Koenig also elects to launch a survival Eagle with a crew of six, in the hope that they might escape the pull of the sun and find a planet to live on. Helena, Carter and Sandra are among the six Alphans with the best potential for survival who are selected for the mission and the Eagle leaves Alpha shortly before the Moon plunges into the black sun. There, Koenig and Bergman experience strange phenomena as they become intangible, age rapidly and meet an omnipotent being who reveals the secrets of the universe...

Notes

David Weir's original script contained enough material for a two-hour episode and was extensively rewritten by Christopher Penfold. Filming on the episode overran by five days and brought director Lee Katzin's problematic association with the show to an end. *Black Sun* was intended to be shown very early in the series' run (ideally as episode two) as the conclusion throws the Moon out of the Solar System and hundreds of light years from Earth into a region of space where stars and planetary systems are much closer together. Unfortunately, on original transmission, *Black Sun* was screened as episode ten (both in the UK and the USA), by which time viewers had already seen the Alphans visiting other star systems and habitable planets. It is revealed in this episode that Victor Bergman has a mechanical heart, which saves his life when he is electrocuted. The episode also introduces the concept of an omnipotent being guiding the Alphans' journey towards some unknown destiny. Some of the themes of *Black Sun* were later explored by Gerry Anderson in the 1975 TV pilot THE DAY AFTER TOMORROW.

RING AROUND THE MOON

Prod. No. 04

Screenplay by **Edward di Lorenzo** Directed by **Ray Austin**

Regular Cast

Cdr. John Koenig	**Martin Landau**
Dr. Helena Russell	**Barbara Bain**
Prof. Victor Bergman	**Barry Morse**
Paul Morrow	**Prentis Hancock**
Capt. Alan Carter	**Nick Tate**
Sandra Benes	**Zienia Merton**
David Kano	**Clifton Jones**
Dr. Bob Mathias	**Anton Phillips**
Tanya Alexander	**Suzanne Roquette**
Operatives	**Andy Dempsey**
	Robert Phillips / Mike Stevens
Guards	**Tony Allyn / Quentin Pierre**

Guest Cast

Ted Clifford	**Max Faulkner**
Voice of Triton	**Prentis Hancock**

First UK Transmission

Thursday, January 15th, 1976
7.00pm (ATV)

As he works near a viewport, maintenance engineer Ted Clifford is struck by an energy beam which transforms his brain into a computer relay station for an alien probe. The probe captures the Moon within an energy ring and a voice announces that the Alphans are captives of the planet Triton. When Clifford's mind burns out, the probe seeks a new relay, and after Carter's reconnaissance Eagle is struck by the energy beam and crashes on the lunar surface, a medical rescue mission provides the probe with the opportunity to capture Helena. She later returns to Alpha, apparently unharmed, but is revealed to be relaying information from the Alpha computer through an energy implant in her brain. In an attempt to free Helena from the probe's control, Koenig and Carter board the probe and discover that the device is on a pre-programmed mission to destroy the human race!

Notes

Although former Christie band member Vic Elms is credited as Music Associate on all 24 Year One episodes, this episode features his only composition for the series. As Elms was unable to read music or understand the requirements of scoring to cues for film incidentals, the majority of the work was actually completed by music editor Alan Willis. Elms also arranged the electric guitar sections of the theme music and for a track in the score of *Matter Of Life And Death*, but he did not contribute to any further episodes. This episode first aired in the USA on January 6th, 1976, nine days before its first screening in the UK.

Oops!

When Carter recovers from the Eagle crash in Medical Centre, a long shot shows his pyjama jacket wide open exposing his whole chest, but in the close-up, the jacket only reveals the middle of his chest. Mathias examines Helena's thermograph from the wrong side: her name and the figures on the chart are only legible on the side facing the camera.

EARTHBOUND — Prod. No. 05

Screenplay by **Anthony Terpiloff** Directed by **Charles Crichton**

A Kaldorian spaceship *en route* to Earth crashes on the Moon and the Alphans find a crew of six on board in suspended animation. Their attempt to revive the crew accidentally kills one, but the surviving Kaldorians are understanding and a peaceful cultural exchange takes place. Captain Zantor explains that they have been travelling in space for 350 years to make their new home on Earth after the destruction of their home planet. Koenig proposes that one Alphan could accompany the Kaldorians to Earth in the now vacant casket, and Zantor agrees to the plan, stipulating that the chosen Alphan will have to be tested for compatibility with the Kaldorian suspended animation technology. The computer is set the task of choosing the one person who will return home, but Commissioner Simmonds takes matters into his own hands, breaking into the power station and threatening to destroy Alpha unless he becomes the Kaldorians' passenger!

Notes

The white wig worn by Christopher Lee in his role as Captain Zantor was later also worn by Peter Cushing (in *Missing Link*), Margaret Leighton (in *Collision Course*), Leo McKern (in *The Infernal Machine*) and Joan Collins (in *Mission Of The Darians*). June Bolton makes her series debut as Operative June here. She later changed her name to Emily Bolton for starring roles in *Moonraker* (1979) and the BBC series TENKO. Female Kaldorian Rhonda Parker previously portrayed Mother's assistant Rhonda in the last season of THE AVENGERS.

Oops!

Christopher Lee's wig starts to fall off as Zantor lies down in his casket towards the end of the episode. During the chilling final scene when Simmonds awakens to find himself trapped in the casket, two of the Kaldorians in the background appear to react to Simmonds' screams: one turns his head while the other sits up.

Regular Cast

Cdr. John Koenig	**Martin Landau**
Dr. Helena Russell	**Barbara Bain**
Prof. Victor Bergman	**Barry Morse**
Paul Morrow	**Prentis Hancock**
Capt. Alan Carter	**Nick Tate**
Sandra Benes	**Zienia Merton**
David Kano	**Clifton Jones**
Dr. Bob Mathias	**Anton Phillips**
Tanya Alexander	**Suzanne Roquette**
Operative Kate	**Sarah Bullen**
Operative June	**June Bolton**
Operative Lee	**Loftus Burton**
Operatives	**Andy Dempsey**
	Robert Phillips
Guards	**Tony Allyn / Quentin Pierre**
Voice of Computer	**Barbara Kelly**

Guest Cast

Captain Zantor	**Christopher Lee**
Commissioner Simmonds	**Roy Dotrice**
Female Kaldorian	**Rhonda Parker**

First UK Transmission

Thursday, December 4th, 1975
7.00pm (ATV)

ANOTHER TIME, ANOTHER PLACE — Prod. No. 06

Screenplay by **Johnny Byrne** Directed by **David Tomblin**

The Moon passes through a rift in space, travelling millions of kilometres in seconds. The Alphans experience a peculiar duplication effect before everything returns to normal, but Regina Kesslann is badly effected by the experience. She develops the symptoms of sunburn and suffers a breakdown when she discovers that Carter – to whom she believes she is married – and Koenig are still alive. Incredibly, the Moon returns to Earth, but an identical Moon is already in the planet's orbit. Regina dies suddenly and an X-ray reveals that she has two brains. Koenig and Carter visit the doppelgänger Moon where they find an abandoned Moonbase Alpha and a crashed Eagle with their own bodies at the controls. Realising that they have travelled through time and caught up with their future selves, Koenig leads a team to Earth to discover the final fate of the Alphan survivors...

Notes

A visual effects shot of the Santa Maria settlement showing a large illuminated geodesic dome appears in the 'This Episode' section of the opening titles, but not within the body of the episode. A deleted scene in the script featured Koenig, Helena and Carter discovering the Santa Maria satellite tower buried under hundreds of feet of ash, leaving only the tip protruding. For split-screen scenes on the future Earth, Zienia Merton played the duplicate Helena opposite Barbara Bain on the studio floor – her side of the screen was masked off and then double-exposed when the two actresses swapped position to create the effect of two Helenas talking to each other. This episode first aired in the USA on September 23rd, 1975, 12 weeks before its first screening in the UK.

Oops!

The X-ray of Regina's skull after her death is actually a thermographic scan similar to those previously seen in *Breakaway*, *Matter Of Life And Death* and *Ring Around The Moon*, and it seems to indicate that Regina's two brains are still quite hot.

Regular Cast

Cdr. John Koenig	**Martin Landau**
Dr. Helena Russell	**Barbara Bain**
Prof. Victor Bergman	**Barry Morse**
Paul Morrow	**Prentis Hancock**
Capt. Alan Carter	**Nick Tate**
Sandra Benes	**Zienia Merton**
David Kano	**Clifton Jones**
Dr. Bob Mathias	**Anton Phillips**
Tanya Alexander	**Suzanne Roquette**
Operative June	**June Bolton**
Operative Lee	**Loftus Burton**
Operatives	**Andy Dempsey**
	Robert Phillips / Mike Stevens
Guard	**Tony Allyn**
Voice of Computer	**Barbara Kelly**

Guest Cast

Regina Kesslann	**Judy Geeson**

First UK Transmission

Thursday, December 18th, 1975
7.00pm (ATV)

MISSING LINK

Prod. No. 07

Screenplay by **Edward di Lorenzo** Directed by **Ray Austin**

Regular Cast

Cdr. John Koenig	**Martin Landau**
Dr. Helena Russell	**Barbara Bain**
Prof. Victor Bergman	**Barry Morse**
Paul Morrow	**Prentis Hancock**
Capt. Alan Carter	**Nick Tate**
Sandra Benes	**Zienia Merton**
David Kano	**Clifton Jones**
Dr. Bob Mathias	**Anton Phillips**
Tanya Alexander	**Suzanne Roquette**
Operative June	**June Bolton**
Operatives	**Andy Dempsey**
	Robert Phillips
Guard	**Tony Allyn**

Guest Cast

Raan	**Peter Cushing**
Vana	**Joanna Dunham**

First UK Transmission

Thursday, January 22nd, 1976
7.00pm (ATV)

Koenig, Bergman, Carter and Sandra are returning from an abortive reconnaissance mission to a nearby planet when their Eagle suddenly loses power and crashes on the lunar surface. Bergman and Carter are unhurt but Koenig and Sandra are critically injured and do not respond to treatment. Apparently in a coma and relying on life-support to sustain him, Koenig awakens to find himself transported to a City of Light on the planet Zenno where Raan, an alien scientist, believes him to be the missing link in the evolutionary ascent of the loveless Zennite people. Initially reticent to comply with Raan's experiments, Koenig is seduced by the scientist's beautiful daughter Vana, and begins to have second thoughts about returning to Alpha, opting for a peaceful, immortal existence on Zenno. Back on Alpha, however, Koenig's body is dying and the command structure is breaking down – without Koenig to lead the Alphans, the base is falling apart!

Notes

A visual effects shot of Zenno City appears in the 'This Episode' section of the opening titles, but within the body of the episode this scene only appears on the Main Mission screen and a floating 'screen' created by Raan. Planet Zenno's solar system Cryton is named after series director Charles Crichton whose surname is pronounced in the same way. Some of the incidental music in this episode was composed for the STINGRAY episode *Ghost Of The Sea*. The track of electronic organ music used for 'Vana's Theme' was originally composed as a theme for establishing shots of Moonbase Alpha, but it makes its sole appearance in the series here.

Oops!

A close-up shot of the medical monitors on the duplicate Alpha shows Koenig's name incorrectly spelled 'Keonig', although the spelling is correct in long shot as Koenig approaches the monitor display.

GUARDIAN OF PIRI

Prod. No. 08

Screenplay by **Christopher Penfold** Directed by **Charles Crichton**

Regular Cast

Cdr. John Koenig	**Martin Landau**
Dr. Helena Russell	**Barbara Bain**
Prof. Victor Bergman	**Barry Morse**
Paul Morrow	**Prentis Hancock**
Capt. Alan Carter	**Nick Tate**
Sandra Benes	**Zienia Merton**
David Kano	**Clifton Jones**
Dr. Bob Mathias	**Anton Phillips**
Tanya Alexander	**Suzanne Roquette**
Ken Johnson	**James Fagan**
Operative June	**June Bolton**
Operative Lee	**Loftus Burton**
Operatives	**Andy Dempsey**
	Raymond Harris / Mike Stevens
Guard	**Tony Allyn**
Voice of Computer	**Barbara Kelly**

Guest Cast

Servant	**Catherine Schell**
Peter Irving	**Michael Culver**
Ed Davis	**John Gleeson**
Sarah Graham	**Anne Hanson**
Eagle Pilot	**Gareth Hunt**
Eagle Co-Pilot	**John Lee-Barber**

First UK Transmission

Thursday, November 13th, 1975
7.00pm (ATV)

When an Eagle crew goes missing during a reconnaissance mission to the planet Piri, it appears that the Alpha Main Computer has supplied incorrect flight data. Then Alpha's atmosphere and medical control is effected and Koenig suspects that the computer is being influenced by something on Piri. To find out how, Kano agrees to have his mind linked to the computer, but during the procedure, he suddenly vanishes. Koenig takes an Eagle to Piri and finds the planet completely lifeless, but when he locates the missing men, he finds them in a trance-like state and unwilling to leave. A beautiful woman appears, introducing herself as the Servant of the Guardian, a powerful control computer created by the long-dead inhabitants of the planet. Koenig refuses her invitation to accept the dominion of the Guardian but back on Alpha, he is betrayed by his colleagues who have succumbed to the Guardian's influence...

Notes

The original story outline for this episode, entitled 'Nobody's Perfect', was written by David Weir. Catherine Schell makes her SPACE:1999 debut in this episode, albeit in a different role from that in which she later appeared as a regular in Year Two. The incidental theme for Piri is a piece entitled 'Undersea' composed by Chuck Cassey. Actor Gareth Hunt was originally cast as Pete Irving, but he had a disagreement with director Charles Crichton during filming and was replaced by Michael Culver. Hunt can still be briefly seen in his role as Irving as the Alphans escape from Piri in the episode climax. *Guardian Of Piri* first aired in the USA on October 21st, 1975, three weeks before its first screening in the UK.

Oops!

Although he is credited as Story Consultant, Christopher Penfold receives no credit for the screenplay of this episode on the in-show titles.

FORCE OF LIFE — Prod. No. 09

Screenplay by **Johnny Byrne** Directed by **David Tomblin**

A strange ball of blue light approaches Alpha and the entire base personnel are suspended in time, except for reactor technician Anton Zoref. The blue light enters the base and envelops Zoref, invading his body and causing him to pass out. Everything apparently returns to normal, but Bergman is curious about an inexplicable energy discharge that was recorded at the same moment that Zoref passed out. Then Zoref's colleague Mark Dominix is discovered frozen to death in Nuclear Generating Area 3, massive power losses are recorded and Koenig begins to suspect that Zoref may be the cause of both. Possessed with a consuming need for heat, Zoref draws it from any source, human or otherwise, as he rampages through the base leaving a trail of dead bodies and useless equipment in his wake. Koenig orders power supplies to be cut from the reactors in an attempt to deprive Zoref of any source of light and warmth, but Zoref heads for the Nuclear Generating Area...

Notes

The working title of this episode was 'Force Of Evil'. Although it was screened as episode five during the original transmission of the series on American television, *Force Of Life* was considered to be such a strong episode that it was selected to be shown as episode two in the UK. The episode relies heavily on electronic library music for its incidental score: 'Cosmic Sounds No. 1' and 'Cosmic Sounds No. 3' by Georges Teperino and 'Videotronics No. 3' by Cecil Leuter. The source music heard in the solarium is a piece entitled 'The Latest Fashion' composed by Giampera Boneschi. The Nuclear Generating Area set built for this episode was also utilised in *Alpha Child* before being dismantled. When the nuclear reactor explodes, some of the footage of Alphans being thrown about is lifted from *Breakaway*. Former Junior Mr Britain runner-up John Hamill (Mark Dominix) was, at the time of production, making a name for himself as the male lead in a series of British sex comedies such as *The Over Amorous Artist* (1974).

Regular Cast

Cdr. John Koenig	**Martin Landau**
Dr. Helena Russell	**Barbara Bain**
Prof. Victor Bergman	**Barry Morse**
Paul Morrow	**Prentis Hancock**
Capt. Alan Carter	**Nick Tate**
Sandra Benes	**Zienia Merton**
David Kano	**Clifton Jones**
Dr. Bob Mathias	**Anton Phillips**
Tanya Alexander	**Suzanne Roquette**
Operative Kate	**Sarah Bullen**
Operative June	**June Bolton**
Operative Lee	**Loftus Burton**
Operatives	**Andy Dempsey / Raymond Harris / Mike Stevens**
Guards	**Tony Allyn / Quentin Pierre**
Voice of Computer	**Barbara Kelly**

Guest Cast

Anton Zoref	**Ian McShane**
Eva Zoref	**Gay Hamilton**
Mark Dominix	**John Hamill**
Jane	**Eva Rueber-Staier**
Medic	**Vincent Wong**
Nurse	**Maureen Tan**

First UK Transmission

Thursday, September 11th, 1975
7.00pm (ATV/Yorkshire)

ALPHA CHILD — Prod. No. 10

Screenplay by **Christopher Penfold** Directed by **Ray Austin**

Sue Crawford gives birth to the first child to be born on the Moon, but the baby boy inexplicably grows to the size of a five-year-old within a matter of minutes. Koenig believes that the child's unnatural development could be linked to the death of his father, a technician in the nuclear generating plant, but the Alphans soon warm to the apparently deaf-mute Jackie, treating him like a normal five-year-old and showing him around the base. Then four spaceships appear over Alpha, resisting all attempts to repel them. Jackie suddenly grows into a mature adult, revealing himself to be Jarak, one of 120 alien travellers who seek physical forms in which to conceal their identities so as to escape the rigorously imposed genetic conformity of their home planet. Together with Sue, now transformed into his partner Rena, Jarak and his companions intend to inhabit the Alphans' bodies, which they can only do at the moments of birth and death...

Notes

The original script of this episode was written by Edward di Lorenzo from a story by Gerry Anderson, but it was entirely re-written by Christopher Penfold, who receives sole credit. The story was inspired by John Wyndham's classic science-fiction novel *The Midwich Cuckoos* (filmed as *Village Of The Damned* in 1960 and 1995). Sue Crawford was written as 'Cynthia' Crawford in the script. Some of the incidental music in this episode was originally composed for the THE SECRET SERVICE episode *Last Train To Bufflers Halt*. Prentis Hancock (Paul Morrow) has a bruise under the nail of his forefinger which was still visible during filming of the next episode, *The Last Sunset*. The design of the alien spacecraft used by Jarak's pursuers was inspired by the *Discovery* spaceship designed by Harry Lange for *2001: A Space Odyssey* (1968). The model later reappeared in the series as the Alien bomber in *War Games*, the Deltan battleship in *The Last Enemy* and a ship in the spaceship graveyard in *Dragon's Domain*. This episode first aired in the USA on October 14th, 1975, two days before its first screening in the UK.

Regular Cast

Cdr. John Koenig	**Martin Landau**
Dr. Helena Russell	**Barbara Bain**
Prof. Victor Bergman	**Barry Morse**
Paul Morrow	**Prentis Hancock**
Capt. Alan Carter	**Nick Tate**
Sandra Benes	**Zienia Merton**
David Kano	**Clifton Jones**
Dr. Bob Mathias	**Anton Phillips**
Tanya Alexander	**Suzanne Roquette**
Ken Johnson	**James Fagan**
Operative Kate	**Sarah Bullen**
Operative Lee	**Loftus Burton**
Operatives	**Andy Dempsey / Raymond Harris / Mike Stevens**
Guards	**Tony Allyn / Quentin Pierre**

Guest Cast

Jarak	**Julian Glover**
Sue Crawford / Rena	**Cyd Hayman**
Jackie Crawford	**Wayne Brooks**
Joan Conway	**Rula Lenska**
Operative	**Maureen Tan**
Medic	**Vincent Wong**
Guard	**Alf Joint**

First UK Transmission

Thursday, October 16th, 1975
7.00pm (ATV/Yorkshire)

THE LAST SUNSET — Prod. No. 11

Screenplay by **Christopher Penfold** — Directed by **Charles Crichton**

As the Moon approaches the Earth-like planet Ariel, which offers the Alphans hope for colonisation, an alien device attaches itself to Eagle One during a reconnaissance flight. Then hundreds of similar devices land on the lunar surface and Koenig fears an attack by the inhabitants of Ariel, but the Alphans are surprised when the devices emit oxygen and turn the Moon into an atmosphere-rich world with blue skies and a warm sun. The Alphans enjoy their new-found freedom on the lunar surface and Helena leads a reconnaissance team to scout for a new settlement on higher ground, but their Eagle is caught in a violent storm and crashes, stranding them miles from Alpha. As search parties attempt to locate the missing Eagle, Koenig and Bergman realise that the Moon is not going into orbit around Ariel and, without sunlight, the atmosphere will shrink into an ice-cap and Alpha will be crushed!

Notes
The scenes of the Alphans greeting the Moon's first rainfall were filmed on the Pinewood backlot two weeks after principal photography on the episode had been completed, during the filming of *Voyager's Return*. Much of the incidental music in this episode was originally composed for earlier Gerry Anderson productions including SUPERCAR, STINGRAY, *Thunderbird 6* (1967), JOE 90 and THE SECRET SERVICE.

Oops!
Scenes deleted from the finished episode would have shown Alpha technicians fitting the viewport in the Technical Section with an opening window so as to allow the fresh air into the base, and Koenig later ordering all the new windows to be replaced by the original sealed viewports after the first signs of corrosion are discovered. Unfortunately, without these scenes, when Koenig slides open the one in the Technical Section it appears that the Alpha viewports have always been designed that way.

Regular Cast

Cdr. John Koenig	**Martin Landau**
Dr. Helena Russell	**Barbara Bain**
Prof. Victor Bergman	**Barry Morse**
Paul Morrow	**Prentis Hancock**
Capt. Alan Carter	**Nick Tate**
Sandra Benes	**Zienia Merton**
David Kano	**Clifton Jones**
Dr. Bob Mathias	**Anton Phillips**
Tanya Alexander	**Suzanne Roquette**
Ken Johnson	**James Fagan**
Operative Kate	**Sarah Bullen**
Operative Lee	**Loftus Burton**
Operatives	**Andy Dempsey**
	Robert Phillips / Mike Stevens
Guard	**Quentin Pierre**

Guest Cast

Operatives	**Maureen Tan**
	Lynda Westover
Alphans	**Richard Adams / Janet Allen**
	Guy Francis Groen / Jack McKenzie
	Linzy Scott / Anita West

First UK Transmission
Thursday, January 1st, 1976
4.50pm (ATV)

VOYAGER'S RETURN — Prod. No. 12

Screenplay by **Johnny Byrne** — Directed by **Bob Kellett**

Voyager One, an Earth probe ship launched in 1985, approaches Moonbase Alpha and Bergman realises that it poses a very serious threat. Due to a miscalculation in the design of the ship's Queller Drive, *Voyager* has spent the last 15 years polluting space with toxic fast neutrons which will destroy Alpha unless the Drive can be shut down. Koenig turns to Dr. Ernst Linden to override the probe's security codes and deactivate the Queller Drive. Linden confesses that he is the only man capable of doing so, for he is really Ernst Queller, designer of the drive unit which wiped out a whole community on Earth when the engines of a second ship, *Voyager Two,* cut in too soon. Linden is assaulted by his assistant Jim Haines, whose parents were amongst those killed by *Voyager Two*, but he manages to shut down the probe's engine in time. Then three Sidon spacecraft arrive, seeking revenge for the destruction that *Voyager One* has wrought upon their worlds...

Notes
Bergman says that 1985 was 15 years ago, so this episode is set in 2000, at least four months after the events of *Breakaway*. In dialogue cut from the script, Morrow says that the community destroyed by *Voyager Two* was a scientific colony on the Moon. As revealed in the episode, Morrow's father was among those killed in the disaster. Of the three scientists who designed *Voyager*, only the names of Ernst Queller and Neill Cameron are legible on the wall of the probe, but the script reveals that the third was Charles Borges. The episode was originally written to end with a chilling speculation from Helena: "We've been sending things like *Voyager One* into space for decades. Who knows what damage they've done, or how many worlds like Sidon are looking for us right now?" Barry Stokes (Jim Haines) was previously seen as a Skydiver Engineer in the UFO episodes *Destruction* and *Reflections In The Water*. Some of the incidental music in this episode was originally composed for THUNDERBIRDS, *Thunderbird 6* (1967) and THE SECRET SERVICE.

Regular Cast

Cdr. John Koenig	**Martin Landau**
Dr. Helena Russell	**Barbara Bain**
Prof. Victor Bergman	**Barry Morse**
Paul Morrow	**Prentis Hancock**
Capt. Alan Carter	**Nick Tate**
Sandra Benes	**Zienia Merton**
David Kano	**Clifton Jones**
Dr. Bob Mathias	**Anton Phillips**
Tanya Alexander	**Suzanne Roquette**
Operative Kate	**Sarah Bullen**
Operative Lee	**Loftus Burton**
Operatives	**Andy Dempsey**
	Robert Philips / Mike Stevens
Guards	**Tony Allyn / Quentin Pierre**

Guest Cast

Dr. Ernst Linden	**Jeremy Kemp**
Jim Haines	**Barry Stokes**
Chief Justifier Aarchon	**Alex Scott**
Steve Abrams	**Lawrence Trimble**
Technicians	**Laurie Davis**
	Al Flemyng / Anita West

First UK Transmission
Thursday, October 9th, 1975
7.00pm (ATV/Yorkshire)

COLLISION COURSE — Prod. No. 13

Screenplay by **Anthony Terpiloff** — Directed by **Ray Austin**

During an operation to destroy an asteroid that is on a collision course with the Moon, Carter experiences problems with his Eagle and is caught in the explosion when nuclear charges planted on the asteroid are detonated. He is saved by the intervention of an aged alien woman named Arra, but when Koenig and Morrow recover his Eagle, they discover that the Moon is now on a collision course with the planet Atheria, 34 times the size of the Moon. Bergman determines that the only way to avoid the collision is to detonate a chain of nuclear mines in space so that the resulting shockwave will alter the Moon's course. Then an alien ship appears between the Moon and the planet and when Koenig investigates he meets Arra, the Queen of Atheria, who tells him that their destinies are predetermined and her people have awaited the Moon's arrival for millennia: to bring about a great mutation in Arra's people, the Moon and Atheria must be allowed to collide!

Notes

This episode features one of the last performances of Margaret Leighton, one of Britain's most prolific and respected stage and screen actresses. Towards the end of filming she told director Ray Austin, "You'd better get this shot, because I'm not going to last long." After SPACE:1999, her only screen role before her death in 1976 was in Kevin Connor's *Trial By Combat* (1976). Arra's ship is later seen in the spaceship graveyard in *Dragon's Domain* and also in the spaceship graveyard on Psychon in *The Metamorph*. Arra's throne later appears as Companion's bed in *The Infernal Machine* and The Archon's throne in *The Dorcons*. Much of the incidental music in this episode was originally composed by Barry Gray for the CAPTAIN SCARLET AND THE MYSTERONS episode *Codename Europa*, *Thunderbird 6* (1967) and the JOE 90 episodes *Operation McClaine*, *Big Fish*, *Business Holiday*, *Arctic Adventure* and *Trial At Sea*. Official ITC promotional information for the series incorrectly gave the name of Arra's planet as 'Astheria' – it appears as Atheria both in the script and on screen.

Regular Cast

Role	Actor
Cdr. John Koenig	**Martin Landau**
Dr. Helena Russell	**Barbara Bain**
Prof. Victor Bergman	**Barry Morse**
Paul Morrow	**Prentis Hancock**
Capt. Alan Carter	**Nick Tate**
Sandra Benes	**Zienia Merton**
David Kano	**Clifton Jones**
Dr. Bob Mathias	**Anton Phillips**
Tanya Alexander	**Suzanne Roquette**
Operative Kate	**Sarah Bullen**
Operative Lee	**Loftus Burton**
Operatives	**Andy Dempsey / Annie Lambert / Robert Philips / Mike Stevens**
Guards	**Tony Allyn / Quentin Pierre**

Guest Cast

Role	Actor
Arra	**Margaret Leighton**
Operative	**Vic Armstrong**
Nurse	**Laurie Davis**

First UK Transmission

Thursday, September 18th, 1975
7.00pm (ATV/Yorkshire)

DEATH'S OTHER DOMINION — Prod. No. 14

Screenplay by **Anthony Terpiloff & Elizabeth Barrows**
Directed by **Charles Crichton**

Alpha receives a signal from a planet where the temperature drops to 200 degrees below zero. The message invites the Alphans to visit Ultima Thule but a second voice warns them to stay away. Koenig, Helena, Bergman and Carter land on the surface and soon find themselves lost in a blizzard and in danger of freezing to death. Carter manages to make his way back to the Eagle while the others are rescued by the survivors of the Uranus Expeditionary Probe of 1986, long believed to have been lost in a proton storm. The Alphans meet Dr. Cabot Rowland, who reveals that his group has survived on Ultima Thule for 880 years and no one has aged a single day. Now they are attempting to rebuild their damaged ship and Rowland fosters dreams of travelling the stars as an immortal god. He invites the Alphans to give up their lunar home and join them on Thule, but Koenig learns his terrible secret...

Notes

Bergman says that 1986 was 14 years ago, so in the Alphans' timescale it is 2000, although to the Thulians the year is 2870. During filming, Martin Landau and Barbara Bain flatly refused to work on the ice cavern set until specialists confirmed that fumes from the formaldehyde used to make the snow were non-toxic. Apart from the actors listed on the right, other Thulians were played by Barbara Bermel, Jenny Devenish, Carolyn Hudson, Annette Linden and Suzette St. Clair. The Revered Ones were played by Adrienne Burgess, Lesley Collet, Robert Driscoll, Margaret Lawley, Terry Rendle, Ian Ruskin and Ellen Sheehan. Brian Blessed (Dr. Rowland) later reappears in the series as Maya's father Mentor in *The Metamorph* and also starred as Dr. Tom Bowen in Gerry Anderson's THE DAY AFTER TOMORROW pilot episode. Some of the incidental music in this episode was originally composed for the THUNDERBIRDS episode *30 Minutes After Noon* and the JOE 90 episode *Big Fish*.

Regular Cast

Role	Actor
Cdr. John Koenig	**Martin Landau**
Dr. Helena Russell	**Barbara Bain**
Prof. Victor Bergman	**Barry Morse**
Paul Morrow	**Prentis Hancock**
Capt. Alan Carter	**Nick Tate**
Sandra Benes	**Zienia Merton**
David Kano	**Clifton Jones**
Dr. Bob Mathias	**Anton Phillips**
Tanya Alexander	**Suzanne Roquette**
Operative Kate	**Sarah Bullen**
Operative Lee	**Loftus Burton**
Operatives	**Andy Dempsey / Annie Lambert / Robert Philips / Mike Stevens**

Guest Cast

Role	Actor
Dr. Cabot Rowland	**Brian Blessed**
Colonel Jack Tanner	**John Shrapnel**
Freda	**Mary Miller**
Ted	**David Ellison**
Thule Girl	**Valerie Leon**
Thulians	**Glenda Allen / Laurie Davis / John Lee-Barber / Tony Houghton / David Murphy / Eddy Nedari / Michael Ryan / Jack Shepherd**

First UK Transmission

Thursday, October 2nd, 1975
7.00pm (ATV/Yorkshire)

THE FULL CIRCLE

Prod. No. 15

Screenplay by **Jesse Lasky Jnr.** & **Pat Silver** Directed by **Bob Kellett**

Eagle Six returns to Alpha after a reconnaissance mission to the planet Retha, but the crew are missing and the only occupant is a dead cave man. Koenig and Helena lead a rescue team to the planet but they too go missing. Carter is attacked by primitive humans and Sandra is kidnapped and taken to the primitives' cave dwelling, where the cave chief takes an interest in her. As a fight breaks out over her, Sandra realises with horror that the chief and his mate are Koenig and Helena, somehow regressed to a primitive Cro Magnon state. She smashes a rock on the chief's head and escapes into the woods, pursued by the primitives. Discovering the cave dwelling, Bergman, Kano and Carter disturb a ceremony for the injured cave chief. The cave people scatter and Carter gives chase, unaware that the primitives he intends to shoot down to rescue Sandra are his Alphan colleagues...

Notes

Scenes on the planet Retha were shot on the backlot at Pinewood Studios and in the adjacent Black Park. This was the only location filming during SPACE:1999's first season and the only exterior filming apart from the rainfall sequence in *The Last Sunset*. Martin Landau and Barbara Bain were reluctant to film outside the studio grounds, so all of their exterior scenes were shot on the backlot behind the studio's ornamental garden. The percussive incidental music featured in this episode was composer Barry Gray's final contribution to the series and his last work for Gerry Anderson, bringing to an end a collaboration that had lasted for 18 years. Oliver Cotton (Spearman) later appeared as Tylan Gershom in the SPACE PRECINCT episode *Protect And Survive*.

Oops!

When Kano lands Eagle Three next to Eagles One and Two, Eagle Two (on the left) is very obviously a flat cardboard cut-out.

Regular Cast

Cdr. John Koenig	**Martin Landau**
Dr. Helena Russell	**Barbara Bain**
Prof. Victor Bergman	**Barry Morse**
Paul Morrow	**Prentis Hancock**
Capt. Alan Carter	**Nick Tate**
Sandra Benes	**Zienia Merton**
David Kano	**Clifton Jones**
Dr. Bob Mathias	**Anton Phillips**
Operative Kate	**Sarah Bullen**
Operatives	**Andy Dempsey**
	Annie Lambert / Robert Philips
	Mike Stevens
Guard	**Tony Allyn**

Guest Cast

Spearman	**Oliver Cotton**
Nurse	**Chai Lee**
Alphan	**Laurie Davis**
Caveman	**Alan Meacham**

First UK Transmission

Thursday, December 11th, 1975
7.00pm (ATV)

END OF ETERNITY

Prod. No. 16

Screenplay by **Johnny Byrne** Directed by **Ray Austin**

Investigating a passing asteroid which appears to have an internal atmosphere, the Alphans blast their way into a living chamber inside. The explosion critically injures the only occupant, who is taken back to Alpha even though Helena feels that he cannot be saved. However, the alien makes a miraculous recovery and introduces himself as Balor, a Progron scientist who has achieved immortality. Unfortunately, Balor is also a dangerous psychopath who lives for the pleasure of inflicting fear and pain. He requests that Koenig allow him free rein to terrorise the Alphans, promising to use his powers of regeneration to keep them alive indefinitely for his eternal amusement, but Koenig refuses so Balor embarks on a rampage of death and destruction...

Notes

The 'This Episode' sequence in the opening titles includes several shots that do not appear within the body of the episode, including a scene with Balor holding a security guard over his head with one hand. Another deleted scene featured Koenig lying on the floor of Baxter's apartment after Baxter's attack on him, his face covered in blood. The incidental score comprises the electronic music tracks 'Experiments In Space – Malus' and 'Experiments In Space – Dorado' by Robert Farnon, 'Stratosphere' by David Snell, 'Videotronics No. 3' by Cecil Leuter and 'Cosmic Sounds No. 1' by Georges Teperino. This episode first aired in the USA on November 18th, 1975, two days before its first screening in the UK.

Oops!

As Koenig's team enter the asteroid, their first view of the corridor leading to Balor's chamber appears upside down. After attempting to shoot open the door with his laser, Koenig moves past Baxter saying, "Excuse me, Jim," but the character's name is Mike – Jim is the name of the actor playing him.

Regular Cast

Cdr. John Koenig	**Martin Landau**
Dr. Helena Russell	**Barbara Bain**
Prof. Victor Bergman	**Barry Morse**
Paul Morrow	**Prentis Hancock**
Capt. Alan Carter	**Nick Tate**
Sandra Benes	**Zienia Merton**
David Kano	**Clifton Jones**
Dr. Bob Mathias	**Anton Phillips**
Tanya Alexander	**Suzanne Roquette**
Operative Kate	**Sarah Bullen**
Operatives	**Binu Balini**
	Andy Dempsey / Raymond Harris
	Mike Stevens / Andrew Sutcliffe
Guards	**Tony Allyn / Quentin Pierre**

Guest Cast

Balor	**Peter Bowles**
Mike Baxter	**Jim Smilie**
Operatives	**Laurie Davis**
	Jan Rennison
Astronaut	**Anthony Scott**
Medics	**Robert Atiko / Paul Kirby**
	Christopher Williams
Nurses	**Judith Hepburn**
	Kathy Mallory

First UK Transmission

Thursday, November 20th, 1975
7.00pm (ATV)

WAR GAMES — Prod. No. 17

Screenplay by **Christopher Penfold** Directed by **Charles Crichton**

As the Moon approaches a new planet, Alpha is inexplicably menaced by a trio of Mark Nine Hawk Warships and, believing them to be about to attack the base, Koenig orders a flight of Eagles to open fire. The three Warships are destroyed but then further Hawks appear and suddenly the Alphans are fighting a war against alien forces that devastate the base, leaving it uninhabitable. With 128 dead, Koenig's only hope for the survivors is to seek peaceful co-existence with the enemy, so he and Helena journey to the planet to plead their case. They meet two remote aliens who refuse their request on the grounds that the Alphans carry contaminants which would destroy a civilisation that has lasted for billions of years. Helena is held captive by the aliens while Koenig returns to Alpha, now left with no choice but to prepare for an invasion of the planet...

Notes

The incidental music accompanying the Hawk attack on Alpha is a track entitled 'The Astronauts' composed by Mike Hankinson. The Hawk models were originally painted white all over, but test footage revealed that they appeared too similar to the Eagles to tell them apart in the battle sequences, so the Hawks were repainted with orange markings. The Alien Bomber was previously seen in *Alpha Child*. Female Alien Isla Blair also appears as Carla Cross in the Year Two episode *Journey To Where*. The gown worn by Helena on the alien planet is the same one that she wore while captured by Triton in *Ring Around The Moon*. As Koenig floats helpless in space, his voice-over reveals that he is the ninth commander of Moonbase Alpha.

Oops!

During the Hawk attack on Alpha, two very obviously flat cardboard cut-out Eagles are blown up in consecutive shots, one suspended over a launch pad, the other (with red stripes on the service pod) riding up on the launch pad elevator.

Regular Cast

Cdr. John Koenig	**Martin Landau**
Dr. Helena Russell	**Barbara Bain**
Prof. Victor Bergman	**Barry Morse**
Paul Morrow	**Prentis Hancock**
Capt. Alan Carter	**Nick Tate**
Sandra Benes	**Zienia Merton**
David Kano	**Clifton Jones**
Dr. Bob Mathias	**Anton Phillips**
Tanya Alexander	**Suzanne Roquette**
Ken Johnson	**James Fagan**
Operative Kate	**Sarah Bullen**
Operatives	**Binu Balini / Andy Dempsey / Raymond Harris / Andrew Sutcliffe**

Guest Cast

Male Alien	**Anthony Valentine**
Female Alien	**Isla Blair**
Alphans	**Robert Atiko / Paul Weston**

First UK Transmission

Thursday, September 25th, 1975
7.00pm (ATV/Yorkshire)

THE LAST ENEMY — Prod. No. 18

Screenplay by **Bob Kellett** Directed by **Bob Kellett**

When the Moon falls into an orbit that places it directly between two planets on opposing sides of their sun, a huge spacecraft from the planet Betha takes up a position on the Moon and begins to launch an offensive against the other planet, Delta. Koenig soon realises that the two planets are at war, and that their relative positions make it impossible for them to fire directly at each other, but now the Moon has provided the Bethans with an ideal gun platform. Missiles from Delta apparently destroy the Bethan craft, but an escape vehicle makes its way to Alpha and the occupant, the Bethan commander Dione, seeks asylum on the base. When a Deltan battlecruiser takes up position on the Moon to launch an offensive on Betha, Koenig desperately attempts to negotiate a cease-fire, but the cunning Dione has other plans...

Notes

The script for *The Last Enemy* was based on an idea by Barbara Bain who suggested the scenario as a metaphor for the War of the Sexes. The episode went into production as 'The Second Sex' but the title was changed to 'The Other Enemy' during filming before finally ending up as *The Last Enemy*. Deleted scenes set in the Control Centre on Betha featured actor Alan Bennion as an Alien Man who appeared on a monitor screen to provide Dione with data on the rogue Moon. Although principal photography was completed in November 1974, the episode was found to run short and additional scenes were written by Johnny Byrne and shot in February 1975 after filming had finished on *The Testament Of Arkadia*. As a result, *The Last Enemy* was the last episode of the series to be completed in post-production. The incidental score includes the track 'Cosmic Sounds No. 3' by Georges Teperino. *The Last Enemy* first aired in the USA on December 9th, 1975, ten weeks before its first screening in the UK. Many UK broadcasters assumed that the title indicated that the episode should be shown at the end of the series, although in the US it appeared as episode 14.

Regular Cast

Cdr. John Koenig	**Martin Landau**
Dr. Helena Russell	**Barbara Bain**
Prof. Victor Bergman	**Barry Morse**
Paul Morrow	**Prentis Hancock**
Capt. Alan Carter	**Nick Tate**
Sandra Benes	**Zienia Merton**
David Kano	**Clifton Jones**
Dr. Bob Mathias	**Anton Phillips**
Tanya Alexander	**Suzanne Roquette**
Operative Kate	**Sarah Bullen**
Operatives	**Andy Dempsey / Raymond Harris / Mike Stevens / Andrew Sutcliffe**
Guards	**Tony Allyn / Quentin Pierre**

Guest Cast

Dione	**Caroline Mortimer**
Theia	**Maxine Audley**
Talos	**Kevin Stoney**
First Girl	**Carolyn Courage**
Second Girl	**Linda Hooks**
Third Girl	**Tara Faraday**
Operatives	**Laurie Davis / Claire Lutter**
Voice of Eagle Pilot	**Shane Rimmer**

First UK Transmission

Thursday, February 19th, 1976
7.00pm (ATV)

THE TROUBLED SPIRIT — Prod. No. 19

Screenplay by **Johnny Byrne** Directed by **Ray Austin**

A strange force sweeps through Alpha, apparently generated in the Hydroponics Unit by botanist Dan Mateo's seance-like experimental attempt to communicate telepathically with his plants. When Mateo collapses, the force dissipates. Investigating, Koenig learns that Mateo believes that man has some affinity with plants, an affinity that can be exploited by tapping into certain wave patterns in the human brain that are identical to those generated by plant life. Mateo quickly recovers, but is forbidden from conducting any further experiments by hydroponics head Dr. Warren. A heated argument ensues and later Warren is confronted by a horribly scarred ghost figure that oddly resembles Mateo. Warren is found dead shortly after and Bergman realises that Alpha is being terrorised by a psychic manifestation which seeks atonement for a death which has yet to take place!

Regular Cast

Cdr. John Koenig	**Martin Landau**
Dr. Helena Russell	**Barbara Bain**
Prof. Victor Bergman	**Barry Morse**
Paul Morrow	**Prentis Hancock**
Capt. Alan Carter	**Nick Tate**
Sandra Benes	**Zienia Merton**
David Kano	**Clifton Jones**
Dr. Bob Mathias	**Anton Phillips**
Tanya Alexander	**Suzanne Roquette**
Operative Kate	**Sarah Bullen**
Operative Lee	**Loftus Burton**
Operatives	**Binu Balini / Andy Dempsey / Andrew Sutcliffe**
Guards	**Tony Allyn / Quentin Pierre**

Guest Cast

Dr. Dan Mateo	**Giancarlo Prete**
Laura Adams	**Hilary Dwyer**
Dr. James Warren	**Anthony Nicholls**
Botanists	**Vernon Morris / Xanthi Gardner**
Medic	**Christopher Williams**
Nurses	**Jeannie Galston / Judith Hepburn / Jan Rennison**
Technicians	**Robert Atiko / Eddy Nedari / Richard Shore**

First UK Transmission

Saturday, December 27th, 1975
5.20pm (Yorkshire)

Notes

Former stuntman Giancarlo Prete (Dan Mateo) was originally cast in a regular co-starring role in SPACE:1999 as chief Eagle pilot Alphonso Catani and shot screen tests with Martin Landau at Pinewood before it was discovered that he was not able to commit to 15 months of filming in the UK. The sitar music which features prominently in this episode was composed and recorded by Jim Sullivan, who is seen performing the sitar recital in the pre-credits sequence. In Johnny Byrne's script, the recital was performed by a quintet of musicians which included Bergman. For the fight between the two Mateos, stuntman Val Musette portrayed whichever Mateo had his back towards the camera in each shot.

Oops!

In-camera superimposition of the Spirit Mateo using a half-silvered mirror results in his image being reversed on his first appearance at the seance (his yellow sleeve is on his right arm and his face is scarred on the left). Later, the Spirit Mateo forces Mateo's left side into the force field, yet Mateo's right side is burned.

SPACE BRAIN — Prod. No. 20

Screenplay by **Christopher Penfold** Directed by **Charles Crichton**

Alien hieroglyphics appear on all of Alpha's screens and an Eagle sent to investigate their origin becomes covered by a white glutinous substance. Contact with the Eagle is lost, but after a small meteorite impacts on the lunar surface, analysis reveals it to be the compacted remains of the Eagle and its two pilots. Meanwhile, Carter has set out in a second Eagle in search of the first and when his co-pilot Kelly spacewalks in the vicinity of the Eagle's disappearance, he too is covered by the glutinous substance. Carter recovers Kelly's body, but the pilot has become a conduit for a huge alien space brain that is attempting to communicate with the Alphans. Unable to understand its messages and with Alpha on a collision course, Koenig has no choice but to attempt to destroy the brain with nuclear explosives...

Regular Cast

Cdr. John Koenig	**Martin Landau**
Dr. Helena Russell	**Barbara Bain**
Prof. Victor Bergman	**Barry Morse**
Paul Morrow	**Prentis Hancock**
Capt. Alan Carter	**Nick Tate**
Sandra Benes	**Zienia Merton**
David Kano	**Clifton Jones**
Dr. Bob Mathias	**Anton Phillips**
Tanya Alexander	**Suzanne Roquette**
Operative Kate	**Sarah Bullen**
Operative Lee	**Loftus Burton**
Operatives	**Andy Dempsey / Mike Stevens / Andrew Sutcliffe**
Guards	**Tony Allyn / Quentin Pierre**

Guest Cast

Kelly	**Shane Rimmer**
Melita Janni	**Carla Romanelli**
Wayland	**Derek Anders**
Cousteau	**James Snell**
Operatives	**Laurie Davis / Jacqueline Delhaye**
Nurses	**Judith Hepburn / Diana Reeves / Erica Svenson**
Alphans	**Robert Atiko / Michael Sirett**
Patient	**Carol Dee**

First UK Transmission

Thursday, January 29th, 1976
7.00pm (ATV)

Notes

This episode features the longest pre-credits sequence of any SPACE:1999 episode, lasting nearly seven minutes. The script originally began with Wayland and Cousteau approaching the space brain – everything prior to that in the episode was added just before filming began. A scene filmed for the episode but deleted from the final edit would have appeared after Carter recovers Kelly from space: back in the Eagle, Kelly wakes and tries to take control of the Eagle to pilot it back to the brain, forcing Carter to stun him with his laser. The incidental music features an arrangement by Malcolm Sargent of Gustav Holst's 'Mars, the Bringer Of War' from 'The Planets' suite. Although principal photography on the episode was completed in December 1974, additional scenes were shot over three days at the end of February 1975. These were the last scenes filmed for SPACE:1999's first season.

Oops!

As Koenig's Eagle rendezvouses with the robot Eagle, the two vehicles overlap.

THE INFERNAL MACHINE — Prod. No. 21

Screenplay by **Anthony Terpiloff** & **Elizabeth Barrows** Directed by **David Tomblin**

A strange craft which breaks every known law of aerospace propulsion appears over Moonbase Alpha and a friendly voice appeals for help and permission to land. Koenig, Helena and Bergman reluctantly accept an invitation to visit the craft, where they meet an old man who calls himself Companion. Companion requests supplies for Gwent, the owner of the voice which is revealed to be the ship itself, a vast cybernetic mobile computer programmed with Companion's own memories and personality which has taken control of the Alpha Computer. Helena realises that Companion is seriously ill and requires urgent medical attention, but Gwent refuses to allow them to leave and return to Alpha. Then Companion collapses and dies and Gwent becomes enraged, blaming his death on the Alphans. Imprisoning them inside himself, Gwent demands that Koenig and Helena will replace the old man as his new Companions...

Notes

Although his character appeared in the original script, Prentis Hancock (Paul Morrow) was replaced in this episode by Gary Waldhorn, whose character Winters was assigned all of Morrow's lines. In a scene that was a last-minute addition to the script, Morrow is said to be recovering from fractured ribs and a broken ankle but Hancock was actually undergoing emergency surgery to remove a small tumour on his neck. This was the only Year One episode in which he did not appear. Episode authors Anthony Terpiloff and Elizabeth Barrows had Sir Ralph Richardson in mind to play Companion, but the part ultimately went to Leo McKern. The incidental score includes compositions by a variety of musicians: 'Outer Space' by Robert Farnon, 'Lunar Landscape' by Roger Roger, 'Mission Control' by Harry Sosnik, 'The Monsters' by Ivo Vyhnalek, 'Dark Suspense No. 1' by Beda Folten and 'Subterranean' by Joe Venuto. One very distinctive piece (accompanying Winters's attack on Gwent) was originally composed by Barry Gray for the THUNDERBIRDS episode *Terror In New York City*.

Regular Cast

Cdr. John Koenig	**Martin Landau**
Dr. Helena Russell	**Barbara Bain**
Prof. Victor Bergman	**Barry Morse**
Capt. Alan Carter	**Nick Tate**
Sandra Benes	**Zienia Merton**
David Kano	**Clifton Jones**
Operative Kate	**Sarah Bullen**
Operative Lee	**Loftus Burton**
Operatives	**Andy Dempsey / Mike Stevens / Andrew Sutcliffe**
Guards	**Tony Allyn / Quentin Pierre**
Voice of Computer	**Barbara Kelly**

Guest Cast

Companion / Voice of Gwent	**Leo McKern**
Winters	**Gary Waldhorn**

First UK Transmission

Thursday, January 8th, 1976
7.00pm (ATV)

MISSION OF THE DARIANS — Prod. No. 22

Screenplay by **Johnny Byrne** Directed by **Ray Austin**

A colossal spaceship, the *Daria*, 20 miles long and five miles wide, drifts near the Moon and Alpha receives a desperate message for help which reveals that the ship has been devastated by a major catastrophe. Koenig leads a rescue party comprising Helena, Bergman, Morrow, Carter and security guard Lowry and they board the ship. Separated into three groups, the Alphans discover a vast world of startling contrasts, the result of the explosion of the ship's nuclear reactor 900 years before. Koenig and Bergman meet the sophisticated and intellectual original Darians, including the ship's commander Neman and the beautiful Kara, Director of Reconstruction, whose lives have been prolonged by transplant surgery. However, the rest of the party encounter the savage descendants of the survivors of Level 7, whose religious beliefs make them intolerant of physical deformity, rewarding imperfection with execution!

Notes

This episode was inspired by the harrowing story of the 1972 South American plane crash which left the surviving members of a rugby team lost in the Andes for ten weeks and forced to eat the bodies of their colleagues. The script originally detailed the *Daria* as being 50 miles long and two miles wide, but these dimensions were altered in order to make the ship appear more imposing on screen. A hand double was used for the close-up shot of Lowry's hand as actor Paul Antrim actually owned a full set of fingers. The Darian radiation suits were revamped from spacesuit costumes originally made for the British space western feature film *Moon Zero Two* (1969), although one of the helmets was originally made for *Doppelgänger* (1968) and was also used in UFO. The episode's incidental music features the introductory passage from 'The White Mountain' by Frank Cordell and 'Experiments In Space – Vega' by Robert Farnon. Other tracks heard in the episode were originally composed by Barry Gray for the STINGRAY episode *Ghost Of The Sea* and the JOE 90 episode *King For A Day*.

Regular Cast

Cdr. John Koenig	**Martin Landau**
Dr. Helena Russell	**Barbara Bain**
Prof. Victor Bergman	**Barry Morse**
Paul Morrow	**Prentis Hancock**
Capt. Alan Carter	**Nick Tate**
Sandra Benes	**Zienia Merton**
David Kano	**Clifton Jones**
Operative Kate	**Sarah Bullen**
Operative Lee	**Loftus Burton**
Operatives	**Binu Balini / Andy Dempsey / Mike Stevens**
Guards	**Tony Allyn / Quentin Pierre**

Guest Cast

Kara	**Joan Collins**
Neman	**Dennis Burgess**
High Priest	**Aubrey Morris**
Bill Lowry	**Paul Antrim**
Hadin	**Robert Russell**
Male Mute	**Gerald Stadden**
Female Mute	**Jackie Horton**
Hirsute Darian Guard	**Ron Tarr**
Blonde Darian Girl	**Linda Hooks**

First UK Transmission

Thursday, October 30th, 1975
7.00pm (ATV/Yorkshire)

DRAGON'S DOMAIN — Prod. No. 23

Regular Cast

Cdr. John Koenig	**Martin Landau**
Dr. Helena Russell	**Barbara Bain**
Prof. Victor Bergman	**Barry Morse**
Paul Morrow	**Prentis Hancock**
Capt. Alan Carter	**Nick Tate**
Sandra Benes	**Zienia Merton**
David Kano	**Clifton Jones**
Dr. Bob Mathias	**Anton Phillips**
Tanya Alexander	**Suzanne Roquette**
Ken Johnson	**James Fagan**
Operative Kate	**Sarah Bullen**
Operative Lee	**Loftus Burton**
Operatives	**Andy Dempsey / Andrew Sutcliffe / Mike Stevens**
Guards	**Tony Allyn / Quentin Pierre**

Guest Cast

Tony Cellini	**Gianni Garko**
Commissioner Dixon	**Douglas Wilmer**
Dr. Monique Bouchere	**Barbara Kellerman**
Dr. Darwin King	**Michael Sheard**
Professor Juliet Mackie	**Susan Jameson**
Space News Newsreader	**Bob Sherman**

First UK Transmission

Thursday, October 23rd, 1975
7.00pm (ATV/Yorkshire)

Screenplay by **Christopher Penfold** — Directed by **Charles Crichton**

Eagle pilot Tony Cellini experiences a strange alien visitation in his quarters and then attempts to steal an Eagle, forcing Koenig to stun him with his laser. The incident encourages Helena to review Earth medical records concerning Cellini's involvement in the ill-fated Ultra Probe mission of 1996, in which Cellini and three science experts were dispatched on the longest ever manned space flight to investigate a new planet, Ultra, discovered by Bergman outside the solar system. Cellini was the only survivor of the mission and on his return, he related a fantastic story about a spaceship graveyard guarded by a horrific creature which killed his companions. The disbelieving authorities rejected Cellini's tale but now, incredibly, the Moon has arrived at Cellini's spaceship graveyard and he senses the presence of the monster guardian...

Notes

This is the only Year One episode apart from *Breakaway* that is specifically dated: February 6th, 2002. Tony Cellini was originally written as 'Jim Calder' in the script and Monique Bouchere was originally written as 'Olga Vishenskya'. The incidental music that accompanies the flight of the Ultra Probe is an arrangement by Allain Lombard of 'Adagio for Organ and Cello in G Minor' by Tomaso Albinoni.

Oops!

The date of the launch of the Ultra Probe is detailed by Helena as June 6th, 1996 but in the pre-launch scene with Koenig, Bergman and Cellini, the SPACE NEWS newsreader gives the current date as September 3rd, 1996 (the newsreader's date was written in the British date format as "nine, three, ninety-six" – March 9th, 1996 – in the script, but actor Bob Sherman interpreted this in the American format of month, day, year). As the Ultra Probe approaches the spaceship graveyard, one shot of the graveyard shows the Dragon Ship with the Ultra Probe already attached.

THE TESTAMENT OF ARKADIA — Prod. No. 24

Regular Cast

Cdr. John Koenig	**Martin Landau**
Dr. Helena Russell	**Barbara Bain**
Prof. Victor Bergman	**Barry Morse**
Paul Morrow	**Prentis Hancock**
Capt. Alan Carter	**Nick Tate**
Sandra Benes	**Zienia Merton**
David Kano	**Clifton Jones**
Dr. Bob Mathias	**Anton Phillips**
Tanya Alexander	**Suzanne Roquette**
Operative Kate	**Sarah Bullen**
Operative Lee	**Loftus Burton**
Operatives	**Andy Dempsey / Mike Stevens / Andrew Sutcliffe**
Guards	**Tony Allyn / Quentin Pierre**

Guest Cast

Luke Ferro	**Orso Maria Guerrini**
Anna Davis	**Lisa Harrow**
Operative	**Ann Maj-Britt**
Voice of Operative	**Shane Rimmer**

First UK Transmission

Thursday, February 12th, 1976
7.00pm (ATV)

Screenplay by **Johnny Byrne** — Directed by **David Tomblin**

Without warning, the Moon stops dead in space and Alpha experiences an unexplained power loss which will render the base uninhabitable within a few days. Suspecting that a nearby planet may be the cause, Koenig leads an investigation team which includes Helena, Bergman, Carter and two specialists, Luke Ferro and Anna Davis. The Alphans discover a cave containing human skeletons and a message written in Sanskrit 25,000 years before. Trees on the planet which are native to Earth confirm the content of the ancient writings, that life on Earth began here on Arkadia, but Koenig does not believe that the planet offers a new home for the Alphans and he cancels evacuation procedures. However, Ferro and Anna are determined to carry out the wishes of their distant forebears and take matters into their own hands: holding Helena hostage, they demand supplies and an Eagle to transport them back to Arkadia...

Notes

Johnny Byrne's script reveals the names of the two security guards played by Tony Allyn and Quentin Pierre who have been seen throughout the Year One episodes: they are Irwin and N'Dole, although the latter appears to contradict the character's appearance in a space helmet marked 'Quinton' in *Earthbound*. The episode's incidental music includes two very distinctive pieces: the Arkadia theme is 'Suite Appassionata – Adagio' by Paul Bonneau & Serge Lancen, while the track which accompanies Ferro and Anna's revelation in the cave is 'Picture Of Autumn' by Jack Arel & Pierre Dutour. Italian actor Orso Maria Guerrini is dubbed throughout by Robert Rietty. The team's disembarkation from the Eagle on Arkadia is lifted from *Another Time, Another Place*. This episode first aired in the USA on December 2nd, 1975, ten weeks before its first screening in the UK.

Oops!

Actress Lisa Harrow is mis-credited as 'Liza' Harrow on the in-show titles.

PRODUCTION CREDITS (Year Two)

Executive Producer **Gerry Anderson***
Producer **Fred Freiberger**
Production Executive **Reg Hill**
Associate Producer **F. Sherwin Green**
Technical Director **David Lane**
Lighting Cameraman **Frank Watts BSC** *(1-7, 9-11, 13-15, 17-20, 22-24)*
Brendan Stafford *(8, 12, 16, 21)*
Production Designer **Keith Wilson**
Special Effects Designed and Directed by **Brian Johnson**
Music by **Derek Wadsworth**
Production Manager **Donald Toms**
Casting Director **Lesley de Pettitt**
Editor **Mike Campbell GBFE** *(1, 3, 5, 7, 10, 13, 15, 19, 20, 23)*
Alan Killick *(2, 4, 6, 9, 12, 14, 17, 18, 22, 24)*
Alan Pattillo *(8)*
Bill Blunden *(11)*
Archie Ludski *(16)*
Ray Lovejoy *(21)*
Sound Supervisor **Roy Baker** *(2-24)*
Sound Editors **Peter Pennell** *(1-6, 8-10, 12-24)*
Jack T. Knight GBFE *(1, 3-6, 8-24)*
Charles Crafford *(7)*
Ted Bond *(11)*
Costume Designer **Emma Porteous**
Financial Director **Terence Connors** *(1-13)*
Music Editor **Alan Willis** *(2-24)*
Sound Recordist **Claude Hitchcock** *(1-7, 9-11)*
John Brommage *(8, 12, 21)*
Brian Marshall *(13-15, 17-20, 22, 23, 24)*
Peter Sutton *(16)*
Camera Operator **Neil Binney** *(1-7, 9-11, 13-15, 17-20, 22-24)*
Tony White *(8, 12, 16, 21)*
Assistant Director **Ken Baker** *(1, 3, 5, 7, 10, 12, 13, 15, 20, 21, 23)*
Robert Lynn *(2, 4, 6, 8, 9, 17-19, 22, 24)*
Jack Causey *(11)*
Dominic Fulford *(14, 16)*
Continuity **Gladys Goldsmith** *(1-6)*
Doreen Soan *(7, 9, 10, 12-15, 17-21, 23, 24)*
Doris Martin *(8, 11, 16, 22)*
Construction Manager **Bill Waldron** *(2-24)*
Make-up **Basil Newall** *(1, 3-7, 9, 10, 12-20, 22-24)*
Connie Reeve *(2-6, 8-11, 13-21, 23, 24)*
Eddie Knight *(7)*
Eileen Fletcher *(8)*
Hairdresser **Patrick Grant** *(1)*
Jan Dorman *(2-7, 9, 12-19, 23)*
Jeannette Freeman *(3-6, 8-11, 13-21, 23, 24)*
Marsha Lewis *(8)*
Michael Lockey *(20, 22, 24)*
Wardrobe **Masada Wilmot** *(1-6, 8)*
Eve Faloon *(7, 12, 16)*
Barbara Gillett *(8)*
Eileen Sullivan *(9-11, 13-15, 17-24)*
Assistant Art Director **Michael Ford**
Movements Arranged by **Lionel Blair** *(3)*
SPECIAL EFFECTS
Lighting Cameraman **Nick Allder**
Camera Operator **David Litchfield**
Electronics **Michael S.E. Downing**

Processed by **Rank Film Laboratories**
SPACE:1999 Based on a Format by *(1)*/
SPACE:1999 Created by *(2-24)*
Gerry and **Sylvia Anderson**

Filmed at Pinewood and Bray Studios, England
A Gerry Anderson Production
From ITC Television

* uncredited

Episode Titles (Year Two)

(Listed in production order)

1. **The Metamorph**
2. **The Exiles**
3. **One Moment Of Humanity**
4. **All That Glisters**
5. **Journey To Where**
6. **The Taybor**
7. **The Rules Of Luton**
8. **The Mark Of Archanon**
9. **Brian The Brain**
10. **New Adam New Eve**
11. **Catacombs Of The Moon**
12. **The AB Chrysalis**
13. **Seed Of Destruction**
14. **The Beta Cloud**
15. **Space Warp**
16. **A Matter Of Balance**
17. **The Bringers Of Wonder part 1**
18. **The Bringers Of Wonder part 2**
19. **The Lambda Factor**
20. **The Seance Spectre**
21. **Dorzak**
22. **Devil's Planet**
23. **The Immunity Syndrome**
24. **The Dorcons**

Episode Running Time

50 minutes approx.

Aside from cosmetic changes to the costumes and sets, the most notable differences in SPACE:1999's second season were the cast changes. The producers were unable to resolve a pay dispute with Barry Morse so he was not invited to reprise his role as Victor Bergman and in his place, Catherine Schell was cast as the Psychon metamorph Maya. She was accompanied by former THE PROTECTORS star Tony Anholt as security chief Tony Verdeschi. First season regulars Prentis Hancock and Clifton Jones also disappeared from the line-up while Anton Phillips appeared in only two second season episodes before leaving of his own volition. Apart from Martin Landau and Barbara Bain, the only members of the Year One cast retained for Year Two were Nick Tate, Zienia Merton, Kate Bullen, Quentin Pierre and Annie Lambert.

THE METAMORPH
Prod. No. 01

Screenplay by **Johnny Byrne** Directed by **Charles Crichton**

During an encounter with a space warp, one of the life support systems has been severely damaged so a survey Eagle is dispatched to the nearby planet Psychon in search of titanium that will be essential to repairs. Suddenly, the Eagle is enveloped by a ball of light and dragged to the planet's surface. A Psychon named Mentor contacts the Alphans, offering to return the pilots at a rendezvous in space, but the rendezvous is a trap and Koenig is forced to land his Eagle on the planet. There, he finds that Mentor seeks to transform his barren, volcanic world by molecular transformation, using a biological computer, Psyche, created from the minds and bodies of the Psychon people. But Koenig learns that Psyche is powered by energy from the minds of intelligent beings and Mentor intends to feed the Alphans to his machine. Koenig's only hope to save his people lies with Mentor's daughter Maya who possesses the power of molecular transformation...

Notes
Johnny Byrne's original script, 'The Biological Soul', was written for the first season format and characters. It was revised as 'The Biological Computer' to introduce Maya and retitled *The Metamorph* just before filming began. In the shooting script, the roles of Verdeschi and Carter were initially written as 'Simon Hays' and 'Mark MacInlock', the events were dated 108 days after leaving Earth orbit, and the survey Eagle was searching for tiranium. The population of Alpha is described by Helena as stable at 297. Scenes filmed for the episode but deleted from the final edit included Maya turning into an orange tree and Verdeschi and Sandra discussing the death of Bergman.

Oops!
Recording her Alpha Log, Helena states that it is 342 days after leaving Earth orbit (August 20th, 2000), placing the events of this episode before those of *Dragon's Domain*. Titanium is not rare and is readily available on the lunar surface.

Regular Cast

Cdr. John Koenig	**Martin Landau**
Dr. Helena Russell	**Barbara Bain**
Maya	**Catherine Schell**
Tony Verdeschi	**Tony Anholt**
Capt. Alan Carter	**Nick Tate**
Sandra Benes	**Zienia Merton**
Dr. Bob Mathias	**Anton Phillips**
Bill Fraser	**John Hug**
Operative Kate	**Sarah Bullen**
Operative Peter	**Robert Reeves**
Operative	**Pam Rose**

Guest Cast

Mentor	**Brian Blessed**
Annette Fraser	**Anouska Hempel**
Lew Picard	**Gerard Paquis**
Petrov	**Peter Porteous**
Ray Torens	**Nick Brimble**
Overseers	**George Lane Cooper**
	Alf Joint
Small Chipping Alien	**John Dixon**
Zombie Chipping Alien	**Neil McCaul**
Coloured Chipping Alien	**Roy Stewart**
Alphans	**Chris Figg / Nina Mitchen**
Operative	**Andy Cummings**
Gorilla	**Reuben Martin**

First UK Transmission
Saturday, September 4th, 1976
11.30am (LWT)

THE EXILES
Prod. No. 02

Screenplay by **Donald James** Directed by **Ray Austin**

53 cylindrical objects which initially appear to be missiles take up orbit around the Moon. One of the cylinders is recovered from space and brought to Alpha where it is found to contain Cantar, a young alien man exiled from the planet Golos. Once revived from cryogenic suspension, he implores Koenig to recover the remaining cylinders – each containing one of his fellow exiles – before the gravitational pull of the Moon destroys them, so Koenig cautiously allows a second cylinder to be brought to Alpha. It contains Cantar's wife Zova and together they set about increasing the capacity of Alpha's life support systems to cope with the additional strain that the 53 Golosians would place upon it. However, the pair have ulterior motives and, forcing their way into the power section, they generate a transporter beam and escape to Golos, taking Helena and Verdeschi with them as hostages!

Notes
Donald James's original script was written for the first season format and characters. In the revised shooting script, the role of Verdeschi was written as 'Simon Hays' and the events were dated 280 days after leaving Earth orbit. Although post-production work on this episode was initially completed in April 1976, additional work was required in June to redub Peter Duncan's voice with that of another actor (to give Cantar an American accent) and to insert an extra sequence in which Maya rescues Petrov after an explosion traps him under a girder. These scenes were directed by Kevin Connor and shot during filming on *Seed Of Destruction* early in June 1976. A sequence with Helena and Maya discussing Sixties and Seventies fashions was deleted to make room for the new scenes.

Oops!
Recording her Alpha Log, Helena states that it is 403 days after leaving Earth orbit (October 20th, 2000), placing the events before those of *Dragon's Domain*.

Regular Cast

Cdr. John Koenig	**Martin Landau**
Dr. Helena Russell	**Barbara Bain**
Maya	**Catherine Schell**
Tony Verdeschi	**Tony Anholt**
Capt. Alan Carter	**Nick Tate**
Sandra Benes	**Zienia Merton**
Dr. Bob Mathias	**Anton Phillips**
Operative Kate	**Sarah Bullen**
Operative Peter	**Robert Reeves**
Operative	**Pam Rose**
Guard	**Quentin Pierre**

Guest Cast

Cantar	**Peter Duncan**
Zova	**Stacy Dorning**
Mirella	**Margaret Inglis**
Stal	**Anthony Blackett**
Old Lady	**Peggy Ledger**
Petrov	**Peter Porteous**
Operative	**Andy Cummings**
Guards	**Roy Everson / Ron Nichols**
Decontamination Crew	**Vic Armstrong**
	Frank Maher
Nurses	**Jenny Cresswell**
	Tracey Hudson / Maryanne

First UK Transmission
Saturday, September 11th, 1976
11.30am (LWT)

ONE MOMENT OF HUMANITY — Prod. No. 03

Screenplay by **Tony Barwick** Directed by **Charles Crichton**

Alpha is stricken by a mysterious power loss and then visited by Vegan woman Zamara, who mistakes Helena and Verdeschi for lovers and demands that they return with her to the planet Vega. Travelling to Vega by positronic transfer, the pair are greeted with hostility by the beautiful Vegans but Helena is warned by a masked servant, Number Eight, that if they show aggression, the Vegans will kill them. Taunted and insulted by the Vegans, Helena and Verdeschi remain calm even when they are imprisoned, but they escape from their cell to track down Number Eight. In caves beneath the city, Number Eight reveals that the Vegans are androids while he and his fellow servants are the true Vegans, hiding their faces beneath masks to conceal their emotions. The androids do not possess the necessary emotions that will enable them to kill so they intend to spur the Alphans to violence that they can emulate...

Notes

This episode was filmed with the working title 'One Second Of Humanity'. In the shooting script, the events were dated 415 days after leaving Earth orbit. The visual effects shot of the surface of Vega is lifted from *Death's Other Dominion* where it appeared as the surface of Ultima Thule. The erotic dance performed by Helena and Zarl was choreographed by Lionel Blair, assisted by Hilary Ding. The whole of the episode's original epilogue sequence was filmed but deleted from the final edit. In this sequence, Number Eight tells Koenig that he and the other Vegans will have to learn to live on the planet's surface, Carter arrives in an Eagle to recover the Alphans and Koenig and Helena discuss Zarl's aggressively masculine qualities.

Oops!

Recording her Alpha Log, Helena states that it is 515 days after leaving Earth orbit (February 9th, 2001), placing the events before those of *Dragon's Domain*.

Regular Cast

Cdr. John Koenig	**Martin Landau**
Dr. Helena Russell	**Barbara Bain**
Maya	**Catherine Schell**
Tony Verdeschi	**Tony Anholt**
Capt. Alan Carter	**Nick Tate**
Sandra Benes	**Zienia Merton**
Operative Kate	**Sarah Bullen**
Operative Peter	**Robert Reeves**
Operative	**Pam Rose**

Guest Cast

Zamara	**Billie Whitelaw**
Zarl	**Leigh Lawson**
Number Eight	**Geoffrey Bayldon**
Operative	**Andy Cummings**
Vegans	**Jurgen Anderson**
	Zena Clifton / Hilary Ding
	Paul Hastings / Maggie Henderson
	Laraine Humphreys / Jason Mitchell
	Barry Rohde
Number	**Micky Clarke**

First UK Transmission

Saturday, September 25th, 1976
11.00am (LWT)

ALL THAT GLISTERS — Prod. No. 04

Screenplay by **Keith Miles** Directed by **Ray Austin**

Koenig leads a geological survey to a dry, waterless planet in search of milgonite, a rare mineral vital to the Alphan life support system. Geologist Dave Reilly discovers a glowing rock formation in a cave and breaks a piece off to test in Eagle Four's specially adapted laboratory section, but there is a sudden blinding flash of light and Verdeschi is apparently killed. However, he soon returns to life and, acting under some form of hypnotic control, collects a second piece of rock and returns with it to the Eagle where the two pieces fuse into one. Then communications with Alpha are cut off, the Eagle is immobilised and the party discover that the rock is an intelligent life-form which has deliberately drawn them to the planet by misleading the computer sensors. Helena is trapped inside the Eagle with the rock and when it absorbs their water supplies, she realises that it desperately needs water to survive...

Notes

There were considerable problems with the script during the filming of this episode which required numerous rewrites by producer Fred Freiberger. The cast hated it, particularly Martin Landau who threatened to terminate his contract over it. In a scene deleted from the script, Reilly surmised that the rocks arrived on the planet 50,000 years ago during the fall-out from a cosmic storm. Guest star Patrick Mower (Dave Reilly) previously appeared as Cass Fowler in the UFO episode *The Square Triangle* and as Raphael Santana in the *Implicado* episode of THE PROTECTORS. Unusually, *All That Glisters* features no scenes set on Moonbase Alpha.

Oops!

Recording her Alpha Log, Helena states that it is 565 days after leaving Earth orbit (March 31st, 2001), placing the events before those of *Dragon's Domain*. When the rock engineers the launch of Eagle Four, the vehicle's laboratory section suddenly vanishes.

Regular Cast

Cdr. John Koenig	**Martin Landau**
Dr. Helena Russell	**Barbara Bain**
Maya	**Catherine Schell**
Tony Verdeschi	**Tony Anholt**
Capt. Alan Carter	**Nick Tate**
Voice of Computer	**Barbara Kelly**

Guest Cast

Dave Reilly	**Patrick Mower**

First UK Transmission

Thursday, October 28th, 1976
4.45pm (ATV)

JOURNEY TO WHERE

Prod. No. 05

Screenplay by **Donald James** Directed by **Tom Clegg**

Alpha receives a neutrino transmission from Space Station One in Texas City on the Earth of 2120. Dr. Logan reveals that experimental transference technology will enable the Alphans to return to Earth, but the movement of a constellation means that contact is only possible between Earth and Alpha for 72 hours. With no time to lose, Koenig, Helena and Carter make the first trip, but during their journey an earthquake hits Texas City and the trio fail to re-materialise. They find themselves in a cold, wooded area quite unlike the conditions that they have been led to expect on 22nd century Earth. Helena contracts pneumonia and they are attacked by savage warriors who take them prisoner. As Dr. Logan and his team attempt to track down the Alphans, Koenig and Carter come to the realisation that they have travelled through time and arrived in 14th century Scotland in the midst of a bitter conflict between the Highland clans and English forces!

Notes

Other actors considered for the role of Dr. Logan included Patrick Troughton, Bernard Hepton, Colin Blakely and Ronnie Barker. Scenes on the Earth of 1339 were filmed on the backlot at Pinewood Studios. Yasuko Nagazumi makes her first appearance as Command Center operative Yasko, temporarily replacing Zienia Merton (Sandra Benes). The wife of series director Ray Austin, she had previously appeared in the regular role of Suki in the first series of THE PROTECTORS.

Oops!

Dr. Logan responds to Koenig's first test question by saying that Yuri Gagarin was unmarried, but the Russian astronaut married trainee nurse Valentina Ivanovna Goryacheva in November 1957 (four years before his space flight) and they had two daughters Lenochka and Galochka, so the first married man in space *was* Gagarin, not Alan Shepherd.

Regular Cast

Cdr. John Koenig	**Martin Landau**
Dr. Helena Russell	**Barbara Bain**
Maya	**Catherine Schell**
Tony Verdeschi	**Tony Anholt**
Capt. Alan Carter	**Nick Tate**
Dr. Ben Vincent	**Jeffery Kissoon**
Yasko	**Yasuko Nagazumi**
Operative Kate	**Sarah Bullen**
Operative Peter	**Robert Reeves**

Guest Cast

Dr. Charles Logan	**Freddie Jones**
Carla Cross	**Isla Blair**
MacDonald	**Roger Bizley**
Jackson	**Laurence Harrington**
1st Operative Texas	**Norwich Duff**
The Old Crone	**Peggy Paige**
Highlander	**Terry Walsh**

First UK Transmission

Saturday, September 18th, 1976
10.20am (LWT)

THE TAYBOR

Prod. No. 06

Screenplay by **Thom Keyes** Directed by **Bob Brooks**

Alpha is visited by Taybor, an itinerant trader from Pinvith the Lesser, who lands on the Moon in his jump-drive spaceship, the *S.S. Emporium*. Unfortunately, his gifts – intended to illustrate his good will – have proven to be too advanced for the Alphans, blinding a hydroponics assistant and placing a weapons technician in a catatonic trance, but Taybor assures Helena that neither is permanently harmed and the effects will soon wear off. Koenig is interested in the *Emporium*'s jump-drive which could return the Alphans to Earth, and Taybor is willing to trade. Koenig offers him Moonbase Alpha with fixtures and fittings intact but Taybor has designs on Maya, intending to add her to his collection of the galaxy's most beautiful objects. Koenig refuses but offers Taybor a perfect robot replica of Maya, sculpted by Helena, as a substitute. Taybor appears to accept the replica as a fair trade, but he later kidnaps Maya and makes a hasty escape in the *Emporium*...

Notes

In actor Thom Keyes's script, the role of Fraser was written for Carter. The girth of guest Willoughby Goddard (Taybor) was so large that costume designer Emma Porteous had to join two tape measures together to measure around him. Footage of the solarium was lifted from the start of this episode and added to *The Exiles* which, despite being filmed before *The Taybor*, was not completed until after it. As *The Taybor* features a fat, bearded man bearing gifts, the episode was billed as a Christmas special when screened for the first time in the Yorkshire Television region in December 1977.

Oops!

Helena describes Taybor's memory amplifier as a cylindrical object, but it is a polyhedron. Koenig tells Taybor that Earth is in Galaxy M104, but M104 is the Sombrero Galaxy (also called NGC 4594) some 40 million light years from Earth beyond the constellation Virgo.

Regular Cast

Cdr. John Koenig	**Martin Landau**
Dr. Helena Russell	**Barbara Bain**
Maya	**Catherine Schell**
Tony Verdeschi	**Tony Anholt**
Dr. Ben Vincent	**Jeffery Kissoon**
Bill Fraser	**John Hug**
Yasko	**Yasuko Nagazumi**
Operative Kate	**Sarah Bullen**

Guest Cast

Taybor	**Willoughby Goddard**
Karen	**Laraine Humphreys**
Slatternly Woman	**Rita Webb**
Andrews	**Mel Taylor**
Barbara	**Vickie Michelle**
Model Girl 1	**Jenny Clare**
Model Girl 2	**Chai Lee**
Model Girl 3	**Penny Priestley**

First UK Transmission

Thursday, November 4th, 1976
4.45pm (ATV)

THE RULES OF LUTON — Prod. No. 07

Screenplay by **Charles Woodgrove** | Directed by **Val Guest**

Koenig and Maya are exploring a planet in the North Quadrant when Verdeschi reports a malfunction in their Eagle and returns to Alpha for repairs. Examining the planet's lush vegetation, Koenig eats some berries and Maya picks a flower but they are suddenly accused of violating the laws of the sentient plant life by the Judges of Luton, a trio of talking trees. The Judges decree that the Alphans must prove their innocence in trial by combat against other alien 'criminals', three strange aliens each of whom has unusual powers and abilities. Forced into a defensive position, Koenig is badly injured after dispatching two of their opponents so Maya turns into a bird to find water with which to clean his wound, but she is captured by the third alien who places her in a cage. Koenig realises that he must face the alien in a final duel to save Maya before she loses control of her form and is crushed to death!

Notes

Charles Woodgrove was a pen name used by producer Fred Freiberger, who decided on the name for the planet in this episode after seeing it on a signpost on the M1. Here, it is pronounced "Loo-tarn". Virtually the entire episode was shot on location, enabling it to be filmed in tandem with *The Mark Of Archanon*. These were known as 'Double Up Scripts' by the production team: pairs of episodes that split the main cast so that they could be shot simultaneously, thereby reducing the filming schedule for the whole series. Three other pairs of episodes were filmed in this way: *Catacombs Of The Moon* and *The AB Chrysalis*, *Space Warp* and *A Matter Of Balance*, and *Dorzak* and *Devil's Planet*. For the only time in the entire series, Martin Landau left the confines of Pinewood Studios for location filming on this episode (all of his exterior scenes in *The Full Circle*, *Journey To Where* and *A Matter Of Balance* were shot within the studio grounds). The Luton exteriors were filmed in nearby Black Park and at the Wapsey's Wood Landfill Site in Gerrards Cross, Buckinghamshire.

Regular Cast

Cdr. John Koenig	**Martin Landau**
Dr. Helena Russell	**Barbara Bain**
Maya	**Catherine Schell**
Tony Verdeschi	**Tony Anholt**
Yasko	**Yasuko Nagazumi**
Operative	**Annie Lambert**

Guest Cast

Alien Strong / Voice of Judges	**David Jackson**
Alien Transporter	**Godfrey James**
Alien Invisible	**Roy Marsden**

First UK Transmission

Thursday, October 21st, 1976
4.45pm (ATV)

THE MARK OF ARCHANON — Prod. No. 08

Screenplay by **Lew Schwartz** | Directed by **Charles Crichton**

Carter and mineralogist Andy Johnson are surveying the catacombs beneath Alpha for dylenide crystals when they discover a stasis chamber containing two aliens, Pasc and Etrec. Revived in the Medical Center, the newcomers introduce themselves as emissaries from Archanon, the planet of peace. Pasc explains that he and his son were imprisoned in the stasis chamber by their own people, who had been affected by a contagion of evil while visiting Earth. The Archanons are welcomed into the base and Carter takes a shine to young Etrec, teaching him how to play Australian football, but Helena discovers the presence of a strange living virus in Pasc's blood cells and the same virus, as yet dormant, in Etrec's blood. Unknown to the Alphans, this virus is a genetic sickness, handed down through generations of Archanon males, which overwhelms them with the urge to kill...

Notes

Specifically written under producer Fred Freiberger's guidelines so that it could act as a 'Double Up' episode shot in tandem with *The Rules Of Luton*, the script of this episode minimised the involvement of Koenig and Maya to a few short scenes in Eagle One. The script originally featured Carter teaching Etrec how to play soccer rather than Australian football. The script also introduced the character of Dr. Ben Vincent, but the part was rewritten as Dr. Raul Nunez when Raul Newey was cast in the role. Michael Gallagher (Etrec) is dubbed throughout by another actor using an American accent.

Oops!

Recording her Alpha Log, Helena states that it is 640 days after leaving Earth orbit (June 14th, 2001), placing the events before those of *Dragon's Domain*. Some shots of Eagle One show the port bow leg bent at an angle, while in others it is in its normal position. When Pasc holds Helena hostage in Eagle Three, Verdeschi orders Eagle One to take up a position over the launch pad, but Koenig and Maya are in Eagle One, far from the base.

Regular Cast

Cdr. John Koenig	**Martin Landau**
Dr. Helena Russell	**Barbara Bain**
Maya	**Catherine Schell**
Tony Verdeschi	**Tony Anholt**
Capt. Alan Carter	**Nick Tate**
Bill Fraser	**John Hug**
Yasko	**Yasuko Nagazumi**
Operative	**Annie Lambert**
Guard	**Quentin Pierre**
Voice of Computer	**Barbara Kelly**

Guest Cast

Pasc	**John Standing**
Etrec	**Michael Gallagher**
Lyra / Maurna	**Veronica Lang**
Andy Johnson	**John Alkin**
Carson	**Anthony Forrest**
Dr. Raul Nunez	**Raul Newey**
Rescue Eagle Pilot	**Terry Walsh**

First UK Transmission

Saturday, October 16th, 1976
11.30am (LWT)

BRIAN THE BRAIN

Prod. No. 09

Screenplay by **Jack Ronder** — Directed by **Kevin Connor**

Records of the Moon's journey are being transferred to the Main Computer memory bank when the computer suddenly records a change in course. Then a Swift spaceship from a 1996 Earth mission lands on Alpha and the pilot is revealed to be a mobile computer called Brian. He explains that his creator, Captain Michael, and his entire crew have died in mysterious circumstances on the nearby Planet D and he has been orbiting the planet alone ever since. He offers to try and pinpoint the source of the Moon's course change, but then Brian reveals his true colours, eradicating the Alpha computer's memory core during a visit to Command Center and abducting Koenig and Helena on the Swift, taking them to Planet D. There Brian forces Koenig to recover nuclear fuel from the Swift's mothership while he holds Helena hostage, but once on board the mothership, Koenig discovers that Brian has murdered his own crew in a jealous rage...

Notes

In the original version of the script, Koenig, Helena and Maya attempted to confuse Brian by each offering to provide him with maintenance and then encouraging him to choose between them. Rather than simply pre-recording his dialogue as Brian, guest star Bernard Cribbins preferred to deliver his lines live on set, enabling the other actors to develop a proper rapport with Brian. Maya's ears are brown in the first nine Year Two episodes but after this they were left white so as to cut down on Catherine Schell's make-up time and discomfort. Marc Zuber (Security Lieutenant) previously appeared as one of Kahan's henchmen in the THE PROTECTORS episode *...With A Little Help From My Friends.*

Oops!

During his visit to Command Center, Brian compares himself with the Alpha Computer describing it as a 'he' and saying that it doesn't talk, although the computer has been heard speaking in many previous episodes with a voice provided by Barbara Kelly.

Regular Cast

Cdr. John Koenig	**Martin Landau**
Dr. Helena Russell	**Barbara Bain**
Maya	**Catherine Schell**
Tony Verdeschi	**Tony Anholt**
Bill Fraser	**John Hug**
Yasko	**Yasuko Nagazumi**
Operative	**Annie Lambert**
Guard	**Quentin Pierre**

Guest Cast

Voice of Brian / Captain Michael	**Bernard Cribbins**
Security Lieutenant	**Marc Zuber**
Brian Robot	**Michael Sharvell-Martin**

First UK Transmission

Saturday, October 2nd, 1976
11.00am (LWT)

NEW ADAM NEW EVE

Prod. No. 10

Screenplay by **Terence Feely** — Directed by **Charles Crichton**

After the Moon passes through an area of turbulence, an omnipotent figure arrives on Alpha and introduces himself as Magus, the creator of all life on Earth. Materialising in Command Center, he announces that he intends to give the Alphans a chance to begin again in a New Eden and transports Koenig, Helena, Maya and Verdeschi to his planet aboard Eagle Four. There, they learn that Magus expects them to be the progenitors of a new human species, but for biological reasons he pairs Helena with Verdeschi and Maya with Koenig, confining them to a glade and enforcing the pairing with positive/negative magnetic field cocoons. Then the Alphans discover a cave which hides strange, mutated creatures, the results of Magus's attempts to learn the secret of creation. Magus is forced to admit that he is the last of a race of cosmic magicians and threatens to destroy the Moon if the Alphans do not co-operate with his plans!

Notes

Former STAR TREK producer Fred Freiberger was not averse to plundering that earlier series for his story ideas: just as *The Rules Of Luton* was inspired by the STAR TREK episodes *Arena* and *The Savage Curtain*, so *New Adam New Eve* was a close re-working of STAR TREK's *Who Mourns For Adonais?* episode. The episode title is punctuated with a comma in the script but not on screen. The incidental score includes a track entitled 'How Beautiful Is The Night' composed by Robert Farnon in 1947, heard during the night-time scene in which Koenig and Maya find it difficult to resist attraction.

Oops!

When Magus transports Koenig's laser to his own hand, a clumsy edit briefly shows a crewmember's hand and arm in shot placing the laser in actor Guy Rolfe's hand. As Koenig climbs into the pit, his commlock falls off his belt and can be heard landing on the studio floor.

Regular Cast

Cdr. John Koenig	**Martin Landau**
Dr. Helena Russell	**Barbara Bain**
Maya	**Catherine Schell**
Tony Verdeschi	**Tony Anholt**
Capt. Alan Carter	**Nick Tate**
Yasko	**Yasuko Nagazumi**
Operative Peter	**Robert Reeves**
Operatives	**Annie Lambert**
	Pam Rose

Guest Cast

Simon Magus	**Guy Rolfe**
Humanoid	**Bernard Kay**
Maya Creature	**Albin Pahernik**
Beautiful Girl	**Barbara Wise**
Ape Man	**Terry York**

First UK Transmission

Saturday, October 9th, 1976
11.30am (LWT)

Above: Joe McClaine, the World Intelligence Network's Most Special Agent in JOE 90.

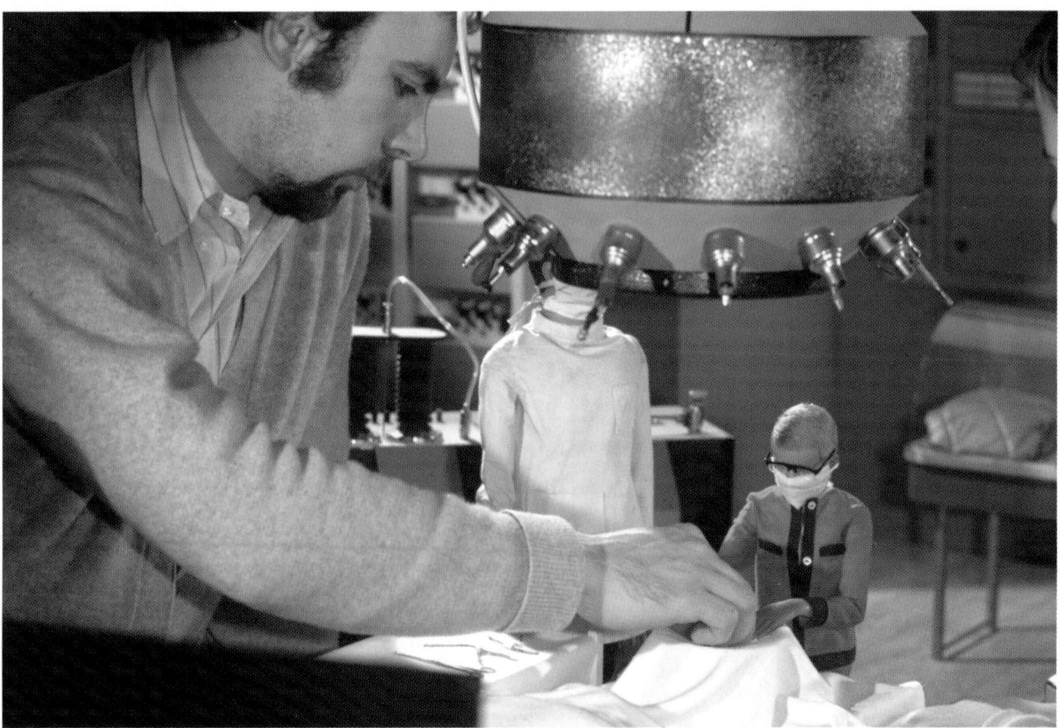

Top: A floor puppeteer holds the Joe puppet in place during filming of a brain pattern transfer sequence for JOE 90.
Above: Director Ken Turner prepares to film the operation scene in JOE 90 – *Operation McClaine*.

Top: Roy Thinnes, Lynn Loring and Franco Derosa arrive in the UK to film *Doppelgänger* at Pinewood Studios.
Above: John Kane (Ian Hendry) and Lisa Hartman (Loni Von Friedl) in a deleted scene from *Doppelgänger* (1968).

Top: Father Unwin sets off from the Vicarage in Gabriel, his vintage Model T Ford, in The Secret Service.
Above: Mrs. Appleby, Father Unwin and Matthew in The Secret Service – *The Cure*.

Top: Commander Ed Straker (Ed Bishop) and Colonel Alec Freeman (George Sewell) at SHADO HQ in UFO – *Exposed*.
Above: Director Ken Turner (left) with Michael Billington and Quinn O'Hara on the set of UFO – *Ordeal*.

Top: Director Ken Turner (centre) with Ed Bishop and George Sewell in Straker's office during filming on UFO – *E.S.P.*
Above: Lt. Joan Harrington (Antonia Ellis) and Lt. Nina Barry (Dolores Mantez) in the Moonbase Control Sphere in UFO.

Above: Harry Rule (Robert Vaughn) entertains a girlfriend (Joanna Lumley) at his apartment in a scene deleted from the second series THE PROTECTORS episode *Petard*.

Above: Aarchon (Alex Scott), Chief Justifier of the Federated Worlds of Sidon, seeks justice for the destruction wrought by *Voyager One* in SPACE:1999 – *Voyager's Return.*

Top: Catherine Schell discusses a scene with director Charles Crichton during filming on SPACE:1999 – *The Metamorph*.
Above: Freddie Jones and Isla Blair on the Space Station One set during filming on SPACE:1999 – *Journey To Where*.

Above: Nick Tate and Albin Pahernik (in creature costume) rehearse a fight scene on the set of SPACE:1999 – *The AB Chrysalis*, observed by director Charles Crichton.

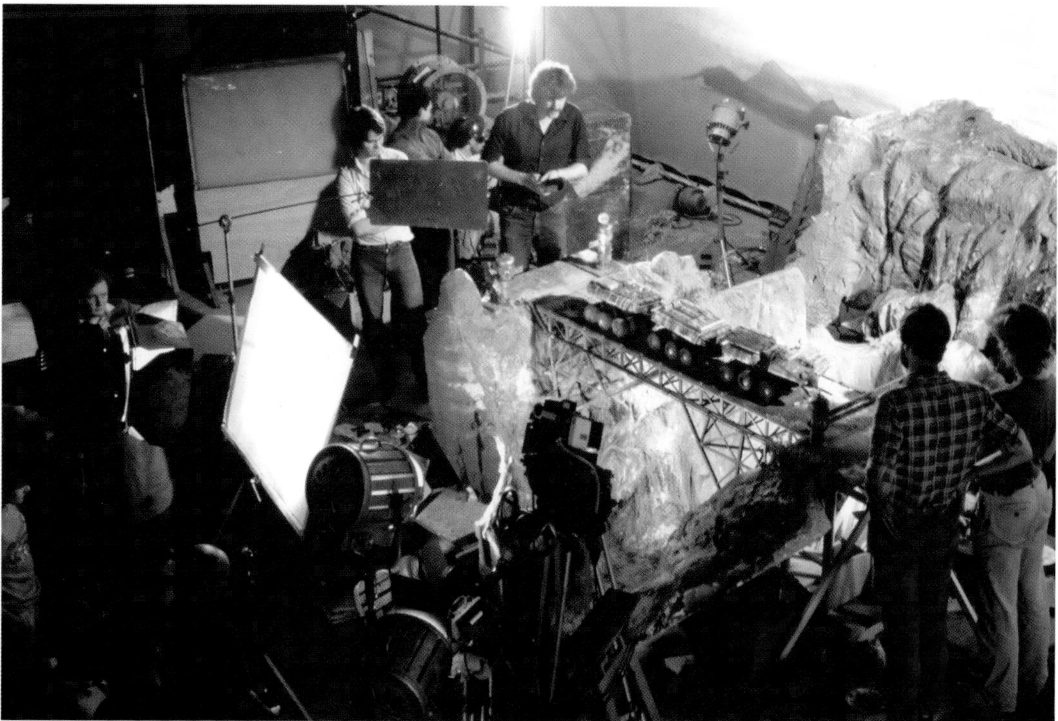

Top: Hudson collects Kate Kestrel and Stew Dapples from Anderburr Records in TERRAHAWKS – *Ten Top Pop*.
Above: Steven Begg (centre in black shirt) supervises the filming of a model effects scene for TERRAHAWKS – *Thunder Path*.

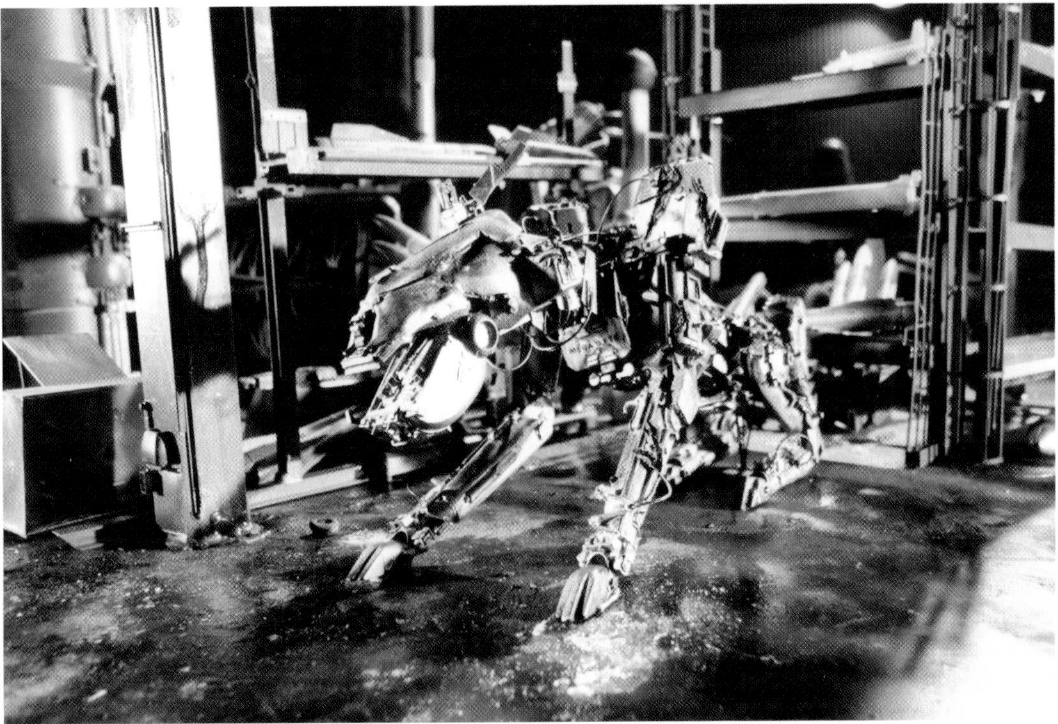

Top: Harry, Tom, Dick and Bats, the alien officers of Precinct 44 East in SPACE POLICE – *Star Laws*.
Above: Megabyte, V. Lann's robotic guard dog, stop-motion animated for SPACE POLICE – *Star Laws*.

Top: Dick's life is on the line in DICK SPANNER – *The Strange Affair Of The Maltese Parrot*.
Above: Writer, director and producer Gerry Anderson, photographed in 1991.

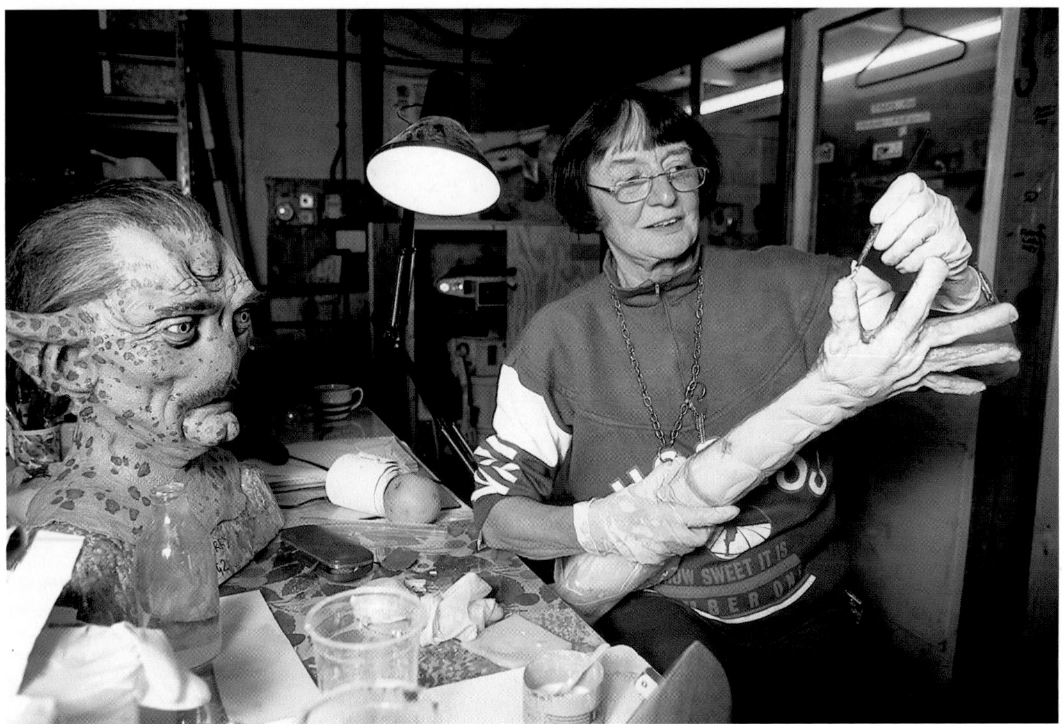

Top: Ted Shackelford and Rob Youngblood with guest star Frances Barber during filming on SPACE PRECINCT – *Hate Street*.
Above: In the tarn and creon workshop, Christine Glanville paints Dag Jomore's arm for SPACE PRECINCT – *Body & Soul*.

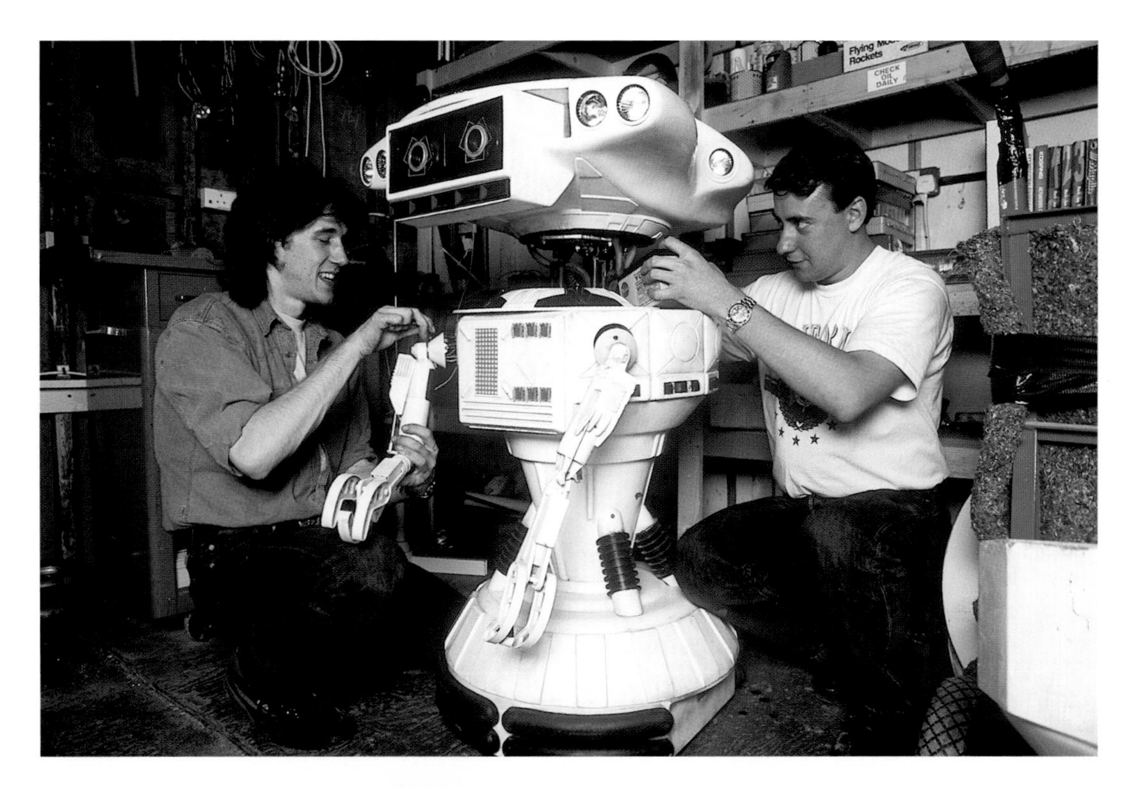

Top: Animatronic technicians make adjustments to Slomo in preparation for filming on Space Precinct.
Above: The alien meteor is collected from the ruins of Roetem Towers in Space Precinct – *Deathwatch*.

Above: The Dank, strange inhabitant of the Great Swamp on planet Quagmire in LAVENDER CASTLE – *Duelling Banjos*.

CATACOMBS OF THE MOON — Prod. No. 11

Screenplay by **Anthony Terpiloff** Directed by **Robert Lynn**

In the catacombs beneath Alpha, chief engineer Patrick Osgood leads a desperate search to find tiranium, a rare metal vital to Alpha's life support functions and the manufacture of an artificial heart that will save his wife Michelle's life. Caught in the blast of his mining explosives, Osgood has visions of Alpha being destroyed by fire and becomes convinced that he is Michelle's saviour. Losing faith in Helena's ability to cure Michelle, Osgood steals explosives and straps himself up as a human bomb to force Helena and Verdeschi to release Michelle from Medical Center, taking her deep into the catacombs where he believes they will be safe from the coming holocaust. As Verdeschi leads a security team to follow Osgood through the tunnels in an attempt to rescue Michelle, it seems that Osgood's visions are coming true when Koenig discovers a massive firestorm heading straight for Alpha!

Notes

Written as 'The Catacombs Of The Moon', the script for this episode was structured to minimise the involvement of Koenig and Maya, thereby enabling it to be filmed in tandem with *The AB Chrysalis*. The original version of the shooting script included dialogue in which Helena and Vincent reveal that the artificial heart they have developed for Michelle has exactly the same specifications as the late Professor Bergman's heart ("Victor might have lived forever – given the chance," says Vincent). Anton Phillips can be briefly seen in his role as Dr. Mathias in a short scene featuring a pair of decontamination technicians (Frank Maher and Vic Armstrong) lifted from *The Exiles*.

Oops!

It was unbelievably shortsighted of the Moonbase Alpha designers to saddle the base with a life support system that relies on so many rare minerals: titanium (*The Metamorph*), milgonite (*All That Glisters*) and now tiranium.

Regular Cast

Cdr. John Koenig	**Martin Landau**
Dr. Helena Russell	**Barbara Bain**
Maya	**Catherine Schell**
Tony Verdeschi	**Tony Anholt**
Sandra Benes	**Zienia Merton**
Dr. Ben Vincent	**Jeffery Kissoon**
Operative Peter	**Robert Reeves**
Operative	**Pam Rose**
Guard	**Quentin Pierre**

Guest Cast

Patrick Osgood	**James Laurenson**
Michelle Osgood	**Pamela Stephenson**
First Engineer	**Lloyd McGuire**
Guard	**Brendan Price**
Co-Pilot Bill	**Alan Hunter**
1st Alphan Woman	**Nova Llewellyn**
Second Engineer	**Saul Reichlin**
Nurse	**Karen Ford**
2nd Alphan Woman	**Felicity York**

First UK Transmission

Saturday, November 27th, 1976
10.55am (LWT)

THE AB CHRYSALIS — Prod. No. 12

Screenplay by **Tony Barwick** Directed by **Val Guest**

Alpha is travelling towards a series of spatial explosions which detonate at precise 12-hourly intervals, sending massive shockwaves through the base. The source of the explosions appears to be a nearby planet so Koenig, Maya and Carter investigate in Eagle One. Discovering a ring of moons surrounding the planet, they land on one of them and encounter self-propelling Voice Probes which cryptically inform the Alphans that their Creators, the Masters, are not yet in existence. Travelling to the planet, they find more Voice Probes which explain that the Masters have a unique life-cycle: after growing old, they enter a chrysalis stage and are reborn but, while in this phase, the Masters are helpless and must be protected by a computer defence system which perceives Alpha as a threat. Only the Masters can countermand the computer's instructions but the Guardian, the last of the Masters, has already entered his chrysalis phase...

Notes

Written as 'The Chrysalis A-B-C', the script for this episode was structured to minimise the involvement of Helena and Verdeschi, thereby enabling it to be filmed in tandem with *Catacombs Of The Moon*. Danish actress Ina Skriver (A) was not averse to appearing naked on screen as she does here (albeit tastefully shrouded by long hair and clouds of gas): she had previously bared all in *Percy's Progress* (1974) and *Take An Easy Ride* (1976) and shortly after her SPACE:1999 appearance, she stripped off for a lesbian romp with Koo Stark in *Emily* (1977). She later changed her name to Christina World for a starring role in the James Bond spoof *Golden Lady* (1979).

Oops!

When the shock wave hits Alpha at the start of the episode, Quentin Pierre's security guard manages to be in two places at once: in a spacesuit on board Eagle One and crouching on a corridor floor wearing a hardhat.

Regular Cast

Cdr. John Koenig	**Martin Landau**
Dr. Helena Russell	**Barbara Bain**
Maya	**Catherine Schell**
Capt. Alan Carter	**Nick Tate**
Bill Fraser	**John Hug**
Yasko	**Yasuko Nagazumi**
Operative Kate	**Sarah Bullen**
Operative Peter	**Robert Reeves**
Operative	**Pam Rose**
Guard	**Quentin Pierre**

Guest Cast

A	**Ina Skriver**
B	**Sarah Douglas**
Sphere Voice	**Robert Rietty**
Guardian's Brother	**David Sebastian Bach**
Creature	**Albin Pahernik**

First UK Transmission

Thursday, November 18th, 1976
4.45pm (ATV)

SEED OF DESTRUCTION — Prod. No. 13

Screenplay by **John Goldsmith** — Directed by **Kevin Connor**

Regular Cast

Cdr. John Koenig	**Martin Landau**
Dr. Helena Russell	**Barbara Bain**
Maya	**Catherine Schell**
Tony Verdeschi	**Tony Anholt**
Capt. Alan Carter	**Nick Tate**
Sandra Benes	**Zienia Merton**
Dr. Ben Vincent	**Jeffery Kissoon**
Operative Peter	**Robert Reeves**
Operative	**Pam Rose**
Guard	**Quentin Pierre**

Guest Cast

Operative Cranston	**Martha Nairn**
Guards	**Jack Klaff / James Leith**
Creature	**Albin Pahernik**

First UK Transmission

Thursday, November 11th, 1976
4.45pm (ATV)

During a reconnaissance mission to a bizarre jewel-like asteroid, Koenig is trapped in a hall of mirrors and replaced by an evil doppelgänger. The duplicate Koenig returns to Alpha with a chunk of crystal and proceeds to organise the directing of an energy beam at the asteroid, apparently to neutralise an energy screen that surrounds the Moon. Maya becomes concerned at Koenig's unscientific and illogical behaviour when he refuses to allow her to examine the crystal or investigate alternative methods of piercing the screen, and after she questions his decisions, he confines her to her quarters. Maya finds allies in Helena and Verdeschi and the trio discover that the crystal is a complex form of living matter that lies dormant, awaiting rejuvenation. Alpha's energy beam will provide the necessary infusion to awaken the Kalthon, a dormant civilisation on the asteroid, but the energy drain threatens Alpha's life support systems...

Notes

In the shooting script, the events were dated 508 days since leaving Earth orbit which would have placed the story between *The Exiles* and *One Moment Of Humanity* (and before *Dragon's Domain*). The date became 1608 days after leaving Earth orbit (February 7th, 2004) in Helena's log in the finished episode. In order to keep track of which Koenig was which, the script designated the real Koenig as 'Koenig-1' and his evil twin as 'Koenig-2'.

Oops!

As Eagle One travels away from the Moon *en route* to the asteroid at the start of the episode, the vehicle is fitted with a booster pod, but the pod has vanished by the time the Eagle touches down on the asteroid. It seems unbelievable that no one on Alpha (even Helena) notices that Koenig has switched the parting in his hair to the right side of his head while exploring the hall of mirrors on the asteroid.

THE BETA CLOUD — Prod. No. 14

Screenplay by **Charles Woodgrove** — Directed by **Robert Lynn**

Regular Cast

Cdr. John Koenig	**Martin Landau**
Dr. Helena Russell	**Barbara Bain**
Maya	**Catherine Schell**
Tony Verdeschi	**Tony Anholt**
Capt. Alan Carter	**Nick Tate**
Sandra Benes	**Zienia Merton**
Bill Fraser	**John Hug**
Operative Peter	**Robert Reeves**

Guest Cast

Cloud Creature	**Dave Prowse**
Space / Kreno Animal	**Albin Pahernik**
Voice of Cloud	**Mark Smith**

First UK Transmission

Thursday, December 16th, 1976
4.45pm (ATV)

A strange cloud appears in Alpha's East Quadrant and lassitude, depression and loss of will incapacitates most of the personnel. Sent to investigate the cloud, Eagle Six returns to Alpha bringing with it a huge, hideous creature that rampages through the base, completely unharmed by the Alphans' weapons. With Koenig, Helena and Carter incapacitated, Verdeschi seals the Command Center personnel in Medical Center for their own safety, instructing the computer to lock all doors and only to open them on his command. Assisted by Maya and Fraser, Verdeschi makes various attempts to stop the creature, but it proves to be immune to vacuum, chlorine and high voltage current. A voice emanating from the cloud announces that the creature has been sent to Alpha to take the Alphan life support core which will prevent the cloud's extinction, so Verdeschi, Maya and Fraser make their last stand outside the life support centre...

Notes

This episode was specifically written by Fred Freiberger to minimise the involvement of Koenig and Helena, thereby enabling Martin Landau and Barbara Bain to take a week's holiday in the South of France. Certain scenes were filmed seven weeks after the completion of the episode's principal photography, during filming on *The Bringers Of Wonder* in mid-September 1976. As initially written in the script, during the closing sequence in Medical Center, Maya discovers Tony looking at a magazine photo of Catherine Schell. Maya changes into the actress before tearing up the photo and storming out. One of Maya's transformations is the Kreno creature from *The AB Chrysalis*, although it doesn't need to breathe chlorine here.

Oops!

The cloud creature appears to have been built by Renault: their logo appears on the circuits inside its head.

SPACE WARP

Prod. No. 15

Screenplay by **Charles Woodgrove** Directed by **Peter Medak**

While Koenig and Verdeschi investigate a derelict spaceship in Alpha's Third Quadrant, Maya is struck down by a mysterious illness and deliriously relives the last days of Psychon. Suddenly, the Moon falls through a space warp which transports the Alphans five light years from their previous position, marooning Koenig and Verdeschi on the other side. Maya transforms into a scaly space animal and breaks out of Medical Center in a feverish attempt to return to Psychon. Making her way to a launch pad, she boards an Eagle, but Carter has the vehicle lowered into the hangar. When Maya tries to lift off, she is unable to control the Eagle in her creature form and the ship crashes inside the hangar. Maya is badly injured and Helena attempts to operate on her but the biology of the space animal that she has turned into is outside Helena's medical experience. Then Maya breaks free, turns into another creature and rampages through the base...

Notes

Fred Freiberger's script for this episode was structured to minimise the involvement of Koenig, Verdeschi and Maya, thereby enabling it to be filmed in tandem with *A Matter Of Balance*. The model of the Betanon Scout-Cruiser *Menon* is revamped from the Archanon spaceship seen in *The Mark Of Archanon*. Maya's transformation into a Psychon warrior was originally intended to be an additional space creature. The second Maya creature is adapted from the cloud creature costume made for *The Beta Cloud*.

Oops!

Captain Duro is listed as 'Grasshopper' on the closing titles, although he looks nothing like one. (The script suggested that the character's head might resemble a grasshopper while pointing out that this description was not intended to be taken literally. Ultimately, it was decided that a new creature head for this character would be too expensive, so Duro ended up as actor Andrew Lodge in a perspex helmet.)

Regular Cast

Cdr. John Koenig	**Martin Landau**
Dr. Helena Russell	**Barbara Bain**
Maya	**Catherine Schell**
Tony Verdeschi	**Tony Anholt**
Capt. Alan Carter	**Nick Tate**
Sandra Benes	**Zienia Merton**
Dr. Ben Vincent	**Jeffery Kissoon**
Operative Peter	**Robert Reeves**
Guard	**Quentin Pierre**

Guest Cast

Petrov	**Peter Porteous**
1st Security Guard	**Tony Osoba**
2nd Security Guard	**John Judd**
Refuel Eagle Pilot Gary	**Trevor Thomas**
Captain Duro	**Andrew Lodge**
Guard	**Jack Klaff**
Technician	**Terry Walsh**

First UK Transmission

Thursday, December 2nd, 1976
4.45pm (ATV)

A MATTER OF BALANCE

Prod. No. 16

Screenplay by **Pip** and **Jane Baker** Directed by **Charles Crichton**

Teenage botanist Shermeen Williams has a crush on Verdeschi but he makes it clear that he has no romantic interest in her. Feeling rejected, Shermeen readily accepts the help of Vindrus, an alien from the planet Sunim who materialises in the Hydroponics Centre and arranges for Shermeen to join Koenig's landing party. On Sunim, the team find a temple guarded by a monstrous creature and inside, Vindrus explains to Shermeen that he requires her help to enable his corporeal body to cross over to this world. When the party returns to Alpha, Vindrus encourages Shermeen to steal a mobile nuclear generator so as to effect this process. He then reveals that he is from a universe of anti-matter where the evolutionary process is in reverse, moving towards extinction. Vindrus and his people wish to cross into the matter universe but for every anti-matter person that crosses over, an Alphan must cross back!

Notes

The script for this episode was designed to minimise the involvement of Helena and Carter, thereby enabling it to be filmed in tandem with *Space Warp*. As described in the original version of the script, the authors envisaged Vindrus as "a handsome man in his late thirties attired in slacks and a simple tunic" wearing a hypnosis-inducing medallion on a silver chain around his neck. Somehow this became Stuart Wilson in a bald wig and gold swimming trunks. The latter caused embarrassing problems for continuity lady Doris Martin who had to establish a uniform side for Wilson to 'dress'. Scenes on the planet Sunim were filmed on the backlot at Pinewood Studios. The head of the Thaed monster was previously part of the cloud creature in *The Beta Cloud*.

Oops!

The fox that Maya transforms into is obviously just a dog made-up to look a bit like a fox. During the transformation, the fox seen in Maya's eye is clearly stuffed.

Regular Cast

Cdr. John Koenig	**Martin Landau**
Dr. Helena Russell	**Barbara Bain**
Maya	**Catherine Schell**
Tony Verdeschi	**Tony Anholt**
Bill Fraser	**John Hug**
Operative Peter	**Robert Reeves**

Guest Cast

Shermeen Williams	**Lynne Frederick**
Vindrus	**Stuart Wilson**
Eddie Collins	**Nicholas Campbell**
Chris Potter	**Brian Osborne**
Whispers	**Olive Greg**

First UK Transmission

Thursday, November 25th, 1976
4.45pm (ATV)

THE BRINGERS OF WONDER Part 1 Prod. No. 17

Screenplay by **Terence Feely** Directed by **Tom Clegg**

While piloting Eagle Ten, Koenig becomes irrational and unresponsive, eventually crashing the spacecraft near the Nuclear Waste Domes. Dragged unconscious from the wreckage, he is taken to Medical Center and hooked up to a cerebral wave machine which will electronically massage his brain, countering the effects of a severe concussion. Then a Superswift faster-than-light spacecraft arrives from Earth and the Alphans are reunited with their friends and relatives, including Verdeschi's brother Guido, Helena's mentor Dr. Shaw and Koenig's old flame Diana Morris. During the reunion, two of the new arrivals exert some form of influence over a medical orderly who attempts to kill Koenig, but he is rescued by Helena and Vincent. Koenig makes a complete recovery and is delighted to learn of the arrival of the Superswift, but when he joins the party in Command Center he sees the newcomers as hideous Plasma Aliens...

Notes

Author Terence Feely was commissioned to write SPACE:1999's only two-part story on the basis of his script for *New Adam New Eve*, which had greatly impressed both Gerry Anderson and Fred Freiberger. However, much of *The Bringers Of Wonder* was rewritten by Freiberger while Feely was away on holiday and the writer was very annoyed when he saw the changes on his return. In the original script, the true form of the Plasma Aliens was hidden from viewers until the end of the episode (what Koenig saw in Command Center would not have been seen on screen) when the pilot ship sets off for Earth. To combat Sandstrom, Maya originally turned herself into a python rather than a Kendo warrior. One of Maya's transformations is the Kreno creature from *The AB Chrysalis*, last seen in *The Beta Cloud* and painted blue for its appearance here. Stuart Damon (Guido) previously appeared as Parks in *Matter Of Life And Death*. Drewe Henley (Ehrlich) was also seen as Steve Maddox in UFO's *Conflict* episode and as Clark in the THE PROTECTORS episode *The Tiger And The Goat*.

Regular Cast

Cdr. John Koenig	**Martin Landau**
Dr. Helena Russell	**Barbara Bain**
Maya	**Catherine Schell**
Tony Verdeschi	**Tony Anholt**
Capt. Alan Carter	**Nick Tate**
Sandra Benes	**Zienia Merton**
Dr. Ben Vincent	**Jeffery Kissoon**
Operative Kate	**Sarah Bullen**
Operative Peter	**Robert Reeves**

Guest Cast

Diana Morris	**Toby Robins**
Guido Verdeschi	**Stuart Damon**
Jack Bartlett	**Jeremy Young**
Joe Ehrlich	**Drewe Henley**
Dr. Shaw	**Patrick Westwood**
Louisa	**Cher Cameron**
Ken Burdett	**Al Lampert**
Professor Hunter	**Billy J. Mitchell**
Sandstrom	**Earl Robinson**
Henry	**Robert Sheedy**
Peter Rockwell	**Nicholas Young**
Clive Kander	**Nick Hobbs**
Lizard Animal	**Albin Pahernik**
Space Animal	**Roy Scammel**
Kendo Warrior	**Okimitsu Fujii**
Plasma Voice	**David Jackson**

First UK Transmission

Thursday, August 4th, 1977
7.30pm (ATV)

THE BRINGERS OF WONDER Part 2 Prod. No. 18

Screenplay by **Terence Feely** Directed by **Tom Clegg**

Helena and Maya discover Dr. Shaw in Medical Center, unaware that they have just saved Koenig from being smothered by a Plasma Alien. When Koenig recovers consciousness, he tries to convince Helena and Maya that he has not gone mad, persuading Maya to undergo the cerebral wave machine treatment which enables her to see the visitors in their true form. Meanwhile Carter, Ehrlich and Bartlett apparently arrive back on Earth in the pilot ship but in reality, the trio have landed near the Nuclear Waste Domes and are being influenced by the Aliens to insert atomic fuel into the nuclear waste core. To find out why, Maya turns into one of the Aliens and learns that they thrive on radiation which has run out on their planet. Now starving, the Aliens intend to feed on the intense radiation that will result from the detonation of the waste dumps...

Notes

Although up to eight Plasma Aliens are seen at any one time, only three full costumes were made (from latex coated in grease) – the other five Aliens are illuminated flat cut-out photographs. The costume for the Laren creature that Maya transforms into on the lunar surface is revamped from the cloud creature costume from *The Beta Cloud*. In 1978, the two parts of this story were edited together to form the SPACE:1999 feature film *Destination Moonbase Alpha*, which was released theatrically in the UK and Europe.

Oops!

Helena's Alpha Log states that it is 2515 days since the Moon left Earth orbit, although part one was set 1912 days after Breakaway. (In the script, Helena gave the date as 1915 days after Breakaway for this part of the story, which would have made more sense.) The pilot ship is shown landing by the Nuclear Waste Domes, but viewers should see the Eagle landing there. When Helena looks at the monitor in Medical Center and still sees the pilot ship, she should be seeing it in New York, not by the Nuclear Waste Domes.

Regular Cast

Cdr. John Koenig	**Martin Landau**
Dr. Helena Russell	**Barbara Bain**
Maya	**Catherine Schell**
Tony Verdeschi	**Tony Anholt**
Capt. Alan Carter	**Nick Tate**
Sandra Benes	**Zienia Merton**
Dr. Ben Vincent	**Jeffery Kissoon**
Operative Kate	**Sarah Bullen**
Operative Peter	**Robert Reeves**
Guard	**Quentin Pierre**

Guest Cast

Diana Morris	**Toby Robins**
Guido Verdeschi	**Stuart Damon**
Jack Bartlett	**Jeremy Young**
Joe Ehrlich	**Drewe Henley**
Dr. Shaw	**Patrick Westwood**
Louisa	**Cher Cameron**
Ken Burdett	**Al Lampert**
Professor Hunter	**Billy J. Mitchell**
Sandstrom	**Earl Robinson**
Henry	**Robert Sheedy**
Peter Rockwell	**Nicholas Young**
Lizard Animal	**Albin Pahernik**
Plasma Voice	**David Jackson**

First UK Transmission

Thursday, August 11th, 1977
7.30pm (ATV)

THE LAMBDA FACTOR — Prod. No. 19

Screenplay by **Terrance Dicks** Directed by **Charles Crichton**

Alpha is plagued by petty disagreements and instrument malfunctions, but when medical technician Sally Martin dies in mysterious circumstances, Koenig suspects murder and questions Mark Sanders, Sally's ex-fiancé, and his new lover Carolyn Powell. However, Koenig's investigations are hampered by personal difficulties as he is troubled by the manifestations of two long-dead friends which appear when he tries to sleep. Helena conducts experiments to test the Alphans' powers of extra-sensory perception and discovers that latent paranormal abilities are being boosted by Lambda Variant waves transmitted from a strange space cloud. Then Sanders is found dead and Helena realises that the murderer is Carolyn, who has become psychotic under the influence of the space cloud. But Carolyn uses her psychic powers to take control of Command Center, forcing Maya to turn into a caterpillar and imprisoning her inside an airtight box...

Notes
In the shooting script, the events were dated 928 days since leaving Earth orbit (between *The Rules Of Luton* and *New Adam New Eve*) but this was changed to 2308 days after Breakaway (January 7th, 2006) in the finished episode. The events surrounding the deaths of Tessa and Sam on the Venus space station were previously mentioned in *The Exiles*. The chimpanzee that Maya is forced to transform into was an unpopular visitor to the Command Center set as it peed on the consoles and the smell lingered for weeks afterwards. Antony Stamboulieh (Crato) appeared as the Greek Protector Yanos in the THE PROTECTORS episodes *Brother Hood* and *One And One Makes One*.

Oops!
In-camera superimposition of Tessa and Sam using a half-silvered mirror results in their reversed appearance in some shots (their badges move to the opposite side of their uniforms).

Regular Cast

Cdr. John Koenig	**Martin Landau**
Dr. Helena Russell	**Barbara Bain**
Maya	**Catherine Schell**
Tony Verdeschi	**Tony Anholt**
Capt. Alan Carter	**Nick Tate**
Sandra Benes	**Zienia Merton**
Operative Peter	**Robert Reeves**

Guest Cast

Carolyn Powell	**Deborah Fallender**
Mark Sanders	**Jess Conrad**
George Crato	**Antony Stamboulieh**
Carl Renton	**Michael Walker**
Peter Garforth	**Gregory de Polnay**
Sally Martin	**Lydia Lisle**
Tessa	**Lucinda Curtis**
Sam	**Dallas Adams**
Operative	**Harry Fielder**
Maintenance Technician Voice	**Shane Rimmer**

First UK Transmission

Thursday, December 23rd, 1976
4.45pm (ATV)

THE SEANCE SPECTRE — Prod. No. 20

Screenplay by **Donald James** Directed by **Peter Medak**

So as not to raise false hopes that a weather belt the Alphans have named Tora might contain a habitable planet, Koenig places Command Center off limits to all but essential personnel. Greg Sanderson and his surface exploration team accuse Koenig of deliberately hiding the planet's existence because he fears losing control over Alpha. After an attempt to usurp control of Command Center ends with the quartet placing themselves in a state of autohypnosis, Helena diagnoses that Sanderson is suffering from greensickness, an extreme manifestation of tension resulting in hallucination and disorientation, so he is confined to Medical Center. Penetrating Tora in Eagle Four, Koenig and Maya discover a planet on a collision course with the Moon which threatens to destroy Alpha, but then Sanderson breaks out of Medical Center and engineers a malfunction in Main Computer, causing Eagle Four to crash-land on the planet...

Notes
The working title of this episode was 'The Mutiny' and Sanderson was originally written as 'Sandor'. In a scene filmed for the episode but deleted from the final edit, Maya teased Verdeschi and Carter by turning into a scantily clad black girl played by actress Venicia Day. Only the start of this scene, in which Verdeschi and Carter admire a photograph of Navy Rum model and actress Caroline Munro, remains in the episode. Ken Hutchison (Sanderson) previously appeared in THE PROTECTORS as Mark Jenner in *Burning Bush*. James Snell (Stevens) was previously seen in SPACE:1999 as Eagle pilot Cousteau in *Space Brain*.

Oops!
Actor Ken Hutchison is incorrectly credited as Ken 'Hutchinson' on the in-show titles. Barbara Bain fluffs her lines in a scene with Sanderson and Eva in Medical Center ("What we're dealing *here* with here is an extreme manifestation of tension...").

Regular Cast

Cdr. John Koenig	**Martin Landau**
Dr. Helena Russell	**Barbara Bain**
Maya	**Catherine Schell**
Tony Verdeschi	**Tony Anholt**
Capt. Alan Carter	**Nick Tate**
Sandra Benes	**Zienia Merton**
Operative Peter	**Robert Reeves**
Guard	**Quentin Pierre**

Guest Cast

Greg Sanderson	**Ken Hutchison**
Eva	**Carolyn Seymour**
Cernik	**Nigel Pegram**
Stevens	**James Snell**
Guards	**Christopher Asante**
	Harry Fielder / Terry Walsh
	Paul Weston
Maya Child	**Christine White**
	Candy Wilson

First UK Transmission

Thursday, August 18th, 1977
7.30pm (ATV)

DORZAK
Prod. No. 21

Screenplay by **Christopher Penfold** Directed by **Val Guest**

While Koenig is investigating a belt of asteroids in the North Quadrant, a Croton spaceship arrives on Alpha and its commander Sahala requests assistance, following an accident on board that has left one crew member dead and another injured. The ship is revealed to contain the Psychon philosopher Dorzak imprisoned in stasis. Sahala is ferrying him to exile on Thesalena, claiming that he arrived on their world seeking asylum and then incited the Norvahn people to violence after thousands of years of peace. Maya refuses to believe Sahala's story as she remembers Dorzak as a compassionate man, but Sahala tells how, during their journey, Dorzak used his mind power on her colleagues, Clea and Yesta. However, when Yesta recovers she is still under Dorzak's influence and accuses Sahala of Clea's murder. On this evidence, Verdeschi allows Maya to free Dorzak from stasis and the real murderer is on the loose in Alpha...

Notes
The script for this episode was structured to eliminate the involvement of Koenig thereby enabling it to be filmed in tandem with *Devil's Planet*. It is, therefore, the only episode of SPACE:1999 in which Martin Landau does not appear (other than in the opening titles). Christopher Penfold's original script was completely rewritten by Fred Freiberger. As portrayed by Sam Dastor, Dr. Ed Spencer was initially going to be called Ed 'Spandau'. Jill Townsend (Sahala) previously appeared as Monica Davies in the THE PROTECTORS episodes *WAM Part One* and *WAM Part Two*. She was suffering from appendicitis during filming, but refused to be admitted to hospital until all of her scenes were completed. Dorzak's costume was previously seen as the Psychon warrior's costume in *Space Warp*.

Oops!
The character of Sam Malcolm is listed as 'Ed' Malcolm (as he was named in the shooting script) on the end titles.

Regular Cast

Dr. Helena Russell	**Barbara Bain**
Maya	**Catherine Schell**
Tony Verdeschi	**Tony Anholt**
Capt. Alan Carter	**Nick Tate**
Yasko	**Yasuko Nagazumi**
Guard	**Quentin Pierre**

Guest Cast

Dorzak	**Lee Montague**
Sahala	**Jill Townsend**
Dr. Ed Spencer	**Sam Dastor**
Yesta	**Kathryn Leigh Scott**
Clea	**Seretta Wilson**
Sam Malcolm	**Richard Le Parmentier**
Guards	**Paul Jerricho / John Judd**

First UK Transmission
Thursday, August 25th, 1977
7.30pm (ATV)

DEVIL'S PLANET
Prod. No. 22

Screenplay by **Michael Winder** Directed by **Tom Clegg**

Responding to a distress signal from Alpha's East Quadrant, Koenig and medical rescue specialist Blake Maine journey in Eagle One to the planet Ellna, where they find that the entire population has been poisoned by a nerve-killing pathogen. Witnessing the arrival via matter transporter of a man dressed in overalls, the Alphans realise that the pathogen is still active when the man falls dead, although the Alphans appear to be immune. Detecting humanoid life-forms on Ellna's moon, Entra, Koenig and Maine are about to land when their Eagle suddenly goes out of control and crashes. Unhurt, they go to the aid of a man being chased by a group of women armed with whips, but Maine runs into a force-field and is vapourised while Koenig is captured and taken to a vast, spartan complex. There Koenig discovers that Entra is a penal colony for exiles from Ellna run by sadistic amazon guards, and he has become their latest prisoner!

Notes
Written and filmed as 'Devil's Moon', the script for this episode was structured to focus entirely on Koenig thereby enabling it to be filmed in tandem with *Dorzak*. Barbara Bain, Catherine Schell and Tony Anholt are only seen in footage from earlier episodes (*The Exiles*, *New Adam New Eve* and *The Bringers Of Wonder Part 1*) projected on the screen in the Security Ward on Entra. The script detailed additional library shots from *A Matter Of Balance* and *Journey To Where* to be seen on the screen. The role taken by new character Alibe was originally written for Sandra (or 'Sahn' as she was renamed for Year Two). Roy Marsden previously appeared as Alien Transport in *The Rules Of Luton*.

Oops!
Helena's Alpha Log states that it is 2306 days since the Moon left Earth orbit (January 5th, 2006) which conflicts with *The Lambda Factor*: Koenig is absent from Alpha for over three days here, yet he is back on the base by January 7th in the earlier episode.

Regular Cast

Cdr. John Koenig	**Martin Landau**
Dr. Helena Russell	**Barbara Bain**
Maya	**Catherine Schell**
Tony Verdeschi	**Tony Anholt**
Bill Fraser	**John Hug**
Operative Peter	**Robert Reeves**

Guest Cast

Elizia	**Hildegard Neil**
Crael	**Roy Marsden**
Dr. Ed Spencer	**Sam Dastor**
Alibe	**Alibe Parsons**
Interrogator	**Dora Reisser**
Sares / Controller	**Cassandra Harris**
Jelto	**Angus MacInnes**
Kinano	**Arthur White**
Blake Maine	**Michael Dickinson**
Hunted Man	**Del Baker**

First UK Transmission
Thursday, September 1st, 1977
7.30pm (ATV)

THE IMMUNITY SYNDROME Prod. No. 23

Screenplay by **Johnny Byrne** Directed by **Bob Brooks**

While surveying an Earth-type paradise planet in Alpha's West Quadrant, Verdeschi apparently goes mad and attacks Koenig, three members of the survey team are poisoned by previously harmless fruit and water, Eagle controls and commlocks become subject to corrosion and fall apart, and the Alphans find themselves stranded. Koenig realises that everything made of metal is disintegrating, although equipment made of plastic seems to be holding up. Discovering a mysterious structure with sophisticated molecular bonding, Carter locates an entrance powered by solar cells and, gaining access, he and Koenig find a holographic message from Zoran, the last survivor of an alien survey team. Zoran tells them that the planet is inhabited by an immortal being who only wishes to communicate with others, but the being's communication methods have killed all those that it has contacted...

Notes

The original script for this episode, titled 'The Face Of Eden', was written for the first season format and characters. In this early version, it was Koenig who went mad after making the initial contact with the lifeform on the planet, a creature named Kwali, and much of the rest of the story involved the other members of the survey team nursing Koenig back to mental health and encouraging him to remember what happened to him. In the revised script written by Fred Freiberger, Jerry Travis was written as 'Yuri Salkov'. Helena's psychological profile reveals Verdeschi's biographical details, but the full text of the final monitor page is not visible on screen. It reads: "Graduated B.A. Hons University of Rome 1990, Ph.D Cambridge England 1993, Commissioned into Space Service 1994." According to Helena's Alpha Log (dated 2310 days after leaving Earth orbit), the unnamed planet was discovered two days ago, which would place the discovery during the events of *The Lambda Factor* (dated 2308 days after leaving Earth orbit).

Regular Cast

Cdr. John Koenig	**Martin Landau**
Dr. Helena Russell	**Barbara Bain**
Maya	**Catherine Schell**
Tony Verdeschi	**Tony Anholt**
Capt. Alan Carter	**Nick Tate**
Bill Fraser	**John Hug**
Operative Peter	**Robert Reeves**
Guard	**Quentin Pierre**

Guest Cast

Zoran	**Nadim Sawalha**
Jerry Travis	**Karl Held**
Dr. Ed Spencer	**Sam Dastor**
Alibe	**Alibe Parsons**
Voice	**Hal Galili**
Les Johnson	**Walter McMonagle**
Joe Lustig	**Roy Boyd**
Guard	**Jack Klaff**
Survey Team Member	**Harry Fielder**

First UK Transmission

Saturday, October 29th, 1977
11.00am (LWT)

THE DORCONS Prod. No. 24

Screenplay by **Johnny Byrne** Directed by **Tom Clegg**

A spacecraft radiating an intense energy field scans the Command Center personnel, focusing on Maya and causing her to pass out. The craft reforms and when Maya recovers, she recognises it as a Dorcon spaceship, crewed by people who have hounded the Psychons for centuries, stealing their brain stems to achieve immortality. Now, the Dorcon leader Archon sets his sights on Maya, threatening Alpha with destruction unless Koenig gives her up. Koenig refuses and Alpha is subjected to a devastating barrage by the Dorcons, whose use of a Meson Converter to transform matter and energy makes them invincible. Transporting to Alpha, Consul Varda captures Maya and takes her back to the Dorcon ship, but Koenig leaps into the transporter beam and, arriving on the ship, is immediately thrown into a cell. However, the prospect of the Archon's immortality displeases his heir Malic, who enlists Koenig's aid in his treacherous plans...

Notes

In Johnny Byrne's original script for this episode, titled 'Return Of The Dorcons', it was suggested that Archon be pronounced 'Arch-on' not 'Ark-on' so as to avoid confusion with *The Mark Of Archanon* (this suggestion was removed from the final version of the script as rewritten by Fred Freiberger). The Archon's throne previously belonged to Arra in *Collision Course* before becoming Companion's bed in *The Infernal Machine*. Patrick Troughton (Archon) was previously seen as Bela Karoleon in the THE PROTECTORS episode *Brother Hood*. Laurence Harrington was previously seen in the series as Jackson in *Journey To Where* (arguably, he is playing the same character here, named either Jackson Stewart or Stewart Jackson). Byrne's earlier version of the script featured different dialogue between the members of the regular cast in the closing scene and, recognising that this would be the series' final episode, ended with the following speech from Koenig: "What's in the past has gone... fate has played us some strange hands but we've won through in the end. As for the future... that starts right here and now."

Regular Cast

Cdr. John Koenig	**Martin Landau**
Dr. Helena Russell	**Barbara Bain**
Maya	**Catherine Schell**
Tony Verdeschi	**Tony Anholt**
Capt. Alan Carter	**Nick Tate**
Guard	**Quentin Pierre**

Guest Cast

Archon	**Patrick Troughton**
Consul Varda	**Ann Firbank**
Malic	**Gerry Sundquist**
Alibe	**Alibe Parsons**
Stewart	**Laurence Harrington**
1st Dorcon Operative	**Kevan Sheehan**
1st Dorcon Soldier	**Michael Halsey**
Command Center Alphan	**Hamish Patrick**
Female Medical Officer	**Hazel McBride**
Guards	**Peter Brayham**
	Frank Henson
Alphan	**Cliff Digging**
Dorcon Soldiers	**Del Baker / Les White**
Maya Creature	**Roy Scammell**

First UK Transmission

Saturday, November 12th, 1977
11.00am (LWT)

THE INDEPENDENT TELEVISION SERIES

1982-1998

TERRAHAWKS
DICK SPANNER
SPACE PRECINCT
LAVENDER CASTLE

TERRAHAWKS

Format

By the end of the second decade of the 21st century, mankind has developed technology capable of interstellar travel, bringing the Earth into contact with a variety of alien civilisations for the first time. However, in anticipation that certain alien contacts might prove hostile, in 2014 the United Nations High Command authorised the creation of the Terrahawks Earth Defence Squadron, an elite international fighting force operating from the Hawknest top-secret base situated beneath the White House somewhere in South America. The force saw action for the first time during a devastating alien attack in 2017, but following the occupation of Mars in 2020 by androids from the planet Guk, the Terrahawks have proved an invaluable asset in defending the Earth from the witch-like android commander Zelda and her collection of hideous monsters.

Led by experienced military commander Dr. Tiger Ninestein, one of nine identical clones of Professor Gerhard Stein, the Terrahawks maintain a fleet of sophisticated weaponry and vehicles to combat the new Martians:

Battlehawk, a heavy transporter and mass deployment unit piloted by Captain Mary Falconer. With a maximum velocity of Mach 5 at 78,000 feet, Battlehawk carries a crew of 100 Zeroids (spherical robot soldiers with unique personalities and emotions) and the Battletank ground attack vehicle operated by Megazoid robots. The vehicle incorporates the Terrahawk, a detachable flight deck that operates as a mobile command control craft.

Hawkwing, an atmospheric interceptor aircraft armed with fireflash particle accelerators, stingwing missiles and a high energy laser cannon. Piloted by Captain Kate Kestrel and Lieutenant Hawkeye, Hawkwing flies at Mach 7 and separates into two units, the wing and the egg, that can be flown independently.

Spacehawk, an advanced early warning and first line defence space station positioned in geostationary orbit. Under the command of Lieutenant Hiro, the station is armed with 100 Space Zeroids and doubles as an interplanetary spacecraft. Personnel and supplies are ferried to Spacehawk from Hawknest aboard the Treehawk space shuttle craft.

Production

In 1977, Gerry Anderson and Reg Hill were approached by Banjiro Uemara, head of Tohoku Shinsha, the Japanese arm of ITC, to create a new animated series for Japanese television. The development process for this series, entitled 'Thunderhawks', resulted in two different sets of outlines, one distinctly English with vehicle designs by Hill, and the other designed by Yoshikazu Yasuhiko in the established Japanese anime style. Although the project eventually collapsed due to network rescheduling, Uemara revamped the Japanese proposal and designs in 1981 as TECHNOVOYAGER, a short-lived animated series which later aired in America and the UK as THUNDERBIRDS 2086.

Meanwhile, Anderson had entered into a business partnership with financial expert Christopher Burr to form Anderburr Pictures. Changes in personnel at ITC had left Anderson without Lew Grade's financial backing for his productions after the cancellation of SPACE:1999, but with Burr's assistance he secured finance from London Weekend Television and Time-Life in America to rework the British 'Thunderhawks' proposal as a puppet production entitled TERRAHAWKS, with new vehicle designs by novice visual effects director Steven Begg and model-maker Philip Rae.

On a budget of £5 million for 26 episodes, filming began on January 10th, 1983 at Bray Studios near Windsor in Berkshire following six months of pre-production work. In marked contrast to the marionettes of Anderson's earlier Supermarionation productions, the characters for TERRAHAWKS were created as sophisticated hand puppets which stood just under three feet tall and featured rubber faces, remote-controlled eyes and underneath control systems. This new puppetry process was dubbed Supermacromation.

Although the series was not an immediate success when it premiered on British television in September 1983, it was soon being watched by more than nine million viewers. As a result, a further 13 episodes were jointly financed by London Weekend Television, Japan's Asahi Tsushin Advertising Agency and Anderburr Pictures at a cost of £1.4 million. Filming was finally completed on the last of these in August 1984.

Main Characters

Dr. Tiger Ninestein
Terrahawks commander, Terrahawk pilot and one of nine clones of Professor Gerhard Stein

Captain Mary Falconer
British astrophysicist, Battlehawk pilot and Groundhawk operator

Sergeant Major Zero
Welsh-accented commander of the Terrahawks' Zeroid forces

Captain Kate Kestrel
(Katherine Westley) Pilot of Hawkwing egg section and international recording artist

Lieutenant Hiro
Japanese technology expert, pilot of Treehawk and Spacehawk operator

Lieutenant Hawkeye
(Hedley Howard Henderson) Pilot of Hawkwing wing section, formerly an Olympic Decathlete

Space Sergeant 101
Camp-voiced commander of the Terrahawks' Space Zeroid forces

Hudson
Heuristic Universal Driver with Sensory and Orbital Navigation fitted into a vintage 1985 Rolls-Royce

Zelda
Imperial Queen of planet Guk, an evil android intent on the domination and slavery of humanoids

Yung-Star
Zelda's incompetent android son

Cy-Star
Zelda's android sister

Dix-Huit
French-accented Zeroid

Zeroid 21
Stuttering American-accented Zeroid

Colonel Johnson
NASA liaison

Stewart 'Stew' Dapples
Anderburr Records A&R man

Chic King
Anderburr Records producer

Zeroid 55
Zeroid personal assistant to Kate Kestrel who always speaks in rhyme

Sram
Master of Felony with a devastating thunder-roar

Moid
Master of Infinite Disguise

Yuri the Space Bear
Metal-bending Orsino Galactica

Sheriff Cy Bull
Sheriff of Badwater County

Deputy Kilroy
Deputy sheriff of Badwater County

It-Star
Cy-Star's devious android offspring

Episode Titles

(Listed in production order)

1. **Expect The Unexpected**
2. **Expect The Unexpected Part 2**
3. **Gold**
4. **Thunder-Roar**
5. **Close Call**
6. **From Here To Infinity**
7. **Space Samurai**
8. **The Sporilla**
9. **Happy Madeday**
10. **Gunfight At Oaky's Corral**
11. **The Ugliest Monster Of All**
12. **The Gun**
13. **Thunder Path**
14. **Mind Monster**
15. **To Catch A Tiger**
16. **The Midas Touch**
17. **Operation S.A.S.**
18. **Ten Top Pop**
19. **Unseen Menace**
20. **A Christmas Miracle**
21. **Midnight Blue**
22. **Play It Again, Sram**
23. **My Kingdom For A Zeaf**
24. **Zero's Finest Hour**
25. **The Ultimate Menace**
26. **Ma's Monsters**
27. **Two For The Price Of One**
28. **Child's Play**
29. **Jolly Roger One**
30. **Runaway**
31. **First Strike**
32. **Terratomb**
33. **Doppelganger**
34. **Cry UFO**
35. **Space Cyclops**
36. **Timewarp**
37. **Space Giant**
38. **Cold Finger**
39. **Operation Zero**

Episode Running Time

25 minutes approx.

PRODUCTION CREDITS

Produced by **Gerry Anderson** & **Christopher Burr**
Series Creator **Gerry Anderson**
Associate Producer **Bob Bell**
Production Manager **Donald Toms** *(1-9)*
Derek Whitehurst *(10-26)*
Special Effects Director **Steven Begg**
Art Director **Gary Tomkins**
Property Master **Peter Holmes** *(1-26)*
First Assistant Director
Derek Whitehurst *(1-9)*
Bernard Hanson *(10-26)*
Lighting Cameramen **Harry Oakes B.S.C.**
Paddy Seale
Supervising Editor **Alan Killick**
Camera Operators **E. Michael Anderson** *(1-18, 20-39)*
Brian Ellis *(19)*
David Lawrence
Focus **Jonathan Earp** *(1-33)*
Fiona Cunningham-Reid *(1-5)*
Nick Wilson *(6-8)*
Alan Gatward *(9, 10, 19)*
Brian Ellis *(11-18, 20-39)*
Paul Cave *(34-37)*
Lee Manders *(38, 39)*
Special Effects Supervisor *(1-26)* / Pyrotechnics Supervisor *(27-39)*
Malcolm King
Special Effects Technicians **Gus Ramsden** *(1-13, 17)*
Peter Farr *(1-13, 17)*
Ross King
Terry Adlam *(14-16, 18-39)*
Editor **Alan Killick**
(1, 2, 5, 9, 11, 13, 15, 17, 20, 21, 23, 25-27, 29, 31, 33, 35, 37, 39)
Tony Lenny *(3, 4, 6)*
Desmond Saunders *(7)*
Tony Hunt
(8, 10, 12, 14, 16, 18, 19, 22, 24, 28, 30, 32, 34, 36, 38)
Dubbing Editor **Alan Willis** *(1, 2, 4-14)*
Brian Lintern *(3, 16-39)*, **Max Hoskins** *(15)*
Dialogue Editor **Roy Hyde** *(3, 16-26)*
Brian Lintern *(13-15)*
Video Game & Titles by **Kevin Davies**
Production Accountant **Ernie Shepherd** *(1-26)*
HOD Model Workshop **Nick Finlayson** *(1-26)*
Simon Deering *(27-39)*
'Hudson' Designed & Built by
Space Models Ltd
Chief Puppeteer **Christine Glanville**
Puppet Maker **Richard Gregory**
Aliens by **Susan Moore**
Puppeteers **Jan Kendall**, **Judy Preece**
Zena Relph *(1-26)*, **Tina Werts**
Wardrobe **Zena Relph** *(27-39)*
Voices **Denise Bryer**, **Windsor Davies**
Jeremy Hitchin, **Anne Ridler**, **Ben Stevens**

Music Composed & Performed by
Richard Harvey
Music Sound Engineer **Steven Rance**
Additional Music Composed by
Gerry Anderson & **Christopher Burr**
Music Published by **Terrahawks Ltd**
Dialogue Recording by *(1-21)* / Dialogue Recording & Re-Recording *(27-39)*
Adam Francis *(1-35)*
Stewart Eales *(27-39)*
Anderburr Recording Studios *(22-26)*
Anderburr Studios, Bray *(27-39)*
Re-Recording **Trevor Pyke** *(1-14, 16-21)*
Ian Turner *(15)*
Kate's Songs Sung by **Moya Griffiths**
'I've Got The Power' *(2, 4, 12, 18, 33)*
'Be My Star Tonight' *(13, 29, 35, 38)*
'It's So Easy' *(14, 16*, 24*)*
'Electra City' *(15, 20)*
'I Won't Let You Hold Me (Responsible)' *(16, 28)*
'Faster Than The Speed Of Love' *(18, 31)*
'I Believe In Love This Christmas' *(20)*
'Don't Take My Heart' *(27, 29)*
Composed by **Richard Myhill**
(2, 4, 12-16, 18, 20, 24, 27-29, 31, 33, 35, 38)*
'I Tune In To You' Composed by
David Barnes & **John Howard** *(11, 12)*
'Need You Tonight' Composed by
David Clifton *(17)*
'You're The One' Composed by
Vicky Watson *(19)*
'S.O.S.' Composed by
Lionel Robinson & **Harry Robinson**
(21, 22, 32, 34)
'Zelda Rap' Composed by **Adam Francis** *(22)*
'Fighting For A Phone Box' Composed by
Ray Russell *(23, 37)*
'Silver Blue Roller' Composed by
Tony Lyons & **Gordon Reaney** *(24, 34)*
'Living In The 21st Century' Composed by
Lionel Robinson & **Harry Robinson**
(26, 30, 35, 36)*
Production Secretary **Mary Anderson***
Art Assistants **Mark Harris***
Simon Melrose*
Assistant Editors **Paul Conway***
Peter Culverwell*
Assistant Accountant **Sarah Robins***
Models **Peter Bohanna***, **Simon Deering***
John Lee*, **Peter Tilbe***, **Ben Tuszynski***
Steven Woodcock*
Miniature Props Buyer **Kaye Moss***
TERRAHAWKS Filmed at Bray Studios, England
With Acknowledgements to
Lloyd Evans, **Yoji Yamamoto** *(1-26)*,
Asatsu Inc. (27-39), **Rolls-Royce Motors Ltd**,
Pearce Studios Computer Graphics
Produced by Anderson Burr Pictures in Association with London Weekend Television

* uncredited

EXPECT THE UNEXPECTED Prod. No. 01a

Written by **Gerry Anderson** Directed by **Alan Pattillo**

Alien invaders destroy a NASA research station on Mars before setting up their own base on the planet. At Hawknest, the Terrahawks prepare to defend Earth when an energy source is detected approaching the planet, but the source evades the Zeroid defences aboard Spacehawk so Tiger dispatches Kate and Hawkeye in Hawkwing to intercept it as it enters the atmosphere. However, they are unable to make visual contact with the source and when Hawkeye opens fire, he hits nothing. Sergeant Major Zero tracks the source to a landing site 100 miles north of Bangkok so Battlehawk heads for the danger zone...

Notes

The end titles of this episode feature the series' only unique game of nought and crosses. It is also the only game in which the expressions on the 'faces' of the Zeroids and Cubes change as the game progresses.

Oops!

Mary asks Zero to load 100 of his 'men' aboard Battlehawk, but only 48 Zeroids are seen boarding from the Zeroid Bay.

Regular Voice Cast

Dr. Tiger Ninestein	**Jeremy Hitchin**
Cpt. Mary Falconer	**Denise Bryer**
Sgt. Major Zero	**Windsor Davies**
Cpt. Kate Kestrel	**Anne Ridler**
Lt. Hiro	**Jeremy Hitchin**
Lt. Hawkeye	**Jeremy Hitchin**
Space Sgt. 101	**Ben Stevens**
Zelda	**Denise Bryer**

Guest Voice Cast

NASA Mars Expedition	**Anne Ridler**
Zeroid 13	**Ben Stevens**

First UK Transmission

Saturday, October 8th, 1983
10.00am (Central)

EXPECT THE UNEXPECTED Part 2 Prod. No. 01b

Written by **Gerry Anderson** Directed by **Alan Pattillo**

101's Zeroids completely destroy Zelda's ship, Mary is released from her paralysis and Tiger reappears on board Terrahawk. He explains to Mary that he had a theory that if the ship was destroyed, Zelda's power to hold him would also be destroyed. Back at Hawknest, the Terrahawks celebrate their success with a party, but then Hiro calls from Spacehawk to warn that Zelda is returning to Earth in her Hub ship. Claiming to be on a goodwill mission bringing a gift from her people, Zelda requests safe passage to Earth. Prepared to give her the benefit of the doubt, Tiger and Mary set off for the rendezvous point in Battlehawk, while Zelda prepares her 'gift' – a horde of Cubes...

Notes

During production, both parts of *Expect The Unexpected* were given the same production number and the subsequent 24 episodes of the first production block were numbered from 2 (*Gold*) to 25 (*Ma's Monsters*). The closing scenes of this second part introduce Sram, Lord of Felony and are intended to lead into *Thunder-Roar*. Kate's song 'I've Got The Power', credited on the end titles, is not actually sung by Kate during the episode: it is performed only as an instrumental at the White House party.

Regular Voice Cast

Dr. Tiger Ninestein	**Jeremy Hitchin**
Cpt. Mary Falconer	**Denise Bryer**
Sgt. Major Zero	**Windsor Davies**
Cpt. Kate Kestrel	**Anne Ridler**
Lt. Hiro	**Jeremy Hitchin**
Lt. Hawkeye	**Jeremy Hitchin**
Space Sgt. 101	**Ben Stevens**
Hudson	**Ben Stevens**
Zelda	**Denise Bryer**

Guest Voice Cast

Narrator	**Ben Stevens**
Zeroid 35	**Ben Stevens**

First UK Transmission

Saturday, October 15th, 1983
10.00am (Central)

GOLD Prod. No. 02

Written by **Cubby Dreistein** Directed by **Desmond Saunders**

A meteorite enters Earth's atmosphere, inexplicably changing course to fall on New York. Kate and Hawkeye intercept the meteorite in Hawkwing and deflect it from its course so that it lands in the desert. Believing that the meteor may not be a natural phenomenon, Tiger sends Zero and Zeroid 21 into the impact crater to investigate. There, 21 discovers a huge gold nugget which he believes is the humans' God and, anticipating a promotion, Zero takes it back to Hawknest without Tiger's knowledge. When the two Zeroids proudly display the nugget in the lounge for Tiger, Mary and Kate, Tiger suddenly realises that it is a bomb that could destroy Hawknest at any moment!

Notes

Although filmed third, this episode was intended to be seen as episode four, as on its original transmission in Japan on April 23rd, 1985. In the UK however, *Gold* was held back to air as the final episode of the original broadcast run, so that viewers apparently saw the death of the Ninestein who had appeared in all of the previous 38 episodes, rather than just the Ninestein seen in both parts of *Expect The Unexpected* and *Thunder-Roar*. The episode title appears on screen as 'G O D' with the 'L' captioned as an inserted letter.

Regular Voice Cast

Dr. Tiger Ninestein	**Jeremy Hitchin**
Cpt. Mary Falconer	**Denise Bryer**
Sgt. Major Zero	**Windsor Davies**
Cpt. Kate Kestrel	**Anne Ridler**
Lt. Hiro	**Jeremy Hitchin**
Lt. Hawkeye	**Jeremy Hitchin**
Space Sgt. 101	**Ben Stevens**
Hudson	**Ben Stevens**
Zelda	**Denise Bryer**
Yung-Star	**Ben Stevens**
Cy-Star	**Anne Ridler**
Zeroid 21	**Ben Stevens**

Guest Voice Cast

TIM	**Ben Stevens**

First UK Transmission

Saturday, July 26th, 1986
11.30am (ITV Network)

THUNDER-ROAR — Prod. No. 03

Written by **Cubby Dreistein** Directed by **Alan Pattillo**

Hiro tracks an unarmed alien ship piloted by Sram approaching Earth, but as 101's Zeroids open fire on it, Sram's thunder-roar rocks Spacehawk, lifting it 45° and spoiling the Zeroids' aim. Kate and Hawkeye race to intercept the craft but the thunder-roar sends Hawkwing spiralling out of control. Kate takes Hawkwing in again and Hawkeye opens fire, disabling Sram's ship and bringing it crashing down into the desert. Tiger heads for the crash site in Battlehawk and drops the Battletank to examine the wreckage, but Sram has disappeared. Then Tiger discovers a trail of green blood leading to a cave nearby...

Notes

Although filmed fourth, this episode was intended to be seen as episode three and follows on directly from the end of *Expect The Unexpected Part 2. Thunder-Roar* introduces Zelda's son Yung-Star, although he had already appeared in *Gold*. Sram appears to die at the end of this episode, but is alive and well again when he reappears in *Thunder Path*.

Oops!

Zelda states that her powers are exhausted, but then uses them to reclaim Sram's ship.

Regular Voice Cast

Dr. Tiger Ninestein	**Jeremy Hitchin**
Cpt. Mary Falconer	**Denise Bryer**
Sgt. Major Zero	**Windsor Davies**
Cpt. Kate Kestrel	**Anne Ridler**
Lt. Hiro	**Jeremy Hitchin**
Lt. Hawkeye	**Jeremy Hitchin**
Space Sgt. 101	**Ben Stevens**
Zelda	**Denise Bryer**
Yung-Star	**Ben Stevens**

Guest Voice Cast

Sram	**Ben Stevens**
TIM	**Ben Stevens**

First UK Transmission

Saturday, October 22nd, 1983
10.00am (Central)

CLOSE CALL — Prod. No. 04

Written by **Cubby Dreistein** Directed by **Desmond Saunders**

After WNTV reporter Mark Darrel promises to expose the Terrahawks operation on live television, he is visited in his country cottage by Zelda and Yung-Star, who offer him to play an active role in a plan that will reveal the secrets of the Terrahawks. Shortly after, Tiger and Mary set off in Battlehawk to rendezvous with the remote-driven supply Overlander, but with the help of one of Zelda's cubes, Darrel halts the vehicle, climbs aboard and alters its course. When Battlehawk arrives at the rendezvous point, Darrel drives the Overlander directly at the Terrahawks' ship and attempts to ram it!

Notes

Colonel Johnson is named in the script for *Close Call*, but not named on screen until *From Here To Infinity*. Cubby Dreistein is a pseudonym for script-writer Tony Barwick.

Oops!

After the commercial break, the Overlander is seen knocking a boulder from a ridge as it passes, and as the boulder falls away, the prod used to push it off the model set can be seen moving back into place. The Security Zeroid is unnumbered.

Regular Voice Cast

Dr. Tiger Ninestein	**Jeremy Hitchin**
Cpt. Mary Falconer	**Denise Bryer**
Sgt. Major Zero	**Windsor Davies**
Lt. Hiro	**Jeremy Hitchin**
Space Sgt. 101	**Ben Stevens**
Hudson	**Ben Stevens**
Zelda	**Denise Bryer**
Yung-Star	**Ben Stevens**
Colonel Johnson	**Jeremy Hitchin**

Guest Voice Cast

Mark Darrel	**Ben Stevens**
WNTV Announcer	**Jeremy Hitchin**
Space Control	**Ben Stevens**
Security Zeroid	**Ben Stevens**

First UK Transmission

Saturday, November 12th, 1983
10.00am (Central)

FROM HERE TO INFINITY — Prod. No. 05

Written by **Katz Stein** Directed by **Alan Pattillo**

When Space Probe Alpha mysteriously returns to Earth after 21 years, Colonel Johnson assigns the Terrahawks to take charge of the tricky salvage operation and prevent the Probe's Mark 24 Nuclear Rocket from contaminating the atmosphere during re-entry. On board Spacehawk, Tiger plans to convert the Probe into a re-entry vehicle by using a remote-controlled Delta Wing to control the Probe's flight to Hawknest. Zero and 101 take charge of the Delta Wing and Zero boards the Probe to install a computer guidance system, but once the Probe has been set on course, Zero discovers that Zelda has converted the Probe into a gravity-triggered bomb which will destroy Hawknest!

Notes

Space Probe Alpha, launched in 1999, is named in reference to Moonbase Alpha in SPACE:1999. 'Space Probe 1999' was an early working title for that series. *From Here To Infinity* formally introduces Cy-Star as Zelda's sister, although she had already appeared in *Gold*. Kate composes a piece of music titled 'Lift Off' which turns out to be the Treehawk launch theme when she plays it on her synthesiser. Katz Stein is a pseudonym for script-writer Donald James.

Regular Voice Cast

Dr. Tiger Ninestein	**Jeremy Hitchin**
Cpt. Mary Falconer	**Denise Bryer**
Sgt. Major Zero	**Windsor Davies**
Cpt. Kate Kestrel	**Anne Ridler**
Lt. Hiro	**Jeremy Hitchin**
Lt. Hawkeye	**Jeremy Hitchin**
Space Sgt. 101	**Ben Stevens**
Hudson	**Ben Stevens**
Zelda	**Denise Bryer**
Yung-Star	**Ben Stevens**
Cy-Star	**Anne Ridler**
Colonel Johnson	**Jeremy Hitchin**

Guest Voice Cast

Helijet Pilot	**Ben Stevens**

First UK Transmission

Saturday, December 10th, 1983
10.00am (Central)

SPACE SAMURAI — Prod. No. 06

Written by **Cubby Dreistein** Directed by **Desmond Saunders**

For 36 hours, Spacehawk has been under attack by wave after wave of alien missiles, but Kate confirms that the missiles are too small to be effective against the Terrahawk ship. The space samurai Tamura has agreed to help Zelda in her latest plan, believing that it will bring peace, so he telepathically contacts Hiro, introducing himself as an emissary and requesting a meeting with Tiger. Spacehawk rendezvouses with Tamura's starcruiser *Ishimo* and Tamura beams aboard to explain that he wishes to open negotiations between Tiger and Zelda. Tiger agrees to meet with Zelda, but only on his own terms...

Notes

Tony Barwick's script for this episode erroneously featured Zelda describing Yung-Star as her brother. In a scene deleted from the script, Hiro tells Ninestein that his tranquillity is like the first flush of cherry blossom, and in return, Ninestein tells Hiro that he is like 20-year-old scotch – a rare spirit. Although *Space Samurai* was produced early in the series' first production block, the episode was screened in the UK as part of the third season in 1986, by which time it had already been broadcast in the USA (on January 10th, 1985) and Japan (on July 16th, 1985).

Regular Voice Cast	
Dr. Tiger Ninestein	**Jeremy Hitchin**
Cpt. Mary Falconer	**Denise Bryer**
Sgt. Major Zero	**Windsor Davies**
Cpt. Kate Kestrel	**Anne Ridler**
Lt. Hiro	**Jeremy Hitchin**
Space Sgt. 101	**Ben Stevens**
Zelda	**Denise Bryer**
Yung-Star	**Ben Stevens**
Cy-Star	**Anne Ridler**

Guest Voice Cast	
Tamura	**Ben Stevens**

First UK Transmission

Saturday, June 28th, 1986
11.30am (ITV Network)

THE SPORILLA — Prod. No. 07

Written by **Leo Pardstein** Directed by **Tony Bell**

Zelda releases a ferocious sporilla from cryogenic slumber, controlling it with a device that she has developed. Penetrating the Terrahawk tracker station on Callisto, Zelda destroys a vital piece of equipment there, leading Tiger and Kate to investigate with Zero and Zeroid 55 when 101 notices that the tracker station has gone off line. Tiger and Kate are puzzled to find that Zelda's sabotage is only minimal when she could have destroyed the whole station, but just as Tiger realises that they have been deliberately drawn into a trap, the two Zeroids discover a set of massive footprints on the corridor floor...

Notes

Leo Pardstein is a pseudonym for script-writer Donald James. 101's remark about having another argument with Zero over which of them is in command on Spacehawk is a direct reference to James's earlier script for *From Here To Infinity*. First time director Tony Bell is the son of associate producer Bob Bell. Although *The Sporilla* was produced early in the series' first production block, the episode was screened in the UK as part of the third season in 1986, by which time it had already been broadcast in the USA (on January 4th, 1985) and Japan (on May 14th, 1985).

Regular Voice Cast	
Dr. Tiger Ninestein	**Jeremy Hitchin**
Cpt. Mary Falconer	**Denise Bryer**
Sgt. Major Zero	**Windsor Davies**
Cpt. Kate Kestrel	**Anne Ridler**
Lt. Hiro	**Jeremy Hitchin**
Space Sgt. 101	**Ben Stevens**
Zelda	**Denise Bryer**
Yung-Star	**Ben Stevens**
Cy-Star	**Anne Ridler**
Zeroid 55	**Ben Stevens**

Guest Voice Cast	
Sporilla	**Ben Stevens**

First UK Transmission

Saturday, July 19th, 1986
11.30am (ITV Network)

HAPPY MADEDAY — Prod. No. 08

Written by **Kit Tenstein** Directed by **Tony Lenny**

On Mars, Zelda introduces Yung-Star and Cy-Star to Moid, Master of Infinite Disguise, who has an incredible talent for mimicry. Shortly after, as Hiro travels to Spacehawk in Treehawk, 101 tracks a Zeaf hiding in the tail of Bell's Comet. The Zeaf opens fire on Treehawk and damages the craft, but Hiro manages to crash-land in an ice field. He takes shelter in a cave, where Moid appears masquerading as Tiger and injects the Lieutenant with a knockout drug. When Hawkeye and Kate arrive to take Hiro back to Hawknest, they are unaware that the man they have rescued is actually Moid in disguise...

Notes

Kit Tenstein and all subsequent writer credits ending in 'stein' are pseudonyms for script-writer Tony Barwick. Bell's Comet is named after series associate producer Bob Bell. The episode is set on Zero's fourth made-day, which would be October 2022 according to the character's official biography in the series' promotional information. Additional scenes deleted from the script featured Tiger and Hiro leaving the ice fields: Hiro cannot understand how Tiger arrived there until the doctor reveals that Hudson has been using his chameleon function to make the car appear invisible against the snow.

Regular Voice Cast	
Dr. Tiger Ninestein	**Jeremy Hitchin**
Cpt. Mary Falconer	**Denise Bryer**
Sgt. Major Zero	**Windsor Davies**
Cpt. Kate Kestrel	**Anne Ridler**
Lt. Hiro	**Jeremy Hitchin**
Lt. Hawkeye	**Jeremy Hitchin**
Space Sgt. 101	**Ben Stevens**
Zelda	**Denise Bryer**
Yung-Star	**Ben Stevens**
Cy-Star	**Anne Ridler**
Moid	**Ben Stevens**

First UK Transmission

Saturday, October 29th, 1983
10.00am (Central)

GUNFIGHT AT OAKY'S CORRAL — Prod. No. 09

Written by **T.I. Gerstein** Directed by **Tony Bell**

After a battle in the desert of Badwater County against six of Zelda's Cubes, Tiger orders the remains of the Cubes to be collected for examination back at Hawknest. However, the pieces only account for five Cubes, so Tiger returns to Badwater in Battlehawk to find out what has become of the missing Cube. That evening, Badwater's Sheriff Cy Bull receives a telephone call from hillbilly Sam Oaky, who lives in a remote cabin on the edge of the desert. Oaky has found something strange in the desert so Bull agrees to take a look at it in the morning, but Oaky's discovery is the missing Cube and when it is accidentally reactivated, it presents Zelda with an opportunity to take control of the hillbilly and use him to lay a trap for Tiger...

Notes

This episode introduces the Badwater County Police Department in the form of Sheriff Cy Bull and Deputy Kilroy, although the latter is only heard speaking from his patrol car and is not seen on screen here. Both characters are later seen in the episodes *Child's Play*, *Runaway* and *Cry UFO*. The animated noughts and crosses game on the end titles of this episode is also seen at the end of *Zero's Finest Hour* and *Space Giant*.

Regular Voice Cast

Dr. Tiger Ninestein	**Jeremy Hitchin**
Cpt. Mary Falconer	**Denise Bryer**
Sgt. Major Zero	**Windsor Davies**
Lt. Hiro	**Jeremy Hitchin**
Hudson	**Ben Stevens**
Zelda	**Denise Bryer**
Yung-Star	**Ben Stevens**
Cy-Star	**Anne Ridler**
Zeroid 21	**Ben Stevens**
Sheriff Cy Bull	**Jeremy Hitchin**
Deputy Kilroy	**Ben Stevens**

Guest Voice Cast

Sam Oaky	**Ben Stevens**
Billie-Jean Hollins	**Anne Ridler**

First UK Transmission

Saturday, November 26th, 1983
10.00am (Central)

THE UGLIEST MONSTER OF ALL — Prod. No. 10

Written by **P.U. Mastein** Directed by **Tony Lenny**

On Mars, Zelda releases Yuri the Space Bear, a monster with the appearance of a cuddly teddy bear, from cryogenic suspension and sends him to Earth aboard a space capsule. When the capsule is detected approaching Earth, Tiger gives Hiro orders to destroy it, but 101 detects a sound coming from inside so the capsule is brought aboard Spacehawk. When Yuri is discovered he is taken to Hawknest where Kate identifies him as an Orsino Galactica. Mary is captivated by the creature but Tiger assigns Hawkeye and Hudson to take Yuri to the zoological institute. However, Yuri uses his strange metal-bending powers to jam the garage doors and then causes Hudson to have a seizure...

Notes

This is the first episode in which Kate Kestrel is seen singing one of her songs as she performs 'I Tune In To You' to entertain Yuri at Hawknest. Yuri, the metal-bending space bear, is named after the world-famous Israeli spoon-bending psychic Uri Geller. Dr. Kiljoy was originally written as Zeroid 8 in the script while his Zeroid Nurse was Zeroid 9. Kiljoy's number is later revealed in *Zero's Finest Hour* to be 50. He is the only character in the series apart from Sergeant Major Zero to be voiced by Windsor Davies.

Regular Voice Cast

Dr. Tiger Ninestein	**Jeremy Hitchin**
Cpt. Mary Falconer	**Denise Bryer**
Sgt. Major Zero	**Windsor Davies**
Cpt. Kate Kestrel	**Anne Ridler**
Lt. Hiro	**Jeremy Hitchin**
Lt. Hawkeye	**Jeremy Hitchin**
Space Sgt. 101	**Ben Stevens**
Hudson	**Ben Stevens**
Zelda	**Denise Bryer**
Yung-Star	**Ben Stevens**
Cy-Star	**Anne Ridler**
Zeroid 55	**Ben Stevens**

Guest Voice Cast

Dr. Kiljoy	**Windsor Davies**
Zeroid Nurse	**Anne Ridler**

First UK Transmission

Saturday, November 5th, 1983
10.00am (Central)

THE GUN — Prod. No. 11

Written by **Koo Garstein** Directed by **Tony Bell**

After Yung-Star discovers that two Cubes working in tandem can generate an immensely powerful force beam, Zelda transfers a force of 20 Cubes to the unmanned Auto Space 4 Transporter which is returning to Earth. 101 tracks the Transporter veering off course and Tiger learns that it is carrying high-grade titanium ore, so he dispatches Kate and Hawkeye in Hawkwing to intercept the craft as it enters the atmosphere. The Cubes abandon ship as the Transporter crashes near the Richardson Dam and as night falls, they gather together and assemble into a single structure to become an irresistible force...

Notes

The closing scene includes the first appearance of French Zeroid Dix-Huit, although he has yet to adopt his trademark moustache. Dialogue cut from the script made an oblique reference to FAB 1 from THUNDERBIRDS when Hudson turns pink to match Kate's outfit.

Oops!

Yung-Star states that the Cube Gun combines the power of 20 Cubes, but when it is assembled, the Gun only features 19 Cubes.

Regular Voice Cast

Dr. Tiger Ninestein	**Jeremy Hitchin**
Cpt. Mary Falconer	**Denise Bryer**
Sgt. Major Zero	**Windsor Davies**
Cpt. Kate Kestrel	**Anne Ridler**
Lt. Hiro	**Jeremy Hitchin**
Lt. Hawkeye	**Jeremy Hitchin**
Space Sgt. 101 / Hudson	**Ben Stevens**
Zelda	**Denise Bryer**
Yung-Star	**Ben Stevens**
Cy-Star	**Anne Ridler**
Dix-Huit / Zeroid 21 / Zeroid 55	**Ben Stevens**
Colonel Johnson	**Jeremy Hitchin**

Guest Voice Cast

Ed Collins	**Jeremy Hitchin**
Zeroid 66 / Zeroid 13	**Ben Stevens**

First UK Transmission

Saturday, November 19th, 1983
10.00am (Central)

THUNDER PATH — Prod. No. 12

Written by **Effie Linestein** Directed by **Tony Lenny**

Zelda uses her power of control over matter to transport Sram directly to Earth. Sram arrives in the desert and causes a landslide with his thunder-roar that halts the remote-controlled supply Overlander in its tracks. When Mary discovers that the Overlander has left the laser rail, Tiger realises that something has taken over the vehicle and dispatches Kate and Hawkeye in Hawkwing to intercept it. Kate locates the Overlander but Zero reports that the vehicle is heading directly for the shale refinery at Santa Verona, where the storage tanks hold over a hundred million gallons of high octane aviation fuel!

Notes

This episode introduces the staff of Anderburr Records in the form of recording engineer Stew Dapples and producer Chic King, although the latter is only ever seen in silhouette. Kate's Cliff House is also seen for the first time while Zeroid 55 and Hudson adopt new roles as her personal assistants, with Hudson taking on the fictitious persona of her manager F.W. Runkin. Anderburr Records (named after producers Gerry Anderson and Christopher Burr) was originally written as Galaxy Records in Tony Barwick's script. The footage of the butte being destroyed by Sram is lifted from *Thunder-Roar*.

Regular Voice Cast

Dr. Tiger Ninestein	**Jeremy Hitchin**
Cpt. Mary Falconer	**Denise Bryer**
Sgt. Major Zero	**Windsor Davies**
Cpt. Kate Kestrel	**Anne Ridler**
Lt. Hawkeye	**Jeremy Hitchin**
Hudson	**Ben Stevens**
Zelda	**Denise Bryer**
Yung-Star	**Ben Stevens**
Cy-Star	**Anne Ridler**
Dix-Huit	**Ben Stevens**
Stew Dapples	**Ben Stevens**
Chic King	**Jeremy Hitchin**
Zeroid 55	**Ben Stevens**

First UK Transmission

Saturday, December 3rd, 1983
10.00am (Central)

MIND MONSTER — Prod. No. 13

Written by **Tom Katstein** Directed by **Tony Bell**

Zelda sends a transparent box to Earth aboard the Rhino, ejecting it into space as the ship approaches Spacehawk. 101 and 55 recover the container and bring it aboard Spacehawk for examination. It apparently contains only water vapour but when Kate looks into the box as it is opened, she hears a strange noise and sees Zelda laughing at her. Hiro suggests that she might be suffering from space sickness so Kate returns to Hawknest in Treehawk. Mary meets her in the lounge but Kate feels tired and heads straight for her quarters. Then Mary hears a strange noise and is suddenly confronted by Sram!

Notes

The final track that Kate is seen recording for her album is 'It's So Easy', which was commercially released by the real Anderburr Records in 1983 as the B-side of the Kate Kestrel vinyl single 'S.O.S.' (HX 1020).

Oops!

Mary has not met Sram yet and Hawkeye has never encountered Moid so the mind force should not be able to conjure images of Sram and Moid from their minds.

Regular Voice Cast

Dr. Tiger Ninestein	**Jeremy Hitchin**
Cpt. Mary Falconer	**Denise Bryer**
Sgt. Major Zero	**Windsor Davies**
Cpt. Kate Kestrel	**Anne Ridler**
Lt. Hiro	**Jeremy Hitchin**
Lt. Hawkeye	**Jeremy Hitchin**
Space Sgt. 101	**Ben Stevens**
Hudson	**Ben Stevens**
Zelda	**Denise Bryer**
Yung-Star	**Ben Stevens**
Cy-Star	**Anne Ridler**
Dix-Huit	**Ben Stevens**
Stew Dapples	**Ben Stevens**
Chic King	**Jeremy Hitchin**
Zeroid 55	**Ben Stevens**
Moid	**Ben Stevens**

First UK Transmission

Saturday, December 17th, 1983
10.00am (Central)

TO CATCH A TIGER — Prod. No. 14

Written by **Claude Backstein** Directed by **Tony Lenny**

Zelda captures the two-man crew of an Earth Transporter ship when they make an unscheduled detour to Mars in the belief that the planet has been placed off limits by the World Government because gold and diamonds have been discovered there. Zelda demands that Tiger is handed over in return for the men so Tiger, Mary, Hawkeye, Zero and Dix-Huit set off for Mars, leaving Kate behind on Earth to take a vital role in Tiger's plan to escape from Zelda's clutches after the hostages are exchanged. Meanwhile on Mars, Zelda reveals to Yung-Star and Cy-Star that she has appointed Moid as Tiger's executioner and he promises a lingering painful death for the Terrahawks' leader...

Notes

This episode features the first appearance of the MEV (Martian Exploration Vehicle), named after the Zero X vehicle seen in *Thunderbirds Are Go* (1966) and the CAPTAIN SCARLET AND THE MYSTERONS episode *The Mysterons*. It is seen again in *The Ultimate Menace* and *Space Cyclops*. The animated noughts and crosses game on the end titles of this episode is also seen at the end of *Expect The Unexpected Part 2*, *Midnight Blue* and *Doppelganger*.

Regular Voice Cast

Dr. Tiger Ninestein	**Jeremy Hitchin**
Cpt. Mary Falconer / Zelda	**Denise Bryer**
Sgt. Major Zero	**Windsor Davies**
Cpt. Kate Kestrel / Cy-Star	**Anne Ridler**
Lt. Hiro / Lt. Hawkeye	**Jeremy Hitchin**
Space Sgt. 101 / Hudson	**Ben Stevens**
Yung-Star / Dix-Huit	**Ben Stevens**
Stew Dapples / Zeroid 55	**Ben Stevens**
Colonel Johnson / Chic King	**Jeremy Hitchin**
Moid	**Ben Stevens**

Guest Voice Cast

Davis	**Jeremy Hitchin**
Cole	**Ben Stevens**

First UK Transmission

Saturday, December 31st, 1983
10.20am (ITV Network)

TERRAHAWKS

THE MIDAS TOUCH

Prod. No. 15

Written by **Trevor Lansdown & Tony Barwick** Directed by **Alan Pattillo**

Using his Ferret to monitor Earth radio signals, Yung-Star learns that the Space Fort Knox satellite is carrying 85 per cent of the Earth's gold reserves so Zelda plans to destroy the satellite to undermine the planet's economy. While the Terrahawks celebrate Tiger's birthday at Hawknest, Zelda tests the destructive power of the Krell, a creature that lurks beneath the Martian sand, and then sends it to Earth aboard a Zeaf. The Zeaf evades the Spacehawk defences but Kate and Hawkeye manage to track it to Egypt in Hawkwing. Tiger is puzzled as to what Zelda's target could be, but the Krell has buried itself in the desert sand to wait until Space Fort Knox passes directly overhead...

Notes

This episode is set on December 20th, the date of Tiger's birthday according to the character's official biography in the series' promotional information. Kate sings 'I Won't Let You Hold Me (Responsible)' at the party, but 'It's So Easy' is also heard during the closing scene. Yung-Star's Ferret makes its first appearance here and Kate Kestrel is seen with her natural black hair for the first time. The animated noughts and crosses game on the end titles of this episode is also seen at the end of *Close Call* and *Terratomb*.

Regular Voice Cast

Dr. Tiger Ninestein	**Jeremy Hitchin**
Cpt. Mary Falconer	**Denise Bryer**
Sgt. Major Zero	**Windsor Davies**
Capt. Kate Kestrel	**Anne Ridler**
Lt. Hiro	**Jeremy Hitchin**
Lt. Hawkeye	**Jeremy Hitchin**
Space Sgt. 101	**Ben Stevens**
Zelda	**Denise Bryer**
Yung-Star	**Ben Stevens**
Cy-Star	**Anne Ridler**
Dix-Huit	**Ben Stevens**

First UK Transmission

Sunday, December 23rd, 1984
11.45am (Grampian)

OPERATION S.A.S.

Prod. No. 16

Written by **Tom Angeristein** Directed by **Tony Lenny**

Yung-Star learns that the World President is making an orbital flight in the Presidential Space Shuttle so Zelda agrees to let him journey to Earth to carry out a devious plan of his own, providing he takes Yuri the Space Bear with him. Evading the Spacehawk defences by using the Presidential Shuttle as a shield, Yung-Star then attacks Hudson as he is ferrying Kate and Stew Dapples to Anderburr Records. Hudson leaves the road and takes off across country but Yuri is waiting for them and uses his powers to force Hudson into a crash. Yung-Star lands his Zeaf and takes Kate and Stew prisoner...

Notes

John S. Franklin is stated to be the 6th World President and the first to venture into space. Yuri the Space Bear was previously seen in *The Ugliest Monster Of All*. Yung-Star's torture chamber is the same device created by Moid to execute Tiger in *To Catch A Tiger*. The animated noughts and crosses game on the end titles of this episode is also seen at the end of *Thunder-Roar* and *Jolly Roger One*. At the time of production, the British SAS (Special Air Service) was very much at the forefront of public consciousness following the assault on the Iranian Embassy in London in May 1980.

Regular Voice Cast

Dr. Tiger Ninestein	**Jeremy Hitchin**
Cpt. Mary Falconer	**Denise Bryer**
Sgt. Major Zero	**Windsor Davies**
Cpt. Kate Kestrel	**Anne Ridler**
Lt. Hiro	**Jeremy Hitchin**
Lt. Hawkeye	**Jeremy Hitchin**
Space Sgt. 101 / Hudson	**Ben Stevens**
Zelda	**Denise Bryer**
Yung-Star / Dix-Huit	**Ben Stevens**
Cy-Star	**Anne Ridler**
Stew Dapples / Zeroid 55	**Ben Stevens**
Colonel Johnson / Chic King	**Jeremy Hitchin**

Guest Voice Cast

Commentator	**Jeremy Hitchin**
Newsreader	**Ben Stevens**

First UK Transmission

Sunday, September 23rd, 1984
4.30pm (ITV Network)

TEN TOP POP

Prod. No. 17

Written by **L. Inkstein** Directed by **Tony Bell**

Zelda discovers Yung-Star using his Ferret to listen to a radio broadcast of Kate Kestrel performing her latest song. She is about to destroy the device when Cy-Star suggests that it could be used as part of a devious plan. Tuning in to the source of the Earth broadcast, Zelda transmits hypnotic commands to Stew Dapples's headphones and takes control of his mind. While Zelda sets off for Earth in the Rhino, Kate collects Stew from Anderburr Records in Hudson to take him to a party at the Cliff House but *en route*, he pulls a gun and orders the car to pull over. Hudson covertly sends out a distress signal but as Tiger and Mary locate the car in Hawkwing, Kate and Stew are captured by Yung-Star...

Notes

Yung-Star's Ferret has been repaired after it was broken by Yuri in *Operation S.A.S.* The other bands listed under Kate Kestrel on Yung-Star's pop chart are Ann and the Droids, The Bray Boys, Cantina Band, Rich Clifford and Simon & Dave. Yung-Star crashes the Hawkwing Wing section into a warehouse belonging to Anderson Cash & Carry. The animated noughts and crosses game on the end titles of this episode is also seen at the end of *Space Samurai*, *Two For The Price Of One* and *Operation Zero*.

Regular Voice Cast

Dr. Tiger Ninestein	**Jeremy Hitchin**
Cpt. Mary Falconer	**Denise Bryer**
Sgt. Major Zero	**Windsor Davies**
Cpt. Kate Kestrel	**Anne Ridler**
Lt. Hiro	**Jeremy Hitchin**
Lt. Hawkeye	**Jeremy Hitchin**
Space Sgt. 101	**Ben Stevens**
Hudson	**Ben Stevens**
Zelda	**Denise Bryer**
Yung-Star	**Ben Stevens**
Cy-Star	**Anne Ridler**
Dix-Huit	**Ben Stevens**
Stew Dapples	**Ben Stevens**
Chic King	**Jeremy Hitchin**
Zeroid 55	**Ben Stevens**

First UK Transmission

Sunday, September 30th, 1984
4.30pm (ITV Network)

UNSEEN MENACE — Prod. No. 18

Written by **Felix Stein** Directed by **Tony Bell**

Zelda sends Moid to Earth in a Zeaf to terrorise the Terrahawks in the guise of the Invisible Man. Approaching Spacehawk, Moid avoids being hit when the Space Zeroids open fire on the Zeaf and then adopts the persona of the Red Baron to try and evade Kate and Hawkeye in Hawkwing. However, Kate and Hawkeye are still better pilots and the Zeaf is shot down, crash-landing in the desert, but when Battletank investigates the crash site, the Megazoids can find no sign of the pilot. That night, Moid's presence at Kate's Cliff House disturbs Zeroid 55 but he can see no sign of the intruder. Moid enters Kate's bedroom to watch her sleeping but when she suddenly wakes up, there is no one there...

Notes

This is Moid's fourth appearance in the series following *Happy Madeday*, *Mind Monster* and *To Catch A Tiger*. Here he impersonates German WW1 flying ace Baron von Richthofen (the Red Baron) and the nameless Invisible Man from H.G. Wells's classic 1897 novel *The Invisible Man*. Kate Kestrel's appearance while asleep in bed confirms that her natural hair colour is black. The animated noughts and crosses game on the end titles of this episode is also seen at the end of *Happy Madeday* and *Runaway*.

Regular Voice Cast

Dr. Tiger Ninestein	**Jeremy Hitchin**
Cpt. Mary Falconer	**Denise Bryer**
Sgt. Major Zero	**Windsor Davies**
Cpt. Kate Kestrel	**Anne Ridler**
Lt. Hiro	**Jeremy Hitchin**
Lt. Hawkeye	**Jeremy Hitchin**
Space Sgt. 101	**Ben Stevens**
Hudson	**Ben Stevens**
Zelda	**Denise Bryer**
Yung-Star	**Ben Stevens**
Cy-Star	**Anne Ridler**
Dix-Huit / Stew Dapples	**Ben Stevens**
Zeroid 55 / Moid	**Ben Stevens**

Guest Voice Cast

Howard Druff	**Jeremy Hitchin**

First UK Transmission

Sunday, November 25th, 1984
4.30pm (ITV Network)

A CHRISTMAS MIRACLE — Prod. No. 19

Written by **Kate Noweestein** Directed by **Tony Lenny**

It is Christmas Eve at Hawknest, but while Mary and Kate decorate the tree, Tiger works on a battle plan that he has been preparing for weeks. He falls asleep at his desk and is woken on Christmas morning by Zero wishing him a Merry Christmas. However, on Mars, Zelda announces that while the Earthlings celebrate Christmas, she will launch a massive attack against them. Expecting just such an attack, Tiger mobilises the Terrahawks personnel aboard Spacehawk and they set off for the Moon where the final showdown will take place. Zelda's fleet arrives in orbit and Zelda eagerly anticipates the coming war of attrition that will end in the total destruction of one side or the other!

Notes

This special Christmas episode has, to date, only ever been broadcast once in the UK, on Christmas Eve 1984. It was omitted from all later repeat runs of TERRAHAWKS on ITV in the 1980s. At the end of the episode, Zero, Tiger, Mary, Kate, Hiro and Hawkeye speak directly to camera to wish viewers a Happy Christmas. Uniquely, the end titles do not feature a noughts and crosses game. Instead, the captions roll over a photo of Zero dressed as Father Christmas while Kate sings 'I Believe In Love This Christmas'.

Regular Voice Cast

Dr. Tiger Ninestein	**Jeremy Hitchin**
Cpt. Mary Falconer	**Denise Bryer**
Sgt. Major Zero	**Windsor Davies**
Cpt. Kate Kestrel	**Anne Ridler**
Lt. Hiro	**Jeremy Hitchin**
Lt. Hawkeye	**Jeremy Hitchin**
Space Sgt. 101	**Ben Stevens**
Zelda	**Denise Bryer**
Yung-Star	**Ben Stevens**
Cy-Star	**Anne Ridler**
Dix-Huit	**Ben Stevens**

First UK Transmission

Saturday, December 24th, 1984
11.30am (ITV Network)

MIDNIGHT BLUE — Prod. No. 20

Written by **Andre Le Chatstein** Directed by **Tony Lenny**

Zelda creates a Zeaf that is one-tenth normal size and sends it to Earth as part of her latest plan. 101 makes contact with the approaching Zeaf and the Space Zeroids lock on target, but their firepower misses the craft completely. Tiger dispatches Kate and Hawkeye in Hawkwing to intercept the Zeaf in the upper atmosphere. Tiger warns Kate that she is approaching Hawkwing's operational limit but Kate cannot understand why they have no visual contact with the Zeaf at such close range. Tiger orders her to break off pursuit as Hawkwing is in danger of going into orbit. The Zeaf is tracked to a landing in New York, but Pentagon officials insist that no alien vehicles have flown into their airspace...

Notes

Kate sings a song entitled 'S.O.S.', which is the series' most blatant homage to THUNDERBIRDS with its references to Mr. Tracy and International Rescue in the lyrics. The song was commercially released on a vinyl single (HX 1020) by the real Anderburr Records in 1983. Hawkwing is not designed for space flight: it can climb to an altitude of 104 miles but no higher. The Zeroids' attack on Yung-Star's Zeaf is accompanied by the Overlander incidental theme composed for *Thunder-Roar*.

Regular Voice Cast

Dr. Tiger Ninestein	**Jeremy Hitchin**
Cpt. Mary Falconer	**Denise Bryer**
Sgt. Major Zero	**Windsor Davies**
Cpt. Kate Kestrel	**Anne Ridler**
Lt. Hiro	**Jeremy Hitchin**
Lt. Hawkeye	**Jeremy Hitchin**
Space Sgt. 101	**Ben Stevens**
Zelda	**Denise Bryer**
Yung-Star	**Ben Stevens**
Cy-Star	**Anne Ridler**
Dix-Huit	**Ben Stevens**
Zeroid 55	**Ben Stevens**

Guest Voice Cast

Bernie the drunk	**Ben Stevens**

First UK Transmission

Sunday, October 28th, 1984
4.15pm (Grampian)

PLAY IT AGAIN, SRAM — Prod. No. 21

Written by **B.O. Garstein** — Directed by **Tony Bell**

After Kate wins the World Song Contest in TV City, Zelda challenges Kate's right to represent the solar system in the Interstellar Song Contest, demanding to compete against her in a new contest on behalf of the inhabitants of Mars. Zelda's challenge is upheld by the United Planets and the new contest is arranged to take place on the remote asteroid Yazgur. The Terrahawks travel to Yazgur aboard Spacehawk together with Stew Dapples, who will compere the contest, but when they arrive at the asteroid, they discover that Zelda's backing group includes Sram, the demon of the drums!

Notes

Kate Kestrel's competitors at the World Song Contest are Hevor Olsen (performing 'Long Nights With You'), Rod Stalwart ('Outback Blues') and Kay, Gee & Bee ('Katriona'). Although Kate's song is introduced as 'S.O.S., Mr. Tracy', it appears as just 'S.O.S.' on the scoreboard. The script originally detailed that she would sing a different song, 'Silver Blue Roller', first heard in *Zero's Finest Hour*. The performance of 'Zelda Rap' is credited to Moya Griffiths on the end titles, but the song is actually performed by Denise Bryer as Zelda.

Regular Voice Cast

Dr. Tiger Ninestein	**Jeremy Hitchin**
Cpt. Mary Falconer	**Denise Bryer**
Sgt. Major Zero	**Windsor Davies**
Cpt. Kate Kestrel	**Anne Ridler**
Lt. Hiro	**Jeremy Hitchin**
Lt. Hawkeye	**Jeremy Hitchin**
Space Sgt. 101 / Hudson	**Ben Stevens**
Zelda	**Denise Bryer**
Yung-Star / Dix-Huit	**Ben Stevens**
Cy-Star	**Anne Ridler**
Colonel Johnson	**Jeremy Hitchin**
Stew Dapples	**Ben Stevens**
Chic King	**Jeremy Hitchin**

Guest Voice Cast

Compere	**Jeremy Hitchin**

First UK Transmission

Sunday, October 14th, 1984
4.30pm (ITV Network)

MY KINGDOM FOR A ZEAF — Prod. No. 22

Written by **Sheik Spearstein** — Directed by **Tony Lenny**

Zelda sends Yung-Star to Earth in a Zeaf accompanied by Lord Tempo, the Master of Time, on a mission to find and destroy Hawknest. Tempo uses his temporal powers to evade Spacehawk's defences by taking the Zeaf back to a time before Spacehawk existed. He lands the Zeaf in Bosworth Field in 1485 where Richard III has just lost his last battle. Yung-Star takes a liking to the king and insists on bringing him along when they journey back to the future. Making their base on the construction site of a recently opened bridge, Yung-Star suggests that Kate Kestrel might lead them to Hawknest, so they send Richard to Anderburr Records to determine her movements...

Notes

The sound effect of Lord Tempo's time-warping power was previously heard as a space warp sound in several episodes of SPACE:1999. The effect was originally created for the appearance of the Grand Lunar in the film adaptation of H.G. Wells's *First Men In The Moon* (1964). The events of this episode take place in 2020: Tempo and Yung-Star travel 535 years forward in time from 1485. The noughts and crosses game on the end titles of this episode is also seen at the end of *The Ugliest Monster Of All* and *Space Cyclops*.

Regular Voice Cast

Dr. Tiger Ninestein	**Jeremy Hitchin**
Cpt. Mary Falconer	**Denise Bryer**
Sgt. Major Zero	**Windsor Davies**
Cpt. Kate Kestrel	**Anne Ridler**
Hudson	**Ben Stevens**
Zelda	**Denise Bryer**
Yung-Star	**Ben Stevens**
Cy-Star	**Anne Ridler**
Stew Dapples	**Ben Stevens**
Chic King	**Jeremy Hitchin**
Zeroid 55	**Ben Stevens**

Guest Voice Cast

Lord Tempo	**Ben Stevens**
Richard III	**Ben Stevens**

First UK Transmission

Sunday, November 4th, 1984
4.30pm (ITV Network)

ZERO'S FINEST HOUR — Prod. No. 23

Written by **Otto Von Lowstein** — Directed by **Tony Bell**

At the Overlander warehouse, employee Harry Blake has been bribed by Yung-Star to place a special package for Tiger aboard the vehicle on its next delivery run. Then Yung-Star and Pluto try to follow the Overlander back to Hawknest but their car gets stuck in mud. After the supplies are transferred to Battlehawk and delivered to Hawknest, Tiger runs two security scans on the mystery package but they both check out negative. He opens the package to find only a pot of flowers inside and, assuming that they are from a secret admirer, Mary puts the flowers on the table as she and Tiger sit down to dinner. Shortly after, 21 reports to Zero that Tiger and Mary are both dead!

Notes

The Overlander was previously seen in *Thunder-Roar* and *Thunder Path*. Kate can be heard singing 'It's So Easy' during Tiger and Mary's romantic dinner, although the song is not credited on the end titles. Zero had the last laugh in Tony Barwick's shooting script where his dialogue at the end of the episode originally continued, "Hang on... he's bound to find out it's the truth in the end. I'll make sure that he do. That'll really have him... he won't know what to believe after that. I'll be able to tell him some real whoppers!"

Regular Voice Cast

Dr. Tiger Ninestein	**Jeremy Hitchin**
Cpt. Mary Falconer / Zelda	**Denise Bryer**
Sgt. Major Zero	**Windsor Davies**
Cpt. Kate Kestrel / Cy-Star	**Anne Ridler**
Lt. Hawkeye	**Jeremy Hitchin**
Hudson	**Ben Stevens**
Yung-Star / Dix-Huit	**Ben Stevens**
Zeroid 21 / Stew Dapples	**Ben Stevens**
Chic King	**Jeremy Hitchin**

Guest Voice Cast

Dr. Kiljoy	**Windsor Davies**
Harry Blake	**Ben Stevens**
Foreman	**Jeremy Hitchin**
Zeroid 04	**Ben Stevens**

First UK Transmission

Sunday, November 11th, 1984
4.30pm (ITV Network)

THE ULTIMATE MENACE — Prod. No. 24

Written by **Ivor Purstein** Directed by **Tony Lenny**

The Terrahawks travel to Mars aboard Spacehawk for a meeting with Zelda. A truce has been declared so that the opposing parties can work together to face the threat of the greatest menace in the known universe: the Zyclon, a powerful computer over a mile long which is programmed to destroy all lifeforms.To learn all they can about the Zyclon, Hiro launches a Hawkspy probe information gatherer, but it is destroyed as it approaches the Zyclon. Tiger confides in Mary that the Zyclon is supposed to be unstoppable and if they fail in their mission, Mars and then the Earth will be totally destroyed...

Notes

Tiger, Kate and Mary travel to the Martian surface in the MEV, previously seen in *To Catch A Tiger*. The electronic background noises emitted by the Zyclon were previously heard in SPACE:1999. In a scene deleted from the shooting script, while Kate and Hawkeye are waiting in Zelda's ship on Mars, Yung-Star persuades Kate to give a performance miming to one of her songs that he has recorded on his Ferret. The animated noughts and crosses game on the end titles of this episode is also seen at the end of *Thunder Path* and *Cry UFO*.

Regular Voice Cast

Dr. Tiger Ninestein	**Jeremy Hitchin**
Cpt. Mary Falconer	**Denise Bryer**
Sgt. Major Zero	**Windsor Davies**
Cpt. Kate Kestrel	**Anne Ridler**
Lt. Hiro	**Jeremy Hitchin**
Lt. Hawkeye	**Jeremy Hitchin**
Space Sgt. 101	**Ben Stevens**
Zelda	**Denise Bryer**
Yung-Star	**Ben Stevens**
Cy-Star	**Anne Ridler**

Guest Voice Cast

Zyclon	**Ben Stevens**

First UK Transmission

Sunday, October 21st, 1984
4.30pm (ITV Network)

MA'S MONSTERS — Prod. No. 25

Written by **Rory Peetstein** Directed by **Tony Bell** & **Tony Lenny**

On Mars, Cy-Star announces that she has some wonderful news but Zelda tells her that it will have to wait as she wishes to review the ways in which her monsters have confronted the Terrahawks. Zelda's crystal shows Sram's attempt to destroy the shale refinery at Santa Verona with the Overlander, the Terrahawks trapped on Callisto with the Sporilla, and Kate Kestrel held hostage by Yung-Star and Yuri. Recognising the need for change, Zelda unveils her new cryogenic store which contains a collection of monsters with horrific powers beyond imagination. As the trio toast their inevitable victory over the Terrahawks, Cy-Star reveals that she is going to have a baby...

Notes

This was the last episode to be filmed in the series' first production block. Only four minutes of new footage was shot for the episode by Tony Bell as the rest comprises material recycled from *Thunder Path*, *The Sporilla* and *Operation S.A.S.* The original script also included scenes from *Happy Madeday*. Tony Lenny is credited as director for his work on the footage from *Thunder Path* and *Operation S.A.S.* The original screening of *Ma's Monsters* in the UK actually preceded the first broadcast of *The Sporilla*.

Regular Voice Cast

Dr. Tiger Ninestein	**Jeremy Hitchin**
Cpt. Mary Falconer	**Denise Bryer**
Sgt. Major Zero	**Windsor Davies**
Cpt. Kate Kestrel	**Anne Ridler**
Zelda	**Denise Bryer**
Yung-Star	**Ben Stevens**
Cy-Star	**Anne Ridler**
Dix-Huit	**Ben Stevens**
Stew Dapples	**Ben Stevens**
Zeroid 55	**Ben Stevens**

First UK Transmission

Sunday, December 30th, 1984
9.30am (Grampian / Border)

TWO FOR THE PRICE OF ONE — Prod. No. 27

Written by **Kay Itstein** Directed by **Tony Lenny**

Kate and Hawkeye test-drive the new Spacetank on the lunar surface in preparation for an assault on Zelda's Martian complex. Unusually high solar flare activity is producing a powerful solar wind that provides cover for Spacehawk to approach Mars and land at a safe distance without alerting Zelda. Zero and Dix-Huit join Kate and Hawkeye aboard the Spacetank and they set off across the surface towards Zelda's base. Meanwhile, Zelda and Yung-Star make preparations for the birth of Cy-Star's baby in the Delivery Room, but when complications arise, Zelda calls for a crow-bar...

Notes

This was the first episode of the series' second production block. The episode production numbers were reorganised at this stage to match the actual number of episodes that had been produced with the result that the series has no episode 26. *Two For The Price Of One* begins with a reprise of the last minute of *Ma's Monsters*. Some two minutes of footage featuring Zelda helping to deliver Cy-Star's baby with a crow-bar was cut from this episode for its original transmission in the UK and has, to date, never been seen on British television.

Regular Voice Cast

Dr. Tiger Ninestein	**Jeremy Hitchin**
Cpt. Mary Falconer	**Denise Bryer**
Sgt. Major Zero	**Windsor Davies**
Cpt. Kate Kestrel	**Anne Ridler**
Lt. Hiro	**Jeremy Hitchin**
Lt. Hawkeye	**Jeremy Hitchin**
Space Sgt. 101	**Ben Stevens**
Zelda	**Denise Bryer**
Yung-Star	**Ben Stevens**
Cy-Star	**Anne Ridler**
Dix-Huit	**Ben Stevens**
It-Star	**Jeremy Hitchin / Anne Ridler**

First UK Transmission

Saturday, May 3rd, 1986
11.30am (ITV Network)

CHILD'S PLAY — Prod. No. 28

Written by **Sue Donymstein** Directed by **Tony Bell**

It-Star develops a super derivative of TNT and suggests a plan that will put the explosive to good use. Shortly after, a strange alien device explodes in Badwater County and Colonel Johnson receives a warning of a second, much larger device which will detonate in ten hours. Flying to the location of the second device in Battlehawk, Tiger is puzzled as to Zelda's motive in planting a bomb in the middle of the desert, but then a sub-terra scan of the area reveals that the TransAmerica Pipeline, which supplies a million cubic feet of gas per hour to half of South and Central America, runs 20 feet below the surface!

Notes

The animated noughts and crosses game on the end titles is also seen at the end of *Gold* and *Mind Monster*.

Oops!

Both here and in subsequent episodes, It-Star refers to Zelda as 'Grandmother', yet it has previously been established that Cy-Star is Zelda's sister, so Zelda is It-Star's aunt, not his grandmother. Similarly, Yung-Star is It-Star's cousin, not his uncle.

Regular Voice Cast

Dr. Tiger Ninestein	**Jeremy Hitchin**
Cpt. Mary Falconer	**Denise Bryer**
Sgt. Major Zero	**Windsor Davies**
Cpt. Kate Kestrel	**Anne Ridler**
Hudson	**Ben Stevens**
Zelda	**Denise Bryer**
Yung-Star	**Ben Stevens**
Cy-Star	**Anne Ridler**
Colonel Johnson	**Jeremy Hitchin**
Stew Dapples	**Ben Stevens**
Chic King	**Jeremy Hitchin**
Sheriff Cy Bull	**Jeremy Hitchin**
Deputy Kilroy	**Ben Stevens**
It-Star	**Jeremy Hitchin / Anne Ridler**

First UK Transmission

Saturday, June 7th, 1986
11.30am (ITV Network)

JOLLY ROGER ONE — Prod. No. 29

Written by **Fred Barestein** Directed by **Tony Lenny**

With the assistance of barmy space pirate Captain Goat, Yung-Star and It-Star take up residence in an abandoned Earth space station. They set up a pirate radio station, Jolly Roger One, to broadcast pop music and threatening messages from their sponsor Zelda, but their transmissions are intercepted at Hawknest and Mary broadcasts a jamming signal. Tiger, Mary, Kate and Zero join Hiro and 101 aboard Spacehawk and set a course for the space station to evict the pirate DJs, but It-Star uses his Goybirl voice to send a message that gives the impression that the androids are holding a young girl hostage...

Notes

Zero gives the date as Tuesday, October 21st so this episode must be set in 2025, the only year between 2014 and 2031 in which October 21st will fall on a Tuesday. The noughts and crosses game on the end titles is also seen in *Thunder-Roar* and *Operation S.A.S.*

Oops!

When Yung-Star's Zeaf docks with the space station, the station's docking clamps overlap with the Zeaf.

Regular Voice Cast

Dr. Tiger Ninestein	**Jeremy Hitchin**
Cpt. Mary Falconer	**Denise Bryer**
Sgt. Major Zero	**Windsor Davies**
Cpt. Kate Kestrel	**Anne Ridler**
Lt. Hiro	**Jeremy Hitchin**
Space Sgt. 101	**Ben Stevens**
Zelda	**Denise Bryer**
Yung-Star	**Ben Stevens**
Cy-Star	**Anne Ridler**
Stew Dapples	**Ben Stevens**
Chic King	**Jeremy Hitchin**
It-Star	**Jeremy Hitchin / Anne Ridler**

Guest Voice Cast

Captain Goat	**Ben Stevens**

First UK Transmission

Saturday, June 14th, 1986
11.30am (ITV Network)

RUNAWAY — Prod. No. 30

Written by **Frank Instein** Directed by **Tony Bell**

After feeding Yung-Star with a special graphite sauce that acts as an undetectable bugging device, It-Star encourages Yung-Star to run away from home. As It-Star explains to Zelda, once Yung-Star arrives on Earth, he will soon be captured, handed over to the Terrahawks and taken to Hawknest, enabling them to pinpoint the location of the Terrahawk base. Sure enough, when Yung-Star walks into the Pete's For Eats diner in Badwater County, the Terrahawks are alerted and arrangements are made to collect the android and ferry him to Hawknest. However, Tiger is suspicious of Yung-Star's motives and recognises an alternative course of action when he is contacted by a film producer...

Notes

Pete and Sue Ellen of Pete's For Eats in Badwater County are also seen in *Cry UFO*. Sue Ellen was originally written as Edith in Tony Barwick's script but she was renamed after Linda Gray's character in the American TV series DALLAS (1978-1991). Film producer Harry Salzburg is named after Harry Saltzman, the Canadian co-producer of the first nine Eon James Bond films. A sign at the abandoned film studios shows that it was previously the home of a company by the name of Century 21 Productions.

Regular Voice Cast

Dr. Tiger Ninestein	**Jeremy Hitchin**
Cpt. Mary Falconer / Zelda	**Denise Bryer**
Sgt. Major Zero	**Windsor Davies**
Cpt. Kate Kestrel / Cy-Star	**Anne Ridler**
Lt. Hiro / Lt. Hawkeye	**Jeremy Hitchin**
Space Sgt. 101	**Ben Stevens**
Yung-Star / Dix-Huit	**Ben Stevens**
Stew Dapples / Deputy Kilroy	**Ben Stevens**
Colonel Johnson / Chic King	**Jeremy Hitchin**
Sheriff Cy Bull	**Jeremy Hitchin**
It-Star	**Jeremy Hitchin / Anne Ridler**

Guest Voice Cast

Pete / Harry Salzburg	**Ben Stevens**
Sue Ellen	**Anne Ridler**

First UK Transmission

Saturday, June 21st, 1986
11.30am (ITV Network)

FIRST STRIKE — Prod. No. 31

Written by **Polly Phillestein** Directed by **Tony Lenny**

Tiger and Kate are contacted by military commander General Rip Cord who announces that he has been authorised by the World President to assume command of the Terrahawks organisation, effective immediately. This is confirmed by Colonel Johnson on board Spacehawk where Cord reveals his intention to initiate a first strike nuclear attack on Zelda's complex from Big White 1, the most powerful space carrier ever built. However, Cord discovers to his cost that he has underestimated Zelda's abilities when she sends Sram, Lord Tempo and Yuri into combat against Big White 1's Interceptors...

Notes

The elevator in Kate's Cliff House illustrates that the building has four floors and the lounge is on the top floor. Tiger travels from Spacehawk to Big White 1 aboard Hawklet, a space shuttle previously seen in *Jolly Roger One*. The Big White 1 Interceptors and their launch sequence are modelled after the Viper starfighters in the 1978 American TV series BATTLESTAR GALACTICA. Hiro and Space Sergeant 101 appear in the episode but neither of them has any dialogue. The noughts and crosses game on the end titles is also seen at the end of *From Here To Infinity.*

Regular Voice Cast

Dr. Tiger Ninestein	**Jeremy Hitchin**
Cpt. Mary Falconer	**Denise Bryer**
Sgt. Major Zero	**Windsor Davies**
Cpt. Kate Kestrel	**Anne Ridler**
Lt. Hawkeye	**Jeremy Hitchin**
Hudson	**Ben Stevens**
Zelda	**Denise Bryer**
Yung-Star / Stew Dapples	**Ben Stevens**
Colonel Johnson / Chic King	**Jeremy Hitchin**
It-Star	**Jeremy Hitchin / Anne Ridler**

Guest Voice Cast

General Rip Cord	**Jeremy Hitchin**
Lord Tempo	**Ben Stevens**
Sergeant	**Jeremy Hitchin**

First UK Transmission

Saturday, May 10th, 1986
11.30am (ITV Network)

TERRATOMB — Prod. No. 32

Written by **Edward E. Barestein** Directed by **Tony Bell**

Zelda sends Yung-Star and Yuri to Earth with a powerful new Supermacro Bomb developed by It-Star. Piloting their Zeaf, Yuri manages to evade the Space Zeroids but feigns a crash-landing to draw Tiger and Mary to the area in Battlehawk. Battletank searches the crash site and the Megazoids locate the two aliens but Yuri uses his powers to disable them. Then Yung-Star takes off in the Zeaf to distract the Terrahawks while Yuri hides aboard Battletank and plants the Supermacro Bomb. With Battletank back aboard Battlehawk, Tiger and Mary return to Hawknest unaware that they are carrying an explosive device which will completely destroy the base!

Notes

The Supermacro Bomb is named after the series' Supermacromation puppetry technique. Hudson can travel at speeds up to 762 mph (Mach 1). This was the last of eight episodes from the series' second production block that premiered in the USA on weekdays between January 15th and January 24th, 1985, 16 months before their first UK broadcast. The other episodes were *Two For The Price Of One*, *Jolly Roger One*, *Runaway*, *Space Cyclops*, *Doppelganger*, *First Strike* and *Timewarp*.

Regular Voice Cast

Dr. Tiger Ninestein	**Jeremy Hitchin**
Cpt. Mary Falconer	**Denise Bryer**
Sgt. Major Zero	**Windsor Davies**
Cpt. Kate Kestrel	**Anne Ridler**
Lt. Hiro	**Jeremy Hitchin**
Space Sgt. 101	**Ben Stevens**
Hudson	**Ben Stevens**
Zelda	**Denise Bryer**
Yung-Star	**Ben Stevens**
Cy-Star	**Anne Ridler**
Stew Dapples	**Ben Stevens**
Chic King	**Jeremy Hitchin**
It-Star	**Jeremy Hitchin / Anne Ridler**

First UK Transmission

Saturday, May 17th, 1986
11.30am (ITV Network)

DOPPELGANGER — Prod. No. 33

Written by **Albert Zweistein** Directed by **Tony Lenny**

It-Star's hypnotism experiments succeed in sending Yung-Star into a trance and turning him into a lifeless statue. Soon after, a nightwatchman at the Museum of Antiquities on Earth discovers a statue of Yung-Star in Gallery 4 and the Terrahawks learn of it when the story is published in Mary's newspaper. Johnson arranges to have the Museum cleared so that Zero and Dix-Huit can scan the statue but they report that it is a completely lifeless inanimate object. Tiger instructs Zero to take the statue out to a safe distance and destroy it, but as the Zeroids detonate explosives which completely obliterate the statue, Zelda and It-Star set the second part of their plan in motion...

Oops!

Kate plays an instrumental version of 'I've Got The Power' on the piano at Hawknest but contrary to the credits given on the end titles, she does not actually perform the song. When the statues of Yung-Star and Cy-Star appear in the Museum of Antiquities, the 'before' and 'after' shots are edited together as a jump cut so that the statues appear very suddenly; the two shots were supposed to be cross-faded so that the statues gradually materialised in the style of previous matter transferences effected by Zelda.

Regular Voice Cast

Dr. Tiger Ninestein	**Jeremy Hitchin**
Cpt. Mary Falconer	**Denise Bryer**
Sgt. Major Zero	**Windsor Davies**
Cpt. Kate Kestrel	**Anne Ridler**
Zelda	**Denise Bryer**
Yung-Star	**Ben Stevens**
Cy-Star	**Anne Ridler**
Dix-Huit	**Ben Stevens**
It-Star	**Jeremy Hitchin / Anne Ridler**

Guest Voice Cast

Nightwatchman	**Ben Stevens**

First UK Transmission

Saturday, May 31st, 1986
11.30am (ITV Network)

CRY UFO

Prod. No. 34

Written by **Ewan Istein** Directed by **Tony Bell**

Living under the thumb of his doting mother, reality is far removed from Stew Dapples's glamorous fantasies of life as a major player in the record industry. Another routine day at Anderburr Records goes from bad to worse and he is at the end of his tether when a rehearsal with Kate Kestrel is interrupted by his mother calling to let him know that they are having steak and kidney pudding for supper. Telling her that he has to work late, Stew instead visits Pete's For Eats for his meal but he is alone in the diner when a huge brilliantly lit spaceship passes overhead before vanishing into the desert. Afterwards, no one believes him when he says that he has seen a UFO – no one, that is, except Kate...

Notes

Denise Bryer's voice for Stew's mother is a spot-on impersonation of the late character actress Irene Handl, perhaps best known for her starring role in the 1970 ITV sitcom FOR THE LOVE OF ADA. Stew's view from the diner as the UFO appears is a pastiche of the poster image and teaser trailer for *Close Encounters Of The Third Kind* (1978). The design of the UFO itself pays homage to the Mother Ship from the climax of that film. This is the only episode in which neither Zelda nor her family appear.

Regular Voice Cast

Dr. Tiger Ninestein	**Jeremy Hitchin**
Cpt. Mary Falconer	**Denise Bryer**
Sgt. Major Zero	**Windsor Davies**
Cpt. Kate Kestrel	**Anne Ridler**
Lt. Hiro	**Jeremy Hitchin**
Stew Dapples	**Ben Stevens**
Chic King	**Jeremy Hitchin**
Sheriff Cy Bull	**Jeremy Hitchin**
Deputy Kilroy	**Ben Stevens**

Guest Voice Cast

Pete	**Ben Stevens**
Sue Ellen	**Anne Ridler**
Mrs. Dapples	**Denise Bryer**
Ultra City Announcer	**Ben Stevens**

First UK Transmission

Sunday, December 16th, 1984
4.30pm (ITV Network)

SPACE CYCLOPS

Prod. No. 35

Written by **Lita Beerstein** Directed by **Tony Lenny**

When a manned NASA probe is sent to investigate a meteorite in lunar orbit, the meteorite suddenly sprouts tentacles which grasp the probe and drag it down to crash on the lunar surface. Johnson shows Tiger and Kate photos of the crash site which show a large mound of moondust growing amongst the probe wreckage. Suspecting that something has hatched from the meteor and is feeding on the wreckage as it grows, Tiger and Mary journey to the Moon aboard Spacehawk. As they scan the crash area from the MEV, the mound of dust shifts and reveals a hideous one-eyed monster. The MEV experiences a power loss and Tiger and Mary are helpless as the creature closes in...

Notes

Kate's song 'Living In The 21st Century' can be heard in the background at La Tour d'Or before Kate performs on stage. Also heard in *Ma's Monsters*, *Runaway* and *Timewarp*, this song replaced the regular end titles theme on an alternate end title sequence used for screenings of the series on American television. The drunken heckler at La Tour d'Or was previously seen as Bernie the drunk in *Midnight Blue*. *Space Cyclops* features the final appearance of Stew Dapples.

Regular Voice Cast

Dr. Tiger Ninestein	**Jeremy Hitchin**
Cpt. Mary Falconer	**Denise Bryer**
Sgt. Major Zero	**Windsor Davies**
Cpt. Kate Kestrel	**Anne Ridler**
Lt. Hiro	**Jeremy Hitchin**
Space Sgt. 101	**Ben Stevens**
Zelda	**Denise Bryer**
Yung-Star / Dix-Huit	**Ben Stevens**
Colonel Johnson	**Jeremy Hitchin**
Stew Dapples	**Ben Stevens**
It-Star	**Jeremy Hitchin**

Guest Voice Cast

NASA Commander	**Ben Stevens**
Cooper / Heckler	**Jeremy Hitchin**
Computer Voice	**Anne Ridler**

First UK Transmission

Saturday, May 24th, 1986
11.30am (ITV Network)

TIMEWARP

Prod. No. 36

Written by **Major Daystein** Directed by **Tony Bell**

Mary has a vivid nightmare in which Hawknest is destroyed by Zelda's Zeafs. The nightmare has been caused by Lord Tempo's attempt to transmit a timewarp into the Terrahawks organisation through Spacehawk, with Mary as a carrier to hold the timewarp in her mind until Tempo is ready to unleash it. However, Mary's mind was too strong and she rejected the timewarp, so Tempo selects a more suitable subject in the form of Sergeant Major Zero. Tiger and Mary are puzzled to discover that there is an eight-second time-lag in Zero's responses to commands so he is sent to the Zeroid Sick Bay for a check-up. Meanwhile, Zelda launches her entire fleet in preparation for battle and as the fleet nears Earth, Zelda tells Tempo to unleash the timewarp...

Notes

Lord Tempo was previously seen in *My Kingdom For A Zeaf* and *First Strike*. *Timewarp* features the final appearance of It-Star. He uses only the dominant Birlgoy (male) personality here: the Goybirl (female) personality was last seen in *Doppelganger*. The animated noughts and crosses game on the end titles is also seen at the end of *The Gun* and *Play It Again, Sram*.

Regular Voice Cast

Dr. Tiger Ninestein	**Jeremy Hitchin**
Cpt. Mary Falconer	**Denise Bryer**
Sgt. Major Zero	**Windsor Davies**
Cpt. Kate Kestrel	**Anne Ridler**
Lt. Hiro	**Jeremy Hitchin**
Space Sgt. 101	**Ben Stevens**
Zelda	**Denise Bryer**
Yung-Star	**Ben Stevens**
Cy-Star	**Anne Ridler**
Dix-Huit	**Ben Stevens**
It-Star	**Jeremy Hitchin**

Guest Voice Cast

Lord Tempo	**Ben Stevens**

First UK Transmission

Saturday, July 5th, 1986
11.30am (ITV Network)

SPACE GIANT — Prod. No. 37

Written by **Manny Pheakstein** Directed by **Tony Lenny**

At a titanium mining outpost on Zeta Four, miners Miller and Cass discover a small sporilla trapped inside the bars of the mine elevator cage. Cass sees an opportunity to make a fortune out of the creature so they smuggle it to Earth and sell it to circus owner The Great Alonzo. However, Cass is unhappy with Alonzo's low payment for the sporilla and anonymously alerts NASA. Johnson contacts the Terrahawks and soon Tiger and Mary are on their way to the circus in Battlehawk. However, the creature is actually a giant sporilla that has been miniaturised by Zelda and when she returns it to its full size, it goes on a rampage, destroying the circus and crushing Alonzo...

Notes

This episode is Gerry Anderson's homage to *King Kong* (1933) with the sporilla as Kong, Mary in the Ann Darrow role (played by Fay Wray in the film) and Hawkwing in place of the biplane that attacks Kong at the top of the Empire State Building. TERRAHAWKS model-maker Ben Tuszynski takes the role of the giant sporilla, appearing in a sporilla suit on the model set in the style of Toho Studios' *Godzilla* (1954). Other Sporillas were seen in *The Sporilla* and *Mind Monster*.

Regular Voice Cast

Dr. Tiger Ninestein	**Jeremy Hitchin**
Cpt. Mary Falconer	**Denise Bryer**
Sgt. Major Zero	**Windsor Davies**
Cpt. Kate Kestrel	**Anne Ridler**
Lt. Hiro	**Jeremy Hitchin**
Lt. Hawkeye	**Jeremy Hitchin**
Space Sgt. 101	**Ben Stevens**
Zelda	**Denise Bryer**
Yung-Star	**Ben Stevens**
Colonel Johnson	**Jeremy Hitchin**

Guest Voice Cast

The Great Alonzo	**Ben Stevens**
Cass	**Jeremy Hitchin**
Miller / Fan	**Ben Stevens**
Sue Ellen	**Anne Ridler**

First UK Transmission

Sunday, December 9th, 1984
4.30pm (ITV Network)

COLD FINGER — Prod. No. 38

Written by **I.C. Bergstein** Directed by **Tony Bell**

Zelda enters into a pact with Cold Finger, the master of ice, who promises to create a new Ice Age on Earth. He launches a huge space iceberg and sets it on a collision course with Earth. Tracking the spaceberg, 101 reports that it is accelerating and Tiger realises that it is not a natural phenomenon. When the Space Zeroids open fire on the berg, it breaks down into an ice storm that threatens the Moon but additional firepower destroys the largest pieces. Tiger, Mary and Zero head for Spacehawk to coordinate a search for the source of the attack but then Cold Finger launches ten more spacebergs...

Notes

Kate Kestrel sings 'Be My Star Tonight' at the White House but has no actual dialogue in this episode. The animated noughts and crosses game on the end titles is also seen at the end of *The Sporilla* and *Ma's Monsters*.

Oops!

As Zelda's Hub ship approaches Cold Finger's ice ship, the two vehicles overlap. They overlap again when Zelda returns to Mars later on.

Regular Voice Cast

Dr. Tiger Ninestein	**Jeremy Hitchin**
Cpt. Mary Falconer	**Denise Bryer**
Sgt. Major Zero	**Windsor Davies**
Lt. Hiro	**Jeremy Hitchin**
Space Sgt. 101	**Ben Stevens**
Zelda	**Denise Bryer**
Yung-Star	**Ben Stevens**
Cy-Star	**Anne Ridler**
Dix-Huit	**Ben Stevens**

Guest Voice Cast

Cold Finger	**Ben Stevens**

First UK Transmission

Sunday, November 18th, 1984
4.30pm (ITV Network)

OPERATION ZERO — Prod. No. 39

Written by **Anne Teakstein** Directed by **Tony Lenny**

Zero has skipped having a major check-up but when it becomes apparent that there is something seriously wrong with the Zeroid, Tiger orders him to the Zeroid Sick Bay for an examination. Dr. Kiljoy decides that he must operate at once so the Zeroid Nurse uncouples Zero's currents to put him to sleep. He awakens to the sound of a 10-40 battle stations alert signal as Zelda's entire fleet approaches Earth for a final assault. Against Dr. Kiljoy's orders, Zero discharges himself from Sick Bay and takes charge of the search operation when he discovers that Zelda's Hub has landed within a mile of Hawknest. Now Zelda, Yung-Star and Cy-Star are at large in the base...

Notes

Dr. Kiljoy was previously seen in *The Ugliest Monster Of All* and *Zero's Finest Hour*. One of the injured Zeroids in the Sick Bay is the unlucky Zeroid 13 who is presumably the same Irish-accented Zeroid 13 seen at the end of *The Gun* (he does not speak here). A previous Zeroid 13 was destroyed during the first battle with Zelda in *Expect The Unexpected*. Footage of Zelda's fleet leaving Mars and approaching Earth is lifted from *A Christmas Miracle*, where it also appeared as part of a dream sequence.

Regular Voice Cast

Dr. Tiger Ninestein	**Jeremy Hitchin**
Cpt. Mary Falconer	**Denise Bryer**
Sgt. Major Zero	**Windsor Davies**
Cpt. Kate Kestrel	**Anne Ridler**
Lt. Hiro	**Jeremy Hitchin**
Space Sgt. 101 / Hudson	**Ben Stevens**
Zelda	**Denise Bryer**
Yung-Star	**Ben Stevens**
Cy-Star	**Anne Ridler**
Dix-Huit	**Ben Stevens**

Guest Voice Cast

Dr. Kiljoy	**Windsor Davies**
Zeroid Nurse	**Anne Ridler**
Zeroid 27	**Ben Stevens**

First UK Transmission

Saturday, July 12th, 1986
11.30am (ITV Network)

Feature Film Titles

(Listed in production order)

1. **Expect The Unexpected**
2. **Menace From Mars**
3. **Terror From Mars**
4. **Hostages Of Mars**
5. **Flaming Thunderbolts**
6. **Zero Strikes Back**

Feature Running Time

86 minutes approx.

COMPILATION FEATURE FILMS

In tandem with post-production on the later episodes of the first production block and production of the final 13 episodes of TERRAHAWKS, 24 episodes from the first production block were reformatted by Anderson Burr Pictures into six feature-length television movies. Primarily, these compilation feature films were intended for release in the UK's fledgling home video market, but were also offered to overseas broadcasters as an alternative format to the original episodes. The six features were released on VHS, Betamax and Video 2000 videotape by Precision Video in the UK in 1983 and 1984 and the first, *Expect The Unexpected*, won the Best Creative Children's Video award at the 1983 UK Video Awards. The films were subsequently re-released on VHS by Channel 5 Video in 1986 but have not, to date, been broadcast in the UK.

EXPECT THE UNEXPECTED

Compilation of *Expect The Unexpected*, *Expect The Unexpected Part 2*, *Thunder-Roar* and *Close Call*.

MENACE FROM MARS

Compilation of *Space Samurai*, *The Sporilla*, *Happy Madeday* and *From Here To Infinity*.

TERROR FROM MARS

Compilation of *Thunder Path*, *The Ugliest Monster Of All*, *Gunfight At Oaky's Corral* and *The Gun*.

HOSTAGES OF MARS

Compilation of *To Catch A Tiger*, *Mind Monster*, *Operation S.A.S.* and *Ten Top Pop*.

FLAMING THUNDERBOLTS

Compilation of *My Kingdom For A Zeaf*, *Play It Again, Sram*, *Gold* and *Midnight Blue*.

ZERO STRIKES BACK

Compilation of *The Midas Touch*, *Unseen Menace*, *Zero's Finest Hour* and *The Ultimate Menace*.

Regular Voice Cast

Dr. Tiger Ninestein	**Jeremy Hitchin**
Cpt. Mary Falconer	**Denise Bryer**
Sgt. Major Zero	**Windsor Davies**
Cpt. Kate Kestrel	**Anne Ridler**
Lt. Hiro	**Jeremy Hitchin**
Lt. Hawkeye	**Jeremy Hitchin**
Zelda	**Denise Bryer**
Yung-Star	**Ben Stevens**
Cy-Star	**Anne Ridler**
Stew Dapples	**Ben Stevens**

First UK Transmission

Monday, October 1st, 1984
to Wednesday, October 31st, 1984
4.00 – 5.15pm (ITV Network)

TERRAHAWKS PRESENT CHILDREN'S ITV

In September 1984, Anderson Burr Pictures produced a series of over 70 short linking sequences for the ITV Network's CHILDREN'S ITV strand, in which various TERRAHAWKS characters introduced the children's programmes that would be broadcast on weekdays between 4.00pm and 5.15pm during October that year. Each of the characters appeared on an appropriate set from the series (Tiger and Mary in Battlehawk, Kate and Stew at Anderburr Records and so on) and a simple plotline was established in which the Terrahawks attempted to prevent Zelda from usurping CHILDREN'S ITV and broadcasting her own programmes as Zelda Network Television. The links varied in length from five to 30 seconds with a total running time of approximately 16 minutes.

Monday, October 1st, 1984

Tiger, Zero, Mary, Yung-Star, Zelda and Hawkeye introduce FLICKS, TOWSER, HE-MAN AND THE MASTERS OF THE UNIVERSE, EDUCATING MARMALADE and DANGER MOUSE.

Tuesday, October 2nd, 1984

Hiro, Tiger, Mary and Kate introduce PORTLAND BILL, TOWSER, ON SAFARI and ADVENTURE OF A LIFETIME and Kate previews THOMAS THE TANK ENGINE & FRIENDS.

Wednesday, October 3rd, 1984

Zelda and Yung-Star introduce ROD, JANE & FREDDY, TOWSER, SAM'S LUCK and HOLD TIGHT!

Thursday, October 4th, 1984

Tiger, Mary and Stew introduce BUTTERCUP BUSKERS, TOWSER, PASSPORT TO TREASURE and SPOOKY.

Friday, October 5th, 1984
Zero, Hiro, Hawkeye and Tiger introduce RAINBOW, TOWSER, INSPECTOR GADGET and TIME TO TIME.

Monday, October 8th, 1984
Zelda, Tiger, Hawkeye, Yung-Star and Cy-Star introduce FLICKS, TOWSER, HE-MAN AND THE MASTERS OF THE UNIVERSE, EDUCATING MARMALADE and DANGER MOUSE.

Tuesday, October 9th, 1984
Zero, Hiro, Mary and Kate introduce THOMAS THE TANK ENGINE & FRIENDS, TOWSER, ON SAFARI and ADVENTURE OF A LIFETIME.

Wednesday, October 10th, 1984
Tiger, Mary, Zelda and Cy-Star introduce ROD, JANE & FREDDY, TOWSER, SAM'S LUCK and HOLD TIGHT!

Thursday, October 11th, 1984
Zero, Kate, Tiger and Hawkeye introduce BUTTERCUP BUSKERS, TOWSER, PASSPORT TO TREASURE and SPOOKY.

Friday, October 12th, 1984
Tiger, Mary and Zelda introduce RAINBOW, TOWSER, INSPECTOR GADGET and TIME TO TIME and Tiger and Mary preview ROYAL CHILDREN.

Monday, October 15th, 1984
Tiger, Zero, Mary and Stew introduce FLICKS, TOWSER, HE-MAN AND THE MASTERS OF THE UNIVERSE, EDUCATING MARMALADE and DANGER MOUSE.

Tuesday, October 16th, 1984
Zelda, Hawkeye, Kate, Zero and Tiger introduce THOMAS THE TANK ENGINE & FRIENDS, TOWSER, ON SAFARI and CBTV and Kate previews RUB A DUB DUB.

Wednesday, October 17th, 1984
Tiger, Zero and Hawkeye introduce ROD, JANE & FREDDY, RUB A DUB DUB, SAM'S LUCK and HOLD TIGHT!

Thursday, October 18th, 1984
Stew and Zelda introduce BUTTERCUP BUSKERS, RUB A DUB DUB, PASSPORT TO TREASURE and SPOOKY.

Friday, October 19th, 1984
Zero and Mary introduce RAINBOW, RUB A DUB DUB, INSPECTOR GADGET and ROYAL CHILDREN and Tiger warns viewers to stay space alert.

Monday, October 22nd, 1984
Stew introduces FLICKS, RUB A DUB DUB, HE-MAN AND THE MASTERS OF THE UNIVERSE, EDUCATING MARMALADE and DANGER MOUSE.

Tuesday, October 23rd, 1984
Zero and Yung-Star introduce THOMAS THE TANK ENGINE & FRIENDS, RUB A DUB DUB, ON SAFARI and CBTV.

Wednesday, October 24th, 1984
Zelda takes over CHILDREN'S ITV and broadcasts programmes from the Zelda Television Network. She, Yung-Star and Cy-Star introduce ROD, JANE & FREDDY, RUB A DUB DUB, SAM'S LUCK and RAZZMATAZZ.

Thursday, October 25th, 1984
Zelda, Yung-Star and Cy-Star introduce BUTTERCUP BUSKERS, RUB A DUB DUB, PASSPORT TO TREASURE and SPOOKY.

Friday, October 26th, 1984
Zelda, Yung-Star and Cy-Star introduce RAINBOW, RUB A DUB DUB, INSPECTOR GADGET and ILLUSIONS.

UK Broadcast Seasons

On original broadcast in the UK, the 39 episodes of TERRAHAWKS were broken down into three seasons of 13 episodes apiece for screening by ITV, as follows:

SEASON ONE (1983)
1. **Expect The Unexpected**
2. **Expect The Unexpected Part 2**
3. **Thunder-Roar**
4. **Happy Madeday**
5. **The Ugliest Monster Of All**
6. **Close Call**
7. **The Gun**
8. **Gunfight At Oaky's Corral**
9. **Thunder Path**
10. **From Here To Infinity**
11. **Mind Monster**
12. **A Christmas Miracle**
13. **To Catch A Tiger**

SEASON TWO (1984)
1. **Operation S.A.S.**
2. **Ten Top Pop**
3. **Play It Again, Sram**
4. **The Ultimate Menace**
5. **Midnight Blue**
6. **My Kingdom For A Zeaf**
7. **Zero's Finest Hour**
8. **Cold Finger**
9. **Unseen Menace**
10. **Space Giant**
11. **Cry UFO**
12. **The Midas Touch**
13. **Ma's Monsters**

SEASON THREE (1986)
1. **Two For The Price Of One**
2. **First Strike**
3. **Terratomb**
4. **Space Cyclops**
5. **Doppelganger**
6. **Child's Play**
7. **Jolly Roger One**
8. **Space Samurai**
9. **Runaway**
10. **Timewarp**
11. **Operation Zero**
12. **The Sporilla**
13. **Gold**

Although it was initially announced that TERRAHAWKS would be the first Gerry Anderson series to be fully networked in the UK since FOUR FEATHER FALLS, several regions ultimately decided to opt out of the network broadcast when the first season started in October 1983. Episodes premiered on Central on Saturday mornings from October 8th and were then screened by the majority of other regions on Sunday afternoons, although Granada held back their start date until October 23rd. In the Tyne-Tees region, *Expect The Unexpected* was shown on Thursday, October 13th, but then no further episodes were broadcast until five weeks later when the series began again with a repeat screening of the first episode on November 17th. However, the two episodes shown over the Christmas period, *A Christmas Miracle* and *To Catch A Tiger*, were both fully networked on Saturday mornings.

From the start of the series' second season on September 23rd, 1984, the episodes were almost fully networked by the ITV regions with Central, LWT, Granada, Yorkshire, Tyne-Tees, Anglia and Border all showing the same episodes on Sunday afternoons. Grampian screened the same episodes on the same days, but usually an hour behind the other regions, although the station broadcast *Midnight Blue* 15 minutes before it was seen in the other regions. Grampian also scheduled earlier screenings for the two episodes shown over the 1984 Christmas period, *The Midas Touch* and *Ma's Monsters* – both episodes were shown there over an hour before they were seen by the rest of the network.

The remaining 13 episodes that comprised the third broadcast season of TERRAHAWKS were held back until 1986 when they were fully networked by the ITV regions on Saturday mornings from May 3rd. By this time, all 13 episodes had been shown in Japan and the majority of them had also been seen in America.

Monday, October 29th, 1984

Zelda and Yung-Star introduce FLICKS, RUB A DUB DUB, HE-MAN AND THE MASTERS OF THE UNIVERSE and MURPHY'S MOB and then preview Thursday's episode of MURPHY'S MOB.

Tuesday, October 30th, 1984

Tiger and Mary introduce THOMAS THE TANK ENGINE & FRIENDS, RUB A DUB DUB, ON SAFARI and CBTV and begin to plan how to wrest control of CHILDREN'S ITV from Zelda.

Wednesday, October 31st, 1984

During the night, Hiro has installed an interceptor beam to jam Zelda's transmissions and Tiger has recovered the programmes that she stole. Mary, Stew and Hiro introduce ROD, JANE & FREDDY, RUB A DUB DUB, SAM'S LUCK and RAZZMATAZZ and Kate previews CHISH & FIPS. Tiger, Mary, Hawkeye, Kate and Zero introduce the next CHILDREN'S ITV presenter Bonnie Langford before saying goodbye.

Overseas Versions and Further Adventures

Following the relative success of the screenings of the first season of TERRAHAWKS on British television, Anderburr Pictures appointed Richard Price Television Associates to offer the series for overseas sales. They very quickly negotiated sales to broadcasters in France, Holland, Australia and New Zealand, before striking a deal with the NHK network in Japan, which dubbed the dialogue into Japanese and added a new animated opening title sequence directed by Satoshi Dezaki.

The series was also bought for American television by the Tribune Broadcasting Company, owners of independent television stations in New York, Chicago, Denver, New Orleans and Atlanta, which decided to premiere the series on its flagship station WPIX-TV New York. The Tribune executives requested a new opening title sequence that would better explain the series' concept to American viewers and plans were made to edit action footage of the various vehicles and characters into the existing animated material. Then Tribune changed their minds and the sequence was abandoned, although a new end title sequence was produced to replace the existing noughts and crosses games on the American prints. This featured an animated Zeroid bouncing up and down at the side of the screen next to one of Zelda's Cubes and then landing squarely on top of the Cube and smashing it. The original end title music was replaced by one of Kate Kestrel's songs, 'Living In The 21st Century', performed by Moya Griffiths.

Tribune were so pleased with TERRAHAWKS that they also expressed an interest in acquiring an additional 26 episodes to bring the total number to 65. This would enable episodes to be shown every weekday for a year by screening the entire series four times. With barely enough time to complete the new episodes before they would be required for broadcast, Gerry Anderson immediately began commissioning new scripts so that filming could get underway as soon as the contracts were signed.

The first of these scripts, 'Number One Seed', was written by Anderson himself under the pseudonym Gerry Anderstein and tells of a plot by Zelda to disable the Terrahawks with a giant pumpkin. She sends a packet of Gargantuan pumpkin seeds to Earth as a birthday gift for Hiro and although it is intercepted by Colonel Johnson and passed to Tiger for examination, the packet is accidentally given to Hiro by Zero. Hiro plants the seeds on Spacehawk and the pumpkin grows to an enormous size overnight, filling the control room and crippling Spacehawk. The situation is resolved when Hiro blows the entire contents of the Spacehawk control room out into space, hurling the pumpkin directly at Yung-Star's Zeaf as he prepares to attack.

Further scripts, including 'Attempted Moider' by Tony Barwick (as D.I. Skeistein) and an untitled script by David Nightingale, were also completed but Tribune ultimately opted not to bankroll the additional instalments.

In December 1984, TERRAHAWKS title sequence and video game animator Kevin Davies submitted a proposal for an animated spin-off series, 'The Zeroids & Cubes'. This would have focused on Zero, 101 and new Zeroids Brigadier 'Bill' Billion and Space Sergeant Thousand (*aka* 'Grandad') as they battled against Zelda's Cubes led by Cube Roots, Cube Ridge and femme fatale Ruby Cube. However, Anderson and Burr had decided to move on to new projects and the idea went no further.

DICK SPANNER

Format

Not so long ago in a parallel universe not far from here, robot private investigator Dick Spanner walks the mean streets of the Big Pear in a world of strange aliens, even stranger humans, rampaging dinosaurs, giant apes and terrible puns. Working from an office on the 15th floor of a crummy block on the East Side of the wrong side, Dick takes on the cases that other gumshoes don't want to touch, the ones that are too dangerous, too bizarre or simply don't pay enough. The voluminous pockets of his coat contain a variety of devices that can help to extricate him from any sticky situation if he gets into a jam, but the problem is finding the right device for the right situation at the right time. Dick cannot stand heights, which is unfortunate as he invariably finds himself falling from them, but no matter what life-threatening situation he might face, Dick always manages to land on his feet – or occasionally his head.

Dick's closest friend is the sultry and curvaceous engineer Mae East, a dab hand with a soldering iron who gives the best lube jobs and never misses an opportunity to get her hands on Dick's nuts. Hankering for a change of direction, she later adopts the name Mae South in an attempt to break into the movie industry. Dick is often at odds with the law in the form of Lieutenant O'Grady from the 10th Precinct, a man who has little time for private eyes and would like nothing better than to see Dick banged up in the slammer. However, he recognises that Dick has an uncanny knack of getting to the bottom of even the most complex and incomprehensible mysteries, and is usually on hand to clean up after Dick exposes the culprits.

Production

Stop-motion animation had been used in the Gerry Anderson productions as early as SUPERCAR in 1960 but was employed to greater effect for a number of visual effects sequences in TERRAHAWKS. Terry Adlam, one of Steven Begg's visual effects assistants on TERRAHAWKS, conceived the idea of a stop-motion animated comedy series featuring a down-at-heel private eye who would narrate each story in the style of Raymond Chandler's Philip Marlowe novels, popularised by Humphrey Bogart in the film noir classic *The Big Sleep* (1946). Anderson was intrigued so he and Christopher Burr decided to finance the production of a six-minute pilot episode which was shot at Bray Studios in April 1985. Using puppet figures primarily made from modelling clay, the animation was achieved by making minute adjustments to the figures between exposures of one frame of film for each set-up.

DICK SPANNER was eventually sold to the relatively new British station Channel 4 who felt that the pilot's odd mixture of slapstick comedy, over-literal puns and double-entendres was perfect to form part of a new two-hour Sunday magazine programme aimed at 18- to 24-year-olds, NETWORK 7. Channel 4 commissioned an additional 21 episodes so that they could slot one instalment into each of the 22 NETWORK 7 programmes, and filming on the new episodes resumed in February 1987. Although the wise-cracking dialogue was all pre-recorded by former THUNDERBIRDS voice artist Shane Rimmer as detailed in the script, many of the series' visual gags were created during filming by director Terry Adlam, cameraman Steven Begg and art director Mark Harris.

Presented as a single multi-part story, the series actually comprised two 11-part stories which, although untitled on screen, were officially documented as *The Incredible Case Of Harry The Human Cannon-Ball* and *The Strange Case Of The Maltese Parrot*.

Alternative Format

For repeat screenings of the DICK SPANNER segments, Channel 4 also commissioned Anderson Burr Pictures to re-edit the existing six-minute episodes into four 24-minute instalments with each story presented in two parts. Dropping the opening and closing title sequences and the story recap sequence from the original episodes still left each story with a running time of 55 minutes, so fully seven minutes had to be trimmed from both before they could be split into the requisite parts. The story titles were slightly truncated for captions overlaid on the start of each instalment.

Main Characters

Dick Spanner
Cynical wise-cracking robot private investigator, a traditional gumshoe with no head for heights

Mae East
Curvaceous robotics engineer with a soft spot for Dick

Lieutenant O'Grady
Pig-headed police officer from the Big Pear's 10th Precinct

Too Tall Tim Johnson
A former basketball player squashed to a height of two feet by a falling elevator

Tall Tim 2
Too Tall Tim's very tall brother

Sidney Sidestreet (*aka* The Fat Man)
A consultant know-all and the true identity of mob boss Mendoza and circus owner Signor Allova

Eric Von Strongbow
Strawberry jam magnate and Ivywood film producer who employs only short actors

Gloria Vamp
Ivywood sex symbol and a legend in her own bi-line

Wild Man Carew
Circus strongman who later becomes an Ivywood lighting cameraman

Episode Titles

(Listed in production order)

ORIGINAL FORMAT

The Incredible Case Of Harry The Human Cannon-Ball

1. **Part One**
2. **Part Two**
3. **Part Three**
4. **Part Four**
5. **Part Five**
6. **Part Six**
7. **Part Seven**
8. **Part Eight**
9. **Part Nine**
10. **Part Ten**
11. **Part Eleven**

The Strange Affair Of The Maltese Parrot

12. **Part One**
13. **Part Two**
14. **Part Three**
15. **Part Four**
16. **Part Five**
17. **Part Six**
18. **Part Seven**
19. **Part Eight**
20. **Part Nine**
21. **Part Ten**
22. **Part Eleven**

ALTERNATIVE FORMAT

1. **The Case Of The Human Cannon-Ball Part 1**
2. **The Case Of The Human Cannon-Ball Part 2**
3. **The Case Of The Maltese Parrot Part 1**
4. **The Case Of The Maltese Parrot Part 2**

Episode Running Time

Original Format:
6 minutes approx.

Alternative Format:
24 minutes approx.

Regular Voice Cast

Dick Spanner **Shane Rimmer**

PRODUCTION CREDITS

Produced by **Gerry Anderson & Christopher Burr**
From an idea by **Terry Adlam**
Creative Supervision **Gerry Anderson**
Music Composed and Performed by **Christopher Burr**
Associate Producer **Bob Bell**
Production Co-ordinator **Mary Anderson**
Photography **Steve Begg** *(1-14, 20)*
Paddy Seale *(15-19, 21, 22)*
Animation **Mark Woollard**
Editor **Jack Gardner**
Sound **Russell Shaw***
Model Designer **Barry Jones**
Modelmakers **Ben Tuszynski**
John Weller
Chris Harper

Produced by The Anderson Burr Partnership
in association with Channel 4
An Anderson Burr Picture

* uncredited on 6-minute version

THE INCREDIBLE CASE OF HARRY THE HUMAN CANNON-BALL Prod. No. 01-11

Written by **Harry Bolt**

Directed by **Steve Begg** *(Parts One and Eight)*
Terry Adlam *(Parts Two to Seven and Nine to Eleven)*

Dick Spanner is hired by a mysterious woman to find a man named Harry who worked in a circus as a human cannon-ball before he was fired. Harry has now disappeared, so Dick agrees to take the case – the woman's very heavy suitcase – and searches the streets of the Big Pear for a lead. At the Crow Bar, he contacts an informant named Squealer but someone bumps him off with a demolition ball. When Dick returns to his office, he is arrested by Lieutenant O'Grady on a charge of murder Juan after a dead Mexican is found in his cupboard and, realising that he has been framed, Dick makes a run for it. Then mob boss Mendoza puts a price on Dick's head and, after avoiding a number of assassination attempts, Dick is caught red-handed with another dead Mexican by O'Grady. A bit of fast-talking persuades O'Grady to let him go and eventually Dick's investigations lead him to Signor Allova's Flying Circus...

Notes

Harry Bolt is a pseudonym for writer Tony Barwick. One of Zelda's Cubes from TERRAHAWKS appears on the street in *Part Three*. A Police Cruiser from SPACE POLICE is seen driving past the 16th Precinct at the start of *Part Four*.

Oops!

In *Part One*, Dick reveals that his office is on the 15th floor of the East Side tower block, but in *Part Six* he says it is on the 10th floor. Dick introduces O'Grady as a Lieutenant from the 10th Precinct, but after Dick is caught red-handed, O'Grady takes him to the 16th Precinct for questioning. Mary Anderson is credited as 'Poduction' Co-ordinator on the end titles of every episode.

First UK Transmission (Original Format)

Part One Sunday, May 3rd, 1987, 1.20pm (approx.) (Channel 4)
Part Two Sunday, May 10th, 1987, 1.20pm (approx.) (Channel 4)
Part Three Sunday, May 17th, 1987, 1.20pm (approx.) (Channel 4)
Part Four Sunday, May 24th, 1987, 1.20pm (approx.) (Channel 4)
Part Five Sunday, May 31st, 1987, 1.20pm (approx.) (Channel 4)
Part Six Sunday, June 7th, 1987, 1.20pm (approx.) (Channel 4)
Part Seven Sunday, June 14th, 1987, 1.20pm (approx.) (Channel 4)
Part Eight Sunday, June 21st, 1987, 1.20pm (approx.) (Channel 4)
Part Nine Sunday, June 28th, 1987, 1.20pm (approx.) (Channel 4)
Part Ten Sunday, July 5th, 1987, 1.20pm (approx.) (Channel 4)
Part Eleven Sunday, July 12th, 1987, 1.20pm (approx.) (Channel 4)
All episodes screened as part of NETWORK 7 programme.

First UK Transmission (Alternative Format)

Part One Sunday, December 13th, 1987, 11.30pm (Channel 4)
Part Two Sunday, December 20th, 1987, 11.30pm (Channel 4)

THE STRANGE AFFAIR OF THE MALTESE PARROT

Prod. No. 12-22

Written by **Harry Bolt** Directed by **Terry Adlam**

After flying back from Mexico, Dick returns to his office to find a huge jar of strawberry jam jammed in the door jamb and his office walls covered in the same jam. Then he learns that he is being sued by Too Tall Tim Johnson and his brother Tall Tim Two, who agree to drop their lawsuit if Dick helps them to find their missing pet Maltese parrot. As the pair work as stuntmen in Ivywood, the film capital, Dick goes there to investigate and drops in on former silent screen siren Gloria Vamp. Later, at the Brown Trilby Restaurant, pint-sized film stars George Lifeboat and Edward G. Hobson hold him at fingerpoint and take him to the top of the RUOK tower where they demand that he hand over the missing parrot. Dick escapes by leaping from the tower to land safely on an old moose head, but then a misunderstanding with the members of a Moose Hunting Lodge lands him in the Sing A Song Penitentiary...

Notes

Harry Bolt is a pseudonym for writer Tony Barwick. Gloria Vamp's house is a homage to Alfred Hitchcock's *Psycho* (1960), being a miniature version of the Bates house seen in that film. The footage of King Kong climbing a tower block that Von Strongbow watches on a home movie projector at Gloria Vamp's house in *Part Three* is lifted from *The Incredible Case Of Harry The Human Cannon-Ball Part Two*. A photo of Gerry Anderson appears prominently on the wall of Von Strongbow's office. Anderson himself (or rather, a plasticine version of him) appears as film producer Sam Silverwyn in *Part Nine*.

Oops!

In *Part Six*, Dick says that he made the front page of the *Big Pear Times* with the headline 'Spanner Hammers Washers & Bolts', but the newspaper shown bearing this headline is the *Ivywood Excess*. In *Part Ten*, Dick says that O'Grady has taken him to the Ivywood station house, but the establishing shot shows the 16th Precinct station house in the Big Pear. Mary Anderson is again credited as 'Poduction' Co-ordinator on the end titles of every episode.

First UK Transmission (Original Format)

Part One Sunday, July 19th, 1987, 1.20pm (approx.) (Channel 4)
Part Two Sunday, July 26th, 1987, 1.20pm (approx.) (Channel 4)
Part Three Sunday, August 2nd, 1987, 1.20pm (approx.) (Channel 4)
Part Four Sunday, August 9th, 1987, 1.20pm (approx.) (Channel 4)
Part Five Sunday, August 16th, 1987, 1.20pm (approx.) (Channel 4)
Part Six Sunday, August 23rd, 1987, 1.20pm (approx.) (Channel 4)
Part Seven Sunday, August 30th, 1987, 1.20pm (approx.) (Channel 4)
Part Eight Sunday, September 6th, 1987, 1.20pm (approx.) (Channel 4)
Part Nine Sunday, September 13th, 1987, 1.20pm (approx.) (Channel 4)
Part Ten Sunday, September 20th, 1987, 1.20pm (approx.) (Channel 4)
Part Eleven Sunday, September 27th, 1987, 1.20pm (approx.) (Channel 4)
All episodes screened as part of NETWORK 7 programme.

First UK Transmission (Alternative Format)

Part One Friday, March 18th, 1988, 6.00pm (Channel 4)
Part Two Friday, March 25th, 1988, 6.00pm (Channel 4)

Regular Voice Cast

Dick Spanner **Shane Rimmer**

DICK SPANNER was originally broadcast in the UK as a short segment of a longer programme, NETWORK 7, a magazine programme aimed at 18- to 24-year-olds presented by Janet Street-Porter. Running from noon to 2.00pm every Sunday on Channel 4 for five months from May 1987, NETWORK 7 provided an eclectic mixture of under-prepared celebrity interviews, amateurish current affairs reports on subjects of special interest to the target audience (various aspects of clubbing and drug culture were the primary topics) and live performances by obscure 'indie' bands.

DICK SPANNER very quickly became the show's only reason for many viewers to continue watching, but schedulers resolutely refused to pin down the programme's start time to anything other than 'between 1.00 and 1.30pm'. When the episodes *did* finally appear (usually any time after 1.20pm), the picture was often overlaid with intrusive graphics advertising the forthcoming items in a vain attempt to dissuade viewers from switching off as soon as DICK SPANNER ended. Clearly NETWORK 7 was about 16 years ahead of its time.

SPACE PRECINCT

Format

Two hundred years ago, planet Altor in the Epsilon Erandi System was completely uninhabited, but by the year 2040 it has been colonised by alien species from the planet's neighbouring worlds, primarily creons from the planet Danae and tarns from the planet Simter. Considerable poverty on their homeworlds and numerous trading opportunities on Altor have encouraged large numbers of creons and tarns to settle on Altor alongside smaller communities of alien life-forms from other solar systems. A community of humans from Earth is the planet's third largest group of settlers and is growing fast.

Demeter City is Altor's largest population centre, a major refuelling point and stopover for interplanetary freight. Consequently, the city has become home from home to a large transient community and crime is rife. Keeping order in this unpredictable environment are the officers of Space Police Precinct 88, under the command of creon Captain Rexton Podly and based in a space Station House which sits in geostationary orbit over Demeter City. The officers' primary mode of transport is the Police Cruiser, a high-speed patrol vehicle that is equally at home in a planetary atmosphere or the depths of space.

Recently transferred from the New York Police Department on Earth are Lieutenant Patrick Brogan and his rookie partner Officer Jackson Haldane, posted on a law enforcement exchange programme. After 20 years with the NYPD, Brogan felt in need of a change and volunteered to join the Space Police. He has been accompanied to Altor by his wife Sally, their 10-year-old daughter Liz and 14-year-old son Matt who all live with him in an apartment in a huge orbiting Space Suburb, a friendly mixed community in a residential orbit around Altor. Since arriving on Altor, Liz has acquired an alien pet named Zil and learned to understand its strange language.

Practically all of Brogan and Haldane's colleagues at Precinct 88 are creons and tarns but there are two other humans, former ECPF (European Community Police Force) Officer Jane Castle and forensics specialist Lionel Carson, the station's science officer. They are assisted by the station's RSA (Robot Secretarial Assistant) Slomo who has instant access to all police files and records.

Production

Following Gerry Anderson and Christopher Burr's failure to find backing for a full series of SPACE POLICE based on their 1986 pilot episode (see separate entry for SPACE POLICE), the project was shelved until 1991 when Anderson collaborated with John Needham of Mentorn Films on a short promotional film for the Birmingham Motor Show. Needham and Mentorn's managing director Tom Gutteridge were keen to develop new television projects with Anderson and entered into partnership with an American company, Grove Television Enterprises (GTV), to raise the finance for a series based on SPACE POLICE. They secured a commission from the BBC to develop a 13-episode series on a budget of £750,000 per episode and a new pilot script, 'The Max Factor', which radically reworked the original pilot's concepts, was written by Gavin Scott.

Production was set to begin early in 1993 when the BBC suddenly backed out of the project citing budget cuts in the drama department, but Gutteridge and Needham were undeterred and commissioned the production of a new two-minute trailer to show the potential of the revised concepts and the new aliens, the creons and the tarns. This trailer enabled Mentorn and GTV to arrange funding from the Gilman Securities Corporation for a 24-episode series on a budget of £20 million.

Pre-production began at Pinewood Studios in Buckinghamshire in March 1994 to develop revolutionary animatronic head appliances for the alien characters that would enable each actor to be fully made-up in just 20 minutes. Pinewood's L & M soundstages were re-modelled with split-level stages which enabled them to accommodate permanent sets for Brogan's apartment and the two-tier Station House and still leave space for sets that would be required on an episode-by-episode basis. The series' visual effects sequences were shot by a separate crew working at Shepperton Studios in Surrey. Working on a ten-day shooting schedule for each episode, filming began on May 9th, 1994 and occupied a crew of over 350 until April 28th, 1995.

Main Characters

Lieutenant Patrick Brogan
43-year-old former New York police officer, married to Sally with two children Matt and Liz, recently transferred to Altor as part of a police exchange programme

Officer Jackson Haldane
26-year-old Tennessee-born former New York police officer, transferred to Altor with Brogan, his police partner for the last five years

Officer Jane Castle
Beautiful 27-year-old former ECPF officer who transferred to Altor over a year ago, partnered with Officer Took who is also her flat-mate

Sally Brogan
Patrick Brogan's 40-year-old wife, an occupational therapist in alien post-operative care at Demeter City Hospital and mother to Matt and Liz

Captain Rexton Podly
Avuncular 55-year-old creon police captain, married to Fama with two grown-up daughters

Matthew Brogan
14-year-old son of Patrick and Sally Brogan

Elizabeth Brogan
10-year-old daughter of Patrick and Sally Brogan

Officer Silas Romek
30-year-old creon officer, partnered with Officer Orrin

Officer Hubble Orrin
23-year-old creon officer, initially partnered with Officer Beezle and then with Officer Romek

Officer Aurelia Took
21-year-old tarn officer, partnered with Officer Jane Castle who is also her flat-mate

Sergeant Thorald Fredo
45-year-old tarn station sergeant, married to Yolanda with a six-year old daughter Estes

Officer Lionel Carson
36-year-old Cincinnati-born station science officer, divorced with a 12-year-old son, J.J., and partnered with Slomo

Slomo
The station's Robot Secretarial Assistant

Officer Beezle
30-year-old creon officer, initially partnered with Officer Orrin

Zipload
Streetwise creon informant

PRODUCTION CREDITS

Series Creator and Producer **Gerry Anderson**
Executive Producer **Tom Gutteridge**
Co-Executive Producers **Roger Lefkon**
John Needham
Line Producer **Tom Sachs**
Associate Producers **Richard Grove** *(1-12)*
Jeffrey Brunner
Producers **J. Larry Carroll** *(1, 5)*
David Bennett Carren *(1, 5)*
Visual Effects Director **Steven Begg**
Director of Photography **Alan Hume BSC**
(1-6, 8-15, 17, 21-24)
Tony Spratling BSC
(7, 16, 18-20)
Special Effects Photography
Harry Oakes BSC *(1-9)*
Peter Talbot *(10-24)*
Live Action Design **Tony Curtis**
Bill Alexander *(6-24)*
Model Design *(1-3, 7-24)* / Models *(4-6)*
Bill Pearson
Creature Effects Design **Neill Gorton**
Tarn & Creon Design **Richard Gregory**
Film Editor **Sue Robinson**
(1, 3, 5, 7, 10, 12, 14, 18, 20, 24)
Jason Krasucki
(2, 4, 6, 8, 11, 13, 15, 17, 21, 22)
Robin McDonell *(9)*
Brian Freemantle *(16)*
Matthew Glen *(19, 23)*
Post Production Supervisor **Mark Sherwood**
Sound Editor **Max Hoskins** *(5)*
Phil Bothamley *(9-24)*
Music **Crispin Merrell**
Executive Story Editor **Philip Morrow**
Executive Story Consultant **Chris Hubbell**
Story Editor **Sam Graham** *(10-24)*
Casting Director (USA) **Lynn Stalmaster** *(1-3)*
Casting Director (UK) *(1-5)* /
Casting Director *(6-24)* **Rebecca Howard**
Production Supervisor **Hugh Harlow**
Costume Design **Raymond Hughes**
Make up & Hair Supervisor **Pam Meager**
Special Effects Supervisors **Alan Whibley**
Ross King *(1-12)*
Ian Biggs *(13-24)*
Post Production Sound **Cliff Jones** *(1-3)*
Paul Langwade *(4-24)*
First Assistant Director **Marcia Gay**
(1, 4, 7, 10, 13, 16, 18, 20, 24)
Christopher Dando
(2, 5, 8, 11, 14, 17, 21, 22)
Clive Reed *(3, 6, 9, 15, 19, 23)*
Barry Langley *(12)*
Second Assistant Director **Julie Davies** *(1-3, 9)*
Paul Morris *(13-16, 19, 24)*
Camera Operator **Jamie Harcourt**
(1-16, 19-23)
Bernard Ford *(17)*
Neil Binney *(18)*
Malcolm Vinson *(24)*

Focus **John Fletcher** *(5-24)*
Chief Electrician **Dennis Brock** *(1-8, 11-24)*
William Pochetty *(9, 10)*
Stunt Co-ordinator *(11)* / Stunts *(18)*
Glenn Marks
(4, 7-9*, 11, 13-17*, 18, 19-24*)*
Production Mixer **Tony Dawe** *(1-22)*
David Allen *(23, 24)*
Dialogue Editor **Max Hoskins** *(6-24)*
Art Director **Bill Alexander** *(1-5)*
Storyboard Artist **Jim Cornish** *(9-24)*
Sculpture Designer **Gary Pollard** *(9-24)*
Construction Manager **John Godfrey** *(5-24)*
Senio Model Maker **Steve Howarth** *(1-4)*
Slomo Designer **David Dunsterville**
Property Master **Brian Wells**
Special Props **James Machin** *(1-6)*
Roy Scott *(7-24)*
Computer Creature Control
Alistair Walsh *(2, 4)*
Visual Effects Co-ordinator *(17, 21, 22)* /
Special Effects Co-ordinator *(18-20)*
Angus Bickerton *(17-22)*
Motion Control **Angus Bickerton** *(1-6)*
Rick Mietkowski
(7, 8, 10, 12, 14, 16, 18, 20, 23, 24)
Nigel Stone
(9, 11, 13, 15, 17, 19, 21, 22)
Digital Effects **Alan Marques** *(1-16, 24)*
Angus Cameron *(17-23)*
Script Supervisor **Cheryl Leigh**
(1-10, 12-19, 21-24)
Sharon Mansfield *(11, 20)*
Production Co-ordinator **Christine Fenton**
Legal Affairs **Catriona Hoolahan**
Production Accountant **John Wall**
Assistant to the Producer **Mary Anderson**
Executive Assistant **Alison Kerr**
Assistant Editor **Charlotte Serpell**
Sound Design *(1)* /
Sound Effects Design *(2-24)* **Beady** *(1-22)*
Eddie Jones *(23, 24)*
Special Visual Effects
Magic Camera Company
Edited on **Lightworks**
Special Thanks to **Hurco Europe**
Eastman Color Film from **Kodak**
Original Processing by **Technicolor®**
Translites by **Stilled Movie Ltd.** *(10-24)*
Produced in Association with
The Space Precinct L.P.
Grove TeleVentures *(13-24)*
and Gilman Securities Corporation
Made at Pinewood and Shepperton Studios
London, England
Country of First Publication -
United States of America
Mentorn Films / Gerry Anderson
Presented in Dolby Surround by
Grove Television Enterprises *(1-12)* /
GTV *(13-24)*

* uncredited

Episode Titles

(Listed in production order)

1. **Double Duty**
2. **Protect And Survive**
3. **Enforcer**
4. **Flash**
5. **The Snake**
6. **Body & Soul**
7. **Time To Kill**
8. **Deadline**
9. **The Power**
10. **Seek And Destroy**
11. **Illegal**
12. **Divided We Stand**
13. **Two Against The Rock**
14. **Takeover**
15. **Predator And Prey**
16. **The Witness**
17. **Hate Street**
18. **Friends**
19. **Smelter Skelter**
20. **Deathwatch**
21. **The Fire Within** (Part One)
22. **The Fire Within** (Part Two)
23. **The Forever Beetle**
24. **Deathwatch Conclusion**

Episode Running Time

43 minutes approx.

SPACE PRECINCT was the first Gerry Anderson production in which all 24 episodes were screened on American television prior to transmission on British television. Syndicated across the United States from October 3rd, 1994, the series suffered from being screened in graveyard timeslots - either very late at night or very early in the morning.

In the UK, the series first appeared on the satellite channel Sky One from March 18th, 1995, broadcast in a primetime 7.00pm timeslot where it regularly became one of the channel's top five programmes. A full terrestrial television screening followed on BBC2 in a 6.00pm slot from September 18th, 1995.

Complete lists of the first US and BBC2 transmission dates appear overleaf. (The Sky One dates accompany the individual episode entries.)

First USA Transmissions

(Listed in production order)

Double Duty October 24th, 1994
Protect And Survive October 3rd, 1994
Enforcer October 10th, 1994
Flash May 29th, 1995
The Snake October 31st, 1994
Body & Soul October 17th, 1994
Time To Kill November 7th, 1994
Deadline November 14th, 1994
The Power January 9th, 1995
Seek And Destroy November 21st, 1994
Illegal January 16th, 1995
Divided We Stand January 30th, 1995
Two Against The Rock February 6th, 1995
Takeover February 13th, 1995
Predator And Prey February 20th, 1995
The Witness April 24th, 1995
Hate Street May 1st, 1995
Friends May 8th, 1995
Smelter Skelter May 15th, 1995
Deathwatch July 17th, 1995
The Fire Within (Part One) June 26th, 1995
The Fire Within (Part Two) July 3rd, 1995
The Forever Beetle July 10th, 1995
Deathwatch Conclusion July 24th, 1995

In May 1994, only days after filming began on *Double Duty*, the producers were forced to drop their original series title, 'Space Police', when they discovered that it had recently been registered as a trademark in the United States by toy manufacturers Lego. Several alternative titles for the series, such as 'Precinct 88' and 'Demeter City Blues', were considered before the producers finally settled on SPACE PRECINCT.

UNCREDITED PRODUCTION PERSONNEL

PRODUCTION DEPARTMENT
Producer's Secretary **Claire Higgins, Suzanne Moulou**
Assistant Co-ordinator **Sharon Mansfield**
Production Runner **Paul Derrick, Simon Emanuel, Sara-Jane Valentine**
Script Co-ordinator **Doreen Coop, Gay Whelan**
Post-Production Co-ordinator **Suzanne Moulou, Louisa Shepherd**
Second Assistant Editor **Mags Arnold**
Assistant Dialogue Editor **Sara Gillian Dodders**
Post-Production Runner **Ian Chitson, Virginia Murray**

MAIN UNIT
Stunt Artists **Lucy Allen, Andrew Bradford, Crystal Chabbert, Abbi Collins, Jonathan Paul Cohen, Gerry Crampton, David Dee, Stuart Fell, Neil Finnighan, Sarah Franzl, Colin Groves, Paul Heasman, Tom Hegarty, Sy Holland, Andrew Hucklesby, Mark Anthony Newman, Adrian O'Neil, Terry Richards, Tony Van Silver, Roderick Woodruffe**
Stand-ins **Katie Allett, Janet Aspinall, Jon Baker, Damien Cleall, Fran Hunter, David Oliver, Anita St. John**
2nd Camera Operator **Neil Binney, Bernard Ford, John Simmons, Malcolm Vinson**
2nd Camera Focus **Neil Brown, Mike Evans, Jason Wren**
Clapper Loader **Sean Connor, Paul Evans, Paul Hanning, David Hedges, Spencer Murray, Robert Palmer, Nick Penn, Clive Pittman**
Grip **John Etherington**
Video Playback Operator **Nicholas Daly**
Boom Operator **Chris Gurney**
Special Effects Technician **Matthew Harlow**
Third Assistant Director **Olivia Lloyd**
Unit Drivers **Douglas Lister, John Newey, Billy Turner**
Unit Nurse **Rosie Bedford-Stradling, Jane Lawrence**

2ND UNIT
Director of Photography **Dennis Brock, Terry Coles, Jimmy Devis, Tony Spratling**
Camera Operator **Martin Menzie, Peter Versey**
Focus **David Hilton, Clive Mackay, Simon Mills, Keith Thomas**
Grip **Harry Eckford, Bob Langridge, Dickie Lee, Adrian McCarthy**
Clapper Loader **David Atkinson, Gavrick Devis, Nienke Hendricks, Helen Williams**
Sound Recordist **David Allen, Rene Borizewitz**
Video Playback Operator **Charles Barter, Nick Coward**
Boom Operator **Jaya Bishop, Stan Phillips, John Samworth, Tommy Staples**
Third Assistant Director **Simon Emanuel, Robert Grayson, Sara-Jane Valentine**

VISUAL EFFECTS UNIT
Camera Operator **David Litchfield**
Focus **Gerry Altman, David Hilton, Peter Talbot, Keith Thomas**
Technician **Tracey Curtis, Graham Riddell**
Gaffer Electrician **Michael McGillivray**
Electrician **Shaun White**
Models **David Allum, Alan Brannan, Andy Hopkinson, Stephen Howarth, Paul Knight, Peter Lee, John Payne, David Poole, Chris Trice, John Weller, Terry Whitehouse, Mark Woollard**
Model Shop Runner **Henry Davis**

ART DEPARTMENT
Art Director **Ken Wheatley**
Assistant Art Director **Simon Lamont, Su Whitaker**
Production Buyer **Jane Cooke, Krissi Williamson**
Set Decorator **Sharon Cartwright**
Draughtsman **David Wood**
Junior Draughtsman **James Hambidge**
Graphics Artist **Carol Kupisz**
Sculptor **Roger Walker**
Art Assistant **Dina Young**

ACTION PROPS DEPARTMENT
Model Designers **Kevin Gilmartin, Steven Scott**
Properties Modeller-Maker Chargehand **Peter Holmes**
Properties Modeller-Makers **Richard Van Den Bergh, Paul Stephenson, Elizabeth Vaughan-Richards**
Drapes Man **Barry Wilson**
Art Department Runner **Katie Gabriel**

WARDROBE & MAKE UP
Wardrobe Master **Paul Vachon**
Wardrobe Mistress **Mary Bridgman**
Tailor/Cutter **Christopher Stevens**
Costume Buyer **Charlotte Sewell**
Wardrobe Assistants **Sheila Cullen, Bryan Davies, Sarah Higbid, Kirsten Marshall**
Costume Makers **Lorraine Cooksley, Chantelle Cox, Jenny Graham, Catherine Hill, Penny King, Brian North, Cheryl-Jane Regan, Sue Stevens**
Make up & Hair Assistants **Julieanne Chapman, Veyatie MacLeod**

TARN & CREON WORKSHOP
Animatronics Model Designer **Chris Barton**
Animatronics Floor Supervisor **Nigel Trevessey**
Animatronics Creature Operator **Christine Glanville**
Animatronics Assistants **Tamzine Hanks, Lindsay Harris**
Assistant Sculptor **Ivan Manzella**

Designer/Modeller **Tacy Kneale**
Modeller **Nigel Blake**
Designer **George Chamberlain**
Catherine Goodley
Sculptor/Painter **Sharon Robbins**
Sculptor/Modeller **Kate Hill**
Mould-Making Supervisor **John Schoonraad**
Mould-Making Assistant **Veronique Keys**
Mould-Makers **Ian Morse**
Tristan Schoonraad
Foam Technician **Adrian Getley**
Animatronic Technicians **Simon Hewitt**
Jamie Jackson-Moore
Slomo Modeller **Alexander Morgan**
Animatronics Unit Runner **Alan Andrews**
John Lewis

CREATURE EFFECTS WORKSHOP
Sculptor Supervisor **Stuart Sewell**
Sculptors **Duncan Brown, Paul Catlin**
Stuart Conran, Daniel Frye
Andrew Hunt, Diane Staniforth
Foam Technician **Daniel Nixon**
Animatronic Modeller **Adrian Parish**
Creature Effects Co-ordinator **Kristian Evans**
Vicki Harvey-Piper
Creature Effects Assistants **Laurence Hallier**
Susan Howard
Creature Effects Runner **Maria Cork**

PROPERTY DEPARTMENT
Dressing Prop Storeman **Paul Humbles**
Dressing Props **David Clarke**
Winston Depper, Albert Gadsen
Lawrence Wells
Standby Props Chargehand **Steven Allett**
Standby Props **Nicolas Stubbings**

CONSTRUCTION DEPARTMENT
Supervising Carpenter **Bert Long**
Chargehand Carpenter **John Marsella**
Carpenters **Bob Archbold, Norman Baker**
Michael Biesty, Lee Biggs, Richard Brown
Robert Brown, Michael Bryant
Laurence Burns, Stanley Catlin
Noel Campbell, John Clarke, John Cole
Michael Davis, Leonard Day
Ciaran Donnelly, Martin Duffy, Gary Fisher
Raymond Fox, Simon Furneaux
Ben Fursewicz, Kenneth Godfrey
Raymond Grant, Leslie Hall, Arthur Healy
John Healy, Martin Hubbard, David Kelly
Adam Kyriakou, Matthew Langley
David Lowen, Stephen McGregor
James McNeil, Eddie Murphy
Anthony Musk, Brian Neighbour
Paul Nott-Macaire, Douglas Phillips
Harry Portlock, Lee Reilly, Steven Rogers
Paul Sansom, Richard Shackleton
Paul Wellbelove, Stephen Williams
Tony Youd, Edwin Young
Machinist **Norman Baker**
Chargehand Plasterer **Ronald Fowler**
Plasterers **Martin Fowler, Anthony Vice**
Supervisor Painter **Steve Williamson**
Chargehand Painter **William Brown**
Painters **Nicholas Bowen, Trevor Eve**
Peter Harrington, Anthony Hanafin
John Hersey, Robert Mason
John McGuigan, Brian Morris
Peter Mounsey, Julian Murray, Jason Reilly
Albert Roper, Glen Start, David Thompson
Paul Whitelock, Bradley Woodbridge
Painter's Labourer **Robert Hartnell**
Standby Painter **Derek Walker**
Chargehand Stagehand **Keith Muir**
Stagehands **Kevin Day, Michael Driscoll**
Derek Ede, Kevin Huse, Richard Law
Gary Malin, Steve Malin, James Muir
Laurence Wells, William Wells
Chargehand Rigger **Edwin Hawkins**
Frankie Webster
Standby Rigger **Sidney Skinner**

ELECTRICAL DEPARTMENT
Best Boy **Andy Hebden**
Electricians **Martin Bloye, Ronald McKay**
Paul Shirley, Tom Shirley, Nigel Woods

ACCOUNTS DEPARTMENT
Assistant Accountant **Sarah Dean**
Accounts Assistants **Claire Browning-Young**
Sue Jenvey

Unfilmed Episodes

Gavin Scott's 1992 'Space Police' pilot script, 'The Max Factor', told how Captain Dave Brogan's arrival in the Demeter System to assume command of the local police force met with the disapproval of crimelord Heironymous Maxul, who kidnapped Brogan and attempted to feed him into a compactor at a space junkyard. However, when the series went into production in 1994, the producers abandoned 'The Max Factor' and commissioned a new introductory story, 'Demeter City' by Paul Mayhew-Archer. In this script Lieutenant Chuck Brogan and Officer Eddie Haldane applied for an operational transfer from New York to planet Alitorp to trace a gang of arms smugglers controlled by alien businessman Mr. Flex. Unfortunately, constraints on the series' shooting schedule caused by the unexpected early screening of episodes in the US prevented 'Demeter City' from being filmed, leaving SPACE PRECINCT without a proper opening episode.

Several other story ideas (with titles such as 'Manhunt' and 'The Guardian') were dropped very early in production, either because they were unworkable, too expensive to produce, or simply not very good. Alan Whiting's 'Stand And Deliver', in which Brogan and Haldane investigated hi-jackings of medical supply trucks, was worked up into a full script before being cancelled, primarily because it lacked any interesting science-fiction elements and no longer suited the format of the series.

First UK Terrestrial Transmissions (BBC2)

(Listed in production order)

Double Duty	November 20th, 1995
Protect And Survive	September 18th, 1995
Enforcer	October 30th, 1995
Flash	January 8th, 1996
The Snake	September 25th, 1995
Body & Soul	October 16th, 1995
Time To Kill	October 2nd, 1995
Deadline	October 23rd, 1995
The Power	November 27th, 1995
Seek And Destroy	November 13th, 1995
Illegal	February 16th, 1996
Divided We Stand	February 12th, 1996
Two Against The Rock	November 6th, 1995
Takeover	December 4th, 1995
Predator And Prey	October 9th, 1995
The Witness	December 18th, 1995
Hate Street	December 11th, 1995
Friends	December 24th, 1995
Smelter Skelter	January 15th, 1996
Deathwatch	February 26th, 1996
The Fire Within (Part One)	January 22nd, 1996
The Fire Within (Part Two)	January 29th, 1996
The Forever Beetle	February 6th, 1996
Deathwatch Conclusion	March 4th, 1996

Almost all of the episodes screened by the BBC appeared in different versions from those that had aired in the US and on Sky One. These 'BBC Six O'Clock' versions were specially prepared by the series' post-production department under instructions from the BBC to tone down or completely delete scenes of violent, threatening or sadistic behaviour, remove all traces of blood and optically enhance all bladed weapons to appear as laser-style instruments. Among the episodes most affected by these changes were *Double Duty*, *Enforcer*, *Flash*, *Time To Kill*, *Seek And Destroy*, *Two Against The Rock* and *The Witness*, but certain episodes even included scenes specially reshot for the 'BBC Six O'Clock' versions according to the BBC's guidelines (see the individual entries for *Illegal* and *The Fire Within*).

DOUBLE DUTY

Prod. No. 01

Written by **J. Larry Carroll** & **David Bennett Carren** Directed by **Colin Bucksey**

Black Crystal dealer Oturi Nissim is savagely murdered in his apartment along with his colleagues Torrance and Piru. The only witness is Aleesha Amyas, a resident of Talos Three who met Nissim at the Kafka Club earlier in the evening. However, she is unable to describe the assassin to Brogan and Haldane as she was hiding behind curtains during the attack. Captain Podly learns that the Gemini Gang are trying to take control of the Black Crystal market, assassinating dealers from Altor to Earth, and it seems that Nissim is their latest victim. After another dealer is found in District 9, Brogan and Haldane track down a courier who delivered Crystal to both dealers shortly before their deaths, but he is unable to lead them to his supplier Zanoc, the biggest Crystal smuggler on Altor who keeps changing his face to avoid arrest. Then Aleesha contacts Haldane to tell him that when she met Nissim at the Kafka Club, he was having an argument with Zanoc. As she knows what Zanoc looks like this week, Aleesha offers to identify him...

Notes

The first scene shot for this episode (and, therefore, for the series) was the sequence with the Brogan family sitting down to dinner and Liz bringing Zil to the table. Additional scenes for this episode were directed by Gerry Anderson during the filming of *Protect And Survive*, and by John Glen during the filming of *Enforcer*. Lana Citron (Aleesha) is dubbed throughout by Moir Leslie while Idris Elba (Pizza Delivery Man) is dubbed by former Supermarionation voice artist David Healy (Shane Weston in JOE 90). A single gram of Black Crystal will extend a human's life by three years or a creon's life by 20 years. Aleesha says that her home planet is Talos Three, an oblique reference to the 1964 STAR TREK pilot episode *The Cage* (later incorporated into *The Menagerie*) which takes place on Talos IV. Orrin and Beezle have been partners for seven years. Inazy's family live in a Caruthian commune where they are tending the egg incubators for the next two years until their indentured service is completed.

Regular Cast

Lt. Patrick Brogan	**Ted Shackelford**
Off. Jack Haldane	**Rob Youngblood**
Off. Jane Castle	**Simone Bendix**
Sally Brogan	**Nancy Paul**
Capt. Rexton Podly	**Jerome Willis**
Matthew Brogan	**Nic Klein**
Elizabeth Brogan	**Megan Olive**
Officer Hubble Orrin	**Richard James / Kieron Jecchinis**
Officer Beezle	**Tom Watt / Gary Martin**
Officer Aurelia Took	**Mary Woodvine / Collette Hiller**
Sgt. Thorald Fredo	**David Quilter**
Voice of Slomo	**Gary Martin**

Guest Cast

Oturi Nissim	**Nickolas Grace**
Aleesha Amyas	**Lana Citron / Moir Leslie**
Bag Lady	**Matyelock Gibbs**
Delivery Man	**Idris Elba / David Healy**
Inazy	**Nitzan Sharron**
Retainer #1	**Richard Ashton**
Aleesha (Alien Killer)	**Leigh Tinkler**
Torrance / Zanoc	**Rob Thirtle**
Piru / Pizza Manager	**Andy Dawson**

First UK Transmission

Saturday, May 27th, 1995
7.00pm (Sky One)

PROTECT AND SURVIVE

Prod. No. 02

Written by **Paul Mayhew-Archer** Directed by **John Glen**

Informant Slik Ostrasky leads Brogan and Haldane to the drop-off point for a shipment of illegal Xyronite immigrants smuggled to Altor by Tylan Gershom. The officers pursue the courier's astravan as he attempts to escape, but the courier is killed during a shootout at a meat store. Jane and Took question the immigrants but Took contracts Xyron fever from them and collapses. As she is placed in quarantine, Podly orders his officers to find a way to stop Gershom before he spreads Xyron fever across the planet. Meanwhile, Gershom has learned of Slik's part in the death of his courier and arranges a fatal 'accident' in a car park, but the murder is witnessed by Melazoid business executive Armand Loyster, who agrees to testify against Gershom. Brogan and Haldane are assigned to Loyster's protection at the Hotel Nirvana but Gershom plants a bug in the main office at the Station House to learn of the witness's whereabouts...

Notes

Ted Shackelford's right cheek was cut in an accident during the filming of the meat store shootout, so his injury was written into the script. The scar can be seen on Shackelford's face in all subsequent episodes. Armand Loyster and Gershom's creon associate Mephistes are both voiced by former Supermarionation voice artist David Healy. Oliver Cotton (Gershom) previously appeared as Spearman in the SPACE:1999 episode *The Full Circle*. Matt reveals that he is 14 years old. He bought the remote transmitter in Ripley Mall, a reference to Sigourney Weaver's character in *Alien* (1979) and its sequels. The painting on the wall of the Brogans' dining room, seen behind Liz in the dinner scene, is a print of *Yellow, Red, Blue* painted in 1925 by Vasily Kandinsky (1866-1944). The original is in the Musée National d'Art Moderne at the Georges Pompidou Centre in Paris. Stuntman Stuart Fell doubled for David Shaw-Parker (as Gershom's lawyer) for the court scene in which he is assaulted by Gershom. Other stunts in this episode were performed by Andrew Bradford, Gerry Crampton and Paul Heasman.

Regular Cast

Lt. Patrick Brogan	**Ted Shackelford**
Officer Jack Haldane	**Rob Youngblood**
Officer Jane Castle	**Simone Bendix**
Sally Brogan	**Nancy Paul**
Capt. Rexton Podly	**Jerome Willis**
Matthew Brogan	**Nic Klein**
Elizabeth Brogan	**Megan Olive**
Officer Hubble Orrin	**Richard James / Kieron Jecchinis**
Officer Beezle	**Tom Watt / Gary Martin**
Officer Aurelia Took	**Mary Woodvine / Collette Hiller**
Sgt. Thorald Fredo	**David Quilter**
Voice of Slomo	**Gary Martin**

Guest Cast

Slik Ostrasky	**Burt Kwouk**
Tylan Gershom	**Oliver Cotton**
Lawyer	**David Shaw-Parker**
Armand Loyster	**Rob Thirtle / David Healy**
Judge / Xyronite #1	**Andy Dawson**
Medic #1	**Leigh Tinkler**
Mephistes	**Ken Whitfield / David Healy**

First UK Transmission

Saturday, March 18th, 1995
7.00pm (Sky One)

ENFORCER — Prod. No. 03

Written by **Marc Scott Zicree** Directed by **Sidney Hayers**

After mugging creon repairman Skeevan, Nick Roberts, a member of Skall Street's notorious Hydra Gang, apparently dies from a massive heart attack when he is approached by a tarn named Trask and his young alien assistant Vala. A medical examination of Roberts's body reveals that some form of severe internal trauma shredded his heart without leaving any external injuries, so Brogan and Haldane treat the death as suspicious and question Hydra Gang leader Andy Sturgeon. The man is unable to offer them any leads but he later visits Skeevan and threatens the old creon. Trask and Vala appear and warn Sturgeon off by telekinetically speeding up his heartbeat, but Sturgeon and his gang corner the pair in a warehouse after they leave Skeevan's shop. Brogan and Haldane are alerted by reports of gunfire, but by the time they arrive at the warehouse, Sturgeon and his gang members are dead and Trask and Vala have made their escape...

Notes

Orrin has a new look with thicker, darker hair. The character's head was modified between filming scenes on *Protect And Survive* and *Enforcer* as it had been noted from rushes of the first two episodes that Orrin and Beezle appeared to be too similar for viewers to make an instant distinction between them. Podly reveals that he was born on Skall Street. Brogan reminds Matt of the time he came home from school with a bruise the size of a Horta's egg – a reference to the 1967 STAR TREK episode *The Devil In The Dark*. The framed photograph of the Brogan family at a lakeside that appears at the end of the episode was taken at Black Park Lake in Black Park, next door to Pinewood Studios.

Oops!

When Vala speaks for the first time, a shot of Brogan shows the top of the apartment set in the top left of the frame.

Regular Cast

Role	Actor
Lt. Patrick Brogan	**Ted Shackelford**
Officer Jack Haldane	**Rob Youngblood**
Officer Jane Castle	**Simone Bendix**
Sally Brogan	**Nancy Paul**
Capt. Rexton Podly	**Jerome Willis**
Matthew Brogan	**Nic Klein**
Elizabeth Brogan	**Megan Olive**
Officer Hubble Orrin	**Richard James / Kieron Jecchinis**
Officer Beezle	**Tom Watt / Gary Martin**
Officer Aurelia Took	**Mary Woodvine / Collette Hiller**
Sgt. Thorald Fredo	**David Quilter**
Voice of Slomo	**Gary Martin**

Guest Cast

Role	Actor
Trask	**Rob Thirtle**
Andy Sturgeon	**Andrew Tiernan**
Vala	**Jade Punt**
Nick Roberts	**Tom Radcliffe**
Madam	**Kazia Pelka**
Skeevan	**Andy Dawson**
Lurzan	**Leigh Tinkler**
IDMP Woman	**Leigh Tinkler**
Creon Officer / Hydra	**Andy Dawson**

First UK Transmission

Saturday, April 22nd, 1995
7.00pm (Sky One)

FLASH — Prod. No. 04

Written by **James Hendrie** Directed by **Alan Birkinshaw**

Brogan and Haldane stop tarn driver Marcus Droon for speeding but before they can arrest him, Droon spontaneously explodes. Jane suggests that Droon's death was caused by an overdose of Altor's latest designer drug HE-11, also known as Flash, so the officers visit Interchem to question company director Dr. Henry Jansen about their use of tetrachriline, a key component of the drug. Meanwhile, an alien named Morgo arrives at the Station House to report that his girlfriend Pola Vad Moonacki is dealing Flash. Slomo traces Pola to a flophouse in the wharf district but when Orrin and Beezle go there, they are followed by Morgo who breaks down the door, knocks out the two officers and kidnaps Pola. At Interchem, Jansen admits that his company developed Flash and when he suggests that the drug might be being made independently by his former chief chemist, Pola Vad Moonacki, Brogan realises that her kidnapping is no coincidence...

Notes

The working title of this episode was 'Blue Hell' from the script's original street name for the HE-11 drug. The photograph of Pola that Morgo presents to Beezle was taken at the entrance to Pinewood Studios' L & M Stage administration block, previously seen as the entrance to Harville Hospital in the UFO episode *The Long Sleep*. Liz states that she is nearly 11 years old. Her favourite screen programme, DEMETER CITY BLUES, comprises footage from the SPACE POLICE pilot episode. 'Demeter City Blues' was an alternative title suggested for the series when the producers learned that the original 'Space Police' title had already been trademarked by Lego. Flash-user Mrs. Sitruc is named after production designer Tony Curtis. Former EASTENDERS regular Tom Watt asked to be released from his contract as Beezle on completion of this episode when he discovered that the character's voice was being dubbed by Gary Martin, leaving nothing that he felt was recognisable as his own performance. Watt also asked for his name to be removed from the credits of the four episodes in which he appeared.

Regular Cast

Role	Actor
Lt. Patrick Brogan	**Ted Shackelford**
Officer Jack Haldane	**Rob Youngblood**
Officer Jane Castle	**Simone Bendix**
Sally Brogan	**Nancy Paul**
Capt. Rexton Podly	**Jerome Willis**
Matthew Brogan	**Nic Klein**
Elizabeth Brogan	**Megan Olive**
Officer Hubble Orrin	**Richard James / Kieron Jecchinis**
Officer Beezle	**Tom Watt / Gary Martin**
Officer Aurelia Took	**Mary Woodvine / Collette Hiller**
Sgt. Thorald Fredo	**David Quilter**
Voice of Slomo	**Gary Martin**

Guest Cast

Role	Actor
Dr. Henry Jansen	**Michael J. Shannon**
Carmel Matthews	**Pippa Guard**
Morgo	**Anthony Venditti / Gary Martin**
Pola Vad Moonacki	**Leigh Tinkler**
Marcus Droon	**Rob Thirtle**
Landlady / Mrs. Sitruc	**Leigh Tinkler**
Forensic / Newsreader	**Andy Dawson**
Creon Officer	**Rob Thirtle**

First UK Transmission

Saturday, July 1st, 1995
7.00pm (Sky One)

THE SNAKE

Prod. No. 05

Written by **J. Larry Carroll** & **David Bennett Carren** Directed by **John Glen**

After the chief executive of Brett Interplanetary is murdered in his own apartment by the Snake, an extortionist who has terrorised victims on seven planets, the 88th Precinct becomes a temporary task force to track down and capture the Snake before he strikes again. The officers are joined by ECPF Sergeant Bill Gray, a specialist on the Snake who previously worked with Jane as part of an ECPF bomb disposal unit back on Earth. Then Podly receives word from the Talon Corporation that they have received a threat from the Snake which targets their Omega Class tanker *Talon Princess*, *en route* to Altor with 200 million gallons of liquefied hydrogen. Brogan, Haldane and Slomo rendezvous with the *Princess* and meet Captain Tecopa and her tech chief Asuza. Slomo soon tracks down one of the Snake's explosive devices in an airlock, but an examination of it activates a trip switch which primes this device and three others to detonate in 13 hours...

Notes

This episode pays homage to Ridley Scott's *Alien* (1979): Dallas, Kane and Brett Interplanetary are all named after characters in the film, and the Snake's acid blood is a straight lift from the biology of the film's title character. Joseph Mydell (Kane) later appears in the series in a regular role as Lionel Carson. Ken Drury (Azusa) was the producers' original choice to play Sergeant Fredo, but after tests with the tarn head, Drury declined the part as he found the appliance too claustrophobic. At the end of the episode, Haldane invites Jane to have a meal at the Royal Straker – a reference to Ed Bishop's character in UFO. Production designer Tony Curtis left the series after this episode and was replaced by Bill Alexander. Curtis continued to be credited on all subsequent episodes for his designs of the standing sets (the station house and Brogan's apartment).

Oops!

En route to the *Talon Princess*, Slomo refers to the tanker as the 'Princess Talon'.

Regular Cast

Lt. Patrick Brogan	**Ted Shackelford**
Officer Jack Haldane	**Rob Youngblood**
Officer Jane Castle	**Simone Bendix**
Sally Brogan	**Nancy Paul**
Capt. Rexton Podly	**Jerome Willis**
Matthew Brogan	**Nic Klein**
Elizabeth Brogan	**Megan Olive**
Officer Silas Romek	**Lou Hirsch**
Officer Hubble Orrin	**Richard James / Kieron Jecchinis**
Officer Aurelia Took	**Mary Woodvine / Collette Hiller**
Sgt. Thorald Fredo	**David Quilter**
Voice of Slomo	**Gary Martin**

Guest Cast

Sgt. Bill Gray	**David Baxt**
John Kane	**Joseph Mydell**
Azusa	**Ken Drury**
Stephen Dallas	**Paul Humpoletz**
Captain Tecopa	**Leigh Tinkler**
The Snake	**Ken Whitfield**
Driver / Creon Officer	**Rob Thirtle**
Military General	**Andy Dawson**
Medic	**Joanna Berns**
Creon News Interviewer	**Joanna Berns**

First UK Transmission

Saturday, March 25th, 1995
7.00pm (Sky One)

BODY & SOUL

Prod. No. 06

Teleplay by **Marc Scott Zicree** Directed by **Sidney Hayers**
Story by **Mark Harris**

Merlin's Asteroid only approaches Altor once every 20 years so Brogan takes Matt in the hopper to see it close up. Flying over the far side, they discover a derelict Humes Interspace Prototype SK90 spaceship on the surface so they board it to investigate. The ship still retains full power but Matt finds a badly decomposed body in a locker and a blaster burn on its chest suggests foul play. As Brogan pilots the SK90 back to Altor, Haldane contacts Humes Interspace and speaks to Dag Jomore, assistant to the reclusive chairman Alden Humes. Shortly after, the SK90 receives a transmission from Altor which activates the ship's self-destruct mechanism and Brogan and Matt barely have time to escape in the hopper before the ship explodes. Back at the Station House, Jane takes a tissue sample of the body from under Matt's fingernails in the hope that a DNA analysis might reveal the dead man's identity...

Notes

Merlin's Asteroid was originally written as Merlin's Comet in the script. The Berkoff radiation surrounding the asteroid is named after actor Steven Berkoff, later seen as Dr. Jorry in *Deadline*. The Humes Interspace SK90 spaceship was originally written as a Prototype 00023. The interior sets of the SK90 are revamped from the sets of the *Talon Princess* built for *The Snake*. One of the fuel storage tank models constructed for the climax of *Protect And Survive* appears on Jomore's desk. Bob Sherman (Humes) was previously seen in uncredited roles as a launch operative in the UFO episode *Close Up* and the SPACE NEWS newsreader in the SPACE:1999 episode *Dragon's Domain*. Megan Olive (Liz), Richard James (Orrin), David Quilter (Fredo) and Mary Woodvine (Took) are all credited on the end titles, but do not appear in the episode. Similarly, Gary Martin is credited as the voice of Slomo, but even though Slomo does not appear, Martin can be heard dubbing the voice of Will Barton as Dag Jomore's underling.

Regular Cast

Lt. Patrick Brogan	**Ted Shackelford**
Officer Jack Haldane	**Rob Youngblood**
Officer Jane Castle	**Simone Bendix**
Sally Brogan	**Nancy Paul**
Capt. Rexton Podly	**Jerome Willis**
Matthew Brogan	**Nic Klein**
Officer Silas Romek	**Lou Hirsch**

Guest Cast

Alden Humes	**Bob Sherman**
Dag Jomore	**Rob Thirtle**
Forensic #1	**Leigh Tinkler**
Underling	**Will Barton / Gary Martin**
Forensic #2	**Will Barton**
Secretary	**Joanna Berns**
Creon Officer	**Will Barton**

First UK Transmission

Saturday, April 8th, 1995
7.00pm (Sky One)

TIME TO KILL
Prod. No. 07

Written by **Hans Beimler** & **Richard Manning** Directed by **Alan Birkinshaw**

After Brogan leads a police raid on a counterfeiting operation run by creon forger Drako, a powerful Cyborg suddenly appears in Drako's warehouse and opens fire on the officers and criminals alike. In the confusion, Drako and Tamsin escape but Took is shot down and an innocent young man named Ross is hit by a stray discharge from Brogan's gun which knocks him into an acid bath. The Cyborg disappears as Took and Ross are rushed to hospital in critical condition. Brogan and Haldane hit the streets to question their usual informants but no one is able to provide a lead as to the whereabouts of Drako or the Cyborg. That night, the Cyborg appears in the hospital, injects the critically ill Ross with drugs and kills Took when she raises the alarm. The officers are stunned by Took's death but then Brogan learns that an analysis of a piece of the Cyborg's armour has revealed it to be made of a metal alloy that has yet to be invented...

Notes
This episode was inspired by James Cameron's cult feature film *The Terminator* (1984). Cyborg Glenn Marks was also the series' stunt co-ordinator and appears unmasked as Dexkor guard Albert Vint in *The Forever Beetle*. Ross's fall into the acid bath was performed by stuntman Jonathan Paul Cohen while Podly's fall from the station house balcony was performed by Mark Anthony Newman. Roderick Woodruffe doubled for Brogan in the fight scenes with the Cyborg. Nigel Gregory (Tamsin) previously appeared in two episodes of UFO, as Ben Culley in *The Sound Of Silence* and as a security man at the Skydiver pens in *The Psychobombs*. He is perhaps better known for his regular role as Frank Mills in CORONATION STREET. This episode was the screen debut of Stephen Billington (Ross), who later went on to appear as Greg Kelly in CORONATION STREET and the title character in *Dracula II: Ascension* (2003) and *Dracula III: Legacy* (2004). The metal chip from the Cyborg is sent for examination to the Hawking Laboratories on Earth, named after the renowned cosmologist Professor Stephen W. Hawking.

Regular Cast

Lt. Patrick Brogan	**Ted Shackelford**
Officer Jack Haldane	**Rob Youngblood**
Officer Jane Castle	**Simone Bendix**
Sally Brogan	**Nancy Paul**
Capt. Rexton Podly	**Jerome Willis**
Matthew Brogan	**Nic Klein**
Elizabeth Brogan	**Megan Olive**
Officer Silas Romek	**Lou Hirsch**
Officer Hubble Orrin	**Richard James / Kieron Jecchinis**
Officer Aurelia Took	**Mary Woodvine / Collette Hiller**
Sgt. Thorald Fredo	**David Quilter**
Voice of Slomo	**Gary Martin**
Zipload	**Rob Thirtle**

Guest Cast

Ross	**Stephen Billington**
Tamsin	**Nigel Gregory**
Dr. Grant	**Alison Rose**
Cyborg	**Glenn Marks**
Drako / Tomb	**Will Barton**
Nurse	**Leigh Tinkler**
Prisoner	**Joanna Berns**
Lab Tech / Creon Officer	**Rob Thirtle**
Tarn Cab Driver	**Will Barton**

First UK Transmission

Saturday, April 1st, 1995
7.00pm (Sky One)

DEADLINE
Prod. No. 08

Written by **David Bennett Carren** & **J. Larry Carroll** Directed by **John Glen**

Brogan and Haldane are in pursuit of an unregistered limo when it releases a missile onto a collision course with Ivory Towers. Brogan manoeuvres the Police Cruiser to knock the missile off course and it lands in the street nearby, disgorging the body of a tarn male. An autopsy shows that the body is missing certain vital organs – heart, liver and all three kidneys – and Podly realises that organ leggers from Danae are at work on Altor. Brogan and Haldane visit Dr. Paul Jorry at his transplant clinic to question him about the donor organs that he uses in transplant surgery but Jorry assures them that his donor organs all come from legitimate sources, illustrating the point with his next patient, Mrs. Vork, a four-armed clyben grandmother who is to receive a new liver courtesy of a mining accident on Asteroid A-16. Meanwhile on Paradise Street, creons Rik and Pike abduct Udo Wirt, a clyben pickpocket with the exact blood and tissue match to Mrs. Vork...

Notes
The advertising dirigible in this episode was inspired by the very similar advertising blimp in Ridley Scott's cult feature film *Blade Runner* (1982). Steven Berkoff (Dr. Jorry) previously appeared as Captain Steve Minto in UFO. Pike is played by Richard James, whose own voice is heard in the series for the first time: in his regular role as Orrin, he is dubbed throughout by Kieron Jecchinis. In the final chase scene, James appears as both pursuer and pursued in dual roles as Orrin *and* Pike.

Oops!
As Jane, Took and Haldane trail the limo ferrying Jorry to the dirigible, a quick shot of the limo's occupants shows clyben pickpocket Wirt sitting in the back seat instead of Jorry (the scene is lifted from earlier in the episode). While Brogan is fighting with Rik inside the dirigible, the top of the set is clearly visible in the the top left of frame in three separate shots of Brogan as he tries to choke Rik with the staff.

Regular Cast

Lt. Patrick Brogan	**Ted Shackelford**
Officer Jack Haldane	**Rob Youngblood**
Officer Jane Castle	**Simone Bendix**
Sally Brogan	**Nancy Paul**
Capt. Rexton Podly	**Jerome Willis**
Matthew Brogan	**Nic Klein**
Elizabeth Brogan	**Megan Olive**
Officer Silas Romek	**Lou Hirsch**
Officer Hubble Orrin	**Richard James / Kieron Jecchinis**
Officer Aurelia Took	**Mary Woodvine / Collette Hiller**
Sgt. Thorald Fredo	**David Quilter**
Voice of Slomo	**Gary Martin**

Guest Cast

Dr. Paul Jorry	**Steven Berkoff**
Speedy	**Truan Munro**
Rik	**Ken Whitfield**
Pike	**Richard James**
Udo Wirt	**Rob Thirtle**
Prosperous Creon	**Will Barton**
Nurse	**Leigh Tinkler**
Mrs. Vork	**Joanna Berns**
Receptionist	**Alexa Rosewood**
Mime Artist	**Jason Maverick**

First UK Transmission

Saturday, April 15th, 1995
7.00pm (Sky One)

THE POWER

Prod. No. 09

Teleplay by **Sam Graham**
Story by **Mark Harris**
Directed by **Sidney Hayers**

While Brogan and Haldane investigate the death of reformed jewel-thief Vella Sugoi, whose body has been found in an alley, Podly insists on supervising the security arrangements when Solartek chief executive Numar and her security chief Rodan announce that they are bringing Luxorian Ice worth four billion credits into the precinct for a presentation to the Energy Commission. The Commission is considering bids for Demeter's lucrative energy franchise, held for the last ten years by Maxx Zeller's Fusion Power Company, but Numar intends to offer a clean solar energy system using Luxorian Ice. Then Rodan is found dead outside a bar and Slomo discovers a link to Vella's death when he reviews the bar's security tapes: a high-class call-girl named Sylvain made contact with both tarns shortly before their bodies were found...

Notes

Podly explains that sentric mind probes were originally used by the sentrans on creon prisoners in the Thalassic Wars to gain vital strategic information. When Brogan accesses Haldane's mind with the sentric mind probe, he sees a clip of Jane from *Enforcer* and hears a line of dialogue from *Body & Soul*. Stunt co-ordinator Glenn Marks doubled for Simone Bendix in the scene where Jane jumps through the skylight into Sylvain's apartment. The control console aboard the Solartek satellite was previously seen in the control room of the Precinct 88 Station House in *Enforcer*. Tom Chadbon (Maxx Zeller) previously appeared as Vent in the THE PROTECTORS episode *Chase*.

Oops!

When Jane jumps through the skylight into Sylvain's apartment, there is already a lot of broken glass lying around on the floor before Jane (and a shower of glass from the broken window) lands there.

Regular Cast

Lt. Patrick Brogan	**Ted Shackelford**
Officer Jack Haldane	**Rob Youngblood**
Officer Jane Castle	**Simone Bendix**
Sally Brogan	**Nancy Paul**
Capt. Rexton Podly	**Jerome Willis**
Matthew Brogan	**Nic Klein**
Officer Silas Romek	**Lou Hirsch**
Officer Hubble Orrin	**Richard James / Kieron Jecchinis**
Officer Aurelia Took	**Mary Woodvine / Collette Hiller**
Sgt. Thorald Fredo	**David Quilter**
Voice of Slomo	**Gary Martin**

Guest Cast

Numar	**Sheila Ruskin**
Sylvain	**Alison Fielding**
Maxx Zeller	**Tom Chadbon**
Paramedic	**Mark Carey**
Vella Sugoi	**Ken Whitfield**
Lindo Sugoi	**Alexa Rosewood**
Nurse	**Leigh Tinkler**
Rodan	**Rob Thirtle**
Commissioner	**Will Barton**
Businessman	**Wayne Forester**
Protester	**Joanna Berns**

First UK Transmission

Saturday, June 3rd, 1995
7.00pm (Sky One)

SEEK AND DESTROY

Prod. No. 10

Written by **J. Larry Carroll** & **David Bennett Carren**
Directed by **Jim Goddard**

Brogan and Haldane respond to a 911 call from the Space Suburb, but by the time they arrive, creon business executive Jonita Styles has been savagely murdered in her own apartment. The officers also find the body of her dog in the garden, apparently killed by a gunshot to the head. Haldane and Jane question Styles's business partner Noah Ingram, who recalls seeing a strange man hanging around their office and a memory-fit picture of the man identifies him as an ulred from Nevin Three, a planet in the throes of civil war. The next day, Ingram is found dead in his apartment and his landlord Mr. Douglas confirms seeing the ulred in a hopper on the wharfside nearby. Later, Brogan and Haldane receive a sighting of the hopper from an informant and set off in pursuit but lose the vehicle in a subway tunnel. Then, when Haldane leaves their Cruiser to grab a coffee, Brogan is approached by the ulred and led away at gunpoint...

Notes

Brogan visits Demeter Dogs Inc. posing as a Mr. Needham, named after series co-executive producer John Needham. For the scenes at Demeter Dogs, six adult labradors and six labrador puppies were provided by Animals Okay of Aldbury Common in Hertfordshire, who also provided the labrador playing Sophie. The poem which Liz writes for her competition entry was actually written by Megan Olive. In the original script, Liz named her dog Trevor, but this was changed to Sophie when the producers learned that a bitch would be better behaved on set.

Oops!

At the end of the episode, Demeter Dogs' much-hyped Aladine 50 vaccine turns out to be fake and Brogan tells Liz that all of the dogs have to be returned to Earth or they will catch creon fever and die. Yet Earth dogs have previously been seen wandering the streets of Demeter City in *Double Duty*, *Enforcer* and *Time To Kill*.

Regular Cast

Lt. Patrick Brogan	**Ted Shackelford**
Officer Jack Haldane	**Rob Youngblood**
Officer Jane Castle	**Simone Bendix**
Sally Brogan	**Nancy Paul**
Capt. Rexton Podly	**Jerome Willis**
Matthew Brogan	**Nic Klein**
Elizabeth Brogan	**Megan Olive**
Officer Silas Romek	**Lou Hirsch**
Officer Hubble Orrin	**Richard James / Kieron Jecchinis**
Officer Aurelia Took	**Mary Woodvine / Collette Hiller**
Sgt. Thorald Fredo	**David Quilter**
Voice of Slomo	**Gary Martin**
Zipload	**Rob Thirtle**

Guest Cast

Vachel	**David Burke**
Slan Nuri	**Paul Brennan**
Noah Ingram	**John Warnaby**
Mr. Douglas	**Sidney Livingstone**
Exeter	**Wayne Forester**
Koprov / Garbarge Man	**Ken Whitfield**
Creon Hooker	**Leigh Tinkler**
Jonita Styles	**Alexa Rosewood**
Forensic / Sketch Artist	**Will Barton**

First UK Transmission

Saturday, May 13th, 1995
7.00pm (Sky One)

ILLEGAL — Prod. No. 11

Written by **Marc Scott Zicree** Directed by **John Glen**

Illegal snuff fights are being organised at a warehouse in Demeter City by creon showman Coe Barner, but after the latest bout, his Saganian champion fighter Tildon Alreeuh escapes from the ring and goes on the run. Hunted through the streets by Barner's henchman Seegur, Tildon accidentally knocks down Brogan as he and Haldane are arresting a drunk driver. Chasing after him, Brogan corners Tildon in an alley, but the fighter saves his life when Brogan is targeted by Seegur. Tildon disappears but later, Sally calls from the Demeter City Hospital where the Saganian has been treated for a blast wound. As Brogan and Haldane arrive at the hospital, Tildon steals an ICC astravan and when they set off in pursuit, he leads them back to the alley near the warehouse. There, he explains that his son Nillim is being held prisoner by Barner and calls on the officers' help to rescue him...

Notes

Richard James appears in dual roles as Orrin and Coe Barner although neither has James's own voice: Barner's voice is provided by Wayne Forester. Romek has a sister named Leemek and his grandfather Zaydek was the desk sergeant at the 3rd Precinct downtown. Tony Haygarth was previously seen as one of Mario's henchmen in the THE PROTECTORS episode *See No Evil*. He was doubled by stuntman Colin Groves for the wrestling scenes here and by Tom Hegarty for other stunts. Fearing imitation by younger viewers, the BBC asked the producers to shoot an alternative version of the scene in which Haldane uses a length of wire to short-circuit the fusebox at Barner's warehouse. Originally shot in October 1994, the scene was remounted in April 1995 during filming of *The Forever Beetle* to show Haldane and Jane struggling to throw a lever on the junction box in order to turn off the power. Unfortunately, Rob Youngblood's hairdresser was unable to match his hair to the style seen in the original scenes and the change is very noticeable in the 'BBC Six O' Clock' version originally screened in February 1996.

Regular Cast

Lt. Patrick Brogan	**Ted Shackelford**
Officer Jack Haldane	**Rob Youngblood**
Officer Jane Castle	**Simone Bendix**
Sally Brogan	**Nancy Paul**
Capt. Rexton Podly	**Jerome Willis**
Matthew Brogan	**Nic Klein**
Elizabeth Brogan	**Megan Olive**
Officer Silas Romek	**Lou Hirsch**
Officer Hubble Orrin	**Richard James / Kieron Jecchinis**
Officer Aurelia Took	**Mary Woodvine / Collette Hiller**
Sgt. Thorald Fredo	**David Quilter**
Voice of Slomo	**Gary Martin**

Guest Cast

Tildon Alreeuh	**Tony Haygarth**
Nillim Alreeuh	**Tim Matthews**
Coe Barner	**Richard James / Wayne Forester**
Seegur / Ogree	**Pat Roach**
Zaydek Romek	**Wayne Forester**
Durl	**Ken Whitfield**
Guard #1 / Drunk Tarn	**Will Barton**
Guard #2	**Terry Richards**
Tarn Girl	**Alexa Rosewood**
Hostess	**Joanna Berns**

First UK Transmission

Saturday, May 20th, 1995
7.00pm (Sky One)

DIVIDED WE STAND — Prod. No. 12

Written by **Arthur Sellers** Directed by **Alan Birkinshaw**

Creon organised crime boss Vintul 'Vinny' Artak is running as the Pride Party candidate in the forthcoming city council elections. Brogan and Haldane are on security detail at the Party Headquarters when Vinny's closest friend Junna Kazar assassinates him in front of dozens of witnesses. The officers apprehend Junna while Vinny's personal physician Dr. Lazlo Kyte takes the crimelord's body to a private care facility. Jane and Took are called to Demeter Memorial Hospital to defuse a situation with the parents of a tarn egg-sac that has been stolen from the maternity incubators, the third tarn egg-sac to have been taken from city hospitals in the last month. Then Vinny miraculously turns up alive and well at the Party Headquarters and his lawyer posts bail to release Junna from custody. However, when Junna is reunited with Vinny at the crimelord's luxurious apartment, Vinny murders him in cold blood...

Notes

The original title of this episode was 'Mob Wars' but it was filmed as 'Carbon Copy'. The title was changed again to *Divided We Stand* during post-production. Vinny Artak is played by David Quilter, who is also seen in the episode in his regular role as Sergeant Fredo. The scene in which Jane is pushed off the fire escape by Dr. Kyte was filmed outside the L & M Stage buildings at Pinewood Studios on an existing fire escape between the two stages. The fall was performed by stunt co-ordinator Glenn Marks. During the filming of this episode, a collection amongst the members of the crew raised £414 for Toby Tyler, an electrician who had been seriously hurt while working on *First Knight* (1995) on Pinewood's 007 Stage.

Oops!

In the opening scene, some members of the crowd are seen reacting to Vinny's assassination before it has actually happened.

Regular Cast

Lt. Patrick Brogan	**Ted Shackelford**
Officer Jack Haldane	**Rob Youngblood**
Officer Jane Castle	**Simone Bendix**
Sally Brogan	**Nancy Paul**
Capt. Rexton Podly	**Jerome Willis**
Matthew Brogan	**Nic Klein**
Elizabeth Brogan	**Megan Olive**
Officer Silas Romek	**Lou Hirsch**
Officer Hubble Orrin	**Richard James / Kieron Jecchinis**
Officer Aurelia Took	**Mary Woodvine / Collette Hiller**
Sgt. Thorald Fredo	**David Quilter**
Voice of Slomo	**Gary Martin**

Guest Cast

Vinny Artak	**David Quilter**
Dr. Lazlo Kyte	**Christopher Baines**
Regina Baylek	**Suzanne Bertish**
Vacua Taz	**Alexa Rosewood**
Reporter #1	**Kate Beckett**
Drak	**Rebecca Steele**
Hospital Administrator	**Dominic Letts**
Junna Kazar	**Ken Whitfield**
Mr. Dodvek	**Wayne Forester**
Forensic	**Will Barton**

First UK Transmission

Saturday, August 12th, 1995
7.00pm (Sky One)

TWO AGAINST THE ROCK — Prod. No. 13

Written by **Paul Robert Coyle** Directed by **Peter Duffell**

At the maximum security prison on Asteroid A-5, popularly known as The Rock, prisoners Eric Volker, Cranston and Smike engineer a breakout by releasing a fatal virus into the ventilation system. Taking control of the prison, they await the arrival of convicted creon crime boss Ariset Gagnon, due to be sent from Altor on the next police escort run. However, Gagnon's ill health delays his departure so Brogan and Haldane are dispatched to The Rock with notorious escape artist Wyndham 'Houdini' Derrit instead. Despite suffering from Altorian flu, Jane replaces Brogan at the last minute so that he can watch the World Series with Matt. When they arrive at Asteroid A-5, Haldane, Jane and Houdini are captured by Volker and locked in a cell with the prison doctor, who reveals that they were all exposed to Volker's deadly virus as soon as they set foot on The Rock...

Notes

Jerome Willis (Podly) appears in the opening title sequence for the first time. Paul Robert Coyle receives sole writer credit in the in-show titles although the script was actually written by Sam Graham and Philip Morrow from a story by Coyle. The episode was specifically written to minimise Ted Shackelford's role, enabling him to return to the United States for a short holiday. The change in Orrin's appearance between *Protect And Survive* and *Enforcer* is explained when it is revealed here that he has been using hair restorer. Haldane's hallucinations feature the Aleesha Killer (from *Double Duty*), the decomposed body of Alden Humes (*Body & Soul*), Dr. Jansen overdosing on HE-11 (*Flash*) and a labrador attack (*Seek And Destroy*). Actor Kerry Shale was originally set to play Houdini but he backed out after having a cast taken of his head. He was replaced by former BROOKSIDE and CARDIAC ARREST regular Danny Webb. Stephen Greif was previously seen as a policeman in the THE PROTECTORS episode *Implicado*. He is best known for his role as the original Travis in BLAKE'S 7. Convict Ray Winstone's voice is dubbed by Wayne Forester, although his own voice can still be heard in some scenes.

Regular Cast

Lt. Patrick Brogan	**Ted Shackelford**
Officer Jack Haldane	**Rob Youngblood**
Officer Jane Castle	**Simone Bendix**
Capt. Rexton Podly	**Jerome Willis**
Matthew Brogan	**Nic Klein**
Elizabeth Brogan	**Megan Olive**
Officer Silas Romek	**Lou Hirsch**
Officer Hubble Orrin	**Richard James / Kieron Jecchinis**
Officer Aurelia Took	**Mary Woodvine**
Sgt. Thorald Fredo	**David Quilter**
Voice of Slomo	**Gary Martin**

Guest Cast

Wyndham 'Houdini' Derrit	**Danny Webb**
Eric Volker	**Stephen Greif**
Con #1	**Ray Winstone**
Dr. Elliss	**Richard Huw**
Sportscaster	**John Chancer**
Warden Bronkov	**Ken Whitfield**
Ariset Gagnon / Cranston	**Will Barton**
Smike	**Wayne Forester**
Tarn Officer	**Leigh Tinkler**
Newscaster	**Alexa Rosewood**
Officer	**Joanna Berns**

First UK Transmission

Saturday, April 29th, 1995
7.00pm (Sky One)

TAKEOVER — Prod. No. 14

Written by **J. Larry Carroll** & **David Bennett Carren** Directed by **John Glen**

At an Internal Affairs hearing following an incident at Magma Park which resulted in the death of bank robber Naxus Simi, creon witness Miles Yorba testifies that Brogan and Haldane blasted Simi's hopper out of the sky without any warning or provocation. The tarn bailiff confirms that Yorba is telling the truth, despite Yorba's earlier statement that Simi had opened fire on the officers with a blaster. Haldane believes that Yorba is part of a conspiracy to discredit them in advance of the trial of crime boss Vanus Olvera, at which they are to be the star witnesses, but Brogan is sceptical until Slomo is infected by a polymorphic virus which prevents the robot from giving his own unimpeachable account of the Magma Park incident. The hearing resumes with Jane's testimony but Brogan and Haldane are astounded when her version of the events matches Yorba's, branding them both as cold-blooded murderers!

Notes

J. Larry Carroll and David Bennett Carren receive sole credit for the script although the teleplay was actually written by Philip Morrow and Chris Hubbell from Carroll and Carren's story. Joseph Mydell makes his debut as Officer Lionel Carson although he previously appeared as John Kane in *The Snake*. The scenes of Yorba in Magma Park were filmed by the 2nd Unit under the direction of Gerry Anderson. Commissioner Tev is revamped from an animatronic alien created by Neill Gorton for a promotional trailer produced late in 1993, which was used to secure finance for the series at the annual NATPE (National Association of Television Producers Entertainment) television industry event in Las Vegas in January 1994. Affectionately known as Cyril, the head appeared as an alien criminal in the trailer but was repainted in brighter colours for his role as Tev. The submarine seen briefly during the pursuit of Naxus Simi's hopper was dubbed the 'STARSKY & HUTCH Submarine' by the model crew due to the similarity of its red and white markings to those of the Ford Torino in the 1970s American police series.

Regular Cast

Lt. Patrick Brogan	**Ted Shackelford**
Officer Jack Haldane	**Rob Youngblood**
Officer Jane Castle	**Simone Bendix**
Sally Brogan	**Nancy Paul**
Capt. Rexton Podly	**Jerome Willis**
Officer Silas Romek	**Lou Hirsch**
Officer Hubble Orrin	**Richard James / Kieron Jecchinis**
Officer Aurelia Took	**Mary Woodvine**
Sgt. Thorald Fredo	**David Quilter**
Officer Lionel Carson	**Joseph Mydell**
Voice of Slomo	**Gary Martin**

Guest Cast

Cambria Elon	**Maryam D'Abo**
Damon Reseda	**Clive Merrison**
Commissioner Tev	**Rob Thirtle / Wayne Forester**
Miles Yorba	**Andy Dawson**
Vanus Olvera	**Wayne Forester**
Bailiff	**Ken Whitfield**
Medic	**Leigh Tinkler**
Mr. Brill	**Will Barton**
Officer	**Joanna Berns**
Creon Officer	**Ken Whitfield**

First UK Transmission

Saturday, June 10th, 1995
7.00pm (Sky One)

PREDATOR AND PREY — Prod. No. 15

Written by **Nicholas Sagan** Directed by **Sidney Hayers**

Chloe Vincent, a police officer from the 79th Precinct, is murdered by the vampire-like Enil Kmada while working undercover at The Taunt nightclub. Brogan, Haldane and Jane meet Vincent's belligerent partner Lieutenant Verro Walker, who reveals that they were investigating a series of recent homicides in the club district. Walker suddenly spots Kmada on the dance floor and sets off in pursuit followed by Haldane, but when the cloaked figure vanishes, it transpires that Walker was the only person who saw him. In common with Kmada's other victims, the autopsy on Vincent shows no physical cause of death – she simply lost the will to live – and Took realises that Kmada is a Meki, a legendary creature who feeds on lifeforces and hibernates within a host body without the host's knowledge. That night, Sally has a nightmare in which she is attacked by a hideous cloaked creature and wakes with a terrible feeling that it was Kmada in her dream...

Notes

The Taunt nightclub is on East Parallel Road which, according to the street map of Demeter City's West Side seen in *Hate Street*, places it in close proximity to Magma Park (seen in *Takeover*). Enil Kmada is played by Richard James, who is also seen in his regular role as Officer Orrin. The bookshelves at Peri's Tarn Antiquarian Books include volumes of history, modern literature, orbit philosophy, tarn telepathy, pyroastrology, tarn mythology, foreign languages, empathetic biology, tarn games and art & aliens. The records of Kmada's previous victims list Massayo Figgis (a tarn), Yoon Gushen (a creon), Mytee Ponnari (a creon) and Solange Belcher (human). Took reveals that she has a sister, but does not name her. The meeting with tarn hooker Mags Serpell in the scrap metal yard at 1420 Jupiter Wharf was filmed in a night shoot on the Pinewood Studios lot adjacent to the 007 Stage – the west wall of the stage can be seen behind Mags Serpell when she meets the officers. Charmingly, the tarn hooker is named after the series' assistant editors Charlotte Serpell and Mags Arnold.

Regular Cast

Lt. Patrick Brogan	**Ted Shackelford**
Officer Jack Haldane	**Rob Youngblood**
Officer Jane Castle	**Simone Bendix**
Sally Brogan	**Nancy Paul**
Capt. Rexton Podly	**Jerome Willis**
Matthew Brogan	**Nic Klein**
Elizabeth Brogan	**Megan Olive**
Officer Silas Romek	**Lou Hirsch**
Officer Hubble Orrin	**Richard James / Kieron Jecchinis**
Officer Aurelia Took	**Mary Woodvine**
Sgt. Thorald Fredo	**David Quilter**
Officer Lionel Carson	**Joseph Mydell**
Voice of Slomo	**Gary Martin**

Guest Cast

Lt. Verro Walker	**Rolf Saxon**
Chloe Vincent	**Natalie Roles**
Enil Kmada	**Richard James**
Zwellin / Peri	**Rob Thirtle**
Bouncer	**Ken Whitfield**
Mags Serpell	**Alexa Rosewood**
Mrs. Kroze	**Leigh Tinkler**
Timmons	**Wayne Forester**
Man #1	**Andy Dawson**
Bartender	**Sonja Mindt**

First UK Transmission

Saturday, May 6th, 1995
7.00pm (Sky One)

THE WITNESS — Prod. No. 16

Written by **Eric Gethers** Directed by **Peter Duffell**

Romek and his new partner Morgan are dispatched to investigate a purse-snatching incident at The Gilmore bar while Brogan, Haldane, Jane, Sally and Took are enjoying a pleasant evening at Fredo's house. The evening is interrupted when Fredo's young daughter Estes has a nightmare vision of a vicious attack on a tarn man with a light lance and only minutes later, Romek and Morgan discover their tarn purse-snatcher Danny Cav stabbed to death in an alleyway. Morgan sees a suspect fleeing the scene and a memory-fit picture identifies the man as Mas Maharg. His picture is circulated to all units but that evening, Estes is practicing for her exams when she experiences another vision in which she sees the murder of creon bookmaker Lam Sidney. Unknown to her parents, Estes's paramental eye enables her to see through the eyes of the serial killer, but the visions are so horrific to the little tarn that she suffers a severe mental trauma...

Notes

At Fredo's house, the officers watch a Slamball match featuring a team called The Stingrays. The script originally featured dialogue detailing that their opponents are The Fireballs. Murder suspect Mas Maharg is named after SPACE PRECINCT's story editor Sam Graham. Maharg is revealed to be a sentran, a member of the race who fought the creons in the Thalassic Wars referred to in *The Power*. According to Sally, slasher movies have been outlawed on Earth. The murder of Mas Maharg was filmed in a night shoot on the Pinewood Lot on a gantry over a series of oil tanks adjacent to the studio's Power House.

Oops!

Sally appears to be employed at Demeter Memorial Hospital in this episode, yet she was working at Demeter City Hospital in *Illegal* and is seen back there again in *Hate Street*. The name of Fredo's wife is spelled 'Yolander' on the end credits instead of Yolanda, as in the script and all production documentation.

Regular Cast

Lt. Patrick Brogan	**Ted Shackelford**
Officer Jack Haldane	**Rob Youngblood**
Officer Jane Castle	**Simone Bendix**
Sally Brogan	**Nancy Paul**
Capt. Rexton Podly	**Jerome Willis**
Officer Silas Romek	**Lou Hirsch**
Officer Hubble Orrin	**Richard James / Kieron Jecchinis**
Officer Aurelia Took	**Mary Woodvine**
Sgt. Thorald Fredo	**David Quilter**
Officer Lionel Carson	**Joseph Mydell**
Voice of Slomo	**Gary Martin**
Zipload	**Rob Thirtle**

Guest Cast

Morgan	**Todd Boyce**
Iona Datch	**Kate Harper**
Mas Maharg	**Peter-Hugo Daly**
Estes Fredo	**Kiran Shah**
Yolanda Fredo	**Alexa Rosewood**
Mr. Chantel	**Wayne Forester**
Danny Kav	**Rob Thirtle**
Lam Sidney	**Ken Whitfield**
Soup Server	**Leigh Tinkler**
Sketch Artist	**Andy Dawson**
Officer	**Joanna Berns**

First UK Transmission

Saturday, June 24th, 1995
7.00pm (Sky One)

HATE STREET

Prod. No. 17

Written by **Steve Brown** Directed by **Piers Haggard**

Xyronite storekeeper Tropek and his two small children are killed when his shop is attacked by a racist gang led by Burl Flak. Bounty hunter Erika Brandt attempts to help Tropek but is beaten to the ground and ends up in Demeter City Hospital with Tropek's widow Maya. There, she is reunited with her old flame Patrick Brogan and attempts to rekindle their relationship of two decades earlier, much to Sally's annoyance. At the Station House, Erika explains that she is in pursuit of Flak, who is wanted on Danae for a series of hate crimes including murder. But Podly is determined that Flak should be tried and prosecuted on Altor so he assigns Brogan and Haldane to catch him before Erika can do so. While they question rabid anti-Xyronite Dr. Taiko Chan, who is believed to have links to Flak, Erika visits sleazy junk dealer Tate and purchases a cryogun, a weapon that will stun and freeze any target inside a block of ice within seconds...

Notes

Burl Flak's record shows that he is wanted by the Danae PD (Terrahawk District). Xyronites were previously seen in *Protect And Survive*. Erika's line, "Well, it's been just this side of paradise," references the 1967 STAR TREK episode *This Side Of Paradise*. The set of Tate's junk shop is dressed with items from the Pinewood Studios prop store including the Atlantean Lens, a crystal helmet which shows Peter Gilmore the future of mankind in Kevin Connor's *Warlords Of Atlantis* (1978). CYBER COWBOYS, the screen programme watched by Matt and Liz, comprises footage from the SPACE POLICE pilot episode. The 'STARSKY & HUTCH Submarine' seen briefly in *Takeover* is visible in Demeter Bay when Dr. Chan's body is recovered from the water. The departure board at the Cargo Terminal shows flights bound for Megalon 7 (home of the Bag Lady in *Double Duty*) and Talos Three (home of Aleesha Amyas in *Double Duty*). Joe Mydell is credited as Carson on the end titles but does not appear in the episode: a scene in which he examined Erika's cryogun was filmed for the episode but deleted from the final edit.

Regular Cast

Lt. Patrick Brogan	**Ted Shackelford**
Officer Jack Haldane	**Rob Youngblood**
Officer Jane Castle	**Simone Bendix**
Sally Brogan	**Nancy Paul**
Capt. Rexton Podly	**Jerome Willis**
Matthew Brogan	**Nic Klein**
Elizabeth Brogan	**Megan Olive**
Officer Silas Romek	**Lou Hirsch**
Officer Hubble Orrin	**Richard James / Kieron Jecchinis**
Officer Aurelia Took	**Mary Woodvine**
Sgt. Thorald Fredo	**David Quilter**
Voice of Slomo	**Gary Martin**

Guest Cast

Erika Brandt	**Frances Barber**
Burl Flak	**Christopher Fairbank**
Sandoff	**David Quilter**
Dr. Eastman	**Jeff Harding**
Tate	**Robert Hamilton**
Tropek	**Rob Thirtle**
Maya Tropek	**Kate Harper**
Tanni Tropek	**Kiran Shah**
Skog Tropek	**Peter O'Farrell**
Dr. Taiko Chan	**Wayne Forester**
Mrs. Chan	**Alexa Rosewood**
Barco	**Andy Dawson**
Tarn Nurse	**Leigh Tinkler**

First UK Transmission

Saturday, June 17th, 1995
7.00pm (Sky One)

FRIENDS

Prod. No. 18

Teleplay by **Chris Hubbell** & **Philip Morrow** and **Carl Jahnsen**
Story by **Carl Jahnsen** Directed by **Peter Duffell**

Karel Tarik Brigade leader Reeve Pataki is arrested by Jane in an undercover operation when he tries to sell an illegal mainframe access key to a representative of Zenek Intergalactics. Reeve's colleagues and close friends Lynn Dilfer and Tong Coop resolve to spring him from police custody, accessing the station house mainframe to set off a fire alert on Level 7. While the officers are responding to the alarm, Tong opens the door to Reeve's cell and Lynn uses the screen system to direct him to the docking bay. However, Brogan realises that they have been decoyed and orders Fredo to seal the docking bay while Jane apprehends Reeve for a second time. Lynn swears revenge on Jane but when Tong discovers the officer's address in the station's personnel files, Lynn decides that the only way to secure Reeve's release is to take a hostage of their own...

Notes

Karel Tarik was the leader of a group of obstructionists in the early days of Altor's colonisation who has subsequently become a figurehead for a revolutionary student movement. The Precinct 88 personnel files downloaded by Tong detail the forenames of some of the regular characters: Rexton Podly, Silas Romek and Hubble Orrin. The characters' addresses are also detailed: Brogan's apartment in the Space Suburb is listed as Apartment 9751, Satellite 3, Nebula Suburb; Haldane lives at 9021 Cherry Hills, Bushland County, Metropoia; Jane lives with Took at 312 Warehouse Road, Demeter City; Captain Podly lives at 1055 Dublin Mews, Gibbon Avenue, Demeter City. Among the other officers listed is one Tracy Virgil.

Oops!

Violent shaking is not a recommended technique for reviving oxygen-starved police officers. Mouth-to-mouth resuscitation would have been better in the circumstances.

Regular Cast

Lt. Patrick Brogan	**Ted Shackelford**
Officer Jack Haldane	**Rob Youngblood**
Officer Jane Castle	**Simone Bendix**
Capt. Rexton Podly	**Jerome Willis**
Matthew Brogan	**Nic Klein**
Officer Silas Romek	**Lou Hirsch**
Officer Hubble Orrin	**Richard James / Kieron Jecchinis**
Officer Aurelia Took	**Mary Woodvine**
Sgt. Thorald Fredo	**David Quilter**
Officer Lionel Carson	**Joseph Mydell**
Voice of Slomo	**Gary Martin**

Guest Cast

Lynn Dilfer / Sprite	**Jacqueline Defferary**
Glen Pataki	**Christopher Thomas**
Reeve Pataki	**Ben Walden**
Tong Coop	**Wayne Forester**
Arrak Gushen	**Rob Thirtle**
Female Officer	**Joanna Berns**
Creon Guard	**Andy Dawson**

First UK Transmission

Saturday, July 8th, 1995
7.00pm (Sky One)

SMELTER SKELTER — Prod. No. 19

Written by **Arthur Sellers** — Directed by **Peter Duffell**

Sally and Liz are shopping at the Jewellery Center when the store is raided by an armed gang who use a strange energy device to punch a hole in the vault door. The masked leader of the gang threatens Sally and Liz with his gun and then takes Sally's wedding ring before escaping with the contents of the vault. Although traumatised, Sally and Liz are able to give details of the raid back at the station house: Sally provides a memory-fit picture of the energy device's tarn operator while Liz recalls markings on the device's case which lead Brogan and Haldane to Dr. Naru Reece, a physicist who was working on a small beam accelerator before the Demeter University Research Institute cancelled his funding. Arriving at his address, the officers find Reece dead, his head obliterated by the accelerator. Meanwhile, Zanadu Mining chief executive Alvin Zann is planning an audacious scheme to plunder the gold vault at the Bank of Altor...

Notes

Peter Duffell is credited as sole director of this episode although nearly half of it was actually directed by Silvio Narizzano. Unable to reconcile creative differences with members of the regular cast, Narizzano left the production after five days of filming and was replaced by Duffell. Narizzano directed the scenes in the station house and the Police Cruisers, the attack on the armoured van and some scenes on the foundry deck of Zann's mining vessel. Duffell directed the scenes in the Brogans' house, the Jewellery Center, the station's forensic room, the bank vault, vault anteroom and Demeter University as well as the death of Reece in the alley and the final shoot-out on the mining vessel. The yellow hopper used by Zann is described as a Humes Coupe, presumably manufactured by Humes Interspace (*Body & Soul*). The painting on the wall of Zann's office is Steven Begg's original design for the Rock Snatcher mining drone. The Rock Snatcher itself was made in two sizes: one model was over 3½ feet long while the other was barely five inches.

Regular Cast

Lt. Patrick Brogan	**Ted Shackelford**
Officer Jack Haldane	**Rob Youngblood**
Officer Jane Castle	**Simone Bendix**
Sally Brogan	**Nancy Paul**
Capt. Rexton Podly	**Jerome Willis**
Matthew Brogan	**Nic Klein**
Elizabeth Brogan	**Megan Olive**
Officer Silas Romek	**Lou Hirsch**
Officer Hubble Orrin	**Richard James / Kieron Jecchinis**
Officer Aurelia Took	**Mary Woodvine**
Sgt. Thorald Fredo	**David Quilter**
Officer Lionel Carson	**Joseph Mydell**
Voice of Slomo	**Gary Martin**

Guest Cast

Alvin Zann	**Bradley Lavelle**
Bank Manager	**Rob Thirtle**
Dr. Rudd	**Alexa Rosewood**
Dr. Naru Reece	**Rob Thirtle**
Ann Drog	**Melissa Knatchbull**
Saleswoman #1	**Alexa Rosewood**
Bank Assistant	**Leigh Tinkler**
Driver / Bank Tech	**Wayne Forester**
Dar / Sketch Artist	**Andrew Dawson**
Lak	**Robert Fisher**

First UK Transmission

Saturday, July 15th, 1995
7.00pm (Sky One)

DEATHWATCH — Prod. No. 20

Written by **Michael Berlin** & **Eric Estrin** — Directed by **Piers Haggard**

A rift opens in space near Altor, disgorging an alien meteor which is tracked to a landing on Altor by MIA officers Major Graffa and Captain Tara Weldon. A meteor fragment is discovered on a farm outside Demeter City by Randall Butler and his farmhand Enro Skyles, but when Butler touches the fragment he is affected by a blast of light and decapitates Skyles with a spade. Some weeks later, the elderly residents of Roetem Towers are being terrorised into leaving their homes by a pair of tarn thugs, Skid and Gullis. Former teacher Bertha Fluss is chased onto the roof, but Brogan and Haldane are alerted by her creon neighbour Virginia Lewton and the tarns disappear into the building when the officers arrive. Bertha gives a statement at the Station House and when Brogan and Haldane return her to Roetem Towers later, they meet her duplicitous landlord Randall Borden, a new identity adopted by the alien-possessed Randall Butler...

Notes

Originally written and filmed as 'Graveyard', this episode was retitled *Deathwatch* in post-production. The 'This Episode' sequence includes several scenes from *Deathwatch Conclusion*. The console at the MIA tracking station was previously seen in *Enforcer*, *The Power* and *Two Against The Rock*. The establishing shot of Demeter City after Skyles's murder is taken from the start of *Smelter Skelter*. Roetem (meteor spelled backwards) Towers was originally written as Gorton Terrace, named after creature effects designer Neill Gorton. Dando at the coroner's office is named after first assistant director Chris Dando. Bertha and Rocky play a board game that was previously seen in *Two Against The Rock* (in the prison control room) and *Hate Street* (on Tate's desk). Virginia Lewton's fall from the roof and Borden's flaming death were both cut from the BBC screening in 1996. During production, the episode was intended to remain open-ended, with the mystery of the alien meteor left unresolved, but the producers then decided to turn the story into a two-part finale and a script for a conclusion was commissioned.

Regular Cast

Lt. Patrick Brogan	**Ted Shackelford**
Officer Jack Haldane	**Rob Youngblood**
Officer Jane Castle	**Simone Bendix**
Capt. Rexton Podly	**Jerome Willis**
Elizabeth Brogan	**Megan Olive**
Officer Silas Romek	**Lou Hirsch**
Officer Hubble Orrin	**Richard James / Kieron Jecchinis**
Officer Aurelia Took	**Mary Woodvine**
Sgt. Thorald Fredo	**David Quilter**
Officer Lionel Carson	**Joseph Mydell**
Voice of Slomo	**Gary Martin**

Guest Cast

Bertha Fluss	**Anne Kristen**
Captain Tara Weldon	**Cecilia Noble**
Randall Butler/Borden	**Ken Farrington**
Major Graffa	**Andy Dawson**
Skid / Enro Skyles	**Rob Thirtle**
Gullis	**Wayne Forester**
Virginia Newton	**Alexa Rosewood**
Anza Valentine	**Alexa Rosewood**
Radar Technician	**Wayne Forester**
Sketch Artist	**Andy Dawson**
Secretary / Shopper	**Leigh Tinkler**
Voice of Rocky	**Wayne Forester**

First UK Transmission

Saturday, August 19th, 1995
7.00pm (Sky One)

THE FIRE WITHIN (Part One) — Prod. No. 21

Written by **Steve Brown** & **Burt Prelutsky** — Directed by **John Glen**

Took attends the consecration ceremony at a new Pyrist Temple. During the ceremony, Sister Nevik Brok appears to become possessed and accuses her fellow priest Brother Tendall Kalike of being a heretic motivated by power and greed. When she points him out to the assembled worshippers, Kalike spontaneously combusts and is consumed by fire. Haldane is on leave in New Hawaii so Jane partners Brogan as they investigate Kalike's death. Sister Nevik assures Brogan that they have experienced a miracle of divine intervention and that Kalike's heart burst into flame because his thoughts were impure, as foretold by The Daskell, the Pyrist spiritual guide. However, the Icar Vedra, the Pyrist spiritual leader, refuses to believe the accusations against Kalike and insists that he be honoured in death. The honour ceremony proceeds and this time Sister Nevik is apparently possessed by Kalike's spirit, confessing his sins from beyond the grave...

Notes

Both episodes of this story are captioned on screen as *The Fire Within* without any supplementary captions to differentiate the two parts. The 'This Episode' sequence at the start of *Part One* includes several scenes from *Part Two*. The temple control console is the familiar console prop seen in previous episodes (last used in *Deathwatch*). Podly's Shakespearean quotation, "To sleep, perchance to dream," is from *Hamlet* Act 3 Scene 1. Kalamandro's police record gives the address of the Pyrist Temple at 42936 Glenjohn Boulevard in Zone 22c. The news footage that Brother Kem obtains to determine Haldane's identity is coverage of the Artak affair from *Divided We Stand*. An alternative version of the closing scene was filmed for the 1996 BBC screening in which Haldane did not set fire to Samina: she was seen to simply fall from the cliff into the water.

Oops!

Tendall Kalike is erroneously captioned as 'Kaliki' on the end titles.

Regular Cast

Lt. Patrick Brogan	**Ted Shackelford**
Officer Jack Haldane	**Rob Youngblood**
Officer Jane Castle	**Simone Bendix**
Sally Brogan	**Nancy Paul**
Capt. Rexton Podly	**Jerome Willis**
Matthew Brogan	**Nic Klein**
Elizabeth Brogan	**Megan Olive**
Officer Silas Romek	**Lou Hirsch**
Officer Hubble Orrin	**Richard James / Kieron Jecchinis**
Officer Aurelia Took	**Mary Woodvine**
Sgt. Thorald Fredo	**David Quilter**
Officer Lionel Carson	**Joseph Mydell**
Voice of Slomo	**Gary Martin**

Guest Cast

The Icar Vedra	**Jack Hedley**
Sister Nevik Brok	**Lisa Orgolini**
Kalamandro	**David Quilter**
Samina Podly	**Alexa Rosewood**
Fama Podly	**Kate Harper**
Dorek Kyyster	**Wayne Forester**
Kem Flexen	**Rob Thirtle**
Sister Fancher	**Alexa Rosewood**
Tendall Kalike	**Andy Dawson**
Sister Anna	**Mary Ordish**

First UK Transmission

Saturday, July 22nd, 1995
7.00pm (Sky One)

THE FIRE WITHIN (Part Two) — Prod. No. 22

Written by **Steve Brown** & **Burt Prelutsky** — Directed by **John Glen**

Following the mysterious disappearance of Samina Podly, the Precinct 88 officers conduct a search of the Pyrist Temple and are surprised when Haldane offers Podly his resignation, stating that he wishes to pursue his calling to the Pyrist faith. Later, Took attends a rededication ceremony at the temple which is interrupted when a hideous tridra three-headed serpent emerges from the eternal flame on the altar. Sister Nevik announces that this is another omen that the Day of Immolation is approaching and that the congregation should prepare for the end of the world, offering their riches to the Icar before taking refuge in the Temple's Cave of Winds. However, the Icar is not convinced, recognising that Nevik and Kalamandro are plotting to discredit him, but when Nevik challenges the Icar's right to lead in a trial by fire, he is consumed by the eternal flame and Kalamandro declares Sister Nevik to be the new Icar Vedra...

Notes

There is no 'This Episode' sequence at the end of the main titles. Kalamandro is said to have recently visited Megalon 7, home of the Bag Lady seen in *Double Duty*. Apart from his appearance in *Part One* of this story, Jack Hedley was previously seen as Foster's defence council Webb in the UFO episode *Court Martial*. Kalamandro is played by David Quilter, who is also seen in the episode in his regular role as Sergeant Fredo. The fiery deaths of both the Icar Vedra here and Tendall Kalike in *Part One* were performed by stunt co-ordinator Glenn Marks. Fellow stuntman Rod Woodruffe, two fire officers and a pair of paramedics from the Heathrow Air Ambulance Service were on set in case anything went wrong. Insert shots of Brogan operating the controls of the Pyrist ship were filmed on the series' last shooting day under the direction of editor Jason Krasucki.

Oops!

Dorek Kyyster is erroneously captioned as 'Kyster' on the end titles.

Regular Cast

Lt. Patrick Brogan	**Ted Shackelford**
Officer Jack Haldane	**Rob Youngblood**
Officer Jane Castle	**Simone Bendix**
Sally Brogan	**Nancy Paul**
Capt. Rexton Podly	**Jerome Willis**
Matthew Brogan	**Nic Klein**
Elizabeth Brogan	**Megan Olive**
Officer Silas Romek	**Lou Hirsch**
Officer Hubble Orrin	**Richard James / Kieron Jecchinis**
Officer Aurelia Took	**Mary Woodvine**
Sgt. Thorald Fredo	**David Quilter**
Voice of Slomo	**Gary Martin**
Zipload	**Rob Thirtle**

Guest Cast

The Icar Vedra	**Jack Hedley**
Sister Nevik Brok	**Lisa Orgolini**
Kalamandro	**David Quilter**
Samina Podly	**Alexa Rosewood**
Fama Podly	**Kate Harper**
Dorek Kyyster	**Wayne Forester**
Kem Flexen	**Rob Thirtle**
Judge Lasik Zorine	**Rob Thirtle**
Sister Anna	**Mary Ordish**
Husband	**Gary Dean**

First UK Transmission

Saturday, July 29th, 1995
7.00pm (Sky One)

THE FOREVER BEETLE — Prod. No. 23

Written by **Peter Dunne** — Directed by **Peter Duffell**

The Brogan family's dinner is interrupted by the unexpected arrival of Brogan's best friend Tommy Murphy, who is very popular with Matt and Liz. Murphy is less popular with Sally who believes he is a freeloader, but she agrees to allow him to spend the night on the couch. The next day, Brogan and Haldane are dispatched to Dexkor Laboratories where a rare *pteronarcys eternicum*, a forever beetle, has been stolen. Project leader Dr. Long explains that the female forever beetle was the last of its kind and goes on to show them the miraculous cell regeneration effects of a drug developed from chemicals found in the beetle's womb. Brogan and Haldane realise how valuable the beetle could be to Dexkor's competitors, but they are unaware that the thief is Murphy, who turns up at the Station House asking to borrow Brogan's hopper. Brogan hands over the ignition card but minutes later, the hopper explodes on Docking Bay 4 and Murphy is killed!

Notes

The working title of this episode was 'Quick Thinking'. In the original script, Murphy's raid on Dexkor Laboratories appeared after Brogan's interrogation of Amory Wolf. Matt's red dot tarantula was played by both a real tarantula provided by Animal Actors and by a duplicate animatronic tarantula made by Neill Gorton's creature effects department. Tarn scientist Dr. Long is voiced by former Supermarionation voice artist David Graham, best-known for his vocal performances as Parker and Brains in THUNDERBIRDS. Tarn girl Sena M is revamped from Estes Fredo, Sergeant Fredo's daughter seen in *The Witness*. Actor and stuntman Kiran Shah (Sena M) previously appeared in the series as Estes in *The Witness* and as Tanni Tropek in *Hate Street*. Very much in demand for work in science-fiction and fantasy films, Shah has been seen in *Superman* (1978), *Return Of The Jedi* (1983), *Indiana Jones And The Temple Of Doom* (1984), *Legend* (1985), *Aliens* (1986) and the *Lord Of The Rings* trilogy (2001-2003). He also appeared as Miss Piggy's stunt double in *The Great Muppet Caper* (1981).

Regular Cast

Lt. Patrick Brogan	**Ted Shackelford**
Officer Jack Haldane	**Rob Youngblood**
Officer Jane Castle	**Simone Bendix**
Sally Brogan	**Nancy Paul**
Capt. Rexton Podly	**Jerome Willis**
Matthew Brogan	**Nic Klein**
Elizabeth Brogan	**Megan Olive**
Officer Silas Romek	**Lou Hirsch**
Officer Hubble Orrin	**Richard James / Kieron Jecchinis**
Officer Aurelia Took	**Mary Woodvine**
Sgt. Thorald Fredo	**David Quilter**
Officer Lionel Carson	**Joseph Mydell**
Voice of Slomo	**Gary Martin**

Guest Cast

Tommy Murphy	**Sam Douglas**
Amory Wolf	**Constantine Gregory**
Thunder Cole	**Glen McCrory**
Dr. Long	**Andy Dawson / David Graham**
Nardo	**Wayne Forester**
Rupp / Drover Pike	**Rob Thirtle**
Bartender	**Alexa Rosewood**
Female Officer	**Joanna Berns**
Creon Hooker	**Leigh Tinkler**
Sena M	**Kiran Shah**
Albert Vint	**Glenn Marks**

First UK Transmission

Saturday, August 5th, 1995
7.00pm (Sky One)

DEATHWATCH CONCLUSION — Prod. No. 24

Written by **Arthur Sellers** — Directed by **Piers Haggard**

Captain Weldon and Major Graffa transport the small meteor fragment from Butler's farm to a warehouse in Demeter City where the large meteor recovered from the ruins of Roetem Towers has been secured inside a biohazard container. Weldon wants the thing destroyed, but Graffa has orders to transport it to Site R for examination. Suddenly, the close proximity of the meteor fragment causes the large meteor to flare, bathing Graffa in beams of light. Weldon realises that he has been possessed by an alien force and flees with the meteor fragment. She contacts Brogan and shows him footage of the planet Nayji, where a thriving civilisation has been completely wiped out by a space-born parasite within two months. Now the parasite has come to Altor and Weldon enlists Brogan's help to find Site R and destroy the alien spore before it can germinate...

Notes

The script for this episode was originally titled 'Graveyard II' but the episode was filmed as 'Deathwatch II' before being changed to *Deathwatch Conclusion* in post-production. There is no 'This Episode' sequence at the end of the main titles. The script indicates that the events of this episode take place one week after the final scene of *Deathwatch*. Sally's favourite film, the fictional *One Night Of Love* starring Clint Noble and Diana More, is a Haggard Bros. Pictures Inc. presentation. The script suggested that this film should be *Casablanca* (1942) if the rights to use clips from it could be obtained. The scene where Brogan kills the spore with the TZ8 enzyme was the last scene shot for the series. Gary Martin is credited as the voice of Slomo on the end titles, but Slomo does not appear.

Oops!

When Brogan and Weldon escape from the station house with the alien spore, the electric cable powering the spore prop's internal lights can be seen trailing from the bottom of the spore canister as they walk down a corridor.

Regular Cast

Lt. Patrick Brogan	**Ted Shackelford**
Officer Jack Haldane	**Rob Youngblood**
Officer Jane Castle	**Simone Bendix**
Sally Brogan	**Nancy Paul**
Capt. Rexton Podly	**Jerome Willis**
Matthew Brogan	**Nic Klein**
Elizabeth Brogan	**Megan Olive**
Officer Silas Romek	**Lou Hirsch**
Officer Hubble Orrin	**Richard James / Kieron Jecchinis**
Officer Aurelia Took	**Mary Woodvine**
Sgt. Thorald Fredo	**David Quilter**
Officer Lionel Carson	**Joseph Mydell**

Guest Cast

Captain Tara Weldon	**Cecilia Noble**
Major Graffa	**Rob Thirtle**
MIA Commander	**Burnell Tucker**
Nox	**Wayne Forester**
Reimer	**Alexa Rosewood**
Pawldo	**Andy Dawson**
Shadow	**Glenn Marks**
Arresting Officer	**Lindsay Harris**
Reporter	**Alexa Rosewood**
Duty Officer / Tech #1	**Andy Dawson**

First UK Transmission

Saturday, August 26th, 1995
7.00pm (Sky One)

THE MAKING OF SPACE PRECINCT

Written by **John Needham** Directed by **Ben Robinson** & **Julian Phillips**

A behind the scenes documentary which examines the making of SPACE PRECINCT, visiting the soundstages at Pinewood and Shepperton Studios during production of *Protect And Survive*, *Two Against The Rock*, *The Forever Beetle* and *Deathwatch Conclusion*. Mime artist Rob Thirtle has a plaster cast taken of his head, the animatronic head of Drover Pike (*The Forever Beetle*) is made in the tarn and creon workshop, animatronics operator Christine Glanville explains how she works with actor Jerome Willis to make Captain Podly come alive and model designer Bill Pearson conducts a guided tour of the Scorpion Bomber cockpit set created by the model team for *Deathwatch Conclusion*. Members of the cast and crew are interviewed including Gerry Anderson, Ted Shackelford, Rob Youngblood, Richard Gregory, John Glen, Steven Begg, Jim Cornish, Nigel Stone, Angus Cameron and Paul Langwade.

Notes

Narrator Nickolas Grace appeared as Oturi Nissim in *Double Duty*. This documentary was originally broadcast on Sky One at the end of a repeat run of the whole series on weekday evenings. It was released on VHS home video in 1995 by PolyGram Video (together with *Protect And Survive* and *Time To Kill*) and on DVD in 2000 by Digital Entertainment (as a special feature on SPACE PRECINCT Volume 1).

Cast

Narrator	**Nickolas Grace**

First UK Transmission

Friday, September 29th, 1995
6.30pm (Sky One)

Programme Running Time

25.5 minutes approx.

PRODUCTION CREDITS

Executive Producers	**Tom Gutteridge**, **Gerry Anderson**
Producers	**John Needham**
Music	**Crispin Merrell**
Camera	**Sam Montague**, **Alan R. Wright**
Sound	**Renato Ferrari**, **Simon Clark**
Dubbing Mixer	**Eddie Jones**
Editor	**Richard Halliday**
Production Assistant	**Alison Kerr**

With thanks to The Magic Camera Company
Air Studios
Mentorn Films / Gerry Anderson

COMPILATION FEATURE FILMS

SPACE PRECINCT's two two-part stories, *The Fire Within* and *Deathwatch*, were also prepared by the series' post-production department in an alternative feature-length format, offering individual stations who purchased the series the option to broadcast each as a special event in conjunction with screenings of the other 20 regular-length episodes. It was suggested to broadcasters that *The Fire Within* could be shown as the series' opening episode – providing a spectacular series premiere – or as a Hallowe'en, Christmas or mid-season special, while *Deathwatch* would be the series finale. To date, neither film has been transmitted in the UK, but both were released on DVD in 2001 by Digital Entertainment.

Feature Film Titles

(Listed in production order)

1. **The Fire Within**
2. **Deathwatch**

Feature Running Time

83 minutes approx.

THE FIRE WITHIN

Compilation of *The Fire Within (Part One)* and *The Fire Within (Part Two)*. The title caption at the start of *Part One* was revised to remove the 'This Episode' portion of the caption. The closing titles were revised to reflect the credits of both episodes.

DEATHWATCH

Compilation of *Deathwatch* and *Deathwatch Conclusion*. The opening and closing title sequences were revised to reflect the credits of both episodes. The title caption at the start of *Deathwatch* was revised to remove the 'This Episode' portion of the caption. The closing scene of *Deathwatch*, in which Weldon and Graffa supervise the excavation of the alien meteor in the ruins of Roetem Towers and see it placed inside a secure container, was deleted.

LAVENDER CASTLE

Format

Lavender Castle is a place of mystery and legend, fabled throughout the universe, a floating city of light, a place of peace, harmony and all the things that have ever been dreamed of. It is the centre of the universe and the greatest source of power – should it be destroyed, the universe would be plunged into darkness forever. Evil scientist Dr. Agon plans to do just that. A lonely megalomaniac with technology-assisted powers of transmutation, he yearns for darkness and has pledged to destroy Lavender Castle from his fortress spaceship, the Dark Station, the most awesome destructive power in the universe, crewed by unseen slaves working deep in its bowels.

In order to prevent this, Captain Thrice has set out on a quest to find the elusive Lavender Castle before Dr. Agon. A previous encounter with Lavender Castle gave life to Thrice's walking stick and left the Captain with a special knowledge of its power and abilities. Travelling in his cottage spaceship, the *Paradox*, Thrice assembles a crew of misfits to join him in his quest, combating evil wherever they find it as they travel the universe searching for clues that will lead them to Lavender Castle. But Lavender Castle works in mysterious ways and lends its lavender power to the *Paradox* crew to protect them when they most need help.

The *Paradox* is a half-timbered spaceship with a thatched roof that helps to keep the ship warm and cosy as it travels through space. Powered by a temperamental old MD 646 engine, the *Paradox* is remarkably agile and capable of speeds up to 20 times faster than light (SOL 20). The ship is equipped with an automatic pilot, Transvision communications systems and remote control steering, but has no defensive weaponry whatsoever. When things break down and require replacement parts, the crew visit the planet Thestal to obtain the necessary equipment from junkyard dealers Twaddle Duff and Twaddle Dim, three-handed twins with teleportation abilities.

Production

In 1989, Gerry Anderson was approached by artist Rodney Matthews, who showed him a portfolio of his highly imaginative science-fiction and fantasy paintings. Prompted by Anderson, Matthews developed the concept and characters for LAVENDER CASTLE and in 1991, Anderson secured backing from the BBC to produce a 26-part animated series. However, the BBC then withdrew their support without explanation, so Anderson offered the project to Carlton Television, who rejected it on the grounds that the children's department head didn't like science-fiction.

LAVENDER CASTLE was shelved until 1996 when Anderson met Craig Hemmings, production executive of Carrington Productions International, who agreed to finance a full series made with stop-motion animation produced at the internationally renowned Cosgrove Hall Films in Manchester and CGI animation produced at White Horse Films in London. Rodney Matthews's highly detailed character designs were meticulously crafted into fully articulated puppets by specialist puppet-makers Mackinnon & Saunders, fitted with glass eyes made by a professional optician and clothed in costumes that were specifically designed for stop-motion work by Cosgrove Hall's in-house costume department.

Following six months of pre-production work, 80 weeks of stop-motion filming began at Cosgrove Hall on March 1st, 1997, with each episode scheduled for three weeks of filming followed by four weeks of post-production work. In a first for Anderson (who had, until now, always shot his productions on film), LAVENDER CASTLE was 'filmed' entirely on digital video. The stop-motion animation of the puppet characters was shot with Sony DXC D30 PL digital cameras and recorded onto an adapted PC hard disk using a Perception Video Recorder running in conjunction with Animate software. The CGI imagery of spaceships and planets was created on Silicon Graphics Indigo 2 computers using Softimage software, while the backgrounds were generated on Apple Mac computers. Filming was completed at the end of February 1998 and the various elements were then blended together in post-production by 4:2:2 Manchester using Quantel Editbox, a non-linear editing, digital compositing and paint system.

Main Characters

Captain Thrice
Three-eyed captain of the *Paradox* cottage spaceship with a special knowledge of Lavender Castle

Walking Stick
A walking stick carved by Captain Thrice from laplon wood and given life by Lavender Castle

Roger
Australander pilot of the *Paradox*, formerly a decorated starfighter pilot

Isambard
Scottish-accented engineer with a passion for inventing gadgets and playing the bagpipes

Lyca
Floran biologist and medical specialist with butterfly wings that give her the power of flight

Sir Squeakalot
Ship's robot fitted with an Outel processor and HK (housekeeping) technology, knighted by Queen Zarla

Sproggle
The Paradox's navigator, a simple orphan with a child-like innocence who cannot tell left from right

Dr. Cedric Agon
Evil scientist and commander of the Dark Station who will let nothing stand in the way of his plans to destroy Lavender Castle

Trump
Dr. Agon's faithful falcon

Short Fred Ledd
One-legged pirate who sails the Galak Sea in his ancient galleon, the *Cutting Snark*

Tin Lizzy
Short Fred Ledd's faithful tin parrot

Twaddle Duff
Junkyard proprietor of Twaddle & Twaddle Rocket Engines Inc. and twin to Twaddle Dim

Twaddle Dim
Junkyard proprietor of Twaddle & Twaddle Rocket Engines Inc. and twin to Twaddle Duff

LAVENDER CASTLE was originally broadcast in the UK as part of the fully networked CHILDREN'S ITV strand, making it the first Gerry Anderson series to receive a first-run UK network screening since FOUR FEATHER FALLS in 1960. The 26 episodes were screened as two series: the first 17 episodes from January 1999 and the last nine from January 2000.

Episode Titles

(Listed in production order)

1. **In The Beginning**
2. **Flower Power**
3. **The Twilight Tower**
4. **High Moon**
5. **The Lost Starfighter**
6. **A Stitch In Time**
7. **Double Cross**
8. **Bird Of Prey**
9. **Collision Course**
10. **The Black Swat**
11. **Raiders Of The Planet Zark**
12. **Swamp Fever**
13. **The Galacternet**
14. **Brightonia On Sea**
15. **The Traitor**
16. **The Collector**
17. **Lost In Space**
18. **Duelling Banjos**
19. **The Legend**
20. **Cloud Of Chaos**
21. **Diamonds Aren't Forever**
22. **Galactic Park**
23. **Wearizy**
24. **Supernova**
25. **Interface**
26. **Birds Of A Feather**

Episode Running Time

10 minutes approx.

The episodes listed above were also prepared by CPI in an alternate format as 22-minute double-bills with extra linking material. Further details of these episodes and the linking material appears at the end of this section, although some background information about the characters and vehicles revealed during the link sections is listed in the 'Notes' for the appropriate episodes on the following pages.

PRODUCTION CREDITS

Produced by **Gerry Anderson**
Executive Producer **Craig Hemmings**
Designed by **Rodney Matthews**
Executive Producer for Cosgrove Hall Films **Brian Cosgrove**
Line Producer **Chris Bowden**
From an original concept by **Rodney Matthews**
Featuring the Voices of **Jimmy Hibbert**, **Rob Rackstraw**, **David Holt**, **Kate Harbour**
Dialogue Recording **Alfasound** *(1-6)*, **The Bridge** *(7-10)*, **Angelsound** *(11-26)*
Music by **Crispin Merrell**
Banjo Playing by **Paul Bishop** *(18)*
Supervising Animator **Sue Pugh** *(1-13)*
Animators **Matthew Palmer**, **Tim Collings** *(1-15, 17-20, 23, 25, 26)*, **Stuart Sutcliffe** *(1, 2, 4, 6, 10)*, **Monica McCartney** *(1, 2, 5)*, **Barry Purves** *(4, 6, 7)*, **Philip Dale** *(5)*, **Bill Martin** *(7, 8, 9, 11, 13)*, **Tobias Fouracre** *(10)*, **Haydn Secker** *(11, 14, 17, 23, 26)*, **Lucy Gell** *(13)*, **Lisa Goddard** *(14-26)*, **David Grove** *(15)*, **Justin Exley** *(16, 21, 22, 24-26)*, **Andy Joule** *(20)*, **Mike Cottee** *(21)*
Puppets by **Mackinnon & Saunders**
Maintenance **Patricia Brennan**
Sculptors **Noel Baker**, **Darren Marshall**, **Alison Lloyd**, **Joe Holman**, **Justin Exley**, **Richard Johnson**
Painter **Astrid Askeralian**
Trim & Scam **Bethan Jones**, **Emma Boyson**
Foam Technician **Michelle Scattergood**
Armatures **Georgina Hayns**, **Stuart Sutcliffe**, **Shannon O'Neil**, **Caroline Wallace**, **Haydn Secker**
Mouldmakers **Bridget Smith**, **Vilija Kontrimas**, **Robbie Manning**, **Mark Thompson**, **Gavin Jones**
Fabrication **Christine Keogh**
Production Supervisor **Christine Walker**
Props **Owen Ballhatchet** *(1-10, 12-26)*, **Jon Fletcher** *(1-12)*
Costumes **Clare Elliott**, **Geraldine Corrigan**, **Karen Betty**, **Barbara Biddulph**
Visual Effects **Stephen Weston**
Art Director **Peter Hillier**
Lighting Camera **Joe Dembinski** *(1-11)*, **Tim Harper** *(11-26)*
Editor **Zyggy Markiewicz** *(1-3, 5-12)*
Off Line Editing **Flix Facilities** *(4, 13-26)*
Visual Effects Assistant **Manfred-Dean Yürke**
Production Controller **Phil Slattery** *(1-3, 5)*
Production Manager **Laura Duncalf** *(4, 7, 8, 13-26)*, **Laura Cosgrove** *(6, 9-12)*
Co-ordination **Mary Anderson**
Production Assistant **Debbie Peers**
Audio Post Production **Hullabaloo Studios**
On-line Editor **Martin Dixon***
On-line Facilities **4:2:2 Manchester**

Produced at Cosgrove Hall Films Limited
Carrington Productions International

* uncredited

IN THE BEGINNING — Prod. No. 01

Script by **Gerry Anderson** & **Pauline Fisk**
Story by **Pauline Fisk**
Directed by **Chris Taylor**

Captain Thrice, Walking Stick and Isambard set out on their quest to find Lavender Castle before Dr. Agon can destroy it and plunge the universe into darkness forever. Realising that they will need a full crew for the starship *Paradox*, Thrice sets course for the Galax Sea to rescue Roger, Lyca and Sir Squeakalot, who are prisoners of the pirate Short Fred Ledd on his galleon, the *Cutting Snark*. Ledd plans to sell the trio as slaves to Dr. Agon who boards the galleon in his Mammoth Machine. The *Paradox* arrives just in time for Thrice to effect a rescue, but Dr. Agon has a few tricks up his sleeve...

Notes

This episode does not feature the regular title sequence. The shooting script originally included dialogue for Fred's parrot Tin Lizzy, and an additional scene in which Walking Stick argues with Isambard, accusing him of taking her stocking and describing his kilt as a skirt. Roger is revealed to be a starfighter pilot who was ferrying Lyca on a mission to collect rare plants for medical research when they were captured by Short Fred Ledd. Sir Squeakalot is an RM96 robot who previously served on the *QZ3*.

Regular Voice Cast

Captain Thrice	**David Holt**
Walking Stick	**Kate Harbour**
Roger	**Rob Rackstraw**
Isambard	**Rob Rackstraw**
Lyca	**Kate Harbour**
Sir Squeakalot	**Jimmy Hibbert**
Sproggle	**David Holt**
Dr. Agon	**Jimmy Hibbert**
Trump	**Jimmy Hibbert**
Short Fred Ledd	**Jimmy Hibbert**

Guest Voice Cast

Nice Old Lady	**Kate Harbour**

First UK Transmission

Thursday, January 7th, 1999
4.00pm (ITV Network)

FLOWER POWER — Prod. No. 02

Script by **Gerry Anderson** & **Pauline Fisk**
Story by **Pauline Fisk**
Directed by **Chris Taylor**

The *Paradox* picks up an Intergalactic Distress Call and Sproggle traces it to the Dragon's Planet. The signal is tracked to one of the giant flowers which cover the planet and the crew discover a dilapidated old house built inside the flower pod. Investigating, they discover a sick old lady who has been confined to her bed for longer than she can remember. The crew help to clean up the house and the old lady gathers them all together so that she can thank them, but she is suddenly revealed to be Dr. Agon in disguise. He locks them in the house and traps the *Paradox* inside the flower pod when it closes for the night...

Notes

The sick old lady that the Paradox crew meet here is portrayed by the same old lady puppet that Dr. Agon transformed into in an attempt to fool Captain Thrice at the end of *In The Beginning*. Dr. Agon also uses his transformation medallion to masquerade as Twaddle Duff in *Galactic Park*. Lyca is revealed to have butterfly-like wings which she uses to fly up into the roof of the flower pod.

Regular Voice Cast

Captain Thrice	**David Holt**
Walking Stick	**Kate Harbour**
Roger	**Rob Rackstraw**
Isambard	**Rob Rackstraw**
Lyca	**Kate Harbour**
Sir Squeakalot	**Jimmy Hibbert**
Sproggle	**David Holt**
Dr. Agon	**Jimmy Hibbert**
Trump	**Jimmy Hibbert**

Guest Voice Cast

Sick Old Lady	**Kate Harbour**

First UK Transmission

Thursday, January 14th, 1999
4.00pm (ITV Network)

THE TWILIGHT TOWER — Prod. No. 03

Script by **Gerry Anderson** & **Pauline Fisk**
Story by **Pauline Fisk**
Directed by **Chris Taylor**

Investigating a strange red mist in the atmosphere of a nearby planet, the *Paradox* is caught in a light beam projected from a dark tower. The beam drags the ship towards the tower and deposits it on the cliff top outside, so Captain Thrice, Roger and Isambard decide to explore. Entering the tower, they are welcomed by the Guardian, who invites them to drink cola and view the Most Fabulous Object in the Universe. This turns out to be a television set which mesmerises Roger and Isambard, but when Thrice realises what is happening, he is overpowered by the Guardian, who reveals that he intends to keep them all in the tower forever – as souvenirs!

Notes

The programme that Roger and Isambard watch on the Most Fabulous Object in the Universe is Gerry Anderson's previous stop-motion animation series DICK SPANNER ("Ripper! I haven't seen this for years," says Roger). Although it seems unlikely that he could have survived the destruction of the Twilight Tower at the end of this episode, the Guardian turns up again alive and well in *Raiders Of The Planet Zark*.

Regular Voice Cast

Captain Thrice	**David Holt**
Walking Stick	**Kate Harbour**
Roger	**Rob Rackstraw**
Isambard	**Rob Rackstraw**
Lyca	**Kate Harbour**
Sir Squeakalot	**Jimmy Hibbert**
Sproggle	**David Holt**

Guest Voice Cast

The Guardian	**Rob Rackstraw**

First UK Transmission

Thursday, January 21st, 1999
4.00pm (ITV Network)

HIGH MOON

Prod. No. 04

Story & Script by **Gerry Anderson** & **Pauline Fisk** Directed by **Chris Taylor**

Regular Voice Cast

Captain Thrice	**David Holt**
Walking Stick	**Kate Harbour**
Roger	**Rob Rackstraw**
Isambard	**Rob Rackstraw**
Lyca	**Kate Harbour**
Sir Squeakalot	**Jimmy Hibbert**
Sproggle	**David Holt**
Dr. Agon	**Jimmy Hibbert**
Trump	**Jimmy Hibbert**

First UK Transmission

Thursday, January 28th, 1999
4.00pm (ITV Network)

In his Mammoth Machine, Dr. Agon chases the *Paradox* in the vicinity of the egg-shaped planet Draco. Roger manages to manoeuvre the ship out of the path of Agon's missile, but then the engine breaks down, leaving the *Paradox* motionless in space. Savouring the defeat of his enemies, Dr. Agon informs Captain Thrice that his destruction will be poetic, commencing when Draco's Moon reaches its zenith in one hour's time. As they wait to be sent to oblivion, Thrice tells the others how he first discovered Lavender Castle and how the Castle gave life to Walking Stick. But as time runs out for the *Paradox* crew, it seems that only Lavender Castle can save them now...

Notes

Captain Thrice reveals that he made Walking Stick from the branch of a laplon tree which he had picked up in the Delerian star system. In his introduction to *High Moon* in the alternate format episode *The Twilight Tower/High Moon*, Isambard proudly tells how the *Paradox* engine never breaks down, and then urges viewers not to watch this episode when he remembers that it's the one in which the engine breaks down ("Look, don't watch this one. Don't watch it. You don't need to see it. Take it from me, all right?").

THE LOST STARFIGHTER

Prod. No. 05

Script by **Gerry Anderson** & **Chris Trengove** Directed by **Chris Taylor**
Story by **Chris Bowden**

Regular Voice Cast

Captain Thrice	**David Holt**
Roger	**Rob Rackstraw**
Isambard	**Rob Rackstraw**
Lyca	**Kate Harbour**
Sir Squeakalot	**Jimmy Hibbert**
Sproggle	**David Holt**
Dr. Agon	**Jimmy Hibbert**
Trump	**Jimmy Hibbert**

First UK Transmission

Thursday, February 4th, 1999
4.00pm (ITV Network)

The *Paradox* comes across the *Firefly*, Roger's Starfighter, floating adrift in space. Recognising that it could come in handy against Dr. Agon, Isambard floats across to the craft to see if he can repair it, unaware that he is being observed from a distance by Dr. Agon. Sproggle expresses an interest in the Starfighter so Lyca flies him across to sit in the cockpit, but Dr. Agon arrives in his Mammoth Machine and targets the *Firefly* with his laser cannons. Under Roger's instructions, Sproggle activates the *Firefly*'s controls to escape the laser beams, but he is pursued by Dr. Agon and, in his panic, starts pressing all the buttons in the cockpit, sending the vehicle spiralling out of control!

Notes

In the shooting script, the Mammoth Machine was damaged by the *Firefly*'s accidental laser fire, rather than by the Machine's own lasers, and after Sproggle ejects from the Starfighter, he was caught by the *Paradox* crew in a giant butterfly net. Roger reveals that he was flying the *Firefly* when he was captured by Short Fred Ledd. The ship makes a return appearance in *Lost In Space*.

A STITCH IN TIME

Prod. No. 06

Script by **Gerry Anderson** Directed by **Chris Taylor**
Story by **Chris Bowden**

Regular Voice Cast

Captain Thrice	**David Holt**
Walking Stick	**Kate Harbour**
Roger	**Rob Rackstraw**
Isambard	**Rob Rackstraw**
Lyca	**Kate Harbour**
Sir Squeakalot	**Jimmy Hibbert**
Sproggle	**David Holt**
Dr. Agon	**Jimmy Hibbert**
Trump	**Jimmy Hibbert**

First UK Transmission

Thursday, February 25th, 1999
4.00pm (ITV Network)

As the *Paradox* enters an asteroid belt, Isambard is attempting to fix an experimental time machine although Captain Thrice has misgivings about ever using it, explaining to Roger that it could destroy the fabric of the entire universe. Suddenly, the Dark Station appears from hiding behind a large asteroid and opens fire on the *Paradox*. Roger takes the ship into cover behind another asteroid, but Agon destroys the asteroid and his next salvo causes an explosion on the *Paradox* which kills Captain Thrice. The Dark Station closes in and just as it looks as though the *Paradox* is about to be obliterated, Lyca activates the time machine...

Notes

The shooting script details that Sproggle's bauble changes colour depending upon his mood: sickly yellow if he is unhappy, dark blue if he is sad, red when he is frightened. This aspect of Sproggle's appearance was abandoned before filming began. Although the previous five episodes were originally broadcast in the order in which they were produced, *A Stitch In Time* was screened as episode eight.

DOUBLE CROSS — Prod. No. 07

Script by **Gerry Anderson** & **Pauline Fisk** Directed by **Chris Taylor**
Story by **Gerry Anderson**

As part of a plot to capture the *Paradox* crew, Dr. Agon commissions scrap merchant Twaddle Duff to find a rare MD 646 engine for him. Duff knows that the *Paradox* has just such an engine so he contacts Captain Thrice claiming to have information about Lavender Castle. He invites the *Paradox* crew to a rendezvous on planet Thestel where he offers to swap the information for the ship's engine, but when Isambard objects, Duff uses his teleportation abilities to steal the engine and transport it to Dr. Agon's Mammoth Machine. With the *Paradox* crew powerless to resist, Dr. Agon tells them to surrender or face being obliterated by the Mammoth Machine!

Notes

The shooting script suggested an Arthur Daley (the character portrayed by George Cole in ITV's MINDER television series) sort of voice for Twaddle Duff, but voice artist Jimmy Hibbert provides the character with a voice that is a very creditable impression of Harry H. Corbett as Harold Steptoe in the 1960s/70s BBC sitcom STEPTOE AND SON. Thunderbird 1 is visible in the background at Twaddle & Twaddle Rocket Engines Inc.

Regular Voice Cast

Captain Thrice	**David Holt**
Roger	**Rob Rackstraw**
Isambard	**Rob Rackstraw**
Lyca	**Kate Harbour**
Sir Squeakalot	**Jimmy Hibbert**
Sproggle	**David Holt**
Dr. Agon	**Jimmy Hibbert**
Trump	**Jimmy Hibbert**
Twaddle Duff	**Jimmy Hibbert**
Twaddle Dim	**Rob Rackstraw**

First UK Transmission

Thursday, February 18th, 1999
4.00pm (ITV Network)

BIRD OF PREY — Prod. No. 08

Story & Script by **Chris Trengove** Directed by **Chris Taylor**

The *Paradox* is lying low behind an asteroid when a cleaning accident causes Captain Thrice to manoeuvre the ship into the range of Dr. Agon's sensors. Agon sends Trump to follow the *Paradox* but the bird falls into a black hole and when she emerges, the falcon has grown to a gigantic size. Spotting the *Paradox*, Trump attacks, grasping the ship in her mouth and then accidentally swallowing it, but the ship gets stuck in her throat. Believing that she has failed to capture the *Paradox*, Agon sends Trump back to the black hole where she returns to normal size, but the *Paradox* and its crew have been shrunk to minuscule size and are still stuck in Trump's throat!

Notes

The giant-sized Trump is animated with CGI so as to more easily interact with the CGI *Paradox*. The sneezing powder that Lyca developed (with Lavender Castle's help) to escape from the flower pod in *Flower Power* is employed again here to escape from trump's throat. In the linking material in the alternate format episode *Bird Of Prey/ Collision Course*, Sir Squeakalot reveals that he is fitted with an Outel processor and HK (housekeeping) technology. He also reveals that Roger is an Australander.

Regular Voice Cast

Captain Thrice	**David Holt**
Roger	**Rob Rackstraw**
Isambard	**Rob Rackstraw**
Lyca	**Kate Harbour**
Sir Squeakalot	**Jimmy Hibbert**
Sproggle	**David Holt**
Dr. Agon	**Jimmy Hibbert**
Trump	**Jimmy Hibbert**

First UK Transmission

Thursday, March 4th, 1999
4.00pm (ITV Network)

COLLISION COURSE — Prod. No. 09

Script by **Chris Trengove** & **Gerry Anderson** Directed by **Chris Taylor**
Story by **Chris Trengove**

The *Paradox* is headed for planet Thestal in search of a spare part so Isambard decides to test his latest invention, a jet-propelled powerpack, with Sir Squeakalot as test pilot. Arriving on Thestal, Captain Thrice places an order with Twaddle Duff for a new Transvision while Isambard takes an interest in a consignment of rocket fuel. Then, the *Paradox* picks up a distress call from Lyca's home planet Flora: an asteroid is on a collision course with the planet and will hit the atmosphere in just seven hours. Captain Thrice proposes a daring scheme to deflect the asteroid using Twaddle Duff's rocket fuel and Isambard's jetpack...

Notes

This episode introduces Isambard's jetpack which also proves invaluable in the later episodes *The Galacternet*, *Cloud Of Chaos* and *Interface*. Viewers are also reintroduced to the Twaddle Twins, now presented as more sympathetic characters after being double-crossed by Dr. Agon in *Double Cross*. Duff and Dim appear again in *Lost In Space* and *Wearizy* while Duff is impersonated by Dr. Agon in *Galactic Park*.

Regular Voice Cast

Captain Thrice	**David Holt**
Walking Stick	**Kate Harbour**
Roger	**Rob Rackstraw**
Isambard	**Rob Rackstraw**
Lyca	**Kate Harbour**
Sir Squeakalot	**Jimmy Hibbert**
Sproggle	**David Holt**
Twaddle Duff	**Jimmy Hibbert**
Twaddle Dim	**Rob Rackstraw**

First UK Transmission

Thursday, March 11th, 1999
3.50pm (ITV Network)

THE BLACK SWAT — Prod. No. 10

Regular Voice Cast

Captain Thrice	**David Holt**
Walking Stick	**Kate Harbour**
Roger	**Rob Rackstraw**
Isambard	**Rob Rackstraw**
Lyca	**Kate Harbour**
Sir Squeakalot	**Jimmy Hibbert**
Sproggle	**David Holt**
Short Fred Ledd	**Jimmy Hibbert**
Tin Lizzy	**David Holt**

First UK Transmission

Thursday, February 11th, 1999
4.00pm (ITV Network)

Story & Script by **Pauline Fisk** Directed by **Chris Taylor**

To avoid a space storm, Short Fred Ledd steers the *Cutting Snark* to the planet Scull where he spots the *Paradox* on the beach. On board, Sproggle attempts to persuade his crewmates that there is buried treasure on the planet as he has seen an 'X' marking the spot during their approach from space. The others are sceptical so Sproggle goes off on his own to explore a cave nearby in search of the treasure, but Lyca follows him to make sure that he is all right. While they are gone, Short Fred Ledd opens fire on the *Paradox*, completely destroying the ship. Captain Thrice, Roger, Isambard and Sir Squeakalot are taken prisoner aboard the *Cutting Snark* guarded by an electronic spider, the Black Swat!

Notes

This episode reintroduces Short Fred Ledd, previously seen in *In The Beginning*. The pirate goes on to become the *Paradox* crew's second most prominent adversary (after Dr. Agon) and is seen again in *Brightonia On Sea*, *Traitor*, *Diamonds Aren't Forever* and *Birds Of A Feather*. In his introduction to this story in the alternate format episode The *Lost Starfighter/The Black Swat*, Roger reveals that the *Paradox* travels many times faster than the speed of light but has no armaments of any kind.

RAIDERS OF THE PLANET ZARK — Prod. No. 11

Regular Voice Cast

Captain Thrice	**David Holt**
Walking Stick	**Kate Harbour**
Roger	**Rob Rackstraw**
Isambard	**Rob Rackstraw**
Lyca	**Kate Harbour**
Sir Squeakalot	**Jimmy Hibbert**
Sproggle	**David Holt**

Guest Voice Cast

The Guardian	**Rob Rackstraw**
Voice of Morg	**Kate Harbour**

First UK Transmission

Thursday, March 25th, 1999
3.50pm (ITV Network)

Script by **Chris Trengove** Directed by **Chris Taylor**
Story by **Chris Bowden**

Sproggle intercepts a message which invites the *Paradox* crew to the Mountain of Morg on the planet Zark in search of a lavender compass that will lead them to Lavender Castle. The crew arrive on Zark and enter the caves of Morg, unaware that they have been drawn to the planet by the Guardian who wants the compass for his own: once the *Paradox* crew have located the compass, the Guardian intends to snatch it from them. The tunnels prove to be full of traps for the *Paradox* crew and they soon become separated, leaving only Isambard free to follow the cryptic clues issued by the Voice of Morg, which lead him to the compass and a final puzzle to win the prize...

Notes

The Guardian, previously seen in *The Twilight Tower*, has escaped apparent death at the end of that episode to reappear here: Captain Thrice refers to the events of *The Twilight Tower* when they meet up with him. Crushed under a stone block at the end of this episode, the Guardian threatens to inflict retribution upon the *Paradox* crew, but he is not seen again.

SWAMP FEVER — Prod. No. 12

Regular Voice Cast

Captain Thrice	**David Holt**
Walking Stick	**Kate Harbour**
Roger	**Rob Rackstraw**
Isambard	**Rob Rackstraw**
Lyca	**Kate Harbour**
Sir Squeakalot	**Jimmy Hibbert**
Sproggle	**David Holt**

Guest Voice Cast

The Dank	**Jimmy Hibbert**

First UK Transmission

Thursday, March 18th, 1999
3.50pm (ITV Network)

Story & Script by **Chris Trengove** Directed by **Chris Taylor**

Captain Thrice has contracted the life-threatening galactic fever and without treatment he will die within days. The cure is made from an extract of wumbo leaves, but the wumbo plant can only be found in the Great Swamp on the planet Quagmire and is fiercely protected by the indigenous danks, who use the wumbo leaves to make dank juice, their favourite drink. Arriving on Quagmire, Lyca and Sproggle set out to find the wumbo plants, but Lyca is captured by a dank who accuses her of trespassing and holds her prisoner at his shack in the swamp. It is left to Sproggle, masquerading as a poisonous doodoo, to rescue her...

Notes

This episode introduces the Dank, a four-armed frog-like creature with an extendible tongue and a Southern accent who plays the banjo and lives on insects and dank juice. He appears again in *Duelling Banjos* and agrees to join Dr. Agon's coalition in *Birds Of A Feather*. Lyca describes a doodoo as a creature that spits deadly poison and then eats its victims, especially the female of the species. However, it seems likely that she is making this up as she goes along.

THE GALACTERNET — Prod. No. 13

Story & Script by **Gerry Anderson** Directed by **Chris Taylor**

Isambard discovers that Lavender Castle has its own website on the Galacternet which gives the co-ordinates of how to find it. Captain Thrice is extremely sceptical of this information and suspects a hoax, but the other *Paradox* crewmembers vote to fly to the co-ordinates to check it out. Roger pilots the *Paradox* to the planet Trimbo and aims for the twin peaks that occupy the co-ordinates on the website, but the ship is suddenly caught in a huge spider's web spun between the peaks. Alerted by the impact, a robotic monster spider appears and menaces the *Paradox* as Captain Thrice realises that they have fallen into a devious trap set by Dr. Agon. Using Isambard's jetpack, Sir Squeakalot attempts to free the *Paradox* from the web before Dr. Agon arrives in his Mammoth Machine...

Notes

Dr. Agon later uses the giant mechanical spider as part of his plan to capture the Paradox crew in *Interface*. Sir Squeakalot uses the jetpack that was introduced in *Collision Course*. Trump has managed to recover his normal size: the bird was last seen shrunk to the size of a canary in *Bird Of Prey*.

Regular Voice Cast

Character	Voice
Captain Thrice	**David Holt**
Roger	**Rob Rackstraw**
Isambard	**Rob Rackstraw**
Lyca	**Kate Harbour**
Sir Squeakalot	**Jimmy Hibbert**
Sproggle	**David Holt**
Dr. Agon	**Jimmy Hibbert**
Trump	**Jimmy Hibbert**

First UK Transmission

Thursday, April 1st, 1999
3.50pm (ITV Network)

BRIGHTONIA ON SEA — Prod. No. 14

Story & Script by **Gerry Anderson** Directed by **Chris Taylor**

Following the suggestion of an electronic holiday brochure that they have received, the *Paradox* crew decide to holiday on the planet of Brightonia On Sea. After Captain Thrice is late returning to the ship for lunch, Sproggle then goes missing while he is picking nomel fruit. Leaving Squeakalot to recharge on the *Paradox*, the other crewmembers go looking for Sproggle, but they are all captured by Short Fred Ledd, who sent the holiday brochure to lead them into a trap. Chaining them up in the hot sun without water, Ledd leaves the *Paradox* crew to die while he steals their ship and returns to the *Cutting Snark*, but he has not counted on Isambard's new remote control device...

Notes

More by accident than design, this episode is a remake (after 38 years) of the SUPERCAR episode *False Alarm* in which the Supercar team are drawn to a remote spot by a bogus radio message, captured and tied up by Masterspy and Zarin who then steal Supercar. In both episodes, the villains are foiled by the use of a new remote control device which manoeuvres the stolen vehicle through a variety of high-speed twists and turns until the villain finally surrenders.

Regular Voice Cast

Character	Voice
Captain Thrice	**David Holt**
Walking Stick	**Kate Harbour**
Roger	**Rob Rackstraw**
Isambard	**Rob Rackstraw**
Lyca	**Kate Harbour**
Sir Squeakalot	**Jimmy Hibbert**
Sproggle	**David Holt**
Short Fred Ledd	**Jimmy Hibbert**
Tin Lizzy	**David Holt**

First UK Transmission

Thursday, April 8th, 1999
3.50pm (ITV Network)

TRAITOR — Prod. No. 15

Script by **Gerry Anderson** Directed by **Chris Taylor**
Story by **Rodney Matthews**

Short Fred Ledd sends Tin Lizzy to the *Paradox* where she disguises herself as an ornament until the opportunity arises to focus her eye beams on Sir Squeakalot. The beams disrupt Squeakalot's programming, causing him to turn on his colleagues. Holding them captive with his laser beams, Squeakalot pilots the *Paradox* to a rendezvous with the *Cutting Snark*. Their arrival is observed by Trump who has been sent by Dr. Agon to find out what is going on after Ledd announces that he has captured the *Paradox* crew. When Trump signals that Ledd is not exaggerating his achievement, Dr. Agon sets a course for the *Cutting Snark* to collect his newly captured slaves...

Notes

The last time a robot (as opposed to a mobile computer, such as SPACE:1999's Brian the Brain and TERRAHAWKS' Zeroids) was seen piloting a spaceship in a Gerry Anderson series was in FIREBALL XL5. By a strange coincidence, Squeakalot reports to Short Fred Ledd that he is approaching the *Cutting Snark* from Sector 24: *Fireball XL5* patrols Sector 25. Dr. Agon reveals that his forename is Cedric.

Regular Voice Cast

Character	Voice
Captain Thrice	**David Holt**
Walking Stick	**Kate Harbour**
Roger	**Rob Rackstraw**
Isambard	**Rob Rackstraw**
Lyca	**Kate Harbour**
Sir Squeakalot	**Jimmy Hibbert**
Sproggle	**David Holt**
Dr. Agon	**Jimmy Hibbert**
Trump	**Jimmy Hibbert**
Short Fred Ledd	**Jimmy Hibbert**
Tin Lizzy	**David Holt**

First UK Transmission

Thursday, April 15th, 1999
3.50pm (ITV Network)

THE COLLECTOR

Prod. No. 16

Story & Script by **Chris Trengove** Directed by **Chris Taylor**

The Paradox arrives at Doodlebug's Supermarket to shop for supplies, but the ship is trapped by restraining arms on the landing pad and Captain Thrice is unable to contact Doodlebug to find out what is going on. Roger, Lyca and Sir Squeakalot enter the supermarket to investigate and find the place deserted but in a terrible mess, as if there has been a fight going on. Squeakalot decides to start tidying up and discovers Doodlebug in a state of suspended animation hidden in a cleaning cupboard. Then Roger and Lyca are captured by the android Colonel Clump, who intends to add them to his collection of living space creatures...

Notes

Sir Squeakalot recalls Colonel Clump from the factory where he was made: Clump was a prototype android with a heat-seeking detector system, but it had a faulty master switch and escaped. The character reappears in *Birds Of A Feather* where it seems that he has made Doodlebug's Supermarket his permanent base. Squeakalot's escape from the supermarket with Doodlebug in a shopping trolley is a pastiche of the iconic 'over the Moon' sequence in *E.T. The Extra-Terrestrial* (1982).

Regular Voice Cast

Captain Thrice	**David Holt**
Roger	**Rob Rackstraw**
Isambard	**Rob Rackstraw**
Lyca	**Kate Harbour**
Sir Squeakalot	**Jimmy Hibbert**
Sproggle	**David Holt**

Guest Voice Cast

Colonel Clump	**David Holt**

First UK Transmission

Thursday, April 22nd, 1999
3.50pm (ITV Network)

LOST IN SPACE

Prod. No. 17

Story & Script by **Gerry Anderson** Directed by **Chris Taylor**

Dr. Agon purchases Roger's Starfighter, the *Firefly*, from Twaddle Duff and asks for it to be delivered as a gift to Captain Thrice from an anonymous benefactor. Duff does so and Roger is delighted to see his old ship once more. He takes the *Firefly* for a test flight around an asteroid belt, but Dr. Agon has sabotaged the controls and the ship goes through hyperlight to end up lost in space on the other side of the galaxy. When he recovers consciousness, Roger is amazed to find that he is close to Lavender Castle, so Captain Thrice urges him to go there for help to get back to the *Paradox*, but the *Firefly* is completely out of fuel. With Roger out of the way, Dr. Agon puts the second part of his plan into operation and captures the *Paradox* with his Mammoth Machine...

Notes

Thunderbird 1 is again visible in the background at Twaddle & Twaddle Rocket Engines Inc. The *Firefly* previously appeared in *The Lost Starfighter*, but it makes its final appearance here as it is destroyed in the final battle with the Dark Station. This was the last episode to be screened in LAVENDER CASTLE's first broadcast season. The remaining nine episodes were held back for eight months to form a second season early in 2000.

Regular Voice Cast

Captain Thrice	**David Holt**
Walking Stick	**Kate Harbour**
Roger	**Rob Rackstraw**
Isambard	**Rob Rackstraw**
Lyca	**Kate Harbour**
Sir Squeakalot	**Jimmy Hibbert**
Sproggle	**David Holt**
Dr. Agon	**Jimmy Hibbert**
Trump	**Jimmy Hibbert**
Twaddle Duff	**Jimmy Hibbert**
Twaddle Dim	**Rob Rackstraw**

First UK Transmission

Thursday, April 29th, 1999
3.50pm (ITV Network)

DUELLING BANJOS

Prod. No. 18

Story & Script by **Chris Trengove** Directed by **Chris Taylor**

Due to an oversight on Sproggle's part, the *Paradox* runs out of fuel and crash-lands in the Great Swamp on planet Quagmire, close to the Dank's shack. Lyca hurts her wings in the crash and is unable to fly across the swamp to get help, so Captain Thrice calls across to the Dank for his assistance. The Dank refuses as he believes that the Paradox crew are just after his dank juice, so Captain Thrice challenges him to a banjo-playing contest: if the Dank wins, the Paradox will be his, but if he loses, he must help them to get the ship flying again. The Dank accepts the challenge, but then Captain Thrice admits to his crewmates that he hasn't played the banjo in years and is a bit out of practice!

Notes

This was the most complicated episode of LAVENDER CASTLE to animate as it required the hand and finger movements of Captain Thrice and the Dank to synchronise with the frenzied string-plucking of the pre-recorded banjo music. The banjo playing was performed specially for the episode by Paul Bishop, whose performance was recorded on video in order to give the animators a visual reference for the puppet characters. The Dank previously appeared in *Swamp Fever* and is seen again in *Birds Of A Feather*.

Regular Voice Cast

Captain Thrice	**David Holt**
Roger	**Rob Rackstraw**
Isambard	**Rob Rackstraw**
Lyca	**Kate Harbour**
Sproggle	**David Holt**

Guest Voice Cast

The Dank	**Jimmy Hibbert**

First UK Transmission

Thursday, January 6th, 2000
3.50pm (ITV Network)

THE LEGEND — Prod. No. 19

Story & Script by **Gerry Anderson** Directed by **Chris Taylor**

Captain Thrice takes the *Paradox* to the planet Bharron where the twin suns eclipse only once every thousand years. Legend has it that during the eclipse, Lavender Castle can be seen in the desert and as this is the millennium year, Thrice and Walking Stick set out on an expedition to find it while Roger takes the *Paradox* back into space. Three days later, Thrice is walking along a ledge when he loses his balance and falls ten feet down a cliff. He is knocked unconscious but the fall activates his emergency radio beacon. Unfortunately, the signal is picked up by Dr. Agon aboard the Dark Station and he decides to investigate...

Notes

The episode title appears as the engraved title on the cover of Captain Thrice's book, rather than as a caption superimposed on the screen.

Oops!

Thrice has a map of the location where Lavender Castle can be seen, but instead of landing the *Paradox* there, he lands the ship miles away and spends days walking to it.

Regular Voice Cast

Captain Thrice	**David Holt**
Walking Stick	**Kate Harbour**
Roger	**Rob Rackstraw**
Isambard	**Rob Rackstraw**
Lyca	**Kate Harbour**
Sir Squeakalot	**Jimmy Hibbert**
Sproggle	**David Holt**
Dr. Agon	**Jimmy Hibbert**
Trump	**Jimmy Hibbert**

First UK Transmission

Thursday, January 13th, 2000
3.50pm (ITV Network)

CLOUD OF CHAOS — Prod. No. 20

Script by **Chris Trengove** Directed by **Chris Taylor**
Story by **Chris Taylor**

From his Mammoth Machine, Dr. Agon fires a missile at the *Paradox* which shuts down the cottage ship's systems and central computer, leaving the crew without external vision and sensors. Sproggle opens the door hatch and looks out to establish visual contact with the Mammoth Machine, but when Roger swerves to avoid Agon's ship, Sproggle falls out into a cloud of strange blue gas. Dr. Agon takes the Mammoth Machine into the cloud to capture Sproggle, but the gas switches Sproggle's personality into Dr. Agon's body – and vice versa!

Notes

Isambard searches for Sproggle using the jetpack that was introduced in *Collision Course*. At the end of the episode, as Isambard rescues Sproggle from the Dark Station, their personalities are switched by the cloud gas and the shooting script detailed that the final line, "Sproggle said that well, didn't he?", should be spoken by Sproggle from his own body to show that their personalities had finally been restored, but in the finished episode, the line is spoken by Isambard from Sproggle's body.

Regular Voice Cast

Captain Thrice	**David Holt**
Roger	**Rob Rackstraw**
Isambard	**Rob Rackstraw**
Lyca	**Kate Harbour**
Sir Squeakalot	**Jimmy Hibbert**
Sproggle	**David Holt**
Dr. Agon	**Jimmy Hibbert**
Trump	**Jimmy Hibbert**

First UK Transmission

Thursday, January 20th, 2000
3.50pm (ITV Network)

DIAMONDS AREN'T FOREVER — Prod. No. 21

Story & Script by **Gerry Anderson** Directed by **Chris Taylor**

Isambard is testing his latest invention when Sproggle suddenly spots Short Fred Ledd heading for the planet Icestar in his dinghy. Captain Thrice reveals that Ledd can only be after one thing on the planet: the Icestar Diamond, the largest diamond in the universe, which can absorb the energy of a sun and then unleash it with devastating results. Pursuing Short Fred Ledd to Icestar, the Paradox crew follow him to an ice cave but Sproggle loses his footing on the ice and slides into Ledd's clutches. When the others catch up with them, Ledd gives them just 30 minutes to locate the Icestar diamond for him or he will cut off Sproggle's bauble!

Notes

In the shooting script for this episode, Icestar was originally 'Icesester' but the name was changed as it proved too much of a tongue-twister for the voice artists. As with several of LAVENDER CASTLE's other episode titles, *Diamonds Aren't Forever* is an obvious film title parody, but this one is, perhaps, more poignant: *Diamonds Are Forever* (1971) was the James Bond film made by Albert R. Broccoli and Harry Saltzman after they rejected an adaptation of Ian Fleming's *Moonraker* written by Gerry Anderson and Tony Barwick.

Regular Voice Cast

Captain Thrice	**David Holt**
Walking Stick	**Kate Harbour**
Roger	**Rob Rackstraw**
Isambard	**Rob Rackstraw**
Lyca	**Kate Harbour**
Sproggle	**David Holt**
Short Fred Ledd	**Jimmy Hibbert**
Tin Lizzy	**David Holt**

First UK Transmission

Thursday, January 27th, 2000
3.50pm (ITV Network)

GALACTIC PARK — Prod. No. 22

Regular Voice Cast

Captain Thrice	**David Holt**
Roger	**Rob Rackstraw**
Isambard	**Rob Rackstraw**
Lyca	**Kate Harbour**
Sir Squeakalot	**Jimmy Hibbert**
Sproggle	**David Holt**
Dr. Agon	**Jimmy Hibbert**
Trump	**Jimmy Hibbert**
Twaddle Duff	**Jimmy Hibbert**

First UK Transmission

Thursday, February 3rd, 2000
3.50pm (ITV Network)

Script by **Gerry Anderson** Directed by **Chris Taylor**
Story by **Craig Hemmings**

Weeks have gone by without incident and the members of the *Paradox* crew are starting to get on each other's nerves. Lyca diagnoses that they are all suffering from space fatigue, so Sproggle suggests a visit to the Galactic Theme Park on planet Themea that he has seen in an advertisement. When they get there, it seems that there is only one ride, a ghost train manned by Twaddle Duff, but he explains that this is the biggest theme park in the universe and there are rides scattered all over the planet. The crew board the ghost train and set off, unaware that Duff is actually a disguised Dr. Agon who has an unpleasant surprise waiting for them at the end of the line...

Notes

The script originally had the *Paradox* crew singing 'Who's Afraid Of The Big Bad Wolf?' when the Dark Station appeared during the ghost train ride, but this was cut to avoid expensive performance rights payments to Frank Churchill, Ted Sears and Ann Ronell, who wrote the song for the Walt Disney animated short *Three Little Pigs* (1933). This was also the first script to name Dr. Agon's Falcon as Trump.

WEARIZY — Prod. No. 23

Regular Voice Cast

Captain Thrice	**David Holt**
Roger	**Rob Rackstraw**
Isambard	**Rob Rackstraw**
Lyca	**Kate Harbour**
Sir Squeakalot	**Jimmy Hibbert**
Sproggle	**David Holt**
Dr. Agon	**Jimmy Hibbert**
Twaddle Duff	**Jimmy Hibbert**
Twaddle Dim	**Rob Rackstraw**

First UK Transmission

Thursday, February 10th, 2000
3.50pm (ITV Network)

Story & Script by **Gerry Anderson** Directed by **Chris Taylor**

On the day before Sproggle's birthday, Captain Thrice takes him to the Twaddle Twins' junkyard on planet Thestal to find a present for him. Twaddle Dim suggests a pet dog, but Thrice rejects the idea as he refuses to allow any animals on board the *Paradox*, despite Sproggle's protests. That night, Twaddle Duff materialises on the *Paradox*, bringing with him a pet dog called Wearizy which he guarantees that Captain Thrice will never see, since the dog is invisible! Then Dr. Agon commissions the Twaddle Twins to teleport him to the *Paradox* so that he can gatecrash Sproggle's birthday party and take the entire crew prisoner...

Notes

The episode title (and the invisible dog's name) is pronounced 'where-is-he'. As before, Thunderbird 1 is visible in the background at Twaddle & Twaddle Rocket Engines Inc. Galactic currency appears to have changed since *Lost In Space*: here, Dr. Agon pays the Twaddle Twins 5,000 spaceos to transport him to the Paradox whereas in *Lost In Space*, he paid the twins 10,000 dollars to write off his previous debt and purchase the *Firefly*. This is Dim and Duff's final appearance in the series.

SUPERNOVA — Prod. No. 24

Regular Voice Cast

Captain Thrice	**David Holt**
Walking Stick	**Kate Harbour**
Roger	**Rob Rackstraw**
Isambard	**Rob Rackstraw**
Lyca	**Kate Harbour**
Sir Squeakalot	**Jimmy Hibbert**
Sproggle	**David Holt**
Dr. Agon	**Jimmy Hibbert**
Trump	**Jimmy Hibbert**

First UK Transmission

Thursday, February 17th, 2000
3.50pm (ITV Network)

Story & Script by **Gerry Anderson** Directed by **Chris Taylor**

From the Dark Station, Dr. Agon causes a chain reaction which destroys a nearby sun. The crew of the *Paradox* watch helplessly as they realise that only Dr. Agon can be responsible for destruction on this scale. Then, to everyone's amazement, Lavender Castle appears within the sun's planetary system. Dr. Agon sends Trump to hide in a tree in Lavender Castle and report when it is in the vicinity of another sun which he can destroy, thereby vapourising the Castle. Spotting Trump flying towards Lavender Castle, the *Paradox* crew intercept Dr. Agon's radio frequency and Lyca makes a desperate attempt to dissuade Trump from going through with Agon's evil plan...

Notes

The script for this episode was specifically designed to give the audience more information about Lavender Castle. The opening titles are modified slightly at the end to show the Mammoth Machine blowing up the Firefly (from *Lost In Space*) in place of the Dark Station destroying a sun (from *In The Beginning*). The removal of the exploding sun section was specified in the script so as to offer a contrast with the opening scene of the story, although it was only suggested that it be replaced with additional shots of Dr. Agon.

INTERFACE — Prod. No. 25

Script by **Gerry Anderson** Directed by **Chris Taylor**
Story by **Craig Hemmings**

The *Paradox* crew investigate a message that they have received reporting a massacre on the planet of Barrenette. Finding bodies of the planet's inhabitants littering the desert floor, Roger lands the *Paradox* and the crew set out to search for survivors, but the 'bodies' turn out to be just flat painted cut-outs, part of a devious trap set by Dr. Agon. From a plateau overlooking the desert, Agon launches a mortar which explodes amongst the *Paradox* crew, releasing a gas which knocks out everyone except Sir Squeakalot. The plucky robot drags his sleeping crewmates back inside the *Paradox*, but then Dr. Agon activates his giant robot spider and programmes it to destroy Squeakalot!

Notes

Dr. Agon's giant robot spider was previously seen in *The Galacternet*. This was the last of five episodes that actually premiered at a special preview screening for over 80 Fanderson club members at Center Parcs' Elveden Forest Holiday Village in Brandon, Suffolk on Saturday, November 21st, 1998. The other episodes screened were *Brightonia On Sea*, *Traitor*, *The Collector* and *Duelling Banjos*.

Regular Voice Cast

Captain Thrice	**David Holt**
Roger	**Rob Rackstraw**
Isambard	**Rob Rackstraw**
Lyca	**Kate Harbour**
Sir Squeakalot	**Jimmy Hibbert**
Sproggle	**David Holt**
Dr. Agon	**Jimmy Hibbert**
Trump	**Jimmy Hibbert**

First UK Transmission

Thursday, March 2nd, 2000
3.50pm (ITV Network)

BIRDS OF A FEATHER — Prod. No. 26

Script by **Gerry Anderson** Directed by **Chris Taylor**
Story by **Rodney Matthews**

Dr. Agon organises a conference on board the Dark Station, inviting Short Fred Ledd, the Dank from planet Quagmire and renegade android Colonel Clump to attend in order to discuss ways of capturing the *Paradox* crew. Each of Dr. Agon's guests recall previous encounters in which Captain Thrice and his colleagues have outwitted them: Colonel Clump's attempt to add Roger and Lyca to his collection of living beings, Short Fred Ledd's theft of the *Paradox* and the Dank's banjo-playing contest with Captain Thrice. Dr. Agon proposes an evil alliance between them all to defeat the *Paradox* crew!

Notes

In the tradition of many previous Gerry Anderson series, LAVENDER CASTLE ends with a 'flashback' episode featuring extracts from previous stories, in this case the episodes *The Collector*, *Brightonia On Sea* and *Duelling Banjos*. The shooting script featured an additional opening scene in which Dr. Agon almost strangles Trump while conceiving his alliance plans. The Dank's shack and Doodlebug's supermarket (now occupied by Colonel Clump) are both revealed to be spaceships.

Regular Voice Cast

Captain Thrice	**David Holt**
Roger	**Rob Rackstraw**
Isambard	**Rob Rackstraw**
Sir Squeakalot	**Jimmy Hibbert**
Dr. Agon	**Jimmy Hibbert**
Short Fred Ledd	**Jimmy Hibbert**
Tin Lizzy	**David Holt**

Guest Voice Cast

The Dank	**Jimmy Hibbert**
Colonel Clump	**David Holt**

First UK Transmission

Thursday, March 9th, 2000
3.50pm (ITV Network)

Episode Titles

(Listed in production order)

1. **In The Beginning / Flower Power**
2. **The Twilight Tower / High Moon**
3. **The Lost Starfighter / The Black Swat**
4. **Double Cross / A Stitch In Time**
5. **Bird Of Prey / Collision Course**
6. **Swamp Fever / Raiders Of The Planet Zark**
7. **The Galacternet / Brightonia On Sea**
8. **Traitor / The Collector**
9. **Lost In Space / Duelling Banjos**
10. **The Legend / Cloud Of Chaos**
11. **Diamonds Aren't Forever / Galactic Park**
12. **Wearizy / Supernova**
13. **Interface / Birds Of A Feather**

Episode Running Time

22 minutes approx.

ALTERNATIVE FORMAT EPISODES

The 26 episodes of LAVENDER CASTLE were also compiled into 13 double-bill episodes linked by 2½ minutes of new material to fill a half-hour timeslot on commercial television. In each linking sequence, one or more of the regular characters talk about aspects of the series which are illustrated by brief extracts from the episodes. To date, LAVENDER CASTLE has not been broadcast anywhere in the world in this alternate format, so these linking sequences (detailed below) remain unseen.

IN THE BEGINNING / FLOWER POWER

Dr. Agon and Trump reveal the secrets of the Dark Station and the Mammoth Machine illustrated by clips from *A Stitch In Time*, *Double Cross*, *Supernova*, *Traitor*, *The Lost Starfighter*, *Wearizy*, *Lost In Space* and *High Moon*.

THE TWILIGHT TOWER / HIGH MOON

Isambard introduces Sproggle and talks about himself illustrated by clips from *Swamp Fever*, *The Galacternet*, *A Stitch In Time*, *Collision Course*, *Brightonia On Sea* and *Double Cross*. The Guardian also appears, threatening to return.

THE LOST STARFIGHTER / THE BLACK SWAT

Sproggle and Roger reveal the secrets of the *Paradox*, illustrated by clips from *Collision Course*, *Flower Power*, *A Stitch In Time*, *Duelling Banjos* and *High Moon*.

DOUBLE CROSS / A STITCH IN TIME

Twaddle Dim and Twaddle Duff explain how their business operates, illustrated by clips from *Collision Course*, *Lost In Space* and *Bird Of Prey*.

BIRD OF PREY / COLLISION COURSE

Sir Squeakalot talks about his relationship with his crewmates, illustrated by clips from *A Stitch In Time*, *Bird Of Prey*, *Galactic Park*, *Brightonia On Sea*, *Collision Course*, *Duelling Banjos*, *The Twilight Tower*, *The Collector* and *Swamp Fever*.

SWAMP FEVER / RAIDERS OF THE PLANET ZARK

Captain Thrice and Walking Stick discuss the *Paradox* crew, illustrated by clips from *The Legend*, *Diamonds Aren't Forever*, *The Galacternet*, *Raiders Of The Planet Zark*, *In The Beginning*, *Bird Of Prey*, *Swamp Fever*, *Collision Course* and *The Twilight Tower*.

THE GALACTERNET / BRIGHTONIA ON SEA

Dr. Agon and Trump discuss their relationship illustrated by clips from *The Legend*, *A Stitch In Time*, *Supernova*, *Galactic Park* and *In The Beginning*.

TRAITOR / THE COLLECTOR

Sproggle is frightened by Short Fred Ledd who reveals the secrets of the *Cutting Snark* and his vendetta with the *Paradox* crew, illustrated by clips from *The Black Swat*, *In The Beginning* and *Brightonia On Sea*. Then Dr. Agon arrives.

LOST IN SPACE / DUELLING BANJOS

Roger and Lyca talk about life on the *Paradox*, illustrated by clips from *Swamp Fever*, *In The Beginning*, *Flower Power*, *High Moon* and *Supernova*, before they are joined by Captain Thrice and Walking Stick.

THE LEGEND / CLOUD OF CHAOS

Captain Thrice and Walking Stick discuss their many adversaries, illustrated by clips from *High Moon*, *The Black Swat*, *Raiders Of The Planet Zark*, *Swamp Fever*, *The Collector*, *The Galacternet*, *Flower Power*, *Supernova* and *Double Cross*.

DIAMONDS AREN'T FOREVER / GALACTIC PARK

Repeat of the linking sequence from *Traitor/The Collector*.

WEARIZY / SUPERNOVA

Repeat of the linking sequence from *Lost In Space/Duelling Banjos*.

INTERFACE / BIRDS OF A FEATHER

Repeat of the linking sequence from *Bird Of Prey/Collision Course*.

THE FEATURE FILMS

1960-1968

CROSSROADS TO CRIME
THUNDERBIRDS ARE GO
THUNDERBIRD 6
DOPPELGÄNGER

CROSSROADS TO CRIME

Screenplay by **Alun Falconer** Directed by **Gerry Anderson**

Policeman Don Ross sees transport café owner Connie Williams being bundled into a Ford Zephyr by garage owner Diamond and his colleague Johnny, but when he tries to stop them by hanging on to the door as they drive away, Diamond fights him off and he falls into the road. Diamond tries to pass the incident off as an accident, but Ross realises that he has stumbled upon something going on at the café, possibly related to a recent series of lorry hi-jackings on the A1. His superior, Sergeant Pearson, refuses to take his suspicions seriously so the next morning, Ross goes to the café to investigate. There he is offered a bribe by Diamond to distract his attention while Diamond's gang steal £10,000 worth of cigarettes from a van at the back of the café. In order to give the appearance of being corrupt, Ross accepts the bribe and Diamond invites him to take part in their next operation, the theft of a consignment of nickel alloy ingots worth £20,000!

Production

As filming was coming to an end on FOUR FEATHER FALLS, Gerry Anderson was invited to make a low-budget live-action B-movie by Stuart Levy and Nat Cohen of Anglo Amalgamated, one of Britain's leading film distributors. The film would act as a support feature to one of Anglo's major releases, such as Joseph Losey's crime thriller *The Criminal* (1960), so the budget was meagre – just £16,250 – but Anderson jumped at the opportunity, believing that this could be his ticket to major motion picture production.

Deciding to direct the film himself, Anderson commissioned a script from Alun Falconer, the writer of crime dramas such as *Never Let Go* (1960) and *The Unstoppable Man* (1960), and cast Welsh actor Anthony Oliver in the lead role, having been impressed with his performance on stage in Agatha Christie's *The Mousetrap*. Anderson also cast David Graham in the role of undercover policeman Johnny, remembering him from *Film Studio Story*, an episode of the MARTIN KANE, PRIVATE INVESTIGATOR television series that Anderson had directed in 1957. The film was shot on location in Slough, Buckinghamshire and Maidenhead, Berkshire in May and June 1960, with one day's interior filming on a soundstage at Halliford Studios in Shepperton, Surrey.

Notes

Most of the film's location photography was shot in the vicinity of the AP Films Studios in Slough, making much use of the main Bath Road (A4). Barton's Café on Dover Road, just off the A4 and opposite the studio building in Ipswich Road, doubled for Connie's café while the studios themselves were used for the gang's warehouse. Connie's menu offers bacon, egg and chips for two shillings and ninepence (about 14p) with a cup of tea for threepence (about 1½p). At one point, a pair of youths are listening to the juke-box and one suggests the theme from FOUR FEATHER FALLS as the next record, but Connie tells him to give it a rest before he can put it on. George Murcell (Diamond) and David Graham (Johnny) both went on to provide voices for characters in SUPERCAR.

Cast

PC Don Ross	**Anthony Oliver**
Miles	**Ferdy Mayne**
Diamond	**George Murcell**
Connie Williams	**Miriam Karlin**
Joan Ross	**Patricia Heneghan**
Sergeant Pearson	**Arthur Rigby**
Johnny	**David Graham**
Paddy	**Harry Towb**
Harry	**Terence Brook**
Phillips	**J. Mark Roberts**
Basher	**Donald Tandy**
Lorry Driver	**Bill Sawyer**
Butler	**Geoffrey Denton**
Youths	**David Sale**
	Terry Sale
Escort	**Peter Diamond**

UK Premiere

November 1960

Running Time

54 minutes approx.

Aspect Ratio

4:3

PRODUCTION CREDITS

Producer	**Gerry Anderson***
Director of Photography	**John Read**
Art Director	**Reg Hill**
Music Composed, Arranged and Conducted by	**Barry Gray**
Editor	**David Elliott**
Assistant Director	**Frank Hollands**
Production Manager	**Arthur Mann**
Camera Operator	**Alan Gatward**
Sound Recordists	**Malcolm Stewart**
	Maurice Askew
Continuity	**Sylvia Thamm**
Dubbing Editor	**John Kelly**
Make-up	**John Alexander**
Hairdressing	**Monty Montsash**
Wardrobe	**John Irwin**
Transport Vehicles and Facilities	**Thamesbrook Ltd.**

Produced by A.P. Films Ltd
Slough, Bucks
Westrex Recording System
Distributed by
Anglo Amalgamated
Film Distributors Limited

* uncredited

Barry Gray's frantic score for *Crossroads To Crime* (1960) was recorded in its entirety on Tuesday, June 21st, 1960. The main theme, heard during the film's opening title sequence, was later prominently used as incidental music for the SUPERCAR episode *The White Line* and the FIREBALL XL5 episode *The Robot Freighter Mystery*. The music can also be heard in the CAPTAIN SCARLET AND THE MYSTERONS episode *Manhunt*, playing on a garage radio as Captain Black murders a mechanic.

THUNDERBIRDS ARE GO

Screenplay by **Gerry** and **Sylvia Anderson** Directed by **David Lane**

The massive *Zero X* space vehicle, commanded by Captain Paul Travers, lifts off from Glenn Field on the first manned space expedition to Mars, but The Hood is secretly on board, photographing the control mechanisms. The ship's elevator controls are jammed when The Hood's foot becomes trapped, but he manages to free himself and bail out as *Zero X* plummets out of control. The crew eject to safety in an escape pod and *Zero X* crashes into the sea. Two years later, the committee of the Space Exploration Center elect to invite International Rescue to organise the security arrangements at the launch of a second mission. Lady Penelope goes undercover as a reporter at Glenn Field and she and Scott successfully unmask The Hood as he attempts to stow away aboard the new *Zero X*. The launch is successful and after a six-week flight, the crew of *Zero X* make a landing on Mars. But as they explore the planet surface in their Martian Exploration Vehicle, they come under fire from Martian Rock Snakes and barely escape with their lives. Then, on their return to Earth, *Zero X*'s locking gear is damaged when one of the vehicle's lifting bodies goes out of control and the crew are trapped on board as *Zero X* heads for a crash-landing on the American town of Craigsville...

Production

The phenomenal success of the initial 26 episodes of THUNDERBIRDS on British television prompted Gerry Anderson to ask ITC chairman Lew Grade if he would be prepared to finance the making of a THUNDERBIRDS feature film which could be shot back-to-back with additional television episodes. Grade immediately agreed and the budget for the film was set at £250,000. As the existing models and puppets would not stand up to scrutiny on the big screen, much of the film's pre-production work involved constructing new, larger, more detailed models of the Thunderbird craft and Tracy Island settings, and making new, smarter puppets of many of the main characters. The most unusual new puppets were replicas of pop stars Cliff Richard and The Shadows (Hank Marvin, Brian Bennett, Bruce Welch and John Rostill), who appeared in cameo roles during a dream sequence performing a new song, 'Shooting Star', that their real-life counterparts specially composed and recorded.

Filmed alongside the last six episodes of the television series for five months from March 3rd, 1966, *Thunderbirds Are Go* (1966) was the first feature film to be shot using the Livingston Electronic Viewfinder Unit, also known as Add-a-Vision. This was an electronic viewfinder which could be used in conjunction with a Mitchell BNC Camera to take a television picture directly from the camera, enabling the entire unit to watch any scene being filmed on the television monitors. The monitored pictures could also be recorded on tape and played back to the director to check that a take was satisfactory.

The film's premiere at the London Pavilion cinema in Piccadilly on December 12th, 1966 was a massive success and executives at United Artists, the film's distributors, told Anderson that they anticipated that the THUNDERBIRDS film series would soon rival James Bond. Unfortunately, the film was a box-office disaster, and United Artists were so surprised and confused by its failure that they put it down to a fluke and immediately commissioned a second film, *Thunderbird 6* (1968).

Notes

Gerry Anderson's first choice of director, Alan Pattillo, declined the job as he felt that he had had enough of puppets, having working on all of the AP Films television series since FOUR FEATHER FALLS. He was replaced by David Lane who was, at the time, the youngest feature film director working in the UK. Voice artist Paul Maxwell (Captain Travers) was previously heard as the voice of Colonel Steve Zodiac in FIREBALL XL5. Actor Alfred Marks was originally selected to provide the voice of Travers's colleague Greg Newman but he rejected Anderson's pay offer and was replaced by Bob Monkhouse. The puppet of Captain Travers was specifically modelled after actor Sean Connery by sculptor Terry Curtis. Several familiar puppets from the THUNDERBIRDS television episodes made background guest appearances in the film: the members of the Space Exploration Center committee include London airport chief Commander Norman (from *Trapped In The Sky*

Voice Cast

Jeff Tracy	**Peter Dyneley**
Scott Tracy	**Shane Rimmer**
Lady Penelope	**Sylvia Anderson**
Virgil Tracy	**Jeremy Wilkin**
Alan Tracy	**Matt Zimmerman**
Brains	**David Graham**
Aloysius Parker	**David Graham**
Tin-Tin Kyrano	**Christine Finn**
Gordon Tracy	**David Graham**
John Tracy	**Ray Barrett**
The Hood	**Ray Barrett**
Captain Paul Travers	**Paul Maxwell**
Space Captain Greg Martin	**Alexander Davion**
Space Navigator Brad Newman	**Bob Monkhouse**
Dr. Ray Pierce	**Neil McCallum**
Dr. Tony Grant	**Charles Tingwell**
Commander Casey	**Ray Barrett**
Space Colonel Harris	**Jeremy Wilkin**
Public Relations Officer	**Charles Tingwell**
Messenger	**Matt Zimmerman**
Angry Young Man	**Charles Tingwell**
Swinging Star Compére	**Bob Monkhouse**
Cliff Richard Jr.	**Cliff Richard**
Goldstone Tracking Station	**Sylvia Anderson**
Woomera Tracking Station	**Charles Tingwell**
Washington Control	**Jeremy Wilkin**

UK Premiere

Monday, December 12th, 1966
8.30pm (London Pavilion, Piccadilly, London)

Running Time

89 minutes approx.

Aspect Ratio

2.35:1

amongst others), Commissioner Garfield (from *30 Minutes After Noon*) and reporter Eddie Kerr (from *Danger At Ocean Deep*); Kerr also appears at the *Zero X* press conference while the press officer is the Commander of Matthews Field (from *The Cham-Cham*); and among the other patrons at the real Swinging Star nightclub at the end of the film are the Duchess of Royston (from *The Duchess Assignment*) and fashion designer François Lemaire (from *Alias Mr. Hackenbacker*). Jeff states that 11.00am on Tracy Island is 4.00pm in England which places Tracy Island somewhere just off the coast of Chile or Peru, according to the demarcation of the world's time zones. *Zero X* sets off back to Earth on Friday, July 22nd and returns on Friday, September 2nd, so the year must be 2067 (the only year between 2061 and 2072 in which those dates fall on Fridays), as intended by the producers. Unfortunately, Jeff's Universal Edition of the *News Of The World* newspaper seen earlier in the film is dated June 2066. The back projection footage of the ground beneath *Zero X* that is seen behind Alan while he is attempting to re-wire the escape pod controls was shot on location in Portugal.

PRODUCTION CREDITS

Executive Producer **Gerry Anderson***
Produced by **Sylvia Anderson**
Visual Effects Director **Derek Meddings**
Music Composed, Arranged and Directed by **Barry Gray**
Supervising Art Director **Bob Bell**
Associate Producer **John Read**
Assistant to the Executive Producer **Norman Foster**
Editor **Len Walter**
Assisted by **George Randall**
Characters Photographed by
Lighting Cameraman **Paddy Seale**
Camera Operator **Alan Perry**
Characters Operated by **Christine Glanville**, **Mary Turner**
Assisted by **Wanda Webb**, **Judith Shutt**
Characters Dressed by **Elizabeth Coleman**
Assisted by **Zena Relph**
Wigs by **Wig Creations of London**
VISUAL EFFECTS – MAIN UNIT
Director **Shaun Whittacker-Cook**
Lighting Cameraman **Harry Oakes**
Camera Operator **Ted Cutlack**, **Richard Conway**
VISUAL EFFECTS – 2ND UNIT
Director **Peter Wragg**
Lighting Cameraman **Ted Fowler**
Camera Operator **Ron Gallifant**, **Ron Ashton**
Model Building Supervised by **Ray Brown**
Properties Made by **Tony Dunsterville**, **Plugg Shutt**
Property Master **Arthur Cripps**
Production Co-ordinator **Brian Burgess**
Assistant Directors **Ken Turner**, **Harry Ledger**
Lip Sync Operator **Ian Spurrier**
Art Director **Grenville Nott**
Designers **Keith Wilson, John Lageu**
Titles by **Studio Film Laboratories Ltd.**
Characters Sculpted by **John F. Brown**
Assisted by **Terry Curtis, Tim Cooksey**, **Peter Hayward*, Mike Richardson***
Sound Editors **John Peverill**, **Brian T. Hickin**
Sound Mixed by **Maurice Askew** at G.H.W. on Westrex Sound System
Dialogue Recorded by **Ken Scrivener**
'Thunderbirds Are Go' Played by **The Band of H.M. Royal Marines**
Conducted by **Lt. Col. F. Vivian Dunn**
Character Voices in Alphabetical Order
Sylvia Anderson, Ray Barrett
Alexander Davion, Peter Dyneley
Christine Finn, David Graham
Paul Maxwell, Neil McCallum
Bob Monkhouse, Shane Rimmer
Charles Tingwell, Jeremy Wilkin
Matt Zimmerman
'Shooting Star' Sung by **Cliff Richard**
Written and Accompanied by **The Shadows**
Instrumental 'Lady Penelope' Written and Played by **The Shadows**
Special Effects Designer **Mike Trim***
Models **Peter Aston*, Eric Backman***, **Alan Shubrook*, Brian Smithies***
The Producers Gratefully Acknowledge the Co-operation of:
Space Colonel Harris of the Martian Exploration Center, Cape Johnson
Jim Glenn, President of the New World Aircraft Corporation, Designers and Manufacturers of the Zero X
Commander Casey, Commander in Chief, Glenn Field
without whose help this motion picture would not have been possible
Martian Sequences Filmed by **Century 21 Space Location Unit**
None of the characters appearing in this photoplay intentionally resemble any persons living or dead....
SINCE THEY DO NOT YET EXIST!
Released through United Artists
A Gerry Anderson Century 21 Cinema Production
Filmed in Supermarionation
Technicolor® and Techniscope®

* uncredited

The first edit of *Thunderbirds Are Go* (1966) overran the maximum running time permitted for the film by the distributors by well over 15 minutes, forcing Gerry Anderson, David Lane and editor Len Walter to cut certain scenes that were not vital to the film's narrative.

The most significant portion of the film to be deleted involved the efforts of the Space Exploration Center to persuade Jeff Tracy to offer International Rescue's services at the launch of the new *Zero X*. The committee members decide to issue a public plea to the organisation through the world's newspapers and under pressure from the media, Jeff agrees to take part in a satellite-relayed television interview with the Trans American TV Network, appearing only in silhouette and broadcasting his responses from Tracy Island to explain why the organisation cannot be involved. While the interview proceeds, The Hood makes telepathic contact with Kyrano from his jungle temple, urging him to report International Rescue's movements should they decide to take part in the *Zero X* launch. As this was Kyrano's only scene in the film, its deletion means that he does not appear at all. Jeff's interview comes to a conclusion with the TV interviewer playing his trump card: a personal request from the World President for Jeff to place International Rescue at the disposal of the SEC for the *Zero X* launch.

After Lady Penelope agrees to fly to the USA to assist with the security operation at Glenn Field, a second deleted sequence featured Penelope and Parker flying to New York aboard Fireflash, travelling in the first class passenger lounge in the aircraft's port wing. Parker is uncomfortable in the luxurious surroundings but resolves to put up with it rather than transferring to the tourist class compartment. Penelope calls Jeff to advise him of her ETA at Glenn Field.

A final deleted sequence featured *Zero X*'s arrival in Mars orbit and the crew's preparations to separate the MEV from the ship's main body. Travers then flies the MEV over the Martian landscape before selecting a landing site and taking the MEV down to the surface.

THUNDERBIRD 6

Screenplay by **Gerry** and **Sylvia Anderson** Directed by **David Lane**

Using the pseudonym Mr. X, Brains has designed a revolutionary new automated airship, *Skyship One*, for the New World Aircraft Corporation. Penelope, Alan and Tin-Tin will be aboard the craft on its maiden voyage, but Brains will be tied up designing a new Thunderbird craft for International Rescue, Thunderbird 6. Alan and Tin-Tin travel by Tiger Moth biplane to rendezvous with Lady Penelope and Parker in England and the quartet board the airship, unaware that the entire crew has been gunned down and replaced by impostors. As *Skyship One* is completely automated, the only way that the impostors will be discovered is if anything breaks down. The International Rescue team meet their charming host Captain Foster, but in the gravity compensator room, his men are in contact with The Hood, who is using the codename Black Phantom. They have bugged every part of the ship that will be visited by Penelope in order to record her voice and then rearrange her words to create a false message which will lure Thunderbirds 1 and 2 into a trap at the disused El Hadim airfield. *Skyship One*'s voyage takes it to various exotic locations around the world, enabling Captain Foster to steer conversation and prompt Lady Penelope to say the words that will make up the bogus message...

Production

Perplexed by the commercial failure of *Thunderbirds Are Go* (1966) yet convinced of the concept's feature potential, United Artists commissioned a second THUNDERBIRDS film early in 1967. With a budget set at £300,000, production was scheduled alongside CAPTAIN SCARLET AND THE MYSTERONS, which was already being shot at the Century 21 Studios in Slough. Twelve episodes of CAPTAIN SCARLET were in the can before pre-production work was completed on *Thunderbird 6*, at which point one of the television series' camera and puppet crews was reassigned to principal photography on the movie. Filming commenced on *Thunderbird 6* on Monday, May 1st, 1967 and continued back-to-back with CAPTAIN SCARLET over the next four months.

The recent technical advances in the puppet workshops had now made it possible to reduce the sizes of the puppets' heads to correct human proportions, but the producers were initially uncertain whether the puppets in the new film should retain the proportions of the original television characters or be substituted by the perfectly proportioned style of puppets being used in CAPTAIN SCARLET. In the end, a compromise of the two styles spawned puppets with heads and hands that were still disproportionate to the bodies, but less so than had been seen in the previous THUNDERBIRDS adventures.

Location filming for the film's extensive flying sequences was based at Booker Airfield near High Wycombe in Buckinghamshire, providing convenient access to open countryside and sections of the M40 motorway, then still under construction. However, the location unit ended up in court when a shot involving stunt flying by ace pilot Joan Hughes contravened instructions issued to the unit by the Ministry of Civil Aviation. The scene called for a Tiger Moth biplane to fly under a motorway bridge at Lane End between junctions 4 and 5 of the M40, but a Department of Transport official insisted that the Ministry's regulations only allowed the biplane to pass under the bridge if the wheels were in contact with the road, a stipulation that made the stunt significantly more difficult for Hughes to accomplish. After several successful passes under the bridge as instructed, Hughes was approaching the bridge for a final take when a sudden crosswind prevented her from landing the plane and she was forced to fly under the bridge without touching down, or risk losing control of the Tiger Moth. The Department of Transport prosecuted Hughes and production manager Norman Foster (for aiding and abetting) but both were eventually acquitted. As the crew was refused permission to film any more scenes on the M40, the visual effects unit built a section of the motorway in miniature to complete the necessary shots using radio-controlled Tiger Moth models.

Thunderbird 6 was completed by January 1968 (the date of its British Film Catalogue classification) but was inexplicably shelved for six months, eventually receiving its premiere on the afternoon of July 29th, 1968 at the Odeon Cinema in Leicester Square. Like its predecessor, box-office returns on *Thunderbird 6* were disappointing and spelt the end for dreams of a long-running film franchise.

Voice Cast

Jeff Tracy	**Peter Dyneley**
Scott Tracy	**Shane Rimmer**
Lady Penelope	**Sylvia Anderson**
Virgil Tracy	**Jeremy Wilkin**
Alan Tracy	**Matt Zimmerman**
Brains	**David Graham**
Aloysius Parker	**David Graham**
Tin-Tin Kyrano	**Christine Finn**
Gordon Tracy	**David Graham**
John Tracy	**Keith Alexander**
The Hood	**Gary Files**
Captain Foster (White Ghost)	**John Carson**
NWA President Jim Glenn	**Geoffrey Keen**
Carter (White Ghost)	**Keith Alexander**
Martin (White Ghost)	**Jeremy Wilkin**
Lane (White Ghost)	**Gary Files**
Hogarth (White Ghost)	**Matt Zimmerman**
Captain Foster (NWA)	**Gary Files**
Martin (NWA)	**Matt Zimmerman**
Lane (NWA)	**Jeremy Wilkin**
Carter (NWA)	**Shane Rimmer**
Hogarth (NWA)	**Gary Files**
Indian Fortune Teller	**Christine Finn**
Indian Stallkeeper	**David Graham**
Missile Base Tannoy	**Keith Alexander**
Narrator	**Keith Alexander**

UK Premiere

Monday, July 29th, 1968
2.30pm (Odeon Cinema,
Leicester Square, London)

Running Time

85 minutes approx.

Aspect Ratio

2.35:1

Notes

Several puppet characters from the previous THUNDERBIRDS productions make cameo appearances here: Commander Casey, the Glenn Field controller in *Thunderbirds Are Go* (1966) is Jim Glenn, President of the New World Aircraft Corporation; Colonel Harris, chairman of the Space Exploration Center meeting in *Thunderbirds Are Go* (1966), is one of the designers at the New World Aircraft meeting at the start of the film; *Zero X* Captain Paul Travers from *Thunderbirds Are Go* (1966) is the bogus Captain Foster's henchman Carter; and the diners at the Whistle Stop Inn include Dr. Pringle from *Give Or Take A Million*, Eddie Kerr from *Danger At Ocean Deep* and Cliff Richard Jr. from *Thunderbirds Are Go* (1966) wearing glasses and a moustache. The Tracy Lounge has been redecorated (in green) since its last appearance in *Give Or Take A Million*. Penelope's newspaper is dated June 11th, 2068. Two of the news items on the front page are clipped from covers of *TV Century 21* comic: "Zero X Finds Life On Saturn?" from issue 126 and "Mystery Space Station Sighted" from issue 137 (a report of a sighting of Spectrum Cloudbase from CAPTAIN SCARLET AND THE MYSTERONS). During the evacuation of the missile base, Sam Loover's car (from JOE 90) is seen driving through one shot. It can be inferred that FAB 1 is destroyed when *Skyship One* crashes onto the missile base, as the car is still in the ship's hold. Grandma Tracy appears in a non-speaking role.

Oops!

Model-maker Peter Aston is erroneously credited as Peter 'Ashton' on the opening titles. As *Skyship One* arrives in Egypt, Tin Tin says that she has never seen the Pyramids before, although she saw them from Thunderbird 2 in *Desperate Intruder*.

PRODUCTION CREDITS

Executive Producer	**Gerry Anderson***
Producer	**Sylvia Anderson**
Visual Effects Director	**Derek Meddings**
Music Composed, Arranged and Directed by	**Barry Gray**
Art Director	**Bob Bell**
Production Manager	**Norman Foster**
Assistant Director	**Peter Anderson**
Lip Sync Operator	**Ian Spurrier**
Director of Photography	**Harry Oakes**
Camera Operator	**Peter Nash**
Focus Operator	**Ian Vinson**
Editor	**Len Walter**
Assisted by	**Len Cleal**
Puppet Co-ordinator	**Mary Turner**
Characters Operated by	**Wanda Webb**
Assisted by	**Linda Rutter, Sheena McGregor, Charmaine Wood**
Characters Dressed by	**Kim Martin**
Puppet Workshop	**Terry Curtis, Tim Cooksey, Plugg Shutt**
Model Makers	**Ray Brown, Peter Aston, Eric Backman, Alan Shubrook***
Visual Effects Assistant	**Ian Wingrove**
Model Workshop	**Brian Smithies**
Sets Designed by	**Keith Wilson, John Lageu**
Properties Made by	**Tony Dunsterville**
Property Master	**Peter Holmes**
LOCATION UNIT	
Cameraman	**Ted Fowler**
Operators	**Derek Black, Tommy Fletcher**
Tiger Moth Flown by	**Joan Hughes MBF**
Remote Control Flying	**Eric Faulkner**
Supervising Sound Editor	**John Peverill**
Sound Editors	**Peter Pennell, Brian Hickin**
Sound Recording by	**Anvil Films**
Character Voices	**Keith Alexander, Sylvia Anderson, John Carson, Peter Dyneley, Gary Files, Christine Finn, David Graham, Geoffrey Keen, Shane Rimmer, Jeremy Wilkin, Matt Zimmerman**
Special Effects Designer	**Mike Trim***

Made at Century 21 Studios, Slough, England
Released through United Artists
A Gerry Anderson
Century 21 Cinema Production
Filmed in Supermarionation
Technicolor® and Techniscope®

* uncredited

The full-size Tiger Moth biplane seen in live-action location footage in the film was G-ANFM, a genuine de Havilland DH82A Tiger Moth built in 1940 at the de Havilland factory in Hatfield, Hertfordshire. After service with the RAF at an ordnance unit in Northern Ireland and then at a training school in Cambridge, Tiger Moth Serial No. 83604 was sold to the Association of British Aero Clubs in October 1953. First registered as G-ANFM by the Norfolk and Norwich Aero Club, the Tiger Moth was purchased in 1965 by the Reading Flying Club, which made it available to Century 21 Productions for filming on *Thunderbird 6* in 1968.

A short film career followed with appearances in Stanley Donen's fantasy musical *The Little Prince* (1974), Henry Herbert's *Emily* (1977) and Michael Apted's *Agatha* (1978), but the biplane was involved in a flying accident in Abbeville, France in 1992 and had to have major repair work to make it airworthy again. With a yellow and silver livery (the *Thunderbird 6* red and yellow markings are long gone), Tiger Moth G-ANFM is still flying today as part of the de Havilland Tiger Moth Diamond Nine air display team based at White Waltham, near Maidenhead in Berkshire.

DOPPELGÄNGER

Screenplay by **Gerry & Sylvia Anderson** and **Donald James**
Based on the story by **Gerry & Sylvia Anderson** Directed by **Robert Parrish**

In 2069, an unmanned Sun Probe has discovered a new planet in the solar system, occupying the same orbit as Earth but on the opposite side of the sun. European Space Exploration Council (EUROSEC) chairman Jason Webb proposes a manned flight to the new planet in conjunction with NASA, but the American space agency only agrees to contribute the lion's share of the budget when it becomes clear that the Sun Probe information has been leaked to the East. The launch date is advanced and project director John Kane is joined aboard the *Phoenix* capsule by American astronaut Glenn Ross for a three-week flight to the far side of the sun. Arriving at the new planet, an orbital survey proves inconclusive, so Kane and Ross decide to make a manned landing using the *Phoenix*'s *Dove* shuttlecraft, but as they approach the surface, the shuttle is hit by an electrical storm and crashes. The astronauts are rescued and returned to the EUROSEC complex in Portugal, but Kane has been critically injured and Ross is puzzled to find himself back on Earth, facing questions about why they aborted the mission and returned home after only three weeks. Slowly, it dawns on Ross that he has not returned to his own planet at all, but arrived on a duplicate Earth that is a mirror image of his own...

Voice Cast

Dr. John Kane	**Ian Hendry**
Colonel Glenn Ross	**Roy Thinnes**
Jason Webb	**Patrick Wymark**
Sharon Ross	**Lynn Loring**
Lise Hartman	**Loni Von Friedl**
Paulo Landi	**Franco Derosa**
Mark Neuman	**George Sewell**
David Poulson	**Edward Bishop**
Dr. Pontini	**Philip Madoc**
Dr. Beauville	**Vladek Sheybal**
Monsieur Clavel	**George Mikell**
Dr. Kurt Hassler	**Herbert Lom**
Flight Director	**Keith Alexander**
Pam Kirby	**Norma Ronald**
Dr. Gordon	**Cy Grant**
Control Technician	**Jeremy Wilkin**
Monitoring Station Technician	**Basil Moss**
Ulan-Bator Air/Sea Rescue	**Anthony Chinn**
Control Technician (Medical 2)	**Nicholas Courtney**
Male Nurse	**Jon Kelley**
Nurse	**Annette Kerr**

UK Premiere

Wednesday, October 8th, 1969
(Odeon Cinema, Leicester Square, London)

Running Time

101 minutes approx.

Aspect Ratio

1.85:1

Production

Early in 1968, during production of JOE 90, Gerry Anderson read in a newspaper that Jay Kanter, an executive for Universal Pictures, would be visiting London to set up a European production arm for the American studio. Anderson arranged a meeting and Kanter agreed to finance the production of a live-action science-fiction film from a script entitled *Doppelgänger* that Anderson had co-written with his wife Sylvia. As Kanter was not entirely happy with their first draft, Anderson commissioned Donald James to rewrite it, beefing up the characterisation that was felt to be weak in the Andersons' version. Anderson wanted to assign David Lane to direct the film, but Kanter insisted on a 'bankable' director so the job was offered to Robert Parrish, the American director of *The San Francisco Story* (1952) and certain scenes in *Casino Royale* (1967), when he suddenly became available due the collapse of another project.

Based at Pinewood Studios in Buckinghamshire, 15 weeks of filming began on Monday, July 1st, 1968 but the production was dogged by unexpected difficulties. American actress Gayle Hunnicutt was announced as the female lead, Colonel Ross's wife Sharon, but shortly before shooting began she was taken ill. A last-minute replacement was found in Lynn Loring, former star of the American THE F.B.I. television series and real-life wife of THE INVADERS star Roy Thinnes, who had already been cast as Ross. Once filming was under way, scenes between Patrick Wymark (as Jason Webb) and Peter Dyneley (as NASA liaison David Poulson, previously heard as the voice of Jeff Tracy in THUNDERBIRDS) had to be completely re-shot with Ed Bishop in the Poulson role when rushes illustrated that there was an uncomfortable physical similarity between Wymark and Dyneley that might confuse audiences. Then in September 1968, Parrish took his cast and crew to Albufeira in Portugal for a month's location filming just as Prime Minister Antonio Salazar fell ill and was deposed by Marcello Caetano. Fearing the possible consequences of the coup, Parrish cut short the shooting schedule and quickly completed the necessary scenes within two weeks.

An additional complication for the crew was the filming of scenes set in the EUROSEC complex on the 'mirror' planet: all of these sequences were shot the correct way round and the negative was then reversed to create a mirror-image print for the final edit (a process called 'flop-over'). While this eliminated the need for the expensive creation of mirror-image sets, props and costumes, all picture composition and movement had to be planned for being seen in mirror image. More than 200 visual effects shots were supervised by Derek Meddings back at the Century 21 Studios in Slough. There, a six-foot model of the *Phoenix* rocket was erected on a platform at the back of the studios for the launch sequence which was shot in the open air against a genuine sky background.

Filming wrapped at Pinewood on Wednesday, 16th October, 1968, by which time production had ended on JOE 90 and the puppet and effects crews at Slough had moved on to work on THE SECRET SERVICE. When they saw the finished movie, Universal were less than enthusiastic about *Doppelgänger* and delayed its release until October the following year, a full 12 months after principal photography had ended. Box-office receipts proved disappointing but the Andersons and Donald James won a Blue Ribbon Award for the screenplay while the film's special effects were nominated for an Academy Award (ultimately losing out to John Sturges's high-profile space drama *Marooned*).

Notes

Overseas, the film was released as *Journey To The Far Side Of The Sun* and this title replaced *Doppelgänger* in the title sequence on international prints. British actor Ian Hendry receives top billing on *Doppelgänger* while American actor Roy Thinnes is billed first on *Journey To The Far Side Of The Sun*. George Sewell, Ed Bishop, Philip Madoc, Vladek Sheybal, Keith Alexander, Jeremy Wilkin, Norma Ronald, Basil Moss, Anthony Chinn, Jon Kelley and Annette Kerr all went on to appear in UFO as did the futuristic cars (designed by Ford consultant Len Bailey), the jeeps (British Leyland Mini Mokes adapted by Space Models at Feltham), the spacesuits, medical staff uniforms, most of Loni Von Friedl's wardrobe, the *Phoenix* rocket, *Dove* shuttle and some of Barry Gray's incidental music. Cy Grant (Dr. Gordon) previously provided the voice of Lieutenant Green in CAPTAIN SCARLET AND THE MYSTERONS. Neptune House at the ATV Studios in Borehamwood (later seen as the Harlington-Straker Film Studios in UFO) doubled for the EUROSEC administration building in location photography while Heatherden Hall at Pinewood Studios appeared as the nursing home where Jason Webb ends his life. Several scenes were shot for the film but deleted from the final edit: Kane and Lisa were shown to be in a close relationship in a scene by the pool at Kane's villa and also a later scene on the beach, Sharon and Landi were seen flirting with each other by the pool at Ross's villa, and Ross returned from the survival exercise to find Sharon in bed with Landi. The latter scene ended with Ross throwing Landi and then Sharon into the pool along with their clothes.

Oops!

The terminals for the Heart Lung Kidney machine aboard the *Phoenix* are surgically implanted in the left wrists of Ross and Kane, but when they arrive at the EUROSEC complex on the mirror planet, the implants have moved to their right wrists. One of the shots of Lisa in the interrogation scene is the correct (unflopped) way round so that the white flash on her dress swaps from left to right and back again.

PRODUCTION CREDITS

Produced by **Gerry & Sylvia Anderson**
Associate Producer **Ernest Holding**
Director of Photography **John Read**
Music Composed and Conducted by **Barry Gray**
Art Director **Bob Bell**
Visual Effects Director **Derek Meddings**
Production Manager **Brian Burgess**
Editor **Len Walter**
Sound Editor **John Peverill**
Sound Recordists **Ken Rawkins**, **Ted Karnon**
Additional Designs **Reg Hill**
Instrumentation and Special Props **Don Fagan**, **Century 21 Film Props**
Assistant Director **John O'Connor**
Camera Operator **Godfrey Godar**
Continuity **Joan Davis**
Production Secretary **Julie Leighton-White**
Location Manager **Ivo Nightingale**
Assistant Editor **Margaret Miller**
Assistant Art Directors **Chris Burke**, **Philip Bawcombe**
Make-up Artist **Geoffrey Rodway**
Hairdresser **Barbara Ritchie**
Wardrobe Supervisor **Elsa Fennell**
Wardrobe Mistress **Gloria Barnes**
Special Effects Lighting Cameraman **Harry Oakes**
Special Effects Production Manager **Norman Foster**
Special Effects Designer **Mike Trim***
Models **Peter Aston***, **Ray Brown***, **Tony Day***, **Alan Shubrook***, **Brian Smithies***

Westrex Recording System
Made on Location in Portugal
and at Pinewood Studios, England
by Universal Pictures Limited
139 Piccadilly, London, England
A Gerry Anderson Production
Filmed in Technicolor®

* uncredited

Gerry and Sylvia Anderson's original script for *Doppelgänger* runs to 194 pages and is very different in many respects from the finished film, although the basic story and its progression remained the same. John Kane is written as Philip Kane, a fair-headed astrophysicist married to intelligent but unsophisticated brunette Susan (replaced in the film by Lise Hartman). Jason Webb is described as a former Minister of Technology in the British Government and is seen to be having an affair with his secretary Pam Kirby. Mark Neuman is Mark Hallam, the unemotional German head of security who discovers that Dr. Hassler is working for the Red Chinese. Glenn Ross is written as Stewart Ross, one of America's most famous astronauts and the first man to land on Mars. His wife Sharon is detailed as the daughter of an American Senator and is explicitly seen having an affair with liaison officer Carlo Monetti (renamed Paulo Landi in the finished film). Ross's growing suspicion of their affair causes an embarrassing scene in front of the entire project team at the Eurosec Space Club.

Once Ross and Kane arrive on the mirror planet, the differences in the story are more significant. In this version of the script it is Ross who is badly injured while Kane is left to face interrogation by Webb and Hallam. Dr. Pontini is written as Dr. Bergman, a psychiatrist who arrives at Kane's villa to sedate him after Kane discovers that everything is reversed. His condition is diagnosed as brain damage caused by the HLK machine on the *Phoenix*. Ross recovers consciousness but turns out to have been blinded in the crash and cannot, therefore, see that his surroundings are reversed. However, Susan comes to believe her husband's theory about the two planets and she manages to persuade Webb to send a second *Dove* up to the *Phoenix* to determine the truth. The *Dove*, with Kane aboard, burns up in the atmosphere, leaving Ross alive but blind, unaware that he is actually living on an alien planet. The script ends with Kane's funeral in a Portuguese cathedral attended by Ross, Sharon, Webb and Susan.

ABANDONED FILM PROJECTS

Since the completion of *Doppelgänger* in 1968, Gerry Anderson has made a number of attempts to develop new feature film projects, some with more success than others but all, ultimately, abandoned during the pre-production process. This is, of course, indicative of the film industry as a whole, where the projects that are terminated during development far outnumber those that finally make it to the screen.

YOUTH IS WASTED ON THE YOUNG (1969)

Screenplay by **Gerry Anderson** & **Wilfred Greatorex**

In the 21st century, an ageing dictator plans to cheat death by arranging to have his brain transplanted into a younger body while keeping control over his country. He grooms a young politician to become his successor in the eyes of his people and then engineers a car accident in which the young man is injured. He and the dictator are flown to an advanced medical installation on a remote island where the dictator's brain is surgically implanted in the young politician's body. After years of therapy, the dictator returns to public life in his new host body and is accepted by the people as their new leader. But the young man's beautiful wife begins to suspect that her husband is not the man he once was...

Notes

Announced in the trade press in February 1969, *Youth Is Wasted On The Young* was inspired by the pioneering transplant work of Christiaan Barnard with a title borrowed from George Bernard Shaw. Co-writer Wilfred Greatorex was the acclaimed creator of the ATV business dramas THE PLANE MAKERS and THE POWER GAME and later went on to create the futuristic political drama series 1990 for the BBC. Following a location recce to Portugal to select the hotel that would appear as the dictator's palace in the film, the project stalled, apparently due to problems with the script.

MOONRAKER (1970)

Script Treatment by **Gerry Anderson** & **Tony Barwick**

A sophisticated electronic tracking device that can be used to pinpoint nuclear submarines has fallen into the hands of a villainous megalomaniac who calls himself Zodiac. Operating from a mobile headquarters hidden within an oil tanker vessel, Zodiac threatens to destroy fleets of nuclear submarines with long-range atomic torpedoes launched from the oil tanker's bows. Top British intelligence agent James Bond 007, licenced to kill, attempts to trace Zodiac but finds himself up against Zodiac's henchmen, the sinister triplets Tic, Tac and Toe...

Notes

In 1970, Gerry Anderson was invited by Eon Productions' Harry Saltzman to work on script ideas for *Moonraker*, then planned as the next James Bond 007 film to follow *On Her Majesty's Secret Service* (1969) into production. Anderson and Tony Barwick wrote a 70-page treatment that entirely abandoned the plot of the original Ian Fleming novel in favour of a much more dramatic new story. Saltzman was delighted with the story, telling Anderson that the treatment was 'outstanding' and offering to buy it for $20,000. Not wishing to lose the opportunity to be involved in seeing his script through to production, Anderson rejected the offer but Saltzman subsequently showed no further interest in working with him. Eon went on to make *Diamonds Are Forever* (1971) instead, but when *The Spy Who Loved Me* (1977) went into production at Pinewood Studios in 1976, Anderson recognised elements of the *Moonraker* treatment in the script for the new film by Christopher Wood and Richard Maibaum: primarily the nuclear submarine tracking device and the oil tanker ship that disguised the villain's secret base. Anderson started legal proceedings against Eon and eventually accepted £3,000 from Eon's law firm on the condition that all copies of the *Moonraker* treatment were handed over and all material relating to it was destroyed. Eon produced a James Bond film entitled *Moonraker* two years later, but it bore no resemblance whatsoever to the Anderson and Barwick treatment.

Canadian producer Harry Saltzman was a former co-director (with John Osborne and Tony Richardson) of Woodfall Productions, producers of the highly acclaimed British films *Look Back In Anger* (1959), *The Entertainer* (1960) and *Saturday Night And Sunday Morning* (1960). Prior to their meetings about *Moonraker*, Saltzman approached Gerry Anderson to collaborate on another film project, *Cold War In A Country Garden* based on a novel by British science-fiction author Lindsay Gutteridge, in which government agent Matthew Dilke and his companions are shrunk to half an inch in height and set out to cross a garden to test whether overpopulation could be countered by resettling the world with a miniaturised mankind. Anderson believed that the concept was technically impossible to film at the time, and told Saltzman so. The project did not progress any further. By 1989, visual effects were sufficiently advanced to enable Disney to cover similar ground in *Honey, I Shrunk The Kids* (1989).

OPERATION SHOCKWAVE (1978)

Screenplay by **Gerry Anderson** & **Tony Barwick**

A terrorist gang kidnaps the son of a television interviewer and then orders her to threaten the life of the Israeli prime minister during a live interview scheduled for the next day. As events unfold, watched by millions of viewers around the world, the terrorists prove that they mean business by kidnapping the prime minister's house-keeper's dog, feeding it chopped liver mixed with Semtex and forcing it to swallow a remote-controlled detonator before turning it loose within sight of its home...

Notes

Operation Shockwave would have marked a rare return for Gerry Anderson and Tony Barwick to the contemporary thriller genre that had proved so successful for them with THE PROTECTORS, but months of pre-production work came to nothing when the project was scuppered. Soundstages had been booked at the United Studios in Israel and Anderson was ready to start filming there with a full crew and American actor Bo Svenson in the leading role when the financier called from London to inform him that the finance had fallen through.

FIVE STAR FIVE (1979)

Screenplay by **Tony Barwick** & **Gerry Anderson**

Details of a scanner system which could be used to jam the planet Kestra's defence network are stolen from a surveillance outpost by Zargon raiders operating from a newly constructed asteroid fortress. The asteroid houses six Zargon battlecruisers with the capability to destroy Kestra in a single attack, so Colonel Zana of the Kestran intelligence service enlists the aid of former Earth Star Fleet officer Captain John Lovell to lead a commando raid to destroy the fortress. *En route* to the asteroid, Lovell recruits the members of his raiding party: talking chimpanzee Clarence B. Bond, robot Rudy, oriental Sumara from the planet Pax Semper, and space gypsy Gyp who brings his robotic dog Dash with him. Meanwhile, Colonel Zana is betrayed by one of her own space captains, captured by the Zargons and brought before the Grand Leutna, commander-in-chief of the Zargon attack forces, in the asteroid fortress. Lovell discovers that Zana has been taken prisoner and realises that his five-man task force will have to break into the fortress to rescue her before engineering the asteroid's destruction...

Notes

After production on SPACE:1999 came to an end early in 1977, Gerry Anderson signed with an agent, John Redway, who introduced him to feature film fundraiser Sydney Rose. They collaborated on developing an action-adventure space fantasy loosely based on *The Magnificent Seven* (1960), lining up John Guillermin, director of *The Towering Inferno* (1974), to helm it and Alan Hume BSC to be director of photography. Work progressed on the script for *Five Star Five* over the next two years while Rose arranged the film's projected budget of $11 million and eventually, in 1979, contracts were signed and pre-production began at Pinewood Studios with production designer Michael Stringer preparing dozens of sketches of character, vehicle and planetary settings. Special effects filming was scheduled to start at Bray Studios on October 22nd, 1979 with principal photography at Pinewood set to follow from November 19th, when, once again, the financial arrangements suddenly fell through and the project had to be cancelled. Another space fantasy version of *The Magnificent Seven* (1960) was produced the following year by Roger Corman – Jimmy T. Murakami's *Battle Beyond The Stars* (1980). The fighting style adopted by the *Five Star Five* character Sumara was later used by Wyndham 'Houdini' Derrit in the SPACE PRECINCT episode *Two Against The Rock*.

Tony Barwick and Gerry Anderson's script for *Five Star Five* introduced a disparate cast of characters. The 'five' were led by Captain John D. Lovell, a 40-year-old Earthman who has seen active service in a war with the Centaurians. After the death of his wife in a space accident, he resigned his commission in Earth Star Fleet and now runs a small shipping business from an ex-Federation B156 Transporter. Lovell's business partner is Clarence B. Bond, a sophisticated, intelligent and articulate chimpanzee with a Masters Degree in Aeronautics. At a Robotics Centre, Lovell hires a huge R42 demolition robot, over seven feet tall with self-generating positronic power. The R42's last renter from Earth called him Rudolph Nureyev, so Lovell takes to calling him Rudy. On the free planet of Pax Semper, Lovell recruits his old friend Sumara, the shaven-headed Oriental son of a Malayan mother and a Centran father. Adept at all forms of martial arts, Sumara combines his skills with powers of advanced telekinesis which enable him to inflict blows on his opponents from 20 feet away. Lovell attempts to recruit space gypsy Dorita to help them, but she declines as she feels that she is getting too old. Instead, she suggests that her 11-year-old grandson Gyp should join them. The boy is an electronics genius and has built himself a robotic dog, Dash, with which he shares a telepathic link – whatever Dash sees and hears, Gyp does too.

TELEVISION PILOTS & ONE-OFF PROGRAMMES

1973-2001

THE INVESTIGATOR
THE DAY AFTER TOMORROW
SPACE POLICE
GFI
CAPTAIN SCARLET AND THE RETURN OF THE MYSTERONS
CAPTAIN SCARLET S.I.G.

THE INVESTIGATOR

Screenplay by **Sylvia Anderson**
Story by **Shane Rimmer**
Directed by **Gerry Anderson**

The Investigator, a benevolent alien from a distant galaxy, selects a pair of American youths, John and Julie, to assist him in his mission to make their world a better place. Miniaturised and granted special powers, John and Julie are briefed on Stavros Karanti, a man who has made money easily but at the expense of others. A 14th century Raphael masterpiece is one of the proudest possessions of an island community and because he cannot buy it, Karanti plans to steal it, so John and Julie are assigned to stop him. The Investigator provides them with a special car fitted with a visual scanner and a sonic detector which they use to eavesdrop on Karanti's yacht, the *Borgia*. They tail Karanti to St. John's Cathedral in the island city of Mdina where the Raphael is on display. Karanti donates a valuable icon to the church's art collection and is shown the security arrangements for the icon's safekeeping...

Production

Early in 1973, as production on the second season of THE PROTECTORS was coming to an end and preparations were being made for a second series of UFO, Gerry and Sylvia Anderson decided to make a pilot episode for a new Supermarionation programme, planning to show it to their friend George Heinemann, vice-president of specialised children's programming for the American NBC television network, in the hope that he might commission a full series. Financed by private venture capital, the format of the programme was designed along similar lines to THE SECRET SERVICE with the puppet characters interacting with real people and settings. Unfortunately, the production was beset by problems, including inclement weather and the unpredictability of a radio-controlled model car driven by the puppet characters. Anderson was so unhappy with the finished programme that he felt unable to screen it for anyone, let alone an NBC executive, so the project was abandoned.

Notes

Location filming on Malta took the crew to Malta International Airport at Luqa and the main gates of Mdina, both locations that were previously used in the THE PROTECTORS episode *A Matter Of Life And Death*. The main location was the Cathedral of St. Peter and St. Paul in St. Paul's Square in Mdina, designed by Lorenzo Gafa and built from the rubble of the island's 1693 earthquake. The Julie puppet was sculpted by John Brown to resemble actress Racquel Welch, star of *Fantastic Voyage* (1966) and *One Million Years B.C.* (1966). Both puppets were later seen in Gerry Anderson's *Alien Attack* commercial for Jif Dessert Toppings. The three leading voice artists from THUNDERBIRDS were reunited for the last time in an Anderson production: Peter Dyneley (The Investigator), Shane Rimmer (John) and Sylvia Anderson (Julie) had previously been heard as Jeff Tracy, Scott Tracy and Lady Penelope respectively. Charles Thake (Karanti) previously appeared as a Police Inspector in the THE PROTECTORS episode *Ceremony For The Dead*.

PRODUCTION CREDITS

Producer	**Gerry Anderson***
Devised by	**Gerry Anderson**
Models Created by	**Reg Hill**
'Investigator' Theme by	**Vic Elmes**
Lighting Cameraman	**Harry Oakes**
Editors	**David Lane**
	Len Walter
Camera Operator	**David Litchfield**
Puppet Operators	**John Brown**
	Wanda Brown
Model Operator	**Plugg Shutt**
Lip-Sync Operator	**John Drake**
Dubbing Editors	**Wilf Thompson**
	Terry Rawlings
Sound Mixer	**Dennis Whitlock**
Puppets	**Volliscene Ltd**
Models	**Space Models Ltd**
Sound	**Cine-Sound Post Productions**
Music Composed by	**John Cameron***

A Starkits Production
Filmed Entirely on Location in Malta

* uncredited

Voice Cast

The Investigator	**Peter Dyneley**
John	**Shane Rimmer**
Julie	**Sylvia Anderson**

Cast

Stavros Karanti	**Charles Thake**
Christoph	**Peter Borg**

First UK Transmission

Unscreened to date

Running Time

23 minutes approx.

Such was their faith in the commercial success of any new Gerry Anderson production that die-cast toy car manufacturers Dinky Toys jumped at the opportunity to produce vehicles based on THE INVESTIGATOR as soon as they learned of the project. With a line of highly successful die-cast toys based on the main vehicles from THUNDERBIRDS, CAPTAIN SCARLET AND THE MYSTERONS, JOE 90, THE SECRET SERVICE and UFO behind them, Dinky eagerly set to work preparing to launch toys based on Reg Hill's designs for the Investigator's car and boat, investing thousands of pounds on creating dies and putting together prototypes. They were understandably disappointed when the expected series did not materialise, but decided to release the vehicles anyway. In green livery with military-style decals, the car was issued in 1975 as an 'Armoured Command Car designed by Gerry Anderson' while the boat was launched in 1977 as a 'Coastguard Amphibious Missile Launcher' with no reference to its origins as part of a Gerry Anderson project.

THE DAY AFTER TOMORROW

INTO INFINITY

Screenplay by **Johnny Byrne**

Directed by **Charles Crichton**

The lightship *Altares* leaves Space Station Delta on the first stage of a mission of scientific discovery beyond the solar system, a journey to Alpha Centauri, four light years from Earth. On board are two complete family units: Dr. Tom Bowen with his wife Anna and son David, and Captain Harry Masters with his daughter Jane. Their work at Alpha Centauri completed, the two families elect to continue deeper into space but the computer guidance system malfunctions and as Bowen switches to the back-up systems, the *Altares* is hit by a meteorite shower. The ship's photon drive suddenly cuts in and the *Altares* hurtles into deep space at a constant acceleration of near light speed. Battered by the terrific acceleration forces, the crew pass out and when they regain consciousness they find that the *Altares* is suspended in space near to a red giant star. However, the drive units have burnt out and the space/time co-ordinates have gone too, so the crew have no idea how long they have been unconscious or how far they have travelled...

Cast

Dr. Tom Bowen	**Brian Blessed**
Dr. Anna Bowen	**Joanna Dunham**
Captain Harry Masters	**Nick Tate**
Jane Masters	**Katherine Levy**
David Bowen	**Martin Lev**
Jim Forbes	**Don Fellows**
Narrator	**Ed Bishop**
Spring	**Bones**

First UK Transmission

Saturday, December 11th, 1976
6.00pm (BBC1)

Running Time

47 minutes approx.

Production

In the spring of 1975, as production on the first series of SPACE:1999 was winding down, Gerry Anderson was approached by NBC executive George Heinemann, who wanted to develop a series of seven self-contained one-hour educational specials, each of which would focus on a particular topic. He commissioned Anderson to produce a programme which would explain the premises and effects of Albert Einstein's Special Theory of Relativity in the format of an action-adventure show that would appeal to younger viewers. Together with SPACE:1999 writer and script editor Johnny Byrne, Anderson devised the concept of what became THE DAY AFTER TOMORROW. As it was by no means certain at this time that ITC would commission a second series of SPACE:1999, they designed the new programme with the potential for an ongoing series if the initial episode, titled *Into Infinity*, were to prove successful.

On a budget of £105,000, principal photography was filmed at Pinewood Studios in ten days during July 1975, with a further six weeks spent shooting the numerous special effects sequences at Bray Studios. Anderson's regular production designers were already employed on other television series – Bob Bell on THE NEW AVENGERS and Keith Wilson on STAR MAIDENS – so Reg Hill took on the job of designing the interior of the *Altares*, designing sets for a Gerry Anderson production for the first time since FIREBALL XL5, 14 years earlier. SPACE:1999 model-maker Martin Bower deliberately designed and built the *Altares* model in a style compatible with the Earth spaceships seen in SPACE:1999, apparently because he was under the impression that the lightship was actually for use in SPACE:1999. Two versions of the *Altares* were constructed: one model was six feet long for close-up shots while a smaller one three feet in length was used for long shots. The larger model was equipped with rocket nozzles that could be loaded from gas jets and a high intensity light for the photon drive. Bower also constructed a space shuttle model that was 2½ feet long (for the scene in which the *Altares* crew arrive from Earth) and to create the massive 10-feet wide Space Station Delta model, he re-dressed a section of his model of the *S.S. Daria* from the SPACE:1999 episode *Mission Of The Darians*.

The programme was completed in September 1975 and Anderson then began planning SPACE:1999's second season, ultimately re-using some of the props and set panels from THE DAY AFTER TOMORROW during filming of the second season episodes for economy. THE DAY AFTER TOMORROW – *Into Infinity* premiered in the US as the third programme in NBC's SPECIAL TREAT series on Tuesday, December 9th, 1975, and was first screened in the UK by the BBC almost exactly a year later. Unfortunately, Anderson was unable to secure finance for a full series and no further episodes were made.

For the first of two screenings of THE DAY AFTER TOMORROW on British television, the BBC made minor edits to the programme, primarily removing the main title caption, as it was felt that viewers would be confused by the appearance of an episode title (*Into Infinity*) on what was, to all intents and purposes, a one-off film. The THE DAY AFTER TOMORROW caption was the easier of the two captions to remove without disrupting the action (the *Into Infinity* caption appears alongside the movement of a lift ferrying the crew to the *Altares*), so the programme was simply billed in BBC listings magazine *Radio Times* as INTO INFINITY. The original title and other edits were reinstated for the programme's VHS home video release by Fanderson, the Official Gerry Anderson Appreciation Society, in 1997 and the subsequent multi-regional DVD release by the club in 2002.

Notes

The *Altares* crew come from an Earth where natural resources have been squandered, where pollution and the haphazard destruction of the environment has put the future of humanity into jeopardy. Some of the events in the programme are surprisingly similar to the first half of the FIREBALL XL5 episode *Faster Than Light*, not only the accidental acceleration of the ship to light speed that causes the crew to pass out, leaving them lost in unknown space when they recover consciousness, but also the attempt to repair the ship's main drive, with the engineer working in a protective suit against the clock.

Brian Blessed (Dr. Tom Bowen) had previously been seen as Dr. Rowland in the Year One SPACE:1999 episode *Death's Other Dominion* and he later guested as Maya's father Mentor in the Year Two episode *The Metamorph*. Joanna Dunham (Dr. Anna Bowen) had also previously guested in SPACE:1999 as Vana in *Missing Link*. Nick Tate (Captain Harry Masters) had appeared throughout the first season of SPACE:1999 as chief Eagle pilot Alan Carter and he went on to reprise the role in the series' second season. His father John Tate had provided character voices for THUNDERBIRDS ten years earlier. Katherine Levy (Jane Masters) made her screen debut in THE DAY AFTER TOMORROW and shortly afterwards appeared in a leading role in the ITV children's science-fiction serial CHILDREN OF THE STONES. Martin Lev (David Masters) went on to win acclaim for his role as gangster Dandy Dan in Alan Parker's *Bugsy Malone* (1976). Don Fellows (Jim Forbes) was previously seen in an uncredited role as the GTV newsreader in the closing scenes of the SPACE:1999 episode *Breakaway*. Narrator Ed Bishop previously provided the voice of Captain Blue in CAPTAIN SCARLET AND THE MYSTERONS, appeared as David Poulson in *Doppelgänger* (1968), starred as Commander Ed Straker in UFO and guested as Colonel John Hunter in the first season THE PROTECTORS episode *The First Circle*.

Jane's pet dog Spring, left behind on Space Station Delta, was played by writer Johnny Byrne's mongrel terrier Bones. Although THE DAY AFTER TOMORROW has not been seen on British television since a BBC repeat screening in 1977, excerpts from the programme appeared in Channel 4's 1997 EQUINOX documentary *Black Holes* alongside clips from the SPACE:1999 episode *Black Sun*.

Oops!

Part of Jane's head and left arm disappear briefly when she strays into the star background area of the matte painting as she runs up the causeway with Spring on Space Station Delta. The *Altares* travels to Alpha Centauri (4.3 light years from Earth) at a speed of 178,141 miles per second so the journey should take 4½ years, yet when the crew arrive there, David and Jane do not appear to have aged a day since leaving Earth.

PRODUCTION CREDITS

Producer	**Gerry Anderson**
Special Effects	**Brian Johnson**
Director of Photography	**Frank Watts BSC**
Editor	**David Lane**
Designer	**Reg Hill**
Production Supervisor	**F. Sherwin Green**
Business Management	**Terry Connor**
Scientific Adviser	**Professor John Taylor**
Camera Operator	**Neil Binney**
Sound Recordist	**Claude Hitchcock**
Sound Editor	**Roy Lafbery**
Music Editor	**Alan Willis**
Assistant Director	**Gino Marotta**
Continuity	**Doris Martin**
Music	**Derek Wadsworth** **Steve Coe**
Wardrobe	**Rosemary Burrows**
Make-up	**Connie Reeve**
Hairdresser	**Patrick Grant**
Processed by	**Rank Film Laboratories**
Special Effects Lighting Cameraman	**Nick Allder**
Special Effects Camera Operator	**David Litchfield**
Wardrobe Furnished by	**Boodles, London**
Fire Suit Furnished by	**Bestobell Engineering Products Ltd.** Slough, England
Models	**Martin Bower***

Made at Pinewood Studios
and Bray Studios, London, England
A Gerry Anderson Production
World-Wide Distribution
Richard Price Television Associates Ltd.

* uncredited

A novelisation of Johnny Byrne's script for THE DAY AFTER TOMORROW – *Into Infinity* was written by science-fiction author J. Michael Butterworth for Star Books, a division of W.H. Allen and Co. Ltd., who foresaw an opportunity for on-going novels and novelisations based on the new television series. When it transpired that a series was not forthcoming, publication of the first book was cancelled and it has yet to see print.

Butterworth went on to write six novelisations of Year Two SPACE:1999 episodes for Star Books, although publication of the last of these, *The Edge Of The Infinite*, was also cancelled. It was eventually published in the United States by Warner Books.

SPACE POLICE

Cast

Lt. Chuck Brogan	**Shane Rimmer**
Officer Cathy Costello	**Catherine Chevalier**
Officer Tom	**Christine Glanville**
Officer Harry	**Lyn Beardsall**
Officer Dick	**Jan King**
Officer Bats	**Tina Werts**

Voice Cast

Officer Tom	**David Healy**
Officer Dick	**Jeff Harding**
Officer Harry	**Kate Harper**
Officer Bats	**Desiree Erasmus**
V. Lann	**Gary Martin**

First UK Transmission

Unscreened to date

Running Time

Original Version:
53 minutes approx.

Alternative Version:
24 minutes approx.

Clips from SPACE POLICE appeared in the video for *Gerry Anderson's Project 90*, an Anderson-themed dance record produced by The Tyler Brothers with lead vocals by Venice and backing vocals by Mistress T. The record was released by In Tape Records in 1990 but Anderson's main contribution to it was allowing permission for the producers to reference his earlier work in the track and feature a revamped design for Thunderbird 2 on the sleeve.

STAR LAWS

Screenplay by **Gerry Anderson** & **Tony Barwick** Directed by **Tony Bell**

After 15 years with the New York Police Department, Lieutenant Chuck Brogan has transferred to the Space Police, becoming the commanding officer of Precinct 44 East. Based in an orbiting space station house, Brogan and his fellow alien officers are involved in a campaign to crack down on organised crime on planet Zar XL5. This has led to the arrest of seven associates of crimelord V. Lann and word is out that he is gunning for Brogan. Brogan attends a meeting with the Zar XL5 President and after an attempt is made on the statesman's life by a pair of assassins hired by V. Lann, Brogan urges him to reconsider plans to travel to Ultraville on board his private monorail train. But the President refuses to give way to threats of terrorism. However, V. Lann has kidnapped the family of the President's aide Bron to ensure his co-operation. Bron provides V. Lann with the monotrain's security code, enabling the crimelord to override the train's automatic control system...

Production

In 1983, Gerry Anderson and Christopher Burr met with television executives in the United States to sell TERRAHAWKS to North American television and were constantly blocked by an attitude that puppet shows were unpopular in the USA, despite the massive success of THE MUPPET SHOW and the popularity of puppet characters in films such as *The Empire Strikes Back* (1980) and *E.T. The Extra Terrestrial* (1982). On their way back to London on Concorde, Anderson and Burr realised that what the American television executives were actually objecting to was puppet representations of human beings – puppets of animals and strange alien creatures were perfectly acceptable. With this in mind, they began to develop an idea for a television series which would combine live actors with puppet aliens animated using a variety of both traditional and modern puppetry techniques. As cop shows had proved consistently popular on American television, Anderson struck on the idea of a cop show set in space aboard a New York-style precinct house space station, crewed by both human and alien police officers. The series would be called SPACE POLICE.

In January 1984, visual effects director Steven Begg began designing the precinct house, vehicles and alien characters for a brochure that would be used by Anderson and Burr as part of their presentation to prospective financiers. This design work continued alongside production on TERRAHAWKS throughout 1984 and into 1985. Actor Shane Rimmer was Anderson's first choice as the star of the new series and Rimmer posed as the proposed lead character, Lieutenant Ben Hagen, in photographs that also formed part of the presentation brochure. The character was later renamed Chuck Brogan. Towards the end of 1985, Anderson Burr Pictures secured a co-production deal with ITV franchise operator TVS to produce a one-hour pilot episode of SPACE POLICE that would introduce a proposed series of 65 half-hour episodes, at a cost of some £625,000. However, the terms of TVS's investment proved too expensive for APB and the two producers ultimately opted to sever their ties with TVS and finance the pilot themselves.

Following the recording of the voices of the alien characters on Tuesday, April 1st, 1986, ten days of principal photography on SPACE POLICE began on Stage 2 at Bray Studios near Windsor on Tuesday, May 27th and were completed on Monday, June 9th, 1986. Former Supermarionation puppet supervisor Christine Glanville became supervisor of the new production's 'Galactronic' puppets, a combination of full-size body suits with animatronic heads (for scenes with the live actors) and sophisticated hand puppets similar to those used on TERRAHAWKS (for scenes that did not involve the live actors). In this capacity, Glanville also performed inside the body suit of Officer Tom alongside puppeteers Tina Werts (as Officer Bats), Lyn Beardsall (as Officer Harry) and Jan King (as Officer Dick).

Post-production work took place throughout the autumn and the programme was finally completed on the weekend of January 3rd and 4th, 1987. SPACE POLICE was publicly screened for the first time at *Conspiracy 87*, the 1987 World Science Fiction Convention in Brighton, and has subsequently been shown at most Fanderson conventions over the last 12 years. Although the programme has never received a television broadcast anywhere in the world, SPACE POLICE was released on home video by Fanderson in 2002, paired with THE DAY AFTER TOMORROW on a multi-regional DVD. A full series of SPACE POLICE finally went into production in May 1994 – albeit in a considerably revised format and with a new title – almost exactly eight years after filming had commenced on the original pilot episode (see the entry for SPACE PRECINCT).

Alternative Version

Frustrated by his attempts to raise finance for SPACE POLICE with the 53-minute pilot episode, in 1989 Anderson took the programme to The Moving Picture Company and edited it down to 24 minutes in order to make it faster-moving and more suitable for the kind of timeslots that were available in children's programming. Although this version generally trims material from scenes throughout, several sequences were cut altogether including Bron's visit to Mr. Big's Hideout, the destruction of the first engine coach, and the defusion of the bomb on the monorail support.

Notes

The list of suspects known to be associated with V. Lann includes R. Sonist, I. Balls, Terry Wrist, C. Nile, Bill Stickers and Jay Walker. The script details that V. Lann's forename is Victor. Shane Rimmer (Brogan) previously provided the voice of Scott Tracy in THUNDERBIRDS, voiced other characters in CAPTAIN SCARLET AND THE MYSTERONS, JOE 90 and THE INVESTIGATOR, and guested in the UFO episodes *Identified*, *Computer Affair* and *Confetti Check A-O.K.*, the THE PROTECTORS episodes *Vocal* and *Zeke's Blues*, and the SPACE:1999 episode *Space Brain*. David Healy (voice of Tom) was the voice of Shane Weston in JOE 90, voiced other characters in CAPTAIN SCARLET AND THE MYSTERONS and THE SECRET SERVICE, and guested in the UFO episode *Ordeal*.

PRODUCTION CREDITS

Producers	**Gerry Anderson, Christopher Burr***
Series Creators	**Gerry Anderson, Christopher Burr**
Associate Producer	**Bob Bell**
Visual Effects Director	**Steven Begg**
Music	**Christopher Burr, Gerry Anderson***
Editor	**Alan Killick**
Art Director	**Mark Harris**
Lighting Cameramen	**Alan Hume BSC, Harry Oakes BSC, Paddy Seale**
Galactronics Director	**Christine Glanville***
Galactronics Operators	**Christine Glanville, Tina Werts, Lyn Beardsall, Chris Harper**
Character Voices	**Desiree Erasmus, Jeff Harding, Kate Harper, David Healy, Gary Martin, Kerry Shale, Terry Sibbald, Ian Tyler, Peter Whitman**
Camera Operators	**E. Michael Anderson*, David Litchfield*, Tony Strachan***
First Assistant Directors	**Vic Smith, Bernard Hanson***
Second Assistant Director	**Keith Young***
Video Editor	**Roo Aitken***
Production Manager	**Derek Whitehurst**
Assistant to Producer	**Mary Anderson**
Armpits and Slomo	**Richard Gregory***
Illustrator	**Barry Jones***
HOD Model Shop	**Ben Tuszynski***
Animatronics Designer	**Mikki Labanguitgeirsdottir***
Animatronics Model Designer	**David Hayes***
Animatronics Assistants	**David Dunsterville*, Ian MacKinnon***
Model-makers	**Mark Woollard, Paul Robbens, John Weller, Quentin Plant, Ben Hall, Barry Jones, Philip Gooch**
Camera Assistants	**Jonathan Earp*, Keith Thomas*, Richard Brierly***
Draughtsman	**Simon Lamont***
Friendly Alien	**Julian Bell***
SFX Supervisor	**Malcolm King**
SFX Technician	**Terry Adlam**
Prop Maker	**Jeremy Richards**
Assistant Film Editor	**Max Hoskins**
Grip	**Malcolm Huse***
Sound Mixer	**Neil Kingsbury**
Boom Operator	**Paul Filby**
Continuity	**Doreen Soan**
Make-up	**Basil Newall**
Wardrobe	**Iris Richens**
Hairdresser	**Jeanette Freeman**
With Acknowledgments to	**Hurco International**
Processing	**Rank Film Laboratories**
Video Post Production	**Carlton Television**
Video Editing	**The Moving Picture Company****
Soundtrack Design	**Motion Control****

Filmed at Bray Studios
An Anderson Burr Picture

* uncredited on Alternative Version

**credited only on Alternative Version

Gerry Anderson's initial format for SPACE POLICE featured a very different cast of alien characters policing the East 42nd space precinct. Enrolled from various planets in the galaxy, the four alien officers were loosely based on Earth animals for easy audience identification: Lieutenant Leo, a feline alien with the strength of a lion who stalks his prey relentlessly; Lieutenant Ellie, an elephantine alien who has a phenomenal memory and carries an elephant gun; Captain Wag, a canine alien with an acute sense of hearing and a nose for sniffing out explosives and drugs; and Sergeant Bats, a bat-like alien who can see all wavelengths of light and glide from mountain tops on his bat-like wings. Actor Shane Rimmer was clearly Anderson's first and only choice for the series' lead role as a grizzled former New York cop, as the character was initially named after him – Commander Shane Rimmer.

Using these characters, Anderson's initial story idea for the pilot episode bore no similarity to the programme that was eventually made. Rimmer and his officers receive a threat from local gang boss Mr. Big who has a shipment of stolen gold in transit across space. If the officers intercept it, Big will totally destroy the heavily populated city of Vega which stands at the foot of a volcano on planet Volcan.

The four alien officers are dispatched to Volcan and Wag picks up a trail that leads them to the base of the volcano. Bats detects infra-red emissions from a cave and when they enter, they discover a huge alien brain creature called the Octagon. When the officers refuse to accede to Mr. Big's demands, the Octagon exerts enormous force on the cave floor, which ruptures the rock membrane sealing the volcano and lava pours out towards Vega. Just in the nick of time, Brogan arrives in his police vehicle and fires rockets which divert the lava flow away from the city.

Mr. Big's gold shipment is intercepted and the thieves are captured and locked in the cells. Rimmer and his officers enjoy a celebratory dinner while they wait for the next emergency call.

GFI

WARMING WARNING

Prod. No. 02

Screenplay by **Tony Barwick**

Directed by **Phil Littler**

American scientist Professor James Gee leads G-Force Intergalactic, a rapid response task force formed by the President of the United Planets to combat major crime and large-scale disasters. Operating from Star City, a hidden base beneath the surface of an asteroid orbiting the Myson planetary system, the G-Force team comprises Wungee and Tugee (Professor Gee's two brightest students), electronics specialist Argent and engineering expert D'Or (a pair of aliens from a distant galaxy), and Professor Gee's small dog Megabyte. The team are supported by a group of robots, Franklin, Abraham and Dickie, controlled by a huge central computer, George Washington. When the planet Zeta is affected by massive global warming which melts its polar ice caps, the farmers of Zeta are forced to build boats and take to the ever-rising seas. The only available land is controlled by the evil Tyran and his warriors: to save the farmers and the planet, G-Force must first overcome Tyran and his mighty metallic fortress city...

Production

In 1990, while attempting to interest broadcasters and distributors in financing SPACE POLICE, Gerry Anderson met with representatives of Jim Henson, creator of the Muppets. Henson was delighted with the pilot episode and agreed to raise the finance to produce the series through The Jim Henson Company. Sadly, he died just weeks later and the agreement for SPACE POLICE collapsed, but during the negotiations, Anderson had met businessman Adam Shaw of Actis Ltd., who approached Anderson late in 1991 and suggested that they might collaborate on a cel-animated series that would be produced in Russia. Anderson developed the idea for 'G-Force' (as the series was initially titled) and he and Shaw turned to Bob McKie and Phil Littler at Tomcat Animation in London to prepare pre-production work, including character and vehicle designs and computer-generated animated models of the vehicle movements. These materials were then sent to Videofilm Corp. in Moscow for the completion of all the cel animation.

By the end of 1992, work had progressed on scripts and stories for a series of 13 episodes of GFI, but it eventually became clear to Anderson that the programme was underfunded and that the animation studio in Moscow was ill-equipped to produce a series on the scale that he had envisaged, despite the undeniable skill of the Russian animators. The first episode to be completed, *Warming Warning*, confirmed all his worst fears and he decided to cancel the whole project before any further instalments were made.

Notes

Warming Warning was actually intended to be the second episode in GFI's first season of 13 instalments and does not, therefore, make any attempt to introduce the characters, vehicles and concepts of the series that would have followed. Denise Bryer (Tugee) previously provided voices for THE ADVENTURES OF TWIZZLE and FOUR FEATHER FALLS, but she is better known for her vocal performances as Zelda and Mary Falconer in TERRAHAWKS. Ben Stevens (Argent) previously voiced a number of regular characters for TERRAHAWKS including Space Sergeant 101, Dix-Huit, Hudson, Yung-Star and Stew Dapples. GFI was script-writer Tony Barwick's last work. He completed full scripts for six episodes but became incapacitated by cancer before he could finish work on another seven stories that he had developed for the series with Gerry Anderson. He died in August 1993, aged 59.

Voice Cast

James Gee	**Paul Carrington**
Wungee	**Dave Wade**
Tugee	**Denise Bryer**
Argent	**Ben Stevens**
D'Or	**Gary Martin**
George Washington	**Gary Martin**

First UK Transmission

Unscreened to date

Running Time

24 minutes approx.

Gerry Anderson's initial concept for 'G-Force' was very much patterned after THUNDERBIRDS, projecting the concept of a secret family-operated international rescue organisation into deep space. The lavish original format brochure that Anderson and Shaw created to raise the finance for the series presents team leader James Gee as a 44-year-old retired USAF Lieutenant General with two marriages behind him – the first ended in divorce while his second wife died in an air crash. His intergalactic rescue team is manned by his four grown-up children who have each been assigned a code-name for security purposes: James Gee Jr. (Wungee), a 24-year-old test pilot; John Gee (Tugee), a 22-year-old mechanical and electrical engineering specialist; Deborah Gee (Threegee), a 20-year-old astro-physicist; and Julie Gee (Fourgee), an 18-year-old computer scientist. The team is completed by the family's four-year-old dog Megabyte.

In this version of the concept, G-Force operate three specialised vehicles: Whizz Kid, a single-seater high-speed reconnaissance space vehicle; CADILLAC (Computer Assisted Design with Integral Logic Linked Automated Construction), a long-range space transporter with an on-board construction facility to build any specialised rescue equipment; and Star Car, a multi-purpose light transporter.

These ideas and the designs that were presented with them underwent various modifications before production commenced on the GFI episode *Warming Warning*, as detailed opposite.

PRODUCTION CREDITS

Executive Producers	**Gerry Anderson**
	Adam J. Shaw
Producer	**Bob McKie**
Music	**Dave Stewart**
Script Editor	**Tony Barwick**
Voice Artists	**Denise Bryer**
	Paul Carrington, Gary Martin
	Ben Stevens, Dave Wade

Distributed by Link Licensing Ltd.

A Gosh!/Inimitable Production

ABANDONED EPISODES

GFI was in production as a 13-episode television series for a full six months before the project was abandoned with only one episode, *Warming Warning*, completed. The list below details the remaining 12 episodes that were planned for GFI's first season, although full scripts were only completed by Tony Barwick for *Blow Out*, *Collision Course*, *The Imaginator*, *Supernova* and *Special Weapons And Tactics*.

BLOW OUT — Prod. No. 01

G-Force fights a blazing inferno at a futuristic rocket fuel refinery. A special vehicle will be required to put out the fire but Professor Gee suspects that the fire could be sabotage, a trap deliberately set by android hitman Head Case to enable him to fulfil his mission for the evil insectoid Diados – the annihilation of James Gee and G-Force!

COLLISION COURSE — Prod. No. 03

A gigantic meteorite is under the control of the insectoid Diados and unless the President of the United Planets agrees to their demands, the meteorite will destroy Icem, the Myson System's primary planet. Only G-Force can save the situation, but to divert the meteorite from its collision course will require a controlled nuclear explosion...

THE IMAGINATOR — Prod. No. 04

In this flashback story, the President of the United Planets loses his daughter in an aircrash caused by the evil Diados. He vows to create an organisation to combat the insectoids and with the use of Imaginators he recruits James Gee and his students Wungee and Tugee to his cause.

SUPERNOVA — Prod. No. 05

The *Supernova*, a gigantic starfreighter, is delivering a deadly cargo to one of Icem's moons when a collision with a meteorite turns the starfreighter into a lethal runaway express train. G-Force is sent to stop the starfreighter, but first they have to neutralise the *Supernova*'s inner defence system...

SPECIAL WEAPONS AND TACTICS — Prod. No. 06

James Gee and Tugee are attending the opening of Starplex 1, the very first orbital commercial centre and shopping facility, but they uncover a plot by intergalactic extortionist Quesslan Dahr to seize control of the Starplex. Gee determines to foil Dahr's plans without bloodshed before the military moves in...

LORE OF THE KHOTAN NEBULA — Prod. No. 07

The Khotan Nebula is a mysterious gas cloud in which more than sixty per cent of all space vehicles vanish without trace. A convoy of 30,000 ships is due to pass through the area in less than two weeks and G-Force is sent to solve the mysterious disappearances before the convoy arrives.

YESTERDAY'S WARRIOR — Prod. No. 08

The wreck of the *Dreadnaught*, a warship left over from the space war between Icem and planet Torrida some 50 years earlier, is towed into space dock on Icem. Inside, G-Force find war hero Megahto Sorgh in a state of suspended animation, but once revived they discover that he is not quite what they expected.

THE PLANETECH CRISIS — Prod. No. 09

G-Force goes to the aid of a company of planetary engineers for whom an operation to relocate the orbit of a moon has gone disastrously wrong. A traitor amongst the Planetech crew brings a bomb onto *Galaxy* and James Gee must save his own crew as well as avert the destruction of the moon.

STING — Prod. No. 10

Drugs baron Zarosa is growing a secret supply of the new narcotic Sting, which only requires users to take it once and they are hooked for life. The President assigns G-Force to destroy the growing fields, but Zarosa has bought the protection of the Diados. It means a showdown between the mighty *Galaxy* and the Diados' own spaceship the *Decimator*, the most powerful space battleship ever built!

The main planet in the Myson System is Icem, a very advanced planet with futuristic buildings and high-tech vehicles. Icem's Capital City is home to the President of the United Planets and base of the Centre for Astrophysics, where most research and scientific develop-ments are carried out for the system's planets, making it a natural point of attack for the destructive and aggressive Diados.

The G-Force headquarters, Star City, is hidden beneath the rocky surface of an asteroid orbiting the Myson System. Here, Professor Gee and his team maintain their main space ship, the *Galaxy*, a huge 250,000-ton vehicle which contains a complete automated factory manned by robots capable of building any form of vehicle or equipment needed to help in a mission. The ship also houses a gene laboratory where lifeforms can be created or modified by advanced genetic engineering, and the huge central control computer George Washington, which has tremendous powers of intelligence and deduction and is based within a room known as Washington Square.

G-Force also have other space vehicles at their disposal. *Star Probe* is a small unmanned vehicle which can travel faster than the speed of light to the site of a G-Force mission and report back on the situation in the disaster area. *Star Probe* is also able to create virtual reality images from the information it gathers, which the G-Force team can use to rehearse the more dangerous parts of a mission before arriving at the scene. Back-up reconnaissance is provided by Wungee's vehicle, *Star Streak*, a high-speed, single-seater space vehicle.

G-Force's main opponents are the evil Diados, an insect-like mafia who operate their own spaceship, the *Decimator*. The Diados are angered by the formation of G-Force and assign their android hitman Head Case to destroy James Gee and his team. Head Case always carries a special case containing a stereoscopic mapping gun which he uses to copy any person's face and characteristics, providing him with a foolproof disguise for every mission.

GULLIVER'S TRAVELS — Prod. No. 11

The Diados' Gulliver is the ultimate warrior robot – a hundred feet tall and weighing a thousand tons, it is virtually indestructible and unstoppable. Lured to a remote planet by a false SOS, G-Force find themselves confronting Gulliver. And when James Gee and his team are left for dead it is up to George Washington, Franklin, Dickie and the rest of the robots to face the awesome Gulliver!

GRANDMA AND THE SEVEN ROBOTS — Prod. No. 12

A group of men are trapped in a blazing chemical plant. G-Force comes to the rescue and everyone is saved except one young hero who dies trying to help his friends. Grandma White is now alone and under pressure to sell up and leave. G-Force wants to help her, but James Gee insists that they cannot interfere in the internal politics of any part of the Federation. However, seven of the robots decide that if their Commander won't help Grandma White, they will...

MISSION OF MERCY — Prod. No. 13

The Diados capture the *Galaxy* to use it as a Trojan Horse and destroy an interplanetary peace conference. They enlist the help of G-Force's old enemy Quesslan Dahr, who steals the *Star Streak* reconnaissance vehicle. But Dahr has not counted on Wungee's hot-headed heroics...

CAPTAIN SCARLET AND THE RETURN OF THE MYSTERONS

Voice Cast

Captain Scarlet	**Francis Matthews**
Captain Blue	**Ed Bishop**
Captain Black	**Gary Martin**
Destiny Angel	**Leone Connery**
Voice of the Mysterons	**Gary Martin**

First UK Transmission

Unscreened to date

Running Time

4 minutes approx.

Written and Directed by **Gerry Anderson** & **John Needham**

Captain Scarlet and Captain Blue return to Spectrum after a long absence and are admiring the new Cloudbase control room when Captain Black arrives. He reminds them that he is no longer under the control of the Mysterons and has been cleared for access by the computer, but he is revealed to be still acting as a Mysteron agent when he knocks Blue down and takes control of his mind. Driving at breakneck speed along a mountain road in a new SPV, Scarlet pursues Black and Blue, who are heading for the atomic power station at Drontenon in a new Spectrum Patrol Car filled with explosives...

Production

In November 1999, Gerry Anderson was commissioned by Carlton International Media, the new owners of the ten television series that Anderson produced for Lew Grade's ITC, to examine the possibility of re-creating the Supermarionation titles for a 21st century television audience. CAPTAIN SCARLET AND THE MYSTERONS was selected for trials of an innovative process of computer-graphic imaging and production began in January 2000 at the London-based Moving Picture Company. Miniature busts of the heads of Captain Scarlet, Captain Black and Captain Blue were cyber-scanned to create computer models of the characters and mime actors Andrew Dawson (Captain Scarlet), Rob Thirtle (Captain Black) and Wayne Forester (Captain Blue) performed action sequences with sensors attached to their bodies at key points so that their movements could be recorded digitally and transferred to three three-dimensional computer-generated figures using sophisticated motion-capture technology. Voice artists Francis Matthews, Ed Bishop and Gary Martin were fitted with sensors which recorded their facial movements while performing the dialogue and this information was imposed on the computer-generated character heads so as to match the dialogue to realistic facial expressions. New vehicle designs by Steven Begg were computer-modelled and textured with Maya 3D software before being animated to fulfil the requirements of the script.

The resulting short test film, CAPTAIN SCARLET AND THE RETURN OF THE MYSTERONS, was screened in public for the first time to a packed auditorium of 400 Gerry Anderson fans at Fanderson's *Century 21* convention in Allesley, Coventry, on October 7th, 2000. The enthusiastic reception encouraged Anderson to secure the remake rights from Carlton and pre-production began on a new CGI-animated series of CAPTAIN SCARLET AND THE MYSTERONS on February 3rd, 2003.

The script for the CGI test film (originally planned to run just two minutes) was titled 'Captain Scarlet – The New Millennium' and made it clear that the new adventure was set several years after the end of the Supermarionation series. The Mysterons appear to have lain dormant in the intervening years, apparently releasing their hold on Captain Black who has returned to Spectrum duty. The Cloudbase control room has been extensively refurbished, the Spectrum uniforms updated slightly, and the Spectrum vehicles modified with the latest technological developments.

Notes

Gary Martin (Captain Black) was previously heard as Slomo and other characters in SPACE PRECINCT. He also provided voices for characters in SPACE POLICE and GFI. Leone Connery (briefly heard as Destiny Angel) is Sean Connery's niece.

PRODUCTION CREDITS

Executive Producers	**Gerry Anderson**
	John Needham
Production Designer	**Mark Harris**
Conceptual Design	**Steven Begg**
Voice Artists	**Francis Matthews**
	Ed Bishop
	Gary Martin
	Leone Connery
Movement Models	**Andrew Dawson**
	Wayne Forester
	RobThirtle
Storyboards	**Robin Shaw**
Facial Modelling	**Mackinnon and Saunders**
Digital Animation	**The Moving Picture Company**

An Anderson Entertainment Production
in association with
Carlton International Media

CAPTAIN SCARLET S.I.G.

Written by **John Needham** Directed by **John Needham**

Voice Cast

Captain Scarlet	**Francis Matthews**
Captain Blue	**Ed Bishop**
Voice of the Mysterons	**Dave Finchett**

First UK Transmission

Unscreened to date

Running Time

56 minutes approx.

Captain Scarlet and Captain Blue review some of their most difficult assignments and reveal the techniques used to make CAPTAIN SCARLET AND THE MYSTERONS with the help of some of the programme's creators: Gerry Anderson, Mary Turner, Alan Perry, Iris Richens, Peter Wragg, Francis Matthews and Ed Bishop. Then the Mysterons issue their latest threat, promising the destruction of the power plant at Willendorf within one hour's time, leaving the World Defence Organisation powerless to stop any alien attack. Scarlet and Blue race to Willendorf in an SPV, but time is running out...

Production

In 2001, the 32 episodes of CAPTAIN SCARLET AND THE MYSTERONS were digitally remastered by Carlton International Media to relaunch the series with a network screening on BBC2. Planning to release the episodes on Region 2 DVD, Carlton Video commissioned Gerry Anderson and John Needham to produce a new hour-long documentary about the making of the series which would appear as a special feature with a six-disc DVD box set. New interviews and puppet footage for the documentary were shot at Halliford Studios in Shepperton, Surrey, where Anderson had filmed all of the interior sequences for *Crossroads To Crime* (1960) 41 years earlier.

Notes

Captain Scarlet and Captain Blue introduce excerpts from the CAPTAIN SCARLET AND THE MYSTERONS episodes *The Mysterons*, *Lunarville 7*, *Crater 101*, *The Launching*, *The Heart Of New York*, *Manhunt*, *Winged Assassin*, *Seek And Destroy*, *Point 783*, *Avalanche* and *Fire At Rig 15*.

PRODUCTION CREDITS

Produced by	**Gerry Anderson**
Executive Producer for Carlton Video	**Tina Lorenzo**
Puppeteers	**Mary Turner**
	Dave Finchett
Scenery	**Andy Rolfe**
Puppet Construction	**Richard Gregory**
	Barry Davis
Director of Photography	**Alan Wright**
Assistant Cameraman	**Ian Chisholm**
Gaffer	**Jimmy Russell**
Sound Recordist	**Colin Hood**
Dubbing Mixer	**Peter Hughes**
	The Sound Studio
Stills Courtesy of	**Carlton International Media**
Rostrum Camera	**Steve Edwards**
Offline Editor	**Matthew Glen**
Online Editor	**Adrian Conway**

Thanks to **Fanderson**, **Stephen Brown**, **Lynn Simpson**, **Ralph Titterton**

Filmed at Halliford Studios
An Anderson Entertainment Production
for Carlton Video Limited
Filmed in Supermarionation

ABANDONED TV PROJECTS

In 1976, during production on the second series of SPACE:1999, Gerry Anderson worked closely with SPACE:1999 Year Two producer Fred Freiberger to develop two new science-fiction television series ideas for American television.

RESCUE 4

The four-man crew of a multi-purpose space rescue vehicle, *Rescue 4*, patrol the north-west quadrant of space, ready to act in the event of a space disaster which requires the assistance of their remarkable craft. *Rescue 4* is equipped with pulsed sonic transmitters which can break down planet surfaces, thrusters for clearing debris which also allow the craft to burrow beneath the surface, and a multi-purpose energy generator which charges a turret cannon to disintegrate rocks. The vehicle itself is extremely versatile, launching from a vertical position but with the ability to fly horizontally in a planet's atmosphere as well as in the vacuum of space. With watertight bulkheads, *Rescue 4* can also sail, submerge or hover-skim across water. The hover-skim function can also be applied on dry land, enabling the vehicle to skim across the surface like a hovercraft.

Notes

RESCUE 4 (also known as 'Inter-Galactic Rescue') was conceived by Gerry Anderson and Fred Freiberger as an amalgamation of the earlier SUPERCAR and THUNDERBIRDS series formats, expanding the International Rescue concept to an inter-planetary scale (as in the later GFI series) but combining the functionality of the various Thunderbird vehicles into a single super-vehicle. Planning RESCUE 4 as a live-action series of 13 episodes in a thirty-minute format, Anderson and Freiberger drew on the talents of some of their SPACE:1999 colleagues to prepare a development package for presentation to the American NBC network. While model-maker Martin Bower designed the *Rescue 4* craft itself and constructed a six-inch model to display to the NBC executives, Reg Hill sketched out a series of storyboards with visual effects designer Brian Johnson to illustrate the vehicle's capabilities. Anderson and Freiberger offered RESCUE 4 to NBC as a new series for their 1976 season, but in competition against 40 other new shows, it was not picked up and the idea was abandoned.

STARCRUISER

The representatives of a group of planets engaged in intergalactic trading have formed Interstellar Command to act as a combination police and scientific exploration group. Under the control of Commander Edward Damion, Interstellar Command is based in the Capricorn-Antilles Space Habitat. The organisation's spearhead craft is *Starcruiser 1*, a small multi-unit spacecraft built for faster-than-light travel. The vehicle is commanded by Captain Christopher Stevens, ably assisted by navigator and astrophysicist Lieutenant Andrea Dehner, medical officer Dr. Brian Moore, and technical officer Professor Melita Alterra, who is also responsible for the design and construction of the ship.

Notes

Created by Gerry Anderson and Fred Freiberger, STARCRUISER was planned as a live-action series for the American CBS network. As with RESCUE 4, designs for the series' star vehicle were developed by Martin Bower, who also constructed a model of the craft to form part of a presentation to the CBS executives, but they ultimately rejected the concept for their 1976 season. However, Anderson was unwilling to abandon the project altogether so he and his marketing business partner Keith Shackleton took the designs to model-kit manufacturers Airfix and persuaded them to develop *Starcruiser* as a model-kit based on an original idea, rather than as part of a television tie-in. Airfix modified the craft by adding an Interceptor Unit on top and issued the model in 1977 as a 1/48 scale clip-together plastic construction kit with tiny plastic figures of the crew. Anderson and Shackleton also arranged to promote the model through a *Starcruiser* comic strip in *Look-in* magazine which first appeared in 1977 issue 2 (January 8th, 1977), illustrated by David Jefferis. For the purposes of the strip, the *Starcruiser* concept was slightly modified: the ship now operated as an Interstellar Survey Unit in the year 2051 and was crewed by command pilot David Starr and systems controller Venus Brown.

The design specifications for *Starcruiser* show that the vehicle is composed of three separate units. The first of these is the Main Unit, a ski-equipped thruster unit and power base for the other units which can be piloted both in planetary atmosphere and in space from a one-man cockpit above the nose-cone docking bay. Wing rockets supply power for both atmospheric and orbital flight, whilst seven main boosters at the rear, powered by laser fusion generated by a Kryten Reactor using pellets of deuterium as fuel, provide the main space drive. The second unit is the Command Module, a detachable nose-cone with seats for pilot and co-pilot, capable of flight within planetary atmosphere and short distances in space. This module can be piloted manually, by computer or by remote-control, and features a cabin which can be decompressed for extra-vehicular activity. The third unit is the Command Base, a centrally mounted pod section capable of independent usage, which functions as a combined laboratory and equipment bay. The pod holds a crawler survey buggy and a one-man skycar for aerial reconnaissance which exits the craft via a loading door in the rear section. The Command Base itself is equipped with caterpillar tracks for crossing most types of terrain and the unit can be collected by the Main Unit from a planetary surface in less than 30 seconds.

Look-in's *Starcruiser* comic strip accompanied a series of columns entitled *The Worlds Of Gerry Anderson* in which Anderson responded to questions posed by readers. The semi-educational half-page *Starcruiser* strip ran for over 75 issues, during the course of which the crew tested the ship's laser-fusion motors on a journey around the solar system, ferried a pair of scientists to the Moon, visited Alpha Centauri in search of life on planet Terra Nova, rescued faulty mining robot Vee-One on the surface of Venus, helped the alien occupants of a flying saucer to find water on Mars and visited a prospecting vehicle in the orbit of Jupiter.

MISCELLANEOUS PROJECTS

1946-1993

FEATURE FILM PROJECTS
YOU'VE NEVER SEEN THIS
PENTAGON FILMS COMMERCIALS
MARTIN KANE, PRIVATE INVESTIGATOR
AP FILMS/CENTURY 21 COMMERCIALS
INDEPENDENT COMMERCIALS
MUSIC VIDEOS

FEATURE FILM PROJECTS

After training in all aspects of film production with the Ministry of Information's Colonial Film Unit, Gerry Anderson made his film industry debut in 1946 as a second assistant editor at Gainsborough Pictures in Shepherd's Bush, London, learning the ropes from editor Peter Graham Scott and first assistant editor James Needs. After National Service, Anderson became a dubbing editor at Pinewood Studios in Buckinghamshire and Shepperton Studios in Surrey before leaving to join independent production company Polytechnic Studios as a director. Much later, during the production of THE SECRET SERVICE, he was invited to produce a visual effects sequence for the Roger Moore thriller *Crossplot* (1969).

THE WICKED LADY (US Version - 1946)

Barbara Worth, the Lady Skelton, embarks on a career of crime, donning a mask and cloak as a highwayman. Pursued by her husband, the local magistrate Sir Ralph Skelton, she begins a torrid romance with fellow highwayman Captain Jackson.

Cast: **Margaret Lockwood**, **James Mason**, **Patricia Roc**, **Griffith Jones**, **Michael Rennie**
Director: **Leslie Arliss**
Executive Producer: **Maurice Oster**
Producer: **R.J. Minney**
Screenplay: **Leslie Arliss**, **Gordon Glennon** & **Aimee Stuart**
Based on the novel *The Life And Death Of The Wicked Lady Skelton* by **Magdalen King-Hall**
Director of Photography: **Jack E. Cox**
Music Composed by **Hans May**
Editor: **Terence Fisher**
Art Director: **John Bryan**
2nd Assistant Editor: **Gerald Anderson**
Running Time: 99 minutes

(The original UK version was released in 1945, but Gerry Anderson was involved in re-editing the film for American audiences, toning down the sexual content.)

CARAVAN (1946)

In 17th century Spain, impoverished author Richard is left for dead by assassins hired by his rival for the hand of Lady Oriana. He is nursed back to health by gypsy dancer Rosal, who falls in love with him.

Cast: **Stewart Granger**, **Jean Kent**, **Anne Crawford**, **Dennis Price**, **Robert Helpmann**
Director: **Arthur Crabtree**
Executive Producer: **Maurice Oster**
Producer: **Harold Huth**
Screenplay: **Roland Pertwee**
Based on the novel by **Lady Eleanor Smith**
Director of Photography: **Stephen Dade**
Music Composed by **Walford Hayden**
Editor: **A. Charles Knott**
Art Director: **John Bryan**
2nd Assistant Editor: **Gerald Anderson**
Running Time: 122 minutes

JASSY (1947)

Gypsy servant girl Jassy Woodroffe falls in love with her master but is accused of murder.

Cast: **Margaret Lockwood**, **Patricia Roc**, **Dennis Price**, **Dermot Walsh**, **Basil Sydney**, **Nora Swinburne**, **John Laurie**
Director: **Bernard Knowles**
Producer: **Sydney Box**
Screenplay: **Dorothy** & **Campbell Christie** and **Geoffrey Kerr**
Based on the novel by **Norah Lofts**
Music Composed by **Henry Geehl**
Director of Photography: **Geoffrey Unsworth**
Editor: **A. Charles Knott**
Art Directors: **Maurice Carter** & **George Provis**
2nd Assistant Editor: **Gerald Anderson**
Running Time: 102 minutes

SNOWBOUND (1948)

Script-writer Neil Blair is trapped in a snowbound ski hut with a group of travellers who are all searching for Nazi treasure hidden in the Swiss Alps.

Cast: **Robert Newton**, **Dennis Price**, **Herbert Lom**, **Marcel Dalio**, **Stanley Holloway**
Director: **David MacDonald**
Executive Producer: **Sydney Box**
Producer: **Aubrey Baring**
Screenplay: **David Evans** & **Keith Campbell**
Based on the novel *The Lonely Skier* by **Hammond Innes**
Music Composed by **Cedric Thorpe Davie**
Director of Photography: **Stephen Dade**
Editor: **James Needs**
Art Directors: **Maurice Carter** & **George Provis**
2nd Assistant Editor: **Gerald Anderson**
Running Time: 102 minutes

SO LONG AT THE FAIR (1950)

English girl Vicky Barton visits the Great Paris Exhibition of 1889 with her brother Johnny and they book into a hotel. The next day, Vicky finds that Johnny and his hotel room have both disappeared and his existence is denied by everyone.

Cast: **Jean Simmons, Dirk Bogarde, David Tomlinson, Marcel Poncin, Cathleen Nesbitt, Honor Blackman, Betty Warren**
Directors: **Antony Darnborough & Terence Fisher**
Producers: **Betty E. Box & Sydney Box**
Screenplay: **Hugh Mills & Anthony Thorne**
Music Composed by **Benjamin Frankel**
Director of Photography: **Reginald H. Wyer**
Editor: **Gordon Hales**
Art Directors: **Cedric Dawe & George Provis**
Sound Editor: **Gerald Anderson**
Running Time: 86 minutes

THE CLOUDED YELLOW (1950)

Disgraced Secret Service agent David Somers takes a quiet job cataloguing butterflies on Nicholas Fenton's country estate, but when Jess Fenton's niece Sophie Malraux is framed for murder, he helps her to escape to London.

Cast: **Jean Simmons, Trevor Howard, Sonia Dresdel, Barry Jones, Maxwell Reed, Kenneth More, Geoffrey Keen, Anthony Oliver**
Director: **Ralph Thomas**
Producer: **Betty E. Box**
Screenplay: **Eric Ambler & Janet Green**
Music Composed by **Benjamin Frankel**
Director of Photography: **Geoffrey Unsworth**
Editor: **Gordon Hales**
Art Director: **Richard Yarrow**
Sound Editor: **Gerald Anderson**
Running Time: 96 minutes

NEVER TAKE NO FOR AN ANSWER (1952)

(US Title: *The Small Miracle*)

Seven-year-old war orphan Peppino is convinced that his ailing donkey Violetta will be cured if they visit the crypt of Saint Francis, the patron saint of animals, so he goes to the Vatican to seek permission from the Pope to take Violetta into the tomb.

Cast: **Vittorio Manuta, Denis O'Dea, Guido Celano, Nerio Bernardi, Frank Coulson John Le Mesurier, John Murphy, Riccardo Foti**
Director: **Maurice Cloche & Ralph Smart**
Producer: **Anthony Havelock-Allen**
Screenplay: **Paul Gallico, Pauline Gallico, Maurice Cloche & Ralph Smart**
Based on the novel *The Small Miracle* by **Paul Gallico**
Music Composed by **Nino Rota**
Editors: **Sidney Hayers & Peter Graham Scott**
Directors of Photography: **Robert Day & Otto Heller**
Sound Editor: **Gerald Anderson**
Running Time: 82 minutes

SOUTH OF ALGIERS (1952)

(US Title: *The Golden Mask*)

Archaeologist Dr. Burnet, his daughter Anne and reporter Nicholas Chapman search for the priceless golden Mask of Moloch in the Sahara, hindered by a pair of crooks who want the mask for themselves.

Cast: **Van Heflin, Wanda Hendrix, Eric Portman, Charles Goldner, Jacques François, Jacques Brunius, Aubrey Mather**
Director: **Jack Lee**
Producers: **Maxwell Setton & Aubrey Baring**
Screenplay: **Robert Westerby**
Music Composed by **Robert Gill**
Director of Photography: **Oswald Morris**
Editor: **Vladimir Sagovsky**
Art Director: **Donald M. Ashton**
Sound Editor: **Gerald Anderson**
Running Time: 95 minutes

APPOINTMENT IN LONDON (1953)

Grounded Wing Commander Tim Mason falls in love with Naval Officer Eve Canyon but when his friend Pilot Officer Greeno mysteriously disappears after being caught tinkering with a code machine, Mason decides to investigate.

Cast: **Dirk Bogarde, Ian Hunter, Dinah Sheridan, Bill Kerr, Walter Fitzgerald, Bryan Forbes, William Sylvester, Annie Leon, Richard Wattis**
Director: **Philip Leacock**
Producers: **Maxwell Setton & Aubrey Baring**
Screenplay: **Robert Westerby & John Wooldridge**
Music Composed by **John Wooldridge**
Director of Photography: **Stephen Dade**
Editor: **Vladimir Sagovsky**
Art Director: **Donald M. Ashton**
Sound Editor: **Gerald Anderson**
Assistant Editor: **David Elliott**
Running Time: 96 minutes

THEY WHO DARE (1953)

Lieutenant Graham and Sergeant Corcoran lead a British Boat Service commando raid to knock out airfields on Rhodes that are being used by the Luftwaffe to threaten Allied forces in Egypt, but the island is crawling with German troops.

Cast: **Dirk Bogarde**, **Denholm Elliott**, **Akim Tamiroff**, **Gérard Oury**, **Eric Pohlmann**
Director: **Lewis Milestone**
Producers: **Maxwell Setton** & **Aubrey Baring**
Screenplay: **Robert Westerby**
Music Composed by **Robert Gill**
Director of Photography: **Wilkie Cooper**
Editor: **Vladimir Sagovsky**
Art Director: **Donald M. Ashton**
Sound Editor: **Gerald Anderson**
Assistant Editor: **David Elliott**
Running Time: 107 minutes

ABDULLA THE GREAT (1954)

(US Title: *Abdulla's Harem*)

A wealthy pleasure-loving Egyptian potentate has everything he could possibly want, until he falls in love with a beautiful model and she rejects his advances.

Cast: **Gregory Ratoff**, **Kay Kendall**, **Sydney Chaplin**, **Marina Berti**
Director: **Gregory Ratoff**
Producer: **Gregory Ratoff**
Screenplay: **George St. George** & **Boris Ingster**
Based on the novel *My Kingdom For A Woman* by **Ismat Regeila**
Music Composed by **Georges Auric**
Director of Photography: **Lee Garmes**
Editor: **Maurice Rootes**
Sound Editor: **Gerald Anderson**
Running Time: 103 minutes

DEVIL GIRL FROM MARS (1954)

Leather-clad Martian dominatrix Nyah arrives on Earth armed with a ray gun and accompanied by a menacing robot. She intends to collect Earth's men as breeding stock.

Cast: **Hugh McDermott**, **Hazel Court**, **Patricia Laffan**, **Peter Reynolds**, **Adrienne Corri**
Director: **David MacDonald**
Producers: **Harry Lee Danziger** & **Edward J. Danziger**
Screenplay: **James Eastwood** & **John C. Mather**
Music Composed by **Edwin T. Astley**
Director of Photography: **Jack E. Cox**
Editors: **Brough Taylor** & **Peter Taylor**
Sound Editor: **Gerald Anderson**
Running Time: 77 minutes

When Gerry Anderson was contacted by film director Stanley Kubrick early in 1965 during filming on THUNDERBIRDS and invited to produce the special effects for his new film 'Journey Beyond The Stars', Anderson told Kubrick's production manager that the AP Films team only produced special effects for their own productions. Had he known then that he was turning down the opportunity to be a part of a film that would go on to be recognised as the most significant science-fiction film of the 20th century – 2001: A SPACE ODYSSEY – he might have been more accommodating. Resolving not to make the same mistake again, Anderson was more agreeable to the idea of producing a visual effects sequence for former THE SAINT producer Robert S. Baker on *Crossplot* (1969). The miniature effects sequence involved flying a model helicopter, with an assassin hanging from a harness beneath it, into power cables at the end of an extended chase scene. The assassin was electrocuted by the cables and the charge was conducted up the harness causing the helicopter to explode. Unfortunately, the filming of this sequence did not go as smoothly as hoped: an effects technician was too close to the charge when the helicopter exploded and was very badly burned.

A PRIZE OF GOLD (1955)

German girl Maria wants to take a group of orphan children from their home in Berlin to a new life in South America so American soldier Sergeant Joe Lawrence decides to help her by stealing a load of gold bullion being flown from Berlin to London.

Cast: **Richard Widmark**, **Mai Zetterling**, **Nigel Patrick**, **George Cole**, **Harry Towb**
Director: **Mark Robson**
Producers: **Irving Allen**, **Albert Broccoli** & **Phil Samuel**
Screenplay: **Robert Buckner** & **John Paxton**
Based on the novel by **Max Catto**
Music Composed by **Malcolm Arnold**
Director of Photography: **Ted Moore**
Editor: **Bill Lewthwaite**
Sound Editor: **Gerald Anderson**
Running Time: 100 minutes

CROSSPLOT (1968)

Successful advertising executive Gary Fenn finds the ideal model for a campaign in Hungarian girl Maria Kogash, but when he learns that she has overheard plans of an assassination plot hatched by a sinister political organisation, Fenn goes on the run with the girl, hunted by vicious killers.

Cast: **Roger Moore**, **Martha Hyer**, **Claudie Lange**, **Alexis Kanner**, **Francis Matthews**, **Bernard Lee**, **Gabrielle Drake**
Director: **Alvin Rakoff**
Producers: **Robert S. Baker** & **Roger Moore**
Screenplay: **Leigh Vance** & **John Kruse**
From a story by **Leigh Vance**
Music Composed by **Stanley Black**
Director of Photography: **Brendan J. Stafford**
Editor: **Bert Rule**
Art Director: **Ivan King**
Visual Effects Producer: **Gerry Anderson**
Visual Effects Director: **Derek Meddings**
Running Time: 96 minutes

(A visual effects sequence featuring a helicopter flying into power cables and exploding was produced by Gerry Anderson at the Century 21 Studios in Slough during production on THE SECRET SERVICE in the autumn of 1968. Neither Anderson nor the sequence's director Derek Meddings are credited for their contribution.)

YOU'VE NEVER SEEN THIS

Written by **Max Elliott** Directed by **Gerry Anderson**

A light-hearted documentary series in which globe-trotting reporter Pete Collins visits strange places and meets people and animals with unusual talents: a man with no arms who plays honky tonk music on the piano with his feet, a German circus performer who hypnotises alligators, a man who has lived in a bottle for a year, a man who can ride his bicycle at 109mph, a man who plays the trumpet while balanced on the end of a billiard cue on the roof of the Munich Rathaus, and a man who leaves the driver's seat of a car travelling at 70mph to fetch a packet of cigarettes from a suitcase on the roof-rack. In the one surviving instalment, Collins visits a restaurant where the patrons are made very unwelcome and the food is deliberately disgusting. He is then introduced to a dog that performs magic tricks, meets a man who makes furniture entirely out of matchsticks and visits a woman who makes clothes out of dog hair.

Production

Early in 1955, Polytechnic Studios, a small independent television production company run from a dilapidated house in Taplow, Buckinghamshire, was approached by Pete Collins, a theatrical agent who booked amazing acts for music hall theatre. Collins wanted to make a television series called 'Pete's Freaks' so Polytechnic advertised for a director to work on the series. Gerry Anderson was hired and over the coming months travelled all over the Continent with Collins and camera operator Arthur Provis to film the unusual performers for the series, which was eventually retitled YOU'VE NEVER SEEN THIS. The series was sold to Associated-Rediffusion but only a single instalment was scheduled and screened in October 1955 (other episodes may have been shown as unscheduled 'filler' material). Polytechnic went into liquidation in 1956, but Anderson and Provis decided to go into partnership with another former Polytechnic employee Reginald Hill and his colleague John Read to form their own company Pentagon Films, specialising in commercials.

Cast

Pete Collins	**himself**
Reporter	**Jon Farrell**
Secretary	**Gay McGregor**

First UK Transmission

Tuesday, October 4th, 1955
8.00pm (Associated-Rediffusion)

Running Time

25 minutes approx.

PRODUCTION CREDITS

Devised & Produced by	**Pete Collins**
Lighting Cameraman	**Geoff Williams**
Camera Operator	**Arthur Provis**
Sound Supervisor	**Red Furderer**
Musical Director	**Ted Astley**
Supervising Editor	**Pete Saunders**
Editor	**Desmond Saunders**
Dubbing Editor	**Hugh Marryat**
Art Director	**Ted Clements**
Make-up	**George Turner**
Continuity	**Peggy Anderson**
Location Manager	**P.L. Cecil Gurney**
Assistant Director	**Albert Pearl**
Chief Electrician	**Bob Powell**

A Video Shows Production
for Associated Rediffusion Ltd.
Made at Polytechnic Studios
Taplow, England

PENTAGON FILMS COMMERCIALS

In the early days of UK commercial television, production companies that specialised in filming advertisements were few and far between and it was, therefore, possible for Gerry Anderson and his three Pentagon Films colleagues to land major clients such as Anadin and Kellogg's. Even so, Pentagon Films went bust, prompting Anderson and Arthur Provis to establish a new film and television production company – AP Films.

ANADIN (1956)

Fast-acting tablets bring instant relief for a girl with a headache.
Director: **Gerry Anderson** Director of Photography: **Arthur Provis**
Camera Operator: **John Read** Art Director: **Reg Hill**

KELLOGG'S CORN FLAKES (1956)

Popular Enid Blyton character Noddy starts the day with his favourite breakfast cereal.
Director: **Gerry Anderson** Director of Photography: **Arthur Provis**
Camera Operator: **John Read** Art Director: **Reg Hill**

Pentagon's Noddy commercial for Kellogg's Corn Flakes was Gerry Anderson and Arthur Provis's first experience of working with puppets and gave them some understanding of what was involved when they were later approached by Roberta Leigh to produce THE ADVENTURES OF TWIZZLE for her. The puppet used in the commercial had previously appeared in a 1955 ITV NODDY puppet television series and Anderson and Provis later employed the actress who had provided the voice of Noddy in that series to voice characters in TWIZZLE – Denise Bryer.

One of the guest performers on the MARTIN KANE, PRIVATE INVESTIGATOR episode *Film Studio Story* was a young actor called David Graham, whom Gerry Anderson discovered was a fellow vertigo sufferer when they had to film a scene in which Graham's character ran along the top of some high scaffolding. Anderson later remembered Graham when he was casting voice artists for FOUR FEATHER FALLS and the actor went on to become one of the most durable performers in the Gerry Anderson productions, with subsequent vocal 'appearances' in SUPERCAR, FIREBALL XL5, STINGRAY, THUNDERBIRDS, *Thunderbirds Are Go* (1966), *Thunderbird 6* (1967), THE SECRET SERVICE and SPACE PRECINCT. David Graham is also well known to fans of British telefantasy for his Dalek voices in the early DOCTOR WHO stories *The Daleks*, *The Dalek Invasion Of Earth*, *The Chase*, *Mission To The Unknown* and *The Daleks' Master Plan*.

MARTIN KANE, PRIVATE INVESTIGATOR

Struggling to make ends meet while waiting for AP Films to be commissioned for major film and television productions, Gerry Anderson accepted a directing assignment from his friend Frank Sherwin Green to work on the Towers of London television series MARTIN KANE, PRIVATE INVESTIGATOR. This was a British-made version of a thriller series that had originally run for nine years as MARTIN KANE, PRIVATE EYE (shortened to simply MARTIN KANE in its last two years) in America, broadcast live on NBC. After its cancellation on American television, the format was resurrected in the UK by producer Harry Alan Towers as a filmed series for ABC Television, featuring the original star of the American series, William Gargan. As wise-cracking former New York cop Martin Kane, Gargan co-starred with Brian Reece as no-nonsense Scotland Yard detective Superintendent Page in a series that ran for 39 episodes and was first seen on ATV Midlands between September 1957 and June 1958. Allowed only one day to prepare, Anderson directed the episode *Film Studio Story* at the Associated British Elstree Studios in Borehamwood, Hertfordshire (which later became the EMI/MGM Studios where Anderson made THE PROTECTORS). A few weeks later, he was invited back to complete work on another episode whose previous director had collapsed from nervous exhaustion, but the title of this second episode is unknown.

FILM STUDIO STORY

Martin Kane and Superintendent Page investigate when a number of valuable paintings are stolen and the thieves choose an original hiding place for their loot – a film studio!

Cast: **William Gargan**, **Brian Reece**, **David Graham**
Director: **Gerry Anderson** Producer: **Harry Alan Towers**
Associate Producer: **Frank Sherwin Green** Running Time: 25 minutes approx.
First UK Transmission: Sunday, April 13th, 1958 (Associated-Rediffusion)

AP FILMS/CENTURY 21 COMMERCIALS

At the end of production on FOUR FEATHER FALLS, the AP Films team briefly returned to work in television commercials when actor Nicholas Parsons invited them to film three advertisements that his company had been commissioned to produce by travel agents Blue Cars. Shot on a shoestring budget, the commercials proved to be highly successful and went on to win awards, much to the surprise of everyone involved. Anderson decided to form a subsidiary commercials company, Arrow Productions, but he was later forced to sell the business when AP Films was bought by ATV (British law forbade television organisations like ATV from owning commercials production companies). However, AP Films/Century 21 continued to be involved in commercials throughout the 1960s as the company was contracted by advertising agencies representing Lyons Maid and Kellogg's to film the necessary elements for adverts featuring the puppet characters and vehicles from the various Supermarionation television series.

BLUE CARS – GERMANS (1960)

A busty German spy receives an Iron Cross from a German officer after learning about Blue Cars Travel from MI.5.

Cast: **Nicholas Parsons**, **Denise Bryer** Director: **Gerry Anderson**
Producer: **Nicholas Parsons** Written by **Nicholas Parsons** & **David Ellis**
Director of Photography: **John Read** Art Director: **Reg Hill**

BLUE CARS – GAMBLER (1960)

A gambler has just lost everything at a casino in Monte Carlo and is about to shoot himself when he discovers that a Blue Cars holiday will make life worth living again.

Cast: **Nicholas Parsons**, **Denise Bryer** Director: **Gerry Anderson**
Producer: **Nicholas Parsons** Written by **Nicholas Parsons** & **David Ellis**
Director of Photography: **John Read** Art Director: **Reg Hill**

(This commercial won third prize in the Consumer Services category at the first Television Mail *Commercials Awards in the spring of 1961.)*

BLUE CARS – MARTIANS (1960)

In an alien observatory, a pair of Martians are fascinated by a flurry of activity on Earth and learn that everyone is talking about Blue Cars holidays.

Cast: **Nicholas Parsons, Denise Bryer**
Director: **Gerry Anderson**
Producer: **Nicholas Parsons**
Written by **Nicholas Parsons & David Ellis**
Director of Photography: **John Read**
Art Director: **Reg Hill**

(This commercial won first prize in the Consumer Services category at the first Television Mail *Commercials Awards in the spring of 1961.)*

WALLS' ICE CREAM – SUPERCAR (1961)

Mike Mercury and Jimmy Gibson enjoy a Walls' Ice Cream cornet in *Supercar*.

Voice Cast: **Graydon Gould** (Mike Mercury), **Sylvia Anderson** (Jimmy Gibson)

LYONS MAID – FIREBALL XL5: 1 (1962)

On board *Fireball XL5*, Colonel Steve Zodiac and Dr. Venus enjoy new Lyons Maid Zoom ice lollies and encourage viewers to collect a set of space picture cards.

Voice Cast: **Paul Maxwell** (Colonel Steve Zodiac)

LYONS MAID – FIREBALL XL5: 2 (1962)

In the cockpit of *Fireball XL5*, Steve Zodiac and Professor Matthew Matic enjoy new Lyons Maid Zoom ice lollies and encourage viewers to collect a set of Famous Locomotives picture cards.

Voice Cast: **Paul Maxwell** (Colonel Steve Zodiac), **David Graham** (Professor Matthew Matic)

LYONS MAID – FIREBALL XL5: 3 (1962)

Steve and Venus launch Lyons Maid Zoom ice lolly missiles into space.

Voice Cast: **Paul Maxwell** (Colonel Steve Zodiac), **Sylvia Anderson** (Dr. Venus)

LYONS MAID – THUNDERBIRDS: 1 (1965)

Jeff Tracy introduces Lyons Maid Zoom ice lolly with free Famous Cars picture cards.

Voice Cast: **Peter Dyneley** (Jeff Tracy)

LYONS MAID – THUNDERBIRDS: 2 (1965)

On Thunderbird 5, Jeff and John Tracy come under attack from The Hood's rocket but they launch a Lyons Maid Zoom missile to destroy it.

Voice Cast: **Ray Barrett** (John Tracy), **Peter Dyneley** (Jeff Tracy)

LYONS MAID – THUNDERBIRDS: 3 (1966)

Parker drives FAB 1 over a rickety rope bridge while Lady Penelope sits in the back keeping her cool with a Lyons Maid Fab ice lolly.

Voice Cast: **Sylvia Anderson** (Lady Penelope), **David Graham** (Parker)

LYONS MAID – THUNDERBIRDS: 4 (1966)

An explosion in Monte Carlo is unable to prevent Lady Penelope from keeping her cool with a Lyons Maid Fab ice lolly.

Voice Cast: **Sylvia Anderson** (Lady Penelope), **David Graham** (Parker)

LYONS MAID – THUNDERBIRDS: 5 (1967)

A cool DJ warns viewers to stand by for 'Cool Off' with Lyons Maid: a Zoom ice lolly rocket is launched, *Stingray* fires a Super Sea Jet ice lolly sting-missile and Lady Penelope enjoys a Fab in FAB 1.

KELLOGG'S – THUNDERBIRDS (1967)

Jeff reveals that the members of International Rescue all eat Sugar Smacks for breakfast and Virgil, Alan and Lady Penelope are seen enjoying the honey-sweet puffs of wheat.

Voice Cast: **Peter Dyneley** (Jeff Tracy), **Sylvia Anderson** (Lady Penelope)

LYONS MAID – CAPTAIN SCARLET: 1 (1968)

The Mysterons take control of the Post Office Tower but Captain Scarlet regains control by launching Lyons Maid big Orbit ice lolly.

Voice Cast: **Francis Matthews** (Captain Scarlet)

LYONS MAID – CAPTAIN SCARLET: 2 (1968)

A DJ reports the great new climber from Lyons Maid – the super-sized Orbit ice lolly.

KELLOGG'S – CAPTAIN SCARLET: 1 (1968)

Colonel White, Captain Scarlet and Destiny Angel reveal that Spectrum agents all eat Kellogg's Sugar Smacks for breakfast to give them the energy they need to fight the Mysterons – SIG for Kellogg's Sugar Smacks!

Voice Cast: **Francis Matthews** (Captain Scarlet), **Donald Gray** (Colonel White), **Liz Morgan** (Destiny Angel)

KELLOGG'S – CAPTAIN SCARLET: 2 (1968)

Captain Scarlet introduces a great new offer from Kellogg's Sugar Smacks: one of six free Spectrum badges in every pack. A small boy is delighted when the complete set appears on his school blazer and Captain Scarlet tucks into a bowl of Sugar Smacks.

Voice Cast: **Francis Matthews** (Captain Scarlet)

LYONS MAID – JOE 90 (1968)

Joe, Mac and Sam uncover a plot to destroy London and launch a Lyons Maid Zoom ice lolly rocket to destroy a hidden laboratory

Voice Cast: **Len Jones** (Joe McClaine), **Rupert Davies** (Professor Ian McClaine), **Keith Alexander** (Sam Loover)

KELLOGG'S – JOE 90: 1 (1969)

After another successful WIN mission, Joe McClaine and Sam Loover enjoy a bowl of Kellogg's Sugar Smacks.

Voice Cast: **Len Jones** (Joe McClaine), **Keith Alexander**

KELLOGG'S – JOE 90: 2 (1969)

After another successful WIN mission, Joe McClaine and Sam Loover enjoy a bowl of Kellogg's Sugar Smacks and introduce a great new offer: one of six free JOE 90 badges in every pack.

Voice Cast: **Len Jones** (Joe McClaine), **Keith Alexander** (Sam Loover)

INDEPENDENT COMMERCIALS

Gerry Anderson renewed his commercials career in 1977 when he was approached by Judy Hurst of London advertising agency Collette, Dickinson, Pearce and Partners to produce a commercial for Jif Dessert Toppings in the style of the Supermarionation productions. Anderson accepted the challenge of producing the 40-second film in just five weeks and the result, titled *Alien Attack*, was screened in cinemas and on television. Anderson has subsequently been involved with the production of a number of television commercials for both domestic and international television, and in 1990 he joined The Moving Picture Company as commercials director. The list below details some of the highlights of Gerry Anderson's commercials work between 1977 and the present.

JIF DESSERT TOPPINGS – ALIEN ATTACK (1977)

Intergalactic Rescue Command comes under alien attack by flying saucers full of ice cream, rice pudding and semolina. Realising that the only way to save the Earth is to eat the gooey puddings, the IRC operatives launch JDTs (Jif Dessert Toppings) from their base on the Moon and coat the puddings in raspberry, strawberry and chocolate sauce to make them more palatable.

Voice Cast: **Ed Bishop** (The Man), **Angela Richards** (The Woman), **David Tate** (The Professor)
Director: **David Lane**
Producer: **Gerry Anderson**
Concept: **Collette, Dickinson, Pearce and Partners, Ltd.**
Executive Producer for CDP : **Judy Hurst**
Art Director and Storyboards: **Reg Hill**
Music Composed by **Barry Gray**
Puppet Operators: **John Brown**, **Wanda Brown**
Visual Effects Supervisor: **Brian Johnson**
Visual Effects Director: **Nick Allder**
Models: **Martin Bower**
Filmed at EMI Elstree Studios, Borehamwood and Bray Studios, Windsor

(The puppets of The Man and The Woman previously appeared as John and Julie in THE INVESTIGATOR but The Professor was a new puppet made by John Brown. Musical accompaniment was provided by the theme from THUNDERBIRDS. The commercial was first shown in the UK in December 1977 as part of the supporting programme to George Lucas's Star Wars *(1977).)*

THE ROYAL BANK OF SCOTLAND – SHOES (1985)

In a world where people walk barefoot, one man creates the idea of shoes and with the help of his bank, establishes a highly successful business.

Director: **Gerry Anderson**
Producer: **Barnaby Spurrier**
Concept: **John Webster**
Photography: **Steven Begg**
Animation : **Steven Archer**, **Joan Ashcroft**
Models: **Harry Franchetti**, **Richard Gregory**
An Anderson Burr Picture
Filmed at Bray Studios, Windsor

(Commissioned by Boase Massimi Pollitt Ltd. and stop-motion animated with 20 Giacometti-style bronze figures, Shoes *was shot in three weeks and proved to be a technical nightmare. However, it was exceptionally well-received when it aired for the first time on British television during the ITV News At Ten on February 24th, 1986, acclaimed as Commercial of the Week by* Campaign *magazine and winning a Silver Arrow award. An alternate version was made in 1986 with a different ending in which the successful shoe salesman was seen relaxing in a hammock instead of smoking a cigar. A follow-up commercial, entitled* Hats, *was also made in 1986.)*

TENNANTS PILSNER LAGER – LOU TENNANT (1987)

Robot detective Lou Tennant solves four difficult cases but always chooses his personal safety over a long cold drink of Tennants Pilsner lager – it's good, but not that good!

Voice Artist: **Viv Stanshall** (Lou Tennant)
Director: **Gerry Anderson**
Producer: **Naomi Stern**
Music: **Pete Thomas**
An Anderson Burr Picture
Filmed at Bray Studios, Windsor

(A series of four stop-motion animated commercials inspired by Dick Spanner featuring a very similar robot private eye and a pun-laden laconic voice-over by Viv Stanshall.)

EXCHANGE & MART – SCOTT'S CAR (1987)

Scott Tracy decides to sell his car through *Exchange & Mart* magazine and soon finds an interested buyer.

Cast: **Andrew Dawson**, **Gavin Robertson**
Director: **Gerry Anderson**
Producer: **Naomi Stern**
An Anderson Burr Picture
Filmed at Bray Studios, Windsor

(A live-action commercial featuring Andrew Dawson and Gavin Robertson from the Mime Theatre Project. Dawson appeared as Scott in an International Rescue costume and full-size Scott head mask and both mime artists acted as though operated on strings in the style of their performances in the Thunderbirds FAB *stage show.)*

SWINTON INSURANCE – PARKER'S DAY OFF (1990)

On Parker's day off, Lady Penelope takes FAB 1 for a drive, crashing through the gates of Creighton-Ward Mansion, smashing into a Mini and then causing a transporter truck to crash off the road into an electricity sub-station. Parker comes to the rescue in Thunderbird 2 and airlifts FAB 1 off the road using magnetic grabs, but knocks the steeple off a church as he flies away.

Director: **Gerry Anderson**
Art Director: **Bob Bell**
Puppet Operator: **Christine Glanville**
Visual Effects Supervisor: **Steven Begg**
Models: **Richard Gregory**, **David Sisson**
Music: **Barry Gray**

(Designed to reproduce the look and feel of the original Thunderbirds television episodes as closely as possible, this commercial utilised an original studio Parker puppet, although Lady Penelope was a new puppet made specially for the commercial by Christine Glanville and Richard Gregory. The transporter truck was modelled after the style of the trucks seen in Captain Scarlet And The Mysterons and Joe 90.)

NESTLÉ KITKAT – SCOTT TAKES A BREAK (1993)

Thunderbirds are go but Thunderbird 1 is stalled as Scott is taking a break with a KitKat chocolate wafer biscuit.

Director: **Gerry Anderson**
Art Director: **Bob Bell**
Puppet Operator: **Christine Glanville**
Music: **Barry Gray**
Models: **Richard Gregory, Mark Woollard**, **Bill James**
Assistant Art Director: **Mark Harris**

(This commercial opens with the countdown from the opening titles of Thunderbirds but holds on a freeze frame of Thunderbird 1 in the hangar before the craft launches. The Scott puppet was made specially for the commercial by Christine Glanville and Richard Gregory.)

Other Commercials

1986 Transworld Festival Gardens
Matchbox Toys' Laser Wheels
Matchbox Toys' Cargantua & Gearshift
1987 Early Learning Centre
Johnson & Johnson's Silhouette Tampons
1988 IDM Bank
1990 Burger King's Burger Buddies
McVitie's Hob-Nobs
Johnson's Shout
Scotch Video Tapes
1991 Golden Wonder Ringos
Alpha Bits
Domestos Fresh

WEETABIX - STINGRAY (1993)

Titan finally gets his hands on *Stingray*, by sending off box tops from packets of Weetabix to get a Matchbox die-cast *Stingray* toy.

Director: **Gerry Anderson** Art Director: **Bob Bell**
Camera Operator: **Harry Oakes BSC** Music: **Barry Gray**
Puppet Operators: **Christine Glanville**, **David Ross**, **Peter Holmes**
Models: **Richard Gregory** Scenic Artist: **Steven Begg**

(This commercial was shot in two days at the start of May 1993 at the Bell Studios near Heathrow Airport, London. A new Titan puppet was made for the commercial by Christine Glanville and Richard Gregory while the Aquaphibian puppets were made by former Supermarionation property master Peter Holmes.)

Prior to the production of *Calling Elvis*, Gerry Anderson had been involved in the production of another music video of sorts when he was approached in 1989 by theatre producer André Ptaszynski to produce some filmed special effects sequences that could be used by director Bob Carlton in the staging of a new musical, *Return To The Forbidden Planet*. Intentionally designed to mimic a crude 1950s-era style of visual effects, the footage was produced by Anderson on a budget of just £8,000.

MUSIC VIDEOS

In the spring of 1991, Gerry Anderson was contacted by pop video and feature film director Steve Barron to contribute a THUNDERBIRDS section to the video for Dire Straits' latest single 'Calling Elvis', the first release from their new studio album *On Every Street*. Accepting the challenge, Anderson and his wife Mary had just 12 weeks to co-ordinate the production of new Supermarionation-style puppets and sets for a three day shoot at Pinewood Studios in Buckinghamshire. Art director Bob Bell meticulously recreated the Tracy Lounge set while Christine Glanville and Richard Gregory created puppet versions of the five Dire Straits musicians, much in the style of the Cliff Richard and The Shadows puppets made for *Thunderbirds Are Go* (1966). Puppets of Lady Penelope and Brains made cameo appearances courtesy of new puppets that had been made for the Swinton Insurance commercial *Parker's Day Off* and an associated print campaign the previous year. A new puppet of Jeff Tracy was specially made for the video from an original studio mould. *Thunderbirds FAB* Mime Theatre Project performers Andrew Dawson and Gavin Robertson appeared in International Rescue uniforms and full head masks as the Tracy brothers, but the original puppet characters were also seen in footage from the television series. The 'Calling Elvis' single was released in August 1991 when the video was screened for the first time as part of a special Channel 4 programme DIRE STRAITS, CALLING ELVIS which also featured interviews with Mark Knopfler and Gerry Anderson.

Gerry Anderson chose 'Calling Elvis' as one of his selections of music for the 1999 EMI album *Gerry Anderson – Evocation*, a collection of music of particular significance to the producer issued as part of an experimental range of 'Songbooks'. Anderson's other selections included 'Four Feather Falls' performed by Michael Holliday, a 1971 recording of 'The Thunderbirds March' performed by the Band of the Royal Marines, 'Shooting Star' performed by Cliff Richard and The Shadows from *Thunderbirds Are Go* (1966), a 1974 recording of Albinoni's 'Adagio in G Minor' (a piece popularised by the science-fiction film *Rollerball* (1975) but also heard in the SPACE:1999 episode *Dragon's Domain*), and a full-length recording of the theme to LAVENDER CASTLE.

DIRE STRAITS - CALLING ELVIS

A girl takes a bath while around her a variety of household objects take on the appearance of the International Rescue Thunderbird craft. Jeff Tracy co-ordinates another rescue mission from the Tracy Lounge and Dire Straits perform their latest single live on stage, both in their real-life personas and as their Supermarionation puppet counterparts, observed by Lady Penelope and Brains.

Cast: **Mark Knopfler**, **John Ilsley**, **Guy Fletcher**, **Alan Clark**, **Phil Palmer**, **Andrew Dawson**, **Gavin Robertson**
Produced and Directed by **Steve Barron** Music and Lyrics by **Mark Knopfler**
SUPERMARIONATION SECTION
Director: **Gerry Anderson** Producer: **Mary Anderson**
Art Director: **Bob Bell** Camera Operator: **Paddy Seale**
Chief Puppeteer: **Christine Glanville** Puppet Wardrobe: **Zena Relph**
Property Master: **Peter Holmes**
Puppet Properties: **Brian Cole**, **Kevin Gilmartin**, **Ben Hall**, **Bill James** **Jim Machin**, **Lee Took**, **Mark Woollard**
First UK Transmission: Wednesday, August 21st, 1991 (Channel 4)

CHRONOLOGY (1946-2003)

About the Author

CHRIS BENTLEY was born in Tanzania in 1963 but grew up in West Yorkshire. He graduated from Newcastle Polytechnic in 1985 with a degree in Graphic Design and joined the creative department of the *Yorkshire Post* newspaper. For 14 years, he was the creative director of a Bradford-based commercial graphics company that he co-founded, but is now a freelance writer and designer. Since 1991, he has also been Chairman of Fanderson, the Official Gerry Anderson Appreciation Society, and contributing editor/designer of the club magazine *FAB*.

He is the author of *The Complete Book of Thunderbirds* (Carlton Books, 2000) and *The Complete Book of Captain Scarlet* (Carlton Books, 2001), and the editor of *UFO Original Screenplays Volume 1* (Century 21 Books, 2001), a collection of scripts from the 1969 Gerry Anderson television series. He is currently editing a new SPACE:1999 novel (*Earthbound* by prolific British science-fiction author E.C. Tubb) for Century 21 Books, and writing *The Complete Book of UFO* for Reynolds & Hearn. He is the son of Fifties road and pursuit cycling champion Keith Bentley.